W9-BCR-771

Windows
Into
Organizations

Windows Into Organizations

John W. Newstrom
and
Jon L. Pierce

amacom

American Management Association

This book is available at a special
discount when ordered in bulk quantities.
For information, contact Special Sales Department,
AMACOM, a division of American Management Association,
135 West 50th Street, New York, NY 10020.

Library of Congress Cataloging-in-Publication Data

Newstrom, John W.
    Windows into organizations / John W. Newstrom and
Jon L. Pierce.
      p.   cm.
    ISBN 0-8144-5955-2
    1. Management—Charts, diagrams. etc. I. Pierce,
Jon L. (Jon Lepley) II. Title.
HD38.N42 1990   89-46216
658.4'02—dc20   CIP

To our **fathers,**
both of whom have left us;
both of whom left us with a deep
respect for family, friends, and nature—
that which binds it all together.

Contents

List of Windows

Acknowledgments

Many, many people contributed directly or indirectly to the creation and completion of this book. We would like to gratefully acknowledge the contributions of some of them in particular.

First, paramount recognition goes to the dozens of individuals who explicitly or implicitly developed the various window models included in this book. They had the inspiration and insight to identify the key dimensions and relate them in meaningful ways into a 2×2 framework. Wherever possible, we have acknowledged these persons with a reference on the appropriate grid.

Second, we received immense assistance from nineteen contributing chapter authors. These persons helped us select which grids to include, confirm their accuracy as portrayed here, describe them in sufficient detail, and provide relevant illustrations indicating how they have been used. The "project managers" who capably provided much of the expert input for each chapter include:

Chapter 2—"Conflict and Its Resolution"—Steve Rubenfeld
Chapter 3—"Control"—David Greenberger
Chapter 4—"Crisis Management"—Jack Kartez
Chapter 5—"Decision Making"—David Cherrington
Chapter 6—"Employee Attitudes and Behaviors"—Richard Blackburn
Chapter 7—"Understanding Groups"—David Vollrath
Chapter 8—"Human Resource Management"—Ann Noe
Chapter 9—"Individual Differences"—Gail McGee
Chapter 10—"Interpersonal Influence"—Jane Goodson
Chapter 11—"Leadership Styles"—Bob Ford

Chapter 12—"Motivation"—Kim Boal

Chapter 13—"Organizational Cultures"—Bob Marx

Chapter 14—"Organizational Environments"—John Schermerhorn

Chapter 15—"Participative Management"—Bill Werther

Chapter 16—"Social Responsibility and Ethics"—Sara Morris

Chapter 17—"Strategic Issues"—Cyndy Lengnick-Hall

Chapter 18—"Stress!"—Jean Lundin

Chapter 19—"Training and Human Resource Development"—Mark Lengnick-Hall

Chapter 20—"Transitions and Change"—Ron Gribbins

Third, we are indebted to Jean Jacobson, Connie Johnson, Vicki Alvar, and others who tirelessly prepared many revisions of the manuscript, always under the pressure of tight deadlines. We appreciate their patience, dedication, and support.

Finally, we especially appreciate the editorial assistance, encouragement, and insight provided by our editor, Adrienne Hickey, and by Eva Weiss at AMACOM.

John W. Newstrom
Jon L. Pierce

Windows Into Organizations

Chapter 1

The Nature and Use of Windows Into Organizations

> For every complex problem, there is a
> simple solution, and it's usually wrong.
>
> —*H. L. Mencken*

For many decades managers searched for the "one best way" to manage. More recently, they have begun to recognize that there is *no* one best way. Instead, management needs to be approached from a *contingency* (situation-by-situation) *perspective.* This means that as situations change, managerial approaches to decision making, planning, organizing, directing, and controlling need to change in order to make organizations effective. As managers, therefore, you need to *diagnose* organizational situations before you take action. For example, you need to recognize that an autocratic approach to decision making works well under some conditions, while other situations call for participative decision making. Clearly, you need to be both analytical and flexible in your approach to managing.

To use the contingency approach, you need help in two

1

areas. First, you need to identify and understand the major elements in complex organizational situations. Second, you must examine the available options and then identify the preferred approaches to managing under each of these complex conditions. One extremely helpful visual format for expressing the contingency approach to management is the managerial "window," or "window into organizations."

1-1. "Windows Into Organizations": A Definition

A managerial window is a grid framework that visually depicts different types of conditions faced by managers, varying degrees of these conditions, and their implications. More specifically, the window is a dual classification scheme that identifies and then combines two interrelated dimensions (e.g., two conditions that affect the choice of leadership styles; two conditions that affect an approach to decision making) into a simple graphic image. For the sake of simplicity, both of the classifying variables are divided at their midpoints. This creates two opposing conditions (e.g., high and low people-oriented leadership styles; autocratic as opposed to participative decision making) for each dimension. Each dimension can be expressed in either *quantitative* degrees (such as "low" and "high"), or in terms of *qualitative* differences (such as "internal" vs. "external").

Through a combination of the two related dimensions, some management or organizational issue is portrayed in a grid that provides a four-paned (2 × 2) window into organizations (see Window 1-1).[1] Each windowpane (also referred to as a cell or quadrant) in the grid highlights a distinct category of a particular management phenomenon (e.g., one of four leadership styles; one of four decision-making approaches). In total, the

---

1. The term 2 × 2 (two-by-two) was coined to refer to any grid that has two classes or categories of one dimension, and two classes of a second and related dimension. This differentiates the 2 × 2 window models in this book from any of the more *quantitatively* complex classification schemes (e.g., 2 × 3 or 5 × 6) that would have a large number of resultant windowpanes. It also restricts this book to two-dimensional models, rather than including the more *conceptually* complex three-dimensional models that result from the interaction of three (or more!) dimensions relevant to a particular issue.

Window 1-1. Format of the Windows Into Organizations.

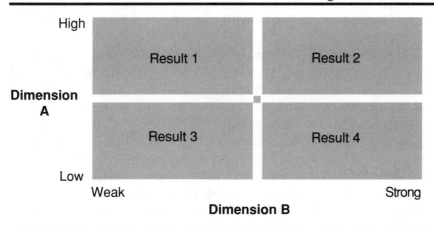

grid and its discussion provide insight into the nature of four different organizational conditions, or the causes of these conditions, or different methods of solving problems.

The Popularity of Windows

The specific origin of this grid format is unknown, but windows into organizations practices have become extremely popular. A detailed search of the management literature reveals that there are several hundred of the 2×2 models capturing a wide array of organization and management situations.

Why have these windows into organizations become so popular? To borrow an old cliche, "The world is divided into two kinds of people—those who divide the world into two kinds of people, and those who don't." A natural tendency exists for people to make simple divisions along dimensions important to them in order to place items into one group or another. This apparently satisfies a need to differentiate things around us and yet retain the intellectual comfort that accompanies relatively simple categorization schemes.

The famed social psychologist Kurt Lewin has had a tremendous influence on the analysis of the human side of organizations. Lewin had the unique capacity to reduce complex relationships to their basic and most central components. His capacity to express complex thoughts in simplified form might be fairly viewed as one stimulus for this trend toward using 2×2 windows.

Regardless of the origin of the grid approach, managers have long been intrigued with visual "grids" as simple yet useful ways to classify organizational situations. For about twenty-five years, for example, managers have been fascinated with Blake and Mouton's classic Managerial Grid® (see our discussion in Chapter 11). Their grid portrays numerous styles of leadership and argues that one style is often the most effective (i.e., the 9,9 style called Team Management).[2] Since the introduction of the Blake and Mouton Managerial Grid, literally hundreds of other grids have been developed. Many have become the focus of highly successful management development programs, managerial consulting practices, and the daily practice of management in public and private organizations.

The combined elegance and simplicity of these grids forms the basis for their popularity. By capturing part of the real world of organizational management in a single portrait, they are highly efficient. These windows into organizations crisply communicate the highlights and the essence of a situation in a combined verbal/visual format that you can grasp, retain, use, and convey to others. Because managers have a strong apparent drive to see their worlds simply, a large number of models that portray important ideas in a 2×2 framework have been developed.

We offer two words of caution, however. First, we echo the lessons of many philosophers who urge you to beware of the hidden limitations in simplified thinking. For example, the opening quote by H. L. Mencken suggests that there needs to be a match or "good fit" between the complexity of a problem to be addressed and the solution to be applied. Similarly, Alfred North Whitehead advised people to "seek simplicity and then distrust it." The message should be clear to you: 2×2 grids are a potentially useful starting point for placing some structure into a situation. However, their inherent simplicity may disguise the richness and complexity that lies within a situation. If these

2. R. R. Blake and J. S. Mouton, *The Managerial Grid* (Houston: Gulf Publishing, 1964).

windows are too rigidly applied, they may actually mislead you into viewing the world narrowly. This would be a tragic misinterpretation and misuse of windows into organizations. Instead of shedding light on a subject and broadening your vision, misuses of a window might actually narrow your perspective!

Second, it is important that you be objective when considering the practical application of the grids. There are limitations. Please keep in mind the following cautions: (1) the arbitrariness involved in always placing the horizontal and vertical dividing lines exactly in the middle of the dimensions used; (2) the need to consider other dimensions as well as the two identified in each grid; (3) the probable difficulty, in practice, of assessing whether a situation is truly "high" or "low" on a given dimension; and (4) the risk that placing a brief descriptive label on each of the four windowpanes may restrict your thinking about what it truly means. In summary, use the windows into organizations when appropriate, but do so with caution.

What You May Gain From This Book

Windows Into Organizations is a pragmatic and systematic presentation of a set of models that can be used to guide managerial practice in several critical areas (e.g., decision making, crisis management, conflict resolution, leadership, and strategic management). Many managers utilize window models such as these to help them organize their thoughts, guide their practices, and interpret their successes and failures in order to generalize from them.[3]

The grids presented in this book are diagnostic tools that portray many of the critical situations that you confront daily. The various windowpanes within each grid help determine which management practice might be best suited for a particular situation.

To supplement the visual portrait of each of the windows into organizations we provide a straightforward presentation, interpretation, and discussion of the model. Numerous practical

3. J. B. Keys, "The Management of Learning Grid for Management Development Revisited," *Management Development Review*, Vol. 8, No. 2 (1989), pp. 5–12.

examples are also included, which are either drawn from our knowledge of actual organizational and managerial experiences or indicate ways in which you can use the grid. In either case, all names used are fictitious in nature.

The book contains several management and organizational grids in each of its nineteen topical chapters (there are twenty chapters in all). Arranged in alphabetical order, each addresses a currently important theme in the practice of management. The presentation of each model follows a standardized format, covering several areas of managerial interest. Each discussion covers (directly or indirectly):

- The primary topic (e.g., managerial decision making) that the model focuses on, and its objective(s) (e.g., what it is designed to do)
- The two dimensions that create the 2×2 grid
- The four situations or products that appear within the windowpanes
- A review of the practical implications suggested by the model ("When to Use the Window")
- A clear illustration of how the window has been, or could be, used ("The Grid in Action")
- Suggestions for additional reading about the topic for those that desire greater details

Experts in each of the nineteen topical areas helped us prepare a chapter covering a set of related 2×2 models that can help to address a particular organizational issue. The specific grids that were selected for presentation in this handbook come from a variety of sources. Some are very popular models that have been used for decades, while others are relatively new. Some were developed by management consultants, and others were created or modified by the editors and chapter authors.

The grids vary dramatically in their scope (macro to micro), complexity (simple to complex), and purpose (descriptive or normative). Some of the grids are very *macro* in nature. They focus on broad features of the organization or its environment. Other grids, more *micro* in nature, help you examine the attitudes, motives, and behaviors of employees.

The windows included here also differ in their complexity. Some are so simple in their presentation, interpretation, and application possibilities that the average reader may yawn and say, "So what?" Others are either subtly or blatantly complex, and the accompanying discussion provides only a frustratingly brief explanation. We have therefore provided, wherever possible, a citation to an original source for most grids, as well as a suggestion or two about additional relevant references. Interested readers may wish to obtain the original source to examine the grid's background in greater detail.

Some of the grids are descriptive in nature, while others are normative. The descriptive grids provide a systematic way to classify major features of environments, organizations, employees, or managers instead of treating all situations, objects, or people in the same way. These descriptive grids enable you to understand and categorize a variety of organizational realities. Although they may not all have immediately practical implications in the applied sense, you will recognize the high value of a solid conceptual foundation for your actions.

The normative grids are more prescriptive in nature. Some of them make predictions about what will happen under certain organizational conditions. These models were developed to help you see the implications of your actions. Other normative models make recommendations regarding how you ought to act under certain conditions.

Readers will quickly recognize that the placement of some windows within one chapter and not another was necessarily arbitrary. Clearly there is topical overlap across several chapters, just as two or more window models may draw on closely similar dimensions and yet reach different conclusions because of their different purpose. We need to remind ourselves that most of the windows were not created for this book (which would have allowed us to make them more distinctly different), but were selected from among a broad array of existing models.

In summary, there are a variety of models presented in the book. What they all have in common, however, is that they can each serve as a useful tool to help increase your effectiveness. Some grids help organize information, while others facilitate the understanding and the diagnosis of organizational situations. Other grids provide portraits of cause-and-effect relationships or provide insight into what is likely to happen, and the normative models offer direct or indirect prescriptions for managerial action.

How to Use This Book

This book is not a novel. There is no single theme that runs from cover to cover. Consequently, you do not need to read this book from start to finish. You can step into it on a theme-by-theme basis. The book is organized topically into major themes of interest to you today, one in each of the next nineteen chapters. Each of these chapters is divided further into a discussion of two to five separate window models that relate to an important management issue. The discussions can stand alone, so that you are not required to read an entire chapter.

For greatest efficiency, you may initially wish to examine the Contents to identify a theme of current interest. After you turn to the relevant chapter, a quick reading of its introduction can provide an overview of the grids to follow. After selecting a particular window, you should then study the graphic portrait of it to see how it focuses on its two dimensions and four products. A detailed reading of the presentation and discussion will then provide a thorough understanding of how the graphic portrait works. Pay particular attention to the applied examples, which portray how other managers have used the grid to guide their actions.

Conclusion

The windows into organizations presented in this book can help improve your analytical skills. However, these windows are not a substitute for continued reading and listening to current developments related to management and organizational understanding. They are also not a replacement for reliance on the art of management. For many situations, intuition (i.e., the art of management) can be a very powerful managerial tool.

These windows—some of which are widely accepted, some of which are provocative and even controversial, some of which have escaped previous attention—should encourage you to think more carefully about your day-to-day managerial practices. They can help you interpret your experiences, organize your thoughts, and generalize your approaches to future events. These windows into organizations are designed to encourage the flexible and situational-driven practice of management.

Chapter 2

Conflict and Its Resolution

One fact of organizational life stands out: Conflict is inevitable. In the 1990s and beyond, the changes necessary to ensure continued organizational competitiveness may actually *increase* the likelihood of conflict. But the news is not all bad. Constructively managed conflict can often stimulate creativity and facilitate change. The historical ideal of avoiding conflict is slowly giving way to the contemporary goal of managing conflict. The challenge that remains is to change the conditions in people and organizations that too often lead to sweeping conflict under the rug or applying cover-up solutions. Simultaneously, conditions must be created that encourage collaboration and problem solving. You must use conflict and learn from it.

The models described in this chapter are learning tools that present somewhat simplified versions of conflict situations. They provide windows through which you can see and explore the forces that influence the choice of a dispute resolution strategy. Not only do the models offer you the chance to learn more about the constructive management of conflict, but they also offer the opportunity to look inwardly at your own values, beliefs, and behaviors.

When viewed as a group, the first three models converge on a common issue. They demonstrate that a variety of dimensions, some situational and others reflecting personal values and goals, may lead to the choice of particular processes for dealing with conflicts. The fourth model, the classical Prisoner's Dilemma, stresses the interdependencies in choices made by the parties to a dispute. In their own way, all of these models offer the opportunity to diagnose situations, to better understand behaviors, and to stimulate thoughtful introspection.

2-1. Managerial Options for Resolving Disputes

When nonproductive conflict erupts in an organization, frustrated participants often ask a third party to alleviate the discord. In most organizational settings, you bear this responsibility for settling conflicts. Clearly, you can use your organizational rank and authority to impose a settlement. However, this may not be the best possible solution to the problem or remove the underlying roots of the conflict. Window 2-1 classifies a variety of paths you can follow. It suggests that the desirability of each available option may vary, depending on the extent of your control of the content and process of conflict resolution.

Applying the Dispute Resolution Window

There are many sources and types of organizational conflict. It may involve individuals or groups, the past or the future, and issues that range from petty to critical. But regardless of the nature of the conflict, the manner in which you intervene in a dispute can be an important determinant of the outcome. If you want to be successful in resolving conflicts (or in constructively using conflict), you should increase your own awareness of the range of available responses to conflict. You would be wise to first diagnose conflict situations and then to select from a broader repertoire of managerial roles.

Many managers are inclined to use the *imposed solution* (arbitration) to deal with work-related conflict. Pulling rank to quickly resolve a dispute often appears to be the expedient path to follow and may be desirable in some situations. But the *imposed solution* may remove the symptoms of conflict without dealing with the underlying issues. Even if it does, it may not yield the best-quality decision. Although chosen less frequently, *delegation* is the other route that is sometimes tempting to

Window 2-1. Managerial Options for Resolving Disputes.

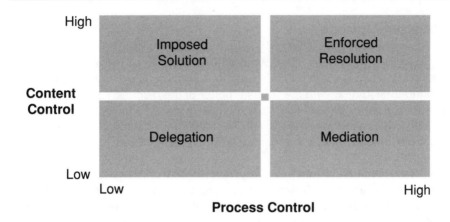

Source: Adapted from Blair H. Shepard, "Managers as Inquisitors," in *Negotiating in Organizations*, Max Bazerman and Roy Lewicki, eds., Beverly Hills: Sage Publications, 1983, pp. 193–213.

Dimensions

Process control. This dimension reflects the extent to which you can affect *how* those in conflict deal with each other during attempts to resolve the dispute. For example, can you effectively impose time limits, regulate access to information, or force the parties to meet face-to-face (or remain separated)? Control of communications, including the ability to specify oral or written responses, impose or prohibit specific rules of conduct, or establish an agenda, is also an essential element of *process control*. The extent of the *process* control may be a product of personalities, authority (rank), managerial style, or the nature of the dispute.

Content control. This dimension measures the degree to which, intervening in the dispute, you can affect *what* is presented, discussed, or debated (as contrasted to *how* the issues are dealt with). *Content control* includes the extent to which you can control the content of communications by establishing norms relating to the type of information or data to be presented. It may also involve limiting tangential discussions, interpreting or editing content, or directing exchanges between parties. Similar to *process control*, personalities, authority, style, and the nature of the dispute may affect your relative effectiveness in *content control*. In addition, expert knowledge may be a critical element.

Window 2-1. (*Continued*)

Managerial Options

Imposed solution. Here, you assume the role of judge and jury and forcefully dictate a decision. In this situation of high content control, you have the confidence to deal with the subject matter of the dispute. At the same time, low process control creates fears that the process of resolution cannot be constructively channeled. This leads you to "pull rank," assert control over the conflict resolution process, and dictate (arbitrate) a solution.

Enforced resolution. Relatively high levels of control of both the content and process of dispute resolution may lead you to a "carrot and stick" approach. The message to the parties in the dispute is "Resolve your differences or I'll resolve them for you." In this scenario you play an active role in helping the parties with the process of conflict resolution. This approach recognizes the potential value of having those involved fashion the resolution to the conflict. In addition it reflects your need to retain control of the situation and to force the parties to solve their problem with the threat of an imposed decision.

Mediation. In a situation of high process control but low content control, you may choose to release some control of the terms of the resolution while still exerting control over the process of resolution. Your role, because you have given up the option of an imposed solution, is to guide the parties to shape a desirable resolution to their differences.

Delegation. Where there is no effective control of either process or content, you may tell the two parties to solve the problem themselves. This managerial reaction to conflict may reflect an unwillingness to get involved for fear of being forced into an undesired or imposed solution situation.

follow. Telling the parties to work out the conflict themselves (or deciding not to decide) may be suitable in some situations, but is often ineffective because it fails to provide the parties with the guidance they require.

True *mediation* is rare in organizational settings, since few managers are willing to give up their authority to resolve conflict. As a consequence, *enforced resolution* is often a desirable compromise between *mediation* and the *imposed solution*. This is particularly true where there is comfort with the level of process and content control. Guiding the parties to resolve their own differences may result in a better settlement than one that is dictated (although this option remains if your initial attempt is not successful). A settlement reached in this way is also more likely to be viewed as a "win-win" outcome, which carries with it a higher commitment to making it work.

When to Use the Window. You will find it productive to use this window when:

- There is a history of unsatisfactory approaches to conflict resolution within your unit.
- You are unsure whether to take an active or passive role in the solution of a conflict.
- You have fallen into a predictable pattern of regularly using a single conflict-resolution approach without preliminary analysis.
- You begin to realize the substantial difference between process control and content control, and the impact those assessments have on the selection of options for dispute resolution.

The Grid in Action. Since his promotion to plant manager, a growing amount of Leonard Rosen's time has been spent resolving technical disputes and rivalries between the engineers in his old work group. Despite assurances that his former colleagues have the utmost confidence in his technical competence and evenhandedness, Leonard is concerned that he is seen as an easy alternative to serious problem-solving efforts. Even though Leonard frequently enjoys the challenges that are presented by technological problems, he firmly believes that these decisions can best be made by the work group itself.

From his vantage point, Rosen is well aware that many of the disagreements that he has been called on to resolve were extremely critical to the company: For example, contractual requirements often impose strict time lines that have to be met. Still, he feels that imposed solutions should be a last resort. Given encouragement, the work group can make better technical decisions and can actually be happier if they settle their own disagreements. Leonard feels that he can play a much more constructive role as a resource person to the work group than as an arbiter of differences. Is it feasible to push for more group decision making?

Leonard assesses the present situation. There is no question about his technical competence (high *content control*). He is fully capable of shaping an appropriate solution. At the same time, his relationship with the engineers, along with the formal authority that comes with his position, gives him considerable control over the rules of conduct, time lines, and other aspects of the decision-making process (high *process control*). He decides that a strategy of *enforced resolution* will therefore be preferable to an *imposed solution*. It will protect his right to make a decision (if necessary) while encouraging group members to resolve their conflicts.

References

Moberg, Dennis J., and David Caldwell. *Interactive Cases in Organizational Behavior.* Glenview, Ill.: Scott, Foresman and Co., 1988, pp. 137–156.

Kolb, Deborah M. *The Mediators.* Cambridge, Mass.: The MIT Press, 1985.

Simkin, William. *Mediation and the Dynamics of Collective Bargaining.* Washington, D.C.: BNA Books, 1971.

2-2. Conflict Resolution Behaviors

When deeply immersed in conflict, two parties may easily believe that their concerns are incompatible. In such situations it is tempting to conclude that the combatants have only two options: Cooperate or compete. But this simple dichotomy doesn't provide enough options when you face complex decisions that have to be made in conflict situations. The model of conflict resolution behaviors described in Window 2-2 demonstrates that there is actually a broader range of options available when you find yourself in conflict situations.

Applying the Conflict Resolution Behaviors Window

Since organizations are partly political systems, it is easy to see that participants will have both conflicting interests and shared interests. From this perspective, conflict is a natural outgrowth of most organizational relationships. To resolve conflict, the popular press has offered a steady diet of descriptive and prescriptive primers. In some, the negative aspects of conflict are stressed and the focus is on avoiding or eliminating conflict. Recently, there has been a shift in attitude, advocating the active management and constructive uses of conflict, a broader view of conflict reflected in this window model of conflict resolution behaviors. The view also relates to a wide range of other applications, including resolving disputes in labor-management relations and choosing strategies to deal with a competing organization.

This model should stimulate introspection, encouraging you to reflect on the conflict handling methods that were followed in a recent dispute. You could speculate about how things might have been different had an alternative approach been chosen. This same process could also help you understand the options for dealing with pending problems.

Of particular interest would be your self-assessment along the defining dimensions of *concern for self* and *concern for others*. This evaluation could be either situation-specific or an overall personal assessment of cooperative attitudes toward others and assertiveness in pursuing selfish goals. It could also be used by two or more individuals who simultaneously share and discuss their assessments of themselves and their interpersonal behaviors.

Another important product of this reflective exercise is the realization that conflict resolution approaches have a higher probability of success if they are well suited to the situation. A few examples will illustrate this point. If the possible disruptive effects of resolution outweigh the expected benefits, it may be acceptable and even desirable to avoid the issue. Where an

(Text continues on page 18)

Window 2-2. Conflict Resolution Behaviors.

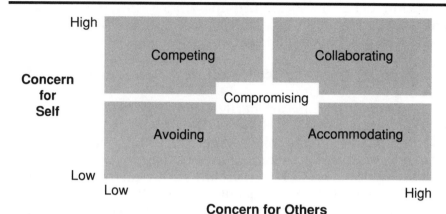

Source: Adapted from K. W. Thomas, "Organizational Conflict," in *Organizational Behavior*, S. Kerr, ed. Columbus, Ohio: Grid , 1979, pp. 151–181.

Dimensions

Concern for self. One important dimension in conflict is the emphasis placed on attempting to satisfy your own concerns. High intensity of *concern for self* is usually associated with high levels of assertiveness in the handling of a conflict situation. On the other hand, where *concern for self* is low (or where there is a willingness to sacrifice self-interest), low levels of assertiveness can be predicted. *Concern for self* reflects your behavioral intentions in a particular situation, intentions that may or may not be consistent with your underlying personal values.

Concern for others. The extent to which a person attempts to satisfy the needs and well-being of the other party is termed *concern for others*. The dimension may be affected by the individual's own values and interpersonal priorities, but it ultimately reflects a situation-specific reaction to conflict. The degree of *concern for others* may be gauged by the level (low to high) of cooperative and supportive behaviors that are present in dealing with the concerns of the other party.

Alternative Conflict Resolution Behaviors

Competing. Competitive managers are assertive in attempting to satisfy self-serving concerns at the expense of the other parties. Any available type of power—threat, argument, authority, or physical intimidation—might be used to enforce an "I'm right and you're wrong" perspective. When using this conflict-handling behavior, you attempt to dominate and persuade, while not listening to others' inputs and positions.

Window 2-2. (*Continued*)

Accommodating. Self-interest is subordinated to the interests of others, and the manager *accommodates* the opponent totally by "throwing in the towel." Whether done as a symbolic gesture, a charitable act, or a tacit admission of defeat, this is the conceptual opposite of competing. An individual's propensity to concede wipes out the necessity for, and validity of, any substantive arguments to be proposed by the opponent. (This is similar to what happens in the U.S. judicial system when a defendant, without admitting guilt, enters a plea of nolo contendere.)

Collaborating. Collaboration attempts to substantially meet the needs of *both* parties. In collaborating, you may find that it is possible to be both assertive and cooperative simultaneously. The objective is to find some alternative that substantially satisfies both you and the other person. Achieving a level of *collaboration* that will result in a win-win outcome requires a shared commitment to solve, not just resolve, a conflict. This represents the ideal way of dealing with many conflicts.

Avoiding . It is possible that, on a given issue, you may have low concern for either yourself or others and therefore totally *avoid* the conflict. You duck, sidestep, or "pass the buck" to escape dealing with the dispute. Avoidance behaviors may also include rigidly "stonewalling" or even tabling the issue. In this case the problem may continue unabated or it may even take care of itself. It is also possible that someone else will step in and take charge of the dispute resolution process.

Compromising. In an unusual fifth window of a 2 x 2 grid, *compromise* suggests a "splitting the difference" approach to conflict resolution behaviors. Being somewhat assertive and cooperative but also pragmatic, you may decide to compromise. In many situations there is merit to the adage "Half a loaf is better that none at all."

integrative solution (through collaborating) is preferred but time is too short to allow it, compromise may be the expedient route to follow. A related and equally useful lesson is the recognition that the basic values and beliefs of the participants (in this case their respective *concerns for self* and *concerns for others*) may lead them to respond differently to a particular situation.

Using the Window. This model, which is truly a "classic" in the area of conflict resolution, should be used to:

- Raise employee awareness that there is more than one way to resolve interpersonal conflicts
- Encourage you to view interpersonal problems from different parties' perspectives, rather than just through your own eyes and only to protect your own interests
- Identify an alternative (backup) conflict resolution style to use when your first preference does not succeed
- Remind participants that compromise is always a viable conflict-resolution strategy when other approaches do not seem to work

The Grid in Action. As a two-term mayor, Becca Winthrop appears to be a "natural" politician. The local newspaper's endorsement of her recent reelection campaign has characterized her as the ideal mayor for Bartsville: "Becca Winthrop can fight with the tenacity of a bulldog, but she is more than a fighter. She has heart and will do what is best for all the citizens of our city."

Over breakfast, Becca thinks back to these words and wonders if her behaviors at the city council meeting last night really do serve the best interests of Bartsville. With a grant application deadline quickly approaching, she had "locked horns" with the president of the city council over the proposed location for a low-income housing project. Neither she nor the councilperson would budge, and the issue was tabled. If they don't resolve the impasse within a week, the deadline will pass and the housing will not be built. Becca is counting on the time pressure working to her advantage.

As she sips her coffee, the mayor thinks about the shortage of low-cost housing in Bartsville and the people who will benefit from this project. She is deeply concerned about the needs of those who elected her. In the privacy of her kitchen, she admits to herself that both of the possible sites are really acceptable. This is a political battle, plain and simple. What if the council president doesn't concede? Becca also concludes that this issue doesn't really carry with it much risk to her future effectiveness as mayor. Why has she felt the need to defeat the council president on this issue? But more importantly, what if she does defeat the president? Will she have "won the battle and lost the war?" Becca deeply wants the president as an ally on future issues.

The more she thinks about it, the more it seems that her competing approach is unnecessary. She has little personal stake (low *concern for self*) and a great deal of concern for not only those who will benefit from this project (high general *concern for others*), but also a genuine concern for the image of the council president. Perhaps she should accommodate his needs and concede, or maybe there is a possibility of some type of compromise. She reaches for the phone and begins to dial.

References

Ferraro, Vincent L., and Sheila Adams. "Interdepartmental Conflict: Practical Ways to Prevent and Reduce It." *Personnel*, July/August 1984, pp. 12–23.

Thomas, K. W. "Toward Multi-Dimensional Values in Teaching: The Example of Conflict Behaviors." *Academy of Management Review*, 1977, pp. 484–490.

Savage, Grant T., John D. Blair, and Ritch L. Sorenson. "Consider Both Relationships and Substance When Negotiating Strategically." *Academy of Management Executive*, Vol. 3, No. 1, pp. 37–48.

2-3. Conflict Resolution Approaches

Most disputes contain the seeds of both conflict and collaboration, but often the seed of collaboration is not given the nourishment it needs to germinate. Disputes and disagreements are typically seen as battles from which only one combatant can emerge victorious. In effect, there must be a winner and a loser. From this perspective the pursuit of self-interests makes it easy to overlook opportunities for cooperation. Through cooperative problem solving, it may be possible for the parties to resolve their differences and both be better off than before (a win-win outcome).

The model of Conflict Resolution Approaches (Window 2-3) demonstrates that you can choose from a variety of strategies for handling disagreements. The probability of success of these strategies is determined by your personal stake in the conflict, skills in using the strategies, and assessment of the prospects for agreement.

Applying the Conflict Resolution Approaches Window

The potential for conflict always exists and, although it is not always obvious, those who disagree often do have interests in common. Labor-management relations is one area where substantial potential for cooperative problem solving exists as an alternative to power-based *win-lose* outcomes. One major historical foundation for this model of conflict resolution approaches is the pioneering work of Richard E. Walton and Robert B. McKersie (see References), who identify two distinct types of bargaining, "integrative" (problem solving) and "distributive" (power based).

Integrative bargaining involves issues that are of common concern—where permanent solutions beneficial to both parties are feasible. A solution would represent a win-win outcome. This relates roughly to the problem-solving and compromise options in the model of conflict resolution approaches. Distributive bargaining, on the other hand, involves issues where one party's goals are in conflict with another's. This creates a situation where a gain to one person results in the other's loss. This would approximate a situation of low agreement possibility, such as the *win-lose* and *acceptance* approaches.

You can use this model as an introspective tool—both to analyze past behaviors and to diagnose situations that are demanding attention. Its value is two-pronged—encouraging you to explicitly consider the defining dimensions (*stake in conflict* and *agreement possibility*), and then suggesting which dispute resolution approach to take.

Window 2-3. Conflict Resolution Approaches.

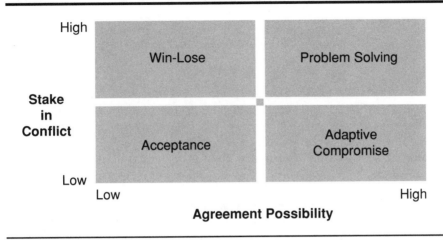

Dimensions

Stake in conflict. This dimension records the extent of your personal interest in the handling or outcome of the dispute. A "high stake" reflects the belief that the way in which this conflict is resolved may have direct personal consequences (promotion opportunities, pay increases) for you, or (because of the importance of the issue) significant consequences for the organization. A "low stake" conflict is not seen as threatening—either to your personal success or to the organization.

Agreement possibility. The extent to which you perceive that the parties have the capability and willingness to work together to reach a negotiated settlement is termed *agreement possibility*. Your evaluation of this dimension, which can range from low to high, may be influenced by factors such as the nature of the contested issue, the initial positions taken by the parties, their personalities, and the time available to resolve the dispute. A high level of *agreement possibility* is a prerequisite to an outcome that is satisfactory for both parties. On the other hand, the assessment of a situation as low in *agreement possibility* makes a competitive relationship almost inevitable.

Four Resolution Approaches

Win-lose. In a situation of low possibility for agreement but high stake in conflict, you may conclude that it is not possible to avoid a *win-lose* outcome. You will then attempt to force a settlement using position power (rank), superiority in bargaining skills or access to information, advantageous rules or

Window 2-3. (*Continued*)

procedures, and other devices to enhance your dominance of the situation. You seek to control the conflict resolution *process* and increase the likelihood of a personally favorable *outcome.*

Acceptance. Some situations present you with a low stake in a dispute and few possibilities for agreement. When this occurs, you are unlikely to expend much energy in trying to resolve the differences that separate the parties, or even in using any available clout to assure a favorable outcome. Rather, you may be inclined to "let the chips fall where they may" and *accept* the inevitable consequences.

Adaptive compromise. *Compromise* reflects a desire to negotiate a desirable mix of gains and losses so that both sides are reasonably satisfied with the outcome. Two conditions encourage compromise. First, the presence of a "low stake" in the conflict makes it palatable for you to "split the difference" or make trade-offs. Second, the belief that an agreement is quite possible provides the encouragement to expend the necessary effort.

Problem solving. Where you feel that there is a good chance for agreement and simultaneously have a high stake in the outcome, the conditions are right for *problem solving*. This win-win approach requires not just a flexible pattern of give-and-take (as in the case of adaptive compromise), but cooperation and understanding to reach a mutually advantageous *solution* to the underlying problem.

The assessment of *stake in conflict* forces you to consider issues of defensive and aggressive reactions to situations, personal risk taking, and the balance between personal and organizational interests. From this, you may be stimulated to think about job or role expectations and the personal values that are brought to (and sometimes challenged by) the job. Too often the "heat of battle" doesn't permit such reflective thinking. It may also be revealing to explore your assessment of *agreement possibility*—not just the judgment of whether or not an agreement seems feasible, but how and why this conclusion was reached. Consideration of the inputs that were used in making this judgment may be a valuable learning experience in itself.

Another important product of Conflict Resolution Approaches and other window models described in this chapter is the realization that there are a variety of factors that may affect the choice of a strategy for handling a dispute. Like the others, this model deals with only two dimensions or sets of influences. Nevertheless, with thoughtful use—along with coaching and encouragement—you may actually outgrow the confines of the model and begin to consider a wider range of variables in making decisions.

Advantages of Using the Window. This window, like many others, has several potential advantages if it is used correctly. For example:

- It encourages you to specifically consider your implicit assumptions regarding whether or not you truly have a high stake in a particular conflict (some people may enjoy conflict and seek it out even if they are not personally involved).
- It stimulates you to "put yourself into the shoes of your opponent" by considering the range of options in which agreement is truly possible (again, some managers may fail to recognize or consider the potential grounds for adaptive compromise).
- It legitimizes the occasional use of an *acceptance* strategy, which may otherwise have negative connotations as inferior to the more active and aggressive strategies.
- Hopefully, it breaks you out of a *win-lose* mentality, in which you may automatically approach conflicts from the perspective of assuming the need for a winner and a loser.

The Grid in Action. "Grievance denied." Brena Lent, Director of Human Resources for Laxwell Pharmaceutical, stares at the words she has just written. It is the same response she has given in countless other cases, yet for some reason she feels uneasy. As she rereads the file, her thoughts wander back to her first job in personnel and the words of her mentor: "Just remember, when you're dealing with unions, if you don't win you lose." She wonders if union-management relations always have to be a *win-lose* proposition.

Brena reviews the facts of the case. She quickly concludes that this grievance, whichever way it is decided, is unlikely to be precedent setting and will have little monetary significance. It is also apparent that the case involves a fairly technical issue and does not challenge the basic values of either the union or the company. In fact, she feels a relatively low *stake in the conflict* and simultaneously senses that there is a high *agreement possibility*. Perhaps a solution (an *adaptive compromise*) can still be fashioned that will satisfy everyone!

Later that morning Bill Holliday, the chief union steward, receives a phone call from Brena Lent inviting him to an informal meeting to discuss the grievance. He had expected a quick denial of the grievance. "Why the meeting?" he wonders. "What is there to discuss?"

References

Baetz, Stephen. "I Win—You Win: Negotiating for Commitment." *Personnel Journal*, March, 1980, pp. 237–239.

Jandt, Fred E. *Win-Win Negotiating: Turning Conflict Into Agreement.* New York: John Wiley & Sons, 1985.

Walton, Richard E., and Robert B. McKersie. *A Behavioral Theory of Labor Negotiations: An Analysis of a Social Interaction System.* New York: McGraw-Hill Book Company, 1965.

2-4. The Prisoner's Dilemma

When individuals or organizations pursue their own goals, they sometimes end up actually cooperating with their competitors. They do this as a means for either increasing their returns or reducing their risk. Alternatively, they may engage in a modern-day version of a duel to the death—continuing the conflict until only one emerges victorious (a win-lose solution). The Prisoner's Dilemma exercise (along with Window 2-4) imitates the real-world choices that may confront organization members who have competing goals. It provides an opportunity to better understand the forces that influence decision makers to compete or cooperate.

Applying the Prisoner's Dilemma Window

Complex interpersonal relationships have often been studied through games or simulations. Game theory analyzes situa-

Window 2-4. The Prisoner's Dilemma.

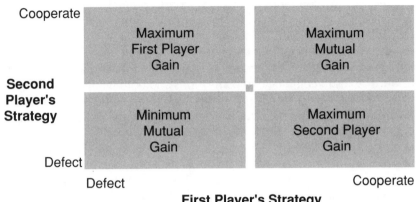

Source: Adapted from D. Luce and H. Raiffa, *Games and Decisions*, New York: Simon & Schuster, 1975, p. 95.

Dimensions

In the classic Prisoner's Dilemma, two parties whose interests are in conflict are presented with a situation where each can choose one of two behavioral alternatives. As the scenario begins, two criminal suspects are arrested and placed in separate cells. The district attorney is convinced they are both guilty, but does not have sufficient evidence to ensure a conviction. Consequently, the prosecutor gives each prisoner the option of confessing to the crime or refusing to confess and taking a chance on a trial. The scenario continues:

> If they both do not confess, then the district attorney states he will book them on some minor trumped-up charge such as petty larceny or illegal possession of a weapon, and they both will receive minor punishment. If they both confess, they will be prosecuted; but he will recommend less than the most severe sentence. If one confesses and the other does not, then the confessor will receive lenient treatment for turning state's evidence, whereas the latter will get "the book" slapped at him.*

It is clear that both prisoners will spend time in prison, but the length of their sentences will be determined by the strategy that each chooses to follow.

First player's strategy. The First prisoner has to decide, without knowing what the other criminal will do, whether to defect (confess) or stick with the

* D. Luce and H. Raiffa, *Games and Decisions,* New York: Simon & Schuster, 1975, p. 95.

Window 2-4. (*Continued*)

earlier agreement to cooperate with the second criminal (not confess). The situation creates complex choices for the prisoner. If he assumes the second prisoner has not confessed, the best outcome for the first prisoner would be to confess—the worst outcome for the second prisoner. But if perceptive, the first prisoner would assume that the second prisoner might have reached the same conclusion. The result could be two confessions and both would suffer long jail terms. With this realization the first prisoner would conclude that cooperation would provide the maximum mutual benefit and minimize individual risk.

Second player's strategy. The strategic alternatives available to the second prisoner are a mirror image of those open to the first prisoner. If one defects, the cooperating prisoner is severely penalized. If both defect, their confessions will result in lengthy sentences for both. The optimal solution then, is to cooperate with each other and stay with their previous decision not to confess. But even this conclusion is dependent on how creative, perceptive, and trustworthy the parties are (and perceive each other to be).

Effects of the Strategies

Maximum first player gain. The first prisoner defects (confesses) and receives the shortest possible sentence. The second prisoner continues to profess innocence (cooperates) and receives the longest possible sentence.

Maximum mutual gain. Where both prisoners cooperate with each other and do not succumb to the divide-and-conquer strategy of the district attorney, they both receive the shortest sentences. While each prisoner acting alone has an ideal scenario, this ideal outcome could be achieved only with substantial risk of the worst possible outcome.

Maximum second player gain. This is identical to the first outcome discussed, but viewed from the perspective of the second prisoner.

Minimum mutual gain. Both prisoners confess and receive fairly lengthy jail terms. Their incarceration is shorter than in the worst-case scenarios, but considerably longer than they would receive in the case of *maximum mutual gain.*

tions where the players in conflict can act independently in choosing from alternative behaviors. The Prisoner's Dilemma is an example of a mixed-motive or nonzero-sum game in which it is possible for either party to win or lose, but also for *both* to win or lose.

Games like Prisoner's Dilemma have been used extensively to explore behaviors—what people *actually* do when confronted with a particular set of circumstances. Simulations of this type, where the players in pursuing their own self-interests must consider both motives and behaviors of their opponent, have been widely used in the areas of negotiation and dispute resolution.

Research into game theory has generated a number of guidelines for players (e.g., "Don't assume there can only be one winner"; "Always reciprocate"; "Play to win the war, not the battle"). But these should not be viewed as rules of conduct in every situation. The size of the possible gain or loss, levels of trust, and a variety of other factors make each situation unique.

While the direct subject matter of this window may appear most relevant to managers under indictment or otherwise fearing incarceration, the Prisoner's Dilemma can readily be adapted to issues of competitive strategy or other important organizational problems. As an illustration, a dentist might use the Prisoner's Dilemma as a framework for helping to make the decision of whether to add evening office hours as a means to gain a competitive advantage over other dentists in the area. In a similar vein, two scientists might use this framework to consider the potential benefits and costs of pooling their efforts and sharing the fruits of research.

Through the study and use of the Prisoner's Dilemma, you can learn much about yourself as a negotiator and decision maker. You are forced to grapple with the interdependencies that exist even when differing goals might lead you to view others as competitors. As a player you may better understand that not only your actions, but competitors' reactions must be considered. As your awareness increases of the extent to which probabilities, trust, communications, perceptions, personalities, and ultimately the behaviors of the players affect outcomes, you may begin to look at decisions to defect or cooperate in a new light. In making decisions to concede, compromise, or stand fast, you will hopefully begin to see that opportunities for win-win solutions may exist where they didn't previously appear possible. Often, in the long run, compromise turns out to be the preferred strategy.

How to Use the Window. The Prisoner's Dilemma Window is very different from most others in this book. Its context is sharply distinct from settings in business or public organizations, and the roles portrayed are totally unique. Nevertheless, for those managers with the capacity to take a concept and adapt it to their own situations, it has powerful implications. You are encouraged to:

- Tally all the situations in which you don't have perfect information about the likely motives and behaviors of your competitors.
- Build multistep scenarios detailing your proposed strategies, the probable responses from your competitors, and the impact of the combinations.
- Recognize that you are not exclusively in control of your own fate, but that the actions of others may diminish or enhance your own outcomes.
- Break away from some of your inherent tendencies to compete, and consider instead the potentially desirable impact of cooperation (implicitly or explicitly) with your competitors.

The Grid in Action. As Bill Procter looks at November's sales figures, his disappointment is evident. Since buying the six Value-One grocery stores in his city last January, Procter has remodeled several of the stores and tried a variety of promotions in an effort to increase market share. Customer comments have been very positive, but market share is virtually unchanged. "There must be *some* way to get more shoppers to try Value-One," he thinks.

Double coupons! What about offering customers double-value rebates on manufacturer's coupons? It isn't a novel idea, but it might get new customers into Value-One stores. Bill knows that there has been some kind of informal agreement among area food store operators to avoid double-coupon promotions. The logic is evident. If one store offers to double the value of coupons, the others will probably feel compelled to follow suit.

In this scenario of minimum mutual gain, market shares will remain unchanged and profits will suffer. All the store owners will be losers.

Procter is confident that if he can just get new shoppers into his stores, many will become regular customers. If his competitors don't follow his lead or even if they react slowly, Value-One will maximize its gain in market share. Of course, there is always the risk that Bill's competitors will offer double value for coupons, and if *he* doesn't, then he will suffer. But clearly the lowest-risk, highest mutual-gain strategy is to conform to the informal agreement and resist the temptation to double coupons. Seeing the unpredictable implications of this marketing strategy, Bill reluctantly decides not to gamble on the coupon idea.

References

Hamel, Gary, Yves L. Doz, and C. K. Prahalad. "Collaborate With Your Competitors and Win." *Harvard Business Review*, January–February, 1989, pp. 133–139.

Lax, David A., and James K. Sebenius. *The Manager as Negotiator: Bargaining for Cooperation and Competitive Gain.* New York: The Free Press, 1986.

Neimark, Jill. "Tit for Tat: A Game of Survival." *Success*, May, 1987, pp. 62–65.

Chapter 3

Control

Nearly three decades ago, Douglas McGregor, in his now classic book *The Human Side of Enterprise*,[1] introduced the idea of Theory Y management thinking. Theory Y attempts to make you aware that employees not only are *capable* of self-direction and self-control within the work environment but *desire* to exercise control. In spite of this capacity, a large number of managers continue to ignore employees' personal need for control and their capacity to exercise control by practicing Theory X-related behaviors. Through this "X" approach to management, you create an organizational structure and a set of processes that closely control the behavior of your peers.

This chapter presents three windows into organizations that are concerned with the exercise of control within organizations. The first window explores the performance outcomes associated with the employee's exercise of personal control. The model suggests that employee performance depends not only on the type of control in the work environment, but also on the employee's capacity to *use* this control. The second window into organizations identifies two types of control—behavioral and output—commonly used by managers. The third window presented in this chapter identifies four different types of control and the conditions under which each should be used. Collectively, these models reinforce the message that you need to

1. Douglas McGregor, *The Human Side of Enterprise* (New York: McGraw-Hill Book Company, 1960).

analyze your situations (e.g., employee needs and capacities) and examine your options (e.g., types of control) before deciding how to proceed with control systems.

3-1. Personal Control Impacts

Although it has taken a variety of different forms over the years, one of the enduring themes in management literature is that offering employees greater control will have positive consequences for them and therefore for the organization. Research in psychology has supported this trend by demonstrating that individuals want control and that different levels of control affect a variety of human psychological and behavioral conditions. Although increasing employee control is expected to make employees more satisfied and more productive, no one has yet discovered whether employees can be given too much control. The model shown in Window 3-1 suggests that a person's performance depends not only on the type of control they have at work, but also on his or her capacity to use the control.

Applying the Personal Control Window

One of the more interesting recent areas of research is that of personal control. Whereas traditional management approaches have emphasized the ways in which you should control your subordinates, interest in personal control emphasizes the innate motivational need for control which most people possess. Current understanding suggests that all people—to lesser or greater degrees—have a desire to see themselves in positions of control. Thus, the focus is on enabling them to satisfy their particular need rather than limiting and constraining what they can do. In fact, the approach taken by many organizations that limits the control of workers may reduce their perceived control enough to cause dissatisfaction and decreased performance.

If organizations continue to limit control, then a state of *learned helplessness* may occur. In this state people learn that their actions are independent of outcomes. For example, they can come to believe that whether or not they work hard on their tasks, they will be equally unsuccessful and will also receive the same reward. This state of helplessness may not only occur in

Window 3-1. Personal Control Impacts.

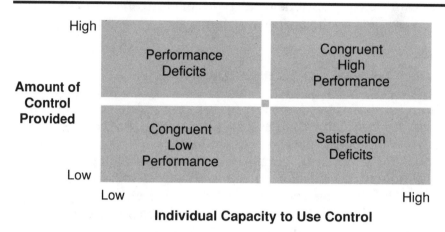

Source: Adapted from Max H. Bazerman,"Impact of Personal Control on Performance: Is Added Control Always Beneficial?" *Journal of Applied Psychology*, Vol 67, No. 4 (August 1982), pp. 472–479.

Dimensions

Amount of control provided. This dimension represents the amount of personal control that the individual perceives himself or herself as having. The most important part of this dimension concerns the fact that control, here, is a perception. For example, observers may believe that a CEO has a large amount of control over a corporation, but in reality the CEO finds that because he has no say over his schedule, what happens in the organization, and customer reaction to his products, he perceives himself as having no control. His behavior is determined by his perception, not necessarily the perceptions of others.

Individual capacity to use control. This dimension refers to the amount of control a person believes that he or she can use. Not all people believe that they want or can use control. Some people want more and more control, whereas others may want very little.

Personal Control Conditions

Performance deficits. Despite the perception that they possess a large amount of control, when employees have a low capacity to use control there is some surplus of control. This surplus may be a constant reminder to them that they are unable to accomplish some of the things they desire. This puts unwanted

Window 3-1. (*Continued*)

pressure on them that, in turn, can have a negative effect on performance. Thus, despite the general admonition to increase their control, if you give employees too much control you can actually decrease their level of performance.

■ **Congruent-high performance.** If employees have a high capacity to use control and perceive themselves as provided with a large amount of control, then there is some congruency. Employees here are expected to perform at a high level. We suggest that this is the optimal situation for the organization. Employees in this quadrant are expected to perform at the highest levels.

■ **Congruent-low performance.** In this quadrant the relationship between the individual's capacity to use control and the amount of perceived control provided is also congruent. However, in this situation, the individual has a comparatively low capacity to use control and the organization matches this capacity by providing little control. These employees should see that they can accomplish their tasks, but that the tasks they accomplish are not as ambitious as those in the congruent-high performance condition. Thus, the performance for employees in this group should lie between *performance deficits* and the *congruent-high* performance condition.

■ **Satisfaction deficits.** When employees have a high capacity for control but perceive themselves as being provided only a low level of control, performance should also suffer. In this state of undercontrol, they are not being permitted to use all of their desires for control. Although they see a link between their actions and the tasks they accomplish, they undoubtedly feel unsatisfied and unhappy at work.

situations like those described in quadrant 4, but may explain why people come to have a low capacity to use control (such as in quadrants 1 and 3).

Most organizations make decisions about participation by weighing two factors: the need to treat employees well and to involve them in decision making; and the common managerial fear that relinquishing control to employees results in decisions worse than those the manager would make and also undermines the manager's position. This window suggests that it is generally desirable to increase people's perceptions of their control. It also suggests that you can provide some people with more control than they can utilize and thereby undermine their performance.

In making certain that control can be used, there are two practical implications. First, you need to discuss the issue of control with employees. You need to ask your subordinates about their wishes to control other employees and/or to have a greater sense of accomplishment in day-to-day tasks. They may need jobs with greater responsibility or even more help in accomplishing existing tasks. In all cases the key is to provide people with the opportunity to believe that their deliberate actions have the intended consequences. Second, as organizations try to increase employee control, they should probably do so in an incremental fashion. If the organization starts to give employees a large amount of control too rapidly, it risks overwhelming the people with control. By slowing increasing control, you have a much better chance of keeping employees' control capacity congruent with their perceived control. The sense of accomplishment at each stage should lead to greater capacity, which in turn should enable them to utilize more control.

When to Use the Window. There are several occasions when you will find it useful to apply the Personal Control Impacts model. Asking yourself questions about an individual's capacity to use control and the amount of control currently provided as well as asking the subordinate about these two issues will help achieve a congruence between his or her need for control and the amount of control exercised under the following conditions:

- A new task (project) comes along and needs to be assigned to someone.
- A decision is reached to increase the level of employee involvement and the amount of participation in organizational activities.
- There is an effort to redesign employee jobs to achieve higher levels of job enlargement and job enrichment.
- There is an opportunity to replace the existing assembly-line technology with a work station-based technology and the concomitant use of autonomous work groups.

Each of these conditions calls for increased personal control and therefore a need to assure a proper match between the individual's capacity to use control and the amount of control provided.

The Grid in Action. Randy Boyer was recently hired by Applied Technology Innovations as Executive Vice-President of Marketing. In his new position, he has to directly supervise four senior vice-presidents. After two meetings with these four people, he has begun to feel that something is wrong. Two of his subordinates appear to be functioning very well; however, serious problems have appeared with the other two.

The first vice-president appears very bored at all meetings. When Randy meets with her, she complains that she just doesn't have enough responsibility and the work is too monotonous. Further, she indicates that she really wants to do more interesting work but that whenever she has made proposals to her previous boss, he has summarily dismissed them and has told her that she is doing a great job.

The second vice-president appears to be completely overwhelmed. Whenever his name comes up at meetings, he turns red and talks about how overwhelmed he is. Rather than wanting more work, he is increasingly delegating his own work to subordinates. Because this delegation means that he has less control over how the work is done, he finds himself getting more and more nervous at work.

Randy concludes that the control perceived by the first vice-president is substantially under her capacity. He immediately gives her more responsibility and tasks to perform. As she accomplishes these tasks, he gives her feedback on how well she has done. For the second vice-president, Mr. Boyer decides that he has a low capacity to use control and that he has been provided too much control. In this case Randy reduces his control by removing some responsibility and allows him to perform his day-to-day work. In both cases there is an immediate positive response.

3-2. Control Methods

A primary concern of organizations is the need to control. The traditional view of control is that it is a process in which the organization monitors employees and their output. The results of this monitoring are compared to some standard that was established during the planning process. The observed behavior and output are then judged as to whether or not they are appropriate. Finally, management provides some kind of selective reward or makes changes based upon these comparisons.

Two common types of control are behavioral control and output control (see Window 3-2). In behavioral control, management attends to the actions of its members, judges how correct these are, and either rewards or changes them. In contrast, in output control, management examines the output of its members. When the output matches some standard, members are rewarded; when output is not consistent with the criteria, organizations make changes. Whether management exercises behavioral control or output control depends on the information available.

Applying the Control Methods Window

Practicing managers need to be aware that they cannot exercise all types of control in all situations. Despite their best intentions to have good control over all components of the organization, the nature of the work itself often dictates which of the four kinds of control is appropriate.

How do you set up control mechanisms within your organization? Very frequently, you look at the way things have been controlled in the past as the best evidence for ways to control future activities. However, it is possible that these controlling mechanisms may be inappropriate. For example, if you use *behavioral* control in situations where only *rituals* can be assessed, then there is need for a change. The first thing that you need to do is to determine whether you know how tasks are performed. Second, you need to determine whether *output* measures are available.

Based on the information, precise control mechanisms can be imposed. The control mechanisms, in turn, have implications for selection and training. In the case of the foreign service, a large amount of resources are placed in the selection process. There is a need for individuals who are extremely capable of the desired ceremonial and ritualistic behaviors—without the normal supervision; that is, since the usual control mechanisms cannot be implemented, management must rely

Window 3-2. Control Methods.

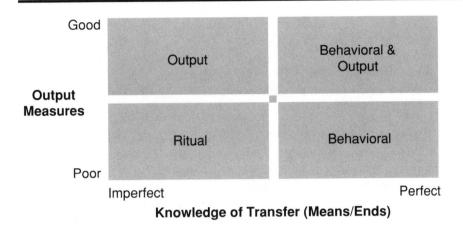

Source: Adapted from "The Relationship Between Organizational Structure and Organizational Control," by William G. Ouchi, published in *Administrative Science Quarterly*, Vol. 22, No.1 (March 1977), p. 98 by permission of *Administrative Science Quarterly*. © 1977 by Cornell University.

Dimensions

Knowledge of transfer. In order to control behaviors, the organization and its members must have some knowledge of the means by which outputs are accomplished; that is, the way in which objects are altered to become outputs varies. Only if the means of transferring objects is known, can supervisors achieve control over the behavior of subordinates. The knowledge ranges from perfect knowledge to imperfect knowledge.

Output measures. The degree to which there exist reliable and valid measures of the desired outputs influences the use of output control. Often the output is fairly easy to assess. However, in cooperative projects, it is sometimes more difficult to discern the output attributable to one person. These measures range from good to poor.

Four Control Methods

Output. In this quadrant, the organization has good measures of the output, but only imperfect knowledge of the transformation process from means to ends. Two examples of organizations fitting in this box are life insurance firms or advertising agencies. In both cases management has a clear measure of the agency's output, while a picture of how this output was achieved is much more ambiguous. Under these conditions organizations should control by focusing primarily on outcomes.

Window 3-2. (*Continued*)

Ritual. In this quadrant the organization and its members possess neither the knowledge of the transfer of the means to ends, nor outcome measures. This is the most difficult box to control. Here there are no objective means to facilitate the control of behavior as outcomes. Organizations neither know that the behaviors are correct, nor are they aware of what output is desired. In this situation only ceremonial or ritualized control is possible.

Behavioral and output. In this quadrant management has perfect knowledge of how means are changed to ends, and it also has good measures of the ends themselves. Because the organization can focus on either the process or the outcome, it can choose either behavioral or output control. Organizations such as those utilizing an assembly line are good examples, because it is really not important which area they choose to monitor. When correct behaviors ensure certain consequences, organizations can focus on either outcomes or behaviors.

Behavioral. Finally, in the last quadrant, organizations have perfect knowledge of the transformation process, but find that only poor measures of output are available. The double play combination in baseball provides a good example for this condition. Although the management of a baseball team has a good measure of the team's double plays, it is difficult to have an adequate measure of the output of a single player; that is, it is difficult to assess the unique contribution of a single player (e.g., the shortstop). On the other hand, the manager does have the ability to monitor the precise behaviors of each member of the double play combination. The reliance on behavioral control in this situation is evident in the number of times teams practice double plays in spring training.

on these persons to exercise the appropriate behaviors and to achieve the goals. The emphasis on selection is critical for a second reason: If these persons commit mistakes in their actions and achieve an undesired outcome, the problem may be uncorrectable.

Using the Window. This window enables you to define four different control strategies—*output, ritual, behavioral,* and a *behavioral/output* combination. In addition to this classification, the window provides insight that can facilitate the *review* of existing control systems in an attempt to answer the question Are we employing the appropriate control system?

The grid can also be used as an aid for the *design* of a new control system. As a design facilitator, you can employ the model when:

- The organization takes on a new set of activities that might accompany the production of a new product or the delivery of a new service.
- The organization adopts a new technology for the delivery of an existing product/service.

Both of these conditions provide the opportunity to examine the nature of output measures and knowledge about the transformation process. These two assessments can serve as a guide to the selection and placement of a control system.

The Grid in Action. Matt Hence has just been hired as the management consultant to provide guidance about control mechanisms to a new specialty steel company. This company has been in existence for only one and one-half years, but serious problems are increasingly in evidence. For example, managers find that they have no idea what the finished products are supposed to look like; they cannot tell their subordinates how to do their work; they cannot reward their subordinates contingently because they cannot determine who has and who has not performed well; the accountants cannot determine how money is disbursed; orders for raw materials are issued irrationally—sometimes they are late and sometimes twice as many things as necessary are ordered. Even a cursory look shows Matt that there are virtually no controls in effect.

Matt immediately sits down with all levels of management to assess what work needs to be done. He carefully describes each job, the output of each job, and how the job is to be performed. When there is no consensus, he restructures the working order to be clear what work needs to be done. Finally, he sits down with all managers to go over the information he has collected.

In general, he finds that most of the workers are paid on an hourly basis and there is both excellent information about the transfer of raw materials into the finished goods and very precise measures of the output. In fact, because the product is highly specialized, these output measures are critical. Matt recommends that the organization can implement controls over either the *behavioral* controls or *output* controls, but because of the importance of the output, it emphasizes *output* controls. The company begins a program of monitoring the quality of its products and finds that many of the problems begin to disappear.

3-3. Control Types

Although many people are anxious to perform well in their organizations, there are rarely assurances that all people will work in the desired ways. You thus have two important missions: to develop short- and long-term plans and to direct the activities of others to make certain that they work in the best interest of the organization. Obviously, there are a variety of different reasons people do not perform in the optimal manner, including personal limitations and poor goal congruence between personal or group goals and organization goals. When people do not perform in an appropriate manner, problems may range from small difficulties in performance to organizational failure. Whatever the source, though, you need to implement control mechanisms to increase the likelihood that individual performance will proceed according to your plans. In Window 3-3, Kenneth Merchant from Harvard University describes the different types of control and the appropriate conditions under which each type of control should be used.

Application of the Types of Managerial Control Window

The research on control is one of the most basic and enduring topics in management. It is quite clear that all managers fear losing control—some worry about losing power, but many correctly believe that management must monitor what is occurring within the organization and behave accordingly. Similar to the discussion pertaining to the other windows in this chapter, research and writing on control has consistently suggested that there are a variety of different ways in which you can influence

Window 3-3. Control Types.

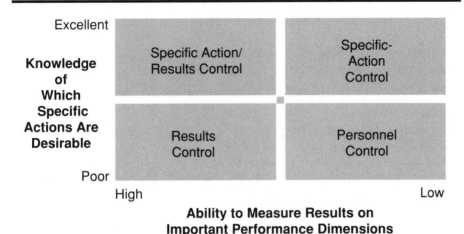

Source: Reprinted from "The Control Function of Management" by Kenneth A. Merchant, *Sloan Management Review,* Summer 1982, pp. 43–55, by permission of the publisher. Copyright © 1982 by the Sloan Management Review Association. All rights reserved.

Dimensions

Ability to measure results on important performance dimensions. This dimension refers to the degree to which you can assess the desired results effectively. Four features of these results-oriented measurements identified are that (1) they must assess the results that the organization really wants, (2) they must be very precise, (3) they must be made on a timely basis, and (4) they must be as objective as possible. The ability to measure results can range from high—where each of these is present—to low—where any or all these features are not present.

Knowledge of which specific actions are desirable. Rather than dealing with the outcome of the employees, this dimension refers to the degree to which you are aware of the specific behaviors that are considered important. This dimension can range from excellent to poor—you can be very much aware of which behaviors you wish to see exhibited by your subordinates, or you can have very poor knowledge of which subordinate behaviors are desirable. Often the desired behaviors are very clear to you, for example, on a production line. However, in jobs that emphasize creativity and innovation, such as those in design areas, the specific desired behaviors are not nearly so clear.

Window 3-3. (*Continued*)

Four Targets of Managerial Control

■ **Specific action/results control**. When managers within organizations have the ability to measure the results of desired performance dimensions and when they also possess excellent knowledge of the specific actions desired, they have a choice of good control tactics. Specifically, you can attempt to control *specific action and/or results*. There are three ways of controlling specific *actions*. First, you can attempt to limit the frequency of undesirable behaviors. Behavioral constraints, such as security guards and separation of duties, are designed to limit the possibility of undesirable *actions* or at least to reduce the likelihood of their occurrence. Second, *action* accountability is a feedback system in which subordinates are held accountable for their behaviors. Work rules, policies and procedures, and descriptions of rules of conduct are examples. Third, preaction review entails monitoring the behavior of others before they complete their activities. These observations can be accomplished by such activities as direct supervision, formal planning reviews, and budget reviews.

You also have the option of focusing on the control of results. Employees are held responsible for accomplishing certain things. In order for this to succeed, the organization must define the results, measure performance on these dimensions, and provide rewards contingent on this performance.

■ **Results control**. In the second quadrant the ability to measure *results* on the important dimensions is high, but you can obtain only a poor knowledge of the desired specific actions. In this quadrant you should attempt to control *results*. Examples of *control of results* include standards for the organization, budgets, and management by objectives.

■ **Specific-action control.** When you have excellent knowledge of the desirable *specific actions* but low ability to assess results of the important dimensions, the organization is limited to *specific-action control*. As indicated, you have a choice of using behavioral constraints, action accountability, and/or preaction review.

■ **Personnel control**. Finally, when the ability to assess results of important performance dimensions is low and when you have only a poor knowledge of which actions are desirable, then control of personnel is most appropriate. In this type of control, the organization relies on the personnel who are involved to perform at the highest level for the organization. Three general types of *personnel control*, are identified. In the first type of control, the capabilities of personnel are upgraded by selection, training, and/or reassignment. In the second type of *personnel control*, you attempt to improve communication. The aim here is to clarify expectations and to provide information for better coordination. Finally, in the third type of *personnel control*, peers are encouraged to control each other. This type of control may be manifest by increasing cohesiveness of work groups and by sharing goals.

the behavior and activities of your employees. Research and writing have concentrated on describing these specific ways of monitoring employee behaviors, the results of employee actions, and the changes that can be made based on these behaviors and results. Naturally, problems often result from control systems. These include poorly defined plans, biased performance appraisal systems, rigid organizational structures, arbitrary budgets, resistance to change by employees, and erroneous reporting of information. Despite the best attempts by management, any of these can undermine even the most carefully developed control system.

The grid helps you decide on a control mechanism in two ways. First, it focuses your attention on two important dimensions: the knowledge of the desirable actions and your ability to measure performance dimensions. After focusing on these dimensions, you can implement the important control systems.

Specifically, this window outlines a series of questions you can ask in order to determine the feasibility of different types of control. First, are other people involved in deciding upon the control mechanisms? The grid does not really indicate what should be done in the event of a group decision. Second, can you avoid people, for example, through an automation process? If you cannot, then you must ask additional questions. Third, can you rely on people? If the answer is yes to either of these questions, or the next question, Are you able to make subordinates reliable? then personnel controls are feasible. Fourth, you must ask if you have specific knowledge of which actions are desirable and whether you can ascertain whether these actions occurred. If the answer to both questions is yes, then specific action controls are feasible. Finally, if you determine that you know which results are desirable and that you are able to measure results, then results controls are feasible.

Using the Window. Managing consists, in part, of planning and controlling. There are several instances when this model, or one similar to it, ought to be applied. For example:

- You review an existing plan. You should also review the control system that has been designed to accompany it.
- You update existing plans (e.g., short-range plans, strategic plans, budgets). Pay attention to the review and updat-

ing of the control systems that were designed to monitor progress toward them.
- You create a plan for a new organizational behavior (venture, activity). Create a control system to accompany the introduction of the plan.

In each of these situations, Kenneth Merchant recommends that you examine the type of information available to you and that you pay attention to the design and implementation of the appropriate type of control system. This window attempts to highlight the importance of designing a control system congruent with both your ability to assess the desired results effectively and the degree to which you are aware of those behaviors that lead to the desired results.

The Grid in Action. Mary Jones, who manages a construction business, is well able to control the construction workers who are building the new corporate headquarters for XNY Technology. She has worked closely with the architect and therefore knows that everything about the project is being done perfectly. Additionally, having been in the business for the last twenty years, she is acutely aware of everything her workers are doing. Thus, she has implemented both *specific-action* and *results* control.

The problem arises with her salespeople who are bidding on other projects. Mary knows that it often take years to reach a final resolution to this process. A salesperson may be exhibiting all of the necessary behaviors and yet find that for reasons outside his control a contract is awarded to another company. Clearly, she could give bonuses to salespeople who are awarded big contracts, but the time delay between these contracts makes this impractical. Thus, Mary has neither the knowledge of specific, desirable actions nor the ability to measure results on important performance dimensions in a timely manner. Because of this, she decides to implement more *personnel controls.* She spends more time in selection, training, and assignment. Further, she establishes better communications with her salespeople and attempts to clarify her expectations. With this new approach, she acquires better control over the work of her sales staff and they are awarded new contracts.

Chapter 4

Crisis Management

Recent events have firmly embedded images of corporate crises and disasters in the minds of management executives and the public. The sudden discovery in 1979 of toxic waste contamination at Love Canal haunted the businesses that had deposited the waste years before. The Tylenol poisoning in 1982 put decades of consumer trust in Johnson and Johnson on the line. The release of deadly gas at Union Carbide's Bhopal, India, plant killed 3,000 people in 1984 and threatened that company's survival. The Exxon tanker's 1989 oil spill off the coast of Alaska had far-reaching environmental impact and organizational consequences. But are there any broadly applicable lessons to be drawn from these dramatic and seemingly unique episodes?

A respected group of management scholars/consultants argue that there are lessons, and they have begun to develop general principles for comprehensive crisis management. *Crises* are events that demand specific, usually nonroutine actions to counter threats to an organization's most important requirements for survival (e.g., profitability, legitimacy, credibility, and freedom of action). Crisis-triggering events can range from a sudden chemical plant accident to the gradual unfolding of a substantial worker health or product safety problem over an extended period of time. These and other types of crises have common roots in managerial failures to diagnose and respond to potential threats from both within and outside the organization. Vulnerabilities to those threats are increasing, due to

45

greater interdependencies between a company's core technology and its external environment, including both direct stakeholders (e.g., customers using the company's products) and indirect ones (e.g., residents adjacent to its production facilities).

The "vulnerability" grid that begins this chapter shows how you can identify crises that could result from a variety of factors. A second and closely related "Window of Opportunities" grid shows how crises can be avoided or their impacts reduced through strategic prevention and preparation efforts. Different organizational styles of crisis diagnosis can support or weaken strategic prevention efforts, as addressed in a third window. The final grid attacks the microlevel problem of how individual decision pathologies under crisislike pressures can contribute to failed organizational-level coping.

4-1. Vulnerability to Corporate Crises

Window 4-1 identifies the organization's "portfolio" of potential threats as the first step in comprehensive crisis management. Organizations are as much the cause of the breakdowns leading to crises as is the apparently uncontrollable external environment. An organization's potential for different types of crises can be identified using this grid, and examples of each will be provided. This identification of vulnerability is the first step in the process of strategic crisis prevention and management.

Applying the Vulnerability to Corporate Crises Window

There are two key concepts for use of the vulnerabilities grid and the others in this chapter. First, you need to identify the dangerous potential conflict between the organization's activities (products, technology, responsibilities) and sources of potential crises. Organizations involved in personal health products, for example, must guard against unpredictable acts of product terrorism and sabotage, which create the most potent type of crisis for them. But a high-technology company producing custom products (e.g., shuttle booster engines or aircraft) has the greatest crisis fit between reliability problems of product

Window 4-1. Vulnerability to Corporate Crises.

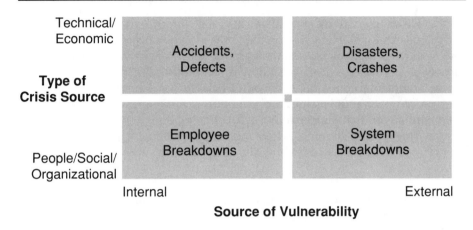

Source: Paul Shrivastava and Ian I. Mitroff, "Strategic Management of Corporate Crises," *Columbia Journal of World Business*, No. 22 (Spring 1987), pp. 5–11.

Dimensions

Source of vulnerability. This dimension identifies the sources of organizational crises as either internal or external. Managers often attribute sudden or chronic threats, and the demands to counter damages, solely to the external environment (e.g., consumers, unions, environmental watchdogs, terrorists, and governmental agencies). However, there is substantial evidence that the seeds of crises are often sown within organizations that fail to act on internal weaknesses, errors of omission, and other problems.

Type of crisis source. This dimension identifies the major types of breakdowns, either internal or external to the organization, that eventually allow crises to erupt. A technical/economic failure, such as a faulty product design (e.g., the Pinto gas tank) is distinguished from a people/social/organizational failure, such as operator errors in using technology at nuclear power plants (e.g., the Chernobyl accident).

Four Organizational Threats

Accidents, defects. Major industrial accidents characterize crises that result from technical/economic breakdowns within the organization itself, as do computer breakdowns and consumer injuries due to product defects. Bankruptcy is an example of the even broader concept of crisis caused by internal technical breakdowns.

Window 4-1. (*Continued*)

Disasters, crashes. Natural disasters (e.g., floods, earthquakes) are easily recognized external/technical-economic breakdowns causing crises. It is not as obvious how conditions outside the corporation can aggravate eventual crisis impacts by becoming system breakdowns. An industrial accident can interact with environmental conditions to become a disaster, for example, when a factory fire turns into a communitywide conflagration due to overcrowded land uses and lack of public fire-fighting capabilities. An emerging crisis potential of this sort exists in Third World countries where the next development project can cause broad collapse of ecological systems due to cumulative abuse (e.g., the Amazon region).

System breakdowns. External social breakdowns are exemplified by terrorism and sabotage (leading to organizational culpability) and kidnappings (leading to organizational loss of autonomy). More traditionally recognized threats to corporate survival are labor strikes or boycotts by interest groups for environmental and political reasons. Multinational corporations face the broadest case of this crisis type when major political/cultural changes take place in the host country (e.g., the Iranian revolution or the efforts by students to "democratize" China).

Employee breakdowns. Internal social/organizational breakdowns arise from a wide variety of incompetencies that include miscommunication or suppression of critical information (e.g., the Challenger disaster) and failures to screen out employees who become saboteurs (as in the Tylenol poisoning) or engage in illegal activities (e.g., insider trading). A general failure of organization members to adapt to changing circumstances is a broad incompetency that can also be legitimately included here.

---

technology and any failures of the communication systems between product engineers, managers, and customers. The Window of Vulnerabilities presents a fuller picture of all quarters in which you should attend to potential or emerging crises. Within that framework what is the organization's "portfolio" of potential types of crises?

The second key concept is the need for your organization to guard against the cultural and personal filters that *prevent* the identification of the risks of crises, a problem expanded on later in this chapter. In sum, organizations can create many of their own disasters through failing to identify their vulnerabilities.

Crises do not "happen" to organizations. Organizations are inevitably vulnerable to crises because of interdependencies between their core technology (products/services) and the environments in which sales or services must be provided. Any case of successful competitive fit also creates the potential for a crisis.

You should also recognize that not all crises "happen" to the organization or originate in the external environment. Even if the triggering event happens "outside," an organization should have been aware that it could happen and should have made preparations to lessen its impacts when it does happen. Crises often have impacts on the organization's external stakeholders as well (customers, suppliers, the general public). The crisis that happens to a company also is happening to other parties that depend on the organization.

Finally, you should identify a portfolio of at least one potential crisis type from *each* part of the window of vulnerabilities, even though the greatest crisis "fit" may come from one specific source/type. There is a great tendency to dwell only on crises that constitute *internal technical/economic* breakdowns such as plant accidents and product safety defects. Although important, and vivid, those breakdowns are only part of an organization's crisis portfolio. Such failures may only be the end result of internal incompetencies (such as operator errors) and can also result from external/social breakdowns, as in the case of criminal product tampering, against which the organization failed to be sufficiently vigilant and for which it is ultimately held responsible (whether fairly or not).

In some cases the magnitude of impacts from an internally based technical/economic accident may be the surprise result of an internal defect interacting with an external system protodisaster. An example would be the case of an ecological disaster resulting from an organization's activities that provides the "last straw" in a history of contamination for which others were previously responsible.

Using the Window. Approximately 50 percent of the Fortune 500 largest companies do *not* have a crisis-management plan in place, even though the vast majority of them recognize that a crisis affecting them might occur. In light of this, the Vulnerability to Corporate Crises Window should be used to:

- Convince other managers in the organization of the importance of engaging in strategic planning for crisis management. Discussion of the window might help a group of managers identify areas of potential threat to the company, better understand the contributing forces, and dramatize the possible impact to those who don't see the need.
- Differentiate between the areas of crisis vulnerability, guiding you to a better analysis of whether the likely sources are internal or external, and their nature.
- Help construct a portfolio of potential crises affecting not only the larger organization, but also each of its major work units.
- Stimulate in-house assessment and discussions of the likelihood that each type of crisis might occur such that reasonable probability estimates and economic assessments of the consequences could be derived.
- Encourage the development of contingency plans detailing the organization's probable response to each major crisis.

The Grid in Action. In the early 1980s a crisis-management consultant is asked to analyze a major oil corporation's crisis vulnerabilities in its Alaskan operations. The consultant knows that internal/technical points of vulnerability—such as faulty shipping facilities or lack of oil spill containment equipment—are only the superficial and final weaknesses leading to a crisis. Internal/people factors can be the *real* cause of either an accident or poor preparations to deal with one. Will emergency containment crews know when to respond quickly? Are personnel at all points in the shipping process—pipeline, ship, and shore—reliable and will they stay reliable over many years? Most important, are executive decision makers prepared to support effective crisis-management preparations over the long term?

Should a spill occur, however unlikely that is in the state-of-the-art Alaskan oil system, factors outside the business could prove crucial to swift and effective crisis resolution. First, the external-technical systems necessary to quickly fight a spill must be on-line, adequate, and willing to cooperate. That includes Alyeska, the oil-company consortium responsible for first-line spill defense. As one of only seven companies funding Alyeska, the subject company needs to know that its personnel and resources will be adequate. Also vital are the resources of the state and federal government (particularly the Coast Guard) and, in a worst-case situation, the president of the United States, who has the power to order major outside support to manage a spill. Futhermore, the Coast Guard's radar navigation and other services are also crucial to preventing accidents at sea in the ecologically fragile Prince William Sound.

The consultant moves on to consider the threats to the company that could arise from external/social-organizational factors. Certainly many executives think of terrorism against the fragile pipeline as the prime culprit in this part of the vulnerabilities window. But the consultant must move beyond that. The greatest long-term threat to the oil firm, he concludes, is complacency about safety among state and federal government agencies, and a retreat from public sector commitments to handle an accident as a backup to Alyeska and the subject company itself. Looking over his portfolio of weak links again, the consultant notes how external complacency could promote blindness on the part of corporate executives years down the line. Less pressure on the corporation can lead to potentially disastrous cutbacks in crisis-response budgets at Alyeska, or loosening of personnel standards for critical individuals on the pipeline or even on the tankers plying Prince William Sound. As the consultant summarizes his analysis, he makes a final, vital note to the company: The greatest weaknesses in crisis-management planning is thinking that the unthinkable—a catastrophic oil spill—will never happen.

Reference

Pauchant, Terry C., and Ian I. Mitroff. "Crisis Prone Versus Crisis Avoiding Organizations: Is Your Company's Culture Its Own Worst Enemy In Creating Crises?" *Industrial Crisis Quarterly*, No. 2 (1988), pp. 53–63.

4-2. Crisis Prevention Strategies

Crises often appear to be surprise events that the organization is little able to prevent or prepare itself to cope with. This is a fatal misconception, however. There are many actions organizations can take before a crisis strikes to reduce its impacts and in some cases even prevent it. Window 4-2 describes the types of strategic actions that organizations can take to prevent and prepare to respond more effectively to crises with different characteristics. Possible actions range from minor internal adjustments to prevent mistakes, to strategies for organizational redesign where the goals include systematically reducing vulnerabilities to shocks and high-liability situations.

Applying the Crisis Prevention Window

Window 4-1 expanded the concept of crisis beyond accidents and technical glitches. This model expands the concept of action beyond one-time technical fixes. Its perspective guards against the fundamental paradox in corporate crisis preparations: The more invulnerable to crises an organization feels itself to be, the less prepared it usually is when calamity does strike. It is also a mistake to view crisis-prevention strategies as limited only to those actions internal to the organization. In some settings it may be crucial for the organization to make strategic investments in the crisis-handling capabilities of other organizations or even the general public (as in consumer education through risk communication). For example, that is what the Chemical Manufacturers Association has done since 1985 and the occurrence of the Bhopal/Union Carbide disaster. This trade group has undertaken a massive technical assistance effort—the Community Awareness and Emergency Response Program—that is attempting to improve the plant accident response abilities of local governments across the United States. Every effort at crisis prevention—through detection of vulnerabilities—can also contribute to swift and effective responses when the worst does happen. Employees given precrisis training can resist stress-induced errors in the real event, and managers involved in identifying likely crisis scenarios are more apt to avoid hasty and disastrous decisions.

Advantages of Using the Window. In the area of crises, as in medicine, "an ounce of prevention is worth a pound of cure." This window encourages you to:

- Focus on preventive management strategies. This directs

Window 4-2. Crisis Prevention Strategies.

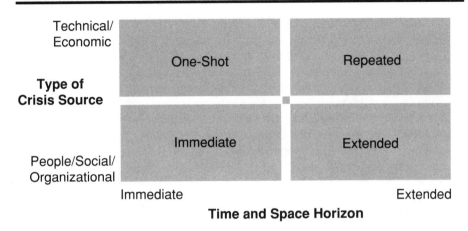

Adapted from: Ian I. Mitroff, Paul Shrivastava, and Firdaus E. Udwadia, "Effective Crisis Management," *Academy of Management Executive*, Vol. 1, No. 3 (1987), pp. 283–291.

Dimensions

Type of crisis source. Knowing the source of a crisis is a necessary step toward identifying strategic action opportunities. Technical/economic sources will involve plant, process, and product designs; production and quality control systems; formal decision procedures; and overall organizational design. People/social/organizational sources include the motivations, loyalties, conflicts, and attitudes of corporate stakeholders (e.g., employees, customers, competitors, regulators). Organizational crises are also likely to affect many of the unorganized individuals who surround the organization.

Time and space horizon. This dimension defines the location of the systems and people to which strategic actions must be directed. The immediate *time and space* environment means the operating systems and people that are *internal* to your organization. *Extended time and space* involves all of the organization's long-term relations with its environment, including customers, regulators, and the innocent victims or malevolent perpetrators of the organization's next crisis.

Crisis-Prevention Strategies

One-shot. These crisis-prevention strategies involve making a specific, one-time resolution of internal, technical/economic systems. The new genera-

Window 4-2. (*Continued*)

tion of tamper-resistant packaging sweeping most other industries in the years after the Tylenol crisis is a good example, as are any efforts to redesign a product that currently invites danger. Other actions that may be less obvious also fall in this area. They include tightening internal production quality controls, modifying plants and equipment to reduce accident potential, or installing chains of command to detect and act on immediate problems (such as poisoning). For example, fixing the O-ring on the NASA Space Shuttle boosters would have been a good *one-shot* (preventive) solution if the Challenger tragedy had never happened. A solution was needed to the chain-of-command problem that let interdependencies between technology, weather, and politics slip by without control to cause the disaster.

     ▩ **Repeated.** These recurrent technical/economic strategies require systemwide changes, rather than a *one-shot* application of specific technologies or system components. *Repeated* crisis-prevention strategies may require the design of entirely new generations of plants or equipment to alter the core technology of the corporation. They can also mean the divestiture of entire classes of products or activities that create too great a potential for crises. The creation of permanent crisis-planning and -management groups to identify and rehearse the worst case is also a repeated, long-term prevention strategy. In this case changes are made to the decision technology of your organization. Permanent crisis-management groups can also aid in swiftly responding to lessen the impacts of the crisis when it does happen. For example, Johnson and Johnson successfully managed the Tylenol crisis by swiftly pulling the product from shelves nationwide and providing continuous information to consumer groups and the press. The majority of companies in similar straits have responded wlth denials, delays, and strictly defensive postures, much to their eventual disadvantage. Every one of those latter organizations could have benefited from developing crisis-anticipation teams before the event actually occurred.

     ▩ **Extended.** These crisis-prevention and management strategies are aimed at external interdependencies with the organization's stakeholders and equally to the other individuals and organizations that may be affected by or create a crisis. One way to visualize *extended* crisis-prevention actions is to consider them as strategic investments in the infrastructure *outside* the organization. If a plant accident happens, such as accidental release of a toxic chemical in a community, are the local fire and police agencies competently prepared and equipped to warn and evacuate potential victims? If not, and if greater harm results, the company owning the facility will still receive the blame. Viewed that way, any effort to improve the community's own crisis-response capabilities ahead of time looks like a wise investment. Other extended strategies of this type include sponsoring mental health programs to identify potential psychotics,

Window 4-2. (*Continued*)

consumer education about product safety, political action groups to change regulatory environments, and special communication preparations for working with the media in a crisis.

Immediate. Prevention actions in the immediate people/social/organizational environment are primarily directed at employees. Crises can be created or amplified when key personnel cave in to stress, succumb to temptations to cut corners to gain personal advantage, or, in the extreme, engage in sabotage. Prevention and preparation in the immediate organizational environment include support for employees through precrisis and postcrisis counseling, training for handling stressful circumstances, enhanced security, and the identification of persons with tendencies toward destructive behavior. As with other approaches, any investment in crisis prevention or preparation in advance also pays dividends in the heat of the event itself.

your attention away from symptom-minimization or curative strategies.
- Incorporate a consideration of time frame into the crisis-prevention anaylsis. This forces you to consider not only forces just around the corner, but those on the far distant time/space horizon.
- Differentiate between four alternative strategies for preventing crises—*one-shot*, *repeated*, *immediate*, and *extended*.
- Consider alternative sources of crises and develop unique crisis-prevention strategies for handling each type.

The Grid in Action. Rocky Forrester is hired by an oil firm to implement a consultant's recommendations for strategies dealing with potential crises. He begins his analysis of prevention/management strategies for a catastrophic oil spill in the company's Alaskan operations with the most obvious actions: *one-shot*/technical fixes. Unfortunately, changing individual pieces of equipment or procedures is more often a treatment of the symptoms rather than the cause of an accident and often occurs only after the fact. In the early 1980s the Alaskan pipeline/tanker transport system represented the state of the art anyway. The question in Rocky's mind is whether or not the system will stay that way and be used properly over a long period of time. To pursue that question, he examines two adjacent cells of the crisis-prevention grid.

Maintenance of the shipping system from North Slope pipeline origins to tanker transports through the fragile Prince William Sound requires a strategy for repeated/technical-economic prevention efforts. Rocky decides to suggest that an executive safety/reliability committee be created. It will consist of top management from Alyeska (the multifirm consortium that runs the pipeline and emergency spill containment efforts), from the company's maritime operations responsible for the tankers plying the sound, and from other central divisions of the company. This is a modest first step toward keeping each of those key actors focused on the need for vigilance. If that group is faithful in its routine reviews of safety and preparedness, this step will also speed effective decision making among group members if a crisis does occur.

The systems and decision procedures are only as effective as the people involved, however. Rocky now considers actions to be taken in the area of immediate/people-organizational factors. An obvious danger of crisis lies in personnel who may not be competent to perform their jobs in sensitive operations that could trigger a spill, or worse, who might be psychologically unstable or drug-dependent. The challenge here is to ensure that personnel are given close scrutiny over the years ahead.

Rocky can see how the portfolio of crisis-management actions begins to work together: The executive-level multidivisional committee is critical to ensure that personnel policies, including crisis readiness and stress training, are maintained. In turn, the better the personnel are, the less likely a major catastrophe is but the better prepared the company will be to cope with one and minimize impacts. But one major area of prevention/coping strategy remains—the external/social environment. Rocky can see that most petrochemical firms have done little in this area except maintain public relations staffs, advertise in newspapers, and prepare to deal with the press if the worst happens. More can be done, however. If an oil spill does occur, for example, the rapid support of the U.S. government through the Coast Guard and by presidential disaster aid could be essential to limiting impacts, as would be actions by the state of Alaska. Will that added muscle be available when it is needed?

In fact, as budget priorities change (and especially if Alaskan oil operations are as routinely safe as everyone hopes), the great danger is that government will cut back on essentials like the Coast Guard navigational and sea-search systems that may be vital to preventing and containing the one-in-a-million disaster. Rocky makes notes to take this up with the company's top management as part of the overall crisis-management plan.

4-3. Organizational Styles of Crisis Management

Window 4-3 describes how organizations develop overall cultural biases and blinders toward recognizing needs for crisis prevention and preparedness. Use of this grid can help anticipate management reluctance to engage in preventive actions, and highlight areas of likely oversights.

Applying the Organizational Styles Window

Certain organizational cultures and biases in strategic thinking can breed "disaster by design" when they result in unwillingness to think about some types of crises—or any at all. *Inactive* organizations assume that their environment cannot hurt them, inviting surprises and catastrophes. The *reactive* organization is only slightly better prepared for one or a few types of crises. They believe that crises "happen" to them, and they focus on technical fixes to problems, not transformation of their relationship with the environment. *Preactive* organizations assume that their environment is in some way unique, because their strategies or products are novel. Though *preactive* organizations work to change those environments, they are often caught by surprise by old problems in new forms.

Only *interactive* organizations are maximal crisis managers. They attend to past and future crises, and they make both internal and external strategic investments to reduce the potential for calamities and to manage those that inevitably occur. For example, in the aftermath of the Bhopal accident, the U.S.

Window 4-3. Organizational Styles of Crisis Management.

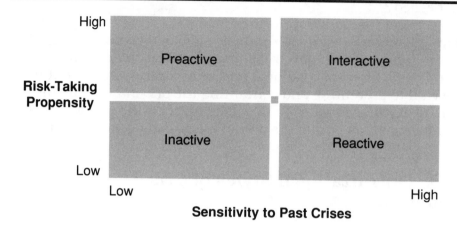

Source: Ian I. Mitroff and Will McWinney," Disaster by Design: And How to Avoid It, " *Training*, No. 24 (August 1987), pp. 33–38.

Dimensions

Risk-taking propensity. Organizations in protected environments (e.g., as regulated monopolies) and in declining markets tend to be strategically risk-averse. Sunshine industries (those that pioneer new technologies or markets) and organizations undertaking strategic renewal have a higher tolerance for risk in their choice of actions to achieve a "tight" environmental fit.

Sensitivity to past crises. This dimension defines the extent to which organizations pay heed to lessons of experience with crises. Insensitive organizations avoid evaluating their present decisions in light of past crises. Sensitive organizations attend to those lessons much more carefully.

Crisis Management Styles

Inactive. Risk-averse organizations that are insensitive to past crises are typically *inactive* crisis managers. A managerial focus on mere survival and minimal effort usually makes crises fatal to such organizations.

Reactive. Organizations that are risk-averse but dwell on crises that have already occurred in their industry are often *reactive*. Defensive over-sensitivity promotes elaborate planning for one narrow type of crisis, and calamitous surprise at new ones.

Window 4-3. (*Continued*)

▨ **Interactive.** Some organizations pay heed to past experience with crises, but they also manage their environments to prevent and respond to new types of crises. These interactive organizations develop human potential and safe systems through both internal and external actions.

▨ **Preactive.** Risk-seeking organizations that are excessively oriented toward the future are labelled *preactive.* Past crises are irrelevant old news to these typically high-technology market pioneers, which only tend to notice novel problems. They are unprepared for crises well-known in older industries.

Chemical Manufacturers Association undertook a massive effort to involve its member companies in open planning for safety with communities. As a result the industry was out ahead of congressional actions that sought to require such planning and it thereby won much public confidence.

When to Use the Window. An assessment of a company's style of crisis management can be done:

- When an organization is in its early development and growth stages and still seeking to establish an internal culture and identity. By making a conscious choice of its crisis-management style, it can guide its own actions toward that objective.
- When an organization begins to mature and gather some important history about itself and its competitors. This allows an examination of its sensitivity to past crises, either directly through its own experiences or indirectly through observation and analysis of the conduct of other companies.
- When a new CEO of a company is named, or when the company is acquired by another oganization. This provides a timely opportunity for reexamination of the company's explicit or implicit risk-taking propensity, which will have a dramatic impact on its overall style of managing crises.

- Just after a major crisis has occurred and been met with an organizational response.

Whether the crisis-management style proves effective or ineffective, the company's management team will undoubtedly want to engage in a detailed postmortem to identify what went well, what went poorly, and what areas could be improved in the future.

The Grid in Action. Issues surrounding crisis prevention can be the most difficult to attack for those advising organizations, like planning consultant Rocky Forrester. Rocky has already heard the arguments from the oil firm's top management: "Sure, there have been oil spills, but this is the best operation, and the chances are small." Nonetheless, Rocky's role is to look most critically at the organizational culture behind crisis-management assumptions. The company is not being *reactive* or *inactive.* Preparations for a spill—however little it is really expected—are still among the best in the world.

But Rocky knows that in Alaska the company is in the ironic position of being *preactive:* one that is so progressive that it discounts the calamities that have befallen its more careless or unlucky predecessors and competitors. All of the company's investments in the pipeline/tanker system minimize the possibility of an oil spill and maximize the response to one should it happen. Nevertheless, the attitude that oil spills are historical rather than potential future problem is the greatest threat of all in the consultant's mind. Furthermore, one cannot discount the importance of external relations in both minimizing chances of a spill (by keeping federal and state government support systems adequately funded) and containing the damage if one happens (by acting in concert with petrochemical industry crisis-response actions). These are all elements of an *interactive* culture of crisis management, which Rocky hopes to sell to management with his crisis-prevention and crisis-management recommendations.

4-4. Crisis Decision Errors

A thorough review of crisis management must consider the impacts of stressful and uncertain events on the decisions made by individual managers. The Crisis Decision Errors Window (Window 4-4) summarizes the problems of decision making that can occur as a result of stress, uncertainty, and their interaction.

Applying the Crisis Decision Errors Window

The first three windows of this chapter explored and attacked the complacency of organizations that fail to consider the potential crises that can strike them. That perspective is equivalent to one cell in the present window, where *adherence* by managers to a view that "it can't happen here" is the greatest problem of crisis decision making (before one happens). The problem of managerial behavior *during* crises has been studied for a long time, however.

Window 4-4 summarizes some additional perspectives. Strong psychological forces are at play when pressure to act and uncertainty interact. A desire to preserve your image (personal or corporate) consistent with past experience can lead to hasty decisions *(premature closure)* when demands are immediate. *Denial* is a process of false rationalization under the highest conditions of stress, while extreme *avoidance* occurs when decisions fail to be made because you have not accepted the need to act.

Using the Window. This window, despite focusing on decisional errors that you can make in crisis situations, can also stimulate you and your organization to examine some key processes. As a result, you should be better prepared if you are willing to do the following things:

- Make managerial selection decisions based partly on the candidate's potential for capable handling of crises. Key managers—for example, those in control of valuable resources or those managing dangerous operations—can be selected for their proven tolerance of stress and their ability to cope calmly with uncertainty.
- Appraise existing managers partly on the basis of their history of handling other organizational crises. If a pattern of dysfunctional behaviors such as *avoidance* or *denial* exists, it may be necessary to transfer these man-

Window 4-4. Crisis Decision Errors.

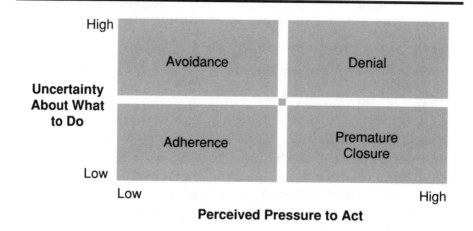

Reprinted from: "A Model of Crisis Perception: A Theoretical and Empirical Analysis," by Robert Billings, Thomas Millburn, and Mary Schaalman, published in *Administrative Science Quarterly,* Vol. 25, No. 2 (June 1980), pp. 300–316 by permision of *Administrative Science Quarterly.* ©1980 by Cornell University; and "Design for Crisis Decision Units," by Carolyn Smart and Ian Vertinsky, published in *Administrative Science Quarterly*, Vol. 22, pp. 640–657 by permission of *Administrative Science Quarterly.* © 1977 by Cornell University.

Dimensions

Perceived pressure to act. This dimension identifies an important aspect of stress on decision makers—the perceived need to move swiftly. A crisis is in part defined by how much pressure a decision maker believes there is to take action. The perception that pressure is high can make even small problems appear to be crises, while low perceived pressure can lead to inaction.

Uncertainty about what to do. The degree of uncertainty that decision makers have about what to do is a second factor that has great impact on managers under crisis conditions. Knowing in advance what to do can reduce the impacts of surprise, while high levels of uncertainty can make appropriate action difficult.

Major Decisional Errors

Adherence. When perceived pressure to act is low and uncertainty about what to do concerning problems is also low, *adherence* to the current course of action is a likely outcome. Unfortunately, this reaction has frequently led to crises like the Space Shuttle O-Ring disaster, which was brought on by a complacent management unwilling to diagnose potentials for calamity.

Window 4-4. (*Continued*)

Premature closure. When perceived pressure to act is high and uncertainty about what to do is low, you may *prematurely close* in on one response to a crisis. This failure to search for and evaluate a set of alternatives may prove harmful in the long run. Corporations that have reflexively "clammed up" to the public when accidents occur, for example, usually pay the price later in larger problems.

Denial. When pressure to act and uncertainty about what to do are both high, *denial* of the need to manage a crisis can take place. Refusals to consider product recalls are an example of this.

Avoidance. When pressure to act is low but uncertainty high, *avoidance* of the crisis predictably takes place. A well-known case of this is failure to confront needs for action when gradual financial deterioration builds into a terminal crisis for an organization.

agers to organizational units that are less subject to crises, or even (at the extreme) to terminate them.

- Establish special crisis-decision procedures and ad hoc groups that can be implemented in conditions where stress and uncertainty could induce severe problems. For example, the Kennedy administration is often credited with using this strategy during the 1962 Cuban Missile Crisis, when the key decision makers were purposely exposed to a wide range of opinions and relentless cross-examination of their assumptions prior to finalization of their response.

The Grid in Action. This illustration continues the exploits of Rocky Forrester, a crisis-management consultant working with a major oil company. Following his earlier advice, a standing executive crisis-managment committee (CMC) was set up for the company's Alaskan North Slope/Prince William Sound oil-shipping operations. The committee consists of key managers from Alyeska, the corporate consortium for pipeline operations/spill containment, the company's maritime and production divisions, and other units of central management. At the first CMC meeting, Rocky begins the process of making these managers learn to think and live the process of crisis decision making.

"A Mayday has just been sent to the Coast Guard from an oil tanker in the Prince William Sound," says Rocky, "indicating that the captain believes they may have breached the hull and are spilling oil. The Alyeska office at Valdez port has been routinely notified." "Let's wait and see what happens before we jump at this," one CMC member from central quickly says. "But if it is a significant spill," says a member from operations, "we need to get Alyeska off the dime and out there into the sound." "But we don't want to panic anybody if it's a minuscule spill— you know that happens all the time. Think of the bad press we'll get if it's a false alarm. I think you're closing in too fast on this."

"Yes, but if it is bad, waiting around could just make it worse. Those are calm seas now, but what about tonight?" "We should be talking to Alyeska now, not arguing," a new voice pops in. "We really don't know what we're dealing with yet, and maybe they don't either."

"This," says Rocky, "is exactly the uncertainty you have to cope with. Just imagine what it would be like without this CMC. Remember, the same thing is going on at Alyeska thousands of miles from you. The last suggestion may be the best immediate action to take: An executive from central should be on the scene to be a sounding board for the crew there and provide clear backward communications to the CMC at all levels. This also minimizes the likelihood of crisis decision errors, such as *denial, avoidance,* and *premature closure.*"

References

Fink, Steven. *Crisis Management: Planning for the Inevitable.* New York: AMACOM, 1986.

Mitroff, Ian, and Ralph Kilmann. *Corporate Tragedies: Product Tamperings, Sabotage and Other Catastrophes.* New York: Praeger, 1984.

Smart, Carolyn, ed. *Studies on Crisis Management.* Toronto: Butterworth, Ltd., 1978.

Janis, Irving. *Victims of Groupthink.* Boston: Houghton-Mifflin, 1972.

Chapter 5

Decision Making

All managers make decisions. Effective decision making requires you to define a problem, gather relevant information, identify and evaluate alternative solutions, and select the best alternative. This decision-making process has often been described as a rational, sequential activity. However, it is greatly influenced by several factors that require your understanding.

This chapter looks at three aspects of decision making. First, it explores the different kinds of problem situations that you may face. Second, it examines the kinds of decision-making styles you typically use. Third, it identifies the kinds of strategies that fit various decision-making situations. A combination of these three should help you make more effective decisions by indicating 1) when to seek additional information, 2) when to consider more alternatives, and 3) when to involve others in the decision-making process.

5-1. Managerial Problem Situations

As a manager, you may sometimes wonder whether to make a decision by yourself or to involve others. Window 5-1 will assist you with this important and delicate issue. Effective decision making requires that you gather relevant information and select the best alternative. However, good decisions must also be *accepted* by those who will implement them. The apparently "best"

(Text continues on page 68)

Window 5-1. Managerial Problem Situations.

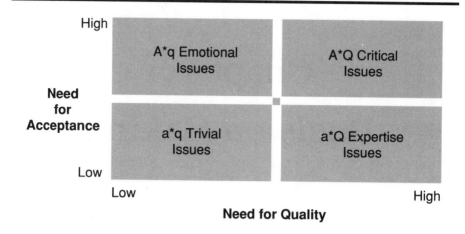

Source: Norman R. F. Maier and Gertrude C. Verser, *Psychology in Industrial Organizations*, 5th ed., pp. 167–181. Copyright © 1982 by Houghton Mifflin Company. Adapted with permission.

Dimensions

Need for acceptance. The first guide to managerial decision making refers to the *need for acceptance.* This factor assesses whether or not the successful implementation of a decision depends on the group's commitment to it. When group members participate in making a decision, they are more cooperative, cohesive, and satisfied with the decision. Participative decision making also stimulates greater initiative and commitment to achieve the group's goals, more positive feelings for you, and greater involvement. Some problem situations demand a very high level of acceptance, especially problems that concern issues of equity and fairness. The *need for acceptance* of the decision is especially important when employees are asked to do something that they are reluctant to do, and when extrinsic rewards or punishments are not apparent to them. On the other hand, the *need for acceptance* is low when (1) the issues are unimportant, (2) the issues do not concern group members, (3) the activity itself is intrinsically satisfying, and (4) group members already want to perform the task.

Need for quality. You also need to consider the *need for quality* in a decision. The *need for quality* refers to the relative importance of incorporating relevant facts, objective data, or logic into a decision. Even where these items are important, the *need for additional quality* may still be judged as low when all decision alternatives are equally good and a bad choice cannot be made. The need for a quality decision is very high when one decision alternative is noticeably better than others. However, the *need for additional* quality would be low if every decision produced about equal consequences.

Window 5-1. (*Continued*)

Four Problem Situations

The combination of high versus low *need for acceptance* and high versus low *need for quality* produces four problem-solving situations, each addressing different types of issues that you are likely to face. Whether you should make the decision alone or whether you should involve others in the decision-making process should largely be determined by the kinds of issues addressed in each quadrant.

A*Q—critical issues. When a problem involves a high *need for acceptance* and high *need for quality* (A*Q), the problem concerns critical issues of central importance to the organization as well as emotional issues within the group. Sample problems include improving work methods, introducing labor-saving methods, increasing production goals, and adopting improved safety standards. These problems should be solved through the use of group decision methods supplemented by strong leadership skills to satisfy both requirements.

A*q—emotional issues. Problems in this quadrant tend to be largely emotional, and their resolution requires a high *need for acceptance* by the group. However, the *need for technical quality* in the decision is unimportant because any alternative would be equally good (from the organization's perspective). Examples of such a situation include who should be asked to work overtime, who should be assigned to various offices, and who should be invited to accept a recognition award for the group. These problems generally involve issues of fairness and equity rather than objective facts. The critical factor determining the effectiveness of these decisions is how well they are accepted, since all of the alternatives are equally good (technically). Therefore, even relatively unskilled leaders can successfully involve subordinates in the resolution of these problems.

a*Q—expertise issues. Where the *need for acceptance* is minimal, but there is a high demand for a quality decision, the situation generally involves issues requiring technical expertise (a*Q). The problems in this quadrant should generally be solved by experts or informed leaders who have the knowledge and background to make a high-quality decision. The acceptance of a decision by group members in this quadrant is usually automatic, either because the group members have no emotional interest in any particular alternative or because every decision is equally acceptable to them. Examples include selecting where the company buys its raw materials, determining how much it charges for its service or products, and selecting the best engineering design for a particular piece of equipment.

a*q—trivial issues. The problem situation involves a low *need for acceptance* and low *need for quality*, and deals with trivial issues (a*q) that should be decided quickly and effortlessly. Very little time or effort should be spent making such decisions. Consequently they could be made either autocratically or by a programmed decision rule (such as the toss of a coin). Employees are not highly concerned about the outcome and hence need not (and should not) be involved.

alternative, however, may not be the best decision if it is rejected by those who must implement it. Autocratic leaders have been criticized for making decisions without allowing input from subordinates. Participative leaders, on the other hand, have been criticized for their lack of decisiveness and for wasting the time of group members on trivial issues. The question of whether you should involve others in decision making should not be determined by your personal preference, but by the *nature of the problem situation* itself. Two criteria are introduced in this window that can be used to determine the appropriate process that you should use for making four types of decisions.

Applying the Managerial Problem Situation Window

The insights and usefulness of this model can be conveniently summarized by noting that "effective decisions are the result of the level of their acceptance and their quality." This suggests that you should never make a decision without considering the need for its acceptance. Most approaches to decision making emphasize the importance of selecting the optimal solution in order to maximize some objective criterion. This window helps you recognize that even the "best" solution will not be effective if those who must implement it are reluctant to do so. In many cases a decision that is less than technically ideal may actually result in the most effective outcome if group members are committed to its success.

When both acceptance and quality are important requirements, the problem situation calls for a high level of conference leadership skills. For these issues group members want to participate openly in the discussion, and they think their opinions should receive strong consideration in the decision outcome. However, you often possess unique information to be shared, or you have an obligation to impose certain constraints on the group's area of freedom. In these situations you must carefully avoid using manipulation or subtle control to create a false sense of participation. At the same time, as a skilled leader, you should share your knowledge by supplying relevant facts and focus the group by carefully stating the problem. Limitations and constraints (the area of freedom for the group) should be made known at the beginning of the discussion process.

The Managerial Problem Situations Window endorses quick and arbitrary decisions when the *needs for* both *acceptance* and *quality* are low. In these situations an immediate decision is useful because it does not waste valuable group time or allow members to choose sides and become personally committed to an alternative. When members participate in a group discussion, they tend to become ego-invested in defending their arguments. Their goal becomes winning the argument rather than making an effective decision. This undesirable situation can be avoided by an immediate decision that comes from a coin toss, objective decision rule, or some other autocratic method.

When to Use the Window. This window can be useful under the following conditions:

- When you fall into a rut in the *problem-classification* process, essentially ignoring one or the other dimension. Reexamination of the window at that point can remind you not to overlook the potential importance of the other factor.
- When you tend to use a single *decision-making process* and find that it is not always equally effective. This may provide a strong clue that there is a poor match between type of problem and type of approach used.
- When an organization's culture shifts sharply toward identification and use of group processes (e.g., autonomous work groups and production teams) and some managers cling to traditional (autocratic) decision-making methods. This window may stimulate them to rethink the need to involve group members in *some* types of decision situations.

The Grid in Action. An example of the Managerial Problem Situations Window can be seen in the experience of Sarah Lepley. Sarah believes that she should show concern for balancing the technical and human sides of her organization. She recognizes that under many circumstances the technically best decisions will be met with resistance, which will ultimately undermine her optimal solution. As a result Sarah always carefully assesses the problem situations facing her. Flexible in her management style, Sarah switches from a participatory decision style to a nonparticipatory style as situations change.

Sarah is confronted with the need to purchase a new piece of machinery. She realizes that those employees who would operate the new device need to accept the job changes that it would impose on them. At the same time, the new equipment has to meet certain technical specifications demanded by the company's consumers. There are several groups whose needs must be considered as she makes this purchase decision.

Sarah recognizes that this is a critical issue (A*Q) with the *need for* both a high-*quality* decision and high employee *acceptance* of the decision. She decides to provide the group with information on the product requirements demanded by customers, the specifications that the competing pieces of equipment are capable of achieving, as well as information about how employees' jobs would be affected by each piece of equipment. Sales representatives from the three competing companies are invited to make a presentation at a group meeting. Following these presentations, she invites employee input regarding the most and least favorable job-design changes. With all of this information in front of them, Sarah and her group discuss the arguments for and against each piece of machinery.

Sarah plays a key role in identifying the criteria for selection of an alternative, facilitating the group's analysis, and making sure that all employees have the chance to be heard. When the group finally arrives at a consensus that everyone can support, she summarizes the agreement and proceeds to order the new machine. Later, when the machine is installed and performs as expected, Sarah congratulates herself on an effective decision reached through simultaneous attention to quality and acceptance.

References

Schoderbeck, Peter P., Richard A. Cosier, and John C. Aplin. *Management.* New York: Harcourt Brace Jovanovich, 1988, Chapter 17.

Vroom, Victor A., and Arthur G. Jago. *The New Leadership: Managing Participation in Organizations.* Englewood Cliffs, N.J.: Prentice-Hall, 1988.

5-2. Decision Styles

Over time, decision makers develop a personal style of making decisions. This tends to become deeply engrained, sometimes to the point of rigidity. *Decision style* represents the decision maker's natural tendency to approach and resolve problem situations. Individuals acquire their decision styles by the way they search for and use information and by the way they develop and select the "best" alternative. Some individuals have a very simple decision style that consists of making quick decisions with limited information. Others display a complex decision style that involves collecting extensive information and considering a large number of alternatives. The way you process information and evaluate alternatives influences your effectiveness in different situations. While some jobs require a simple decision-making approach, others require complex decision styles. To improve your effectiveness, your organization needs to create a match between the decision demands of your job and your preferred style. Window 5-2 depicts four managerial decision styles and the conditions appropriate for each.

Applying the Decision Styles Window

This window emphasizes the need to match, through job assignments, your decision style with the organizational situations you face. *Decisive* managers are best suited for highly programmed jobs that require speed and consistent behavior based on specific procedures. Managers with a *flexible* style, however, are better suited for jobs that require speed, ingenuity, and adaptability, such as the position of insurance claims adjuster. Managers with a *hierarchical* decision style tend to perform best as project managers responsible for developing a unique product and bringing it to market. Managers with an *integrative* style are best suited for highly complex and rapidly changing situations, such as a research and development institute.

Regardless of your characteristic style, you need to remember that extremes in the amount of information used or the number of alternatives considered are usually undesirable. Too much information is overwhelming and creates confusion and chaos. Too little information prevents you from making effective

(Text continues on page 75)

Window 5-2. Decision Styles.

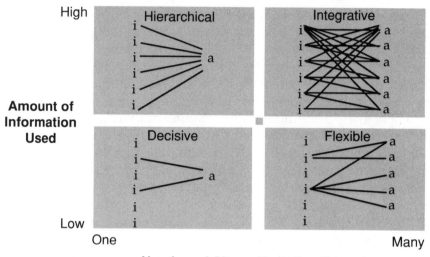

Number of Alternatives Considered

Source: Philip L. Hunsaker and Johanna S. Hunsaker, "Decision Styles—In Theory, in Practice," *Organizational Dynamics*, Vol. 10 (Autumn 1981), pp. 23–36. Reprinted, by permission of the publisher, from *Organizational Dynamics*, Autumn/1981 © 1981. American Management Association, New York. All rights reserved.

Dimensions

Amount of information used. Based on their past experience, managers differ in terms of how much information they generally use to make a decision. Some managers consider very limited information and are willing to make a decision on that basis. These managers assume (1) that additional information will only confirm what they already know, (2) that the data will be too slow in arriving, (3) that additional information will be confusing and distracting. Other managers, however, insist on collecting and using a considerable amount of information before making almost any decision. These managers want to examine all of the relevant data, especially information from independent sources that either refutes or supports other data.

Number of alternatives considered. Because of their past experience and preferences, managers differ in the number of alternatives they prefer to consider when making a decision. Some individuals are called satisficers because they search only long enough to find one satisfactory solution to their problem and then they adopt that solution. Other managers insist on exploring multiple solutions and consider several feasible alternatives to a problem before making a decision.

Window 5-2. (*Continued*)

Four Decision-Making Styles

The combination of high versus low in terms of the amount of information used, and one versus many alternatives considered produces four decision styles. These are called *decisive, flexible, hierarchical,* and *integrative.* Decision styles are related to the way individuals engage in other activities such as planning, goal setting, communicating, and leading.

Decisive. A manager with a *decisive style* uses a minimum amount of data to arrive at a satisfactory decision. Decisive managers focus on the speed, efficiency, and consistency of their decisions. They are highly action-oriented. Their plans tend to accent short-range objectives and they prefer to work in an organizational structure with clearly defined rules and specific plans. They prefer written communications that are brief and to the point; long, detailed reports are either ignored or returned for a summary.

Because they consider only limited information regarding one alternative, managers who use a *decisive* style tend to make decisions that are fast, consistent, and reliable. Furthermore, since they tend to follow existing rules, these managers can be described as loyal and orderly.

Flexible. Managers who use a *flexible decision style* also rely on minimum information. They are willing, however, to consider several alternatives and reinterpret the information to arrive at possibly different conclusions. These managers also value speed, action, and variety, but they are more adaptable in their decision making. They also desire to pursue their own self-oriented goals. *Flexible* managers prefer to work in an organization with a *flexible* structure that allows them to change direction depending on the conditions. *Flexible* managers also prefer to receive from subordinates concise communications that contain a variety of briefly stated solutions from which they may choose. Because of their willingness to adapt to the interests of others, they prefer decision-making settings that invite spontaneous interactions between people. Therefore, they often utilize participative decision making, which considers the needs and feelings of group members. They use their popularity and charm to influence others, and they support their influence by using incentives.

Managers who have a *flexible* decision style also tend to make rapid decisions, but their decisions are more adaptable and spontaneous due to the influence of other people. Because their decisions are adaptable, they tend to be more popular but they may also be perceived as exploitive.

Window 5-2. (*Continued*)

Hierarchical. Managers who use a *hierarchical decision style* consider only one or a very limited number of alternatives. Before deciding, however, they gather an extensive array of facts in support of their decisions. These managers value perfection and thoroughness and want to be in control of what is happening. They tend to adopt a long-range planning perspective that allows them to control both the methods and the outcome. They prefer to work in a *hierarchical* organization with a high degree of structure and a low degree of delegation. They also prefer lengthy and carefully written reports that focus on the merits of the preferred alternative. They base their authority on competence and they prefer using logic and rational explanations to influence others. Because of their desire for control, they tend to make unilateral decisions after consulting with subordinates for additional information.

Managers who follow a *hierarchical* decision style tend to be thorough, logical, and well controlled. Because they are willing to consider extensive information, they tend to have a relatively complete view of the situation. Furthermore, they are particularly sensitive to issues of quality.

Integrative. Managers who use an *integrative decision style* like to process extensive information as they consider several feasible alternatives. These managers value creativity and variety, and they tend to be more contemplative than action-oriented. They adopt a long-range perspective in organizational planning, and their plans are adaptive because of the many alternatives they consider.

Integrative managers prefer to work in organizations that have a flexible structure with a high degree of delegation. Organizations that use a matrix structure or autonomous work teams are well suited for these managers. These managers like to receive long, elaborate reports containing a careful analysis of problems from many viewpoints. They base their authority on trust and information, and they motivate others through mutual understanding and cooperation. Because of their empathy, understanding, and sense of fairness, they are able to use participative decision making effectively, and this maximizes the information available for deciding.

Managers who use an *integrative* decision style tend to be well-informed and open to new information. They possess a broad vision of the organization and its distinctive mission, and they tend to generate creative solutions to organizational problems. Co-workers of *integrative* decision makers are likely to describe them as empathetic and cooperative.

decisions. Refusing to consider more than one alternative almost inevitably limits the quality of your decision. However, it is possible to consider so many alternatives that none of them can be carefully analyzed or executed. Nevertheless, there are times when both of these extremes are appropriate. Some situations call for immediate, simple, decisive answers. Other situations require creative, adaptive, and innovative solutions. Effective managers will recognize the different contexts and adapt to fit the situation (regardless of your primary style preference).

Using the Window. The Decision Styles Window can be a useful guide to self-management in decision situations, as well as a managerial tool for the management of others. In particular:

- The window essentially tells you that there are times when a *decisive, flexible, hierarchical,* or *integrative* decision style is appropriate.
- During the initial selection process, you should attempt to assess (e.g., through in-basket exercises) the candidate's dominant decision-making style in an attempt to achieve a match between job demands and personal decision styles.
- The Decision Styles Window alerts you to the importance of considering a candidate's dominant decision style and fitting it to the dominant demands of the job when you make promotion, transfer, or job rotation decisions.
- When faced with a job (or work unit) redesign, you might want to change the work so that the decision demands of the situation fit the style of the valued employee or work unit manager.

The Grid in Action. Eric Jons, Vice-President of Human Resources for a major midwestern utility company, faces a challenging task. He needs to choose one person to head the company's new organizational development department, and another for the reorganized compensation unit within the human resources department. As he approaches these two personnel decisions, Eric evaluates the nature of the work and the types of problems that would typically be dealt with by a manager in each of the two work units. The compensation department requires someone who can manage basically routine and non-complex issues. By contrast, the manager of the new organizational development department will be confronting essentially nonroutine and complex decision conditions.

Armed with this information, Eric begins to identify candidates with proven decision styles that match these two very different situations. For the organizational development group, Eric seeks someone with an *integrative* decision-making style. In this unit there will be a need for processing large amounts of information and developing several unique solution strategies. He therefore needs someone who can work well in a flexible structure, dealing with complex and highly uncertain organizational conditions.

The compensation unit job calls for a manager with a *decisive* style. Management of routine decisions will be the order of the day in this unit. Therefore, he needs a manager who will be comfortable developing and applying standard operating procedures for the orderly and consistent administration of the company's wage and salary programs.

Once Eric has the job types clearly in mind and a sharp image of the characteristics of the desirable candidates, he is easily able to generate two lists of people to interview. Not surprisingly, the same name never appears on both of his lists.

References

Driver, Michael J., and Alan J. Rowe. "Decision Making Style: A New Approach to Management Decision Making," in Cary L. Cooper, ed., *Behavioral Problems in Organizations*. Englewood Cliffs, N.J.: Prentice-Hall, 1979, pp. 149–155.

Hunsaker, Phillip L., and Johanna S. Hunsaker. "Decision Styles—In Theory, in Practice." *Organizational Dynamics*, Vol. 10 (Autumn 1981), pp. 23–36.

5-3. Decision Strategies

In a rational approach to decision making, decision makers follow a logical and sequential process to solve problems. Several alternatives are identified, the costs and benefits of each alternative are carefully evaluated, and the alternative expected to produce the best outcome is selected and implemented. Identifying the best alternative is supposed to be a simple computational problem that merely requires you to use the appropriate analytical approaches.

Regardless of how appealing this approach seems, however, actual decision making rarely unfolds in this systematic manner. There are important limitations associated with the rational approach: (1) It assumes that everyone involved can agree on what is the best possible decision, and (2) it assumes that everyone knows what has to happen in order to achieve that result. These two limitations dramatically affect the nature of the problem and force you to adopt significantly different strategies for making decisions. The Decision Strategies Window presented here (Window 5-3) identifies four very different conditions that you are likely to confront. In addition, this window proposes that as decision conditions change, the recommended strategy for decision making should also change.

Applying the Decision Strategies Window

The four decision strategies in this window help explain the kinds of decisions that are made at different places in the organization and at different stages in the organization's life cycle. *Computation* is generally appropriate only for problems over which the organization has total control. Such problems tend to be internal matters where there is goal clarity and relative certainty in the causal relationships. Production scheduling and inventory control, for example, require agreement on both dimensions and are therefore prime candidates for a *computational* decision strategy.

Other decision strategies are appropriate for external issues. An organization's diverse environment often does not produce consistent agreement among managers about beliefs of causation or preferences for outcomes. On the input side, organizations face uncertainty regarding the availability of resources (especially human resources), and many decisions are made by *compromise* because of the disagreement surrounding preferred outcomes. On the output side, organizations face uncertainty in knowing the kinds of products they ought to produce and how well these will be accepted by society. Consequently, many decisions regarding marketing and sales are *judgment* decisions

(Text continues on page 80)

Window 5-3. Decision Strategies.

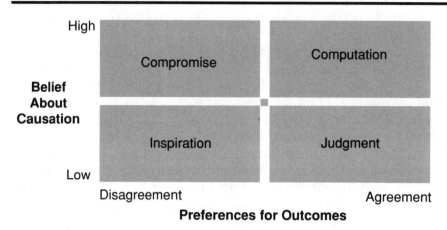

Reprinted from: James D. Thompson and Arthur Tuden's "Strategies, Structures, and Processes of Organizational Decision, " in *Comparative Studies in Administration*, James D. Thompson, et al, editors. Published in 1959 by the University of Pittsburgh Press. Used by permission of the publisher.

Dimensions

Belief about causation. Belief about causation refers to the amount of agreement that exists between relevant individuals regarding what causes what. If everyone believes A causes X, and B causes Y, then there is high agreement regarding causation. However, if people don't know or can't agree on what it is that causes X and Y, then disagreement about causation exists. For example, inflation is widely believed to be a serious social problem, but citizens and legislators do not agree on what causes it. If everyone agreed that the cause of inflation was the relative supply of money, then this dimension would be rated high (for this problem). However, since some people think inflation is caused by other factors such as budget deficits, interest rates, minimum wage increases. and negotiated wage increases, there is substantial disagreement on causation of the problem. Furthermore, as society, business organizations, and problems become more complex, our beliefs about causation become less certain.

Preferences for outcomes. Preferences for outcomes refers to whether people agree or disagree about which results they desire. There would be high agreement if everyone wanted the same outcome. But if some wanted X (e.g., profit maximization), others wanted Y (e.g., a socially responsible company), and others didn't know what they wanted, there would be disagreement in the preferences for possible outcomes.

Window 5-3. (*Continued*)

Four Decision-Making Situations and Associated Strategies

The combination of agreement versus disagreement in *beliefs about causation*, and agreement versus disagreement in *preferences for outcomes* creates four different conditions. These call for four different decision-making strategies: *computation, compromise, judgment, and inspiration.*

Computation. If key persons involved agree on the preferred outcome and they are relatively certain about the methods for achieving it, the appropriate decision strategy becomes one of *computation*. In its extreme form, this situation requires decision makers to calculate the expected value of each alternative and select the one that contributes most to the preferred outcome. Many production problems and job redesign efforts appear to be *computational* problems. Everyone agrees that the goal is to maximize efficiency, and previous experience has indicated that the ideal way to accomplish this is through a division of labor and task specialization. Highly specialized jobs maximize productive efficiency by eliminating wasted motions and time lost when employees change from one task to another. However, highly specialized jobs are also perceived as boring. The resultant dilemma may reduce the agreement that efficiency is the only preferred outcome and force those involved to change their decision strategy on job redesign from *computation* to *compromise*.

Compromise. Sometimes decision makers are certain about the expected consequences of the available alternatives, but do not agree on the relative value of the outcomes. In this case the appropriate decision strategy is *compromise*, where people negotiate for their preferred outcome. The problem of creating an acceptable benefits package illustrates a *compromise* strategy. The cost of insurance, vacations, sick leave, and other benefit options is reasonably certain based on previous experience; but employees may disagree about whether they want more paid holidays, better medical coverage, or an improved pension plan. This problem cannot be solved by computation since it depends on the values of the decision makers. Instead, it requires individuals to negotiate and develop a compromise solution.

Judgment. If the preferences are clear but the means of achieving them are uncertain, *judgment* becomes the relevant decision strategy. This situation occurs when the forces determining a problem become increasingly complex. For example, the problem of excessive turnover indicates that a *judgment* strategy would be appropriate. Managers generally agree that excessive turnover is undesirable and poses a serious economic cost to the organization. Knowing how to reduce excessive turnover, however, requires careful *judgment*. A variety of complex forces cause turnover, such as job dissatisfaction, punitive supervision,

Window 5-3. (*Continued*)

low unemployment levels, and unfair compensation practices. Good *judgment* is required to know which of these or other variables may be contributing to excessive turnover.

■ **Inspiration.** When managers disagree about the consequences of the alternatives or the outcomes they prefer, the decision strategy calls for *inspiration.* Such a situation is very threatening to a group and may cause it to dissolve. There are two reasons why the strategy is called *inspiration.* First, the lack of agreement regarding causation and preferred outcomes forces you to make decisions based on hunches, guesses, or intuition. Second, the lack of agreement creates a need for a charismatic leader who can inspire others. Charismatic leaders use their imaginations to create a new vision, "sell" it internally, and thereby pull together a stagnant organization. Many of the decisions regarding performance appraisals are often made by *inspiration.* You do not always agree about the outcome of the appraisal—whether it is for rewarding employees, for personal development, for promotion purposes, or for some other management function. Likewise, you typically disagree about the type of evaluation method—such as a ranking procedure, graphic rating scales, forced choice items, or management by objectives—that will produce a given result. Only *inspiration* explains the choices made.

---

because of the disagreement over which strategies will produce the best financial results.

At different stages in its life cycle (e.g., formation, growth, maturity, decline), the organization faces different kinds of uncertainties in both its preferred outcomes and beliefs about causation. In the early stages of its life, decisions are largely made by *inspiration* since the product mix is unsure and the methods are uncertain. As the organization grows and matures, its products at first become more certain as a single product or product mix is decided. Eventually, however, the output becomes increasingly uncertain as a mature organization is forced to recognize multiple objectives and various groups that need to be pleased. Likewise, the maturing organization faces a fluctuating state of uncertainty at the input end as it increases its demand for a greater quantity and variety of resources. The kinds of decision strategies at both the input and output ends may fluctuate between *compromise, judgment,* and *inspiration* as the levels of agreement regarding *causation* and *outcome* preferences increase and decrease. Although the growing complexity of the organization forces the decision strategies to move toward increasing reliance on *inspiration*, you continually try to reduce uncertainty through such strategies as coalition formation and cooptation.

The major benefit of this model is that it helps you recognize inappropriate decision strategies and select better ones. You have learned to use various quantitative tools and methods for making financial and administrative decisions. But these methods are only useful when the decision strategy calls for a *computational* decision. If you disagree on the outcomes you are pursuing, a *computational* mind set can interfere with a careful focus on the most appropriate *compromise* (bargaining) strategy. This situation calls for a *compromise* decision through the process of negotiation.

This model also helps to explain why *inspirational* decision strategies are becoming increasingly important. As society and business organizations become increasingly complex, there is a growing need for leaders who have the capacity to create a new vision or belief and thereby inspire the members of a floundering organization. This emphasizes the importance of strategic leadership, in which a distinction is often made between leaders and managers. While managers do things right, leaders focus on doing the right things. Managers use *computational* decisions to allocate resources and control organizational processes. However, leaders use *inspiration* to focus the efforts of a large number of individuals into a unified effort.

Advantages to Using the Window. This window into organizations alerts you to the fact that you are likely to face a variety of highly differentiated decision-making situations, and that each condition may *not* call for the same decision-making strategy. Thus, you need to be sensitive to the need for flexibility in your approach to decision making.

The Decision Strategies model can be used to guide an individual employee in the decision-making process, as well as guide you by signaling when to act unilaterally or participatively. For example:

- You can recognize that different individuals or groups who will be affected by a decision differ in terms of the outcome that they hope will be achieved through the decision-making process (this situation calls for bargaining/negotiations in an effort to find a common solution that is acceptable to all those who will have to live with its consequences).

- You can recognize that there is uncertainty (lack of proof) surrounding how to go about achieving a particular goal (this situation calls for soliciting ideas and information from a group of experts and then basing the decision on their collective judgment).
- If you recognize that there is agreement on the importance of quickly solving a product quality problem, as well as agreement on how to eliminate the cause of the decline in quality, you should act decisively, not bothering with participative meetings.
- When, as an individual decision maker, you confront decisions, you will find that some have clear cause-and-effect relationships and some have unknown causality. This will necessitate the use of a *computational* strategy and a *judgmental* strategy, respectively.

The Grid in Action. Let's examine the use of the Decision Strategies Window by Professor Tanya Morgan, head of a marine biology department at a western university. As a member of the baby boomer generation, Tanya prefers the democratic and participative approach to decision making, yet she recognizes the need to be flexible in her style. She has discovered that there are times when making a decision and directing others in an autocratic fashion is both acceptable and effective. There are other times when decision quality is improved by delegating decision-making authority to someone else within her department. This is often more effective than deciding on her own. There are, however, many times when neither of these two hierarchical approaches to decision making would prove effective, and the use of some form of participative decision making is more effective and accepted.

Called on by the dean of the College of Sciences to make a curriculum change within her department, Tanya finds she needs to make a decision. The dean wants an increase in active learning experiences for the undergraduate and graduate students throughout the entire science curriculum. Tanya recognizes that the outcome that the dean hopes to achieve, an increase in active learning, will most likely be acceptable to all of the members of her department. She senses, however, that there will likely be a lack of consensus on *how* to bring about that desired outcome.

Having diagnosed the situation confronting her as consisting of basic agreement on desirable outcomes and disagreement over the right (appropriate) means to achieve active learning, Tanya turns to a participative decision strategy as opposed to making a unilateral decision. She recognizes that it will be better to rely on the collective *judgments* of her colleagues (that is, to rely on a judgmental decision strategy) because no single individual has "the proven correct" solution.

The next day she notifies members of her department that they will be discussing ways of implementing active learning within their marine biology curriculum. She asks each departmental member to think about the issue and organize his/her opinions and judgments for an upcoming departmental meeting. She also calls on an educational consultant to join in on their discussions, offering insight to the group into different approaches to active learning. Tanya hopes that by pooling these diverse perspectives the departmental members will be equipped to identify and select several approaches that will satisfy their objective. Their ultimate decision will be based on each faculty member offering his/her independent judgment as to the desirability of each alternative generated. Finally, a simple majority rule decision criterion will be applied to identify several desirable alternatives for implementation.

References

Thompson, James D. *Organizations in Action.* New York: McGraw-Hill, 1967, Chapter 10.

Thompson, James D. "Decision Making, the Firm, and the Market" in W. W. Cooper, H. J. Leavitt, and M. W. Shelby II, *New Perspectives in Organizational Research.* New York: John Wiley & Sons, 1964, pp. 334–348.

Thompson, James D., and Arthur Tuden. "Strategies, Structures, and Processes of Organizational Decision" in James D. Thompson et al., eds., *Comparative Studies in Administration.* Pittsburgh: The University of Pittsburgh Press, 1959.

Chapter 6

Employee Attitudes and Behaviors

You want good *performance* from your employees. To perform, employees must participate—come to work regularly and on time, and not quit. Behaviors such as absenteeism, tardiness, and turnover can be described as undesirable types of employee *participation.* What do employees want from their job? They probably want *satisfaction.* These three important outcomes—performance, participation, and satisfaction—are discussed in this chapter.

A dynamic relationship exists between *participation, performance,* and *satisfaction.* To perform, employees must participate (come to work). Recognizing performance with valued rewards leads to satisfied employees. Satisfied employees participate more frequently than do dissatisfied ones.

The four windows presented here offer insights into each of these outcomes. The first window considers the impact of goal setting and feedback on employee performance levels. Behaviors related to various levels of job dissatisfaction are then discussed. One of these behaviors is turnover, and the third window presents different classifications of turnover. The final window examines the types of employees (and how they feel and act) who are involved in their jobs and committed to their organization.

84

6-1. Performance Effects of Goals and Feedback

The phrase "If you don't know where you are going, you will likely end up somewhere else" speaks volumes about the importance of setting goals. Most managers understand that goals can provide direction and guidance. And, human nature being what it is, most employees want feedback about their progress toward those goals. By examining the relations between job-related goals and feedback, you will understand the powerful impact of these factors on employee performance (see Window 6-1).

Applying the Goals and Feedback Window

Knowledge about the impact of goals on performance is substantial and surprisingly consistent in its results. Individuals given specific goals tend to perform better than those provided general goals or no goals. Similarly, challenging goals lead to higher levels of performance than do easy goals. However, if challenging goals (specific or not) are viewed by employees as too difficult or impossible, then these goals will not be accepted and will have little or no effect on individual performance.

Understanding the role of feedback in the motivation and performance of employees requires multiple perspectives. First, we know that jobs providing feedback directly to the employee (without the need for a report from some third party) tend to result in higher levels of motivation than do jobs where the only feedback comes from some other source. Second, we also know that providing feedback to employees about their performance on current goals (or how others have performed in the past on similar goals) allows the employee to make informed judgments about the acceptability and achievability of current goals. To get employees to accept difficult goals, you will be wise to provide knowledge (feedback) about their performance or that of others on this or similar goals. Finally, as suggested by this window, feedback about progress toward an accepted goal can influence the levels of performance an employee will pursue. Thus, feedback can influence (1) motivation levels, (2) the likelihood of accepting difficult goals, and (3) actual performance levels.

The implications for the practice of management and the

Window 6-1. Performance Effects of Goals and Feedback.

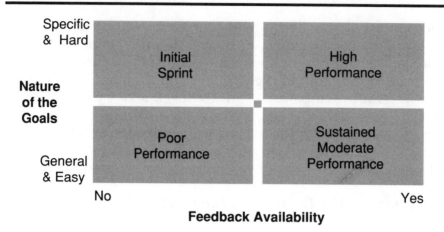

Source: T. Matsui, A. Okada, and O. Inoshita, "Mechanism of Feedback Affecting Task Performance," *Organizational Behavior and Human Performance*, Vol. 31 (1983), pp. 114–122.

Dimensions

The factors affecting the level of employee performance are the nature of goals and the availability of feedback.

Nature of the goals. Goals can be either difficult or easy (running a four-minute mile is difficult; running a twenty-minute mile is easy), and either specific or general ("Increase sales by 10 percent next quarter" is specific; "Do your best" is general). This dimension combines these goal characteristics, putting specific-hard goals at one end and general-easy goals at the other.

Feedback availability. This dimension indicates whether or not feedback is available to an employee on the progress made toward a particular goal. This feedback may come from the job itself (the employee can determine the progress being made) or from some third party (the supervisor or a quality control inspector, for example).

Employee Performance Effects

Initial sprint. When specific and hard goals are set (and these goals are accepted as realistic), most employees will make a good-faith effort to achieve them. This is particularly true if the employees have reason to believe that some type of reward will be provided when goals are achieved. However, this *initial sprint* to higher levels of performance can come to a quick halt if employees receive no feedback on how well (or how poorly) they are progressing toward their goals. They wonder why they should maintain high performance levels if there is no way for them to know how close they are to their goals.

Window 6-1. (*Continued*)

■ **Poor performance.** General and easy goals are not particularly taxing to employees and typically lead to lower levels of performance than do specific and hard goals. In the absence of feedback about progress to those goals, *poor performance* usually results.

■ **Sustained moderate performance.** Performance can be *sustained* at *moderate* levels if feedback is provided about employee progress toward general and easy goals. Since these goals are readily attainable, moderate performance can only be sustained if new goals are again established as old goals are achieved.

■ **High performance.** When feedback is provided on progress toward specific and hard goals, *high performance* is usually the result. Given information about their status relative to these goals, most employees remain motivated to perform to achieve them in anticipation of receiving intrinsic rewards (personal accomplishment) or extrinsic rewards (bonus, time off, and promotion).

---

motivation of employee performance are straightforward. Goal setting is already being used in many organizations through the application of Management by Objectives (MBO). Under such a program, how do you get employees to perform in ways you want them to? You tell them what to do! The answer to increased performance lies, then, in providing employees with clear goals. But as the window suggests, those goals must be specific and challenging (but not so challenging as to be seen as impossible) rather than general and easy. The old advice frequently given to frustrated employees, "Don't worry about it. Just go out and do your best," may actually be doing them a disservice.

Employees will accept goals more readily if you give them feedback about how they are doing on their current goals or how others have done on similar goals. They value ongoing feedback of any sort, including progress reports on goal accomplishment. If the only feedback they receive is bad news, is it any wonder that motivation levels are low?

In some cases you can use participation in goal setting to help employees accept goals as relevant and achievable. But care is in order, because not all employees feel it is their responsibility to participate in goal setting. They may view it as a management task. If a company uses an MBO program, participative goal setting is probably already under way.

When to Use the Window. Most managers find themselves interested in issues pertaining to employee performance. It is not uncommon to hear questions probing for ways to arrest employee motivational problems and to increase performance. This window into organizations should and can be used frequently to address the performance issue. Employ this model:

- Whenever you find yourself interested in understanding low performance levels and/or a sudden shift (e.g., from high to low) in an employee's level of performance
- When you are questioning what can be done to increase the motivation of your employees
- When you are interested in increasing the performance level of one or several employees
- When you are in the process of planning and establishing goals (this model provides insight into the type of goals that are effective motivators of employee behavior)
- When you are considering the implementation of a Management by Objectives (MBO) program (this window will provide you with insight into two important design features [goals and feedback] as well as insight into the potential consequences of the MBO program)

The Grid in Action. Mike Thomas has just taken over as controller at the Novus Corporation. He got the position because his predecessor had been unable to meet performance objectives set by Novus's top management. In his new position, Mike supervises seven financial analysts, all of whom, he believes, have the necessary skills to get their jobs done. What appears to be lacking is motivation.

As a first step in understanding his unit and his subordinates, Mike spends the first few days on his new job interviewing each employee. Reviewing his notes from those interviews, Mike starts seeing comments that sounded familiar:

"I never knew what was expected of me."

"We were never certain where the unit was going, and I didn't understand my role in the group."

"The only news we ever got about our performance was bad news."

"Other units used MBO, and it worked for them. We might have had MBO, but if we did it could only have meant Management by Osmosis. We were expected to figure out both what the boss wanted and how well we were doing. There just wasn't any feedback."

It is clear to Mike that many of the problems in his unit stem from lack of understanding of unit goals and the expected employee contributions to those goals. Similarly, there has been a lack of feedback about how employees and the unit are doing relative to those objectives.

Having diagnosed the problem, Mike sets about implementing a working MBO system. He meets with each employee and jointly establishes a variety of specific and challenging, but realistic, goals that the employee accepts. Mike also devises a variety of formal and informal feedback systems to let employees know how they are doing—computer reports on the formal side and frequent informal discussions with employees, both of which give them both the good news and the bad news about their own and unit performance.

Within six months employee performance and morale in Mike's unit improve, and the controller's office is well on its way to meeting its corporate objectives.

Reference

Matsui, T., A. Okada, and O. Inoshita. "Mechanism of Feedback Affecting Task Performance." *Organizational Behavior and Human Performance*, Vol. 31 (1983), pp. 114–122.

6-2. Employee Responses to Job Dissatisfaction

When dissatisfaction arises on the job, the consequences can range from frustration and feelings of general animosity ("Take this job and shove it!") to very destructive acts of sabotage and physical violence. Window 6-2 depicts responses to dissatisfaction, classifies the various kinds of reactions that can occur, and suggests that from the organization's perspective some outcomes are more desirable than others.

Window 6-2. Employee Responses to Job Dissatisfaction.

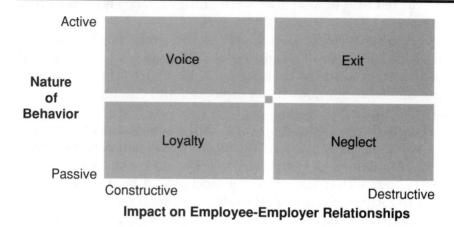

Adapted from: C. Rusbult, et al., "Impact of Exchange Variables on Exit, Voice, Loyalty, and Neglect: An Integrative Model of Responses to Declining Job Satisfaction," *Academy of Management Journal*, Vol. 31, No. 3 (1988), pp. 599–627.

Dimensions

Two critical dimensions that help us organize differing employee reactions to job dissatisfaction are the constructive-destructive nature of the response and the degree to which the behavior is active or passive.

Impact on employee-employer relationships. This dimension records the extent to which employee responses to job dissatisfaction are *constructive* and beneficial or *destructive* and harmful to the ongoing employee-employer relationship.

Nature of behavior. This dimension represents the level of action in employee behaviors. Dissatisfaction on the job can result in a variety of responses ranging from *passive* acceptance of the situation (perhaps in the face of perceived powerlessness to do anything about the situation and/or the inability to leave the situation) to *active* behaviors undertaken to change or leave the situation.

Responses of Dissatisfied Employees

Voice. Given a dissatisfying job, some employees may work in an active and constructive way to reduce their dissatisfaction. Such verbal behaviors could include notification of superiors of the dissatisfaction, identification of the apparent reason for this feeling, and suggestions for improving the problem. The employees actually *voice* their concerns in a constructive fashion.

Window 6-2. (*Continued*)

▨ **Loyalty.** Also constructive but less active is a *loyalty* response to job dissatisfaction. Unwilling or unable to voice complaints about the job setting, the employee nevertheless remains loyal to the company. Evidence of one's loyalty may include optimistically anticipating that eventually the problem will be solved and conditions will improve.

▨ **Neglect.** Equally passive, but far more destructive to the employee-employer relationship, are dissatisfied employees who practice *neglect* in their daily job-related activities. These employees may allow situations to deteriorate by not bringing problems to the attention of superiors. Alternatively, they may respond to what they perceive as an untenable situation by coming to work late, calling in sick more frequently, making more mistakes on the job, or refusing to protect the organization in an emergency.

▨ **Exit.** Sufficiently prolonged dissatisfaction may bring about the most active and destructive behaviors associated with *exit*. This *exit* may be from the job or the organization, and it can occur either physically or psychologically. The relationship between employee and employer is severed by the employee quitting, looking for another job, and/or mentally withdrawing from the current position.

Applying the Employee Responses to Job Dissatisfaction Window

If we assume that you want to continue useful relationships with your employees, then it is important to recognize that job dissatisfaction can have harmful (but also beneficial) effects on these relationships. Some reactions of employees (particularly those with previously high levels of satisfaction and a heavy investment in the job) to dissatisfying conditions can be creative and innovative responses to problem areas on the job. Thus, in many jobs some tension or challenge may well be appropriate. However, ongoing job dissatisfaction, particularly if it is consistent with prior dissatisfaction, low investment in the job, and greater employment alternatives, can lead to actions destructive to the employee-employer relationship and reduce the effectiveness of both the individual and the organization.

Employers should think about ways of assessing employee

satisfaction. Anonymous and confidential attitude surveys are used by many organizations (Sears and IBM, for instance) on a regular basis to determine average job satisfaction levels among employees. While the guarantee of confidentiality is generally needed to get valid information, it also precludes the identification of individual employees who are dissatisfied with their jobs. But clusters of dissatisfied employees complaining about a situation should prompt closer attention by management. If required, changes to reduce dissatisfaction should be implemented, particularly if it is important for certain groups of employees to remain with the company. Employee complaints or suggestions for improvements should not be rejected. They may well be voicing legitimate concerns that should be accepted and investigated.

Three factors tend to influence which responses will occur: (1) the individual's level of overall job dissatisfaction prior to the occurrence of the current situation; (2) the investment the employee has already made in his/her current job (experience, job-specific training, friendships, living arrangements); and (3) the number of alternative employment opportunities inside and outside the organization.

Employees who were previously well satisfied and are heavily invested in their jobs tend to use *voice* and *loyalty* to resolve dissatisfaction. However, employees with higher levels of job alternatives use *voice* and *exit* behaviors more frequently.

Not surprisingly, there appears to be a progression of responses to job dissatisfaction depending on the severity of the problem and the duration of the dissatisfaction. In many cases *voice* reactions occur first. If such actions do not adequately resolve the problem, the employee may then engage in the more passive *loyalty* approach, followed by *neglect*, and finally *exit* as a last recourse.

If responses to job dissatisfaction do follow a pattern, then frequent occurrence of employees voicing their concerns (directly or via attitude surveys) should serve as an early-warning indicator of organizational problems. The model indicates that continued employee dissatisfaction can lead to more serious responses. Failure to deal with the issues causing the dissatisfaction can prompt serious consequences from the organization's perspective.

When to Use the Window. Employee attitudes play a key role in organizations. They are shaped by many elements in the work environment (e.g., job characteristics, pay, leader behavior, co-workers, physical working conditions). They also produce powerful organizational consequences (e.g., employee acts of good organizational citizenship, tardiness, absenteeism, turnover, grievance filing, strikes). In this context this window can be useful when you:

- Counsel and coach a subordinate manager about the importance of employee satisfaction/dissatisfaction, which he/she may have overlooked or underestimated.
- Examine negative employee behaviors within the organization and search for causes as well as consequences.
- Are about to make a decision; you should examine and predict the likely impact on employee attitudes to see if the dysfunctional consequences will exceed the benefits.
- Find that symptoms of employee dissatisfaction emerge within the organization. These can alert you to even more significant problems ahead, because dissatisfaction may spread from verbal complaints to active neglect of job duties to eventual turnover.

The Grid in Action. Amanda has been in management long enough to realize that there are times when a job can just drive you crazy. She has just finished a performance appraisal interview with Tyler Cook, and he is a very dissatisfied employee. Both Amanda and Tyler work for the Advanced Manufacturing Company. Amanda is a second-shift manager in production, and Tyler is a crew chief with twelve years' experience in the company. As Amanda replays the appraisal interview, she realizes that Tyler probably has good reason to be dissatisfied. In addition to some personal concerns that seem to be affecting his attitude on the job (but not his performance), the corporate office has reduced the amount of merit money Amanda can give in raises, and Tyler has gotten less than he expected. Those concerns, combined with an apparent personality conflict with another crew chief, really have Tyler upset with his job, with Amanda, and with the whole company.

Amanda has discussed all of these issues with Tyler, and now she sits in her office trying to make some predictions in her own mind about what Tyler's dissatisfaction may lead to. She does not believe that Tyler will quit. He probably does not have other job opportunities, and his job-related concerns do not seem that important. Tyler is enough of a team player not to simply neglect his job. He may not enjoy his job right now, but he is performing up to expectations—for the time being at least.

Fortunately, Tyler has expressed his dissatisfaction with various aspects of his job during the appraisal interview (voice). Since Amanda is aware of his feelings, she can take actions to deal with some of his concerns. In the meantime it appears that Tyler is willing to live with the current circumstances. His loyalty to the company and his friendships with some of his other co-workers means that Amanda can continue to count on him—at least in the short run. But she also knows that she has to do something about the sources of job dissatisfaction before more serious consequences arise for Tyler, the company, and herself.

Reference

Rusbult, C., et al. "Impact of Exchange Variables on Exit, Voice, Loyalty, and Neglect: An Integrative Model of Responses to Declining Job Satisfaction." *Academy of Management Journal*, Vol. 31, No. 3 (1988), pp. 599–627.

6-3. Analysis of Turnover

One of the measures used to evaluate the efficient use of human resources in many organizations is employee turnover. A single, highly qualified individual leaving an organization can cost upward of $100,000 to replace. At one time managers felt that turnover levels in any organization should be as low as possible. But some turnover (of the right people at the right time) can be beneficial to the company. Window 6-3 examines different types of turnover from the perspective of employee attitudes about the organization and organizational attitudes about the employee.

Applying the Turnover Analysis Window

The impact of satisfaction on employee behaviors has been examined many times and many ways. Unfortunately, the re-

Window 6-3. Analysis of Turnover.

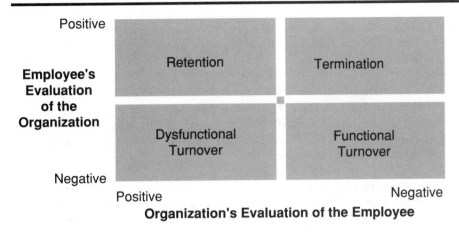

Adapted from: Dan R. Dalton, William D. Todor, and David M. Krackhardt, "Turnover Overstated: The Functional Taxonomy," *Acadamy of Management Review*, January 1982, pp. 117–123.

Dimensions

Employee's evaluation of the organization. Employees develop attitudes about certain aspects of their organization. As suggested in this model, these specific attitudes develop into a generalized attitude about the organization as a whole. Such attitudes can range from negative ("This is the worst place I have ever worked") to positive ("This is the best place I have ever worked").

Organization's evaluation of the employee. Organizations also evaluate their employees. Formal and informal evaluations usually involve some aspects of a performance appraisal system. One result of such an evaluation is a global assessment of employee performance. This assessment can also range from positive to negative.

Effects of Employee-Employer Evaluations

Retention. When both sets of evaluations are positive (and when all else is equal), it is likely that the employee will choose to stay with the company. In addition, the organization will encourage *retention* by providing the employee with appropriate and valued rewards.

Dysfunctional turnover. Problems can arise from the organization's perspective when a valued employee develops negative attitudes about the company. The company would like to retain the individual, but dissatisfaction may

Window 6-3. (*Continued*)

lead to a desire to move on. Since the organization wants to retain the employee but the employee does not wish to stay, *dysfunctional turnover* occurs when the employee leaves.

　■　**Functional turnover.** On occasion, evaluations by the employee and the organization are both negative. The employee is dissatisfied with his/her job, and the organization is dissatisfied with the employee's performance. If the employee leaves, the event is called *functional turnover;* the employee and the organization benefit from the employee's departure.

　■　**Termination.** In the most problematic situation, an employee has a positive attitude about the organization, but cannot or will not perform to the organization's expectations. The organization's evaluation of the employee is negative. In this case the result is most likely *termination*, the unilateral dismissal of the employee by the organization.

search examining the relationship between satisfaction and employee turnover has been inconsistent. In some studies there is a strong association between satisfaction and turnover (high satisfaction associated with low turnover or low satisfaction associated with high turnover). In other studies this association has been zero or even negative (low satisfaction associated with low turnover or high satisfaction associated with high turnover). One possible explanation for some of these results is that researchers (and organizations) have traditionally lumped the three different kinds of turnover together and compared this aggregate turnover figure with employee satisfaction. This model suggests that turnover is the product of *both* employee attitudes about the organization *and* organizational attitudes about the employee. The result of this interaction of attitudes can be retention or three *different* kinds of turnover. From the organization's perspective, issues surrounding *dysfunctional turnover* are probably the most important.

The belief that turnover is necessarily a negative indicator of your organization's effectiveness is largely outmoded, however. It is probably inappropriate to reduce your turnover level to zero. This model reminds us that turnover can actually help an organization or employee (and should be encouraged in some cases). When employees leave an organization, positions for new people with new ideas and perspectives become available. Turnover at upper levels provides promotion opportunities for those at lower levels. This maintains or increases motivation levels. The model also suggests that turnover is not completely under the control of the organization.

The model prompts several questions you may wish to ask in light of your own turnover levels. First, are there currently substantive levels of *dysfunctional turnover* or *terminations* in your company? How do you know? What is the baseline against which you are making your judgments? Are you looking at historical data for your own company? At averages for the industry? Second, which employees are leaving and which staying? If the poor performers are leaving and the good ones are staying, do you really have a problem? If the good ones are leaving and the poor ones are staying, what are the specific reasons? Third, what can you do to minimize *dysfunctional turnover* without artificially suppressing *functional turnover?*

Finally, you should determine how your company measures and classifies turnover. Are all employee departures lumped in the same category? Should they be? Exit interviews might be conducted with those leaving to gain more accurate information about the causes of *dysfunctional turnover.* This knowledge could then be used to develop programs designed to retain valued employees.

Advantages to Using the Window. Turnover can have both positive and negative consequences for the organization (or any work unit within the organization). Like many employee attitudes (e.g., job satisfaction, organizational commitment), work motivation and work-related behaviors (e.g., performance, absenteeism, tardiness), and turnover (i.e., employees leaving the organization or their work unit) should be managed and not left to random events and circumstances. Toward this end, this window into organizations:

- Aids in the conduct of an organization's (or work unit's) turnover review.
- Facilitates a review of the organization's human resource climate—Is low quality of work life producing job dissatis-

faction that ultimately results in costly employee turnover?

- Facilitates a review of the quality-of-work-life differences across organizational units in an attempt to identify desirable units within which to work and undesirable work environments that necessitate managerial attention and quality-of-work-life improvements.
- Identifies which employees are leaving, thereby facilitating an identification of whether the organization is experiencing *functional turnover* (e.g., poor performers leaving) or *dysfunctional turnover* (e.g., good employees exiting).

The Grid in Action. Gregory Dunne, Senior Personnel Specialist at IBT Inc., an information services company, is meeting with Matt Lucas, senior manager for the company's data base development division. Greg and Matt are discussing the 40 percent turnover rate in the data base division. Matt has come to see if Greg can offer any assistance in dealing with this substantial turnover problem.

Greg asks, "Matt, what do you think the turnover rate should be for your group?"

"I would like to see it at zero, but I know that's unrealistic."

"Unrealistic and probably undesirable," Greg suggests. "A little turnover can be healthy. It opens up positions for new people to enter the unit, allows qualified employees to be promoted out of the unit, and provides for the termination of employees who can't cut it. Your first step should be to find out how your turnover rate compares to other units in the company and to similar units in the industry.

"The second issue that you need to be concerned about is the nature of the turnover. In other words, who's leaving and who's staying? If all of your high performers are leaving and your low performers are staying, then you have a problem. If it's the other way around, your problem may not be as serious as you think.

"It's also important, Matt, to get a handle on the type of turnover you are seeing. When you get back to your office, try and classify those people who have left recently to see how much of the turnover is *functional* and how much is *dysfunctional.* That would give us some useful information."

"I'm not sure I understand the difference here, Greg."

"Well, what percentage of those who left in the past year did so because they weren't doing well in your unit, but could do well in a different unit, or left because they got a promotion within the company? That's *functional turnover.* It benefits the company and the employee.

"On the other hand, if you are losing the wrong people and it's the high performers who are going to the competition, that's *dysfunctional turnover.* And you also want to count the number of people in that turnover who left because we had to fire them for poor performance."

Matt's eyes light up. "So if most of my turnover is *functional,* that's fine—that should improve both my unit and the organization as a whole. But if most of my turnover is what you called *dysfunctional* or if we're firing a lot of people, then I need to start looking for what is causing that problem. I might need to go back and start looking at the way I recruit, select, place, and reward my employees. Thanks for the help, Greg."

As Matt turns to leave, Greg offers one other piece of advice. "You know, Matt, it might be useful if you and your managers made sure that we conduct exit interviews with everybody in the unit who leaves. That would give us a better understanding about who is leaving and why and allow us to stay on top of this kind of problem."

"Great idea. I'll do that starting tomorrow."

Reference

Dalton, D. R., W. Todor, and D. Krackhardt. "Turnover Overstated: The Functional Taxonomy." *Academy of Management Review,* No. 7 (1982), pp. 117–123.

6-4. Employee Types

Employees bring widely differing levels of effort to their jobs. Think about the people you interview for a job with your company. Some new job applicants want to work at a particular job regardless of the organization, while others want to work for your organization regardless of the job. Still other individuals have both a particular job and particular organization in mind. Window 6-4 uses two dimensions to categorize these different

Window 6-4. Employee Types.

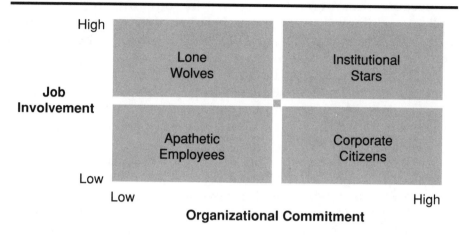

Source: L. Porter, E. Lawler, and J. R. Hackman, *Behavior in Organizations*, New York: McGraw-Hill, 1975, p. 309.

Dimensions

Job involvement. This dimension refers to the extent that the employee identifies with his/her job (as opposed to the organization in which that job is done). This identification is determined by (1) how important the job is to an employee's self-image, (2) an employee's willingness to proactively participate in the job, and/or (3) the extent to which job performance influences an employee's self-esteem. The focus of employee interest and effort is on the job itself.

Organizational commitment. As opposed to focusing on the job, this dimension refers to the extent to which an employee focuses on and has internalized the goals of the organization. The employee with high commitment wants to remain with the organization and help it achieve mutually held goals. The nature of the job undertaken to achieve these goals is immaterial.

Employee Types

Lone wolves. For these employees, the major focus and interest is their job. They are not particularly committed to the goals of the organization and appear to be *lone wolves* from the perspective of other employees. They are totally involved with their jobs.

Window 6-4. (*Continued*)

■ **Apathetic employees**. While lone wolves focus on and have a keen interest in their jobs, other employees lack attachment to or interest in their jobs and their organization's goals. They are *apathetic* employees to the extent that they perform only as needed to maintain employment.

■ **Corporate citizens.** Some employees view the organization as the major focus of their allegiance, even to the point of ignoring certain job requirements. This is particularly true if these requirements are perceived to be in conflict with the goals of the company. The *corporate citizen* is willing to do almost anything for the good of the company.

■ **Institutional stars.** These employees are willing and able to focus their efforts and interests equally on the job at hand and the goals of their organization. These *institutional stars* possess high levels of involvement in their jobs and high levels of commitment to their organization. They are highly valued by the organization.

employee (interviewee) types. It offers insights into why organizations end up with some employees or job applicants who are outstanding and others who are less desirable overall.

Applying the Employee Types Window

To the extent possible, you will surely want to limit the number of apathetic employees in your organization. The best method is by not allowing them into the organization in the first place. It may also be necessary to develop ways to influence levels of involvement and commitment for current employees. Since *job involvement* is a function of the nature of the job, anything that can be done to increase the job's excitement would be helpful. *Commitment to organizational goals* could be enhanced by the extent to which these goals are clearly stated and communicated to all employees. When corporate goals are similar to employee goals and employees perceive that their efforts contribute in some way to goal achievement, *organizational commitment* can be increased. The use of good performance appraisal procedures with a goal-setting component could serve this requirement well.

Astute managers will note that actions designed to increase or decrease levels of *job involvement* may have the opposite effect on *organizational commitment* (and vice versa). You must walk a fine managerial line to maintain optimal levels of interest in both the job and the organization.

When to Use the Window. Not all employees are the same. Some employees have a strong job orientation—they feel good when their work gets done well, they are strongly motivated by the job, and their self-esteem is deeply rooted in the work that they do. Other employees are oriented toward their job's context, such as the development of social relationships at work, leisure-time activities, and family. Some employees internalize the goals and values of the organization as their own, while other employees express almost no loyalty to their employer. Recognizing these individual differences, you can use this window when:

- A new employee joins the organization. Having a vision of what an ideal employee would be like (e.g., *institutional star*) can help guide the socialization process in shaping the new employee's attitudes and behavior.
- An employee exhibits symptoms of being *apathetic.* This may encourage you to develop uniquely different strategies for increasing the employee's *job involvement* (possibly through enrichment strategies) and *organizational commitment* (possibly by explaining the long-term career opportunities available).
- An employee carries the *institutional star* phenomenon to a detrimental extreme. This may occur because the high levels of *job involvement* and *organizational commitment* create a high risk of burnout, or because the employee's extreme behavior antagonizes other employees who have more balanced perspectives. Whatever the cause, you may wish to counsel the employee before significant problems emerge.
- You can stereotype employees as static and either unwilling or unable to change. Recognition of this fixation in perception may awaken you to the fact that change may occur from within the employee or through the stimulation of you and the organization.

The Grid in Action. The deans from a number of the country's top engineering schools are talking at a meeting. The topic of conversation is "retro-education," short courses that allow practicing engineers whose skills have become obsolete to retool. The quickening pace of technological change has greatly reduced the half-life of engineering knowledge and skills.

Offering such updates as part of the school curriculum will require that faculty members also be able to maintain their cutting-edge skills and be willing to teach adult students.

George Welch, an ex-engineer who became a dean only a few months before this meeting, is voicing his concern over the apathy he sees in many of his faculty toward this idea. "Dammit, we give these guys tenure, and they disappear. They could care less about keeping up with the latest in engineering. They just want to teach engineering basics to undergraduates. I haven't yet figured out how to get these people more *involved* in their jobs and more *committed* to the school."

"George, you're not alone. I've got some of those people myself," echoes Kay Seibert, a longtime dean who has come up through the academic ranks. "But I've got a problem with the faculty members who are so concerned with their own professional development that they ignore the needs of the school. These people spend most of their time traveling to meetings to stay at the cutting edge. They are exactly the faculty who should be teaching these 'update' courses, but I don't know how to get them to stay in one place long enough to do that. And they are never around to take any of the committee responsibilities that we have. You can ask for commitment to the school, but these *lone wolves* won't give you any."

"I wish I had one or two of those myself," laments Marcia Harris, one of the most respected deans in the country. "My problem is that I've got too many *corporate citizens.* These folks will do anything I ask them—serve on committees, teach courses, visit sponsors, or meet with recruiters. But they spend so much time on school matters that they are losing touch with the reason we hired them—to keep in touch with recent engineering developments."

All three of the deans agree that they occasionally manage to find a real *superstar*—a faculty member who is willing and able to do it all. Such people are *involved* in their jobs, but they are also *committed* to their school. The deans are not sure how these *superstars* do it or how they can go about getting a whole department of superstars, but they are certain that they have to protect these folks from burnout.

As the discussion winds down, the deans conclude that they would all like to get rid of the *apathetic* employees. They want a faculty composed strictly of *superstars*, but this is unrealistic. Most likely a successful school has a combination of a few *lone wolves* (to keep up with the field), *corporate citizens* (to deal with the bureaucracy), and *superstars* (to act as role models for the others). The key is managing this diversity to maximize the overall performance of the school.

Reference

Blau, G., and K. Boal. "Conceptualizing How Job Involvement and Organizational Commitment Affect Turnover and Absenteeism." *Academy of Management Review,* Vol. 12, No. 2 (1987), pp. 288–300.

Chapter 7

Understanding Groups

Some organizational tasks are too demanding, too difficult, or too important to be performed by individuals. Because of their great potential for diverse perspectives, their combined breadth of member experiences, and the powerful support they can provide for decisions made, groups represent key building blocks for organizations. Consequently, managers at all levels need to understand group behavior whether it occurs in work groups, informal circles of friends, top management teams, or boards of directors. However, you must also note that group behavior can be simultaneously productive, puzzling, and vexing.

Some of the key features of group life include internal and external roles played by members, the ease of entry into a group, a group's cohesiveness, and the products of group effort (performance). This chapter introduces four closely related windows, each providing a different perspective on group behavior.

7-1. Group Reactions to New Members

Window 7-1 can help improve selection decisions for new work-team members. It encourages you to anticipate the reactions of present group members to potential new members. The model identifies four specific reactions that depend on the position to be filled and the group's receptivity to the newcomer. You can

Window 7-1. Group Reactions to New Members.

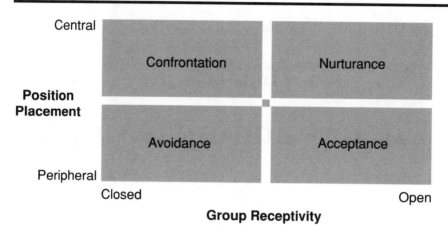

Source: James W. Fairfield-Sonn, "Work Group Reactions to New Members: Tool or Trap in Making Selection Decisions," *Public Personnel Management*, Vol. 13, No. 4 (Winter, 1984), pp. 485–493. Reprinted with permission of the International Personnel Management Association.

Dimensions

Position placement. The position to be filled within a group may be central or peripheral, depending on the information to be controlled and the individual's probable role in decision making. New members who fill central positions will have more power than those occupying peripheral positions.

Group receptivity. This dimension describes how receptive a group will be to a new member, ranging from very closed to very open. Receptivity often reflects how the work group feels about other groups with which a new member is identified.

Four Reactions to New Members

Confrontation. The most actively detrimental response—*confrontation*—occurs when a new member fills a central position in a closed group. The newcomer will encounter more or less active opposition (possibly even sabotage) by the group, especially if members have not been actively involved in the selection decision.

Nurturance. When a group is open and receptive and new members will be placed in a central position, *nurturance* is likely to result. The group will welcome, support, and work with the new members to facilitate their rapid acceptance and productive behavior.

Window 7-1. (*Continued*)

■ **Avoidance.** This represents a closed group's reaction to a newcomer who will occupy a peripheral position. The group may reject or isolate the new employee *avoiding* any contact that is not required.

■ **Acceptance.** This type of result occurs when a newcomer fills a peripheral position in an open group. The new member will be *accepted* and even welcomed, but will play a limited role in the group's decisions.

use the model to predict work group reactions to alternative candidates. Assuming that other qualifications are about equal, those candidates likely to cause positive group reactions should be selected.

Applying the Group Reactions Window

Problems with new employees occur during *socialization*—when newcomers "learn the ropes" of their jobs and organizations—and may produce low performance, job dissatisfaction, and turnover. Some of these problems can be avoided by improving personnel practices of recruitment, selection, placement, and orientation. Because socialization and personnel practices often ignore group reactions to new members, this window can enhance managerial analysis and action.

Groups often react to outsiders in terms of *stereotypes*—simplistic categories of people which are seldom accurate in describing particular individuals. These stereotypes help make each group feel good about itself, often at the expense of others. Work-group reactions to new members, then, reflect group history and image as well as specific assessment of individual newcomers.

A new member's position within the group structure—the norms, roles, and status systems learned during socialization—affect the newcomer's experience and performance as well as the group's reaction. As the specific reactions of the model suggest, centrally placed individuals may affect, and be affected by, the group differently than peripherally placed individuals.

To apply the window, you should predict group reactions to new members by assessing *position placement* and *group receptivity*. Several indicators predict whether the position to be filled is central or peripheral to the group. This can be determined by estimating access to information and influence in decision making that goes with the position. Whether a group will be open or closed to new members includes the leader's receptivity, group stereotypes of outsiders, the members' pride in the group, the group's power relative to other groups, and the openness of the group boundary.

You can also use predicted group reactions with other criteria to make decisions about new employees. Group reactions can be incorporated to screen recruits, to select employees, or to place new hires. Probable reactions can also form part of a *realistic job preview* for potential employees, which informs them of key information in an attempt to increase their future job satisfaction and to reduce turnover.

Finally, you should use the model to monitor the socialization of new members in work groups. The accuracy of predicted group reactions should be checked to improve future predictions. Moreover, you should reexamine access to information, decision making, and the indicators of group receptivity to gain insight into any problems that occur as new members enter their groups. These insights should guide ongoing managerial actions to improve group process or structure, with the aim of facilitating socialization and enhancing group effectiveness.

When to Use the Window. Much of the work that transpires within organizations, whether at top management levels or at the production level, unfolds in groups. This window into organizations—Group Reactions to New Members—should be used:

- To aid in the selection of new employees who will join an existing work team.
- When selecting people for group membership that involves consideration whether their role within the group is central or peripheral.
- When an existing group is being expanded and the group is likely to be closed (not receptive to new members). Here, you may need to confront the group and encourage the members to be more receptive.

The Grid in Action. Chris manages a clerical group in the "back office" of a regional banking firm. The group's newest member has just quit, after several months of struggling to "fit in." Despite excellent qualifications and motivation, the person had continuing difficulties with co-workers which hurt performance and morale. Chris remembers hearing about other problems with newcomers before she arrived. As a consequence Chris resolves to take group reactions into account in selecting a replacement.

Now faced with the task of replacing a member of the clerical group, Chris begins by assessing the position to be filled in terms of access to information and making decisions. She realizes that the position is quite central because it affects so many of the group's transactions. Chris also considers the group's receptivity to new replacements. Her people are a tight-knit group of veteran employees, focused on co-workers and families. "No wonder that young, single, ambitious individuals have had problems getting along in this group!" she thinks to herself.

When the personnel office sends Chris a list of qualified applicants to interview, she actively considers likely group reactions to each person. During her interviews she describes the group and some of the past problems of newcomers in order to provide a more realistic job preview to the applicants. One applicant doubts that he would be satisfied in such a situation, and so he takes a job elsewhere in the company. However, Chris finds a qualified replacement who has much in common with the other members of her group. As the new replacement starts to work, Chris resolves to keep an eye on the newcomer's progress and to help in anyway that she can.

7-2. Boundary Roles in Groups

Groups frequently find themselves exchanging resources with surrounding groups, organizations, and environment. These resources may include information, money, goods, services, status, and even affection. The purpose of Window 7-2 is to identify four boundary roles or functions that *manage* the flow of resources into and out of the group.

Window 7-2. Boundary Roles in Groups.

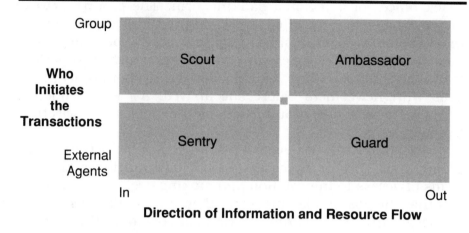

Source: Deborah Gladstein and David Caldwell, "Boundary Management in New Product Teams," *Academy of Management Proceedings*, 1985, pp. 161–165 (Figure 1, p. 162).

Dimensions

Who initiates the transactions. The initiative for an exchange may be taken either by the group or by other (external) agents. From a practical perspective this distinction implies that the group's stance in an exchange will be either proactive or reactive.

Direction of information and resource flow. This dimension describes the primary direction in which resources move. Viewed from the group's perspective, resources move either into or out of the group.

Four Boundary Roles

Scout. A *scout* initiates and facilitates the flow of resources *into* the group. If the group wants some information or needs a resource from the surrounding organization, the *scout's* role is to bring it into the group.

Ambassador. An *ambassador* initiates the flow of resources *out* of the group. If the group wants to convey some information or other resource to the organization, the *ambassador's* role is to present it effectively.

Sentry. A *sentry* regulates the flow of resources that external agents send into the group. If organizational agents want to introduce some information or other resource into the group, the *sentry* controls passage by delaying, expediting, screening, or modifying it.

Window 7-2. (*Continued*)

■ **Guard.** A guard regulates the flow of information or resources that external agents obtain from the group. If organizational agents want something from the group, the *guard* controls its exit.

Applying the Boundary Roles Window

First, you should assess the flow of resources between your group and surrounding organizations using this window. Effective boundary management consists of exchanging the right resources with the right party at the right time. Groups need resources for effective performance, but they also provide resources for organizational purposes.

Second, *scouts, ambassadors, sentries,* and *guards* must all act to get the right resources to the right party at the right time. To achieve such effective boundary management, you need to look for opportunities to perform several roles at once, such as giving (by an *ambassador*) and receiving (by a *scout*) information at a meeting. You may also develop roles or norms to involve group members in boundary management. While the reactive roles of *sentries* and *guards* may already exist in many groups, you should thoroughly examine the possibilities of the proactive roles of *scouts* and *ambassadors*.

Third, the mix of roles needed for such effective boundary management must be constantly updated in response to changing circumstances. Factors such as the present stage of a group project, the degree to which a group may operate autonomously, the extent to which resources are easy to obtain, and the state of relations among group members should be considered in developing an effective mix of boundary role activities.

When to Use the Window. Groups engage in transactions with their environment. Whenever group survival or effectiveness is affected, this window could be used. Examples include:

- Recognizing that there are different roles that group members serve to facilitate the group's task-related activities, and some of these are boundary roles

- Making sure that several necessary boundary roles are performed when the work of a team is being divided up and allocated
- Choosing a person with the skills and personality that will fit the particular boundary-role needs of the group when you select a new member for a work group
- Recognizing that the *scout* and *ambassador* roles become especially important when you attempt to manage the group's relations with external groups

The Grid in Action. Kim works for a software company and has been assigned to lead a new group to develop products for elementary schools. Her previous experience in product development has convinced her that getting resources and using contacts within the company are crucial for the success of such a group. She wonders how she can effectively manage the relations between her group and the organization.

Kim begins by assessing the *flow of information and resources* to and from the group which will be necessary to get started. At first, she plans to be the group's *ambassador,* presenting its case to possible allies throughout the organization. Kim also expects to take the initiative by *scouting* around the company to bring needed resources to the group. Later, the group may need protection from disruptions by helpful, jealous, or curious outsiders. To assure that the group can continue to develop its product ideas, Kim is prepared to serve *sentry* and *guard* duty to prevent interference by others in the company. When the group has developed a product, Kim expects to champion her group's idea as *ambassador* to top management.

As she considers all these efforts to manage group relations with the company effectively, Kim realizes that she will need help. She identifies several group members with good contacts throughout the organization as possible *scouts.* If the group needs to be protected from outsiders at a critical stage of development, Kim imagines that she might enlist all members in an effort to prevent outside interference.

7-3. Member Roles in Groups

In any organization different individuals assume different roles or postures toward other group members and activities. Not all group members, therefore, engage in the same activities or have the same group orientation. Roles are the particular activities that distinguish some group members from others. Window 7-3 describes different types of roles that members play in groups. The model classifies a member's activities in terms of social and task-oriented behaviors. Implicitly, the model prescribes that group members balance their social and task activities, or that a group must have some balance of roles played within it.

Applying the Member Roles Window

You can use the model to understand the roles played by different group members, which can include themselves. By assessing the degree of each member's social and task activities, you can determine the role played by each member. In addition, this evaluation enables you to determine whether or not any role is now missing.

Groups have both a task and a maintenance (social-interpersonal) need if they are going to survive. A group dominated by unchosen members may soon die. There is, therefore, a need for many *stars* or a balance between *social specialists* and *technical specialists.*

When to Use the Window. This window points out that different group members generally assume different organizational roles. The model also suggests that groups have two critical roles that need to be fulfilled—one *social* and the other *task-oriented.* You can use these insights:

- When constructing a group for the very first time. You need to recognize that you should select people with *socially relevant* behaviors and *task-relevant behaviors.*
- When adding to the size of a group. Here you will need to assess the existing group's current social/task composition and future needs, and select new members to fill those needs.
- When group membership is unstable. For example, as task demands call for the rotation of members in and out of a task team, the selection process should in part be guided by the group's *socially relevant/task-relevant* needs.

Window 7-3. Member Roles in Groups.

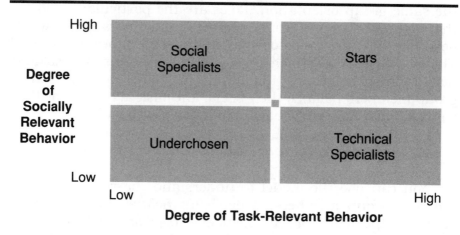

Source: Robert F. Bales, *Interaction Process Analysis: A Method for the Study of Small Groups*, Cambridge, Mass.: Addison-Wesley, 1950.

Dimensions

Degree of socially relevant behavior. A group member's behaviors may demonstrate a high or low degree of concern with social aspects of the group. *Socially relevant behavior* concerns such issues as the members' emotional reactions to events, conflict, support for other members, loyalty, and unity.

Degree of task-relevant behavior. A group member's activities may also show a high or low degree of concern with regard to the task that the group is engaged in. *Task-relevant behavior* concerns such issues as setting and focusing on group goals, establishing procedures, fixing responsibilities, and focusing on the management of time.

Four Member Roles

Stars. The *star* role involves a high degree of both social and task behavior. *Stars* show balanced concern for the members and the work of the group.

Social specialists. The *social specialist* role involves a high degree of social behavior and little task activity. *Social specialists* focus on needs of the members of the group.

Window 7-3. (*Continued*)

■ **Technical specialists.** The *technical specialist* role involves a high degree of task behavior with very little focus on the group's social activities. *Technical specialists* focus on the work of the group.

■ **Underchosen.** The underchosen role involves little social or task activity. *Underchosens* focus on personal concerns, rather than on the members or work of the group.

The Grid in Action. Lee has just been elected chairperson of the board for a local charitable organization. During his coming term he believes that the board expects the executive director to lead the organization through some dramatic changes. In preparing for his new responsibilities, he feels that he needs to understand better how each member contributes to the board.

During the next meeting Lee notes the kind of comments made by each member. Most members seem to specialize in such *social* activities as supporting other members, resolving disagreements, and emphasizing unity. A few, including Lee, concern themselves with the *task* before the board, such as schedules, procedures, and technical details of reports. The outgoing chairperson seems to contribute both *social-* and *task-*related comments.

Lee now considers the balance among the board members' contributions. He admires how well the outgoing chairperson has balanced both *social* and *task* concerns in her role. Lee is happy to see that no board members have limited themselves exclusively to personal concerns. Because relatively few members specialize in *task* concerns, he notes, the board tends to rely often on the executive director and her staff for guidance and assistance. The large proportion of *social* specialists makes serving on this board a pleasant and friendly experience. Such *social* support may also prove to be an asset if the board receives public criticism for allowing unpopular changes by the executive director.

Reference

McGrath, Joseph E. *Groups: Interaction and Performance.* Englewood Cliffs, N.J.: Prentice-Hall, 1984, pp. 154–158.

7-4. Group Performance Predictions

Window 7-4 helps us to see that group performance depends on how well rewards match task requirements. The model predicts higher or lower performance for different combinations of rewards and task requirements for working together. Higher group performance is likely where reward differentials are compatible with task demands for close interaction.

Applying the Group Performance Window

Various reward structures are used to motivate performance. Competitive (very high differential) structures, such as merit pay from a fixed pool of money, reward the best performers at the expense of other group members. Individualistic (high differential) structures, such as piece rate systems, reward employees according to their own levels of performance. Cooperative (low differential) structures, such as group-based incentives, reward members equally. Each type of reward structure has its supporters among managers and workers.

In studies of group performance, however, these reward structures have produced a confusing mix of positive and negative results. This window helps you see through the confusion by illustrating the effect of rewards in light of the tasks being performed. *Only where reward structures and task requirements are congruent is high performance likely.*

You should use the model, then, to assess the congruence of *reward* and *task* structures in your group. Do group members receive approximately equal or substantially different amounts of pay? Do group *tasks* demand close interaction and cooperation among members, or not? Is the existing combination of *reward* and *task* structures a good match or a poor match?

In most cases of a poor match, you should consider changing the *reward* structure to increase congruence with the *task* and thereby motivate higher performance. A competitive or individualistic (high differential) structure should be adopted only where *tasks* require little interaction. A cooperative (low differential) system should enhance performance of *tasks* that demand close interaction. Any reward structure will be more motivational if pay is based on performance rather than on some other (uncontrollable) factor.

Window 7-4. Group Performance Predictions.

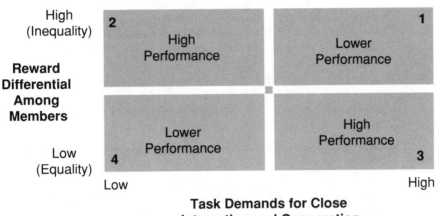

Source: Terence R. Mitchell and James R. Larson, Jr., *People in Organizations: An Introduction to Organizational Behavior*, 3rd ed., New York: McGraw-Hill, 1987, pp. 239–241. Reprinted with permission.

Dimensions

Reward differential among members. An organization can reward group members with similar or different amounts of pay for performing similar tasks. When members are paid equally, the *reward differential* is low. When members are paid very different amounts, the *reward differential* is high.

Task demands for close interaction and cooperation. This dimension reflects how much tasks require group members to *work together* and *coordinate* their efforts. Some tasks demand high levels of *interaction* and *cooperation* of group members, while other tasks require little *interaction* to get the work done.

Performance Predictions

Quadrant 1. High *reward differential* and high *task demands for close interaction* are a poor match, with *lower performance* likely. Differences in pay among members foster destructive competition, which hinders performance of tasks requiring cooperation.

Quadrant 2. High *reward differential* and low *task demands for cooperation* are a good match, making *higher performance* likely. Differences in pay among members recognize individual performance on tasks requiring little interaction.

Window 7-4. (*Continued*)

■ **Quadrant 3.** Low *reward differential* and high task demands for close interaction are a good match, making *higher perfomance* likely. Members are paid equally for performing tasks that require them to cooperate.

■ **Quadrant 4.** Low *reward differential* and *task demands* for cooperation are a poor match, making lower performance likely. Equal pay among members provides little reward for outstanding individual performance of tasks that require little interaction.

In some cases of a poor match, *tasks* might be performed equally well with or without *close interaction and cooperation.* You might then change *task* procedures to increase congruence with the existing reward structure. Employees could complete independent units of work for higher performance under a competitive or individualistic reward system. Members could work together for higher performance under a cooperative reward system.

When to Use the Window. Not all managers have the capacity to modify the existing reward system. Similarly, not all supervisors, especially those in highly automated operations, can independently change the required interactions among their employees. Nevertheless, this model can be useful to you when:

- A new work unit is being formed, and interactions among group members are still being designed. Decisions can be made reflecting your perception of the desirability of *close interaction* or even constraints to interaction.
- The organization's reward system is subject to close scrutiny and the possibility of change. Sometimes this occurs on a recurring cycle, sometimes it is brought about through merger, and sometimes it is the result of either initiatives from staff specialists in human resources or pleas for change from line managers.
- Symptoms of underlying problems begin to appear with some degree of regularity, such as low morale, high turn-

over, or destructive conflict among group members. These may indicate the need to examine the *reward structure-task demands* for interaction "fit" and recommend constructive changes.

The Grid in Action. Leslie manages her own market research firm, employing a small group of people to conduct telephone interviews and process survey data. Her personal philosophy is to pay all her employees the same, providing equal raises reflecting the success of the business and the cost of living. Lately, however, she has begun to question this pay policy. Her hardest workers and those who have been with her the longest have complained about lack of rewards; several have left for better-paying jobs. Leslie also wonders if she could boost performance by adjusting her pay policy.

Leslie begins by assessing *reward differential and task demands.* Her equal-pay policy means that the *reward differential* among employees is very low. The *tasks* of telephone interviewing and data processing *demand* little interaction or cooperation among her employees. She concludes that the existing combination of low *reward differential* and low *task demands for cooperation* is a poor match, limiting group performance.

To improve performance, Leslie decides to increase the *reward differential* among the employees. She considers several alternative criteria for paying employees different amounts, including seniority and performance level; she also considers responding to competing job offers. In the end Leslie decides to develop a performance appraisal (merit) system as a basis for paying employees.

Chapter 8

Human Resources Management

The human resources of any organization are a very valuable component of that operation. The management of those human resources is not only important but often fairly complex. This is reflected in the amount of monetary resources devoted to this part of the organization, which creates pressure to make sure that the money is well spent. The complexity of the human side of the organization is also reflected by the fact that when we are dealing with individuals there are never any absolutes—there are myriad individual differences that characterize how people behave and respond. Consistent with the contingency approach to managing, there is no single best way of dealing with all individuals in all situations. Finally, human resources management is difficult because of the number of functions that fall within that category. Hiring, firing, appraisal of performance, and socializing employees to become the type of individuals who will be both successful and useful for the organization are just a few of the mandates for human resource managers.

This chapter presents models and suggestions for just a few of the issues human resources managers are confronted with daily. The first window introduces a set of guidelines for ensuring that employment practices follow approved legal standards. The second window addresses strategic career systems and the hiring strategies to use given the types of jobs and the market of potential employees. The third window is a model of socialization strategies that describes which strategies to use given certain desired organizational outcomes. Finally, the fourth window matches effective performance-appraisal techniques with the particular employee being appraised.

8-1. Employment Effects

When Title VII of the Civil Rights Act of 1964 became law, the concepts of discrimination and fair employment gained importance for American businesses. It was declared illegal to discriminate against individuals because of their race, color, religion, sex, or national origin. This discrimination is not only illegal in hiring but also in matters of discharge, compensation, or any other terms, conditions, and privileges of employment. The Equal Employment Opportunity Commission (EEOC) was then set up to help monitor and enforce these rules. One of the more important acts of the EEOC has been the publication of the Uniform Guidelines on Employee Selection Procedures (1978). The guidelines attempt to make explicit exactly what is meant by discrimination, adverse impact, and unfairness. They set out detailed descriptions of what measures organizations need to follow in order to ensure compliance. These guidelines have been closely followed by the courts in making several decisions regarding employment discrimination charges. For this reason they correspond very closely to what the courts consider law.

One basic way to analyze a work force to determine if there is any adverse impact is by using a rule of thumb known as the four-fifths rule. Adverse impact occurs when there is a substantially different rate of selection in hiring, promotion, or other employment decisions which works to the disadvantage of members of a race, sex, or ethnic group. This "substantially different rate" occurs when the selection rate for the disadvantaged group is less than four-fifths (or 80 percent) the rate for the group with the highest rate. It should be emphasized that this does not refer to the total number selected, but rather the selection *rate.* An example will clarify this very important point.

Assume that whites are the group with the highest selection rate. In this case, assume 100 whites apply for a job and 60 are selected. This is a selection rate of 60 percent (60/100). Next, assume that the minority group in this example is Hispanics. Forty Hispanics apply for the same job and 20 are selected. This is a selection rate of 50 percent (20/40). Now, the key to determining whether or not there is adverse impact is to compare the two selection rates. The ratio of the selection rate of Hispanics to whites is 83.3 percent (50/60). Because this is greater than 80 percent, there is no evidence of adverse impact in the example, despite the differential selection rates.

Window 8-1 explains when a situation represents fair employment and when it may represent employment that has an adverse impact. Two key factors that aid in this determination are the availability of minorities and the allocation (use) of minorities.

Applying the Discrimination/Fair Employment Grid

All managers should be aware of the need to staff their organizations in a way that gets the best people for the jobs in which they will be most successful, while at the same time not creating an *adverse impact* against any other persons. This model helps to provide a thumbnail sketch of when a situation might be acceptable and when it might be discriminatory. Organizations need to monitor their employment methods both to make sure that societal fairness exists and to avoid costly and time-consuming litigation.

While we generally concentrate on *adverse impact* effects only at the initial hiring time, it is important to remember that Title VII and the Uniform Guidelines both make it clear that discrimination is illegal not only in hiring but also in making layoff decisions and promotions, providing access to special training programs needed for further advancement, and other employment situations. It is important for organizations to monitor their progress at all levels and to use valid instruments and methods in order to ensure fair employment for all.

Guidelines for Using the Window. Although the specific implications of this window may not be immediately apparent, the effects of disregarding this model can be astronomical, as many companies have ruefully discovered. The immediate guidelines for its use follow:

Window 8-1. Employment Effects.

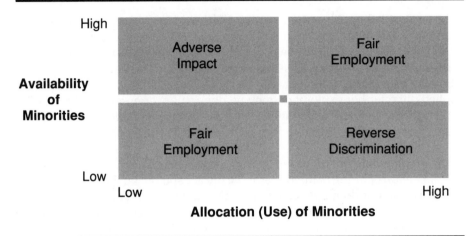

Dimensions

Availability of minorities. The relevant labor market is generally defined as the working population in the relevant employment area or (for jobs of greater specialization) the population of individuals with the necessary (and valid) prerequisites for the job in question. The Uniform Guidelines state that when a group makes up less than 2 percent of the relevant labor market, then no statistics on adverse impact need be kept (although blatant discrimination is still illegal). This dimension ranges from low to high. Low is defined as occasions when a group makes up less than 2 percent of the relevant labor market of the job in question.

Allocation (use) of minorities. This dimension refers to the proportion of available minorities hired, promoted, placed in training programs, discharged, or any other relevant employment decisions. Such use can range from low to high.

Employment Effects

Adverse impact. The most obvious case of *adverse impact* arises when many qualified minorities are *available* but few are *used*. This could be any situation where the four-fifths rule is violated; that is, when the selection rate or the minority group is less than 80 percent of the majority group selection rate. Even if the four-fifths rule is not violated, if it appears that an adequate supply of qualified and minority individuals exist in the relevant labor force who could have applied but did not and therefore the selection rate for minorities appears

Window 8-1. (*Continued*)

to be artificially high, then there might still be evidence of *adverse impact.* For example, if 50 whites apply and 30 are selected (60 percent selection rate), and if 10 minorities apply and 6 are selected (also a 60 percent selection rate), the ratio of selection rates is 100 percent (60 percent/60 percent). However, if the relevant labor market suggests that similar numbers of whites and minorities should have applied, then further exploration may be done. If fewer numbers of minorities applied due to differential recruiting techniques, then *adverse impact* may still be found.

Fair employment. When there is a low *availability* of minorities, then a low *allocation* or hiring of minorities is legally acceptable. In the case of a group that makes up less than 2 percent of the relevant labor market, no employment statistics need to be kept and an organization need not compute the selection rates. However, it should be clear that intentional discrimination against members in this category is still illegal. Further, organizations should be very sure they know what is considered the relevant labor market for the job in question.

Reverse discrimination. When few minorities are *available* but a disproportionately high *use* of minorities occurs, it is possible that reverse discrimination is present. A Supreme Court case in 1978 (Bakke v. Regents of the University of California) disallowed a medical school admission procedure that set aside a specific number of places for economically disadvantaged applicants who were rejected from admission according to the standard combination of test scores and grades. Bakke, a white applicant, complained that he had been denied admission in favor of less qualified minority applicants. The court ruled in favor of Bakke, but made it clear that using race in admission decisions was still permissible, especially in an attempt to remedy past discrimination.

Fair employment. The final cell of the model represents fair employment, which again exists when minority applicants are readily *available* and when they are *utilized* by the organization in a corresponding high degree. Organizations that fulfill the criterion of maintaining a selection ratio of at least 80 percent (as defined earlier) for all relevant groups can be assured that the results of their employment decisions will pass this test.

- Evaluate all human resource policies and practices within the organization, and test them for compatibility with *fair employment* principles.
- Study the locally relevant labor markets to identify legitimate minorities.
- Eliminate any practices (formal or informal) that result in *adverse impact* for any minority group.
- Attempt to balance the risk of creating *reverse discrimination* with the consequences of *adverse impact* so as to minimize both.
- View minorities as the untapped labor resource for the 1990s, and focus future energies on recruiting, hiring, training, and using them in a fair and positive manner.

The Grid in Action. Charlie Stutesman is concerned. He has just completed a course in personnel management at the local university where he has learned about the legal aspects of employment. Charlie has been working at the zipper factory for fifteen years and has a personal stake in the affairs of the company since it is owned by his father-in-law. Charlie goes in to see him and discuss his concerns. "Ray," Charlie says, "I want to talk to you about how you select your employees here." Ray Andrews is a bright man who knows that the way to stay successful is to surround yourself with other bright people, especially those who have expertise in areas other than your own. Besides being his son-in-law, Charlie is also one of those sharp individuals. "Go ahead, Charlie," Ray says, "tell me what is on your mind."

Charlie describes what he has learned about selection ratios, relevant labor markets, the four-fifths rule of thumb, and *adverse impact.* Ray assures Charlie that there is nobody in his company who harbors any discriminatory thoughts toward anyone, women included. Charlie says he is sure that there is no intentional discrimination, but it seems that a fair number of new employees were hired through the recommendations of current employees. Many of these current employees have been with the company for years, and the bulk of them are white males. Ray and Charlie then take a look through the company employment records for the past five years and find that while in most jobs it appears everything is fine, a few jobs appear to show *adverse impact* (the *use* of minorities is low and *availa-*

bility may well be high). Ray thanks Charlie for his information and makes a high-priority note to call in a consultant on *fair employment, adverse impact,* and the validity of selection instruments.

References

Arvey, Richard D. *Fairness in Selecting Employees.* Reading, Mass.: Addison-Wesley, 1979.

Schneider, Benjamin, and Neal Schmitt. *Staffing Organizations.* Glenview, Ill.: Scott, Foresman and Company, 1983.

Uniform Guidelines on Employee Selection Procedures, 43 *Federal Register* 38290–38315 (1978).

8-2. Strategic Career Systems

From the organization's perspective, effective career management means having the proper staffing levels and an uninterrupted flow of qualified individuals into all jobs. The jobs in an organization may be staffed by primarily internal candidates, external applicants, or some combination of both. In addition, each job within the organization consists of projects that are mainly group- or individual-oriented. Window 8-2 relates to an organization's career system. The model provides you with suggestions pertaining to career system priorities and the training and development strategies that will best fit those needs. This window suggests that the supply and assignment flows for a company's work force should fit the company's strategic orientation.

Applying the Strategic Career Systems Window

Strategic career systems encompass a whole range of organization functions. They include recruiting, hiring, performance appraisal, training, retention, and the career system an organization wants to maintain based on its type of industry, level of competition, and corporate mission. An organization in a very competitive, regulation-free industry will be interested in a very different corporate career system than will a company that is basically a monopoly in a very regulated industry. Organ-

Window 8-2. Strategic Career Systems.

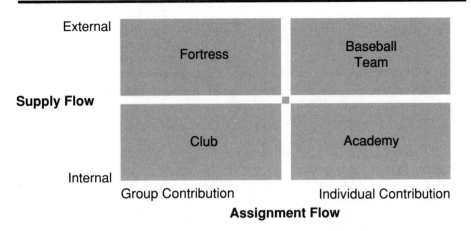

Source: Jeffrey A. Sonnenfeld and Maury A. Peiperl, "Staffing Policy as a Strategic Response: A Typology of Career Systems," *Academy of Management Review*, Vol. 13, No.4 (1988), pp. 588–600.

Dimensions

Supply flow. This dimension records the relative openness of the organization to the external labor market at jobs beyond the entry level. An organization with a very external focus would rarely promote from within but rather look to outsiders to fill open positions. On the other end of the continuum would be an organization's internal focus, making an effort to bring in outsiders only at the entry levels and then letting people work their way up the ladder. IBM is a classic example of a company that has a very internal supply-flow focus.

Assignment flow. The assignment flow dimension captures the way projects are assigned and promotions given. Most organizations operate within the individual contribution side of the dimension; that is, they look for the star performers (the individuals with the best track records) and assign them to the most desirable or important projects. Other organizations (for example the military) want individuals who work primarily toward furthering the goals of the group. An example would be an individual who was willing to help pick up the slack for a co-worker or take an undesirable assignment in order to increase the group's effectiveness.

Types of Career Systems

Fortress. Organizations of this type typically struggle for survival. They are often found in very competitive business sectors or where key resources are

Window 8-2. (*Continued*)

often lacking. Employees work toward the betterment of the group—specifically, to keeping the organization viable. *Fortress* organizations search for individuals who appear to be able to resolve the difficulties that the company faces. They look to generalists who will work toward the group goals and who have the flexibility to help out where needed. No real time or money is spent on training and development; instead, these companies concentrate on hiring people who already have the needed skills.

Club. Organizations with a *club* orientation are found in a competitive situation that is fairly protected because of regulatory constraint or virtual monopoly. Public utilities, museums, and the different military branches are examples of the *club* career system. Employees often work toward what they see as the overriding company goal, which is serving the public interest. These organizations staff internally and attempt to retain individuals who are company-specific generalists. Any training undertaken is usually done for general enrichment.

Baseball team. On a baseball team hitters are kept on the basis of their current batting average, not their historical average. In short, individuals are only as valuable as their current level of contribution. In creative industries such as advertising agencies, consulting firms, and software development companies, innovation is highly important. Individual stars are recruited from outside, and only those internal candidates who achieve star status are retained. Very little training is done, since skills are typically portable and the company is therefore not interested in spending money on developing skills that might then be taken to a competitor.

Academy. Organizations who fit the *academy* category are often the major competitor in an industry. The heavy emphasis on internal staffing promotes an atmosphere where there is little turnover. Such organizations have very complex career ladders and tracks that people follow from entry level positions to the top of the organizational pyramid. IBM is the classic example of an *academy* organization with its "no layoff" policy and work force consisting of many people who have been with the organization for fifteen, twenty, and twenty-five years. *Academy* companies in this quadrant concentrate on developing specialists in company-specific functional areas and rely on continuous retraining as individuals move through their careers and the organization's hierarchy.

izations that choose recruitment and hiring strategies inappropriate to their appraisal and promotion policies will suffer far greater inefficiencies in trying to match persons and jobs.

Organizations should use this grid to help detemine where they fit, and more importantly to see if they are utilizing personnel practices that are all consistent with a given system. For example, an organization that is basically in the *baseball team* windowpane should check its training and development budget. If there is a lot of money being spent on skill or non-company-specific training, the amount should probably be cut, since the return to the company for such training is likely to be very low. In fact, it could be negative if an employee leaves and then puts those new skills to work for a competitor.

While any organization often fits into one career system type, it is likely that an individual department or division may not be the same as the organization as a whole. An example of this might be an advertising or public relations department within an automobile company. Here the company might be an *academy* system while the department is run more like a *baseball team.* It is important for you to assess both the company and department situation to see where they are currently operating and to determine if that is the most efficient way to continue operating.

As policy changes are suggested (ideally before they are implemented), you should ask yourself, "Is this policy going to fit with the sort of strategic career system that I already have in place?" Additionally, you should be constantly monitoring your environment to see if a change to a new quadrant is necessary or even imminent. An industry that becomes increasingly regulated will probably want to adjust its human resources practices to fit the new operating situation.

Using the Window. Organizations can be expected to become increasingly interested in designing the proper career system in the 1990s, when labor force shortages in the U.S. are expected to be severe in some jobs, industries, and geographical areas. In light of this, you should use this window to:

- Analyze and classify your present career system to assess its appropriateness.
- Examine the probable changes in *supply flow* of appli-

cants, and the intended use of *assignments* internally, to determine what type of career system best fits the organization's needs for the future.

- Function as a counseling tool, advising both present and prospective employees to consider carefully the match between their system preferences and the nature of the company and department.
- Examine various units within the organization to identify differences within it, and (if they are present) to explore reasons why such differences might logically exist.

The Grid in Action. After ten years in the work force as a teacher, Joan Walters has returned to college to get her MBA degree. With her final semester of school about to begin, Joan begins to think about where she would like to work after graduation. Through her years of teaching experience and her coursework, she has concluded that the training area is definitely where she wants to locate. The next question is: In what industry? Joan decides to apply some information she has learned in one of her courses.

The matrix of career systems the class has studied has presented different types of organizations categorized by the type of projects and whether the work force came up through the ranks internally or was hired from outside. *Fortress* organizations are those typically in the middle of a major retrenchment with frequent layoffs necessary. Training is considered a luxury and rarely implemented. Joan decides that these companies, such as retailers and publishers, are not for her. *Baseball team* organizations such as advertising and consulting firms and software development companies also do little training, which she feels she will require. *Club* organizations such as utilities and government agencies and banks are usually somewhat interested in training, but provide only general enrichment-type training such as communication skills. This seems a little too monotonous to Joan and is the very reason she left teaching and went back to college in the first place.

Joan finally decides that *academy* organizations will be the best place in which to concentrate her job-search efforts. Automobile, consumer products, electronics, office products, and pharmaceutical companies are all industries that have reputations for concentrating on internal staffing with individual-level project contributions. Because of this, they rely a great deal on continual training and retraining, and moving people within the organization. While not every company in these industries will fit the profile completely, Joan decides that they are the best place to begin her search for further information in order to line up a satisfying job when she graduates.

8-3. Socialization Strategies

Socialization is the process of instilling key organizational values, norms, and practices in a company's employees.

Socialization is typically one of the initiations given to employees in their new company or their new department in the organization following transfer to a new job. Formal socialization programs occur during the first few days on the job (or before the job even begins). They consist of a basic "how-to" introduction to life in the new organization. Topics discussed include organizational philosophy and policies, history of the organization and its products/services, a company tour, and an introduction to new co-workers. In addition, informal socialization occurs on a daily basis as employees learn the ropes from their bosses and co-workers.

Socialization programs should be set up to help create the climate that an organization hopes to maintain. Window 8-3 describes four socialization strategies. Each strategy is associated with a set of outcomes that an organization might hope to achieve.

Applying the Socialization Strategies Window

Socialization strategies should reflect the type of individuals that the organization is interested in developing. The strategies should also maintain their stated mission, philosophy, and culture. Other policies in the organization such as evaluation and compensation should be consistent with the socialization strategies. For example, an organization that values *innovative* behavior should have a performance appraisal system that can accurately assess and reward individuals who show appropriate creativity.

Some organizations simply hand an employee a handbook

(Text continues on page 134)

Window 8-3. Socialization Strategies.

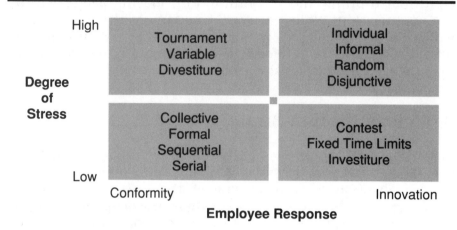

Source: J. Van Maanen, "People Processing: Strategies of Organizational Socialization," *Organizational Dynamics,* Vol. 6 (1978), pp. 19–36.

Dimensions

Degree of stress. Socialization programs and practices can produce variations in *stress* and stress expectations. While many jobs might best be performed under low stress conditions, some jobs, such as that of a Wall Street investment broker, are inherently highly stressful. In those cases a socialization program that is similar in tone might provide the employee with a realistic job preview as well as important training.

Employee response. Depending on the socialization strategies used, employers can encourage job-related behavior that is either highly conforming or highly innovative. In organizations where teamwork is important, an emphasis on conformity might be best, while a research and development-oriented company might prefer innovativeness.

Socialization Strategies

Tournament, variable, and divestiture. This cell consists of three different strategies. The *tournament* strategy separates new employees into different socialization programs on the basis of presumed job differences (e.g., compensation specialists vs. staffing specialists). Rather than being socialized together, new employees are socialized according to homogeneous groups. The *variable* socialization program has no fixed length. New employees have no timetable against which to judge when they should reach different stages in the learning process. The third strategy, *divestiture,* provides very little support for the

Window 8-3. (*Continued*)

newcomers. This socialization program ignores and dismisses any personal characteristics of the new employees. The program is oriented toward molding the employee into the organization's mold.

Use of either the *tournament, variable,* or *divestiture* strategies will generally result in both high *stress* and high *conformity.* Organizations that need individuals who think and act similarly and can deal with stressful situations (e.g., medical student training programs) might find these strategies most effective. While further along in their careers an *innovative* approach might be desirable, initially medical schools might prefer individuals who conform—doing things by the book, recognizing the right way and the wrong way of doing something. The realities of a *stressful* working environment make this socialization strategy highly effective for incoming medical students.

Collective, formal, sequential, and serial. Four different socialization strategies lead to the predicted outcomes of low *stress* and *conformity.* The *collective* strategy puts new organization members through a common set of experiences. These experiences help to produce standardized responses that are reinforced by the observation of other group members doing exactly the same thing. *Formal* tactics, closely related to the collective strategy, separate the recruits from current organizational members during the socialization phase; that is, recruits participate in socialization programs with other recruits, away from the job. This separation from current employees helps to ensure that new recruits will accept definitions of situations and how to respond in the way taught by the socialization program organizers. Consequently, they will not be contaminated by other suggestions (for example, a current employee who says, "Oh yeah, that is the way they tell you to do it, but *nobody* actually does it that way"). *Sequential* tactics give the recruits explicit information on the series or experiences and milestones they will pass while in the organization. For example, a university department might tell new faculty members that they will undergo performance reviews every year and at the end of three years a decision will be made whether or not to renew their contract. Assuming a contract renewal, they will continue to be reviewed yearly and then at the end of six years a decision will be made as to whether tenure will be given. If yes, then promotion to the rank of associate professor will occur. If the decision is no, then the individual will have one final year before employment is terminated. Finally, *serial* tactics involve the use of role models to follow once the individual is on the job. Mentors might serve this purpose in organizations where there is an obvious career progression from one job to the next. These four strategies are likely to result in low *stress* and high *conformity.*

Contest, fixed time limits, and investiture. The tactics in this cell produce outcomes exactly opposite from those used in the first category (*high stress, conformity*). The *contest* strategy emphasizes that "we're all in this together"

Window 8-3. (*Continued*)

rather than the "me against you" attitude present in the *tournament* strategy. An effort is made to avoid big distinctions between groups of new employees. *Fixed time limits* during which the new recruit should complete each stage of experiences are made known. Finally, *investiture* strategies give new members positive social support from individuals already working for the company. In addition, attention is directed toward the unique and useful personal characteristics that each recruit brings to the company.

■ **Individual, informal, random, and disjunctive**. This cell contains strategies that are the polar opposites of those in the second category (*low stress, conformity*). *Individual* socialization programs socialize each recruit in isolation from any other recruits. Each has a unique learning experience and therefore develops some innovative differences in how he/she responds to different situations. Informal methods also help to encourage *innovation. Random* socialization processes are designed to have no particular sequence of steps to be learned or achieved before the next level is reached. Additionally, *disjunctive* processes, by providing no true role model, encourage newcomers to blaze their own trails. A new organization, department, or product group might utilize these strategies. There are no preconceived ideas about how a job is to be defined. Instead the organization lets the nature of the task and the talents of the individuals involved define how things get done.

and say, "Read this and report to work on Monday." Other organizations have lengthy socialization programs conducted on company time. Either approach is fine, provided it yields the outcomes desired by the organization. Organizations that do not attempt to match their socialization strategies with their other human resource programs and organizational philosophy may implement programs that detract from each other. When this happens, good programs fail and employees who would have been successful may leave to join other organizations. Well-integrated programs are imperative, and socialization strategies are an important part of this integration.

Steps to Employ When Using the Window. Socialization can be planned or unplanned, formal or informal, quickly completed or long and sustained. Remembering this, you should:

- Resolve not to leave the socialization of new employees to chance.
- Evaluate the success of current socialization efforts.
- Identify which set of socialization strategies seems most appropriate for your organization and implement a conscious process designed to produce the desired effects.
- Attempt to adapt the socialization process to fit the particular needs of each individual or group of individuals.

The Grid in Action. Mark Hanselman, John Patricks, Mary Gay Dooley, and Teri Schneider all went to college together. When they graduated, they began to work for a new electronics company. The company is growing quickly, based largely on the development of several new products. It has also benefited from an aggressive advertising campaign in the trade journals and trade shows where manufacturers that use electronic components in the production of their own products have learned about the company. Mary Gay and John work in the product development areas, while Mark is in the advertising department and Teri handles recruiting. After about three whirlwind months on the job, they all get together and compare observations.

All four agree that their socialization and early days have been quite stressful, but, they agree, so is working in this industry and this company. All four have undergone their socialization programs separate from one another or any other new recruits. In fact, for the most part they have not been treated much like recruits at all, but have been thrown right into the job along with the employees already working for the company. They are now having new employees assigned to them who are trying to learn the positions. They assume that means they have survived the process, although nothing has ever been formally said.

Most interesting to the four in the group is the way in which they all seem to be learning the job on their own and adapting to it in different ways. Even though they have all gone to school together and taken many of the same courses, they find they approach situations in ways different than the others say they might in the same position. This is even true of John and Mary Gay, who are both in the same product development department, although working on different projects. Because the company is new, there aren't many established experts to explain how things are done, so each does what makes the most sense based on previous knowledge and experience.

This company is using high-*stress*, high-*innovation* strategies to socialize Mary Gay, John, Mark, and Teri. Individual, informal programs where the *disjunctive* and *nonsequential* approaches to socialization are implemented are a good match with this organization, because it is in a fast-moving and somewhat stressful consumer products marketplace. Here the emphasis is on *innovation*, whether it is in new product lines or the campaigns to market them, and there seems to be a good fit with the socialization method.

Reference

Gordon, Judith R. *Human Resource Management: A Practical Approach.* Boston, Mass.: Allyn and Bacon, 1986.

8-4. Employee Behaviors in Performance Appraisals

Conducting performance appraisals is typically a very time-consuming and costly process. However, despite this investment, appraisals are often not very effective. Designed to help employees understand how they have been doing, to point out areas of deficiencies, and to motivate them to improve, the appraisal process sometimes fails because of both the employee and the employer. Employees often become defensive during appraisals and view the process more as confrontation than an exchange of useful information and ideas. The persons conducting the appraisals are also often uncomfortable, disliking the task of evaluating people and passing judgment on their performance. Frequently the two sides misread each other's signals and think the other is being overly critical or stubborn.

This failure to communicate effectively leads to an inefficient appraisal. One way to avoid this is for the appraisers to try to better understand each employee as an individual with different needs and to shape their own behavior during the appraisal to best fit with each employee. Window 8-4 helps classify important individual differences between employees so that employee

Window 8-4. Employee Behaviors in Performance Appraisals.

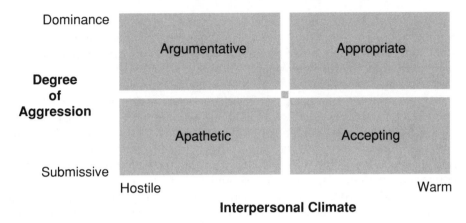

Interpersonal Climate

Source: Adapted from Robert E. Lefton, "Performance Appraisals: Why They Go Wrong and How to Do Them Right," *National Productivity Review* (Winter 1985–1986), pp. 54–63; and R.E. Lefton, V.R. Buzzotta, and M. Sherberg, *Improving Productivity Through People Skills*, Cambridge, Mass.: Ballinger Publishing, 1980, p. 26. Reprinted with permission of Psychological Associates, 8201 Maryland Ave., St. Louis, Mo. 63105.

Dimensions

Interpersonal climate. Some employees like to have good working relationships with their supervisors. They communicate freely and openly on a range of subjects, which creates a warm *interpersonal climate.* In contrast, other employees generally dislike or distrust their supervisors. These employees, who are very cold or slow to open up to others, are more likely to present a hostile *interpersonal climate.*

Degree of aggression. Employees can also vary widely on the *level of aggression* that they exhibit, which can range from dominant to submissive. Some individuals are generally assertive and dominating, preferring to be in charge of all situations. Other individuals are more submissive and unassertive in nature, preferring to take the role of a follower.

Appraisee Types

Argumentative. Some individuals are dominating as well as hostile. They demand to be respected and held in esteem by the boss. They often argue, deny responsibility for any problems, and are stubborn. They are reluctant to explore the record to see what was accomplished and where improvements can be made. In appraising *argumentative* employees, appraisers must be strong and

Window 8-4. (*Continued*)

forceful with their comments in order to make sure that the important information is understood. They must also show respect for the individuals and allow them some independent opinions. Appraisers must focus on the most important areas and not try to point out every single deficiency.

Apathetic. This group of individuals is submissive but still hostile. The combination produces *apathetic* individuals who are more cautious, unwilling to discuss the appraisal content, and reluctant to share their own opinions. The employees are more remote and harder to read, making it difficult to really know how they feel or what they are thinking. They are typically the individuals least comfortable with the appraisal process, and it is difficult to know whether or not they accept the feedback given. They rarely disagree during the appraisal, but they also don't ask many questions or give much input. Here it is important that the appraiser calm many fears the people have about being appraised, and at the same time try to get them to communicate as much as possible. Having the subordinates rate themselves prior to the interview and then comparing appraisals can sometimes be an effective strategy.

Accepting. *Accepting* individuals are submissive and warm. They like to be liked and want everyone to be happy and everything to be okay. They agree with everything the appraiser says, but often they haven't truly listened because they just want to avoid conflict. These appraisal sessions will seem very easy for the appraiser and may seem to have gone well on the surface when actually they were very inffective. With these individuals the appraiser must make a point not to seem harsh or impersonal, yet at the same time provide clear guidance and make sure that it is understood.

Appropriate. Individuals in this quadrant are the type that most appraisal systems assume you are working with. These employees are both dominant and warm. They listen to feedback and respond candidly when appropriate. Managers with such employees should make the performance appraisal process one of joint input. Together you should discuss strengths and weaknesses and make plans to help improve any deficiencies. Simply telling this employee what to do won't work; mutual discussion will be much more effective.

reactions in the performance appraisal process can be better understood.

Applying the Performance Appraisal Window

Companies spend lots of money on appraisal systems and appraisers spend lots of time going through the process. In spite of this, the results are often far short of adequate. Managers who attempt to discover how their employees will be most receptive to performance feedback will find that it is utilized much more effectively to improve performance. Additionally, appraisers will find that the feedback process is a much less dreaded experience for both sides.

Ideally, all appraisers will have the joy of dealing primarily with individuals who operate out of the *appropriate* category. These individuals are the most receptive to constructive feedback and most likely to add their own insightful thoughts about ways to improve performance. Eventually you may help your employees to move into this category as they all become more comfortable with the appraisal process.

Performance appraisals yield information that is useful for compensation purposes, future staffing and training considerations, and career planning. They also help the organization as a whole to improve its performance in order to increase effectiveness. Appraisals that are done incorrectly or even inefficiently are a waste of time and money, and they fail to provide the information necessary for all these other purposes. You need to characterize employees appropriately and tailor your feedback in a way they can best understand and use.

Steps to Employ When Using the Window. This window clearly picks up on a theme from Chapter 9, highlighting the importance of individual differences among employees. However, because of the accent on key human resources management function (performance appraisal), it is most appropriate to discuss the subject here. The implications for you are to:

- Remain constantly on the alert for clues and evidence that suggests whether employees are generally dominant or submissive, warm or hostile. This allows an advance assessment of their predicted behavior within the performance appraisal discussion.

- Engage in frequent and ongoing counseling with employees in an attempt to inform them of their typical behaviors and point out more constructive patterns of interactions.
- Accept the fact that employees are truly different in sometimes significant ways, which creates an obligation for you to treat each of them in a unique fashion.
- Recognize that at least one of the dimensions—*interpersonal climate*—is partially your responsibility in creating a relationship with each employee. Consequently, if this can be improved over time from hostile to warm, the predicted employee response in performance appraisal would change from *argumentative* to *appropriate*, or *apathetic* to *accepting*.

The Grid in Action. It is that time of year again, performance reviews. Stephanie looks forward to appraisal time with mixed feelings. Some of the ten bank tellers she has to appraise are fine. They get along well with each other and accept the review process not just as a necessary evil, but as an opportunity to get feedback about their own performance. They also like to pass along their opinions about the appraisal and other work-related issues to her. However, several of the other tellers are a different story. Stephanie decides to try the new technique she and her colleague learned during the last supervisors' training session. The consultant told them how to get better appraisal results by trying to identify the employee's likely behavior in terms of dominance or submission as well as assessing the *interpersonal climate* between the supervisor and her appraisees as either warm or hostile. Once an employee was characterized, supervisors could adjust the way in which they gave the feedback so it could be best received and acted on by the employees.

As she had thought, several of her tellers fall into the *appropriate* category. They have more dominating personalities, but the warm *interpersonal climate* allows them to exchange information and thoughts about the appraisal process without becoming angry. With them she will approach the appraisal feedback as a joint process. Unfortunately, Stephanie also has one employee, Mike B., who can be considered *argumentative*. His dominating and hostile attitude makes it very difficult to give any constructive commentary without his disagreeing or trying to shift the blame to others. Stephanie decides she will follow the advice of the consultant and focus on only the three biggest areas in need of improvement and stay away from bringing up any little things that might just make him more defensive and hostile.

Both Dennis and Rich seem *apathetic.* They are somewhat hostile, but at the same time seem submissive and in general act like they don't care much one way or another. Stephanie finds them hardest to read and isn't sure whether or not they listen when she makes suggestions. She decides the best strategy will be to have them complete a self-appraisal before the meeting. Then she will sit down with them individually and compare her appraisal with their own, attempting to get them to discuss areas of disagreement or where both have indicated a weak area.

Her final two employees are what she characterizes as *accepting.* Ray Donaldson and Jean MacDonald are both very friendly and try very hard to do their best and please her at all times. She typically has an easy appraisal session with them because they both dislike conflict, are eager to agree to anything, and readily promise to change their behavior just to avoid the discussion. Stephanie decides she will try to avoid coming across as an impersonal boss, but she will make it clear that there are a couple of areas that need improvement. Rather than just seeking promises of change, she wants them to come up with some specific strategies for improvement. With these forethoughts, Stephanie begins setting up appointments with the tellers for their appraisal feedback sessions.

References

Lefton, Robert E. "Performance Appraisals: Why They Go Wrong and How to Do Them Right." *National Productivity Review,* Winter, 1985–86, pp. 54–63.

Lefton, Robert E., and Victor R. Buzzotta. "Performance Appraisal: Why Bother?" *Training and Development Journal,* August, 1978, pp. 49–58.

Chapter 9

Individual Differences

Individual traits or characteristics represent a very important influence on behavior within organizations. Individuals within the same organization are not simply clones produced from the same mold. While organizations may impose many controls designed to produce similarity or consistency in behavior across employees (e.g., uniforms, standard procedures, policies, scheduled working hours), individuality inevitably asserts itself. For the most part, employees do not look alike, talk alike, or act alike; to understand one employee is not to understand them all. Therefore, astute managers must recognize the unlimited potential for individual variation across employee groups and tailor their managerial behaviors accordingly.

This chapter presents four models that are designed to help you better understand yourself and your employees. Each model offers unique insight into individual differences; collectively, the four models provide a broad framework that you may use to understand human interaction in the workplace.

The Johari Window focuses on perceptions; it emphasizes similarities or differences in self-perceptions and others' perceptions of us. The impact of perceptions and, in particular, perceptual "gaps" on behavior, is discussed. The Life Positions Model, a key part of transactional analysis, focuses on our basic attitudes toward ourselves and others. The positive or negative nature of our attitudes toward self and others influences many behaviors, including communication, leadership style, and decision-making style. The third model emphasizes differences in styles of information gathering, information processing, and decision making. This model illustrates different modes of thinking and deciding and points out the potential for misunderstanding and conflict between different types of individuals. Finally, the Social Style model is a framework that helps us understand our own predominant styles of social interaction. How assertive are we in our interpersonal relationships? To what extent are we responsive to others in social relationships? The model helps us identify our own particular social styles, and it emphasizes strengths and weaknesses of each style for building productive interpersonal relationships.

9-1. Johari Window

The Johari Window (Window 9-1), developed by Dr. Joseph Luft ("Jo") and Dr. Harrington Ingham ("Hari"), graphically portrays various states of awareness of oneself and perceptions by others in interpersonal relationships. The model facilitates greater understanding of the behaviors, feelings, and motives (both your own and others') that underlie interpersonal interaction. Although the model may be used to evaluate any type of human interaction, it has special relevance and applicability to ongoing relationships at work.

Applying the Johari Window

Although the Johari Window can be useful for assessing a current interpersonal relationship, a more important benefit is its potential for pointing the way, or building a foundation, for what might evolve. The model itself is dynamic (i.e., the horizontal and vertical dividing lines determining the relative size of each area are movable). This suggests the possibility (and desirability) of periodic self-analysis, which should result in the conscious improvement of information exchange in interpersonal relationships.

The Johari Window can be used in organizations for periodic evaluation of interpersonal dynamics within ongoing work groups. Dorothy Hai (1989) suggested that work group members write down their specific perceptions of each member's assets

(Text continues on page 146)

Window 9-1. Johari Window.

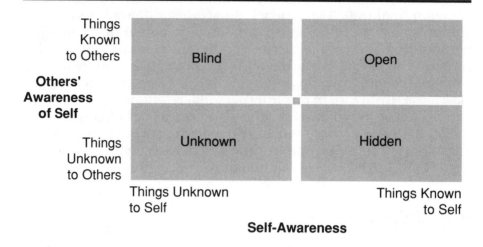

Source: J. Luft and H. Ingham, "The Johari Window, a Graphic Model of Interpersonal Awareness," University of California, Los Angeles, Extension Office, *Proceedings of the Western Training Laboratory in Group Development*, 1955.

Dimensions

Self-awareness. The horizontal dimension of the Johari Window reflects the degree of *self–awareness* that we possess regarding our own behaviors, feelings, and motivations. As individuals, we fully recognize the motives and emotions underlying *some* of our interpersonal interactions (things known to self). However, we remain unaware, or are unwilling to recognize, some other factors underlying our interpersonal relationships (things unknown to self).

Others' awareness of self. The vertical dimension of the model reflects the degree of awareness that others possess concerning our behaviors, feelings, and motivations. At the extremes, other persons may be clearly conscious of our acts, feelings, and motives (things known to others) or totally unaware of such factors (things unknown to others).

Combinations of Awareness Levels

Blind. People who are observant and know us well often discover many things about us which we do not know or do not recognize ourselves. This type of information is labeled the "blind area" or the "blind spot." The *blind* area reflects feelings, acts, or motives that other people see in us, but that we deny or ignore. Feedback from others (whether sought or unsolicited) regarding our

Window 9-1. (*Continued*)

actions and interactions serves to reduce the relative size of the blind quadrant, enabling us to shift information from the *blind* into the open area. However, if we are unwilling to receive personal feedback from others (due to defensiveness, embarrassment, etc.), the *blind* area may remain large and be a significant barrier to free and open interpersonal relationships.

Unknown. The *unknown* quadrant (sometimes labeled the "undiscovered self") refers to behaviors, feelings, and motives that are *unknown* both to ourselves and to others. The items contained within this area exist by inference, are uncovered retrospectively, or can be discovered through such methods as drug therapy, hypnosis, psychological tests, sensory deprivation, or dream analysis. Therefore, it is difficult to know the exact size of the *unknown* quadrant or to evaluate its negative effects on our interpersonal relationships. However, merely acknowledging the existence of this hidden area and being willing to contemplate its contents may enable us to improve the quality and effectiveness of our interpersonal interactions.

Hidden. The third quadrant (also referred to as the "private" area or "facade") reflects information that is known to self but unknown to others. The *hidden* area contains discretionary information that we may voluntarily disclose to others or, conversely, purposely hide from others. Thus, self-disclosure plays a key role in determining the size and impact of the hidden quadrant. Some individuals freely disclose much key information about themselves (resulting in a small hidden area), while others carefully guard or mask such information (producing a very large hidden area).

Open. The *open* quadrant has also been referred to as the "public self," the "open area," the "arena," or the "area of common knowledge." This domain reflects things about ourselves that are known to both self and others. The acts, feelings, and motives within the *open* area form the basis for free interaction and exchange with other individuals. If our self-perceptions and others' perceptions of us are generally in agreement, the *open* quadrant will be large relative to other areas within the grid. A large *open* area should result in healthy interpersonal relationships that are characterized by openness, mutual understanding, and continued growth.

and liabilities (including their own). Individuals then share their lists to provide both self-disclosure and feedback between group members. This process of feedback and self-disclosure should enhance participants' understanding of their own degree of *openness*, their own *hidden* agendas, and their own psychological *blind* spots. An exercise such as this enables group members to see themselves as others see them, eliminate the individual behaviors that create misimpressions among others, and emphasize the behaviors that create accurate impressions. Further, enhanced mutual understanding should lead to better interpersonal communication and smoother working relationships.

The Johari Window could also be effectively applied within an organization to identify your dominant leadership style and to diagnose problems of your influence over subordinates. For example, managers who operate predominantly from the "*hidden* area" predictably would disclose little to subordinates regarding their underlying feelings, goals, or personal "agenda" in the workplace. Because of this tendency to act and react in a private or guarded manner, these managers most likely would use an autocratic or task-oriented leadership style, showing little concern for interpersonal relationships or employee needs. They probably would rely primarily on one-way communication (downward to subordinates).

Managers whose interactions are based largely on *blind* motives or feelings (i.e., those they refuse to acknowledge) are likely to assume a biased stance toward the causes of conflicts and the resolution of problems within the workplace, always assigning the blame or the responsibility to someone else. Furthermore, the *blind* manager's true goals and priorities are not likely to be clearly defined for subordinates. In contrast, a manager who generally operates from the *open* area will emphasize employee needs as well as task requirements, encourage two-way communication, and approach both goal setting and conflict resolution with a cooperative or collaborative style. Managers who experience many interpersonal problems with subordinates might use Johari Window concepts to determine whether or not their own styles of leadership and communication are contributing to their troubled relationships.

With regard to interpersonal communication, the Johari Window offers specific prescriptions regarding the appropriateness of self-disclosure as well as the nature and value of feedback. For example, self-disclosure is most appropriate under the following conditions: (1) It occurs in an ongoing relationship; (2) it is reciprocal (both parties participate actively in self-disclosing); (3) it is timed to fit current events; (4) it does not change the nature of the relationship drastically; (5) it is confirmable by the other party; (6) it accounts for possible effects on the other person; (7) it does not create an unreasonable risk for either party or the overall relationship; (8) it is required by crisis conditions; or (9) the parties have enough in common that the disclosure will be understood similarly by both (Luft, 1984, see References). Our undisclosed feelings, needs, goals, strategies, and expectations can create a formidable "*hidden* agenda" of which only we are aware. Consequently, others cannot respond appropriately to that agenda. Constructive self-disclosure from you to your subordinates should create a "mutual agenda" regarding goals and priorities, and hopefully lead to increased performance effectiveness.

Managerial feedback to employees will generally be most effective when it (1) is direct, (2) is descriptive, (3) is invited, (4) is specific, (5) does not pressure the other party to change, (6) is immediate, and (7) focuses on events shared by both parties (Boshear and Albrecht, see References). Be careful, however, not to force unsolicited feedback onto others. For example, unsolicited, destructive criticism of subordinates is one type of feedback that you should generally avoid. Forced exposure of weaknesses damages an individual's self-esteem and may also destroy rather than improve interpersonal trust.

In summary, the Johari Window offers a potentially useful framework for viewing your relationships with others, including subordinates, supervisors, and peers at work. By becoming more sensitive to your own feelings, motives, and behaviors, and by being willing to learn how others view those same factors, you should be able to improve the interpersonal relationships that are vital to both personal and professional success.

Advantages to Using the Window. The Johari Window is one of the oldest, and most popular, 2×2 models. It has these applications:

- It provides an easy tool for self-analysis. It helps you

understand your own strengths and weaknesses and consequently increases your self-awareness.

- It serves as a foundation for interpersonal growth. The window encourages you to invite feedback from others and clarify others' perceptions of you. The information gained can serve as the basis for an action agenda for behavioral changes.
- It stimulates you to help others (e.g., subordinates and peers) grow through providing key information about them to increase *their open* window areas.
- It reminds you that not only may you be *seen* by others differently, but you may be presenting yourself differentially to persons around you. Consequently, construction of unique Johari Windows for each key interpersonal relationship may be not only desirable but necessary as a basis for your self-improvement.

The Grid in Action. Janet Fielding, Vice-President for Nursing Services at a large hospital, sits back and contemplates the variety of personalities and work styles among the people in her work group. She has just met with the eight directors of nursing to discuss annual performance evaluations for each of their units. The eight directors have completed evaluations of the head nurses and staff nurses within their own units. It is now Janet's responsibility to evaluate the performance of the directors and to give them feedback on their strengths and weaknesses. As she thinks about each director, she realizes what a tough job she has facing her. They are all so different!

Three of the nursing directors clearly typify different quadrants in the Johari Window (Window 9-1). June, who supervises the surgical units and recovery rooms, has a very *open* relationship with her employees. Feedback from June's subordinates about her management style is always consistent with June's own assessments of her strengths and weaknesses as a supervisor. Her subordinates frequently make statements such as "June is a straight shooter" or "You always know exactly where you stand with her." According to the Johari Window, June has a large *open* quadrant relative to the *blind* and *hidden* areas. Her *open* style encourages two-way communication, honesty, and mutual problem solving among employees in her units.

In sharp contrast to June, however, is Ann who supervises

the outpatient clinics and outpatient surgery. Ann often has disputes with her head nurses and staff nurses, which she invariably blames on them. Several of Ann's subordinates have complained directly to Janet, charging that Ann is unduly harsh and critical of them, that she never praises or compliments people, and that she always focuses on the negative. Janet has attempted several times to talk with Ann about her subordinates' perceptions of her, but Ann always reacts defensively. She once told Janet that her subordinates "are just a bunch of babies who expect to be praised every time they do anything right." Ann's total lack of receptivity to feedback about her managerial behavior has crated a large *blind* quadrant that seriously hampers her effectiveness as a supervisor.

Finally, John, director of the emergency room, presents a different problem. He is known to his employees and to others in the hospital as a "very private person." He maintains a relationship with employees that they describe as "cool" (he describes it as "professional"). He rarely discusses overall unit goals with his group, preferring instead to deal with them on an individual, day-to-day basis. One employee told Janet that "John seems to know where we're going, but he doesn't share it with us. We have to figure it out day by day." Another told her, "John is basically a nice guy; he's even willing to listen to our problems and help solve them. It's just that he's so secretive about himself and his goals that it's hard to know where he's coming from." John operates so much from the *hidden* area that his subordinates must play a daily guessing game to figure out his feelings and priorities.

Clearly, June's *open* behavior is the most functional. Janet wonders however, how she can help Ann and John decrease their *blind* and *hidden* areas and become more open with subordinates. She decides to introduce the Johari Window concept to all nursing supervisors in an upcoming management meeting to help each evaluate their self-perception, others' perceptions of them, and to contemplate the impact of these perceptions of their managerial effectiveness.

References

Boshear, W. C., and K. G. Albrecht. *Understanding People: Models and Concepts.* LaJolla, Calif.: University Associates, 1977.

Esposito, R. P., H. McAdoo, and L. Scher. "The Johari Window Test: A Research Note." *Journal of Humanistic Psychology*, Vol. 18, No. 1 (1978), pp. 79–81.

Hai, D. M. *Organizational Behavior: Experiences and Cases* (2nd ed.) St. Paul: West Publishing Company, 1989, pp. 31–34.

Luft, J. *Of Human Interaction*. Palo Alto, Calif.: National Press Books, 1969.

Luft, J. *Group Processes: An Introduction to Group Dynamics*, 2nd ed. Palo Alto, Calif.: National Press Books, 1970.

Luft, J. *Group Processes: An Introduction to Group Dynamics*, 3rd ed. Palo Alto, Calif.: Mayfield Publishing Company, 1984.

9-2. Life Positions

Transactional analysis (TA), introduced by Eric Berne during the late 1950s, originally provided a tool for individual and group analysis within clinical settings. Through the years, however, TA has become a popular training technique for analyzing behavior—both one's own and that of others—in a wide variety of settings. Within organizations, TA concepts have been integrated into managerial training to improve individual understanding of interpersonal dynamics, enhance awareness of individual differences among employees, and encourage more cooperative and effective work performance.

The Life Positions Model (LPM) which is presented in Window 9-2 and is an important part of TA, assumes that everyone adopts a basic psychological perspective (life position) that reflects their attitudes toward both their own and others' abilities to think, feel, and behave effectively. The views taken toward themselves and toward others may range from positive (*OK*) at one extreme, to negative (*not OK*) at the other. Once a dominant life position is established, it exerts a major influence on people's lives and on the quality of their interpersonal relationships.

A life position conditions individuals to approach others and to react to others in a certain way (e.g., defensively if they view their own abilities negatively; arrogantly if they view others' abilities negatively). Some estimates suggest that people operate from a single dominant life position as much as 50 percent to 70 percent of the time. Consequently, the LPM is useful for

Window 9-2. Life Positions.

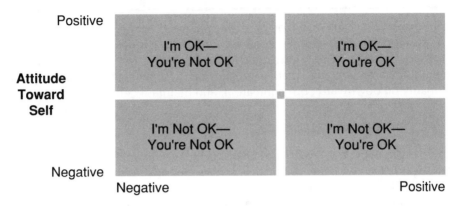

Source: Keith Davis and John W. Newstrom, *Human Behavior at Work: Organizational Behavior* (8th ed.), New York: McGraw-Hill, 1989, p. 264. Adapted from: T. Harris, *I'm OK—You're OK: A Practical Guide to Transactional Analysis*, New York: Harper & Row, 1969.

Dimensions

Attitude toward self. Individuals, in effect, record and store "mental tapes" of their early interpersonal interactions, initially based on relationships with parents and later with a variety of other individuals (peers, friends, bosses). The combined content of these "tapes" eventually results in either positive (*OK*) or negative (*not OK*) attitudes *toward oneself.* Positive (*OK*) feelings include a sense of control over one's own life, competence, well-being, lovableness, and high personal worth. Conversely, *not OK* attitudes are characterized by feelings of personal helplessness, weakness, insignificance, anxiety, and lack of personal worth.

Attitude toward others. Similarly, our interactions with others (particularly relationships occurring during childhood and later interactions with "significant" others) result in a fundamental attitude *toward other people.* We may regard others as *OK* (e.g., basically honest, trustworthy, helpful, kind, lovable) or as *not OK* (e.g., fundamentally dishonest, untrustworthy, destructive, mean).

Major Life Positions

I'm OK — you're not OK. Individuals who develop this life position adopt attitudes of superiority over others, mistrust of others, and, perhaps, hostility toward them. These individuals often blame their problems on others and

Window 9-2. (*Continued*)

at the extreme become suspicious and even paranoid. Managers who acquire this life position have sometimes been labeled "superiority bosses," or "high-pressure managers." They tend to be critical of subordinates, rarely express warm feelings toward them, give them instructions poorly, delegate ineffectively, rely primarily on downward communication, and maintain centralized control systems. Subordinates often perceive "superiority bosses" as domineering and manipulative.

I'm not OK — you're not OK. This life position generally becomes the most destructive of the four. In fact, it has been referred to as the "futility position." Individuals who adopt this life position consider themselves and most others to be essentially worthless and may even view life itself as meaningless. Managers who fit this profile have been called "hopeless bosses" or "unconscious managers" by some critics. "Hopeless" managers exhibit passivity (i.e., they have simply given up and "opted out" of their managerial role) or highly erratic behavior toward subordinates.

I'm not OK — you're OK. This life position reflects feelings of inferiority, powerlessness, and depression. Individuals who adopt this life position generally have low levels of aspiration because they have little confidence in their own abilities. In some cases, they may deny their own needs and give in to the wishes of others in order to obtain approval or cooperation. Managers in this category have been labeled "friendly persuasive managers" or "depressed bosses." They tend to be indecisive, overly reliant on others, and are viewed by others as weak and powerless. The "depressed" manager may be friendly and entertaining at one extreme (in an effort to gain the approval of others) or cool and withdrawn at the other extreme (in an effort to avoid feeling inferior).

I'm OK — you're OK. This, the healthiest life position, facilitates successful individual functioning and productive interpersonal relationships. Individuals who adopt this life position tend to evaluate both their own and others' abilities in a positive light. Therefore, they feel neither arrogant nor inferior. *I'm OK — you're OK* managers have also been called "problem-solving managers" or "confident bossers." They are competent, respectful of others' abilities, open to the ideas of others, effective (two-way) communicators, effective delegators, and cooperative resolvers of conflict.

exposing the basic attitudes that influence interactions with others. It helps people evaluate the impact of their dominant views on their interpersonal effectiveness.

Applying the Life Positions Window

The LPM offers valuable insight to individuals who are interested in serious self-examination and the improvement of interpersonal skills. The LPM encourages awareness of the impact of one's life position on interpersonal interactions with peers, subordinates, and superiors in the workplace. The LPM should stimulate you to address several questions. How do you classify your own dominant life position? Does this dominant life position help or hinder your relationships with others? How would others classify their life position? Do they appear to be overly timid and insecure or are they domineering and aggressive? Are their interactions with others based on respect, consideration, and genuine interest in mutual well-being?

The LPM suggests that you should be aware of the important link between life position and self-concept. Enhancement of your self-concept clearly supports the development of *I'm OK* attitudes. You should consciously strive to recognize and accept both your strengths *and* your weaknesses. You should look for opportunities, within and outside the workplace, that allow you to legitimately display and develop your strengths. You should conscientiously work to improve rather than deny your weaknesses. You should be willing to state important opinions or make decisions without excessive concern for the approval of others. When you accomplish something important, you should not immediately attribute your success to luck, fate, or the help of others, but be willing to take credit when it is deserved.

On the other hand, managers who are in positions of leadership and influence over others should consciously help *them* improve their self-esteem. You need to treat subordinates with respect and consideration and allow subordinates to develop their strengths and abilities, freeing them to try and sometimes fail without undue punishment. You should provide constructive feedback to subordinates concerning their weaknesses, in the form of guidance rather than simply criticism. And you must be willing to listen to the needs and opinions of others, responding in a straightforward manner even when you must deny requests or recommendations. A manager is often viewed as a very powerful role model by subordinates, and you have considerable responsibility for communicating *You're OK* messages to them.

Along the same line, you should consciously avoid stereotyping others, whether they are superiors, peers, or subordinates. Managers who hold many stereotypic assumptions about others (e.g., blonds are dumb; women are too emotional to be managers; older individuals are stubborn and resistant to change; all subordinates are lazy and try to avoid work) are clearly communicating to them a dominant life position of *You're not OK*.

You should try to see the connection between life position and styles of leadership. The *I'm OK—You're OK* position is the only one that leads to productive patterns of communication and influence strategies that are likely to generate cooperative, sustained, supportive responses from co-workers and employees. Without substantial support and cooperation from subordinates and peers, few managers can successfully execute their own assigned tasks.

Finally, you should evaluate the life positions of those significant others with whom you interact. Are responses given in the most effective manner based on the life position of the other party? If others approach you from an *I'm not OK* position, do you attempt to help them change (e.g., "I'd really like to have your opinion"; "Give yourself a break"; "You're being too hard on yourself") or do you reinforce their insecurities? If a boss, peer, or subordinate approaches you from an *I'm OK—You're OK* position (e.g., asks your opinion, expresses appreciation for your assistance, compliments you on a job well done), do you respond from a similar *OK—OK* position or do you react in a self-deprecating (e.g., "It was nothing," "I was lucky") or boastful (e.g., "Of course, it was good") manner?

How to Use the Window. You can use the Life Positions Model in these ways:

- First, you should objectively assess your own life position and validate your assessment by seeking feedback from trusted peers. If it is anything but *I'm OK—You're OK*, you will need to question yourself on your capacity for long-term managerial success.

- Second, you should assess the life positions of your subordinates, give them feedback, and counsel them regarding the images they project and the possible consequences of their life positions for their career success in the organization.
- Third, you should examine the nature of their communications, their decision-making processes, and their patterns of delegation to see if they are truly synchronized with the ideal life position. Sometimes we delude ourselves into believing we are in one life position, but many of our behaviors project a totally different image.
- Finally, you need to continue monitoring your life position across an extended time period as well as in different circumstances (e.g., work, community, home) to see if you are being consistent.

The Grid in Action. Janet Fielding, Vice-President for Nursing Services, is evaluating the performance of all supervisory personnel in the department of nursing. She turns her attention to Mary, director of the general medical units in the hospital. Of the eight directors of nursing, Mary supervises the largest number of units—a total of six. Mary has recently approached Janet to discuss evaluations of her six head nurses and in particular to get Janet's input regarding problems with two of them. The Life Positions Model is a useful aid for understanding Mary's six head nurses.

According to Mary, four of the six head nurses on her units are very effective supervisors. They are clinically competent and are also respectful of their staff nurses' skills. Thus, they are able to develop the nurses by enhancing their self-confidence and their clinical abilities. They provide both positive and negative feedback to the nurses in a way that is productive and nonthreatening. These four head nurses, according to Mary, feel positively toward themselves and toward their subordinates (*I'm OK—You're OK*), which is reflected in their problem-solving orientation and participative management style.

Two of the head nurses are considerably less effective, though their particular problems are quite different. Andrea, a relatively young head nurse, has alienated many nurses on her unit. Andrea has been promoted to head nurse relatively quickly because of her excellent clinical skills, but she doesn't seem to possess equally good interpersonal skills. According to the nurse on her unit, "she doesn't think anyone else is as good as she is." She always insists on doing the more complicated procedures herself and has even commented publicly that she "can't trust any of her nurses to do things right on their own." Not surprisingly, Andrea is autocratic in her managerial style; she relies almost exclusively on downward communication. Her *I'm OK— You're Not OK* attitude has resulted in low morale and loss of self-confidence among some subordinates and hostility and resentfulness among others.

Brenda also has problems with subordinates, but is quite different from Andrea. She appears to lack self-confidence and is consequently reluctant to ever be directive with the nurses on her unit. She is indecisive, insecure, and tries to "win" her subordinates approval by deferring to their wishes. However, her attempts have backfired. She is generally perceived as weak and ineffective by her subordinates. Indeed, she has lost control of the unit to Carla, a particularly dominant staff nurse, which has caused many interpersonal conflicts. One subordinate complained that "Brenda is nice, but she never tells two people the same thing; she's always trying to please everyone." Another told Mary, "Brenda is not really running this unit; Carla is. Unless the situation can be straightened out, I will be requesting a transfer to another unit."

Janet schedules an appointment with Mary to discuss strategies for improving the situation in Andrea's and Brenda's units. She plans to share the LPM with Mary and to use the model as a tool to help Mary understand the management style of each head nurse. If Mary can understand the basis of Andrea's and Brenda's behavior, she can formulate more effective strategies for dealing with each one. Janet Fielding considers performance appraisal to be one of the most challenging and important tasks she faces as Vice-President for Nursing Services. She recognizes the importance of fairness and objectivity in her appraisals of nursing managers, and she also believes that appropriate task-related feedback to employees is critical to ensure effective departmental performance.

References

Albano, C. *Transactional Analysis on the Job.* New York: AMACOM, 1974.

Bennett, D. *TA and the Manager.* New York: AMACOM, 1976.

Berne, Eric. *What Do You Say After You Say Hello?* New York: Grove Press, 1972.

Berne, Eric. *Games People Play.* New York: Grove Press, 1964.

Berne, Eric. *Transactional Analysis in Psychotherapy.* New York: Grove Press, 1961.

James, M. *The OK Boss.* Reading, Mass.: Addison-Wesley, 1975.

James, M., and D. Jongeward. *Born to Win: Transactional Analysis with Gestalt Experiments.* Reading, Mass.: Addison-Wesley, 1971.

Johnson, D. W. *Reaching Out: Interpersonal Effectiveness and Self-Actualization.* Englewood Cliffs, N.J.: Prentice-Hall, 1972.

Jongeward, D. *Everybody Wins: Transactional Analysis Applied to Organizations.* Reading, Mass.: Addison-Wesley, 1976.

Meininger, J. *Success Through Transactional Analysis.* New York: Grosset & Dunlap, 1973.

Wagner, A. *The Transactional Manager: How to Solve People Problems With Transactional Analysis.* Englewood Cliffs, N.J.: Prentice-Hall, 1981.

9-3. Social Styles

The Social Styles model helps you more fully understand the nature of your interpersonal interactions. The model aims at facilitating greater self-understanding by focusing on external, observable behaviors rather than on internal motives or feelings. In addition, the model focuses on *self* rather than others as the key to improving interpersonal relations. Since you cannot control what others do, you must focus on your own behaviors if you are to improve the quality of your interactions. Finally, the model assumes that while your social style may vary to some extent in different relationships or different situations, most managers have a predominant style that remains very stable across time.

The Social Styles Window (Window 9-3) facilitates understanding of your own dominant social style by learning how *others* view you (i.e., your "outer self"). The Social Styles analysis also helps you learn to evaluate the impact of your interpersonal behavior on others. Your ultimate goal is to develop the

(Text continues on page 160)

Window 9-3. Social Styles.

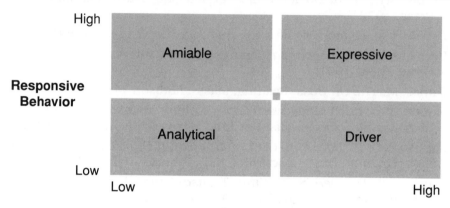

Source: Reprinted, by permission of the publisher, from *Social Style/Management Style*, by Robert Bolton and Dorothy Grove Bolton, p. 22. © 1984 AMACOM, a division of the American Management Association, New York. All rights reserved.

Dimensions

The Social Styles model identifies two important *behavioral* dimensions that affect interpersonal relations. Each dimension represents a continuum, ranging from "less" of the behavior at one extreme to "more" of the behavior at the other.

Assertive behavior. *Assertiveness* is the extent to which someone is directive or forceful in interpersonal interactions. A *less assertive* individual typically "asks" others for opinions, directions, or goals; a *more assertive* person tends to "tell" others his or her opinions or preferred way of doing things. *Highly assertive* people clearly express their opinions and preferences to others, and they typically prefer "directing" over "following." They also generally display a number of observable behavioral cues, such as more rapid speech, louder voice, more rapid body movement, more confrontations with those whose opinions differ, and greater decisiveness. In contrast, *less assertive* individuals are likely to speak more slowly and quietly, move more slowly, be more tentative in making suggestions to others, and display greater indecisiveness.

Responsive behavior. *Responsiveness* ranges in degree from emotionally expressive to emotionally controlled. Individuals who are *less responsive* are likely to be viewed as somewhat serious and reserved in their interpersonal relationships. Behavioral cues indicating *low responsiveness* include little interest in "small talk," more subtle nonverbal behaviors (e.g., fewer gestures, less facial

Window 9-3. (*Continued*)

expressiveness), and relatively little animation during interactions with others. Individuals who are *more responsive* typically display the opposite behavior pattern—friendly and outgoing with others, extensive use of nonverbal cues, and unrestrained expression of emotions.

The Social Styles

The combin of low and high points on the assertiveness and responsiveness dimensions produces four dominant social styles. The four styles are almost equally distributed across the general population (i.e., we would expect to find about 25 percent of the population with each style). None of the four social styles is inherently more effective than the others; all have both positive and negative attributes.

Analytical. These managers combine *low assertiveness* and *low responsiveness* in their interpersonal relationships. Positive traits of *analyticals* include industry, logicality, persistence, orderliness, objectiveness, and good discipline. Less desirable adjectives that describe *analyticals* include such terms as "picky," "stuffy," "moralistic," "cold," "detached," "critical," and "unfriendly."

Amiable. Persons who fall into this pattern are *more responsive* to the needs of others than to their own needs or preferences. On the positive side, *amiables* are described as "friendly," "agreeable," "supportive," "empathic," "understanding," and "warm." However, at the other extreme, *amiables* may be viewed less favorably as conforming, insecure, dependent, yielding, or weak.

Expressive. Individuals who are both *highly assertive* and *highly responsive* fall into the *expressive* category. *Expressives* display the most outgoing or "flamboyant" style in relating to others. Positive terms that are used to describe *expressives* include "friendly," "enthusiastic," "innovative," "charming," "persuasive," "inspirational," and "communicative." At the other extreme, however, *expressives* may be viewed as manipulative, overly excitable, egotistical, and domineering.

Driver. The *driver* combines emotional control with highly forceful behavior in relationships with others. Positive characteristics of the driver include pragmatism, decisiveness, goal orientation, independence, and competitiveness. On the negative side, however, drivers may be viewed by others as pushy, stubborn, cool, noncommunicative, and impersonal.

skills that are necessary to maintain effective interpersonal relationships at work.

Applying the Social Styles Window

The Social Styles model, if used with a sound knowledge base concerning its purposes and with valid assessment methods, offers a method of understanding and improving interpersonal interactions. Whether or not formal training is chosen, however, the Social Styles concept offers useful recommendations to managers who wish to improve the effectiveness of their interpersonal interactions.

First, the model suggests the need for unbiased self-understanding. Your own opinions about your social behavior have less influence on the quality of your relationships than do the opinions of those people with whom you interact. If you view yourself as an *amiable*, but the majority of others (subordinates, peers, superiors) view you as a *driver*, which is more valid? If self-satisfaction is your only goal, self-assessment is probably sufficient. However, if building effective interpersonal relationships is the goal, others' views must be accepted as valid and relevant.

A second recommendation is to develop the skills to *adjust* your behavior temporarily when your dominant style fails. Versatility, independent of assertiveness and responsiveness, is *the* critical key to successful interactions. *Analyticals, drivers, expressives*, or *amiables* can develop and maintain productive relationships *if* they are able to deviate from dominant behavioral patterns when the situation demands it. The idea is not to change your dominant social style, but to add other, less characteristic behaviors.

A third implication of the Social Styles model is that you should recognize the potential weaknesses, as well as the strengths, inherent in each style. Particularly under conditions of stress, people are inclined to intensify their characteristic styles. The behavioral tendencies associated with any of the four styles may become counterproductive if taken to the extreme (e.g., supportive becomes ingratiating; objective becomes detached; forceful becomes assaultive). Hence, you should guard against intense, negative style-related behaviors, especially when you face conflict or stress.

Finally, you must learn to observe and accurately assess others' social styles if you want to develop and maintain more productive relationships. Accepting personal responsibility for the quality of interactions is the first step. It implies that you understand the styles of others and interact with them in a manner that increases their level of comfort with the relationship. For example, when interacting with an *analytical* person, concentrate on factual information, logic, and control in order to make the other individual more comfortable. With an *amiable*, concentrate on more than simply task accomplishment. The importance of personal relationships and emotional expression needs to be recognized, and opportunities provided for the *amiable* person to satisfy those needs. The Social Styles concept does not suggest that you manipulate others through insincere responses. Quite the contrary, it demands understanding and acceptance of others and sincere efforts to make the interaction successful from their point of view.

In summary, the Social Styles model encourages you to obtain feedback from others regarding your own interpersonal behaviors and to examine the impact of those behaviors on your relationships. Understanding how others view you, evaluating others' preferred ways of interacting, and accepting personal responsibility for improving the quality of your interactions will provide a sound basis for developing mutually productive interpersonal relationships.

When to Use the Window. The social styles are particularly useful to assess and use under these conditions:

- When a technical person (e.g., computer analyst, accountant, or engineer) gets promoted to a supervisory position. Here, the focus of job responsibilities would suddenly broaden to include new demands and complex interactions, and therefore social styles would predictably become highly critical.
- When you have been plagued by a pattern of ineffective interpersonal relationships. Dissension, misunderstanding, conflict, and low morale might provide clues to the need for social style examination.
- When a subordinate appears to have become "locked in" to a single social style. Here you have an obligation to

explore with the individual the advantages and disadvantages of that style, as well as encourage the person to consider greater flexibility and capacity to use alternative styles.

- When you become aware that your self-perceived social style is not the same as the way others see you, or not as effective as you would like. Sometimes this insight comes through systematic assessments from colleagues, and other times it arises through informal feedback from supportive friends and co-workers. Whatever the source, it provides a springboard for self-examination and possible change.

The Grid in Action. Janet Fielding, Vice-President for Nursing Services, has finally completed her evaluations of the eight directors of nursing, and she has also done an overall evaluation of each unit's performance as a group. Janet has met with managers and employee groups from each unit to discuss the past year's performance and to set goals for improvement in the coming year. Her next task is to prepare a report for her superior, the executive vice-president of the hospital, discussing the prior performance and outlining future plans for the department of nursing.

The entire evaluation process has forced Janet to think seriously about her own relationships—both within her department and with her peers and superiors in other areas of the hospital. She realizes that as Vice-President for Nursing Services, she is ultimately responsible for maintaining effective relationships and guiding interactions within her department. Janet vaguely remembers an exercise on Social Styles that she participated in during a management training seminar a couple of years ago. Out of curiosity, Janet retrieves the "Social Style Profile" assessment from her files and studies the report with renewed interest. Her social style is labeled as *expressive*, indicating that she is both *highly assertive* and *highly responsive*. According to the report, she is likely to be viewed by others as self-confident, persistent, and persuasive. However, the report cautions that she might be viewed as overly competitive, dogmatic, or aggressive if she doesn't temper her expressive behavioral tendencies. She can do so by listening carefully to others and by allowing others to "win" sometimes. Janet wonders which view of her is dominant among her subordinates, peers, and superiors. Returning to the report, Janet notes that she is most likely to experience interpersonal conflicts with *analyticals*, who are her opposite on the Social Styles Window. (Could *that* explain some of the conflicts with Joanne, director of the intensive and subintensive care units?) Janet speculates that her immediate superior, the executive vice-president, would most likely be catagorized as a *driver*. She wonders how she should structure her written report and what approach would be most effective in her upcoming meeting with him. After about forty-five minutes of reflection on her Social Styles Profile report, Janet concludes that this model could be useful to the entire management staff in the department of nursing. Several of the nursing directors have expressed an interest in team building; this might be the tool they are looking for. She immediately picks up the phone to contact a management consulting group who can administer the Social Styles Inventory. However, she suddenly remembers her profile and, instead, places "Social Styles Assessment" on the agenda for the next nursing directors' meeting so that she can first ask if others are interested in pursuing it.

References

For information on the Social Style Profile instrument, contact The TRACOM Corporation, a subsidiary of Reed Telepublishing, N.A., 200 Fillmore Street, Denver, Col. 80206.

Bolton, R., and D. G. Bolton. *Social Style/Management Style: Developing Productive Work Relationships*. New York: AMACOM, 1984. (The work of Bolton and Bolton generally follows that of Merrill and Reid; however, some specific aspects of their model differ slightly. It is an excellent accompaniment to the original work, offering a somewhat different perspective). For training resources based on the work of Bolton and Bolton, contact Center for Social Style Research and Application, Ridge Consultants, 5 Ledyard Avenue, Cazenovia, N.Y. 13035.

9-4. Psychological Types

How do managers vary in their thought process? A number of models attempt to explain the perplexing phenomenon referred to as "managerial or executive thinking." While these models vary somewhat in their specific emphases, labels, and descriptions (e.g., decision-making style, problem-solving style, cognitive style, strategic thinking), several share a common foundation. Carl Jung's model of Psychological Types has provided the basis for a number of other attempts to explain differences in managerial thinking. During the past few years, interest in Jung's topology has grown considerably within businesses. As a management training tool, Jung's approach offers insight into how people acquire information, process that information, and make decisions. Ultimately, the model may predict who will succeed or fail to perform effectively in a managerial role. Currently, it provides insight into the source of conflicts and communication problems among individuals in work groups. Thus, the Psychological Types Window (Window 9-4) is especially useful in organizational settings.

Applying the Psychological Types Window

Managers who wish to apply the Psychological Types model need to begin by *becoming aware of their own predominant thinking style*. When you have identified your dominant type, carefully consider potential strengths and potential weaknesses associated with that style. No particular style is inherently superior to any other; each type can be good or bad, depending on the situation and how intensely the style-related characteristics are expressed. For example, *intuitives* (N) may provide valuable insight and vision for an organization; however, they may be viewed as absentminded, "head-in-the-cloud" types if taken to the extreme. *Sensation* types (S), though logical and systematic, may be so wrapped up in details that they miss the overall picture. *Thinkers* (T) may be viewed as cold, tactless, or self-absorbed. *Feeling* types (F), in contrast, may be seen as overly emotional and illogical. Enhanced self-knowledge can help individuals see both their own strengths and weaknesses and consciously work to avoid the possible pitfalls associated with each type.

In addition, you should be aware of the relationship of psychological type and specific aspects of your managerial style—such as leadership, communication, and problem-solving approaches. Managers who are *feeling* types (F) are more likely

Window 9-4. Psychological Types.

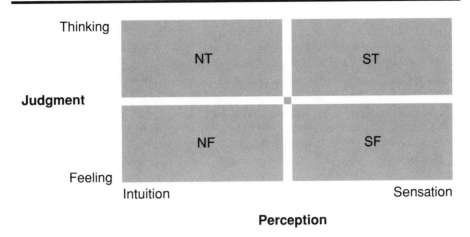

Source: C. G. Jung, *The Structure and Dynamics of the Psyche*, New York: Pantheon, 1955.

Dimensions

Two specific psychological functions are believed to be critical components of individual thinking. These two functions—perception and judgment—produce the four additional specific processes of sensing, intuition, thinking, and feeling.

Perception. *Perception* involves a number of mental activities or processes—scanning the environment for informational cues, selecting those to which we will pay attention, and gathering the selected information. Thus, *perception* is our way of becoming "tuned in" to the world around us. According to the model, all perceptual activities can be placed into two categories—*sensation* (S) and *intuition* (N). These two types of perception are paired opposites lying on a continuum, with *sensation* at one end and *intuition* at the other.

Sensation (S) is *perception* that occurs through the five senses (i.e., seeing, hearing, smelling, tasting, or touching). *Sensation* types are characterized as data-oriented, preferring hard facts, details, specifics, and concrete experiences. They also tend to be "present-oriented," dealing with what *is*. In contrast, *intuition* (N) is a *perceptual* style that is based on less tangible information; it involves considering possibilities, determining the underlying meaning of observations, and contemplating relationships between observed phenomena. *Intuitive* types are described as insightful, introspective, imaginative, abstract, and future-oriented.

Window 9-4. (*Continued*)

Judgment. *Judgment*, the other dimension, includes processes that lead to conclusions after cues are perceived. In short, this is the decision-making dimension; it reflects evaluation, comparison, and choice. According to the model, *thinking* (T) and *feeling* (F) reflect opposite orientations toward the *judging* function. *Thinkers* are described as unemotional, impersonal, and logical. Ideally, they prefer standardized formulas to guide problem solving. *Thinkers* "depersonalize" the decision-making process.

In contrast, *feeling* types rely on personal feelings, values, and other subjective factors when reaching conclusions. Individuals who display this style of *judgment* also consider the feelings and preferences of others when making decisions. They view the personal aspects of a problem situation as more important than the technical aspects. In direct opposition to *thinkers, feeling* types personalize the decision-making process.

Psychological Types

In general, one of the four processes (S, N, T, F) will dominate an individual's cognitive style, but the dominant function will be supported by one of the processes from the other pair of opposites. For example, an individual may be predominantly *intuitive*, backed by *thinking*; or predominantly *intuitive*, backed by *feeling*. By combining the two perceptual types (S and N) with the two judging types (T and F), four pure psychological types are derived.

Sensing-thinking types (STs). *STs* are characterized as matter-of-fact or practical thinkers. They combine a preference for concrete information or "hard" facts (S) with an objective, impersonal approach to decision making (T). When analyzing and solving problems, *STs* tend to be systematic, logical, scientific, and orderly; they think of themselves as realistic.

Sensation-feeling types (SFs). These individuals combine a data-oriented *perceptual* style (S) with a personalized decision-making style (F). Like *STs*, they prefer concrete, verifiable facts. Unlike *STs*, they also consider personal feelings and values when making decisions. *SFs* are characterized as both analytical and humanistic in their approach to problems.

Intuition-feeling types (NFs). *NFs* have the most abstract or insightful cognitive style. They combine a preference for intangible information (N) with a personalized decision-making style (F). Their use of intuition results in attention to symbolic meanings, possibilities, and complex relationships; their feeling orientation directs their intuitive energies toward human relationship issues. Therefore, *NFs* are described as insightful, humanistic, and concerned with broad cultural or social problems.

Window 9-4. (*Continued*)

Intuition-thinking types (NTs). These individuals prefer intangible informational cues (N) and a depersonalized decision-making style (T). Like NFs, they focus on abstract concepts, complex relationships, and theoretical issues. However, unlike NFs, NT types approach such issues or problems with impersonal, logical analysis. When dealing with problem situations, NTs can comfortably handle ill-defined issues or ambiguous information, but they try to change these complex issues into manageable problems by using logic and reason.

to use an employee-oriented leadership style, while *thinkers* (T) are likely to place greater emphasis on task- or job-related matters. At one extreme, ST managers are most likely to display a short-term, task-focused orientation, always using the bottom line as the criterion by which to judge performance. At the other extreme, NF managers are most likely to ignore the "bottom line," focusing instead on long-term outcomes that will do the "most good for the most people." Either approach lacks balance. Thus, you must either strengthen your weak areas in order to provide a balanced approach yourself, or ensure that you are surrounded by different types who can bring new perspectives and different ways of thinking to the organization.

Similarly, you should avoid filling your organization (or your division, or department) with "clones" who share your style of thinking. With respect to psychological type, there is virtue in variety. Too much similarity, though comfortable, may create a myopic view of the world and a stagnant, uncreative approach to solving problems. Thus, you should work toward assembling work groups with *complementary* ways of thinking and deciding.

While variety and complementarity are desirable, you must also recognize the potential for conflict between individuals of different psychological types. The greatest potential for misunderstanding and miscommunication can be found between individuals whose "pure types" are diagonally opposite on the grid (STs with NFs; SFs with NTs). Such pairs of individuals share *neither* perceptual style nor judgment style; thus they are most likely to view the other as odd or wrong. You must, therefore, develop the skills to recognize and accept styles other than your own. You should also help other people within your work group understand the concept of Psychological Type and its effects on communication, conflict, individual attitudes, and, ultimately, group performance.

Furthermore, you should be aware of your own influence on the thinking style of the entire organization (if you are a higher-level manager) or your own employee group (if you are a lower-level manager). For example, strong *ST* managers might inadvertently stifle creativity and individual thinking by their own example, the type of feedback given to employees, and their reward practices. Be careful not to automatically punish employees who are different and reward only those who are similar to yourself.

Finally, managers who can accurately identify others' styles and respond appropriately will be more effective listeners and communicators. You should analyze those groups or individuals with whom you must communicate, and adapt your messages to fit the intended audience. If the communication is to take place with another individual (e.g., a peer or a superior), what is that individual's predominant style of *judging* and decision making? Should the message emphasize facts, feelings, long-term, or short-term goals? If the communication is to occur in a group setting (e.g., group of subordinates), will there be a predominant type in the audience? What kind of message will be most effective with that particular psychological type? For example, management audiences are likely to be predominantly *ST*s; thus, they will be most impressed by facts, logic, or proposed solutions to specific problems. If the audience is likely to be mixed, an effective presentation must incorporate something that will appeal to *each* psychological type.

As a receiver of information, you must also recognize your own type and that of the "sender." A manager who is dominated by *thinking* may hear only words and facts and miss equally important underlying feelings. Conversely, *feeling* managers must concentrate specifically on content or ideas when listening to others. *Sensing* managers, without conscious effort, may disregard too quickly the visions of *intuitives* because they lack the desired concreteness.

For managers who are interested in assessing their psychological type, a number of useful resources are available. The most widely used and well-validated instrument is the Myers-

Briggs Type Indicator (MBTI) developed by Isabel Briggs Myers and Katherine Briggs. The most current version of the MBTI, an accompanying manual, scoring instructions, and other materials related to applications of the MBTI are available from Consulting Psychologists Press.

Advantages to Using the Window. Jung's Psychological Types model has been used by thousands of managers as a way to increase their self-understanding and awareness of their interpersonal effectiveness. Beyond that, however, the model can be linked to a number of other approaches:

- It influences managerial decision making and strategic planning. For example, strategic planners have been labeled (Mullen and Stumpf, see References) as identifiers (*ST*s), convergers (*SF*s), evolvers (*NT*s), and searchers (*NF*s). Knowledge of your type provides clues to whether you would be inclined to focus on short- or long-range issues, tangible or intangible environmental cues, and broad issues or bottom-line details.
- It can be useful for counseling individuals regarding their vocational preference and career choice. *ST*s are best suited for fields that involve impartial, logical analyses of facts, such as accounting, systems analysis, economics, and law; *SF*s combine factual information and human relationships in fields such as nursing, sales, purchasing, or teaching; *NF*s combine conceptual and personal skills in advanced education, counseling, writing, R&D, or public administration; and *NT*s are most suited for fields that utilize both their insight and logic, such as scientific research, mathematics, strategic planning, or advertising.
- It can provide food for thought when correlating it to other 2×2 models to see if there is consistency of interpretation and consistent behavior. For example, Psychological Types bear some similarity to Kolb's Learning Styles model (Window 20-1), as well as various decision-making typologies.

The Grid in Action. As Janet works on the evaluations for her eight nursing directors, she is troubled by her own poor relationship with one of them—Joanne, who is in charge of the intensive care (ICU) and subintensive care units. Janet often feels annoyed by Joanne's "abrupt" style of dealing with others and her "uncooperative attitude," but at the same time she recognizes that Joanne performs her job quite well. Janet is determined not to let her own negative feeling toward Joanne color her performance appraisal. Further, she really wants to understand the basis for their interpersonal problems so that she can improve their interactions.

Joanne acquired her position as director by performing exceptionally well as a staff nurse, and later, head nurse, in the ICU. She is very effective at handling crisis situations and is generally viewed by physicians and nurses as technically competent, objective, and well organized. One head nurse in the ICU stated that "Joanne can analyze complicated information quickly and act decisively, which is important on our unit." The only complaints ever heard from Joanne's subordinates are that "sometimes the patients seem more important to her than employees" or that she "tends to be impatient in dealing with family members of patients." Generally, however, her subordinates feel that her strengths outweigh her weaknesses, and they are proud of their unit's excellent performance.

Janet's conflicts with Joanne center around Joanne's reluctance to use nurses from the "floater pool" to fill staffing gaps in the ICU (she insists that they are clinically "incompetent" when dealing with ICU technology) and her unwillingness to let "her" nurses rotate to other units that are understaffed (she says it "wastes" their technical skills or slows down their mastery of the clinical skills needed in the ICU). Janet recognizes the validity of Joanne's arguments and wants to be sensitive to the ICU's needs, but Janet has to worry about adequate staffing and effective performance on *all* units, not just the ICU. She is irritated with Joanne's "myopic thinking and inflexibility" and wishes that they could work together to solve problems in a way that would benefit the hospital at large.

The Psychological Types model (Window 9-4) could help Janet better understand her problems in dealing with Joanne. According to the model, Joanne's style of thinking and decision making is that of an *ST* (sensing—thinking). She is analytical, fact-oriented, and often impersonal (appropriate attributes given her area of responsibility). Janet, on the other hand, seems to combine intuitive thinking (seeing the "big picture") with personalized decision making. As an *NF* (intuitive—feeling), Janet has the ability to think creatively, to handle complex information, and to generate a "vision" for the entire department of nursing. Further, she combines this ability to "think big" with humanistic concern for both patients and employees. Again, Janet's skills are valuable for effective performance in her role as Vice-President for Nursing Services.

The Psychological Types model could give Janet greater insight into different styles of thinking and acting. She might recognize, for example, that her own style (*NF*) and Joanne's style (*ST*) are diagonally opposite on the grid; hence the potential for conflict and misunderstanding between them is great. She might also recognize the value of complementary styles within her management group and try to develop the different strengths offered by each manager. The model, if shared with the nursing managers as a group, could help them to diagnose their own styles, recognize their potential weaknesses, and develop greater tolerance and appreciation for others whose styles differ.

References

Jung C. G. *Analytical Psychology, Its Theory and Practice.* New York: Vintage, 1968.

Keegan, W. J. *Judgments, Choices, and Decisions: Effective Management Through Self-Knowledge.* New York: John Wiley & Sons, 1984.

Kolb, D. A. "On Management and the Learning Process." In D. A. Kolb, I. M. Rubin, and J. M. McIntyre, *Organizational Psychology: A Book of Readings.* Englewood Cliffs, N.J.: Prentice-Hall, 1974.

Kolb, D. A., I. M. Rubin, and J. M. McIntyre. *Organizational Psychology: An Experiential Approach.* Englewood Cliffs, N.J.: Prentice-Hall, 1971.

McKenney, J. L., and P. G. W. Keen. "How Managers' Minds Work." *Harvard Business Review,* Vol. 51 (1974), pp. 79–90.

Mullen, T. P., and S. A. Stumpf. "The Effect of Management Styles on Strategic Planning." *Journal of Business Strategy,* Vol. 8 (1987), pp. 60–75.

Myers, I. B., and M. H. McCaulley. *A Guide to the Development and Use of the Myers-Briggs Type Indicator.* Palo Alto, Calif.: Consulting Psychologists Press, 1985.

Osborn, A. F. *Applied Imagination*, 3rd ed. New York: Scribner's Sons, 1963.

Rowe, A. J. *Managing With Style*. San Francisco: Jossey-Bass, 1987.

Rowe, A. J., and R. O. Mason. "A Case of Alignment: Tying Decision Styles to Job Demands." *Management Solutions*, April 1988, pp. 15–22.

Chapter 10

Interpersonal Influence

Managers have a continual need to modify the behavior of others. This makes interpersonal influence an essential managerial tool. You must use your influence to correct behavioral problems of employees; to stimulate high motivation and productivity; to convince subordinates, co-workers, or superiors to accept your ideas; and to achieve your own personal objectives. In fact, the accomplishment of most individual and organizational goals hinges on the sophisticated and skillful use of interpersonal influence. The purpose of this chapter is to examine styles, strategies, and approaches for exercising interpersonal influence, to evaluate their effectiveness, and to suggest ways that you can cultivate your skills to influence others.

Each of the grids presented in this chapter sheds a different light on the use of interpersonal influence. One, focusing on Influence Styles, warns you of the dangers of developing an inflexible influence style. The second, a Political Manipulation grid, highlights the strategic decisions you make in selecting influence tactics. Third, Force Field Analysis shows the need to analyze factors contributing to employee behavior before you respond with an influence approach. Fourth, the Interaction Patterns grid recognizes that the individual being influenced ultimately makes the decision about whether or not to change.

Taken together, these grids provide you with valuable insight into the use of interpersonal influence. They each advocate your need to explore your own objectives in influencing others, and to analyze the needs, goals, and behaviors of those you are attempting to influence. You must then guard against unintended side effects of your approaches. With this forethought you can more consciously select influence strategies that are likely to accomplish your goals.

10-1. Styles of Influence

The purpose of Window 10-1 is to describe ways in which you use influence to achieve either personal or organizational objectives. Specifically, the model profiles five dominant styles of managerial influence that develop from your consistent use of hard and soft influence strategies. Use of these styles may (and should) vary, depending on whether you are attempting to influence subordinates, superiors, or co-workers.

Applying the Styles of Influence Window

The model presented here should heighten your awareness of the variety of influence styles and their potential effects on subordinates, supervisors, and co-workers. It is particularly useful for alerting you to consider possible negative side effects of specific influence styles. For example, a *coercer* may be successful in gaining short-term compliance, but may evoke negative attitudes with his or her tactics. Further, *coercive* managers are likely to exercise close control over their employees. As a result, these managers often attribute good employee performance to their own managerial techniques rather than to the efforts and abilities of their employees. Such inappropriate attributions can hurt the future motivation of high performers.

Although the *coercive* style is the most apparent case, the model should also help you see that each of the basic styles of influence may fail to accomplish their intended objectives. *Bootlickers* may lose the respect of others, *shotgunners* may waste resources while never accomplishing their goals, and *bystanders* may unconsciously encourage stagnation in the organization. Recognizing your influence style and understanding its shortcomings are critical steps toward the effective use of managerial influence.

You can either develop your own list of behaviors to use in

Window 10-1. Styles of Influence.

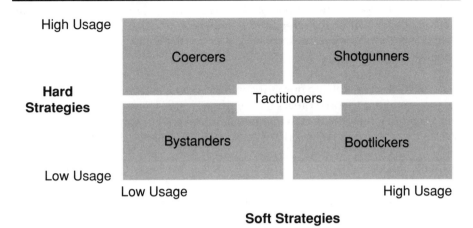

Source: David Kipnis and Stuart Schmidt, "The Language of Persuasion," *Psychology Today*, April 1985, pp. 40–46.

Dimensions

Hard strategies. This dimension reflects the extent to which you employ directive strategies such as orders, sanctions, and appeals to higher authorities to influence behavior. *Hard strategies* are used with greater frequency when the influencer has the relative power advantage over the target.

Soft strategies. This dimension represents the degree to which you attempt to influence behavior through interpersonal and persuasive skills such as friendliness, flattery, and humility. *Soft strategies* are more likely to be used when the influencer has little power over the target.

Influence Styles

Your low and high use of *soft* and *hard* influence *strategies* are combined to form four distinct influence styles. (The moderate use of both *soft* and *hard* *strategies* produces a fifth influence style—the tactitioner—that will also be discussed.)

Bystanders. *Bystanders*, who are below average in the use of both *hard* and *soft strategies*, exercise little organizational influence. Their perceived lack of power over organizational events discourages them from engaging in any

Window 10-1. (*Continued*)

influence attempts, either for personal or organizational reasons. Bystanders are often managers who have directed the same routine work units for a number of years. Research shows that *bystanders* are dissatisfied with their ability to manage effectively.

Coercers. Relying primarily on *hard strategies* (e.g., orders and threats), coercers attempt to force others to comply with their demands. Gaps in power between the influencer and the target often provoke a coercive influence style. While *coercers* may succeed in accomplishing the goal of the immediate influence attempt, their actions may create hostility and draw future resistance from the target.

Shotgunners. *Shotgunners* indiscriminately use any and all means of influence. While they openly seek to influence others for personal and organizational reasons, they are generally ineffective in accomplishing their objectives. Specifically, research shows that they are unsuccessful in selling their ideas, obtaining personal benefits, and motivating others to work effectively. Young, inexperienced staff managers are often *shotgunners.*

Bootlickers. These individuals rely primarily on *soft strategies* to influence behavior, usually because they are unwilling to jeopardize interpersonal relationships. Individuals with limited power may become *bootlickers* when previous influence efforts have met with resistance. With repeated interaction, *bootlickers* run a high risk of losing the respect of others.

Tactitioners. *Tactitioners* are more deliberate in their influence attempts and use both *soft* and *hard strategies* to a moderate extent. They often rely on reason in their initial attempts to influence. If they are unsuccessful, they carefully choose their influence strategies depending on the target, their objectives, and other situational factors. Research indicates that *tactitioners* are generally effective in accomplishing their goals.

attempting to influence others or use tools such as the Profile of Organizational Influence Strategies (POIS) scale to provide a more systematic approach for identifying influence styles. Three separate forms of the POIS are available to measure the frequency with which you use a variety of strategies to influence subordinates, co-workers, and superiors.

The influence styles model should also encourage you to examine your reasons for selecting particular influence strategies. Managers often select strategies without substantial analysis or forethought. Even worse, their choice may be based on their own biases in how they expect or desire the target to respond.

Rather than relying on one unfounded or rigid approach for all situations, the effective manager should analyze the situation carefully and respond with the most appropriate strategy. The *tactitioner*, who is flexible in the use of interpersonal influence, most closely approximates this approach. Self-examination and training can be useful for improving your diagnostic abilities and developing skills needed to vary strategies according to the demands of the situation.

The model has organizational implications as well. In an organizational culture encouraging conformity rather than open expression of ideas, you may fall into a *bystander* mode. While an organization characterized by *bystanders* would be easy to control, it would resist innovation and change. Examination of actual uses of influence in organizations may be helpful in assessing accurately the organization's adaptability, as the case on pages 178–180 illustrates.

When to Use the Window. This window can appropriately be used under these circumstances:

- When you have traditionally used only one (e.g., *hard*) or the other (e.g., *soft*) *strategy* for influencing others. Examination of the window can help illustrate that there are several sharply different methods available to use, each with its own consequences.
- When you need to counsel another person regarding his/her rigid use of a particular influence style. The window can be helpful in pointing out the merits of the *tactitioner style*, which emphasizes flexibility in its approach.
- When you receive clues (either from your superior, or from colleagues and subordinates) that your typical style of influence is not successful. This should encourage you to more systematically seek feedback, while also experimenting with alternative behaviors.
- When you have been largely successful at influencing others, but don't understand why. This can be especially true when you are transferred to a new job and wish to be

equally successful. Analysis of your typical style, and its components, can help you gain cognitive understanding of why something has worked in the past.

The Grid in Action. Eric Gray has been promoted to business manager of a large, urban hospital. He has worked with the hospital for ten years, starting out as an accounting clerk in the business office. He has always placed top priority on his relationships with other people and as a result has typically employed *soft strategies* in his efforts to influence others. With former supervisors, he would make his requests in a very humble manner, usually assuring them that he knew that they would make the best decision for the overall good of the department. If Eric wanted a favor from co-workers, such as substituting for him on a Saturday, he would begin his request by complimenting them on "what a good friend" they were and how the hospital was lucky to have them. Most of the time he was successful in getting his requests honored. His flattering *bootlicking* style also seemed to be a primary reason behind his eventual promotion to manager.

When Eric assumes the role of manager, he has great expectations for enhancing the productivity of the department. One goal that he hopes to accomplish is to reduce the time lag between patient discharge and processing of insurance claims. Accomplishment of this goal requires the coordination of all areas. It is necessary for the admissions office to record insurance information accurately, for the collections department to process bills quickly, and for the insurance clerks to file claims quickly and accurately. Eric continues to rely on his usual *bootlicking* style to influence his subordinates to improve performance in their own areas. He compliments freely, affirms the employees' worth to the department, and makes his requests pleasantly.

Many of the employees respond with greater quantity and quality of output, seemingly glad to have a little flattery thrown their way. Several employees within each area, however, resist Eric's efforts to influence them to improve their performance. Four employees blatantly ignore Eric when he makes his requests. Two employees in admissions seem to deliberately make more mistakes than before. Not knowing how to approach these individuals, Eric backs away from the situation.

To Eric's surprise his *bystander* style seems to result in improved attitudes and work habits for four of the six employees that have been causing him problems. The two employees in admissions, however, continue their downhill slide in performance. Now totally confused, Eric decides to confide in a fellow manager. The manager shows Eric the Influence Styles grid to help him figure out what he should do next.

Using the grid, Eric finds that the influence style that has been so successful for him up until now was *bootlicking,* or reliance on *soft strategies* to influence others. Why has this style worked so well for him as a co-worker, yet seems to fall short in his role as manager? Eric begins thinking about the circumstances in which he has attempted to influence others before now. Before he was a manager, most of his requests were made to supervisors or co-workers for his own personal goals. He has never considered the possibility that his *bootlicker* style may be appropriate when requesting benefits from individuals over whom he has little control, but may not be an effective approach for other subordinates. Examining the grid closer, he finds that even his action in backing away from his problem employees has a label, *bystander.* He recognizes that his *bystander* style is really a response to his lack of knowledge about what to do to influence these subordinates. But why do some of his employees respond positively to the *bystander* style? He thinks about these employees. They are long-term, seasoned employees and a little gruff—perhaps they are the types of employees that would be "turned off" by *soft strategies.* This simply has never occurred to him before.

Finally, he scrutinizes the grid for other styles that he can use to influence his subordinates. He realizes that *hard strategies* are available to him in his new role as manager. He has never considered using a *coercive* style to accomplish his goals, but then again, he has never had the authority that he feels is necessary to use *hard influence* strategies. After thinking about it, he decides that *coercion* may be needed for some subordinates and in some situations. And then it dawns on him that his general strategy should be to use different styles for different subordinates and situations—to be a *tactitioner* who carefully plans his influence strategies to fit the target and the goals of the influence attempt. Not only should his style vary according to the individual he is trying to influence, but he must continually evaluate his goals (e.g., "Do I want conformity or commitment?") before deciding on an influence approach.

References

Kipnis, D., and S. M. Schmidt. "The Language of Persuasion." *Psychology Today,* Vol. 19 (1985), pp. 40–46.

Kipnis, D., S. M. Schmidt, C. Swaffin-Smith, and I. Wilkinson. "Patterns of Managerial Influence: Shotgun Managers, Tacticians, and Bystanders." *Organizational Dynamics,* Vol. 12 (1985), pp. 58–67.

Kipnis, D., S. M. Schmidt, and I. Wilkinson. "Intraorganizational Influence Tactics: Explorations in Getting One's Way." *Journal of Applied Psychology,* Vol. 65 (1980), pp. 440–452.

10-2. Political Manipulation

Political manipulation is the process of one individual attempting to affect the behavior of another. Although the term *manipulation* sometimes carries a negative connotation, it is a legitimate, effective, and frequently used set of tactics to obtain the compliance of some target (a peer, supervisor, or subordinate). This model of political manipulation (Window 10-2) describes four unique forms of manipulation that build on positive or negative uses of power and influence to achieve individual objectives. The model also provides a framework for you to evaluate how your use of specific manipulation forms can either expand your capacity for political action (i.e., the ability to operate politically) or weaken it.

Applying the Political Manipulation Window

The Political Manipulation model has several implications for managers attempting to maintain or increase their political capacity. First, it warns you of the costs, in terms of both material resources and future power and influence, that may be incurred by using particular manipulation forms. An important step is to distinguish manipulation forms requiring no expenditure of resources (*influence* forms) from those requiring actual changes in the target's outcomes (*power* forms). The Political Manipulation model gives you a framework by which to

Window 10-2. Political Manipulation.

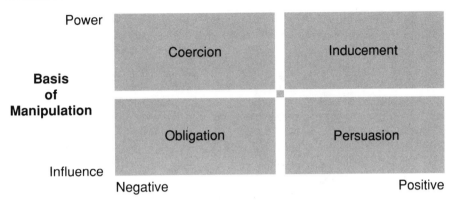

Nature of Manipulation

Source: Don R. Beeman and Thomas W. Sharkey, "The Use and Abuse of Corporate Politics," *Business Horizons*, March-April 1987, pp. 26–30. Copyright © 1987 by the Foundation for the School of Business at Indiana University. Used with permission.

Dimensions

Basis of manipulation. You can manipulate behavior either by altering the outcomes actually experienced by the target (e.g., using *power*) or by altering the perceptions of the target (e.g., using *influence*). The use of influence requires no actual expenditure of resources. Your total capacity for political action is the sum of influence and power.

Nature of manipulation. Both *power* and *influence* have positive and negative uses. If the target benefits in some way by complying, either through actual outcomes (*power*) or feelings of betterment (*influence*), the use of *power* and *influence* is positive. In contrast, if the target actually *is* worse off (*power*) or *feels* worse off (*influence*) from compliance, the manipulation is negative in nature.

Four Political Approaches

Coercion. Through threats and punishment (*negative power*), a *coercive* manipulator actually worsens the situation of the individual who has not behaved as the manipulator desires. By evoking hostility and future resistance, the overuse of *coercion* can quickly deplete your existing supply of *power* and *influence*.

Window 10-2. (*Continued*)

▧ **Obligation.** When using *obligation* (*negative influence*), the manipulator attempts to convince the target that he or she is *obligated* to comply or will be worse off with noncompliance. Often manipulators using obligation center their arguments around the "debt" that the target "owes" the manipulator and/or the organization for past investments in the target.

▧ **Persuasion.** With *persuasion* (*positive influence*), the manipulator attempts to convince the target of the merits and/or benefits of behaving in the desired manner. The manipulator appeals to logic and reason in getting the target to perceive a particular course of action as beneficial.

▧ **Inducement.** The use of *inducement* (*positive power*) involves actually providing the target with some valued outcome for his or her compliance. In this way, the target individual can see an explicit gain.

evaluate the costs of your manipulation decisions. The *power-based* forms are more costly for you to use because they can deplete the stock of resources needed for future *influence* and *power.* For example, the hostility and antagonism that may result from the use of *coercion* may cause subsequent manipulation attempts to be met with resistance. Likewise, the use of inducements may diminish the material resources needed to influence behavior in the future.

As a general rule, you should choose the least costly strategy in your initial attempt to influence. Thus, *persuasion* and *obligation*, in which perceptions rather than actual contingencies are altered, should be considered first. If these forms fail, then you can decide whether or not the target's compliance is worth the costs of using *inducement* or *coercion*.

There must be some words of caution, however, in taking this approach. In choosing between the forms, you must be aware that your past use of *power* will play a part in determining the effectiveness of the present *influence* attempt. At some point, you will cease to have any *influence* over perceptions if the actual experiences of the target never bear out your arguments. For example, if you never actually use inducements in attempting to change behavior, you will eventually lose the ability to persuade others that their own outcomes will be enhanced by a particular action *(persuasion)* or that certain favors are owed *(obligation)*. Similarly, if you never use *coercion*, it would be difficult over time to convince individuals that they would be worse off for failing to change their behavior *(obligation)*.

The past tendency to rely exclusively on one or both of the *power* forms can also sabotage your future attempts to alter individual perceptions. The consistent use of *coercion*, for example, lessens the future effectiveness of *persuasion* or *obligation*. *Coerced* individuals may be less likely to be *persuaded* or feel *obligated*. Even inducements, given freely and irrespective of performance, may become expected and less useful for incurring the future *obligation* of the target.

Some evaluation of how your past use of *power* might affect the target's perceptions will place you in a better position to decide whether to use *persuasion* or *obligation* as an initial influence strategy. It will also give you some indication of the level of effort that will be needed to alter the target's perceptions.

If in doubt, *persuasion, the positive form of influence, is preferred*. Research indicates that managers who are most effective in their *influence* attempts use *persuasion* initially, resorting to other influence strategies only when *persuasion* fails. Individuals who have been *persuaded* to follow a particular course of action are more likely to be committed to that action. In contrast, individuals who are made to feel *obligated* to alter their behavior may react with resentment, future resistance, and power plays of their own. Further, the ability to *influence* using *obligation* is more heavily dependent on your past actions; e.g., doing favors for the target, etc.

You are not, however, guaranteed success by using *persuasion*. The ability to *persuade* requires that you have access to pertinent information, be skilled in communication, and, possibly, have a great deal of time. You should be prepared to approach the target with convincing arguments.

When *persuasion* fails, you should reevaluate the situation to determine if *obligation* could work as a fall-back position. If you have no basis for *obligation* (or *obligation* actually fails), you must decide whether or not the desired behavior is worth the expenditure of resources necessary for compliance.

Given that compliance is desired, you must evaluate

whether the situation calls for *inducement* or *coercion*. This step is especially important since the *power* form chosen can either replenish or drain your future stock of *power* and *influence*. You should consider the present availability of resources, the likelihood of success, and the probable reductions in resources associated with each *power* form. However, in general, *inducements* (if not overused) are more likely to cause positive behavioral change, while building future sources of *influence* and *power* for you. *Inducements*, used appropriately, can lay the groundwork for future *obligation* and generate the clout for effective *persuasion*.

In summary, the Political Manipulation model views the selection of *influence* and *power* forms as a conscious investment decision on your part. Resources should not be expended unnecessarily or without proper cost/benefit analysis. However, when they are used, they should be invested wisely to ensure that they yield maximum returns to your stock of *power* and *influence*.

When to Use the Window. This window model is particularly appropriate for you to consider and apply if:

- You have not previously recognized the difference between actual outcomes and perceived effects. Depending on the objective chosen, you can then choose between using *power* or *influence* to attain your ends.
- You have accepted the occasional societal connotation that the use of *power* is "bad," while the use of *influence* is "good." This window highlights the fact that either technique can be positive or negative in its use, depending on the real or perceived outcome for the target person.
- You do not regularly consider the costs to you, the organization, or the recipients of using *power* and *influence* to attain your objectives. Some techniques may be effective in attaining their narrow goals, but highly wasteful in terms of their other effects.
- You lack either *persuasive* skills or the capacity to convince a target person of the personal merits of compliance. In this way, the model may point the way toward totally new skills you need to achieve your ends.

The Grid in Action. John Powell has been hired as the manager of a new branch of a regional bank chain. Although the traditional approach for selecting branch managers is to hire proven performers from within the bank's system, John was recruited from outside. The primary reason for his selection was his previous sales experience with other financial institutions. The company's president hopes this background will move the branch into an aggressive sales effort and serve as a model for the other branches in the region.

Because of increased competition with other banks and financial institutions, the bank needs to emphasize methods for bringing in more accounts. The branches can no longer depend on walk-in customers for growth. Although John has a sales staff, their duties primarily involve processing new accounts and deposits obtained from walk-ins. In order to focus the attention of the sales staff on sales rather than administrative tasks, John redistributes many of their duties to his operations staff. He tells the sales staff that he wants them to spend at least one-half of their time contacting prospective customers. He personally develops lists of individuals for them to contact and holds training sessions to help them develop their sales techniques.

Despite John's efforts, however, no new accounts are being generated by the sales staff. They resist making the calls and continue to spend the majority of their time on administrative duties. They always claim they are too busy taking care of office business to make calls.

John realizes that he has to use a strategic approach to *influence* his employees to implement the sales-oriented philosophy needed for success. He knows that he does not yet have enough "clout" to accomplish his goals by using *coercion*. He also feels that starting out with *coercive* tactics will create hostility, limiting his ability to be effective with his plan in the future. He does not have the financial luxury of developing elaborate bonus systems to induce the employees to acquire new accounts. He has to be particularly careful about expenses this early in the game. Thus, he rules out using his limited *power* in his initial attempts to influence his employees. He reasons that it will be more cost-effective to first try to change his employees' perceptions of their situation (i.e., *influence*), using *persuasion* and *obligation.*

John knows that the trust and respect of his employees will have a large impact on his ability to *persuade* them. Since he has not had time to earn credibility, he is aware that he must carefully plan his strategy for *persuasion.* He understands that he must appeal to both the minds and emotions of these employees, using logic and reason to support his arguments. He decides to focus primarily on the advantages to the employees of emphasizing an active sales effort. For example, he plans to point out that the bank's growth will eventually translate into financial benefits for the employees. He will mention that he has already discussed with the president the possibility of a stock ownership plan if the branches begin contributing to the bank's growth. He will also appeal to their emotions by saying, "We want to show everyone that we can be a winning team. After all, we are the model every branch will aspire to become." Although he de-emphasizes obligation, he does include the statement "I think growth will be necessary for any bank to stay in business."

John feels that his sales employees will be responsive, but he also knows that he has no guarantee that his plan will work. He does know, however, that he must do whatever is necessary to place the appropriate emphasis on sales. Therefore, he is already considering how he might use his *power* to accomplish his goals if his *influence* fails. As an *inducement* for increased accounts, he might develop a system that ties bonuses to sales goals. While such a plan would be unprecedented in the bank and would also reduce his capacity to engage in other marketing efforts needed for success, he must consider it as a backup strategy. Even if *persuasion* works, an *inducement* plan may be desirable in the future. It would show that John followed through on his promise to reward employees for their contributions to the bank's growth, building the credibility John needed to be successful with future *influence* attempts. John decides that his last resort will be *coercion.* Only if forced will he use his authority to get his employees to "shape up or ship out."

10-3. Force Field Analysis

Force field analysis, originally developed by Kurt Lewin in 1951, provides a framework for analyzing factors that may impede or facilitate your efforts to influence behavioral change in subordinates. Lewin identified two sets of forces affecting individual behavior. One consists of factors that *drive* the individual toward a particular behavior (causal or driving factors) and the other consists of factors that *restrain* the individual from exhibiting the behavior (restraining factors). In order to influence individuals to change their current behavior and move toward a new desired performance, causal and restraining forces must be identified, and methods for altering key factors developed. In the Force Field Analysis Window (Window 10-3), generic strategies (i.e., increasing or decreasing either the causal or restraining factors) for influencing the continuation, enhancement, or elimination of specific employee behaviors are prescribed.

Applying the Force Field Analysis Window

The grid provides some general guidelines for you to follow in attempting to influence employee behavior, yet it depends heavily on force field analysis for the development of specific strategies. As a general approach for changing employee behavior, the model shows that you should emphasize "reduction strategies," e.g., identifying and *reducing causes* of *negative behavior* and barriers to effective behavior. Failure to remove roadblocks to desired behavior will undermine the effectiveness of any influence strategy. For example, if employees low in productivity (*low, positive* behavior) do not know *how* to improve performance, attempts either to force or induce them to do so will be futile. Likewise, if absenteeism is high (*high, negative* behavior) due to employees' avoidance of an unpleasant work environment, coercion by you may only worsen the situation. These examples also suggest that efforts to improve performance or eliminate negative behavior through the pressure tactics typically employed by managers may result in consequences that are detrimental to the accomplishment of organizational goals (e.g., resistance, hostility, turnover, absenteeism, lowered productivity).

Clearly, the model does not do all the work for you. You cannot automatically respond to a particular employee behavior with positive reinforcement or punishment. To explore fully the range of possible reduction strategies, careful force field *analysis* of the factors underlying the present behavior is required.

Force field analysis can be applied to the behavioral prob-

Window 10-3. Force Field Analysis.

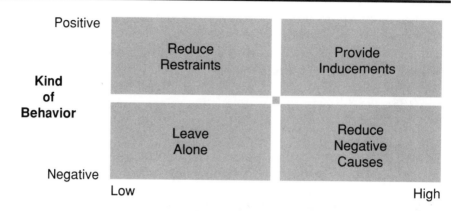

Source: Adapted from *Making the Training Process Work* by Donald F. Michalak and Edwin G. Yager, p. 33. Copyright © 1979 by Donald F. Michalak. Reprinted by permission of Harper & Row, Publishers, Inc.

Dimensions

Kind of behavior. This dimension recognizes that individuals may engage in two extreme kinds of goal-related behaviors of interest to the organization. One type (*positive*) contributes to the accomplishment of organizational goals. The other (*negative*) hinders the accomplishment of organizational goals.

Extent of behavior present. Ranging from low to high, this dimension reflects the degree to which positive or negative behaviors are exhibited. It forces examination of whether the behavior is *mild* or *strong*, or having a *weak* or *powerful* impact.

Methods for Inducing Change

Reduce restraints. When the level of desired behavior is low (*low, positive*), you may attempt to influence higher levels of performance either by increasing causal factors (e.g., applying pressure on subordinates to increase production) or decreasing restraining factors (e.g., identifying and reducing or eliminating factors suppressing the current performance level). You will generally be more effective by identifying and removing barriers to effective performance (in other words, *reducing restraining factors*), than by attempting to force improvements in performance. For example, you may discover that a major

Window 10-3. (*Continued*)

factor restraining performance is the employee's uncertainty regarding job responsibilities. Clarification of performance expectations would be more effective in producing higher levels of performance than would threats and punishment.

■ **Leave alone.** Individuals displaying low levels of dysfunctional behavior such as occasional tardiness or absenteeism (*low, negative*) could be *left alone*, with the anticipation that the near-acceptable behavior will be maintained. Alternatively, employees could be provided with incentives to continue their present (functional) behavior.

■ **Reduce negative causes.** You may attempt to eliminate undesired behavior (*high, negative*) either by reducing factors contributing to it or increasing factors restraining it. You can usually eliminate undesired behavior if causal factors are identified and reduced. Pressure for compliance may temporarily suppress the negative behavior, but may cause it to resurface later in the form of hostility, antagonism, turnover, absenteeism, and other negative outcomes.

■ **Provide inducements.** In situations where there are high levels of desired behavior (*high, positive*), two strategies are available to you. You can either do nothing, thereby running the risk that the behavior will be extinguished, or you can provide the subordinate with inducements to maintain the current performance level. The latter approach is generally recommended.

lems of groups or individuals. For group problems, brainstorming sessions including all group members should be conducted to ensure that all factors influencing the situation are identified. Specifically, you should ask the group to identify a desired outcome (preferably a measurable one) and should encourage members to explore factors moving them toward and away from this goal. These factors should then be ranked or prioritized in order to determine which "key" factors have the strongest impact on behavior.

Once factors have been identified and their relative strength assessed, strategies to reduce major barriers to goal attainment should be explored. Such a problem-identification/problem-solving approach not only produces strategies more likely to influence behavioral change, but also generates the employee support needed to implement the plan.

Steps to Employ When Using the Window. Force field analysis is a *process,* and only its major *implications* are shown in the 2 × 2 window format. Consequently, if you are interested in applying the model, you should:

- Recognize that anyone's behavior is currently either in a state of equilibrium between opposing forces or seeking to regain equilibrium. Therefore, your first task is to identify, and assess the strength of, the competing forces.
- Consider applying the Force Field model to your *own* behavior, which will help you to understand your personal resistance to change under some circumstances.
- Attempt to be creative and flexible while searching for alternative ways to modify the behavior of others. In short, all of the four windowpanes have some merit for use under certain circumstances.
- Remind yourself not to tamper with situations that are mildly negative. If you ignore the situation (leaving the individual alone), it may either disappear or at least not magnify in scope or intensity.

The Grid in Action. June Weaver is a divisional manager of a regional retailing organization. June had risen through the ranks of the organization and was promoted from department store manager to divisional manager after demonstrating her entrepreneurial skills. As department store manager, June was constantly generating new ideas for increasing sales and profits. Now, in her role as manager of twenty department stores, she expects her store managers to develop their own strategies for improving the bottom-line figures in their stores.

June keeps in constant touch with the store managers, sometimes asking them to justify particular expenses or explain sales figures in specified departments. She applies constant pressure to them to improve their profits. Her approach appears to pay off, because in her first year as divisional manager there is a significant increase in profits for all department stores. Then in the first quarter of her second year, she notices a drop in the profits of all but one department store. She sees this as a reason to apply even greater pressure to her store managers. The decline in profits, however, continues into the second quarter. In evaluating the individual statements of each store, June finds that sales are declining slowly but surely for each store, causing profits also to fall.

Although June's entrepreneurial philosophy usually prompts her to deal with each store on an independent basis, she feels that the pervasive nature of this problem calls for a meeting with all store managers. Remembering some of the force field analysis techniques from her earlier training, she decides that she will ask the question What is happening to sales? and just let the store managers talk.

At the meeting the store managers are at first hesitant to speak, but after some encouragement from June a few begin to open up. Several feel that the cuts that they have been forced to make in advertising have hurt their competitive position and caused sales to suffer. A few others have reduced inventory in an effort to cut expenses; however, they have recently caught wind of customer complaints that there are not enough varieties in sizes. Still others are eliminating needed sales clerks, often leaving customers without the attention demanded in department stores today. Most agree that the short-term sacrifices that were made to reduce expenses have finally begun to hurt their sales.

June is shocked. She cannot imagine what would cause these managers to take such a short-term view of retailing. Rather than applying more pressure, she decides to encourage the group to explore factors that might be contributing to their undesired short-term behavior (*high, negative* on the grid). Two factors seem to take top priority: 1) Under pressure from June to increase profits, the store managers have resorted to short-term crisis management—it was quicker for them to reduce expenses than it was for them to figure out ways to increase sales; and 2) because the managers were not sure how they should go about increasing sales, they have tackled expenses instead.

June discovers the value of force field analysis for uncovering causes of problems. She realizes that she has created the negative behavior of the managers by continually pressing them to increase profits. Now she can *remove the factor directly causing the negative behavior* and focus on improving sales.

She already knows that the factor that has been causing the short-term emphasis—the perception that she unintentionally created that "only profits count"—has at the same time been a factor restraining higher sales. However, another restraining factor seems to be the general lack of direction of the managers in knowing the types of strategies they need to employ in order to improve sales. With this in mind, June decides to hold another brainstorming session to explore ideas for increasing sales (currently a *low, positive* behavior).

As a first step, June plans to work with the store managers in setting goals for the upcoming quarter. Then the group will brainstorm factors that may contribute to or impede the accomplishment of these goals. This analysis should allow them to evaluate potential strategies for approaching the sales effort and for removing roadblocks to their goals. Based on the success of their first session, June is optimistic that the department stores will now be headed in a positive direction.

References

Finlay, J. S. "Diagnose Your HRD Problems Away." *Training and Development Journal*, Vol. 38 (1984), pp. 50–52.

Herbert, T. T. *Dimensions of Organizational Behavior.* New York: Macmillan Publishing, 1976, pp. 344–347.

Lewin, K. "Frontiers in Group Dynamics: Concept, Method, and Reality in Social Science." *Human Relations*, Vol. 1 (1947), pp. 5–41.

Lewin, K. *Field Theory in Social Science* (D. Cartwright, ed.). New York: Harper & Row, 1951.

10-4. Interaction Patterns

Window 10-4 views influence as the relationship between two individuals, rather than as a unilateral act of the influencer. One person *(individual A)* may attempt to initiate control over another individual, but the response of the target *(individual B)* determines the success or failure of the influence attempt. The interaction pattern that develops between the two individuals may be *complementary* (individual B accepts *individual A*'s definition of the relationship, e.g., compliance) or *symmetrical* (*individual A*'s control behavior evokes similar behavior

Window 10-4. Interaction Patterns.

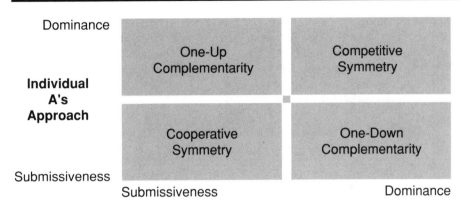

Source: Kathleen M. Watson, "An Analysis of Communication Patterns: A Method for Discriminating Leader and Subordinate Roles," *Academy of Management Journal*, Vol. 25, No. 1 (1982), pp. 107–120.

Dimensions

Individual A's approach. This dimension represents two extreme forms of control behavior taken by *individual A. Individual A* may approach the relationship by restricting the behavioral options of *B* (*dominance*) or may yield control to *B* (*submissiveness*).

Individual B's approach. *Individual B* may respond to *individual A*'s control message either by relinquishing control (*submissiveness*) or by bidding for control in the relationship (*dominance*). Thus, *individual B* may or may not accept *individual A*'s definition of the relationship.

Alternative Relationships

Cooperative symmetry. In *cooperative symmetry, individual A* yields control to *individual B*, and *B* responds with similar uncontrolling behavior. Each is willing to *cooperate* with the other.

Competitive symmetry. In response to (or concurrently with) *individual A*'s attempt to dominate, *individual B* also competes for control. This interaction pattern is more likely to develop if the subordinate attempts to initiate dominance over you, or if two individuals are equally hungry for power.

Window 10-4. (*Continued*)

███ **One-up complementarity.** A *one-up complementary* relationship is characterized by *individual B*'s acceptance of *individual A*'s bid for dominance. *Individual A* assumes the primary "one-up" position, and *individual B* follows with the corresponding position of submissiveness. This interaction pattern is more likely to be found in employer-employee relationships, with the subordinate passively responding to your one-up position.

███ **One-down complementarity.** In *one-down complementarity, individual A* relinquishes control to *individual B,* who exercises dominance over *individual A.*

from *individual B,* e.g., resistance). The nature of the relationship (e.g., employer-employee) significantly affects the interaction pattern that emerges. However, interaction patterns may vary with different subordinates and situations. If you examine your own interaction patterns, you can better evaluate the effectiveness of these relationships for accomplishing organizational goals.

Applying the Interaction Patterns Window

You can use the Interaction Patterns model to evaluate the effectiveness of your control relationships. It should encourage you to examine your patterns of interaction and to consider more productive means by which to influence employees to achieve organizational objectives.

Each pattern of interaction can make a positive contribution to desired work outcomes. However, you should be aware of the consequences to goal attainment when interaction patterns become too rigid over time. You should constantly evaluate the effectiveness of interaction patterns for each unique situation. Additionally, you should develop responses that alter patterns of interaction when they have become dysfunctional.

In *competitive symmetry* (i.e., the high dominance you initiate is met with high dominance from the subordinate), you and your employee need to engage in more frequent discussions and disagreements regarding organizational roles. While this level of interaction would likely enhance both parties' understanding of role expectations, it would be highly inefficient if used for every interaction. Constant negotiation of actions wastes valuable organizational resources, particularly when one party is the expert in the situation. In addition, struggles over dominance can escalate into destructive conflict that causes the parties to focus on "winning the battle" rather than on understanding the issues.

You should use the flexibility inherent in your position to interrupt rigid, ineffective patterns of interaction. For example, rather than automatically responding to employee dominance with more of your own dominance, you should evaluate the needs of the situation. Has the primary concern of the relationship become one of gaining control? Is there information from the employee that you need? You may need to *yield* some control in order to refocus the relationship on work-related, as opposed to personal, outcomes.

You must be particularly careful with *one-up complementary* relationships that typically evolve between you and your subordinates. A *one-up complementary* relationship may be beneficial when you have special expertise needed to enhance employee learning and development. However, if a rigid pattern of managerial dominance develops, the employee may never learn to make independent decisions or share work-related information. Such stagnant relationships would encourage work outcomes of the same quality.

Often managers do not consider alternative behaviors that may be useful. You may need to assume a *one-down* (submissive) position in order to encourage employees to take control. If the employee responds with dominance and the result is a *complementary* pattern of interaction, you would be in a position to benefit from the employee's knowledge. However, you should also look for signals regarding the employee's willingness to take control. An employee response of submissiveness, forming *cooperative symmetry*, may indicate that the employee is not ready to take the lead. A continued *cooperative symmetrical* pattern may result in nothing ever being accomplished. Again, it is up to you to diagnose the effectiveness of the relationship and respond accordingly.

You should also be aware that the way in which dominance and submissiveness are expressed has an impact on the effectiveness of the interaction pattern that emerges. Although a *one-up complementary* relationship may be efficient, quick, and satisfying in certain situations, it is less likely to yield desired outcomes if it is based on threats and punishment. A more positive approach is to nurture the trust and responsiveness needed to initiate productive interaction patterns. This can be accomplished over time by exercising dominance only when it is appropriate (rather than as a power tool) and by using expert power and reward power as the bases for compliance.

Advantages to Using the Window. Your primary advantages in analyzing your patterns of interaction with others are that:

- It encourages you to examine your own propensity to try to control, or dominate, the behaviors of others.
- It forces you to accept the fact that the other party may also have a high or low general inclination to control a situation. In addition, it highlights the fact that your control behavior does not occur in a vacuum, since the other party may *select* a response specifically to combat your behavior. In effect, many interactions are actually consciously interactive.
- It encourages you to consider the long-term benefits and costs of maintaining general relationships of one-up complementary. Is it healthy for the relationship if one party always controls the interactions?
- It raises a question regarding the most desirable relationship to establish over time (often through minimization of dominance). How do you build and nurture a trust-filled relationship?

The Grid in Action. Jackie Palmer manages one of 330 stores in a national record and video chain. Because top management wants each store to tailor its strategies to its own unique market, the store managers have been given a great deal of autonomy in their operations. They are encouraged to develop advertising, promotional, and other marketing strategies to fit the needs of the local clientele, and they only need approval from their regional manager before implementing their plans.

Jackie has little trouble in influencing her regional manager, Tom Burns, to accept her plans. Even if he initially resists her ideas, Tom normally will give in once he has heard her reasoning. Jackie has established a *complementary* interaction pattern with Tom, with Jackie holding the dominant *one-up* position. Jackie's dominant role has been highly effective for the store, primarily because of her skill in gauging and responding to the needs of her market.

Until now, Jackie has also been in *one-up complementary* relationships with each of the five salesclerks reporting to her. The salesclerks are all young and working their way through school. Because of Jackie's position, education, and experience, *one-up complementary* relationships (with Jackie in the dominant role) just seem to emerge. These relationships are pleasant enough; Jackie's employees seem to like and respect her, and they always do what she requests.

With market trends indicating an even younger music and video audience for the store, Jackie feels that she needs to solicit ideas from her young salesclerks. She has noticed in recent weeks that they seem to have a better feel for the needs of the growing group of younger customers. She holds a store meeting with the clerks to solicit ideas for contests and/or specials that will attract the attention of the younger customers. However, she receives little response from her salesclerks. They seem intimidated and a little reluctant to speak. Jackie has not realized that her typical *one-up, dominant* pattern has made her employees reluctant to ask questions or make suggestions.

Once Jackie recognizes how her rigid pattern of interaction prevents her from obtaining needed employee input, she works on establishing other patterns that may help her accomplish her goals. She continues to encourage the salesclerks to share their ideas, assures them that their ideas will be discussed and evaluated, and is careful not to slip into her dominant role by rejecting ideas outright. She needs to play a role much like her own boss does, taking a "backseat" while her employees assume the dominant role in generating ideas (a *one-down complementary* pattern).

Jackie finds that her salesclerks are more than willing to put considerable thought into ideas that can help the store reach its younger clientele. Of course, to maintain the interest of the salesclerks, Jackie knows that she must follow through by implementating the good suggestions. As she anticipates, Jackie finds many of the salesclerks' ideas to be creative, innovative, and worthy of consideration. She focuses subsequent meetings on the implementation of these plans, again being careful not to always assume the dominant role. After hearing from her employees, she discovers that she, like her own boss, is often sold on plans that she initially resisted.

Jackie has found that her willingness to submit to her employees at the appropriate time (i.e., a *one-down complementary* pattern) has resulted in better meeting the needs of her customers. Although her new approach has at times encouraged employees to challenge a plan that Jackie is pushing *(competitive symmetry)*, she sees such discussions as healthy rather than dysfunctional. She approaches these situations in a way that shows the merits behind her plan, rather than asserting her authority. Because she displays expertise and experience in certain areas and flexibility in others, Jackie's employees will usually accept her ideas with enthusiasm.

Chapter 11

Leadership Styles

What style of leadership is "best?" What factors determine which style to use? What are the ways in which leadership styles differ? What styles are most ineffective for achieving results through people? These and other questions surrounding leadership have been debated for decades. Unfortunately, there has been relatively little agreement on defining what leadership even is, much less what it should be.

Early studies of leadership focused on identifying the traits that good leaders were believed to require. That thrust has given way to examination of the behaviors that successful leaders display. These were first believed to exist on a single continuum (e.g., from autocratic to democratic). More recently leadership models have identified two major dimensions on which leaders differ. The four window models in this chapter are similar in some ways, and yet each has subtle differences in its interpretation and implications. Collectively, they span over forty years of thought and study, and they serve as a foundation for further development of our knowledge of effective leadership—a quality so important to the future of our nation's economic and political development.

11-1. Classic Emphases in Leadership

The most famous and oldest of the 2×2 leadership models is introduced here. Window 11-1 represents the work of a group of

Window 11-1. Classic Emphases in Leadership.

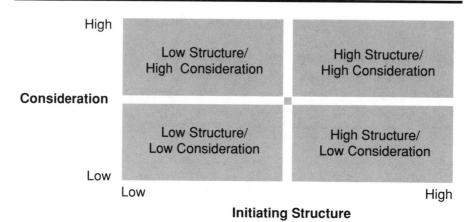

Source: Ralph M. Stogdill and Alvin E. Coons, eds. *Leader Behavior: Its Description and Measurement,* Columbus, Ohio: Bureau of Business Research, Ohio State University, 1957; and J. K. Hemphill, *Leadership Behavior Description,* Columbus, Ohio: Ohio State University Press, 1950.

Dimensions

Initiating structure. The horizontal dimension represents the degree to which the leader *initiates structure* for the subordinates, and this ranges from low to high. The behaviors included within this *structuring* dimension include establishing and maintaining standards, setting deadlines, selecting goals, deciding how tasks will be done, and other direct goal-oriented activity.

Consideration. The vertical dimension represents the degree to which the leader shows *concern* for the welfare of the group members. It includes such factors as treating subordinates with respect, getting subordinate approval or participation on job-related changes, expressing appreciation for good performance, showing a concern for individual job satisfaction, and creating productive interpersonal relationships. These roles directly contrast with the *inconsiderate* supervisor who criticizes employees publicly, shows little respect for employees, expresses no interest in their ideas, and shows *no concern* for interpersonal feelings.

Four Leadership Styles

Low structure/low consideration. One quadrant in this model describes a leader who is *low* on both *consideration* and *initiating structure.* This leader shows no significant interest in either production goals or employee feelings. As a result, such a manager would generally be ineffective.

Window 11-1. (*Continued*)

▨ **High structure/low consideration.** The second quadrant describes a leader who is quite *concerned* with *structuring* the activities of his or her subordinates. This leader emphasizes goals, task completion, and job performance behaviors, but does *not* spend much time or energy on relationships, or show sensitivity to employee feelings or to other *considerate* behaviors. This style is believed to be useful for achieving high levels of production and results, but it may not be appreciated by some subordinates.

▨ **Low structure/high consideration.** The leader described by this quadrant expresses relatively *little concern* with productivity or organizational goal achievement. Instead, this leader spends his or her energies building employee esteem, developing employee job satisfaction, and providing interpersonal warmth and support. This leader may be less effective from a results perspective, although subordinates often find him/her to be terrific to work for.

▨ **High structure/high consideration.** This last quadrant seems, both from an intuitive standpoint and on the basis of research results, to describe the most effective leader. The data from many studies support the belief that the ideal leader is one who strongly cares about production and people and is willing to exert energy to help employees accomplish both personal and organizational goals.

scholars at Ohio State University beginning in 1945. At that time a great deal of research on the traits associated with effective leaders in leadership situations was being reviewed and summarized. The results were discouraging and ambiguous.

There were virtually no leadership traits that clearly and consistently distinguished effective and ineffective leaders. This group of researchers then decided to take a new approach. They investigated the settings in which leadership took place and hoped to discover the *behaviors* (as opposed to traits) of leaders who were successful. After collecting, testing, and analyzing over 1,800 items describing different aspects of leader behavior, these researchers discovered that they could all be grouped under two broad factors that form the dimensions of this grid. Although similar work was performed at the University of Michigan, this window is often referred to as the Ohio State leadership model.

Applying the Ohio State Leadership Model

This model confirms and suggests that there is a need to attend to both major supervisory roles of concern for the worker and concern for the job. Considering the period of time (1940s) that the bulk of the developmental work on it was being done, this model caused a tremendous reconsideration of the then-traditional autocratic supervisory style in post-World War II industry. Besides that, it shifted the focus of leadership research away from seeking the traits of a leader to attempting to define *how leaders behave.*

This important shift stimulated a new look in leadership research and practice. Both scholars and businesspeople began to examine the behaviors that led to effective and ineffective work-group performance. Although the Ohio State model is somewhat outdated today, it did represent a path-breaking approach to the study of leadership which has yielded both practical and theoretical benefits. Today, managers know that if they spend all of their time on task-related issues, they are not helping the organization to achieve its productivity potential. As the work force becomes even more educated and skilled, the kinds of issues that this model introduces become more important for leadership effectiveness.

When to Use the Window. Leadership grids can be productively examined and applied on many occasions. For example, they can be useful when:

- An individual is first promoted to a supervisory position and wonders what general leadership style to use with his/her employees. You can use the Ohio State leadership grid to explain the need for a balanced emphasis on both dimensions.
- Feedback from employees, peers, or your supervisor suggests that one or both dimensions have been under- (or over-) emphasized. Placing yourself on the graphic portrait (in the eyes of others) can have a powerful awakening effect.
- You are being transferred to a new department or joining a new company. These are prime times to engage in

introspection as well as an analysis of your new tasks, to see if the style that was previously successful should still be used.

Overall, the primary benefit of the leadership grid discussed here is to encourage you to make a conscious choice about your behavior on two important dimensions. It also reminds you that your style is not necessarily fixed, but can be changed to match new circumstances.

The Grid in Action. Sally Garcia is reviewing the files of four supervisors being considered for promotion. Each is different, has different responsibilities, and has contrasting work records. The first, Alice, is known as a real taskmaster. She is proud of her department's work record, constantly urges her subordinates to greater efforts, and is famous throughout the Beta Insurance Company for her "can-do" approach. On the other hand, Sally knows that Alice's department has many employee complaints, her department doesn't score well on attitude surveys, and it has one of the higher turnover rates in the company. Alice's explanation, when she was confronted with this information in an earlier performance review, was that these employees are unique in the organization. They are mostly young, entry-level employees who too often find they don't really want to work, or quickly leave to get married. "Turnover and low morale has to be expected with these types of people," Alice claimed.

A second candidate has nominated herself. Betsy is a long-time employee of Beta, with a mediocre work record. During an earlier period of rapid growth, she was given a supervisory position when she was the only experienced person available. Even after this promotion, she continued to be an indifferent employee. It seems as though Betsy is now somewhat reassured by the promotion that her low level of interest in either the job or the people she supervises is perfectly acceptable to the company. With nearly twenty years in the company, she figures she is due another promotion and a pay raise, and so she has applied for the newly available position.

A third candidate, Connie, has also indicated an interest in the position. Connie is loved by her subordinates, always scores at the top in departmental attitude surveys, and is considered one of the kindest, warmest persons in the company. On the other hand, her department is frequently the lowest performing of all. Discussing this at her last appraisal interview, Connie had a variety of explanations as to why her department just couldn't get all the assigned work done. "Various people have been out sick, there are an unusual number of personal problems, and the department picnic has used up some of the work time," she reported. She felt it was important to allocate time to these activities in order to help the employees stay happy with her and the company. She pointed with pride to the high morale ratings and felt that eventually these would turn into higher levels of productivity. "But," as she explained, "these things take time."

The fourth candidate is Debra. Debra is known as a considerate person who leads a productive group. She makes sure she stays in constant touch with her employees and feels she is aware of and sensitive to their unique personality quirks and needs. But at the same time, she reminds her people that work needs to be done.

Sally stacks the files up on her desk. The stark contrast in these four candidates' leadership styles makes an interesting comparison. It also causes Sally to reflect on how she approaches leadership tasks. "Do I," she asks herself, "worry too much about getting the job done and not enough about those employees I supervise, or am I too concerned about people and not enough about quality standards and deadlines?" She has never really thought about the contrast in leadership styles before and she can now see that this question is worth pondering.

References

Stogdill, Ralph M. *Handbook of Leadership.* New York: The Free Press, 1974.

Yukl, Gary A. Leadership in Organizations. Englewood Cliffs, N.J.: Prentice-Hall, 1981.

Bass, Bernard M. *Stogdill's Handbook of Leadership.* New York: The Free Press, 1981.

11-2. Situational Leadership (Life Cycle Theory of Leadership)

The situational leadership model was developed by Paul Hersey and Kenneth Blanchard.[1] They felt there was a major weakness in the Ohio State leadership model (which is the basis for their work). This limitation is the inability of that model to take into account the *situation* in which the act of leadership occurs. To remedy that, the Life Cycle model begins by identifying the level of willingness, readiness, and ability of the subordinates (their task-oriented maturity level) to perform their assigned jobs. Hersey and Blanchard then argue that it is not enough to describe leadership by breaking it into only the two components of *task behavior* (the amount of guidance and direction) and *relationship behavior* (the amount of socioemotional support). The level of maturity (job readiness) that followers have to perform the task also needs to be included for a more complete description of how leadership actually works. Based on this analysis, Window 11-2 describes four unique leadership styles, *all* of which can be effective.

Applying the Situational Leadership Grid

Leader behavior is related to the maturity of subordinates. Maturity is defined in terms of subordinates' experience, achievement motivation, and willingness and ability to accept responsibility. As subordinates' maturity increases, leader behavior should be characterized by a decreasing emphasis on *task structuring* and an increasing emphasis on *consideration.* As maturity continues to increase, there should be an eventual decrease in *consideration.*

You need to assess your subordinates' maturity level accurately in terms of their willingness and ability to perform their assigned *tasks.* At the same time, you need to develop both the willingness and ability to vary your leadership style to match these levels of varying maturity. If you can do both, this model can help you adopt the best style to fit the situation. Most experienced managers know that some employees need a pat on

1. Paul Hersey and Kenneth Blanchard, *Management of Organizational Behavior* (4th ed.) (Englewood Cliffs, N.J.: Prentice-Hall, 1982).

Window 11-2. Situational Leadership.

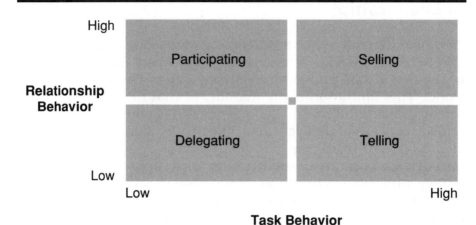

Source: Paul Hersey and Kenneth Blanchard, *Management of Organizational Behavior: Utilizing Human Resources* (5th ed.), Copyright © 1988, pp. 169–201. Adapted by permission of Prentice-Hall., Inc, Englewood Cliffs, New Jersey.

Dimensions

Task behavior. The horizontal dimension of this matrix represents the amount of guidance you must use to help a subordinate accomplish tasks. This guidance ranges from low (where you let the subordinates largely choose their own methods) to high (where you provide specific instruction and direction). *Task*, or *directive, behaviors* include goal setting, organizing, directing, and controlling.

Relationship behavior. The vertical dimension represents the degree to which you interact with subordinates to provide social or emotional support. This ranges from low (where you essentially let people alone to do what they're supposed to do) to high (where you spend time and energy interacting with the subordinates). *Relationship behaviors* include actively listening, giving feedback, using two-way communication, and providing support.

Situational Leadership Styles

Telling. The *telling* leadership style combines high *task behavior* and low *relationship behavior* in the model. This quadrant represents the situation where you provide specific directions, close supervision (i.e., tell people what to do), and spend very little time or effort on relationships. This quadrant describes effective leadership for subordinates who are largely unable and unwilling to do

Window 11-2. (*Continued*)

their jobs because they are either insecure or incompetent. Thus, the effective leadership style in a situation with this type of subordinate would be directive.

Selling. The second leadership style calls for a high emphasis on *task* and a high emphasis on *relationships*. This leadership style (*selling*) is best suited for subordinates who are willing but unable to do the task. Thus, this situation calls for a leader who is directive in telling people what to do, but also supportive in reinforcing their present willingness, confidence, and enthusiasm for doing it.

Participating. The third quadrant (*participating*) calls for a leader who is high in *relationship* behavior and low in *task-oriented* behavior. This matches a situation where there are followers who know what they are doing, but aren't especially willing to do it. Their unwillingness to do what they know needs to be done calls for you to use personal interaction, emotional support, and two-way communication as the optimal strategy. This helps to get these subordinates to buy into the task, develop a commitment to it, and put energy and effort into doing what they know should be done.

Delegating. The last quadrant in this model describes a leader who is low in *task structuring* and low in *interpersonal behaviors*. This describes a leader who *delegates* task accomplishment to the subordinates and leaves them alone while they do it. This is effective in situations where you have subordinates who are both willing and able to do their jobs. Thus, the effective leader who has subordinates with this level of maturity gets out of their way and lets them work.

---

the back and some a more directive approach, that some require close supervision and some can be left alone to do a job, and that some need constant reassurance and some do not. This model affirms this long-known managerial wisdom.

When to Use the Window. The Situational Leadership Window is an appropriate model to use in three ways:

- Whenever a new employee is hired or assigned to a work unit, it is a prime time to evaluate the individual's *task-related* abilities, willingness to exhibit high levels of motivation, and general levels of confidence. Once the employee is assessed as low, moderately low, moderately high, or high on the readiness scale, you can choose an appropriate leadership style to coordinate with it (such as *telling, selling, participating,* or *delegating*).

- Periodically (e.g., every three to six months), you should reassess every employee's readiness and see if changes have occurred. You should note that because readiness can either increase or decrease, a leadership style change in either direction may be called for.
- Use of the grid would suggest that it may be necessary for employees to highlight their own perception of willingness and confidence to you. You may have erred in assessing an employee's readiness and therefore made a conscious error in selecting a leadership style to use with him/her. Alternately, the choice of style may have been an unconscious one, and a frank discussion in which the employee points out his/her capabilities may stimulate a change in the style you use.

The Grid in Action. As the sun pokes up through the eastern sky, it catches Staff Sergeant Sam Lopez reflecting on his combat platoon. He has been with these twenty men now for almost a year. He started with them as a drill instructor when they first came into the army. He worked with them all the way through their basic training and their advanced combat infantry training and was now the field leader for their operational unit.

"These men have learned a great deal since the day I first saw them as raw recruits," he thinks to himself. "I remember when I had to tell them when to stand, when to sit, when to eat, and where to sleep. As time went on and these people got used to the army routine, learned some basic military skills, and learned discipline, it was time to train them in more advanced skills. I'll never forget the day on the obstacle course when I had to convince these men they could do it. And paratrooper training was something else. What a job I had convincing young Nelson he could jump out of that plane and everything would be all right. What a great feeling I had when he did it. He was so pleased with himself that even I could risk a smile on that one.

"Later on, when we went through advanced survival training, these guys really responded. They sat in the middle of that desert site and shared ideas, knowledge, and expertise to find a way to survive. What a feeling of camaraderie. Those were really the great times in this job when you get everyone pulling together and helping each other to do something well that everyone feels good about."

But the biggest test of all lays ahead today. Sam is going to see how good a teacher he has really been over these last months. This is, in his mind, the ultimate test of whether or not he has done his job in bringing them from helpless, raw recruits to capable, well-trained, professional soldiers. Today they will be flown into a remote area to infiltrate and capture an enemy position in a war game exercise. The object of the drill is to see how well these men can take their learning and apply it without a designated leader to tell them what to do and how to do it. Their success or failure will tell Sam's commander how good a job he has done in teaching and training. He looks over the still-sleeping group and thinks, "Well it's time to wake them up and get them going so I can find out how good a leader I am."

Sam has enjoyed the rather unique opportunity to work with an intact group long enough to see them grow from helpless recruits to competent professionals. At various stages of their development, Sam has been able to change his leadership style, too, to fit their needs. When they were unable, unwilling, and insecure, he focused on *directive* behaviors. Later, in keeping with the modern views of leadership and the platoon's task-oriented maturity, he increased his *relationship* orientation. Now he is ready to back off on both dimensions and use a fully *delegating* style.

References

Argyris, Chris. Integrating the Individual and the Organization. New York: John Wiley & Sons, 1964.

Bass, Bernard. *Stodgill's Handbook of Leadership.* New York: The Free Press, 1981.

Fiedler, Fred. *A Theory of Leadership Effectiveness.* New York: McGraw-Hill, 1967.

Reddin, W. J. *Managerial Effectiveness.* New York: McGraw-Hill, 1970.

11-3. Leadership Behaviors

The Leadership Behaviors Window (Window 11-3) is a recent attempt to provide a new and better way of looking at leadership

(Text continues on page 212)

Window 11-3. Leadership Behaviors.

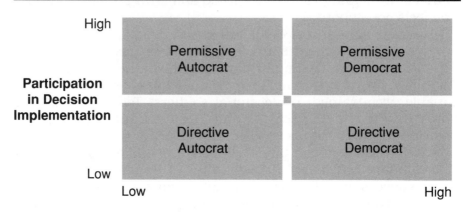

Participation in Decision Making

Adapted from: Jan P. Muczyk and Bernard C. Reimann, "The Case for Directive Leadership," *Academy of Management Executive*, Vol. 1, No. 3 (1983), pp. 301–311.

Dimensions

Participation in decision making. The horizontal dimension refers to the degree of participation you encourage and use in the *making* of organizational decisions. This dimension can be assessed as low (*autocratic*) or high (*democratic*). *Autocratic* leaders believe that their jobs require them to make decisions for subordinates to execute. *Democratic* leaders, by contrast, believe that subordinates should be involved in making significant day-to-day work-related decisions.

Participation in decision implementation. The vertical dimension assesses the amount or direction provided to employees for carrying out a task. It separates the two major styles of implementing (or executing) a decision into *permissive* and *directive*. A *permissive* (or *nondirective*) leader holds subordinates accountable for results but allows them considerable latitude in selecting which course of action they would prefer in reaching those results. This is a highly delegative style. *Directive* leaders, on the other hand, carefully stipulate how they want the subordinate to reach the desired results and then closely oversee the subordinate to ensure that the tasks are done in the stipulated manner.

Leadership Behaviors

Directive autocrat. The *directive autocrat* makes decisions *without participation* and implements them through close and direct supervision. This type

Window 11-3. (*Continued*)

of leader is well suited to a small, entrepreneurial company that is operating in a dynamic, competitive environment with new and inexperienced employees. Since the manager often knows what is going on better than anyone else does, owns the whole business, and can directly supervise a relatively small number of people, this leadership style is appropriate in this set of circumstances and can be readily achieved.

Directive democrat. The *directive democrat* leader solicits input from subordinates in decision making, but will then tightly supervise the implementation or execution of that decision. This may often be an effective style because many organizations lack the trained personnel, support systems, or organizational resources to successfully use both participative decision making and autonomous subordinate decision implementation. Thus, a manager predisposed toward participation, but wary of subordinates' ability or enthusiasm for implementing those decisions on their own, may find this to be a very useful strategy.

Permissive autocrat. The type of leader represented in this quadrant makes the decisions but then allows a considerable amount of leeway to the affected subordinates in how they can implement them. The *permissive autocrat* is willing to trust subordinates to carry out his or her wishes. This leadership style is appropriate in a situation where a decisive manager has subordinates quite capable and very willing to do what they're told. This could be true because the subordinates have an extraordinarily strong commitment to the organization's goal, for which they are perfectly willing to sacrifice their own need for decision involvement. It could also be attributable to the unique characteristics of a manager who has little desire or interest in following up on the decisions made.

Permissive democrat. The last quadrant portrays the leader who is both *highly participative* in decision making and nondirective in the subsequent *implementation* of that decision. In some ways this is the "ideal" leader; he/she is comfortable delegating both decision and execution to subordinates who are ready, willing, and able to handle these responsibilities.

styles. Its creators suggested that too much of the popular and the academic literature pointed strongly toward participative leadership as the one best way to lead. They were uncomfortable with this emphasis, because their research suggested that sometimes participative leadership was not the best leadership style to use in a particular organization or with particular types of decisions.

They developed a typology that distinguished between leading in *making* a decision and leading in *implementing* (or executing) a decision. This model helps to identify the ideal leadership styles for the particular phase of decision making as well as the specific organizational circumstances.

Applying the Leadership Behaviors Window

This model attempts to help managers to consider the leadership style best suited to either *making* a decision or *implementing* a decision. Many modern authorities support the use of *participation* in virtually all situations and in all parts of the decision-making process. This model breaks the decision-making process down into two distinct phases. This allows managers who truly desire to use *participation* (either because they believe in it or because it seems to be an appropriate style for their particular organizational setting and group of people) to do so without completely relinquishing the managerial control over the situation they feel they must retain. It recognizes that most managers are frequently unable or unwilling to let go of the complete decision process because they are concerned about the willingness and commitment of the subordinates to participate. Alternatively, you may be operating under such tight resource constraints that you feel any form of *participation* threatens the company or your own survival.

When to Use the Window. There are three primary occasions in which to use this window:

- When you are first appointed to a managerial position, and wish to make a *proactive* choice of the appropriate leadership style to use. This encourages you to engage in a conscious analysis of the situation and select a style for *making* decisions and a style for *implementing* them.

- *After* you have struggled with a particular leadership style and found it less than adequate. Here, you can evaluate the needs of employees (see also Chapters 5 and 15) and determine whether they are capable and desirous of being involved in one or both stages of decisions—*making* them and *implementing* them.
- In addition, as a counseling tool in providing feedback to a peer or subordinate supervisor. You can point out the two dimensions involved, the resulting style, and the probable consequences in terms of employee satisfaction and commitment.

The Grid in Action. Steve Shapiro has been somewhat nervous about his leadership role ever since his promotion to supervisor six months ago. He knows that this promotion represents a significant recognition and reward by Acme Ball Bearing for his excellent job performance on the ball bearing production line as well as for his loyalty to the company marked by nearly seven years of service. Yet the promotion means new expectations and responsibilities that he isn't quite sure how to meet. He knows that his role as a manager is supposed to be different than that of a line worker, but he isn't yet comfortable with what he is supposed to do. He does know that he is expected to make sure his unit meets high quality and production standards with the ultimate goal of ensuring that every one of the twenty people he supervises meets the production standards. He knows that will be difficult because he does not feel that anyone is quite as good at the job or as hard working as he is. When he first got promoted, therefore, he felt it was necessary to make all the decisions in the department. Then he told those he supervised what he wanted done, explained exactly how he wanted them to do it, and then watched closely to make sure they did it his way.

While the initial reaction in the department to his promotion had been positive ("Old Steve really deserved it") and the early response to his decision-making style was tolerant ("He's new. Humor him. He'll simmer down after a while."), there has been a growing resentment in the unit to his unwillingness to let anyone else have the freedom to make or decide how to implement any decisions in the department. This has begun to frustrate Steve as well as his employees. He senses their unhappiness and wonders how he can let these people *participate in decision making* without losing control. His discomfort is compounded by his belief that he knows he was promoted because he was considered by the company to be the best in the unit. "Why," he wonders aloud, "should I involve them in decision making? After all, if they were that good, why weren't they promoted instead of me?"

While sharing these thoughts one day with Jim Dailey, a fellow supervisor, he asks Jim how he handles these situations and how it works for him. Jim responds that he, too, underwent the same soul-searching after his promotion. Finally, he concluded that his most enjoyable experiences as an employee occurred when he was given the opportunity to contribute to the decisions affecting his job. He figured if his boss felt that he had enough knowledge, training, and ability to *participate in these decisions*, probably he should feel the same way about his own subordinates and let them get involved in decision making without necessarily giving up his ability to make the final choice. What he did was to realize that decision making involves more than just choices and that he can divide the process of decision making into *choice* and *implementation* of that choice. Thus, he can reserve the *final choice* for himself, while comfortably seeking real subordinate involvement in the *implementation*. They feel good and he feels comfortable. Indeed, he finds that this strategy *(permissive autocrat)* gives him an opportunity to share decision making in a way that lets everyone have a part in the final outcome.

Steve is impressed by the conversation and vows he will no longer be a *directive autocrat,* at least.

11-4. The Blake and Mouton Managerial Grid®

The Managerial Grid (Window 11-4) was developed by Robert Blake and Jane Mouton in conjunction with a major organization development project they undertook at Exxon. It was offered as a novel way to develop and provide management training in organization development (OD) concepts. Beyond this, it also provided a means to keep track of whether or not the subsequent training helped managers become effective. As a result the grid could be used as a pre- and post-test for human

Window 11-4. The Blake and Mouton Managerial Grid.®

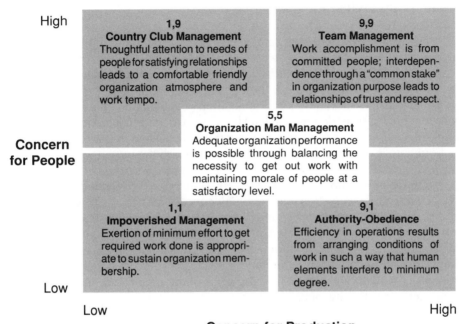

High

1,9
Country Club Management
Thoughtful attention to needs of people for satisfying relationships leads to a comfortable friendly organization atmosphere and work tempo.

9,9
Team Management
Work accomplishment is from committed people; interdependence through a "common stake" in organization purpose leads to relationships of trust and respect.

5,5
Organization Man Management
Adequate organization performance is possible through balancing the necessity to get out work with maintaining morale of people at a satisfactory level.

Concern for People

1,1
Impoverished Management
Exertion of minimum effort to get required work done is appropriate to sustain organization membership.

9,1
Authority-Obedience
Efficiency in operations results from arranging conditions of work in such a way that human elements interfere to minimum degree.

Low

Low **High**

Concern for Production

Source: Robert R. Blake and Jane Srygley Mouton, *The Managerial Grid III*: *The Key to Leadership Excellence,* Houston: Gulf Publishing Company, Copyright © 1985, p. 12. Reproduced by permission.

Dimensions

Concern for production. The horizontal dimension of the grid represents the degree to which you are concerned with getting a job or task accomplished. This may refer to maximizing units, adding new accounts, or generating a number of creative ideas. Your concern is portrayed on a scale from 1 (low) to 9 (high).

Concern for people. The vertical dimension in this model represents the degree to which you have a concern for the human elements of the organization. This can include establishing and monitoring good work relationships, ensuring fair and equitable decisions, and building interpersonal trust. This is also presented on a 1-to-9 scale from low to high concern.

Window 11-4. (*Continued*)

Leadership Styles

▓ **Authority-obedience management (9,1).** The lower right-hand corner represents the leader who is extremely production-oriented and minimally concerned with people. This *authority-obedience* manager believes that there is a fundamental conflict between the needs of the people and the needs of the organization and this requires a minimization of any human *concern* in favor of *production.* These leaders tend to lean heavily on their formal authority, measure their success in terms of production quotas, and believe that an unsupervised subordinate is one who will "goof off" or do the job the wrong way.

▓ **Country club management (1,9).** The *country club manager* has very *low concern for production* and very *high concern for people.* This leader is so focused on the personal, social, and welfare needs of his or her subordinates that production is allowed to take care of itself. This type of leader assumes that happy workers are, by definition, productive ones and that as long as the employees are kept well satisfied they will work hard. The *country club* manager helps subordinates cope with any reasonable demands of the organization. In return this manager wants loyalty, acceptance, and understanding.

▓ **Impoverished management (1,1).** This manager doesn't have an interest in people or production and is the antithesis of the **9,9** manager. The **1,1** manager has accepted defeat, frustration, and powerlessness. This manager sticks to the rules, goes by the book, and does the minimum to survive. This type of leader fits well in a highly bureaucratic setting where decision making is reserved for top managers. Subordinates have little opportunity to contribute their ideas and, consequently, little interest in the organization, its goals, or its people. The *impoverished* manager just does not care to do any more than what it takes to survive.

▓ **Organization man management (5,5).** This manager has an intermediate *concern for production* linked with a moderate *concern for people.* A contradiction between *production* and *people* needs is presumed by this grid style; that is, the **5,5** solution to the *production-people* dilemma is to trade off—to give up half of one in order to get the other half. The underlying assumption is that extreme positions promote conflict and should be avoided. Steady progress comes from compromise and a willingness to yield some advantages in order to gain others. The result is that a **5,5**-oriented manager is unlikely to seek the best position for either *production* or *people,* but to find an equilibrium that is in between both.

Window 11-4. (*Continued*)

▓ **Team management (9,9).** *The team management* leader has a high *concern for people* and a high *concern for production.* This is, in many ways, the ideal. This manager believes that there is not and should not be any conflict between the *human needs* of the employees and the *production needs* of the organization. This leader seeks to fully utilize the potential of the employees in a joint effort to attain the highest possible level of production. Accomplishment and contribution are seen as the driving forces behind both organizational performance and individual satisfaction.

relations-oriented training that was, at the time of its development, very much in need of more precise measurement of effectiveness. Since such training very often had no conclusive evidence to support its effectiveness, the Managerial Grid and its associated measures became a useful way to convince managers that the costs of such OD programs and human relations training were worth the benefits.

Applying the Managerial Grid Window

The Managerial Grid has achieved wide popularity and will likely continue to have a wide range of uses in organizational development. The concept is relatively simple to comprehend and straightfoward in its application. The program for development detailed by Blake and Mouton will, if followed, yield managers who will move closer toward the *9,9* ideal where they should be able to display more of a concern for both *production* and *people.* The program can be utilized by corporate training staffs seeking to improve the general human relations climate through a structured and "proven" development program.

The Managerial Grid is a way of methodically changing the employee orientation of the organization by creating successive waves of trainees who go back to their functional units, implement their new skills, and encourage other co-workers to do likewise. The relatively low cost of this team-based training and the ease with which it can be conducted on-site means that an organization can afford to train all of its managers. This will create the critical mass so necessary to change the prevailing orientation of an organizational culture to a more positive, humane, and sensitive orientation. Through this type of a program, the organization builds a managerial team that has a strong commitment to both *people* and *production.*

How to Use the Window. The Blake and Mouton Managerial Grid has been used in many ways in many organizations over the past quarter-century. Most typically it can be used under the following conditions to:

- Alert a task/production-oriented *(authority-obedience)* manager to the fact that overemphasis on this dimension may result in low morale, low commitment to the organization, absenteeism, and/or turnover.
- Alert a humanistic manager that too much of an emphasis on people's feelings and emotions *(country club)* may result in limited performance by the employees who feel no pressure to produce.
- Alert a manager who is negligent in creating either condition (*impoverished* management) to take some early action to improve both the concern for *people* and the concern for *production.*
- Provide an organization-wide goal for the creation of a *team-oriented* culture that appropriately accents a high degree of both dimensions.

The Grid in Action. Tom Miller is from "the old school." Because his father was raised during the depression years, Tom knows firsthand both the agony of not having a job and the joy the whole family felt when employment finally came. This lesson has been impressed deeply onto Tom. Working is a privilege, holding a good job paying good wages is an honor, and every man who is lucky enough to have a job owes the company both loyalty and a fair day's effort for the right to work there.

Tom joined Amazing Steel in the mid 1960s after high school. He worked hard following these values and within a reasonably short time became a foreman. His supervisory style focuses on getting the job done, and he does. While management respects his hardworking attitude and company loyalty, there is less enthusiasm among those who work for him. The department he runs has many grievances filed on work rule violations and a surprising amount of turnover for such well-paid jobs in the mill.

Tom is a bit mystified by all this because he can't understand why everyone isn't like him. After all, why do people *come* to work, if they don't come to *work?* He certainly doesn't feel that it is any concern of his that some have personal problems or difficulty getting along with either him or other members of the department. If they were unhappy with him or the company, let them go find another job. He just can't understand what these young kids expect from him or the company. They are getting $15 per hour, enjoy great fringe benefits, and have job security. They drive new sports cars, buy flashy gold chains, and take expensive vacations. Tom wonders what his father would think if he could see and hear these fellows talk today as he reads a memo he has received. "All supervisors will report to Room 912 on Monday for training in team management concepts," it says. "Why do I need this stuff?" wonders Tom as he reads the note. "What possible reason is there for me to worry about teamwork?"

The next Monday evening Tom is having a beer with another supervisor, Ed Jones, who started with Amazing Steel the same day he did and who also attended the training. Tom says, "Ed, what do you think about all this stuff on team building?" Ed responds, "Sounds like they want to turn this place into a *country club* for these young fellows. Isn't anyone just happy to have a job anymore?"

"I don't know," says Tom. "Maybe these young folks just expect more out of their work than you and I did when we came here. Maybe that fellow talking to us today had a good point. I think I'll try spending a bit more effort on those interpersonal things he talked about. I've been having some real problems in my department getting some of these fellows to pay attention to the work. Maybe they want more out of this than I do. I guess it's worth a try to find out."

Reference

Blake, Robert R., and Jane S. Mouton. *The New Managerial Grid.* Houston: Gulf Publishing, 1978.

Chapter 12

Motivation

What factors influence an employee's job performance? In broad terms the primary considerations are a person's capacity, the opportunity to perform, and the willingness to expend the energy. The topic of motivation addresses the latter factor—an employee's willingness to engage in some behavior desired by the organization.

Several fundamental questions emerge in considering motivation: 1) Why do some people conform to organizational expectations, while others willfully withhold their effort (e.g., some people almost never miss a day of work and others frequently call in 'sick')? 2) Why do some people choose to work hard, while others choose to hardly work? and 3) Why do people stop doing one thing and start doing another?

Motivation, then, deals with choices employees make, the energy they expend, and the channeling of their efforts. The windows presented in this chapter provide diagnostic clues and preliminary answers to these questions, as well as suggestions for implementing the ideas discussed.

12-1. Changing Employee Behaviors

Some employee behaviors are desirable, and managers seek to continue such actions. Sometimes, however, employees consciously or unconsciously exhibit undesirable behaviors, and these need to be prevented, corrected, or at least diminished. Window 12-1 suggests two ways of increasing the likelihood that a behavior will be repeated and two ways of decreasing the likelihood a behavior will be repeated. In particular, it clarifies 1) the importance of administering or withholding consequences as a result of the employee behavior, and 2) the powerful difference between pleasant and unpleasant consequences and their effect (intended and unintended) on employees.

Applying the Employee Behaviors Window

Many theories of motivation attempt to understand, predict, and control behavior by attempting to identify what goes on inside a person's head in terms of perceptions, cognitions, and beliefs. Operant conditioning, however, states that behavior is often a function of the *consequences* it produces. You can choose when and how to respond to an employee's behavior. Therefore, you can directly affect employee behavior without attempting to psychoanalyze your employees (e.g., identify their motives).

Many useful suggestions have been made regarding how to apply operant conditioning principles. Here are some suggestions and relevant insights:

- Define a Good Job—tell subordinates specifically what behaviors you want and what behaviors you don't want.
- Don't Treat Everybody the Same—make sure rewards are contingent on only desired behaviors.
- Give Big Strokes to Big Folks—make the magnitude of the reward appropriate to the level of behavior observed or desired.
- After, Not Before—make sure the rewards follow, not precede, the desired behavior.
- Too Soon Is Not Soon Enough—reward the person as quickly as is practical.
- Children Are Not Born as Adults—remember that it takes time to learn new behaviors. Therefore, reward small steps of improvement toward a final goal. However, do not reward backsliding (regression to less desirable levels of behavior).
- Money Is Not the Only Game in Town—recognition, praise,

Window 12-1. Changing Employee Behaviors.

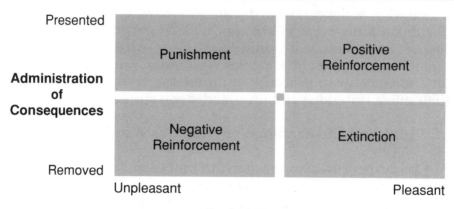

Desirability of Response

Source: Hugh J. Arnold and Daniel C. Feldman, *Organizational Behavior,* New York: McGraw-Hill, 1986, p. 69.

Dimensions

Administration of consequences. This dimension points out that you can respond to an employee's behavior in either of two ways (other than ignoring it). You may choose to *give* the employee something or you may *withhold* (or even remove) something.

Desirability of response. This dimension shows that the consequence that you administer or remove can have either positive value (e.g., a pay raise) or negative value (e.g., a reprimand). The desirability of a response is judged by the recipient, not you.

Four Ways to Affect Behavior

Positive reinforcement. Here you respond to, and reward, desired behavior. This process of *positive reinforcement* is recommended as the best way of increasing the likelihood an employee will continue to perform in a desired manner. It draws on the Law of Effect, which simply means that the behaviors that are rewarded are more likely to be repeated.

Extinction. Here you attempt to eliminate the link between undesired behavior (e.g., low performance) and positive consequences (e.g., a pay raise) by simply not rewarding undesirable behavior. This process should result in the diminution, and eventual *extinction*, of the undesirable behavior. This is recom-

Window 12-1. (*Continued*)

mended as the preferred manner of increasing the likelihood that an undesirable behavior will stop. It should be noted that failing to reward desired behavior can also lead to the *extinction* of a desired practice.

Negative reinforcement. This is the process of *removing* an unpleasant consequence when an employee stops behaving in an undesired way and starts behaving in an appropriate manner. For example, imagine an employee who is sharply reprimanded for every tardy arrival at work. When the employee finally reports for work on time, the reprimand stops. Note that the intent (and the effect) of removing the unpleasant consequence is to increase the likelihood that the employee will exhibit and repeat the desired behaviors (e.g., showing up to work). This is a result of the employee's desire to avoid unpleasant consequences (e.g., having pay docked or being fired).

Punishment. This represents a direct attempt to stop an undesired behavior by *administering* an unpleasant consequence. However, many unintended and organizationally undesired effects often accompany the use of punishment. Therefore you should generally limit your use of this technique.

---

personal interest, favorable job assignments, or allowing personal control of time often mean more than an extra twenty dollars in take-home pay.
- Managers get the behavior they reward, and not the behavior they *want*—don't engage in wishful thinking.

When to Use the Window. A major part of every manager's job is to guide employee behavior toward organizational goals through using one or more of the strategies outlined earlier. This window can prove useful to you when:

- You want to encourage employee behaviors that make a positive contribution toward the organization (e.g., consistent work attendance, quality performance, innovative thinking).
- You want to increase the frequency of a desired behavior that is already being exhibited.
- You want to recognize and reward constructive employee behaviors.

- You need to reduce or eliminate organizationally harmful or undesirable behaviors.

The Grid in Action. John Wells is perplexed. As night shift foreman, he plans to promote Jane Greer to lead person because she is by far his best worker. Unfortunately, recently Jane has been consistently late for work. He has not said anything to her because he hopes it will stop, and he doesn't relish the idea of confronting her. But, if her behavior does not change, John cannot promote her, and he and the company will lose along with Jane. As he thinks about the situation, he realizes that by not saying anything to Jane he has actually reinforced her tardiness.

One day he resolves to act. But how? Should he *punish* her by issuing a reprimand the next time she comes to work late? After all, *punishing* a behavior tends to stop it. But it can also destroy the rapport he has with her. No, John decides to approach the situation by encouraging on-time behavior rather than stopping tardy behavior. Thus, he decides that the next time she comes to work on time he will let her know that he appreciates it because she is an important role model for the other workers. Also, he will continue to do this on a regular basis until Jane's tardiness is no longer a problem. John's application of *positive reinforcement* ultimately contributes to Jane's punctual behavior. Eventually he feels comfortable giving her the promotion.

References

Miner, John B. *Theories of Organizational Behavior.* Hinsdale, Ill.: The Dryden Press, 1980, Chapter 8: "Behavior Modification and Operant Learning," pp. 201–230.

O'Brien, Richard M., Alyce M. Dickenson, and Michael P. Rosow. *Industrial Behavior Modification: A Management Handbook.* Elmsford, N.Y.: Pergamon Press, 1982.

12-2. Reinforcement Schedules

Employee reward systems vary widely across (and sometimes within) organizations. They differ in many respects, including the basis on which rewards are administered and the degree to which they are systematically applied.

Window 12-2 clarifies the effects of making the receipt of rewards contingent on the passage of *time* (e.g., being paid every two weeks), versus tying the rewards to specific *behaviors* (e.g., a piece-rate system). The grid also distinguishes between the effects of a *fixed* versus a *variable* response pattern.

Applying the Reinforcement Schedules Window

Research shows that an employee's behavioral pattern is primarily a result of the type of reinforcement pattern used. Generally speaking, 1) *ratio* schedules are more effective in producing high levels of behavior than are *interval* schedules; and 2) *variable* schedules are more effective, though they take longer, than are *fixed* schedules. However, individuals prefer the predictability of *fixed* schedules more, at least when it comes to pay.

In general, you are advised to (1) recognize that there are a variety of potential rewards that can be administered as opposed to relying solely on money; (2) employ a variable reinforcement schedule; and (3) tie rewards to *behavior* as opposed to *time*, whenever it is possible.

When to Use the Window. Consciously or unconsciously you are continually influencing the behavior of others, through your actions as well as the timing of your responses. This window can help you motivate employees under these conditions:

- You have attempted to change an employee's behavior through the use of one type of schedule, and the effort has been unsuccessful.
- You hear about the use of one or more of the reinforcement schedules and discover that the actual definition is different than you originally believed.
- You have historically used only one of the reinforcement schedules and begin to realize that other options may be available and may be useful.
- You discover that continuous schedules of reinforcement are too time-consuming and of diminishing effectiveness.

Window 12-2. Reinforcement Schedules.

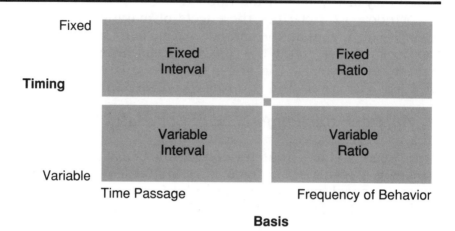

Source: Hugh J. Arnold and Daniel C. Feldman, *Organizational Behavior,* New York: McGraw-Hill, 1986, p. 70.

Dimensions

Basis. Rewards can be administered as a function of either the passage of *time* or the frequency of the desired *behavior.* The former provides the comfort of predictability to the employee (e.g., "I'll receive my weekly check for about $325 next Friday"), but may fail to motivate improvement in productivity. The frequency approach serves to stimulate greater *quantity* of employee performance among those with economic needs, but makes it difficult for the organization to accurately budget for wage costs.

Timing. Rewards can also be administered based on fixed or variable response patterns. The *fixed* approach either bases rewards on time (e.g., receipt of a paycheck every week on Friday at 4:00 P.M.) or follow a predetermined number of occurrences of a behavior (e.g., a bonus awarded following the successful assembly of twenty-eight widgets). Alternatively, a *variable* approach provides rewards after different time periods or after a variety of different numbers of widgets are successfully assembled. Although the timing of the reward varies, the average time period that passes or the average number of widgets produced before rewards are administered is known to (and controlled by) the manager.

Four Reinforcement Schedules

Fixed interval. The most common form of administering a pay system is on the basis of a *fixed interval,* where employees are paid weekly, biweekly, semimonthly, or monthly. These systems have the advantages of simplicity, low

Window 12-2. (*Continued*)

cost, and predictability. Unfortunately, in terms of motivating a high level of performance, they are the least effective.

Variable interval. In a *variable interval* schedule of reinforcement, the reinforcement opportunity is unpredictable, but it varies around some average. A supervisor who checks in with each subordinate to provide work-related praise on an average of once a day, but at different times throughout the week, is an example.

Variable ratio. Under a *variable ratio* schedule, reinforcement occurs after a number of desirable behavioral responses have occurred, with the number required varying around a designated average. The state of Nevada has based its economy on the power of *variable ratio* schedules of reinforcement to sustain high levels of behavior that are not easily extinguished (e.g., tourists playing slot machines). Some companies employ lottery systems in which employees who are present and on time qualify for a potentially winning number. This method tends to reduce tardiness/absenteeism.

Fixed ratio. A *fixed ratio* of reinforcement provides a reward following a predetermined and stable number of occurrences of the desired behavior. Paying salespeople on a commission basis (e.g., a three-dollar commission for every twelve units sold) would be an example.

Here, you may discover that intermittent schedules of reinforcement may work even better and be used more economically.

The Grid in Action. Mary Grey is excited about her promotion to regional manager. She realizes that she will be on the road often, visiting the eight district offices reporting to her. However, she is anxious to get out in the field so she can personally size up the situation in each district. She is concerned, though, that if she announces when she will visit each office she will see each only at its best and not observe its typical behavior. She realizes that if people know when an event is to take place they will be at their best right before the event happens, but will usually slack off right afterward. This she does not want. She wants offices to be at their best all the time.

Analyzing the situation, she concludes this will be more likely to happen if each district cannot anticipate the exact date of her visit. Thus she establishes the policy of visiting each district at least once every three weeks, but she will *vary randomly by order and time* when the visits will take place (*variable interval* reinforcement).

References

Miner, John B. *Theories of Organizational Behavior.* Hinsdale, Ill.: The Dryden Press, 1980, Chapter 8: "Behavior Modification and Operant Learning," pp. 201–230.

O'Brien, Richard M., Alyce M. Dickenson, and Michael P. Rosow. *Industrial Behavior Modification: A Management Handbook.* Elmsford, N.Y.: Pergamon Press, 1982.

12-3. Satisfaction and Dissatisfaction

One stream of provocative and controversial research suggests that the factors that make employees satisfied are not the same factors that, when absent, cause them to feel dissatisfied. This suggests that treating employees well so that they will not be dissatisfied is not the same as using them well so that they will be both satisfied and motivated (see Window 12-3).

Applying the Satisfaction and Dissatisfaction Window

Several theories of human needs suggest that it is useful to dichotomize needs into two "supra" categories, often referred to as higher- and lower-order needs. Lower-order needs are associated with physiological and survival needs, such as the need to avoid pain. This window model equates conditions in the job environment (or context) with pain avoidance and labels them *hygiene* factors. Higher-order needs, such as the need for esteem, achievement, competence, and self-actualization, are associated with psychological growth. This model associates job content factors with the fulfillment of the growth needs and refers to these factors as *motivators*. The distinction is useful because it suggests that an important source of sustained and

Window 12-3. Satisfaction and Dissatisfaction.

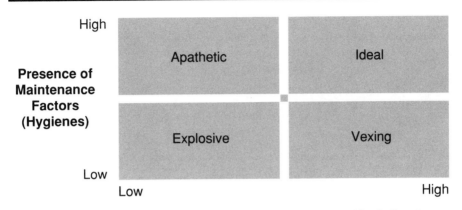

Source: Adapted from Randall B. Dunham, *Organizational Behavior*, Homewood, Ill.: Richard D. Irwin, 1984, pp. 117–123.

Dimensions

Presence of maintenance factors (hygienes). Certain factors in the work *context* or environment (e.g., poor technical supervision, unsatisfactory relations with the boss and co-workers, bad working conditions, low pay) cause a person to feel dissatisfied. Attention to these factors, however, will only reduce feelings of dissatisfaction and will not cause a person to feel satisfied and motivated.

Presence of motivator factors (satisfiers). Other factors in the work *content* (e.g., jobs that provide a sense of achievement, recognition, and responsibility) cause an employee to feel satisfied and motivated. Their presence serves to release employee energy toward acceptable goals.

Employee Attitudinal Responses

Apathetic. Some employees have jobs that provide many *hygiene* factors, but not many *motivators*. These are low in job content, but the job context is good. These employees will not be dissatisfied, but on the other hand they will not be motivated. They might be described as being *apathetic*.

Explosive. In some situations neither the job content nor job context is good. Here the employee experiences both strong negative feelings and a lack of any positive feelings. Such a situation is *explosive.*

Window 12-3. (*Continued*)

▨ **Vexing.** Some employees love their work but hate the company, the boss, or some other aspect of their work environment. Here the job content is good, but the job context is not. As a result, the employee is motivated to do a good job, but miserable at the same time. Such a situation is *vexing*.

▨ **Ideal.** The best of all possible worlds is to have a job that provides challenge, opportunity, and recognition coupled with good working conditions, pay, and interpersonal relations. Such a situation is *ideal*, because the job context is sound and the job is loaded with content.

internal motivation stems from the nature of the job that people perform, and not from the context in which the job is embedded.

This framework reminds you that a major source of employee motivation stems from how the jobs they perform are designed. Building on the job enlargement-job enrichment prescriptions, it offers the following recommendations:

- Allow people greater control over scheduling their own time.
- Provide for greater personal control of resources through the use of individual budgets that make the person accountable for cost.
- Provide opportunities for psychological growth through new and meaningful learning.
- Provide for direct and nonevaluative performance feedback.
- Provide for contact with the persons who use the workers' product or service.
- Allow workers to directly communicate with others, as needed, to get the job done without going through the hierarchy.
- Hold people personally responsible for results.

Steps to Employ When Using the Window. Management has often been defined as the art of getting things done through others. To accomplish this, you must focus on managing employee attitudes, motivation, and behaviors. They are so intertwined that you cannot manage one without seeing the impact on the other two. In light of this, the Satisfaction and Dissatisfaction Window implies that you should:

- Recognize the substantive difference between providing opportunities for satisfaction through managing job content, and removing dissatisfaction through manipulation of job context.
- Seek to provide a balanced set of rewards in the work environment that will appeal to both sets of factors (*hygiene* and *motivator*).
- Actively seek to manage both the work environment for employees, so that it won't distract them, and the job content surrounding them, so that they can receive intrinsic satisfaction from their work.
- Look beyond motivating employees with solely monetary rewards and consider a wide range of noneconomic ways to reinforce desirable behaviors.

The Grid in Action. Susan Dean sits staring at the year-end turnover figures for her division. As Human Resource Manager, she has the responsibility, among many other duties, to develop strategies for managing the selection and retention of employees. And right now those strategies do not look too effective. For the third straight year, turnover is up to almost 40 percent, or 120 out of nearly 300 employees. When she calculates all the costs associated with recruiting, selecting, placing, and training new employees, not to mention productivity losses due to operational disruption, she estimates that her division is spending over a quarter of a million dollars per year.

Thinking back, she runs over the changes that have taken place in the last year and a half. First, the company has greatly improved the physical working environment. After all, not only has the cafeteria been remodeled, but an employee health spa has been built. Second, the division has changed its pay strategy and now, instead of matching the competition, it has become one of the leaders, if not the leader, in the local labor market. And finally, all the supervisors have gone through a human relations training program. Yet, despite all these changes, turnover has not decreased. In fact it has gone up. Silently, Susan sits there pondering what to do.

Looking out the window, she gazes at the green pastures typical of the farm belt where her division is located. She wonders to herself why folks who make such hardworking motivated farmers make such poor factory workers. Then it dawns on her that maybe the work itself is the problem. As farmers, they have high control over what, how, and when they do their jobs. They are personally responsible for what they do and can see the results of their labor. She thinks to herself, "Is it possible to redesign the jobs in the plant to make them more like the work of the farmers?" She resolves to do two things. First, she will interview some of the workers to see if this is the real reason for the turnover problem. Second, assuming the answer to her first question is yes, she will work with the line supervisors and engineering to see what changes can be made. Whether or not this is possible is not yet apparent, but already her mood has changed from despairing to hopeful.

References

Herzberg, Frederick I. *The Managerial Choice: To Be Efficient and to Be Human.* Homewood, Ill.: Dow Jones-Irwin, 1976.

Herzberg, Frederick I., Bernard Mausner, and Barbara B. Snyderman. *The Motivation to Work.* New York: John Wiley & Sons, 1959.

12-4. Predictable Attributions

Employee behaviors are often difficult to understand, much less predict. This process is compounded by the sometimes confusing and erratic responses of managers to the behaviors of their subordinates. A complex situation arises in which employees themselves may not even know why they act as they do, and then you must make assumptions to try to understand that behavior and respond to it.

Whether observing everyday work behaviors of your employees in order to provide spontaneous critique and job-related guidance, or engaging in periodic performance appraisals, you base your conclusions on your perceptions of the causes of employee behavior. Window 12-4 identifies four predictable patterns of explanations often used to explain differences in behav-

Window 12-4. Predictable Attributions.

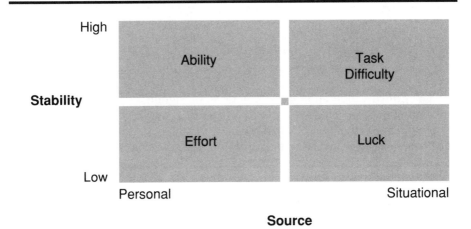

Source: Jean M. Bartunek, "Why Did You Do That? Attribution Theory in Organizations," *Business Horizons*, September-October, 1981, pp. 66–71. Copyright 1981 by the Foundation for the School of Business at Indiana University. Used with permission.

Dimensions

Source. This dimension refers to the probable location of a problem—where you tend to look in a search for behavioral causes. Sometimes people attribute the cause of a person's behavior to something *internal* to the person (e.g., motivation, personality traits, abilities), and other times they attribute the cause to something *external* to the person (e.g., lack of proper tools or training).

Stability. Some employee behaviors occur only once or just infrequently; others are repeated regularly. This dimension assesses whether the behavior seen is *stable* across time (e.g., an employee is habitually late in returning from lunch break), or whether it occurs only occasionally (e.g., an employee landed large sales contracts twice during the year).

Major Attributional Tendencies

Ability. When people examine their own (personal) successful behavior and believe that it occurs regularly (stable), the natural tendency is to attribute it to their own (high) *ability* level. *Abilities* include creativity, problem-solving capacity, motor skills, or even intuition.

Task difficulty. A *stable situation* represents another common target of attributions. For example, some tasks are so easy that almost anyone can do them well every time; others are difficult. The explanations for success or failure may include an assessment of how challenging it was to perform the task.

Window 12-4. (*Continued*)

▓ **Luck.** Some events happen without apparent cause, at least none that can be associated with the individual. When these occur (usually very rarely), people tend to conclude that fate or *luck* caused these random occurrences.

▓ **Effort.** When an employee achieves a significant success, but does it only infrequently, you tend to attribute it to extraordinary *effort* on the part of the individual. Similarly, if an employee who is regularly successful happens to fail once or twice, you may assume that insufficient *effort* was expended.

iors observed and their causes. The tendency to use simple causal patterns as explanations is referred to as *attribution*.

Applying the Predictable Attributions Window

Whether you hold a person responsible for success or failure on a task, and how positive or negative your response is to the level of performance achieved, depends on the causes you attribute to the performance. For example, training is often recommended when poor performance is attributed to a lack of *ability*. On the other hand, a reprimand would be appropriate when a lack of *effort* was the cause. Unfortunately, many people tend to have fundamental biases when assessing the causes of their own versus others' behavior. For example, when assessing the poor performance of others, we tend to make internal attributions for them (e.g., low *ability*, or poor *effort*). But when assessing our own poor performance, we tend to blame the situation. The opposite bias occurs in assessing the causes of success. Differing attributions often lie at the heart of conflict during the performance appraisal process, and they can lead to inappropriate rewards or punishment.

From a performance appraisal viewpoint, the Predictable Attributions Window suggests the following:

1. Determine whether the cause of the performance *should* be attributed to the person or the situation. Ask yourself how the person's current performance compares to a)

his/her past performance, b) performance on other tasks, c) the performance of others on this task.

2. If the person is legitimately assigned responsibility, determine whether the cause is *stable* or *unstable*. If it is *stable*, then past behavior will be the best predictor of future behavior unless action is taken.

3. If the cause is external, continue current policies and reward practices for high (*stable*) levels of performance. But if low levels of performance occur, focus on changing the work environment and not the person.

4. Don't just assign blame, but focus on assigning responsibility for corrective action.

Using the Window. Part of any manager's job is to observe employee performance, monitor it, and attempt to redirect it toward more productive avenues whenever necessary. Assessment, judgment, and appraisal are regular managerial duties, but you rely heavily on the accuracy of explanations given for employee behavior. Therefore, the Predictable Attributions Window can be useful for:

- Encouraging you to accept the fact that not all causes of employee behavior (whether good or bad) lie inside the individual, nor do they necessarily recur regularly. The Predictable Attributions Window encourages you to analyze the *stability* of behaviors as well as identify their realistic *sources*.

- Helping you to look for patterns in employee behavior, which, if *stable*, help to predict future behaviors unless you intervene in some way.

- Stimulating you to explore situations for potential obstacles to improved employee performance.

- Examining your own behaviors (and the perceived causes) and thereby better understanding the ways in which people tend to explain their own successes more favorably (and personally) while attributing others' behaviors to different sets of causes. This will help you to predict possible sources of perceptual disagreement in appraisal interviews and drive you toward developing a more objective basis for your conclusions.

The Grid in Action. It is late as Harve Wilson sits down to the arduous task of preparing for the annual performance appraisal reviews with his subordinates. One of the things he is least looking forward to is his meeting with Jim Coker. Jim was once a solid performer, but this last year his performance has been considerably below par. As a result Harve is not recommending Jim for a merit pay increase. Harve knows telling Jim this will likely provoke a bitter debate that Harve doesn't relish. Of equal importance to him, however, is pinpointing the *cause* of Jim's declining performance. If it doesn't improve, he will have to let him go; and after fifteen years of solid, if not spectacular, performance by Jim, Harve wants to avoid doing that.

Harve realizes that there is a natural tendency to blame the employee for unacceptable levels of performance, e.g., to assume Jim just isn't trying. However, he also realizes that sometimes the reason has nothing to do with the employee, but has to do with the situation, e.g., lack of proper equipment or training. Therefore, he decides to ask himself a series of questions to help him decide whether the problem is in Jim or elsewhere. Harve recalls that prior to this year Jim was a good worker. He takes note of the fact that as a result of a technological development Jim's job has changed during the past year. However, that is true of everyone else's job as well, and the job performance of others has not declined. Thus Harve concludes that the problem has more to do with Jim than with the situation. The next question is whether the problem exists because Jim just isn't trying or whether it is attributable to something more enduring. He notes that Jim is rarely absent, never tardy, and still seems to have a positive attitude. Thus Harve concludes that the decrease in performance is not a motivational problem. That means it has to be something else. Looking at Jim's personnel folder, Harve notes that he did not go to school beyond the eighth grade. While this has never hindered Jim's performance before, Harve wonders if the job change, which involved the use of computer-assisted monitoring devices and simple arithmetic that Jim has never mastered, could be the cause. He decides to explore that possibility with Jim tomorrow. If it proves to be relevant, he can recommend a remedial course of study to bring Jim up to speed. He feels better now that he has a positive course of action to pursue rather than simply letting Jim go.

References

Brickman, Phillip, Vita Carulli Rabinowitz, Jurgis Karusa, Jr., Dan Coates, Ellen Cohn, and Louise Kidder. "Models of Helping and Coping." *American Psychologist*, Vol. 37, No. 4 (1981).

Mitchell, Terence R., Stephen G. Green, and Robert E. Wood. "An Attributional Model of Leadership and the Poor Performing Subordinate: Development and Validation," in L. L. Cummings and B. M. Staw, eds., *Research in Organizational Behavior*, Vol. 3. Greenwich, Conn.: JAI Press, 1981, pp. 197–234.

Chapter 13

Organizational Cultures

Today's managers live in a world of rapid change. New technologies appear even before old methods are fully understood. Mergers and acquisitions necessitate adaptation to new ventures and personnel. Environmental and political events require organizations to react quickly to a changing business environment. The culture of an organization binds its members together and helps them keep the organization's important values intact.

The culture of an organization is a set of values and norms shared by its members. Very similar to the way that members of a religious group or a family unit adhere to a number of beliefs, rituals, and ways of doing things, companies develop a set of accepted values, beliefs, and actions. Effective managers are able to harness the power of technology and corporate strategy to their organization's culture so that all are pulling in the same direction.

The windows in this chapter help you answer the following three questions: 1) What is the most appropriate culture for the social and business environment of this company? 2) What is the most effective way for the cultures of two merging companies to unite? 3) How can you move beyond your preferred values orientation and incorporate the contributions of competing approaches to help you optimally manage organizational problems?

13-1. Organizational Cultures

Culture is a set of important values, beliefs, and understandings shared by members of an organization. It also reflects the unwritten, informal norms that bind an organization together. Norms prescribe behavior and also help explain "the way we do things around here." Culture cannot be seen, but it can be inferred from patterns of office dress, rationales for office layout, stories, logos, and ceremonies. When the organization's culture is strong, values are clear and widely shared by organizational members at all levels. From these shared values flow clear policies whose meaning is shared and endorsed among employees.

An organization's culture must be appropriate for its social and business environment. The Organizational Cultures Window (Window 13-1) describes four different corporate cultures and the environments that offer the best fit for them. By understanding how to identify your own culture, you can be proactive in managing and changing your culture to respond to a changing corporate environment.

Applying the Organizational Cultures Window

The workplace is teeming with change. Employees want more input into their jobs; more women and minorities comprise the work force; automation, computers, and international forces are realities. Culture must be responsive to these powerful changes in the world of work.

Values are the core of culture. Strong values guide you as you make decisions. Organizational values, such as a commitment to retain employees during slow periods or to please a customer, sometimes conflict with financial goals. In strong-culture companies, values are clearly displayed through the organization's heroes, and stories about these role models' heroic acts are shared at all levels of the organization. Symbols, slogans, rites, and rituals complete the building blocks of culture by providing concrete, day-to-day expressions of the corporation's values. The norms and ceremonies spell out for employees how to behave, and dramatize those activities vital to the continuation of culture.

Information exchange in an organization goes far beyond

(Text continues on page 242)

Window 13-1. Organizational Cultures.

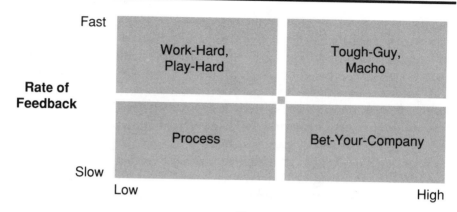

Source: Adapted from Terrence E. Deal and A. A. Kennedy, *Corporate Cultures.* Copyright © 1982, Addison-Wesley Publishing Co., Inc., Reading Massachusetts. Reprinted with permission.

Dimensions

Degree of risk. You always face levels of risk in the company's strategic decisions. The probability that major decisions will result in successful outcomes ranges from low-risk to high-risk. A *high-risk decision* can be one to fund a Broadway extravaganza or an oil well exploration project. A *low-risk decision* can involve whom to call on when you are promoting a product or what computer software you will use to perform a data gathering task. When these activities are not successful, other sales calls can be made or another software package can be tried.

Rate of feedback. The speed with which the company receives feedback on the success of its strategy can be critical. *Fast feedback* occurs when the venture capitalists learn that their Broadway show is a smash hit or when the salesperson's efforts are immediately reinforced by a substantial order. *Slow feedback* is evident when an organization has to wait years to realize whether a decision to research and design a product will pay off in substantial sales. In large, regulated organizations there may be little or no *feedback* on the impact of decisions.

Organizational Cultures

Tough-guy, macho. This culture combines high-risk decisions with *fast feedback* regarding their success. Entrepreneurs, individualists, stars, and gamblers thrive in this environment. A high-pressure culture may result in either fast

Window 13-1. (*Continued*)

fortunes or quick descents. Financial stakes are high, and the constant assessment of whether a project has succeeded or failed results in quick burnout and diverts attention from long-term planning. The entertainment industry and advertising, investment, and consulting positions typify this culture.

Work-hard, play-hard. This culture combines numerous *low-risk* decisions and *fast feedback*. Highly active, energetic people (who are often in sales and promotion) characterize this culture, where a fast pace and creative interventions result in success. Each sales call is relatively *low-risk* because no single sale will dramatically affect the organization. The *feedback* is as quick as a yes or no. Heroes of this culture are excellent salespeople and team players. Conventions, contests, and meetings reinforce the hard work and active life-style of this culture.

Bet-your-company. This culture combines *high-stakes* decisions followed by a long wait for feedback. A major decision such as a plan to build a new airplane can result in years of development. Because the correctness of the decision may not be known for several years, heroes in this culture must have stamina and maturity. They are respected for their technical competence and seniority. This culture often develops breakthroughs for society, but its employers wait patiently for their recognition.

Process. *Low-risk* decisions and a *slow* rate of *feedback* lead to a process culture. In this culture outcomes are hard to measure. Employees in government agencies, insurance companies, and accounting firms focus on accuracy and follow-through of procedures. Their individual efforts rarely make an impact on their larger environment, yet they provide the order and predictability in the world of work that allow others to take *risks* and be creative. Process cultures value reliability. Their heroes devise new, effective procedures or support the employee's needs on the job. When the process culture dominates, overemphasis on procedures can lead companies to lose touch with the external marketplace.

the sterile memo. Behind every communication is the powerful informal network of communicators who give meaning to its content. Storytellers, priests, gossips, and spies exist at all levels of the organization to convey important messages throughout the organization.

Organizational cultures are rooted in their history as well as in their present leadership. Organizations founded by *risk-taking* entrepreneurs are likely to have an autocratic climate geared for fast action. Organizations emerging out of a group of collaborative scientists may display a climate emphasizing democratic collaboration, with creative solutions to complex technical problems as their goal.

The critical question facing managers who are aware of the importance of culture is: Does the organization's culture fit with, and respond to, the prevailing business environment? An autocratic culture that may be desirable for company start-up may later squelch creative ideas necessary for continued success. Similarly, the collaborative culture that effectively developed technical breakthroughs may lack the direction needed to maintain internal stability.

Most organizations, of course, blend the four different cultures. This is logical, especially when the different functions of each department are recognized.

The Organizational Cultures Window serves practicing managers in a number of ways. First, it asks you, "Do you understand your culture?" The Organizational Cultures model offers you an excellent starting point for identifying the culture that is operational in your organization. Second, it prescribes modifications that can transform the prevailing environment into one more consistent with your business. When there is a mismatch between the prevailing culture and its business environment, you can use the Organizational Culture framework to direct your change efforts, but you must not succumb to simplistic solutions simply because of long-standing traditions. Third, the window challenges you to maintain desirable aspects of the culture that are true to the organization's core values. You must, therefore, assess your organization and preserve those aspects of the culture that have been responsible for its success. Values are difficult to change, and those that serve the organization well should be guarded. Fourth, the classification of corporate cultures has implications for acquiring new businesses. When the nature of a new business clashes with a deeply entrenched culture, the parent company may impose its own strategies, which may vary drastically from those necessary for the new acquisition to succeed. Understanding the culture of both the old and the new company can reduce such errors.

While this window provides only a glimpse of the rich content that comprises corporate culture, it encourages deeper understanding of the origins of culture. It also suggests how culture can be reshaped or revitalized to better fit organizational realities.

Using the Window. Some ideas for effectively using the Organizational Cultures Window model include the following:

- Prospective employees might fruitfully assess the culture of a company they are considering joining. If it matches their expectations of a "good place to work," they are more likely to be comfortable there; if not, they should consider employment elsewhere.
- Departmental managers should examine the culture that they have established within their units and see if it is compatible with that of the larger organization.
- Corporate executives should assess their organization's environment in terms of its relative *risk* and rate of *feedback* on key decisions and determine whether they have developed the appropriate organizational culture to fit that environment (according to the window model).
- An organization might begin by developing its preferred culture and then seek ways in which it could at least partially *control* its degree of *risk* and flow of *feedback* in order to make the environment more compatible with its culture. This is a more aggressive approach that refuses to accept the notion that organizations are totally at the mercy of their environments.

The Grid in Action. Darren Johnson is a "numbers" person. Even as a child growing up in the tough inner-city projects, his love for numbers kept him focused while others became distracted. His engineering scholarship to the University of Michigan resulted in graduation with honors and a job with a prestigious aerospace firm. The quality of his work has led to several quick promotions, and at the age of twenty-nine he finds himself the project manager of a major contract with NASA. Despite his successful career, Darren is seeing that his love of numbers, always his greatest ally, is beginning to fail him. This is growing increasingly troublesome to this young man.

Production has been good, turnover low, and the project is on schedule, but Darren sees a glimmer of trouble on the horizon. Two high-quality engineers have been hired away by another company. The project itself is "coming along fine," but there seems to be no passion about it, no peaks or valleys, just data and then more data. When Darren asks his departing engineers why they are leaving, they use terms that seem strange at first, such as *vision, heroes, celebrations,* and *allegiances.* "The job was fine," they say. "You are fine." But they didn't feel a sense of passion for what they were doing. Darren suddenly realizes exactly what they are talking about. His whole life at home was based on his parent's vision for him, the family celebrations of his achievements, their support during his losses. His numbers kept him focused, but the fuel behind this determined young man was his culture, the very meaning of his life.

Darren Johnson moves quickly to put culture into practice in his project. Using the organizational cultures ideas, he examines the ways things are done in the larger organization and makes a point to learn about its founders, heroes, and villains. He begins to lunch with his engineers and support staff and tell stories about previous projects that have made a difference. He slowly establishes regular, celebratory get-togethers that playfully reward those who perform well and provide support to those still learning. He seeks input from his employees on project decisions and builds loyalty and commitment to the project as his team begins to "own" the process. The numbers remain, but in the context of the culture they take on a shared meaning. Several Ohio State graduate engineers challenge the Michigan group to a weekly softball series that proves socially enjoyable. Best of all, production goals are surpassed.

Having established a strong cultural context for work, Darren begins to assess the appropriate culture for his own project within the company. Using the Organizational Cultures model, he determines that his work with NASA is consistent with the larger company's business environment, called the *bet your company* culture. Here, *high-stakes* decisions are made in developing new technologies, and there is a long wait for *feedback* while NASA tests the devices. In this culture technical competence and patience are rewarded. Darren still maintains his love affair with numbers, but his work team is developing the loyalty and commitment to their organization that will make the difference in the years to come.

References

Bower, M. *The Will to Manage.* New York: McGraw-Hill, 1966.

Deshpandi, R., and A. Parasuraman. "Linking Corporate Culture to Strategic Planning." *Business Horizons,* May–June, 1986, pp. 28–37.

Kilmann, R. H., M. J. Saxon, and R. Serpa. "Issues in Understanding the Changing Culture." *California Management Review,* Winter, 1986, pp. 87–94.

Schroeder, D. M. *Implementing Major Strategic Change: A Holistic Perspective.* University of Massachusetts working paper, 1989.

13-2. Forms of Acculturation

Mergers, large and small, have become commonplace in recent years. Much public attention has focused on the financial gains and costs; the degree of a good product, market, and strategic "fit" between the two companies; and the impact on middle management and other employees. However, almost lost in the excitement has been the need for in-depth and advance consideration of the organizational cultures of the merged companies.

When two organizations unite, we may safely predict that changes in both existing cultures will occur. This is true whether there is a clearly dominant merging partner or simply the marriage of two relatively equal organizations. In any case this process is termed *acculturation.* As the two groups try to adapt to each other and work together, members of one culture frequently attempt to dominate members of the other, guided by beliefs that their culture is "best." (A classic example was the difficulty that General Motors had in absorbing Electronic Data Systems in the mid-1980s.)

Window 13-2 focuses on alternative modes of acculturation.

(Text continues on page 248)

Window 13-2. Forms of Acculturation.

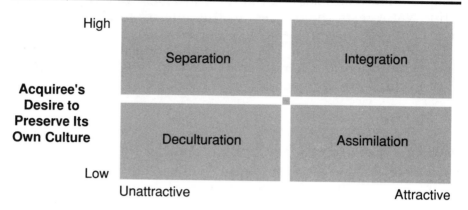

Attractiveness of the Acquirer

Source: Afsaneg Nahavandi and Ali R. Malekzadeh, "The Role of Acculturation in Mergers and Acquisitions," *Academy of Management Review*, Vol. 13, No. 1 (1988), pp. 140–144 (Table 1, p. 141).

Dimensions

Attractiveness of the acquirer. The perception of the *attractiveness* of the *acquiring company* by members of the acquired company is an important determinant of the acculturation process. When the acquirer is perceived as *attractive* (as in a friendly merger), collaborative approaches to merging cultures are predictable. When the perception of the acquirer is *unattractive* (as might be the case in a hostile takeover when the targeted company does not wish to be acquired), resistance to and withdrawal from combining cultures is likely.

Acquiree's desire to preserve its own culture. The degree to which the *acquired company* values and wishes to preserve its own culture and identity is the second important determinant of the acculturation process. When a company is acquired because of its unique strengths such as its innovative management style or strong entrepreneurial spirit, it is likely to place a *high value on preserving the culture* that led to its successful performance. Alternatively, when a company has been acquired for geographical reasons, a single product line, or its bargain price, it is more likely to place a *low value on preserving the culture* that did not serve it well.

Methods for Blending Cultures

The Acculturation model uses these two factors to determine how merging companies can adapt to each other and deal with their differences. The combination of these two factors determines which mode of acculturation will be used. Four modes are suggested.

Window 13-2. (*Continued*)

Integration. When the acquirer is seen as *attractive* by the acquired company and the acquired company strongly *values its own culture*, an *integrative* mode is recommended. In this mode of acculturation, the company that is acquired willingly adopts some of the acquirer's practices, and yet it maintains some of the characteristics that made it unique. In this process, change occurs in the cultures and practices of *both companies*, with neither trying to dominate the other.

Assimilation. *Assimilation* occurs when the *attractiveness of the acquiring company* is perceived as high and the acquired company places a *fairly low value on preserving its own culture*. If the acquired company perceives its own culture as hindering performance and values the culture of the acquirer, the acquired company is willing to be absorbed into the prevailing values and practices of the acquirer. In the process it casts off most features of its former culture.

Separation. When the acquirer is perceived as *low in attractiveness*, and the acquired company *highly values its own culture, separation* is the likely mode of acculturation. Here, the acquired company actively refuses to become connected to the acquirer in any meaningful way. The members prefer to function as a separate operating unit, retaining their previous culture and only blending the financial operations of the two companies. If the acquirer is uncomfortable with this level of autonomy in its acquired unit, cultural stress and disruption are likely.

Deculturation. When the acquirer firm is seen as unattractive, but the acquired company does not value its own identity, *deculturation* results. In this form of acculturation, the acquired company feels resentment toward the values of the acquirer. At the same time it recognizes that its own values were not conducive to success. Typically, there is tremendous resentment toward the acquirer. This results in resistance to adopting the acquirer's culture. In addition, the acquired company has no interest in preserving its own cultural values.

It identifies two key characteristics of the acquiring company and the acquired company and uses these to prescribe the preferred acculturation process. When preferences are compatible, a smooth merger is more likely. Incongruent preferences, however, can yield conflict that may delay the success of (or even defeat) the merger.

Applying the Acculturation Window

Corporations are generally advised to diversify only into related businesses, so that they can take advantage of their operational similarities. However, this "stick to the knitting" philosophy has been challenged by the successful mergers of several unrelated businesses. The Acculturation model predicts that unrelated acquisitions *can* take place successfully if the culture of the acquired business remains intact. Because the unrelated business is typically acquired for financial reasons rather than to achieve operating or managerial synergy, there is little need for the two companies to mesh strategies, people, and structure. In merging with related businesses, synergy is important and the separation mode of acculturation may diminish performance.

Multicultural companies are those that value culture diversity and encourage it. *Unicultural* companies, on the other hand, emphasize conformity and reward adherence to specific company goals and practices. The Acculturation model predicts that multicultural companies would be comfortable acquiring a related business and integrating both cultures. When acquiring an unrelated business, the multicultural company would be comfortable allowing the acquired company to maintain a separate culture.

Unicultural companies would expect related acquisitions to become *assimilated* into the prevailing culture of the parent company. *Deculturation* would be most likely among unrelated acquisitions by the unicultural parent.

The Forms of Acculturation model proposes that when two companies, the acquirer and the one being acquired, agree on the preferred mode of acculturation, then little acculturation stress will occur. Thus, if both companies agree on *assimilation* as the preferred mode, a smooth transition can be expected. The merger will be hindered, however, when the acquired company does not agree with the acculturation strategy of the acquirer. These differences must be considered in choosing which acquisition possibilities stand the greatest likelihood of succeeding.

The Acculturation model alerts you and other decision makers to the importance of meshing people, cultures, and organizational practices in order to make a merger successful. To the extent that mergers approximate marriages, companies cannot be merged solely on financial criteria any more than a spouse can be chosen strictly on the basis of his/her physical attractiveness.

The Acculturation model serves organizational decision makers in a number of ways that help them to predict the cultural aspect of potential mergers. First, it tells them that total absorption of one company into the other is not always desirable or even possible. Decision makers must consider *integration, separation,* and *deculturation* as other viable alternatives.

Decision makers must also realize that the *agreement* between the merging companies about how the merger will take place is crucial for the success of the merger. When companies agree to merge and blend their cultures, minimal stress results. The implementation of the merger will be far easier than it is when conflicting preferences exist.

This model shows decision makers which factors of the acquiring and acquired company make a difference in attempts to reach an agreement. These decision makers must assess the acquired company to determine how much they value their own culture and how attractive the acquirer is to the acquired company. The answers to these two questions will suggest an appropriate mode of acculturation. Finally, decision makers must assess the degree of cultural tolerance in their own organization. When a choice of acquisition targets exists, the Forms of Acculturation Window can help decision makers predict which of the available companies offers the least likelihood of cultural resistance to merging. Better performance can thus be achieved through the smooth meshing of people, systems, and organizational practices.

When to Use the Window. This window applies basically to top-management groups in organizations that are considering a merger. However, it would also provide useful insights to all members of the merging companies, helping them to understand and explain why mergers are (or might be) successes or failures. In particular, you should use the Acculturation Window:

- To redirect your energies away from an exclusive focus on financial, product, market, and other operating issues. It should awaken you to the significance of cultural dimensions as well.
- To stimulate an examination of the strength with which the acquired company's members value their existing culture and perceive that the acquirer has a desirable culture to adopt.
- To initiate the development of a specific strategy for marrying the two merging companies' cultures, whether it is *integration, assimilation, separation,* or *deculturation.*
- To stimulate the reexamination of your own organization's culture, assessing its continued viability in light of the impending merger of two companies.

The Grid in Action. Dr. Beverly Cordova is not only a superb physician and scientist, but she has developed into an exceptional entrepreneur. As the Director of Medical Research at a prestigious New England hospital, she recognized the need for inexpensive and reliable tests for numerous medical problems. She and four of her brightest colleagues left the hospital to form Accu-Test, a research firm that develops tests to diagnose a variety of medical conditions for consumer and medical use.

The company succeeded quickly, and expansion became necessary within eighteen months. She quickly acquired several similar companies based on their recent strong financial performance. However, she is unhappy to discover that some of these mergers are failing to produce the expected synergy with her thriving company. She finds herself spending much of her limited time meeting with the leaders of these companies trying to reduce the conflict that is diminishing the creativity and hard work necessary to succeed in this rapidly changing business.

Dr. Cordova approaches her next acquisition with greater caution and a broader perspective that includes the Acculturation model. She has learned the hard way that financial and technical considerations are not the only factors important to successfully combining two companies. In her haste to expand, she forgot the importance of the cultural norms and values that differentiate one organization from another. In studying the situation, she realizes that her company has a very strong culture that emphasizes creativity, risk taking, and sensitivity to a changing medical environment. She now wants to merge with a production-oriented company to manufacture her test kits. It is important that the company have consistent, high-quality practices and an appreciation for careful work.

She thus seeks out a company that excels in these tasks. Because her research firm is tolerant of different ways to achieve excellent performance and the production objective of the company to be acquired is quite different from the research emphasis of her own company, Beverly concludes that a *separation* mode of acculturation will be most appropriate. The top executives in the production firm agree with this assessment. Even though they are pleased to be a part of this new company, they fiercely value the practices that have resulted in their success. *Integration* or *assimilation* will prove disruptive to the different goals of each company.

References

Buono, Anthony F., and James L. Bowditch. *The Human Side of Mergers and Acquisitions.* San Francisco: Jossey-Bass, 1989.

Malekzadeh, A., and A. Nahavandi. "The Fit Between Strategy and Culture in Mergers." *Academy of Management Best Paper Proceedings,* 1987, pp. 41–45.

13-3. Competing Values Framework

Managers acquire, and exhibit, many key values. However, many of your values have never been consciously chosen and therefore they remain implicit and unexamined. Exploration of your value sets might provide you with viable reasons for selecting alternative values with greater payoffs for you and your organization.

The Competing Values Framework Window helps identify the basic values that exist side by side in organizations. The Competing Values Framework Window (Window 13-3) is based on four different perspectives about what good organizations are and what good managers do. These values not only differ

(Text continues on page 254)

Window 13-3. Competing Values Framework.

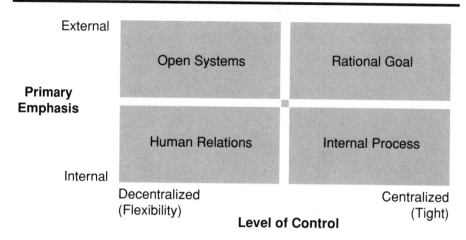

Source: Robert E. Quinn, *Beyond Rational Management.* San Francisco, Calif.: Jossey-Bass, 1988, p. 48.

Dimensions

Level of control. This dimension assesses whether the organization centralizes control at higher levels or decentralizes it at lower operating levels. It contrasts the competing values of flexibility and adaptability with those of tight control and stability. *Flexibility*-oriented values support decentralization, self-management, and differentiation. This allows the organization to adapt quickly to changing environments and to avoid the troublesome elements of bureaucracy. A belief set exemplified by *tight control* supports centralization, hierarchy, and integration. This allows the organization to maintain stable procedures and develop plans that avoid dysfunctional, reactive, or uncoordinated organizational activities.

Primary emphasis. This dimension examines and contrasts the competing values of an external versus an internal emphasis. An *external emphasis* is exemplified by values that support an orientation toward the competition. This posture emphasizes growth, productivity, and short time lines in an effort to respond to the changing external environment. An *internal emphasis* features values oriented toward maintaining the socio-technical system within the organization. This requires coordinating people and technology in a manner that efficiently utilizes the technology while maintaining employee motivation. Socio-technical systems integrate structures for information management, decision making, and clear job descriptions with emphasis on human resources issues such as autonomy, commitment, and fair incentives.

Window 13-3. (*Continued*)

Four Value Systems

The Competing Values framework combines level of control (*flexible* vs. *tight*) and primary focus (*external* vs. *internal*). This yields four different, and contradictory, organizational cultures. *Effective managers do not see these perspectives as mutually exclusive*, but understand that most organizational problems require a delicate blend of contradictory perspectives for effective solutions to occur.

Human relations. This perspective combines the values of *internal* emphasis and *flexibility*. The prevailing concerns in this culture are the team concept and concern for members of the organization. Commitment and morale are maintained by openness, participation, and group discussion. Human resources are valued, and training, autonomy, and delegation are commonplace. Career management, fair salaries, incentives, and matching jobs to the skill of the individual are concrete expressions of this value system. This culture emphasizes the importance of *understanding the needs of employees*. If carried to the extreme, the perspective creates an "irresponsible country club" that encourages laxity and negligence.

Internal process. This perspective represents the values of *internal* focus and control. The prevailing concerns of this value system are maintaining the hierarchy, which provides the organization with the stability and continuity to make effective long-range decisions. In this framework information management and documentation allow for efficient integration. An organization that emphasizes these values has an accessible and comprehensive data base. There are clear job descriptions, role expectations, and procedures for resolving conflicts over unclear procedures. This culture emphasizes an internally oriented company. However, in its extreme form this perspective can be perceived as the "frozen bureaucracy," where the organization becomes atrophied as a result of excessive measurement and documentation. There, everything is done "by the book" regardless of its effectiveness.

Open systems. The values of *flexibility* and an *external* focus define the third cultural perspective. The prevailing concerns of this value system are expansion and adaptation to the changing business environment. The key to growth and resource acquisition lies in readiness to make decisions. The *open systems* perspective helps an organization produce in a competitive market through constant innovation and change. This culture emphasizes *adaptability to the marketplace*. However, when used to the extreme, this perspective could produce a "tumultuous anarchy," where the emphasis on insight and innovation

Window 13-3. (*Continued*)

results in disastrous experimentation, political expediency, and an obsession with competitive advantage at the expense of continuity and *control* over work.

▦ **Rational goal**. This culture combines the values of *external* focus and *control*. The prevailing concerns of this value system are productivity and efficiency, which are achieved through planning, goal setting, goal clarification, and direction. The *rational goal* perspective values the *control* inherent in planning and goal setting and builds in feedback systems to modify procedures when goals are not accomplished. This culture tries to *maximize output* in a competitive environment. At the extreme this cultural value system could create an "oppressive sweatshop" where the emphasis on productivity and effectiveness yields perpetual exertion and eventual burnout with little room for individual differences and employee input.

from one another but are contradictory in nature. For example, "organizations must be highly adaptable and yet implement tight controls." Another value set might suggest that "organizations should emphasize programs that benefit their employees, yet also engage in planning that results in cost-effective products or services." The Competing Values framework makes explicit the underlying values that may otherwise result in dysfunctional conflict. The model then indicates how you can move beyond your *preferred* values orientation and incorporate the contributions of competing and even contradictory approaches.

Applying the Competing Values Framework

The Competing Values framework states that underlying values drive behavior in organizations. However, values sometimes lead to narrow preferences and positions that make it difficult for you to see any merit in contrasting views. Rigid adherence to any set of values will result in your overlooking both the advantages of competing values and the disadvantages of your preferred value systems. By contrast, if you are mature and insightful, you can rise above your preferred value system and develop the capacity to view organizational problems from contradictory frames. This approach to organizational decision making assumes that *maximum values flexibility* helps the organization respond quickly to problems.

This approach differs from other views of corporate culture that see culture as "a set of shared values that reflect the company's mission and help it fit into the marketplace." That notion of values is more fixed and resistant to change. Strong, deeply held values serve the company well by clarifying its identity and building employee loyalty and sense of purpose. Yet, when an environmental change occurs, a new set of shared values may be difficult to instill. For example, when AT&T began to compete with other companies after holding a monopoly for many years, it had great difficulty disengaging from its old value system.

You are thus faced with a question of values. Should your culture emphasize strong *shared* values or *flexible* and competing values? The risks involved with each approach must be understood.

The Competing Values framework should stimulate you to confront one of life's most difficult tasks—*understanding and supporting an opposing viewpoint*. Effective managers must be able to transcend their own values orientation through recognizing that there are weaknesses in their own perspective and advantages in opposing perspectives. This framework emphasizes the contradictory nature of the *human relations* model and the *rational goal* model, with the former emphasizing people and morale and the latter focusing on productivity and efficiency. Similarly, the *internal process* model contrasts with the *open systems* model, with the former maintaining internal stability and the latter emphasizing external adaptability.

You should not view these contradictory perspectives as mutually exclusive, but should attempt to *balance these values* to optimally handle different organizational problems. Thus the Competing Values framework provides a system for you to *become aware* of your intellectual biases and then encourages you to examine alternative perspectives.

This framework can also be used to diagnose actual organizations and design interventions for them. Questionnaires have been developed to help diagnose the orientation of the organization's managers by creating a *group* profile of their prevailing values. You can then use the profile to generate an action plan for change. Finally, the dynamic perspective alerts you to the *changing* values that will need to be addressed as the organization matures.

Steps to Employ When Using the Window. The Competing Values framework encourages you to:

- Examine not only the current relative degree of *centralization/decentralization* (*control* over decision making) that exists in your company, but also whether or not there is a valid basis for maintaining it at its current level).
- Consider whether your organization has established the proper balance between an *internal* and *external* emphasis in its daily operations. Reactive organizations may not have made a conscious choice, but simply reacted to pressures from within or without.
- Identify the organizational values that implicitly or explicitly underlie the organization's operations. When these are examined, they may be found to be less than optimum for producing the results desired.
- Maintain flexibility in the adoption of any one values emphasis. Specifically, you might consider the merit in encouraging the expression of competing values in any major decision process.

The Grid in Action. The board of directors of the Community Crisis Clinic is facing its own crisis once again. In the past six months, the number of volunteers available to staff the crisis telephones has dwindled dramatically. This necessary community service is being staffed by overworked trainers and office personnel rather than community members who have previously turned out in large numbers. One year ago the board met in another emergency session to cope with another crisis of equal magnitude but different causes. At that meeting Leslie Bernstein, the board president, reported that they had too many volunteers! What was missing was predictable community funding and carefully planned crisis line shifts. When the United Way cut its funding, the clinic had to hastily arrange both bake sales and car washes in order to cover operating expenses. When three community-minded volunteers appeared at midnight one night to answer one available phone, something snapped. The board reacted by hiring a new director who could manage finances and develop orderly systems. Immediately, money and clear roles became top priorities, but morale plummeted, and old loyalties gave way to halfhearted participation.

Leslie, armed with the Competing Values framework model for understanding the culture of organizations, explained to the board how they first chose administrators who shared their own strengths (caring for people) and weaknesses (lack of sophistication in planning and finances). They functioned from the extremes of the *human relations* perspective, believing that the control and hierarchy of the *internal-process* perspective and the bottom-line emphasis of the *rational-goal* perspective were inconsistent with the values of trusting people to do their best.

Then, when the lack of structure and controls led to funding and systems problems, the board overreacted under pressure, selecting new administrators who overemphasized a focus on control, but didn't seem to understand the importance of *human relations* values. But, because the Crisis Clinic is not competing with other agencies and its environment is very stable, the *open systems* perspective is not a key to its survival. Leslie realizes the importance of broadened perspectives and recruits new board members who have technical and financial backgrounds. Employment interviews with new administrators are designed to obtain more evidence of people and planning skills, and abilities to handle *internal* and *external* problems.

Finally, the board is beginning to understand the developmental stages of organizational life. The *human relations* values that motivated the creation of this clinic have to be broadened to assure continuity and financial survival of the organization. The Competing Values framework is helping this organization evaluate its own leadership, its hiring decisions, and its future needs.

References

Kilmann, R., J. Saxon, and R. Serpa. "Issues in Understanding and Changing Culture." *California Management Review*, Winter, 1986, pp. 87–94.

Peters, T., and R. Waterman, Jr. *In Search of Excellence.* New York: Harper and Row, 1982.

Chapter 14

Organizational Environments

The external environment exerts a significant influence on any organization. A favorable environment is rich in opportunities and support; an unfavorable environment offers substantial threats and constraints. Enlightened management must be aware of these environmental opportunities and threats and respond to them. If you understand your environment, you can make informed decisions with the potential for substantial contributions to long-run enterprise prosperity. However, if you fail to recognize and properly understand the "signals" in your environment, you contribute to organizational decline and decay.

This chapter introduces three window models through which you can better understand and address organizational environments. The first window offers a way of looking at the external environment with primary attention to its level of complexity and degree of change. The second window views the decision-making risk posed by environments in terms of their perceived uncertainty and degree of change. The third window introduces the performance challenges of interorganizational groups based on the pressure for group formation and degree of external task structure. Taken together, all three windows offer a convenient way for you to frame issues relating to the nature of your organizational environment. Once you identify those issues, you can develop plans for dealing with them in systematic and appropriate ways.

14-1. The Nature of External Environments

Most organizational environments today are increasingly volatile, turbulent, and unpredictable. Window 14-1 highlights the critical impact of uncertain environments. Uncertainty is a function of the complexity and speed of change of an environment's components. By assessing these dimensions, you can better understand that environments differ in their potential implications for planning and action.

Applying the External Environments Window

One of the best ways to understand this grid, as well as the others in this chapter, is to place it in the context of organizations and their "competitive" environments. You recognize that strategies must be developed and implemented in a manner consistent with the opportunities and threats posed by an organization's competitive environment. Not only should you be aware of the challenges posed by these environments; you must identify appropriate strategic and tactical responses to them. Good managers will confront any uncertain environmental conditions by being prepared with backup plans. You should also vigilantly monitor environmental developments that might indicate that changes in strategy and/or tactics are in order.

To begin with, this model forces you to consider the level of *perceived uncertainty* in your environment when you begin the strategic planning process. In this case, use of the grid adds some important discipline to strategic planning and may cause you to formulate strategies differently than you otherwise might. Second, this grid can help you to position your "grand" strategies. For example, if your organization operates in *relatively certain* environments, you can anticipate that a strategy that once proved successful will continue to be successful in the future. That is, a successful strategy can be "programmed" and implemented with a sense of durability and the anticipation of making only minor adjustments over time. If you operate in *more uncertain environments,* by contrast, you cannot be sure

Window 14-1. The Nature of External Environments.

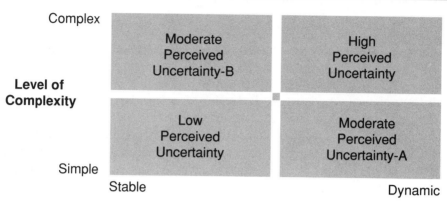

Source: Adapted from James D. Thompson, *Organizations in Action*, New York: McGraw-Hill, 1967, p. 72.

Dimensions

Level of complexity. The complexity of the organization's environment is a function of two elements—the *number* of its significant components and the degree to which these components are *similar or dissimilar* to one another. Environments can be characterized as relatively simple or highly complex.

Degree of change. This dimension records the degree to which the components of an organization's external environment are changing. Some are relatively stable and unchanging, while others are more dynamic and constantly evolving.

Uncertainty Levels in Environments

Low. Some environments consist of relatively few components, many of which are quite similar to one another. These elements also change very little over time. This is a situation of *low perceived uncertainty* for managerial problem solving and decision making. You can readily identify which components are significant in the organization's environment and easily understand them. Because of their relative stability, you can predict with considerable confidence what they will be like in the future.

Moderate-A. Some environments consist of relatively few components, many of which are quite similar to one another, but they do change rapidly over

Window 14-1. (*Continued*)

time. This is a situation of *moderate perceived uncertainty* for managerial problem solving and decision making. You can readily understand which components are significant in the organization's environment, but you may have some difficulty predicting the state of these components in the future.

▓ **Moderate-B.** Some environments consist of many separate components with few similarities to one another. These components change very little over time. This is a situation of *moderate perceived uncertainty* for managerial problem solving and decision making. You have difficulty understanding which of the many components are significant in the organization's environment. Once a component is identified, however, its relatively stable character allows some degree of certainty in predicting its future state.

▓ **High.** Some environments consist of many separate components with few similarities to one another. These components change rapidly over time. This is a situation of *high perceived uncertainty* for managerial problem solving and decision making. You have difficulty understanding which components are significant in the organization's environment and, because they are constantly changing, also have difficulty predicting with any certainty what these components may be like in the future.

that a strategy that is successful today will remain so tomorrow. Once even *moderate uncertainty* is recognized, strategies should be formulated and implemented on a contingency basis. This provides various options designed to deal with the given eventualities. Of course, environments of *very high uncertainty* increase the risk of even contingency planning. However, even this is always preferable to proceeding as if a programmed strategy will prove its worth forever.

When to Use the Window. It is not always easy for you to see the applications of "macro" models like this one, since they do not provide specific guidance or prescriptions for immediate action. However, this model can be used when:

- You wish to alert other managers to the powerful and sweeping forces that affect organizations from the outside—such as the trend toward globalization.

- You have become complacent about the level of complexity and change that exists in your external environment. Here, the window model can force you to confront your environment and at least attempt to assess its overall level of uncertainty.
- You have made the mistaken assumption that environments can only be monitored and not changed. Careful assessment of your situation may convince you that it is possible to exert some control over parts of your environment.
- You have made the assumption that your environment is homogenous, when in reality there may be many unique environments for different products/services and organizational units, each of which has differing degrees of change and levels of complexity.

The Grid in Action. When Ann Pool first begins her management consulting business, she realizes an immediate payoff in both reputation and profits. Ann specializes in helping small retail businesses in her rural community install computerized inventory and financial management systems. In this situation she serves a well-defined clientele with her highly specialized field of expertise. Her initial success is achieved in a competitive environment of *low perceived uncertainty.* Until consulting competitors come along and/or she has served all the available clients in town, Ann's business will prosper if she continues to provide high quality consulting and software in this market.

It is not too long, however, before Ann's aspirations grow. She begins to solicit work in other locations and from some larger retail businesses in larger cities some distance away. In so doing, she is entering quite a different marketplace. In the big city, clients are more diverse and their expectations often exceed the range of her personal expertise. She also faces stiff competition from many other consultants offering similar services.

Ann does not recognize the implications of all this at first. She simply responds to demands of the moment by hiring additional people to work with her whenever a consulting job proves too big. Her payroll and revenues grow quickly, but profits are hard to come by. While still struggling with her new circumstances, Ann meets another consultant who assists her with his expertise in business planning and environmental analysis. Soon thereafter, Ann realizes that her business expansion has involved a move from a competitive environment of *low perceived uncertainty* to one of *moderate (if not high) perceived uncertainty.* Unfortunately, her planning has not changed accordingly.

Her new awareness gives Ann a chance to more systematically analyze the challenges of *uncertainty* in her new environment and make plans to deal with that uncertainty in specific ways. To begin, she decides to examine the field of competitors, the diversity of clients and client demands, and the degree to which new technologies are affecting computer support for retail operations.

14-2. Environmental Risk

The primary objective of Window 14-2 is to portray the degree of decision-making risk as a function of perceived environmental uncertainty and stability. It encourages you to understand that a given organizational environment will vary in the risk presented to organizational decision makers.

Applying the Environmental Risk Window

The degree of risk present in decision-making situations must be assessed and understood. This grid allows you to portray the perceived *degree of uncertainty* in an organization's environment and then interpret its implications in respect to decision-making risk. As the grid shows, *perceived uncertainty* should not be considered the only determining factor. The grid also reinforces the responsibility of organizational decision makers to take appropriate actions to learn as much as they can on a continuing basis about the variety of elements in their external environments. At the very least, you can help reduce the risk present in decision making from *substantial* to *moderate* by giving more attention to identifying and understanding key environmental factors.

One of the possible errors that many managers make is moving into new situations and assuming that the risk conditions of the past still apply. This error is potentially harmful but

Window 14-2. Environmental Risk.

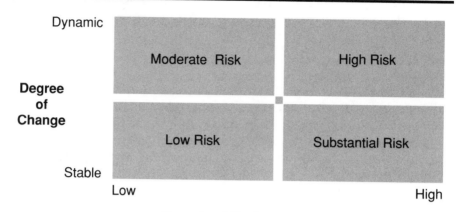

Perceived Environmental Uncertainty

Source: Adapted from Robert B. Duncan, "The Characteristics of Organizational Environments and Perceived Environmental Uncertainty," *Administrative Science Quarterly*, p. 320, by permission of *Administrative Science Quarterly*. Copyright © 1972 by Cornell University.

Dimensions

Perceived environmental uncertainty. This dimension records the degree to which you can obtain useful information regarding the organization's environment. Environments can be perceived to be relatively *certain or uncertain* in terms of your ability to "understand" the environment and establish its implications for decision making.

Degree of change. This dimension records the degree to which the components of an organization's external environment are stable. Some environments are known to be relatively *stable and unchanging*, while others are more *dynamic and constantly changing.*

Degrees of Environmental Risk

Low. Some environments are perceived to be relatively *certain and stable.* This is a *low-risk environment* for managerial problem solving and decision making. You can readily identify the small number of environmental factors of consequence to the organization and understand their implications, both present and future.

Moderate. Some environments are perceived to be relatively *certain and dynamic.* This creates a *moderate risk environment* for managerial problem

Window 14-2. (*Continued*)

solving and decision making. You are at present able to identify the small number of environmental factors of consequence to the organization and understand their implications. Due to the *dynamic* or *changing* nature of these factors, however, there is some risk regarding the future consequences of your current decisions.

    Substantial. Some environments are perceived to be relatively *uncertain and stable.* This provides a *substantial-risk environment* for managerial problem solving and decision making. You have difficulty understanding the large number of environmental factors of consequence to the organization, even though these factors are *relatively stable* over time. Because they are not very dynamic, these elements *can* be understood. But decision making will be risky until this is accomplished.

    High. Some environments are perceived to be relatively *uncertain and dynamic.* This presents a *high-risk environment* for managerial problem solving and decision making. You have difficulty understanding the large number of environmental factors of consequence to the organization. This difficulty predictably continues in the future because of the dynamic nature of the elements themselves.

---

somewhat hard to recognize. Experience in a situation usually builds understandings that reduce the risk of operating in that situation over time. In sum, you learn through past experience and this reduces the risk of present decisions *if* the environment is stable.

Another value of this grid is to enforce self-discipline in trying to understand and deal with the risk in new situations. Past successes should not be misinterpreted as guarantees of future successes. Good managers can benefit, therefore, from systematic *risk assessments* that subject new ventures and future considerations to close scrutiny. A periodic comparison of "here we are now" and "where we may be tomorrow" on this grid can help you meet this particular requirement.

When to Use the Window. You may find the Environmental Risk Window useful when:

- The level of *perceived uncertainty* of your environment is increasing and becoming more and more difficult to understand.

- The nature of the external environment is evolving slowly or rapidly to a more *dynamic* set of surroundings.
- Your company is considering a move into new and unfamiliar markets.
- Your company has relatively little margin for error (e.g., is financially limited or engaged in a highly competitive battle with other organizations for market share).

The Grid in Action. When the call comes from the state Department of Commerce, Bill is ecstatic. As the owner-manager of a small medical products firm, he is excited to learn that a Chinese company is interested in forming a joint venture to manufacture sterile lab kits in China. Bill quickly agrees to meet with a Chinese delegation visiting in the state capital. Soon after that meeting he is on an airplane bound for Beijing and what he hopes will be a major new business opportunity.

Before arriving in Beijing and starting business meetings and negotiations, however, Bill will be well-advised to sit back and systematically consider the implications of the proposed joint venture. At home Bill's company operates with a small but profitable niche in a technologically stable market. Although there are other competitors, each seems to have its own customer base and tends to serve the same clientele from one year to the next. In terms of environmental uncertainty and complexity, Bill is operating in a *low-to-moderate risk situation* with a great deal of experience and understanding at his disposal.

Things in China will be very different. Joint venturing is totally new to Bill's company. Furthermore, he has no personal knowledge regarding the lab kit markets in China and has no prior international experience, let alone any specific experience in China.

Clearly, Bill is moving into a new situation characterized by *high environmental uncertainty* and *rapid change*. If he proceeds with the joint venture, his company will be operating internationally in a *high-risk situation*. Once Bill recognizes this, he should probably slow the process down on this first visit and make it a purely fact-finding trip. Then, if he feels the risk is "potentially" justified, he might engage an international consultant's help in further analyzing the proposed joint venture and deciding whether or not to proceed with a foreign investment.

14-3. Interorganizational Group Outcomes

Window 14-3 explores the alternative products that may emerge when two organizations interact. The grid portrays the nature of interorganizational group outcomes as a function of the forces that encourage *group formation* and the degree of *external task structure.*

Applying the Interorganizational Group Window

Today's business and organizational environments are increasingly characterized by interorganizational relationships—both *voluntary* and *mandated.* More and more businesses are finding that they *can* work beneficially together in joint ventures and other "strategic alliances." More and more public organizations are finding that government regulations and legislative mandates require that they *have to* work together on a variety of issues and problems. Thus, it is appropriate for organizational decision makers to have their horizons expanded to encompass *inter*organizational as well as *intra*organizational thinking.

This grid helps you identify the various outcomes that may be expected under different foundations for interorganizational groups. By being more aware of the likely outcomes and responses of these groups, you may be better prepared to both participate in them as a member and to convene them in ways more conducive to the accomplishment of a desired purpose.

The grid can also help you and participants in interorganizational groups to better understand the conditions under which a given group is operating. Certainly the challenges of leading and participating in groups in each of the four quadrants will be different. Sometimes there will be little that can be done to change just where on the grid a group falls. But by knowing what constraints a given group is operating with, a more informed leadership and membership may be able to improve outcomes through better management of the group processes.

Window 14-3. Interorganizational Group Outcomes.

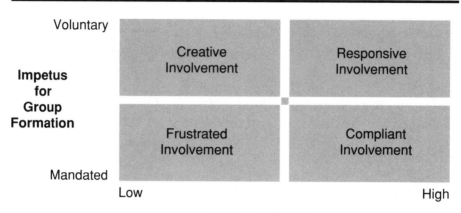

Source: Adapted from Janice H. Schopler, "Interorganizational Groups: Origins, Structure and Outcomes," *Academy of Management Review,* Vol. 12, No. 4 (October 1987), pp. 702–713.

Dimensions

Impetus for group formation. This dimension identifies the sources of the external *impetus for forming* the interorganizational *group.* One possibility is to form the group on the initiative of organizational decision makers (*voluntary*). In other cases, group formation will be stipulated by legislative action or government regulation (*mandate*).

External task structure. This dimension identifies the *nature* of the interorganizational group's *task structure* as a function of *external interests. High external task structure* is associated with an external agent or constituency that identifies group purpose and task activities; *low external task structure* is associated with only a general purpose and little task direction being externally defined.

Group Responses

Creative involvement. Some interorganizational groups are formed through *voluntary* impetus and under a low degree of *external task structure.* This creates a situation that encourages *creative involvement* for the participants. In this situation the group members can be expected to work integratively together to develop appropriate tasks and activities supporting the established purpose.

Responsive involvement. Some interorganizational groups are formed through *voluntary* impetus but with a *high degree of external task structure.* This

Window 14-3. (*Continued*)

creates a situation of *responsive involvement* for members. This type of group can be expected to comply with the externally determined purpose and tasks, but may do so in a perfunctory manner while restricting energies to the domain of the external mandate.

Frustrated involvement. Some interorganizational groups are formed through *mandated* impetus but with a *low* degree of *external task structure*. This creates a situation of *frustrated involvement* for members. In this situation the group can be expected to experience considerable internal conflict as members work together only because they are required to and have to struggle at the same time with a relatively *unstructured task environment*.

Compliant involvement. Some interorganizational groups are formed through *mandated* impetus but with a *high* degree of *external task structure*. This creates a situation of *compliant involvement* for participants. In this situation the group can be expected to respond as required under the confines of the *externally imposed group purpose* and *task structure*.

In many cases the initial management of the interorganizational group's formation can make an important difference in what is accomplished. When people are brought together under *voluntary* as opposed to *mandated* conditions, different results may also be expected. When people are brought together under *low* versus *high task structure*, different results may be expected. If you use this grid to double-check your interorganizational initiatives, you are more likely to recognize opportunities for improving outcome possibilities by changing your approaches to group formation.

When to Use the Window. Contemporary illustrations of interorganizational groups are numerous. A prime example is the labor-management task force, created to identify ways to cut costs and raise efficiency. In other cases two or more companies form joint ventures (sometimes, cross-culturally) to develop and distribute products in new markets. Or a bankruptcy judge may order a company's management and creditors to work together to propose a plan for payment of debts and refinancing of operations.

You can use the Interorganizational Group Outcomes Window to:

- Predict, and understand, the reactions and behaviors of group members who are thrown together under different conditions.
- Explore ways of making the mandate seem less onerous, perhaps by helping the members recognize the implicit or explicit benefits that might accrue through their participation in the group.
- Identify ways of reducing the *externally imposed task structure* in order to allow greater flexibility to the participating members.
- Alert yourself to similar potential reactions of your employees when intraorganizational groups (across departments or divisions) are formed.

The Grid in Action. Health policymakers are always concerned about increasing the "efficiencies" of the health care delivery system. Of particular concern in one state is the duplication of services among hospitals, clinics, and other providers in selected metropolitan areas. Leslie Marshall has just been placed in charge of a statewide effort to promote greater sharing of services and a greater rationalization of the service delivery system.

Leslie's immediate response to this responsibility is to make personal visits to each of the providers in one area and to meet with the person in charge to discuss the general nature of the problem. After meeting one-on-one with all of the providers, she decides to invite them to participate in an interorganizational planning group that will address the whole issue.

At the first meeting Leslie reports on prior individual contacts with the representatives and encourages all those present to work together to arrive at ideas for increased sharing and rationalization of services within their collective delivery area. A task force leader is appointed, and the representatives agree to start meeting formally to work on the idea and to keep Leslie informed about their progress.

In this instance Leslie is approaching the task in a way that is likely to lead to *creative involvement* on the part of members of this interorganizational task force. Each representative has been "invited" to participate on a *voluntary* basis, and the task force has been given only a minimal amount of task structure. On the other hand, Leslie could have "directed" each provider to send a representative to an official state-mandated task force established to determine how they would share services with one another. This would have created a situation where only *compliant involvement* on their parts would have been likely, because they came together by mandate and under highly structured task conditions. Leslie has chosen to approach the problem in a very different manner. More creative outcomes and greater commitment to their implementation are the likely results.

Chapter 15

Participative Management

The continued economic growth of the United States and every other industrial nation depends on tapping the wellspring of employee ideas and motivation. Fierce domestic and international competition, combined with emerging employee needs for autonomy, suggests that you need to apply participative management to simultaneously meet company objectives and employee expectations. The attitudes of employees, values of managers, and the nature of the particular issue to be resolved all affect the use of participative management.

The need to create effective work teams blended from different values, experiences, and expectations has led to widespread interest in, and a greater general use of, participative management. This chapter examines three grids that focus on key elements of participative management. The first window assesses Participative Readiness by evaluating the ability and desire of employees to participate. The second window assesses Participative Match, the fit between your use of participation and the employees' desire for it. The final window in this chapter evaluates Participative Systems by contrasting the significance of the issues with the frequency of participation. Together, these three windows allow you to assess the appropriateness of participation, how well your propensity to use participation matches the employees' desire for it, and the nature of participation relative to the significance of the issues under consideration. Once these factors are considered, the result will be a greater *understanding* of participation and a more appropriate *use* of it.

15-1. Readiness for Participation

Do all of my employees wish to participate in decision making? Are all of my employees equally capable of making useful contributions? These are two vitally important questions that you must confront before choosing a participative leadership approach.

The Readiness for Participation Window focuses on two critical elements within the employee. It encourages you to weigh the ability and desire of participants to contribute to the participative process. Window 15-1 also forces you to recognize and assess the *technical capacity* (e.g., relevant knowledge to share) and *motivation* (e.g., interest and willingness) of employees to participate.

Applying the Participative Readiness Window

The effective use of participative management depends on the *abilities* and *desires* of employees to participate. In evaluating the appropriateness of participative management in any particular situation, consideration must be given to both dimensions. In some cases—especially in dealing with experienced employees or professionals—the *ability* to participate is often assumed, but little consideration may be given to whether employees *desire* to participate. Even when employees have *technical knowledge* about the issues, individuals or groups may lack the *ability* to express their ideas effectively because they lack an understanding of group dynamics or presentation skills. You have an opportunity, and an obligation, to help employees develop these skills. Conversely, with new workers or unskilled ones, the *ability* may be lacking even though the *desire* is present.

Cultural, family, or work experiences may have discouraged individual or group participation. The perceived rewards for participatory behavior may be too low, absent, or inappropriate. The acid test for many employees is not management's claims about participative management, but whether employee ideas

Window 15-1. Readiness for Participation.

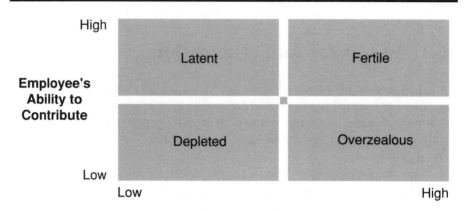

High

Employee's Ability to Contribute

| Latent | Fertile |
| Depleted | Overzealous |

Low

Low   High

Employee's Desire to Contribute

Dimensions

Employee's desire to contribute. This factor captures the degree to which an employee shows interest, concern, and motivation to invest time and effort in the decision-making process. It reflects the employee's attitude, capturing the employee's willingness to be involved in the participative process. It ranges from *low* (where an employee says, "Leave me alone") to *high* (where an employee is hungry to make a contribution).

Employee's ability to contribute. In contrast to an employee's desire or willingness, the second dimension focuses on the intellectual and technical *capabilities* of employees. Can they contribute relevant and meaningful content ideas to a discussion? Can they make useful process comments that will facilitate a high-quality conclusion? *Ability to contribute* refers to both innate and developed abilities of employees—those they were born with and those they have acquired through education and experience. It addresses questions such as Do they have relevant knowledge (about a specific problem) to share? or Can they express themselves adequately? *Ability to contribute* can range from *low* to *high*, reflecting both differences *across* different employees and differences *within* the same employee (relevant to different problems).

States of Relative Readiness

The *desire and ability to participate* combine to create four possible outcomes:

Window 15-1. (*Continued*)

Depleted state. *Low desire* and *low ability* create a depleted state. Neither the *desire* nor the *capability* to contribute to a problem exists, and therefore the use of participative management in this situation will probably fail. When the employee has neither the intellectual nor experiential background to make useful comments and also lacks the interest to do so, the use of participative management is unlikely to be successful, at least in the short run.

Fertile area . At the other extreme, an employee who has *high ability* combined with a *high desire* creates a *fertile* situation. Here, the employee expects to be involved in a participative process and is likely to be successful. This is the target toward which you should guide your efforts to use participative management.

Overzealous area. When employees *strongly desire* to contribute, but their technical *ability* is *low*, they may be considered *overzealous*, because willingness exceeds ability. In this situation you should try not to undermine their enthusiasm in the short run, while gradually guiding their efforts and developing their abilities through long-term training and coaching.

Latent area. A *latent* situation occurs when employees have a *high ability to contribute* and yet surprisingly *little desire* to do so. Reasons for the low desire may include their previous negative experience with another manager, insufficient rewards for participating, or doubts about your intentions to use their ideas. These barriers may have to be overcome to develop their desire to contribute.

---

are actually *implemented.* A lack of implementation (for whatever reasons) of employee ideas sends a clear and unmistakable message: Participation does not exist in reality. The result is *pseudoparticipation.* Often, employees resent the manipulative aspects of pseudoparticipation, where they are asked to suggest ideas and become involved but have little or no impact on the final results. You *can* affect employee attitudes and desires by your consistent use of participative methods.

An employee's current *desire to contribute* is largely affected by the results of previous contributions, which serve to create employee *expectations.* If the previous efforts to participate by employees have been encouraged or discouraged, the likely result is for their current desire to be high or low. A *high level of desire* will often wane if that desire is not met and reinforced. More commonly, the manager who wishes to use a more participatory approach finds that employees have a *low desire to participate.* This result is particularly common when there is a change in leadership from an autocratic or directive manager to one who is more participative. Many employees may have *lowered* their *desire to participate,* since previous participation was neither encouraged nor rewarded.

To enhance the *desire to participate,* the new manager must often solicit individual ideas on specific, and often narrowly focused, issues. Then—and this is crucial—those ideas must be accepted and implemented. If the new manager solicits ideas that are subsequently not used (regardless of why those ideas are rejected), the employees "learn" that to participate is at best frustrating or at worst a sham.

The *ability-to-participate* dimension presents a different set of issues. Employees who are believed to be *low* in their *ability to participate* require *training.* This training usually has two dimensions: knowledge and skills. Knowledge training can provide employees with sufficient information so that they have the basis on which to develop new ideas and suggestions. Asking employees to participate on issues about which they have little information is often frustrating for them and can lead to their reduced *desire to participate* in the future. The other focus of training concerns skills. Many times employees want to contribute but are uncertain as to how to go about contributing.

One of the advantages of quality circles and other structured group-participative approaches is that these techniques are often introduced with extensive training on group dynamics and presentation skills. Regardless of the approach used, however, you must create opportunities that provide employees with a sense of *ownership* in the tasks at hand. By allowing participation, the *autonomy* and *recognition* needs of employees are more likely to be met.

When either *ability* or *desire* is lacking, you should develop strategies to overcome these deficiencies. Coaching, training, delegation, job enrichment, or other means can be used to increase abilities. The implementation of employee ideas and suggestions may increase employee *desires for more participation* opportunities in the future.

Assuming 1) the *technical ability* and the necessary participatory skills are present and 2) employees have a *desire to participate* because they feel their efforts will make a meaningful contribution, the participative readiness of the organization is *fertile.* Managers who have considered both the *ability* and *desire* of employees are more likely to find success in using participative approaches that tap employee ideas and, therefore, their commitment. When neither element is present, participative management is likely to fail completely.

Steps to Employ When Using the Window. This window should stimulate you to engage in a number of behaviors, some of which are analytical and descriptive, and some of which are action-oriented:

- You should maintain an in-depth level of *awareness* about the knowledge, experience, and skills of each employee to make a fairly accurate assessment of each person's capacity to contribute to a decision process for any particular problem.
- You can help employees *improve* their *ability to contribute* by encouraging employee attendance at workshops that provide technical upgrading as well as communication skill development. In addition, informal coaching, counseling, and feedback on past contributions can aid employee development.
- At a minimum, you can monitor a particular employee's *desire to contribute* based on your reaction to previous opportunities. This can take the form of direct inquiry, by asking the employee about his/her desire to be involved on a specific issue or task.
- If the *desire* is *low,* but the *ability* is present (e.g., a *latent* state), you can attempt to induce a greater *desire to contribute* by offering incentives for it, demanding it via a job description, or providing successful role models.
- It may also be necessary for you to rein in *overzealous* employees whose *desires* exceed their *ability.* Here, employees must be cautioned to wait until they have developed sufficient levels of technical expertise before they can expect participative opportunities to arise.

The Grid in Action. The applicability of the participative readiness window can be seen from the experience of Anne-Marie, a supervisor in a claims-processing department of a large insurance company. After Anne-Marie returns from a company-sponsored seminar on participative management, she wants to try out the new ideas for employee involvement that she has learned. Rather than charging ahead, however, she first decides to analyze her work situation to see if participative methods will work.

Three of her claims processors stand out as prime examples of different areas in the window. Seth is a difficult employee for her to deal with, because he has a very limited background in insurance. In addition, he has abruptly dismissed her past invitations to suggest ideas on work-related problems. For the moment, she concludes, it might be wisest to classify Seth as being in the *depleted* state. Consequently, Anne-Marie chooses *not* to invest additional energy into trying to get Seth to do any more than complete his daily quota of claims.

Teresa, on the other hand, regularly provides unsolicited ideas for methods improvement in the department. She clearly likes to immerse herself in the total job and go beyond normal expectations by sharing suggestions. Although Anne-Marie considers Teresa high on the *desire to contribute* scale, the quality of her ideas leaves much to be desired. Apparently, it will take much more work experience before Teresa can differentiate between sound ideas and trivial ones. Teresa, concludes Anne-Marie, is currently in the *overzealous* category. With patience and a structured program of job-related training, she shows promise of moving into the *fertile* area over time.

Damon is a different story altogether. Whenever Anne-Marie questions him on any aspect of insurance, Damon demonstrates a deep understanding of the issue. She has even asked him to serve as the role model and informal trainer for new employees in the department. Clearly, his technical knowledge about insurance is superior to all others. However, when she asks him to serve on departmental task forces to assess current procedures and suggest improvements, he has always found an excuse for refusing in the past. Her motivational challenge with Damon appears to be one of awakening his *latent* interest, but the rewards for the department appear to make this a worthwhile task, she thinks. "Perhaps if I explained to him how a record of constructive ideas offered might help him qualify for Employee of the Month he might become more interested," she muses to herself. "I'll talk with him tomorrow during lunch," Anne-Marie decides.

15-2. Participative Match

Sometimes employee expectations regarding the use of participation in decision making do not match precisely with managerial behaviors. Failure to anticipate these differences may create problems for the organization, as well as unfair criticism of participation in general. The Participative Match Window (Window 15-2) helps you assess your *use* of participation relative to the employee's *desires* for it. This analysis reminds participative managers of the need to create a balance between the manager's and employee's relative motivations to use participative management.

Applying the Participative Match Window

Your use of participation depends on your perception of organizational appropriateness. The *leadership style of your superior* serves as a role model and powerful clue about the acceptable *use* of participative management. Your *use* may be increased or decreased depending on how you perceive the superior's support for participation. Your perceptions about rewards and penalties associated with participation also shape your attitudes. Closely related concerns regarding how errors or mistakes are viewed deal with the *organizational culture.* Some managers feel that participation means losing some degree of control, which leads to mistakes for which they may still be held responsible.

Even when employees are perceived as *desiring* and capable of participative management, you should examine your underlying assumptions about them. These leadership assumptions have historically been referred to as *Theory X* and *Theory Y.* McGregor's Theory X describes a set of implicit assumptions in which employees are believed to have little motivation or capabilities. A manager who holds those values will be unlikely to *use* participative approaches under any conditions. A manager who

Window 15-2. Participative Match.

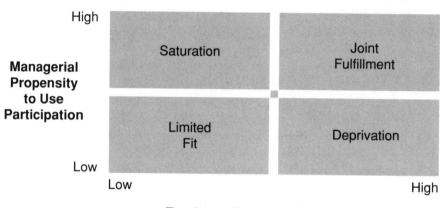

Employee Desire for Participation

Dimensions

Employee desire for participation. Similar to one factor shown previously in the Participative Readiness grid is the level of employee *desire* to participate that you need to assess. This represents an employee's underlying interest in being involved in decisions and sharing ideas for the benefit of the organization. The level of *desire* can range from low to high. It largely stems from an employee's prior experiences, self-confidence, and loyalty to the company.

Managerial propensity to use participation. The second factor—the managerial propensity to *use* participation—also ranges from low to high. This dimension assesses your attitudes about participation, or willingness to *use* it, reflecting past successes and failures with it, its compatibility with the organization's culture, and your assessment of subordinate capabilities.

Fit Between You and Employee

These two dimensions create a grid that connects the two sets of attitudes that affect the success of participation. The four products are:

Limited fit. When your *use* of participation and the employee's *desire* for it are both low, the result is *limited fit*. There is a *fit* or balance because the employees seek little participation and get little opportunity for participation. This congruence is limited, however, because little involvement exists between employees and you in identifying and solving problems. The organization does not gain, and employees do not grow.

Window 15-2. (*Continued*)

Joint fulfillment. The other extreme defines a mutually *fulfilling* situation for both parties, where the employees' *desires* for, and your *use* of, participation are high. This match between you and the employees leads to a very healthy agreement on participative management. The agreement may even be unnoticed because both managerial and employee needs and expectations are met. Satisfied expectations cause little tension, and the participative approach becomes part of the accepted organizational background. It may be noticed only by outsiders from different decision-making cultures or by insiders if you violate the implied contract of participative management.

Saturation. A problem arises when you believe in, advocate, and try to practice participative management when the employee lacks strong motivation to become involved. Any attempts to involve the employee are perceived as overkill and result in a feeling of being *saturated* with the additional demands and expectations. The predictable consequences include limited enthusiasm, low-quality contributions, or even behaviors that may sabotage the participative attempt.

Deprivation. The opposite situation occurs when the employee has a strongly felt need to be involved and contribute useful suggestions, but you use only a low degree of participation. A natural result of this mismatch is that interested employees feel *deprived* of legitimate opportunities to share their expertise, ideas, or enthusiasm. In fact, some contemporary employees actually feel that they have the "right" to participate. As a result, they become angry and eventually alienated when you do not respond with appropriate opportunities.

believes in Theory Y, which assumes employees are capable and motivated, is more likely to *use* participative management. A range of leadership styles from moderately autocratic to highly participatory results. Although most managers will vary their leadership style somewhat across this continuum, their basic assumptions about employees (Theory X or Theory Y) help to steer their *use* of participation toward the low or high end.

Using the Window. This window can be useful to you either before (for predictive purposes) or after (for explanatory and developmental purposes) participation occurs. For example:

- You need to recognize, as a result of the structure of this window, that the best occasion for the use of participation occurs when the needs of both parties—you and employee—are considered.

- You need to assess your own feelings as candidly as possible about the *use* of participation with your employees. This means not just reaching a value-based decision (e.g., "I suppose that I *ought* to allow participation because everyone else is using it"), but one based on individual wants and desires (e.g., "I believe that participation is an appropriate method to use in light of my own assumptions, experiences, and aspirations for the development of my employees").
- Retrospectively, you can look back on your experiences with a participative attempt and try to discover why it did or did not work. Did you approach the interaction half-heartedly while the employee strongly *desired* involvement *(deprivation)*, or was the employee not excited about the opportunity to become involved despite your best efforts *(saturation)?*
- Finally, you need to assess the degree of *fit* between your own inclination to use participation and the explicit or implicit support for the practice from the larger organizational culture. Without this, it will be difficult for any manager to sustain a participative program or set of practices.

The Grid in Action. The Participative Match Window is helping Stan, the executive director of a small medical clinic, change the pattern of leadership behavior that he uses with one of his vice-presidents. Stan endorses Theory Y assumptions about people in general and is convinced that his staff (each of whom he has personally hired and groomed) is highly competent. He also recognizes his own limitations in each of their professional areas, especially in the last few years, because he has turned his attention away from operating details and more toward strategic planning and community relations. Out of both necessity and conviction, he believes that he has a strong basic propensity to use participative management approaches whenever the situation allows them.

Stan also assumes that, because of their technical competence and overall dedication to the clinic, his vice-presidents enjoy the opportunities for participation he provides during both regular staff meetings and one-on-one discussions. This apparent state of *joint fulfillment* is shaken one day, however, when Dominic, the Vice-President of Physical Plant and Maintenance, suddenly vents his frustrations on Stan. "I've got enough problems in my own areas to solve," he says, "without being continually burdened with trying to help out the other vice-presidents. Many of those group problem-solving meetings are really a waste of my time!"

Further exploration of the issue convinces Stan that Dominic is literally overwhelmed *(saturated)* with his expected level of participation. Despite feeling some reluctance at the prospects of treating one member of his staff differently than the others, Stan agrees that he will excuse Dominic from portions of future meetings. Having recognized that Dominic wants less involvement in decision making, Stan wisely adapts his behavior to bring about a better fit between Dominic's expectations and Stan's own leadership behavior. In this case he tempers his own enthusiasm for a participative approach with the reality of his employee's more limited need for it. A *limited fit* turns out to be a more acceptable product with Dominic, while Stan continues to use a high level of participation with his other vice-presidents.

Reference

McGregor, Douglas. *The Human Side of Enterprise.* New York: McGraw-Hill, 1960.

15-3. Participative Systems

Participative decision making may appear to be a simple idea, but it can be complex in practice. For example, employees may judge its presence and value by noting either the *number* of times they are asked to participate or the *nature* of the decisions presented to them. The Participative Systems Window (Window 15-3) contrasts the *frequency of participation* (quantity) with the *significance of the issues* under consideration (quality). This evaluation gives both you and employees an estimate of the overall status of participation.

Window 15-3. Participative Systems.

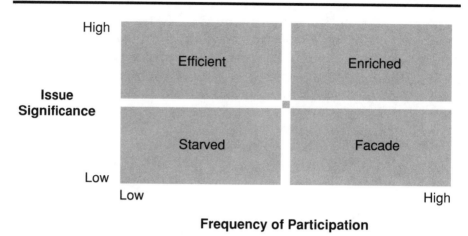

Dimensions

Frequency of participation. One factor assesses the *frequency of participation*, ranging from low to high. The prime question for any one employee is How *often* does my manager use participation (with me)? *Frequency* of use gives insights about the likely attitudes and possible abilities of both you and your employees. It may also be a function of the nature of tasks and decisions that are typically confronted. *Frequent* use with any one employee, of course, naturally builds expectations of future use for not only that person but other workers as well.

Issue significance. The other factor evaluates the *significance of issues* brought to an employee for consultation. The problem under consideration can range from low to high in importance, as judged by its potential impact on the employees involved, resources used, or the overall organization. High-quality participation must involve employees on a wide range of issues, particularly those critical to the department's success.

Systems of Participation

Starved system. When the *frequency of participation* and the *significance of the issues* brought to employees are both low, a *starved* participation system results. Employee talents are underutilized, producing a malnourished

Window 15-3. (*Continued*)

system of participation in an organization. Performance gains are likely if either or both dimensions are appropriately increased.

■ **Enriched system.** When the *frequency* and *significance* of participation are both high, an *enriched* environment emerges. High *frequency* and high *significance* combine to create an environment where participative management is commonly used for a wide range of issues, including those deemed as important to the participants.

■ **Facade system**. When you use participation *frequently*, but only on relatively *insignificant issues,* the result is a *facade.* This illusion (or pseudo participative management) results when employees are allowed to participate only in relatively meaningless or trivial decisions. The condition predictably leads to a low desire by employees to participate in the future, since the significance of their contribution is at best marginal and at worst manipulative.

■ **Efficient system**. Some managers use participation infrequently but selectively, reserving it for highly *significant issues.* This produces an *efficient* participative system. These managers reserve participation only for important matters. Although the environment will not be as enriched participatively as those in which *significance* and *frequency* are both high, the situation may be self-sustaining because employees are likely to feel they are making a noteworthy contribution (when they do get the opportunity).

Applying the Participative Systems Window

Some managers, uncomfortable with the participative approach, may rationalize their underuse of participation by *defining* too few issues as significant. Low utilization of participation despite the presence of *significant issues* may result in a *starved,* or at least a *partially starved,* environment. By contrast, the overuse or indiscriminate use of participation may create the appearance of a *facade* or even an image of indecisiveness. The key implication is that you *must be able to identify the significant issues accurately and then permit (even encourage) participation in these items.*

Many managers actually use a participative approach to evaluate the significance of issues by using key employees as sounding boards. They seek the opinions of informal leaders (influential employees) and others about their potential reactions to a particular *issue* and let the responses about the perceived *significance* guide their behavior.

A partial gauge to the *significance of the issue* can also be obtained from superiors (through upward participation). By suggesting that the *issue* will be discussed with employees before a plan is formulated, you can often assess the superior's view by his/her reaction. Supportive comments or concerns about delays may provide valuable hints about the *significance issue.*

Your need for control is often highest on the more *significant issues*, which creates a paradox. The need for control affects your perceptions of the employees' abilities and desires and may greatly distort your use of participation in *significant* events. For example, in organizations where the corporate culture does not support participation, your *frequency* of use may actually *decline* with *significant issues.* Although this moves the participative system away from the enriched or even efficient outcomes, it may fit your expectations and the organizational culture.

Steps to Employ When Using the Window. This window's dimensions incorporate two fairly common themes in this book—*frequency and significance,* or quantity and quality (for example, see Window 18-1). The importance of the distinction is highlighted by the age-old cliche used to evaluate a job candidate's twenty years of job experience—"Do you truly have twenty years of different, and increasingly progressive, job responsibilities, or do you simply have one year's worth of experience repeated twenty times?" Similarly, you can evaluate your organization's participative systems by:

- Monitoring how often, in the eyes of your subordinates, you are *perceived* to involve them in a variety of job-related decisions.
- Assessing, through the perceptions of your subordinates, the nature of the *issues* taken to them. Are the issues relatively trivial? Are they truly *substantive?* Are they the kinds of problems and issues that, when resolved, *will truly have impact?*

- Committing yourself to changing from your current mode of operation to a desire state reflecting not only your own beliefs but also your employees' capabilities and expectations. This can be accomplished by consciously choosing to vary the *frequency of participation,* as well as more careful selection of *high-significance issues.* Again, you need to very carefully recognize that employee perceptions of each are critically important.

The Grid in Action. Katy Richards, the general manager of a grain milling division, discovers how important perceptions are when she tries to evaluate the participative system in her mill. After her first year as general manager, she schedules individual interviews with her four department heads. Among other topics she asks each of them to assess her approach to decision making in terms of the four systems portrayed in Figure 15-3. To her surprise and dismay, she finds that only the head of the marketing department agrees with her assessment *(efficient),* while the other three suggest that she has basically created a *starved* environment.

On reflection, Katy is pleased that all agree on the level of *frequency* with which she involves them in decisions. This was a conscious strategy on her part at the beginning of the year—not to burden them or distract them from their departmental functions unless it was absolutely necessary.

The disparity in perceptions of the relative *significance of issues* on which they have been consulted really concern her, however. The explanation emerges only after Katy polls each of them regarding which *issues* they considered *important,* and *unimportant,* during the year. She discovers that whereas she has assessed several *issues* as *moderately important* (roughly a 7 on a 10-point scale), most of the department heads see the same *issues* as only *mildly significant* (generally rated as 4s and 5s on the same scale). The problem is a matter of *degree,* or the level of the threshold arbitrarily dividing *high-significance issues* from *low-significance* ones. Had she raised her own threshold just slightly, the group would have been saved from *forced participation* on *issues of little concern* to most of them. "Next year," she resolves to herself, "I will ask at least two of the department heads for their assessment of the *issue's significance* before I try to involve them in a *participative* discussion."

References

Lawler, Edward. *High Involvement Management.* San Francisco: Jossey Bass, 1986.

William B. Werther, Jr. *Dear Boss.* Deephaven, Minn.: Meadowbrook, 1989.

William B. Werther, Jr., William A. Ruch, and Lynne McClure. *Productivity Through People.* St. Paul: West Publishing Company, 1986.

Chapter 16

Social Responsibility and Ethics

Businesses are economic institutions that seek profits for their owners. They achieve this objective through the efficient production of goods and services for external consumption. This chapter addresses your challenge of integrating the organization's *social* function with its *economic* function, given its responsibility to operate legally. Corporate social responsibility and business ethics address this challenge. Today's managers have begun to realize that corporate social responsibility (i.e., the responsibility to maintain the right, proper, fair, and/or just balance between financial performance, legal performance, and social performance) is necessary for the long-term viability of the company. Business ethics attempts to define conduct that is right, proper, fair, and/or just.

The four models in this chapter are windows into various aspects of corporate social responsibility and business ethics. The first window traces the historical evolution of thinking about corporate social responsibility. Then we express corporate social responsibility through two windows. One examines the diverse interests of various kinds of stakeholders, and the second explores corporate philanthropy. While pursuing its economic and social responsibilities, the company is obligated to operate within legal constraints—the second and third windows incorporate the company's legal responsibilities. The last window presents a set of ethical criteria that could help corporate executives resolve conflicts among the company's economic, legal, and social responsibilities.

16-1. Evolving Views of Business Responsibilities

The economic and legal responsibilities of business are quite clear, and widely acknowledged. Whether the company should accept social responsibilities beyond its economic obligations and legal requirements has, however, been the subject of considerable debate. The purpose of Window 16-1 is to stimulate your thought about the historical evolution of business responsibilities in general and corporate social responsibility in particular.

Applying the Evolving Views Window

Over the last twenty-five years, our views of business responsibilities have become more complex than can be expressed by the traditional and philanthropic perspectives, which divorced *social* endeavors from *economic* endeavors. More recent ideas about business responsibilities demonstrate a struggle to *integrate* the *economic* and *social* aspects of business. The *contemporary* view represents a conceptual breakthrough from the historical ways of thinking. It explicitly recognizes the *social consequences* of *economic activity*. Business was encouraged by public pressure, then forced by government regulation, to "clean up its own mess" or "pay for its own mistakes." In other words it needed to absorb the *social* costs it had previously pushed onto society.

While the *contemporary* view was an initial blending of *economic* and *social* concerns, the *emerging* view strives for an even better synthesis. All previous points of view held that profitability and corporate *social* responsibility were incompatible goals for business. The conceptual leap of the *emerging* view, then, is the recognition that becoming *socially* responsible should have a positive effect on profits. Many of the regulatory reformers holding the *contemporary* view tended to disregard the economic viability of a company. In contrast, the *emerging*

Window 16-1. Evolving Views of Business Responsibilities.

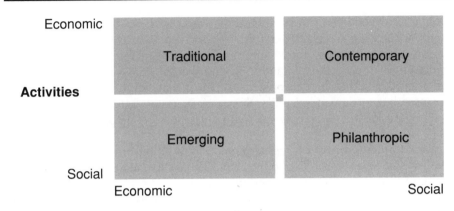

Source: "Corporate Responsibility—Reconciling Economic and Social Goals," by James J. Chrisman and Archie B. Carroll, *Sloan Management Review*, Winter 1984, pp. 59–65, by permission of the publisher. Copyright © 1984 by the Sloan Management Review Association. All rights reserved.

Dimensions

Activities. This dimension refers to business *activities* such as opening a new plant, dropping a product line, declaring a dividend, acquiring a supplier, diversifying into an unrelated line of business, contributing to the United Way campaign, sponsoring a Little League team, or hiring hearing-impaired people. Business activities are classified as either *economic* or *social* in scope.

Consequences. This dimension refers to the major *consequences*, results, or outcomes of business activities. They are classified as either *economic* or *social* in nature.

Alternative Views of Responsibilities

Traditional. The *traditional* view of business responsibilities is captured in the narrow statement, "The business of business is business." According to this view, which was prevalent before the turn of the century, the only responsibility of business is to pursue economic activities that produce economic consequences. A company is believed to serve society best by focusing its energies on efficient internal operation.

Philanthropic. The *philanthropic* view of business responsibilities is based on the idea, "Doing well obligates doing good." This view came into focus

Window 16-1. (*Continued*)

early in the twentieth century when some very successful business people, like Andrew Carnegie, A. Leland Stanford, Henry C. Frick, and Henry Ford, began to endow public libraries, found universities, fund settlement houses for poor people, and support other philanthropic and charitable causes. Two assumptions are important to the philanthropic view. One is that charity may be expected of business, but not demanded; philanthropy is a voluntary act. Another assumption is that only *social*, not *business, activities* produce social consequences.

■ **Contemporary.** The *contemporary* view of business responsibilities is expressed in the premise "Economic activities have to make sense for society, not just for business." This view gained prominence in the 1960s and 1970s when the public, having grown weary of absorbing the social costs of business operations (like environmental pollution, unsafe products, and unequal employment opportunity), increasingly demanded change. A wave of new government regulations resulted, and businesses were forced to seriously consider the *social consequences* of their *economic activities.*

■ **Emerging.** The *emerging* view of business responsibilities can be summarized with the proposition "Social activities must make economic sense." This proposition, which links *social activities* to *economic consequences*, has a double meaning. Such ambiguity would be expected in an emerging perspective, since emerging phenomena are in the formative stages of development. One meaning of the proposition is that *social activities* make *economic* sense for the business. This implies that corporate *social* responsibility yields financial rewards or, at the extreme, that it is even necessary to do good (i.e., be *socially* responsible) in order to do well (financially). Another interpretation of the proposition is that the business should engage in *only* those *social activities* that make good *economic* sense.

---

view assumes that the financial health of a company has paramount importance. Since participation in *social* activities is also considered imperative, the *emerging* view holds that *socially motivated activities* must be carried out in a way that will *increase* corporate resources and profits.

Possible Results from Using the Window. After studying this model, you might:

- Examine your own organization's explicit (or implicit) view of its business responsibilities. You do this by examining public pronouncements and policy documents, by interviewing top executives, or by inference based on prior corporate actions. In effect, you would be seeking answers to the questions: What are we currently doing? How did this posture come about? What is the rationale for our position with regard to business responsibility?
- Set some goals, a timetable, and an action plan for the adoption, if necessary, of a more modern and progressive view of business responsibility (e.g., the emerging or contemporary views).
- Actively seek to encourage other companies in your community to upgrade their own views of business responsibilities. Perhaps you can do this by sponsoring open forums, in which the costs and benefits of various approaches can be debated.

The Grid in Action. By and large, acceptance of the *contemporary* view of business responsibilities is a fait accompli. Consider Marge Choot, CEO of the Acme Brick Company. Compared to the corporate executive of 1965, Marge has relatively little choice but to prevent any negative *social consequences* that could result from Acme's business operations. Because of a vast array of government regulations, Marge's brickworks must protect the natural environment, hire and promote women and minorities without discrimination, provide safe working conditions for employees, and produce safe products for customers.

Whether Marge embraces the *emerging* view is very much a matter of free choice, however. The *emerging* view stresses the *economic consequences* of corporate *social* responsibility. Businesspeople are encouraged to pursue *economic* and *social* goals simultaneously, that is, to engage in *social activities* in such a way as to achieve *economic* rewards.

How might Marge implement the *emerging* view of business responsibilities? One possibility is for Acme Brick Company to scrutinize *social* issues to find their real profit-making potential. Peter Drucker advocates that businesses tackle society's most pressing problems as serious business opportunities.[1] What if Marge wants Acme Brick to maintain its *traditional* line of business (rather than selling remedies to social ills)? What is the link between *social activities* and *economic consequences* then? The *emerging* view holds that *social* responsibility should be treated as an investment that will result in long-term profit maximization. Two strategic planners have called this "doing better by doing good."[2] A more extreme interpretation is that the general public *expects* social responsibility and will penalize companies that do not act responsibly. In other words, "doing good is necessary in order to do well."

16-2. Social Responsibility and Corporate Stakeholders

Both Windows 16-2 and 16-3 classify companies according to how well they execute their social and legal responsibilities. Each pane in these two windows represents the impact on public opinion that results from the social and legal posture taken. The existence of two such windows demonstrates that social responsibility and legal responsibility are complex concepts.

Window 16-2 tries to balance the conflicting interests of various stakeholder groups (owners and others who have a stake in the organization). The aspect of legal responsibility of interest is in compliance with regulations designed to protect stakeholders. You can operate from various positions with regard to stakeholders and regulations. This model distinguishes among these various positions. Every position is subject to public criticism, but some positions are more easily defended than others.

A key to the model is the power that stakeholders wield over organizations. Stakeholder clout became evident during the 1960s and 1970s, the heyday of the contemporary view of business responsibilities, when various coalitions of stakeholders

1. Peter F. Drucker, "Converting Social Problems into Business Opportunities: The New Meaning of Corporate Social Responsibility," *California Management Review*, Winter, 1984, pp. 53–63.
2. Margaret A. Stroup and Ralph L. Neubert, "The Evolution of Social Responsibility," *Business Horizons*, March–April, 1987, pp. 22–24.

Window 16-2. Social Responsibility and Corporate Stakeholders.

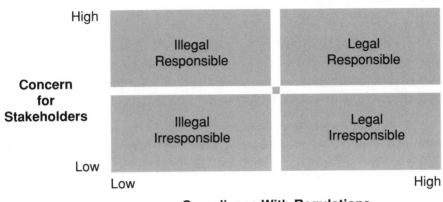

Source: Dan R. Dalton and Richard A. Cosier, "The Four Faces of Social Responsibility," *Business Horizons,* May-June 1982, pp. 19–27. Copyright © 1982 by the Foundation for the School of Business at Indiana University. Used with permission.

Dimensions

Concern for stakeholders. *A stakeholder* is anyone who has a vested interest in a company. (Examples are owners, employees, middle managers, suppliers, competitors, customers, the local community, governments, the media, and special-interest groups like environmentalists, consumer advocates, or civil rights groups.) Social responsibility requires that the interests of *all stakeholders,* not just stockholders, be considered. This first dimension depicts whether there is a high or low *level of concern.*

Compliance with regulations. Most government regulation of business, especially that legislated within the last twenty-five years, tries to protect stakeholders in some way. Sometimes regulations are not effective in protecting stakeholders' interests, however. Therein lies the value of considering both the legal and social aspects of business actions. This dimension depicts two levels of compliance with regulations.

Array of Social Responsibility Positions

Illegal, irresponsible. Some companies simultaneously disregard the interests of some of their stakeholder groups and flout government regulations.

Window 16-2. (*Continued*)

Whether this occurs consciously or unconsciously, the managers in charge are placing their company in an *illegal-irresponsible* position.

Illegal, responsible. Managers who carefully balance *stakeholders' interests*, yet find themselves *out of compliance* with government regulations, hold an *illegal-responsible* position. One reason for operating from this position stems from contradictory government regulations.

Legal, irresponsible. Compliance with existing regulations doesn't always guarantee social responsibility; managers may choose to ignore the *interests* of some *stakeholder* groups, yet remain in *compliance with regulations* designed to protect the interests of other stakeholders. This is a *legal-irresponsible* position.

Legal, responsible. A *legal-responsible* position means not only that the company is law-abiding in terms of *regulatory compliance*, but also that top executives are *sensitive* to the needs of a broad array of company *stakeholders*. It is a sometimes difficult, but socially responsible, strategy to adopt.

---

brought about an unprecedented level of government regulations of business. Not all stakeholder power gets exercised in the political arena, however. For example, employees can choose to work hard or hardly work; consumers can choose to buy more or less; community leaders can choose to be cooperative or uncooperative. In a nutshell, public support for, or criticism of, a company's position really matters.

Applying the Social Responsibility Window

The model identifies four managerial positions on *social and legal responsibility*. In a given situation, your choices are limited to only two of the four positions; you are restricted to one of the diagonals in the model, but free to alter your position on the given diagonal. This means that sometimes the choice is between an *illegal-irresponsible* position and a *legal-responsible* position; other times the choice is an *illegal-responsible* position versus a *legal-irresponsible* position.

The match or mismatch between *government regulations*

and *stakeholder concerns* dictates which diagonal you face. If *government regulations* adequately address *stakeholder's interest*, you operate on the primary diagonal (either *legally* and *responsibly*, or *illegally* and *irresponsibly*). When *regulations* do not accurately reflect the *best interest* of stakeholders, your choices are limited to a *legal-irresponsible* position or an *illegal-responsible* position. There are three conditions under which you may find yourself in this dilemma: (1) a *regulation* passed for the benefit of one group of *stakeholders* overlooks the *interests* of another group; (2) *contradictory regulations* are passed in a piecemeal fashion, to the benefit of different groups; or (3) the law lags behind society's changing view of what is socially *responsible*.

Consider the first case, where some *stakeholder groups* are overlooked. For instance, Global, Inc., a U.S. consumer products firm, may find that it can produce one product line at lower cost with higher quality overseas than it can domestically. Petty bribery of government officials may be a fact of business life in the foreign country where Global wants to locate a plant for this line, but the Foreign Corrupt Practices Act prohibits a U.S. company from engaging in this type of behavior. Several kinds of stakeholders, like Global's customers, suppliers and company stockholders, would be better off if the company could bribe the foreign officials. Unfortunately, Kirsten Kraft, Global's manager in charge of this division, has to choose between a *legal-irresponsible* position (no bribery, no foreign production) and an *illegal-responsible* position (bribing the foreign officials).

Managers who are the victims of contradictory *regulations*, forcing them into an *illegal-responsible* position, may feel blameless, but are likely to suffer serious criticism anyway. For example, the Department of Energy may require a plant to burn coal instead of oil to lessen U.S. dependence on foreign petroleum sources, while the Environmental Protection Agency may require the same plant to use oil instead of coal to minimize certain noxious emissions. The company is subject to major hassles from whichever regulatory agency it must ignore in order to comply with the other relevant regulator. If you seek a legal remedy by asking exemption from one type of *regulation* or by demanding that the conflicting laws be reconciled, stakeholders who support the "losing" *regulations* may put up a wall.

The existence of a *legal-irresponsible* alternative illustrates that, if corporate executives want to behave responsibly, the legality test is not enough. The law sets a minimum standard and typically lags behind the public's evolving view of what is acceptable behavior. It is perfectly legal, though most would argue irresponsible, for instance, to manufacture cigarettes, tell lies in order to obtain information about competitors, or mislead workers about upcoming layoffs. Accordingly, being a law-abiding corporate citizen does not protect a company against scathing public criticism. For example, U.S. corporations can legally operate in South Africa, but American shareholders, churches, and civil rights groups who find apartheid repugnant have strongly pressured many companies to get out.

Consider the more common case, where *government regulations* are well tuned to *stakeholders'* interests. How might the model be used? You look at the primary diagonal in the model and may choose an *illegal-irresponsible* or *legal-responsible* position. You would expect to provoke more public criticism in the first position and would be subject to less criticism in the second case. Although we would expect you to be reluctant to adopt an *illegal-irresponsible* position, in some situations this approach would be an attractive alternative.

Considerations to Make When Using the Window. After studying this model, you might:

- Begin by specifically identifying who your major *stakeholders* are and then assessing the *degree of concern* the organization has for each of them.
- Make a subjective assessment, preferably developed on the basis of a careful longitudinal study, of the degree to which the organization regularly complies with all relevant *governmental regulations.*
- Classify not only your general pattern of behavior, but also the major specific events in your recent history, into one of the four windowpane categories.
- Repeat the preceding step from the perspective of the public at large or key *stakeholder* groups, to see if their external perceptions differ substantially from those of insiders.
- Make a top-management policy decision specifying the windowpane in which the organization intends to operate

in the future, and then transmit this information to all key employees to guide their behavior.

The Grid in Action. Suppose that the Santa Claus Toy Company is required by law to install expensive new equipment that will improve worker safety on its assembly line. The fine that the Occupational Safety and Health Administration (OSHA) can impose for noncompliance with this regulation is apt to be fairly small. Furthermore, the likelihood of an OSHA inspection that could detect noncompliance is remote. These circumstances (high costs of behaving *legally-responsibly*, low penalty for *noncompliance*, and little likelihood of getting caught) could tempt Donald Blixon, head of Santa Claus Toys, to choose to operate *illegally and irresponsibly*. If Santa Claus Toys occasionally commits minor offenses, it may risk no more than "mild tarnishing" of its public image. If Donald Blixon takes an *illegal-irresponsible* position more frequently, he is setting Santa Claus Toys up for severe criticism. Whether the company can survive the public outcry must be carefully weighed against the perceived benefits.

All four managerial positions described in the model are subject to some public criticism. For instance, even if Donald Blixon stakes out a *legal-responsible* position, he may take some heat due to the conflicting *interests* of different *stakeholders*. In other words a *socially responsible* act like meeting the new OSHA standard could alienate customers (if prices had to be raised), could upset some employees (if pay raises were scaled back), or could antagonize the state in which Santa Claus pays taxes (if tax revenues took a noticeable drop). Nevertheless, organizational decision makers like Blixon can best defend their positions from the *legal-responsible* domain.

Reference

Freeman, R. Edward. *Strategic Management: A Stakeholder Approach.* Cambridge, Mass.: Ballinger, 1984.

16-3. Social Responsibility and Corporate Philanthropy

The purpose of Window 16-3 is to classify organizations on the basis of their behavior or conduct relative to social responsibility

Window 16-3. Social Responsibility and Corporate Philanthropy

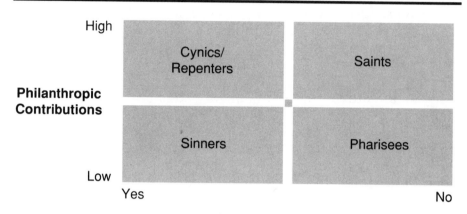

Source: Richard E. Wokutch and Barbara A. Spenser, "Corporate Saints and Sinners: The Effects of Philanthropic and Illegal Activity on Organizational Performance," *California Management Review*, Vol. 30 (Winter 1987), pp. 62–77.

Dimensions

Philanthropic contributions. Corporate *philanthropy* is a widely recognized form of corporate social responsibility. (Another commonly accepted form, balancing the interests of diverse stakeholders with those of stockholders, is discussed in Window 16-2.) Through corporate *philanthropy*, a company voluntarily *contributes* a portion of its profits to the worthwhile social causes of its choice. Corporate giving by an individual company may be high or low, with the average company contributing approximately 1 to 2 percent of pretax net income.

Corporate criminal activity. Crimes are serious offenses—gross violations of the law. Since crimes are defined by the minimum moral standards, avoidance of *criminal activity* (as a measure of social responsibility) is a much laxer standard than is compliance with government regulations protecting the interests of stakeholders (the measure of social responsibility associated with legal responsibility in Window 16-2). This dimension records whether or not the organization has engaged in *criminal activity*.

Window 16-3. (*Continued*)

Types of Organizations

Saints. Corporate *saints* are companies that make high *philanthropic contributions* and avoid *criminal activity*. Their headlines in the popular press evoke praise rather than reveal scandal.

Pharisees. *Pharisees* are companies that obey the letter of the law. Since the law does not require corporate *philanthropy*, they make no charitable contributions.

Cynics/repenters. Companies that commit *crimes* and simultaneously give generously to *philanthropic* causes are labeled *cynics/repenters*. This somewhat confusing label is used because two motives could be involved. Corporations with these behaviors may be headed by *cynics*, who use *corporate contributions* to generate favorable publicity. By doing so, they hope to make the public more tolerant of the company's *legal offenses*. On the other hand, companies caught for *criminal activities* may be run by *repenters*, who are genuinely trying to atone for their transgressions through generous corporate *giving*.

Sinners. *Sinners* are companies that fail both tests of corporate responsibility. They contribute little to *philanthropic* causes and also commit *crimes*.

---

and legal responsibility. Four behavioral profiles result, and each creates a different public image for the company.

Window 16-3 is unusual in that it pairs two fairly extreme measures of corporate social responsibility—*philanthropy* and *criminal activity*. These represent, respectively, the most that can be expected and the least that can be demanded of the corporation. Charitable giving is an age-old idea; those who have been blessed share some of their wealth with those less fortunate. Unlike concern for stakeholder interests (discussed in the previous window), *philanthropy* is not a duty of the corporation; rather, contributing to worthwhile causes is a type of commendable behavior beyond what can reasonably be demanded. While corporate *philanthropy* is praiseworthy, avoidance of *criminal activity* shows no exceptional virtue. Avoidance of *criminal activity* represents the minimally acceptable behavior for a company—the absolute lowest limit on what can be expected and tolerated.

As in the previous model, the relationship between the corporation's social and legal responsibilities is important to this model. Legal responsibility is related to social responsibility because laws reflect moral standards. Criminal laws, however, are based on the minimum ethical standard; it is faint praise to contend that a company refrains from domestic bribery, unfair labor practices, or false advertising, for example.

Applying the Social Responsibility and Corporate Philanthropy Window

Corporate *philanthropy* has acquired a new importance in recent years for both donors and recipients. Recipients have a greater level of need. Profound cuts in federal funding for social programs during the Reagan era prompted a dramatic increase in requests to private industry to pick up the slack. During the 1970s corporate *philanthropy* among major U.S. corporations averaged one percent of pretax net income, while during the 1980s corporate contributions have averaged nearly two percent.

This model illustrates that donors can have multiple motives for corporate giving. The original reason that companies engaged in *philanthropy* may have been altruism (refer to the first window in this chapter; early in the twentieth century, *philanthropy* was viewed as a social activity with social consequences independent of corporate profits). Corporate executives have learned that *philanthropy* can have other effects, however. These include effects on company image and reputation in the marketplace, as well as strategic effects that show up directly on the bottom line.

Accordingly, in recent years we have seen many companies using *philanthropy* as a marketing or advertising tool. For instance, publicity campaigns announce to consumers that a portion of the purchase price of each unit sold will go to a particular cause; consumer products companies carefully select major brands to promote by sponsorship of sports events, concerts, and festivals; and companies increasingly insist on strong corporate name identification when they donate to the arts, in order to impress clients and upscale consumers.

There is some preliminary evidence that, among Fortune 500 companies, *saints* and *cynics/repenters* have better reputations than do *pharisees* and *sinners*. This may indicate that a good public image is associated with high *philanthropic* contributions, and that high corporate giving can overcome the taint of *criminal activity*. While *pharisees* (no *crimes*, but little or no corporate *philanthropy*) cannot be technically faulted, their morally neutral behavior apparently does little to endear them to the public. Among Fortune 500 companies, profitability may be lower for *sinners* than it is for any other group.

Considerations to Make When Using the Window. After studying this model, you should:

- Carefully assess the nature and level of your company's *philanthropic contributions*. Does your company need to be giving more? Less? In addition, you might wish to examine the public's *perception* of the *philanthropic activity* of the organization. Is it getting adequate recognition for its current contributions, or does it need to find ways to obtain greater visibility from its present *philanthropy*?
- Examine the past level of *corporate criminal activity*. This, in the public eye, may be a product of both frequency of illegal actions, as well as the magnitude (of publicity) associated with them. It will also be a function of the length of time that the public clings to past memories of corporate wrongdoing.
- Adopt an official corporate posture proclaiming your intentions with regard to both dimensions (philanthropy and noncriminal, or legal, behavior), and then create programs designed to ensure that both activities occur according to plan.

The Grid in Action. How could a corporate executive put this model to practical use? Consider the case of Samantha Austin, who has just inherited the family fried chicken empire and wants to seriously challenge the bigger players in the industry, Kentucky Fried Chicken and Church's. Samantha's company has poor name recognition and no history of *corporate giving*. However, it also has no *criminal record*. She is pleased not to find her company in the *sinners* category, but somewhat less pleased to realize that it is in the category of *pharisees* (no *crimes*, no *corporate philanthropy*), which offers little help in terms of public image. Moreover, Samantha is concerned about the health risks of her primary product (high cholesterol, high amount of fat in fried chicken) as Americans become increasingly health-conscious. Her solution is to add two new healthy entrees to the product line, to launch these new selections as "heart smart" foods with heavy publicity, and to sponsor a ten-kilometer run with all proceeds going to the American Heart Association. This would move Smanatha's company into the *saints* category and should significantly improve its image and reputation.

16-4. Ethical Criteria for Business Decisions

Window 16-4 identifies a set of ethical criteria that you could use when you evaluate decision alternatives. Managers are generally more comfortable considering the profit potential or legal ramifications of their decisions than the ethical implications. Most people, managers included, have little or no formal training in ethics. An important assumption underlying the model is that you would be more willing to explicitly apply ethical criteria to decision situations if you understood how to go about it.

Ethics determines what is right or proper or fair or just. Conflicts between the company's economic performance (costs, profits, competitiveness in the marketplace) and social performance (obligations to various groups affected by the organization, corporate philanthropy) inevitably occur. These managerial dilemmas, which you are prone to think of as tough calls or hardball decisions, are really ethical problems. Recognizing the ethical principles and/or values that decision alternatives implicitly endorse can help you evaluate options.

Applying the Ethical Criteria Window

Scrutinizing the various alternatives in a decision situation with this model will reveal what ethical trade-offs are being made. A given alternative will likely pass some of the criteria and fail others. Knowing which criteria are being satisfied and which

Window 16-4. Ethical Criteria for Business Decisions.

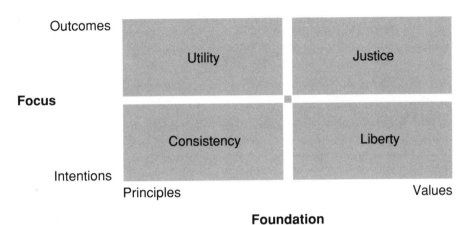

Source: LaRue Tone Hosmer, *The Ethics of Management* , Homewood, Ill.: Irwin, 1987.

Dimensions

Focus. An ethical criterion could *focus* on either the decision maker's *intentions* or on the *outcomes* of the decision. Those who argue that intentions are the proper *focus* can name practical reasons ("Outcomes are too uncertain and uncontrollable") as well as philosophical reasons ("The ends cannot justify the means"). Others can argue that outcomes or consequences are the proper *focus*, on the grounds that "the good that is produced by an act is more important than the act itself," and/or that "good intentions often meet with poor implementation."

Foundation. An ethical criterion could be *founded* on a *principle* (a fundamental, comprehensive rule of conduct) or a *value* (a condition held in high esteem and priority). In classical ethical systems, moral standards tended to be based on a principle, such as the Golden Rule. In modern ethical systems, moral standards tend to be based on the primacy of a single value, such as personal liberty.

Ethical Criteria

Utility. The *utility* criterion is founded on a principle that focuses on the outcome of the decision. The principle here is to do the greatest good for the greatest number. The appropriateness of a decision is measured by its consequences. A decision is right if it creates the greatest benefits for the largest number of people, while generating the least harm to others.

Window 16-4. (*Continued*)

Consistency. The *consistency* criterion is founded on a principle that focuses on the decision maker's intentions. The principle here is that what is right for one is right for all. The appropriateness of a decision is measured by the honesty of the decision maker's intentions. A decision is right if the decision maker wishes that everyone in similar circumstances would reach the same decision.

Justice. The *justice* criterion is based on the primacy of a single value, distributive *justice*, and it is outcome-oriented. A decision is right if it results in an improved situation for the least-advantaged members of society.

Liberty. The *liberty* criterion, which focuses on the decision maker's intentions, is based on the primacy of a different value, personal *liberty*. The appropriateness of a decision is measured by the decision maker's motives; he/she must treat others as ends, worthy of dignity in and of themselves, rather than as means for accomplishing the decision maker's self-interests. A decision is right if it respects people's capacity to choose freely for themselves.

---

are being violated will give the decision maker more confidence in "hardball" situations. An example will illustrate how it might work.

Suppose an urban bank is considering increasing its fees for small checking accounts to reflect the costs of servicing these accounts. Further, suppose that most of the customers who will be affected are retired persons on modest fixed incomes. In other words these customers cannot easily maintain the minimum balance to avoid the service charge and, as elderly people, they are afraid to carry cash. Should the bank president raise the fees?

The bank president should not, according to the *utility* criterion. A large number of elderly customers would be harmed, while a small number of large depositors, stockholders, and employees would be helped by the more complete recovery of costs on little accounts. The *justice* criterion would similarly prohibit the new, higher fees, because the least advantaged customers are made worse off. The *liberty* criterion would also prohibit the higher fees, because they limit the choices available to elderly customers. The *consistency* criterion, however, would allow implementation of higher fees, on the grounds that every banker faced with unprofitable accounts would try to recover the true costs of those accounts.

How would these considerations help the bank president decide? The decision maker would become consciously aware of the fact that imposing the increase in fees runs contrary to most ethical criteria. Knowing this might prompt the banker to look for some creative, less negative solutions to the checking account problem (i.e., designing a new type of account that would be less costly to administer).

Considerations to Make When Using the Window. After studying this model, you should:

- Examine the major decisions made within the organization that have an ethical element. The intentions, as well as the outcomes, of past decisions should be examined to assess the underlying philosophy in place. In short, which receives the greater emphasis in decisions leading up to the significant decisions?
- Study the basis on which your ethical decisions are made to see if they involve broad principles or specifically focused values. It would be even more interesting and useful to discover whether you can even *identify* the underlying principles or values in regular use!
- Analyze the four general ethical criteria (*utility, consistency, justice,* and *liberty*) to see which of those you would *prefer* to use as guiding criteria for your actions, and then use these on a regular basis to provide an ethical context for your decisions.

The Grid in Action. Suppose Smith Widget Company is trying to obtain information about a scientific discovery at another, more innovative company, 21st Century. Smith Widget could gather useful intelligence by paying an "escort" to butter up the 21st Century's crack scientist at a professional meeting. After enough wining and dining and flattery, the scientist may volunteer important technical details. Should Jeri Smith, Smith Widget's CEO, authorize the use of this intelligence-gathering tactic?

The *utility* criterion would allow this tactic, provided that greater dissemination of the scientific information would result in more competition and lower prices to a larger number of consumers, with minimal damage to 21st Century's profits. The *justice* criterion would similarly endorse use of this tactic, if wider knowledge of the scientific discovery somehow produced a better standard of living to those in need. The *consistency* criterion, on the other hand, would disallow pumping 21st Century's scientist for information, unless Jeri Smith was willing to have Smith Widget's staff be pumped for information in the same way. The *liberty* criterion would likewise prohibit pumping 21st Century's scientist for information because this process treats the scientist as a means to an end, rather than as a human being worthy of dignity and respect.

What should Jeri Smith do now, given that the "score" seems to be two "yes" votes and two "no" votes? By use of the model, she would become aware of trade-offs buried in the decision. The two criteria that focus on the decision maker's intentions (*consistency* and *liberty*) argue against use of this intelligence-gathering tactic. The two criteria that focus on the decision outcomes (*utility* and *justice*) argue for it. Jeri must determine whether she is willing to use questionable means (wrong incentives or improper motives) to accomplish desirable ends (good outcomes or consequences).

References

Buchholz, Rogene A. *Fundamental Concepts and Problems in Business Ethics.* Englewood Cliffs, N.J.: Prentice-Hall, 1989.

Clinard, Marshall B. *Corporate Ethics and Crime.* Beverly Hills, Calif.: Sage, 1983.

Chapter 17
Strategic Issues

Strategic issues focus on determining the potential and future direction a company will take within its competitive environment. The scope of strategic concerns ranges from a choice of product/market environment, an analysis of competitive options, and decisions regarding growth patterns within the company, to specific strategic options regarding resource allocation, managerial processes, organization structures, and other strategy implementation concerns. The four windows in this section present a sampling of these issues. The first window, Strategic Adaptation, depicts broad patterns of organizational strategy formulation and strategy implementation choices. This model incorporates issues related to environmental fit and to internal consistency. The second window, Generic Strategies for Competition, presents a range of options for securing competitive advantage. This model describes the distinct organizational competencies that successfully allow a company to maintain a strong position in the marketplace. The model describing Strategic Growth Vector options, the third window in this set, looks at different approaches to expanding the product and market scope of a company.

Product and market domain considerations are often considered one of the key components in strategy formulation. The final window presents a perspective on portfolio management. The "Boston Consulting Group (BCG) Business Portfolio Approach" has popularized four methods of managing resources among a company's diverse business activities.

The Strategic Adaptation Window presents the most global perspective on strategic management issues. Each of the other windows in this section concentrates on one specific type of strategic choice. Taken as a group, these models provide a representative sample of the types of concerns that are typically embedded in a company's strategy.

17-1. Strategic Adaptation

Strategic adaptation is a process by which a company selects and maintains a viable product-market domain and develops internal mechanisms to effectively compete in this strategic target area. Adaptation includes a process of external and internal alignment to achieve congruence or fit. Four different approaches to achieving a two-part alignment are presented in Window 17-1.

Applying the Strategic Adaptation Window

Every organization must develop solutions to three fundamental problems. (1) The *entrepreneurial problem* involves defining a company's product-market domain. This is not done in terms of specific products to be offered or customers to be served, but in terms of domain characteristics such as stability, permanence, and predictability. (2) The *engineering problem* for a company is to operationalize the solution to the entrepreneurial problem by developing appropriate planning and control systems, communication networks, decision-making procedures, and organizational structures. (3) The *administrative problem* involves stabilizing organizational activities, implementing organizational processes, and designing a company's culture. An adaptive cycle reflects an organization's set of choices regarding these three strategic problems. The four organization types presented in the model depict different patterns of behavior with regard to managing the adaptive cycle that reflects internally consistent approaches to defining a company's relationship with its environment.

Several assumptions provide the foundation to the Strategic

Window 17-1. Strategic Adaptation.

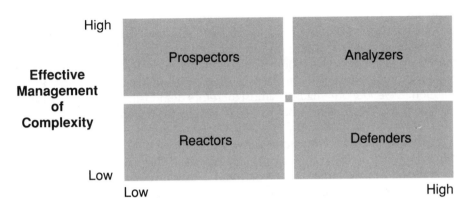

Source: Raymond E. Miles and Charles C. Snow, *Organizational Strategy, Structure and Process,* New York: McGraw-Hill, 1978.

Dimensions

Effective management for efficiency. Effective competition in certain types of market segments, as well as effective implementation of certain organizational processes, requires a company to manage its activities in order to achieve maximum *efficiency* in operations and in its dealings with external forces. In other domains (e.g., prestige-based purchases) or with alternate implementation strategies (e.g., greater concern with innovativeness than with cost), *efficiency* is less important. This dimension rates an organization's attention toward, and effectiveness in, managing for *efficiency* as either high or low.

Effective management of complexity. Some product-market choices and some organizational designs require great skill in managing *complexity*. Diagnostic capabilities, flexibility, synergy, and decision-making competencies are typically seen as necessary skills. This dimension rates an organization as either high or low in terms of its competence to effectively manage *complex* external networks (e.g., multiple suppliers using diverse technologies) and *complex* internal interdependencies (e.g., a large number of vertically integrated activities) and conflicts.

Four Strategic Adaptation Approaches

Defenders. *Defender companies* identify and protect a portion of the total market in an effort to create a stable product-market domain. Growth is

Window 17-1. (*Continued*)

generally achieved through market penetration and some limited product development (see Window 17-3 for additional information). The primary implementation concern is how to produce and distribute goods or services for maximum *efficiency*. This requires strict control of organizational activities and external interactions. Standardization of goods and procedures is a typical solution. *Defender* organizations must therefore demonstrate strong capabilities for managing for *efficiency*, but have a low need for managing *complexity*.

■ **Prospectors**. *Prospector organizations* face demands that are nearly mirror opposites to the conditions facing *defenders*. The product-market domain for *prospecting* companies is in a continual state of development as they seek to locate and exploit new product and market opportunities. As a result of constant redefinition in scope and target market, such companies must manage a great deal of *complexity* in external relationships and in internal operations. *Prospector* companies, therefore, score high on their ability to manage *complexity*, but have a relatively low requirement for managing to achieve *efficiency*.

■ **Analyzers.** *Analyzer companies* play a dual role. They maintain a strong core of stable products and customers, while simultaneously attempting to develop new product and market opportunities. *Analyzer* organizations are required to operate in a highly *efficient* manner to manage their core businesses and to generate sufficient resources to fund modifications in the product-market domain. Yet, these companies must also manage high levels of *complexity* in their efforts to balance conflicting demands, expectations, and competencies and to undertake new ventures. High levels of both *efficiency* and *complexity* management are needed to maintain organizational equilibrium.

■ **Reactors**. Companies that are only able to achieve low levels of *efficiency* and can only manage low levels of *complexity* are generally maladaptive and are termed *reactors*. *Reactor organizations* are basically unsuccessful. They do not establish a clear relationship with their environment, nor do they develop organization structures and processes to fully fit a selected strategy.

Adaptation Window. First, the environment is seen as influencing, but not determining, organizational choices and behavior. This reinforces the importance of management decisions and actions. Second, none of the organizational types are seen as ideal. Each type of solution carries with it an accompanying set of risks. Third, the notion of fit, or congruence, is an important part of adaptation. A company must achieve at least minimal fit with its external environment and simultaneously achieve fit among its internal processes. As a corollary, tight fit is offered as a key to competitive success, and early fit is suggested as a means to achieve competitive advantage.

Two requirements for successful maintenance of a *defender* strategy stand out. First, the industry and the product attributes must be relatively stable. Second, a specific market domain must be identified, and differences between this segment and other portions of the market must be maintained. (Note the similarity between these requirements and the requirements for a successful focus strategy in Window 17-2, the Generic Strategies for Competition Window). If a company is successful as a *defender*, competitors have difficulty undercutting its position in the absence of serious market or technology shifts. The risks associated with a *defender* strategy include the potential for ineffectiveness as a result of undue concern with *efficiency*, and a reduced ability to identify or exploit new opportunities.

For a *prospector* strategy to be effective, success must not depend on efficiency. For example, a *prospector* strategy would be most difficult to implement in an industry dominated by experience-curve management or economies of scale. Product development, market development, and diversification are all viable options for growth (see the Strategic Growth Vector Window, Window 17-3, for additional information). The primary risks of a *prospector* strategy are low profitability due to an excess of cash-user businesses (see the Boston Consulting Group Business Portfolio Approach Window, Window 17-4, for additional information) and resource-allocation errors that result in underutilization, overextension, or misuse of resources. *Prospector* companies are able to respond rapidly to technological and market shifts and thereby capitalize on environmental turbulence. As a consequence, *prospector* organizations are often active in shaping the competitive dimensions of their industries.

Analyzer companies attempt to minimize risk while maximizing the opportunities for profits. These companies should operate in industries that do not have rapid or unpredictable market or technology changes. In addition, *analyzer* companies should support an active applied research group that enables quick adoption of innovations. The pressure placed on balancing *efficiency* and *complexity* makes an organization more vulnerable to ineffective operations, and if internal or external balance is lost, *analyzer* companies may have difficulty reestablishing equilibrium. The information-processing demands on *analyzer* companies are very high. *Analyzer* organizations become *reactors* because they lack a clear, articulated strategy, because they have not developed sufficient congruence between their strategy and their structure, or because they have not made appropriate changes when faced with a shifting environment. These problems identify important pitfalls in strategy formulation and implementation and can serve as important warning signals.

This model is useful in describing categories of strategic patterns of behavior. It also generates a list of specific capabilities that are required for each set of entrepreneurial, engineering, and administrative choices. Further, this model highlights the trade-offs made once a company accepts a given type of product-market domain as its target.

Advantages to Using the Window. A significant number of organizations fail to engage in *any* form of strategic planning. The Strategic Adaptation Window can serve several valuable functions. For example, it:

- Encourages you to think about your ability (effectiveness) to manage organizational *efficiency*
- Encourages you to assess your competence in managing external networks as well as internal processes
- Facilitates the recognition of the type of approach the organization takes in adapting to its external environment by categorizing strategic behaviors
- Identifies the type of managing capabilities needed for four different adaptation strategies
- Illuminates the trade-offs that accompany a given type of product-market domain choice

- Identifies several capabilities required for entrepreneurial, engineering, and administrative problems

The Grid in Action. The board of directors of Ventures Inc. are meeting to elect a new general manager for their consumer products division. Ventures is a growth-oriented high technology firm specializing in finding and capitalizing on new product and market opportunities. Over the years Ventures has boasted a product line that ranges from high-fashion consumer goods, to kitchen appliances, to computer accessories, to scientific instruments and medical equipment. The three primary candidates for the job are Sara, James, and David. Each candidate approaches the job with a different set of assumptions. Selection of the best candidate is crucial, because division managers not only set the tone for their semiautonomous operations; they are considered prospects for the CEO spot.

Sara is a traditionalist. She believes that work is inherently distasteful to many people. Consequently, she assumes that the tasks people perform are less important to them than what they earn. She suspects that most people do not want jobs that require creativity, self-direction, or self-control.

James assumes that people want to feel useful and important. He contends that people want to belong to a group and to be recognized as individuals. He argues that these needs are as important as money in motivating behavior, and as a result he believes a manager's basic task is to make each worker feel useful and important.

David assumes that people want to contribute to meaningful goals that they have helped establish. He asserts that most people can exercise creativity, responsible self-direction, and a great deal of self control. He believes that a manager's role is to make use of untapped human resources. David assumes that work satisfaction is not a reasonable goal in itself, but that satisfaction is often a "by-product" when employees make full use of their capabilities.

Since Ventures Inc. is a typical *prospector* company, the board knows there are two primary managerial concerns. First, a general manager must avoid establishing long-term commitments to a single technology or product arena. Second, general managers must be able to facilitate and coordinate a large number of diverse activities and operations. The board concludes that Sara is too concerned with control to be an effective general manager in this setting. She is a high performer in stable and mature product areas (and might be a strong leader in a *defender* organization), but would not likely be effective with the degree of decentralized decision making and innovation required of upper management at Ventures. James seems a somewhat better fit, but the board finally decides that he is too concerned with people's feelings and with making them feel part of a group to effectively manage the high-risk and very non-routine activities in the consumer products division. It seems to the board that James's concern with shared values and common goals might stifle necessary innovation and diversity. (James might be an ideal general manager for an *analyzer* company.) David is offered the job. It seems to the board that his role will be more that of a "coach" than a traditional manager, which seems likely to foster innovation and appropriate risk taking. David seems comfortable with diversity, and this matches Ventures's need for flexible operations. Since David's background is in marketing, the board feels confident that he will continue to measure performance against competitors.

Reference

Miles, Raymond E., Charles S. Snow, Alan D. Meyer, and Henry J. Coleman, Jr. "Organizational Strategy, Structure, and Process." *Academy of Management Review*, Vol. 3, No. 3 (July 1978), pp. 546–562.

17-2. Generic Strategies for Competition

In order to be an effective competitor, a company must make two important choices. First, it must decide upon the type of *competitive advantage* it intends to pursue. Second, it must determine its *scope* of operations (e.g., the products it will produce and the markets it will serve). This model of Generic Strategies for Competition (Window 17-2) portrays the range of choices a company can make along these two dimensions. Each of the strategies can be successful depending on industry characteristics and a company's areas of competence.

Window 17-2. Generic Strategies for Competition.

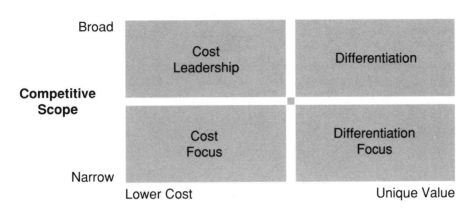

Source: Reprinted with permission of The Free Press, a Division of Macmillan, Inc., from *Competitive Advantage: Creating and Sustaining Superior Performance* by Michael E. Porter, p. 12. Copyright © 1985 by Michael E. Porter.

Dimensions

Competitive advantage. *Competitive advantages* are the sustainable distinct competencies of a company that lead to its favorable position within its industry and permit above-average performance over the long term. *Competitive advantage* refers not only to the specific strengths and weaknesses of a company, but to the purposes toward which these capabilities are directed.

Two basic types of *competitive advantage* are identified. A competitive advantage based on *lower cost* means that a company attempts to be the low-cost producer of a good or service while selling the good or service for a price at or near the industry average. This requires that a good be perceived as roughly comparable to the goods offered by competitors. *Competitive advantage* based on *differentiation* relies on a company's ability to offer something both unique and valued to its customers. A company using a differentiation strategy charges a price premium as a reward for its uniqueness.

Competitive scope. This dimension refers to the breadth of target market segments a company intends to serve. This distinguishes a company that constrains its activities to meet specialized needs from one that attempts to identify the common product-related characteristics that appeal to the entire marketplace. A company choosing a broad target directs its attention toward the industry as a whole. A company selecting a narrow target identifies specialized industry

Window 17-2. (*Continued*)

segments with clearly marked and relatively stable boundaries toward which it directs its efforts.

Four Generic Strategies

Cost leadership. A *cost leadership strategy* means that a company intends to be the preeminent low-cost producer of a product within its industry. A company electing this strategy serves many industry segments, and, at times, may cross industry boundaries in its effort to secure economies of scale or cost advantages from suppliers or within distribution channels. All sources of cost advantage must be used. A cost leader typically sells a standardized product with few, if any, frills. BIC pens provide an example of a successful use of cost leadership. A *cost leadership* strategy cannot ignore differentiation, however. The product must be acceptable to customers at a price roughly equivalent to that of a company's rivals. If such parity is not achieved, any advantage resulting from lower costs of production will be nullified by a need to severely discount market price.

Cost focus. A *cost focus strategy* reflects a company's choice to be the low-cost producer within a structurally attractive segment of the total marketplace. *Structurally attractive* means that the target segment is substantially different from other parts of the industry in its preferences or buying habits. Also, the boundaries of the segment are relatively stable and can be defended from encroachment by more broadly targeted competitors. Thus, a company adopting a *cost focus* strategy is the lowest-cost producer that meets the basic needs of a unique market segment. Kodak disk cameras illustrate this strategic approach.

Differentiation. A company pursuing a *differentiation strategy* attempts to be unique within its industry along attributes that are widely valued by a large proportion of potential customers. Such a strategy involves the identification of one or more dimensions that are seen as important to buyers and then positioning a company to meet those needs. Hewlett-Packard products in the scientific instrument industry rely on this strategy. This quality orientation allows *differentiators* to charge higher prices for their products. The particular product attributes that are important vary by industry.

Differentiation focus. A *differentiation focus strategy* requires a company to identify industry segments with special needs, and to meet these needs more exactly that any other competitor. Thus, a successful *differentiation focus* strategy requires a segment of potential buyers that have quite different needs from the larger industry. Such segments must be poorly served (at present) by more broadly targeted competitors for the segment to be structurally attractive. American Motors' Jeep line illustrates this approach.

Applying the Generic Strategies Window

This view of *competitive advantage* requires an understanding of both the structural forces that shape industry competition and a company's value chain. Five forces dominate the structural characteristics of an industry: (1) the degree of rivalry among participants, (2) bargaining power of buyers, (3) bargaining power of suppliers, (4) threat of entry by new competitors, and (5) threats from substitute products. In combination, these forces determine both the potential for industry-wide profitability and the segmentation, leverage, and stability of an industry. The strength of these forces reflects the underlying technical and economic features of an industry. Understanding industry structure is a prerequisite for identifying the range and number of generic choices that can be successfully maintained within a particular industry.

A value chain depicts the primary (inbound logistics, operations, outbound logistics, marketing and sales, service) and support (company infrastructure, human resource management, technology development, procurement) activities that a company must accomplish to successfully engage in any competitive strategy. A network of activities results. This network identifies the variety of specific avenues through which a company can pursue each of the generic competitive strategies. Successful companies carry out their selected type of *competitive advantage* throughout the value chain. Companies that concentrate their efforts on only a limited portion of the value chain are likely to find that no sustainable *competitive advantage* is obtained.

The most important implication of this model is that organizations must make a choice. The easiest way to guarantee that no *competitive advantage* is obtained is to attempt to pursue two or more of these generic strategies simultaneously. However, this does not mean that cost-based competitors can ignore *differentiation* or that uniqueness-based competitors can ignore *costs.* In each case some degree of parity must be maintained. For a *cost-based* strategy to be effective, the quality of a product must be perceived as acceptable within an industry or a specialized segment. Similarly, an excessive price premium resulting from poor cost management will undermine effective *differentiation.* A number of specific factors are important to achieving *cost leadership* and *cost focus* strategies. These include an awareness of economies or diseconomies of scale and management of learning curves and experience curves. Often overlooked opportunities for managing costs include exploitation of linkages with external organizations and interactions among factors in the value chain. Companies can also capitalize on first-mover advantages or seek gains from being an earlier follower. Finally, selecting appropriate discretionary policies can enhance a company's cost position. Sources of uniqueness can be enhanced by developing *differentiation* throughout the value chain. Unique features can be more readily appreciated by potential customers if a company makes sure that actual product use is consistent with intended product use, employs various signals to reinforce the need for *differentiation,* and bundles information with the product to facilitate both use and marketing distinctions. At times a company can change the rules that govern competition to secure uniqueness.

The risks associated with these strategies should also be noted. *Cost leadership* is difficult to sustain if competitors imitate a company's strategy, if technology is continually changing, or if other bases for *cost leadership* erode. Occasionally, competitors in an industry are so evenly matched in terms of their scale economies and other sources of efficiency that no company is able to gain an advantage over the others. *Differentiation* strategies are difficult to maintain if the unique qualities of a product are easy to copy or if the bases for *differentiation* become less important to customers. At times, features that set a product apart at the early stages of development become common as the product matures. *Focus* strategies are vulnerable to imitation and to erosion or saturation of the target segment. Advantages associated with a broad product line can outweigh the specialized features that were initially attractive to buyers in the segment. As the structural forces of an industry shift, new segments can emerge or early segments can consolidate.

Consideration of the type and scope of a company's *competitive advantage* is a fundamental aspect of developing an effective strategy. This model outlines the range of choices and guides a company's consideration of important portions of its strategic decision making.

Advantages to Using the Window. Planning as a managerial activity should be a systematic and ongoing process. As a part of the planning process, you ought to think about and plan for the placement of your organization in its external environment. This window is intended to facilitate the strategic planning process. Specifically, it:

- Encourages you to ask the question: What competitive advantage do we intend to pursue?
- Encourages you to decide on your scope of operations by answering the questions: What business are we in (e.g., what products/services will we deliver)? and What market(s) will we serve?
- Encourages a reexamination of your existing strategy whenever the organization's external product/service market changes.
- Encourages a reexamination of your existing strategy whenever the organization's competitors make a change in their product, service, or delivery.
- Encourages a reexamination of your existing strategy whenever the organization considers a change in its own structure, products, services, or delivery.

The Grid in Action. Joe-Bob Williams is the owner and manager of the Lone Star Boot Factory. His grandfather started the factory in the late 1800s, but it didn't really take off until his father won a contract to supply "senior boots" to the cadet corps of a nearby land-grant university. Since that first contract, Lone Star has operated as the sole supplier of boots to the corps. The boots are of a standard, conservative military design and are noted for their long wear, consistent high quality, and ability to maintain a highly polished "spit-shine" even during rough weather. For members of the corps, boots are a badge of distinction and a symbol of honor.

In the early years the demand for 2,000 pairs of boots each spring strained the operating resources of the small company. Within ten years, however, an equilibrium was achieved that allowed Joe-Bob's father to maintain entrepreneurial control of the business while obtaining an acceptable, if not exorbitant profit. Joe-Bob assumed the company reins two years ago. He is more interested in growth than either his father or his grandfather was. He also wants to consider branching out in new directions. Making a single product for a single customer seems somewhat risky.

One option that appears on the horizon is the acquisition of a nearby boot manufacturing operation. This company specializes in working boots for the surrounding community. His brother Billy has suggested expanding their own operation to include a line of dress boots in exotic leathers. Billy believes such an expansion would enable Lone Star to capitalize on their expertise in boot making, while maintaining their high-quality image. His wife, Laverne, is a graduate of an Oklahoma university with a similar cadet corps. She suggests a market expansion move and is encouraging Joe-Bob to negotiate a similar supply contract with additional universities. She argues that this type of growth will enable Lone Star to achieve economies of scale and thus lower their cost per boot, and that this will enable them to be a *cost leader* in the market.

Financing is not a problem, but Joe-Bob is keenly aware that the competitive issues require careful consideration. The three family members meet at the local Dairy Queen to discuss the company's future. They agree that their current strategy is one of *differentiation* focus. They have identified a specialized segment of the industry and meet those needs precisely, at an acceptable price. Joe-Bob feels that perhaps the 10 percent price premium they charge might reinforce the quality and uniqueness of Lone Star boots. They all agree that one reason their contract is secure is that unless you are a member of the corps, you cannot purchase a "Corps Special." University students have remarked over the years that an imitation boot is easy to spot. They conclude, as a result, that any strategy intending to make Lone Star a *cost leader* is both impractical and unwise.

Laverne's idea will maintain their attention on the specialized market segment, while enabling them to lower their costs. This could lead to a *cost focus* strategy. After much discussion they decide that pricing is not an important issue to their customers, and further, that lowering their price at this point might undermine their quality image. Billy also argues that since the two universities in question are rivals they might be unwilling to have boots made by the same source. Billy's idea of expanding into dress boots maintains their high-quality *differentiation* approach but for a broad target market. They reluctantly agree, however, that members of the corps might view this move as an inappropriate concern with fashion. This type of expansion might undermine Lone Star's attractiveness as a supplier, because it would allow anyone with the cash to wear a Lone Star boot. This leads the group to realize that expansion into work boots will entail the same disadvantage. The source of their *differentiation* in this target market is not only the quality of their boots, but their specialization and limited clientele. By the end of the meeting, Joe-Bob has concluded that their only viable growth strategy is to encourage members of the corps to buy new boots from Lone Star as their old boots wear out, or to expand their product line to include other leather goods that will be sold only to members of the Corps of Cadets. Perhaps belts for cadets and their spouses would work.

References

Porter, Michael E., *Competitive Strategy: Techniques for Analyzing Industries and Competitors.* New York: Free Press, 1980.

17-3. Strategic Growth Vector

An important aspect of a company's strategy is the identification of a common thread that provides a sense of direction and a unifying feature to its activities. This common thread provides guidance for organizational decision makers and permits outsiders (such as potential investors or competitors) to anticipate where a company is headed. The growth vector describes the direction a company is heading with respect to its current product and market posture (see Window 17-3).

Applying the Strategic Growth Vector Window

Many descriptions of a company's strategy are available. The Strategic Growth Vector offers an important component of strategy that recognizes the need for a unifying concept while avoiding the pitfalls of overspecification. Consideration of *mission* in conjunction with *product scope* makes several contributions to understanding a company's strategy. First, a growth vector approach is more useful than describing a company's strategy

Window 17-3. Strategic Growth Vector.

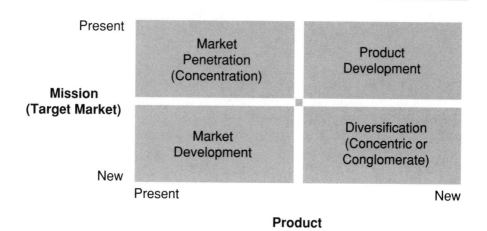

Source: H. Igor Ansoff, *The New Corporate Strategy,* New York: John Wiley & Sons, 1988, Chapter 6, p. 83.

Dimensions

Product. The *product* dimension describes the relationship between future goods and services the company intends to provide and the current range of goods and services. This dimension is segmented into products that fall within the *present* portfolio with only slight modification in product characteristics or price, and *new products* that represent a significant departure from the current goods or services offered by a company. *New products* can reflect an innovative technology, new materials, improved or altered product features, or an entirely different product group from the ones currently being produced.

Mission. The *mission* of a company describes particular uses or needs for a set of products or services. A *mission* is not the same as a target customer. Customers are the actual buyers of a product; thus, customers possess the need and the economic power to satisfy that need, as well as a choice to purchase what a particular company offers. *Mission* is also segmented into *present* and *new* categories. The *present mission* encompasses the current range of needs and uses that are satisfied by the company while a *new mission* represents an expansion or modification of its current capabilities.

Four Growth Strategies

Market penetration. In a *market penetration strategy,* also referred to as a concentration strategy, a company focuses its energies and resources on ex-

Window 17-3. (*Continued*)

panding the current business (sales of present products in present markets). This can be accomplished by increasing the rate at which current customers purchase the present product, by attracting customers away from competitors, or by encouraging nonusers who are similar to current customers to try the existing product.

Market development. With a *market development strategy*, a company relies on its current product offerings, but attempts to expand the range of uses to which these products are put (present product in new markets). This can include market expansion efforts such as extending the geographic territory, introducing a consumer product to industrial markets (e.g., selling bath oil to nursing homes), or selling an industrial product to individual consumers (e.g., offering business computers to the home market).

Product development. A *product development strategy* involves changing the existing products in some significant way or adding related items to be marketed to existing customers (new products for present market). This can include such activities as increased product differentiation (e.g., regular, diet, caffeine-free, vitamin C-added soft drinks) or the development of "families" of products (e.g., shaving cream, after-shave lotion, soap, powder, and deodorant all having the same scent).

Diversification. A *diversification* strategy entails entering new markets with new products. *Concentric* diversification is accomplished through acquiring or developing related product lines or targeting consumers with similar market characteristics. When the new product or market areas are unrelated to current activities, *conglomerate diversification* occurs. In either case a company extends both its mission and its output into new, often innovative territory.

in terms of industry boundaries. Many companies compete in a number of different industries: The boundaries of industries are continually being redefined, segmented, and described from varying perspectives; and new industries can emerge without a change in the *products* or *missions* of participant companies. A growth vector provides direction both within an industry as well as across industries.

Second, strategy refers to an organization's sense of direction and interaction with its marketplace. A growth vector approach reflects both the product/market scope of a company's strategy and the magnitude and direction of its growth expectations.

Third, the growth vector approach incorporates the concept of synergy. In *market penetration* the potential for synergy is strong due to high levels of interdependence and shared expertise. With the two development strategies, synergy often reflects marketing skills or product technology and can be key to identifying new product or market opportunities. Under *diversification*, synergy becomes the basis for an organization's unity of purpose, and understanding the sources of synergy can guide the selection of new product and market arenas.

While the model is intended as a descriptive tool, you will find that each quadrant can be enriched to identify when a particular strategy is appropriate for consideration and what common problems emerge from its implementation. In this way the growth vector can be converted to a planning device as well as a strategic illustration.

Market penetration is a particularly attractive strategy when the market in the primary business is growing or when a company has no resources or expertise to pursue other opportunities. Common problems associated with a concentration strategy include retaliation from competitors (particularly in a maturing marketplace) and increased dependence on a single product line (which often increases strategic vulnerability to technological or market shifts). For many product and market arenas, increased *penetration* is only a short-term option if growth is an important goal. If several companies that are competing for the same product/market segment choose *penetration* strategies, then saturation and dysfunctional rivalry are likely.

A *market development* strategy is an attractive option if new uses are developed for existing products or if new and untapped geographic markets are identified. This strategy is particularly inviting for companies that have demonstrated prior success at product differentiation. Common problems include cultural barriers among diverse geographic regions, unexpected costs in making a product attractive to diverse customers or users, and unanticipated market segment differences that make distribution, service, or product acceptability more difficult or expensive than expected.

A *product development* strategy is desirable when opportunities exist to prolong a product life cycle through rejuvenation or when related products emerge that expand the use of an original product. *Product development* can also be an appropriate vehicle for capitalizing on a company's image or brand association. Similar to *market development*, problems associated with this strategy include unexpected costs, unanticipated competition or retaliation, or unnoticed market differences across product lines.

In general, *diversification* is appropriate when growth potential is low within existing products and markets, when greater opportunities exist in new areas for which a company has needed expertise, and when a company has slack resources. *Concentric diversification* is desirable if a company wants to increase its efficiency or capitalize on existing synergy. *Conglomerate diversification* is attractive when a company wants to reduce the need to actively manage certain types of uncertainty or when it wishes to reduce dependency on an existing business area. Common problems associated with *concentric diversification* include increased risk potential associated with technological change, dependence on certain uncontrollable environmental events, or increased difficulty in executing widespread organizational change. Common problems associated with *conglomerate diversification* reflect increased organizational complexity and conflict. *Concentric diversification* can increase a company's ability to manage uncertainty, while *conglomerate diversification* can reduce a company's need to manage uncertainty.

The growth vector can be a useful tool for generating and describing a company's strategy, particularly when used in conjunction with other depictions of strategic components (see Windows 17-1 and 17-2 for additional information).

Advantages to Using the Window. This window into organizations is both a descriptive tool and an aid to managerial planning because it:

- Helps management analyze its current and planned strategies, leading to a classification of these strategies into *market penetration, market development, product development,* or *diversification.* Thus, the window is a descriptive tool aiding the understanding of your current and planned strategies.

- Helps the management group considering a merger or buyout by examining the relationship between its current and future product/service lines.
- Helps the management group consider expanding or moving into new product/service markets.
- Can provide insight during organizational planning as to when a strategy is appropriate and insight into problems that are likely to emerge from its implementation.

The Grid in Action. Intech Steel is a vertically integrated minimill steel company and joist and structural beam manufacturer. Intech has enjoyed a dominant position in the minimum segment of the industry due to the technological sophistication of its operation, the high levels of productivity among its work force, and strong human resource management policies. Intech has a decentralized structure and encourages shared values among employees. This, in turn, facilitates independent judgment on the shop floor and leads to effective and efficient operations. As much as 50 percent of the paychecks of many workers comes from productivity bonuses, making them among the most highly paid employees in the industry.

Intech realizes that many of its human resource compensation systems are premised on continued growth. While they believe their workers are highly skilled and highly motivated, they are reluctant to test whether or not their competitive position can be maintained during an economic downturn. Further, they are well aware that the steel industry, as well as industries that rely on steel as a raw material, are highly cyclical and often interdependent.

Andrew, who is Staff Assistant for Planning and Development, is trying to generate alternative growth projects to be considered at an upcoming general managers' meeting. The most obvious option is to increase the company's penetration among current customers. Perhaps Intech can offer volume discounts to encourage larger purchases. Since most of its sales go to large industrial users in commercial and home construction, perhaps this offer would increase sales. A shortened delivery schedule might entice some customers away from competitors. This may increase sales in the short run, but since the products are undifferentiated, switching costs are low, and this strategy could be widely copied to the disadvantage of all mini-mill operations.

A *product development* strategy seems attractive. Perhaps they could expand the range of construction products to include bolts, nuts, washers and small steel structural shapes that are similarly undifferentiated and dependent on price and delivery. This would take advantage of Intech's production strengths and would not require learning many new skills. It would provide a potential economy of scale in distribution channels as well.

Market development offers another growth option. With only minor modification, many of Intech's current products could be scaled down for the do-it-yourself homeowner. This would require the development of new marketing approaches as well as new distribution channels. Perhaps Intech's industrial reputation might provide an initial competitive advantage in the consumer market.

Diversification offers both the greatest growth opportunities and the greatest risk. If Intech can transfer its production strengths to products and markets that are independent of steel operations, it can reduce the effects of economic cycles and expand its innovative and technical capabilities. The question is: What will this do to the cohesive corporate culture that provides the underpinning for Intech's current competitive position? Can employees share a common goal and work together in a productive and decentralized way when they know very little about the product characteristics, market conditions, or other events that shape each other's competitive environment? Perhaps *diversification* will provide growth at the expense of competitiveness. Andrew is relieved he only has to make the suggestions, not decide on a course of action.

Reference

Ansoff, H. Igor. *Corporate Strategy.* New York: McGraw-Hill, 1965, Chapter 6.

17-4. Boston Consulting Group Business Portfolio Approach

The purpose of the Boston Consulting Group (BCG) Business Portfolio Approach (Window 17-4) is to categorize the businesses

(Text continues on page 332)

Window 17-4. Boston Consulting Group Business Portfolio Approach.

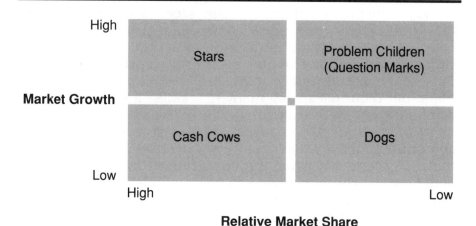

Source: John S. Hammond and Gerald B. Allan, Note on the Boston Consulting Group Concept of Competitive Analysis and Corporate Strategy, 175-175. Boston: Harvard Business School, 1975. Adapted and used with permission.

Dimensions

Market growth. This dimension indicates the *market growth* rate for a product or product group. *Market growth* rates range from low to high, and companies often use a 10 percent growth rate as a divider. Adjustments can be made to either raise or lower this measure to reflect a particular company's situation. The *market growth* dimension is often considered a proxy for industry attractiveness. The assumption is that a rapidly growing market offers greater competitive opportunities than does a market experiencing slow growth. It is also assumed that if a company has not secured a desirable position by the time its *market growth* rate falls below 10 percent, the probability of ever assuming market leadership is very low.

Relative market share. *Relative market share* is calculated by taking a company's annual dollar sales for a product and dividing this by the dollar sales of the industry's largest competitor. (If the company itself is the largest participant, then divide its product sales by the dollar sales of the next largest competitor.) Thus, a ratio of less than 1.0 will result if a company does not have the largest *market share,* and a ratio of greater than 1.0 will occur for markets in which a company is the dominant competitor. *Relative market share* is generally considered a proxy for competitive position. As described below, dominant market share permits capitalization on experience-curve cost reductions, economies of scale, and other size-related advantages.

Window 17-4. (*Continued*)

The Portfolio Matrix Categories

▨ **Problem children** (also known as question marks). Businesses categorized as *problem children* have a low *relative market share* in an industry classified as having high growth. These businesses are expected to require large cash (and other resource) investments to establish or maintain their competitive position, and even larger investment to gain share and become the *stars* of the future. Most often, *problem children* businesses are at the early stages in the product life cycle. (Product life cycles are often characterized as having introduction, growth, maturity, and decline stages.)

▨ **Stars.** Products having high market shares in high-growth industries are classified as *stars*. These businesses may be self-sufficient in terms of resources or may require modest additional investment. Additional funding is common in industries noted for high levels of technological change coupled with growth. A primary concern is to ensure that *stars* maintain their solid market position as the industry life cycle progresses (and industry growth slows), so that these businesses can become the cash generators of the future.

▨ **Cash cows**. Products that have high *market share* in slow-growth industries are classified as *cash cows*. A *cash cow* typically generates large amounts of cash, much more than can be effectively reinvested in the business. Both the product life cycle and the industry life cycle are considered mature. The competitive position does not need improvement, but only maintenance.

▨ **Dogs.** Dogs are businesses that are not expected to generate or to require substantial amounts of cash, given their low *market share* and slow *industry growth*. At times, modest funding is required to maintain even the low competitive position, and a choice must typically be made regarding an appropriate endgame strategy for the business to prevent it from becoming a cash trap (in which the continued investment of funds yields no corresponding benefits for the business or the company).

of a multidivisional company into groupings that reflect their respective competitive positions and the relative attractiveness of the industries in which they compete. This categorization leads to an assessment of the expected resource requirements and resource generating capabilities of each business. In addition, the distribution of a company's total portfolio of businesses among the four classifications suggests appropriate investment or divestment strategies for a company as a whole.

Applying the Business Portfolio Window

This model is permised on an assumed linkage between *high market share* and strong competitive position. There are two important aspects to this linkage. First, *dominant market share* is presumed to be both necessary and sufficient to provide a sustainable competitive advantage. This means that companies using this model will compete, at least in part, on price. (See Window 17-2 for additional information.) Second, profit margins and the amount of cash generated by a business are assumed to depend on *market share.* Both aspects reflect the BCG concept that experience curves link high margins with *high market share* and with low per-unit cost. Several resource-related concepts are important for interpreting the model. An increase in *market share* is presumed to require financial investment to make operations more efficient and thus permit price reductions, or to enhance product quality. Similarly, *market growth* requires financial investment if a company wishes to maintain its *market share,* because additional production capacity, more extensive distribution channels, and increased coordination of activities are often necessary.

Both product-related and industry-related life cycle effects shape a business's classification within the model. Product-related life cycles project a natural movement from *problem child,* to *star,* to *cash cow,* to *dog.* Industry-related life cycles apply vertical pressure and suggest movement from *star* to *cash cow,* and from *problem child* to *dog* if *market shares* are maintained but not improved.

Controllability is a final assumption. *Market growth* is assumed to be the result of uncontrollable, external factors while *market share* is presumed to be the consequence of investment decisions made by the company. Finally, the competitive situation is assumed to be stable, with few major new entrants, unpredictable technology changes, or shifts in industry structure.

The purpose of the BCG model is to aid a company in competitive analysis and resource-allocation decisions. As a first step, product/market business segments must be defined. Next, *product/market growth* and *relative market share* are calculated for each business. Finally, each business is plotted on the grid and portrayed by a circle in which the diameter is proportional to the dollar sales volume for the product. This charting allows for a visual analysis of the company's businesses. A trend analysis that compares past, current, and projected portfolio charts allows a company to examine how well its objectives are being met. If past investments have led to improved *market share,* and if businesses have moved in an expected manner from being cash users to cash generators, you can be confident of your past analytic and judgmental skills. If, however, investments have not led to improved competitive position, or if businesses have unexpectedly slipped from high-growth to slow-growth conditions, this is a signal that you need to reevaluate your environmental scanning and internal corporate assessment practices. Portfolio projections indicate the anticipated cash requirement and cash-generating capabilities of a company.

The distribution of products across the four quadrants indicates the internal balance of a company. Ideally, businesses with large sales volumes will appear in either the *star* or *cash cow* quadrants. There should be relatively few *problem children,* because these businesses require both large cash outlays and a great deal of managerial attention. There should be sufficient cash-generating businesses (e.g., *cows*) to fund cash users (e.g., *problem children*). Correspondingly, there should be enough businesses with cash requirements to make effective use of the resources generated by a company. Companies interested in growth would have a large proportion of businesses in the upper half of the model, while those interested in stable financial returns should have more businesses in the lower half of the model.

A company may wish to gather sufficient information on its competitors to generate portfolio charts for them. Such a competitive analysis allows a company to better anticipate the resource capabilities and investment choices of its competitors. Further, such comparisons allow a company to evaluate the potential for competitor response should it undertake an aggressive growth strategy. For example, retaliation for an attack on a *star* by a company with few other *stars* and *problem children* and a number of *cash cows* is much more likely than an aggressive response by a company with many potential cash users and few cash generators. Because the dimensions of the model are transferrable across a number of different industries, it is more generalizable than are many other portfolio models.

Perhaps the greatest contribution of this portfolio model is its ability to distill and integrate a large amount of complex and diverse information into a visually understandable and manageable format. This model is useful both as a planning tool and a control mechanism. While the resource and competitive implications of a portfolio chart are not a substitute for managerial judgment and instinct, they are a useful place to begin. Moreover, the use of a portfolio model can focus your attention on the most significant questions and areas of uncertainty.

When to Use the Window. An analysis of an organization's *market share* and *relative market share* enables management to place each of its business units into this window, thereby facilitating an analysis of the organization's business holdings. The window should be used:

- If your organization is currently multidivisional
- If your organization is considering internally or externally generated expansion that will result in its becoming multidivisional
- When you are interested in assessing the expected resource requirements of each business unit
- When you are interested in assessing the resource-generating capability of each business
- When you are interested in identifying an appropriate investment or divestment strategy for the organizaion as a whole
- When you are involved in a competitive analysis and resource-allocation decisions
- When you are interested in assessing the nature of your competitors

The Grid in Action. The planning staff of Playtime Toy Company meets to evaluate their current portfolio and to consider resource allocations for the coming year. Across their product line, *market share* seems to be a reliable indicator of profitability. In part this is attributable to lower production and marketing costs associated with higher volumes, and in part it seems to reflect the buying patterns of Playtime's customers. Once a toy reaches a critical mass of purchases, it often seems to sell itself as more children want exactly the toy the neighbor child has. As the toy industry matures, increasing segmentation occurs. Different segments seem to be in different stages of their life cycle and certainly demonstrate widely different growth prospects.

The first step in the process is to plot Playtime's product groups on a growth/share matrix. Their largest revenues come from board games ($3.7 million). Board games have a dominant position in the industry segment, but the *market growth rate* is only about 5 percent. This puts board games in the *cash cow* category. Another *cash cow* is their baby book products. *Pat the Walrus* and other titles generate $2.3 million for Playtime each year. Playtime has a number of product lines in rapidly growing market segments, many of which are growing at a rate of 15 to 18 percent annually. None of these products has established a dominant position as yet, which classifies them as *problem children.* The computer game line ($1 million sales) and the preschool educational toys ($1.5 million) are strong contenders, but facing stiff competition from larger and more well-known companies. The scientific toys ($.7 million) are a relatively new entry and have not had much time to establish their competitive position. The sports equipment line ($.8 million) has been slipping in recent years. The mechanical games ($1.3 million) are improving competitively, but are still way behind the two leading contenders in this segment. Finally, Playtime's dolls ($1.6 million) have captured a small but stable portion of this slow growth segment of the industry. This classifies dolls as a *dog.*

For the most part, the resource characteristics of these businesses are typical for their placement on the growth/share matrix. The *problem children* operations are all heavy cash users. Board games provide a large and sustained cash overflow, but this represents only about half the cash needed by the high-growth businesses. Baby books generate more profits than are needed to maintain their position, but competition is increasing while demand has slowed, requiring high proportions of the revenues to be reinvested each year. The doll line is profitable and able to contribute resources to the growth businesses, but it is not clear whether these profits can be sustained over a long time horizon.

The planning staff identifies two serious problems with Playtime's current portfolio. First, it does not have enough long-term cash-generating businesses to fund all of its current "cash users." As a result, it is often investing too little too late in its growth businesses. This has led to Playtime's second problem area. It does not have a *star* (dominant competitor in a growth business) to become the cash generator of the future. Clearly, if Playtime wants to be successful over the long term, it must consolidate its efforts. The planning staff decide to divest their sports equipment lines, since it is unlikely they will ever achieve a dominant position in this segment. Further, they decide to lease the rights to their computer games. This eliminates the operating costs and provides a modest new source of revenues. Playtime can now concentrate on its remaining high-growth businesses. The staff realize there is a potential for synergy among preschool educational toys, mechanical games that can be refocused toward skill development and learning mechanical and spatial relationships, and the scientific toys that can be marketed as self-education devices.

Since the dolls are profitable, the planning staff decide to maintain their position in this line. Looking to the future, they begin thinking about developing a line of anatomically correct dolls to revitalize this segment and adding a new growth area to their educational toys once the preschool toys and mechanical games move into the *star* quadrant.

References

Christensen, H. Kurt., Arnold C. Cooper, and C. A. DeKluyver. "The 'Dog' Business: A Reexamination." *Proceedings of the 41st Annual Meeting of the Academy of Management*, 1981, pp. 26–30.

Haspeslagh, P. "Portfolio Planning: Uses and Limits." *Harvard Business Review*, Vol. 60 (1982), p. 58.

Hofer, Charles, and Dan Schendel. *Strategy Formulation: Analytical Concepts.* St. Paul: West Publishing, 1978.

Chapter 18

Stress!

Stress is a problem that seriously affects the health of many employees—and the bottom-line performance of numerous organizations. Each year industry incurs an astonishing $150 billion in stress-related costs including higher insurance premiums, absenteeism costs, diminished productivity, and training cost increases when employees leave the organization due to stress.

Employees who feel they have little or no control over their working environment tend to feel the effects of stress. In large organizations with highly detailed job descriptions due to specialization, an individual performing a small part of the overall operation may feel easily expendable. In other situations the employee's work is so standardized and routine that no creative individual input is expected or even desired. Unreasonable deadlines, a heavy workload, or an inability to feel successful no matter how much of an effort is made are other reasons for high stress levels within organizations.

The dilemma you face is that both too much and too little stress is detrimental. In fact, optimal productivity and creativity do not occur when all stress is eliminated, but when you try to find an optimal level of stress. The general relationship between stress and performance is an inverted U-shaped curve, in which the presence of a moderate level of stress actually increases productivity and is psychologically beneficial to the employee. However, the optimum level is difficult to find because it varies from individual to individual. Clearly, beyond a certain point stress becomes counterproductive for both the individual and the organization.

In order to deal effectively with stress among employees, you need to recognize conditions in which it arises, understand it, and anticipate employee reactions to it. This chapter provides two models that focus on employee responses to stress.

18-1. Responses to Stress

Stress arises whenever individuals interact with their environment. The result is a bodily reaction to the demands placed. Although organizational stress has often been viewed by most experts as dysfunctional, a certain level of stress is necessary to stimulate employees to meet objectives. Higher levels of stress may even lead to individual creativity and high levels of productivity. Since stress is a fact of life, the key issue centers around the ability of an individual to control and utilize stress.

The purpose of Window 18-1 is to distinguish between four basic patterns of individual responses to stress. By understanding these patterns in your employees and yourself, you can better promote creativity and productivity in the stressful situations employees face daily.

Applying the Responses to Stress Window

Practically any event or situation in an organization that puts heavy physical or psychological demands on people is a potential source of stress. Some stressors, however, must be present if organizational goals are to be accomplished. Work environments that have extremely *low frequencies* of stress incidents coupled with *low magnitudes* of stress sometimes do not stimulate the attainment of organizational goals. In the absence of some stress, many employees are likely to feel little pressure to achieve and may view the workplace more as a place for socialization and relaxation. An *energizing* level of stress means that attention is paid to attaining organizational goals and that all employees know what is expected of them. It also suggests that adequate time and resources are available to allow goals to be reached. *Destructive* stress may mean that organiza-

Window 18-1. Responses to Stress.

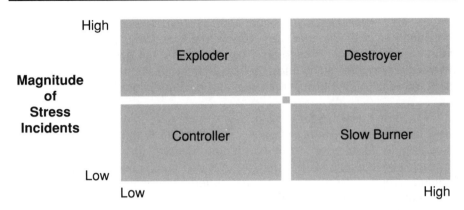

Frequency of Stress Incidents

Source: Adapted from Robert Kreitner, "Managing the Two Faces of Stress," *Arizona Business,* October 1977, pp. 9–14.

Dimensions

Frequency of stress incidents. This dimension examines *how often* stress incidents occur, which ranges from low to high. An employee who is high on this dimension frequently encounters a variety of stressful situations. Although each single incident may be minor, the cumulative effects may produce a destructive response in the individual, which may also be dysfunctional to the organization.

Magnitude of stress incidents. This dimension records the *intensity* of stress incidents. Employees who are high in this dimension encounter highly potent stress situations, such as critical resource shortages, accidents, or mechanical breakdowns. If even a few such incidents accumulate during a short period of time, the employee may become consumed with frustration and "boil over," which leads to destructive responses within the organization.

Four Ways of Responding

Exploder. Some individuals experience *high-magnitude* stress events, but only *infrequently.* When this occurs, they literally *explode* (perhaps vocally) due to the sudden extreme pressure. This *exploder* type of response is destructive and manifests itself in high emotional peaks in which the stress situation becomes so intense that the individual is unable to control an emotional response. Consequently, the *exploder* may either become argumentative, irrational, or even physically violent. Reactions that are unexpected and intense can cause significant personal, interpersonal, and physical damage.

Window 18-1. (*Continued*)

Destroyer. *Destroyers* experience *frequent* stress of a *high magnitude*. Individuals in this category are overwhelmed by stress intensity, and as a consequence they often become programmed for self-destruction. This self-destructive response can manifest itself in physical (i.e., heart attacks, headaches, gastrointestinal difficulties) and/or mental (i.e., depression) problems.

Slow burner. Some individuals experience relatively *low-magnitude* stress incidents, but with *high frequency*. Individuals in this category often lead "lives of quiet desperation" or are considered "martyrs" (because they outwardly appear to be coping well). This type of individual, however, experiences a buildup of repressed responses and often suffers a physical consequence such as a heart attack that occurs for no apparent reason. *Slow burners* may not appear to represent a problem to the organization, but they are certainly a potential danger to themselves.

Controller. A *controller* is an individual who experiences primarily *low-magnitude* stress events, and even those occur only *infrequently*. An individual in this category is experiencing energizing stress, in that these low-to-moderate levels of stress actually increase his/her ability to respond creatively and productively to deadlines or challenging goals. Since stress is created through an individual's interaction with the environment, energizing stress is partially a product of the nature of the individual and partially a product of the employee's surroundings.

---

tional goals are set too high to be readily attainable (and that punishments will follow if goals are not realized), time pressures are excessive, or resources (financial, human, or technical) are not readily available when needed.

Individuals also face stressors in nonwork environments (e.g., death of a spouse, personal financial problems). You should therefore be aware that a cumulative effect is possible even though the *frequency* and *magnitude* of stressors in the workplace is minimal. A manager who thinks that an employee is experiencing dysfunctional stress should attempt to identify what stressors (internal or external to the work environment) are causing this problem. However, don't assume that work environment stressors should be changed. Some stressors may be destructive for some employees and energizing for others.

Considerations to Make When Using the Window. To maximize the energizing stress found in the working environment, you should:

- Allow employees to participate in setting their own work goals and performance standards. Input into these types of decisions has a twofold benefit: (1) Employees know what is expected of them (and why), which in turn makes "individual planning" easier and more relevant to organizational goals; and (2) employees are likely to feel they are an important part of the organization, which in turn minimizes unnecessary stress about job security.
- Attempt to identify an employee who is experiencing excessive stress *before* a destructive response occurs. Warning signs might include difficulty in making decisions, increases in the number of careless mistakes, problems interacting and getting along with others, missing deadlines, working late more than usual, and/or increased tardiness and absenteeism. Your recognition of these warning signs should result in increased communication with the individual and possible adjustments in the work environment (extending deadlines, giving positive reinforcements, clarification of job responsibilities) to minimize the stressors.
- Classify employees as *destroyers, exploders, controllers,* or *slow burners.* Since stress is the product of an individual-environment interaction, prospective employees should also be screened in an attempt to match them with work environment demands. This may, of course, add a whole new dimension to the selection process.

The Grid in Action. "Replacing Janine is more difficult than I ever expected," Mark Denton states at the monthly managers' meeting. "We've hired four payroll clerks in the last seven months and all of them have quit. They all blamed a heavy workload and stringent weekly payroll check deadlines. Janine could always handle the work and never complained. These younger people just expect a 'free ride.' I don't have time to be constantly interviewing job applicants for this clerical position. Any suggestions?"

Sheila Killian, manager of the Fiscal Services Department of the large heavy equipment firm, clears her throat. "Well—it's always been difficult to keep people in those clerical positions that demand overtime almost weekly, because the stress and fatigue do take their toll. Janine was only 48 when she had her heart attack and died. Maybe the job content contributed to her demise. In my department I've tried to take those types of jobs and break up the tasks into two positions. The department's overall productivity may not be higher, but I've reduced the employee turnover rate by 23 percent and training costs are also way down. I'm even experimenting with flextime and job sharing. The atmosphere seems less tense and I haven't been confronted with nearly as many internal interpersonal conflicts. Also, absenteeism is no longer the major problem it once was."

Mark quickly responds, "Now you're accusing me of killing Janine. Her problem was *not* the job but all of the family members living off her. Her sister and her two small children had lived with Janine for over a year and no one even tried to work except Janine. *Plus* I have no budget for additional personnel! Sheila, you're living in a dream world. If I don't have time to interview applicants for one position, how can I *possibly* start splitting jobs and have people coming and going whenever they please? I'm manager of the payroll department, and everyone in the organization is on my back if their payroll checks aren't on time. I just need a dependable person like Janine. Sheila, don't contribute stupid suggestions—I have no time for that either!!!"

As Mark rises and storms out of the meeting, the other six managers sit in stunned silence. Finally Sheila stands and exclaims, "I guess Mark didn't agree with my suggestion. My labor costs have actually decreased due to much less costly overtime even though headcount has increased. Probably, though, Mark won't want to hear about that."

A third manager adds, "Mark's always been hesitant to take advice even though he solicits suggestions. Let's adjourn and see what happens. Maybe he'll get lucky and find a person who will stay with the payroll clerk's job. If not, we'll talk about it at next month's meeting."

Janine, the diligent and conscientious payroll clerk, had apparently been a *slow burner.* Although she never complained and was willing to work long and hard, the stress level was high and frequent in her job. The organization did nothing to alleviate this and now it is faced with replacement problems. Mark, as an *exploder,* finds himself facing a high level of stress in terms of department productivity, and he reacts in a confrontational manner. Sheila, exhibiting the characteristics of a *controller*, has minimized the stress level by solving problems as they occur and now finds herself in an environment with an energizing level of stress.

Reference

Selye, Hans. *The Stress of Life.* New York: McGraw-Hill, 1956.

18-2. Coping With Stress

Stress, in an organizational sense, can be described as a feeling of pressure to fulfill job responsibilities and meet deadlines. Not all stress is harmful, and at least some measure of stress is necessary to meet corporate objectives. The ability to control or reduce high levels of stress down to a manageable level requires the use of coping responses by employees.

The purpose of Window 18-2 is to distinguish between various types of employee reactions to stressful situations. In particular, this framework describes the various actions or psychological reactions that employees use to cope with negative stress in their working environments. By understanding these possible responses among your employees, you can better predict *reactions* to stress. Hopefully, you can also take positive action to affect employee behaviors.

Applying the Coping with Stress Window

You should recognize that although stress will (and should) exist in the workplace to some degree, *excessive* stress can cause dysfunctional responses. Stress can lead to lower productivity, higher absenteeism and/or turnover, job dissatisfaction, and difficulties in communication. Employees will not always identify a stressful environment, nor will they necessarily apply a *problem-solving* response. Instead they may choose to cope with a stressful situation that they feel cannot be changed through *problem toleration, problem minimization* and/or *symptom minimization.*

You can best address stress problems by:

Window 18-2. Coping With Stress.

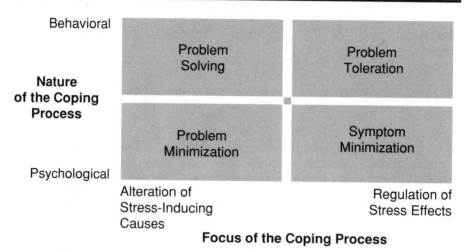

Source: Adapted from David M. Herold and Edward J. Conlon, "Alcohol Consumption as a Coping Response to Job-Induced Stress," *Academy of Management Proceedings*, 1982, pp. 292–296 (Figure 1, p. 292).

Dimensions

Nature of the coping process. This dimension identifies whether the response to stress is behavioral or psychological in nature. Both responses tend to change the situation to reduce the stress experienced by the individual. One approach is by taking direct action, and the other achieves its result by modifying a perception of the situation.

Focus of the coping process. This dimension records whether the employee actively seeks to change the causes or the effects of the stressful situation. It suggests that employees have two major options—addressing the problem or dealing with the symptoms. They can attempt to reduce the discomfort they feel by striving to solve the problem permanently if they are able. Alternatively, they can simply try to minimize the effects if problem resolution is not an available (or desirable) alternative.

Four Coping Responses

Problem solving. This is an action-oriented response to the causes of a stressful situation. Here employees have several options. They may either attempt to clearly identify the problem to others who have the ability to change it, solve the problem unilaterally, or take action (such as leaving the organization) to permanently separate themselves from the cause of stress.

Window 18-2. (*Continued*)

▪ **Problem toleration.** Another overt response toward the problem, but one that more likely addresses symptoms, is *problem toleration.* In this case employees try to minimize the stress experienced by one of two means. They may actively redirect their conscious energies into other activities (such as hobbies, increased physical activity, and/or participation in social organizations). Alternatively, they may learn to better *tolerate* the situation through the use of relaxation techniques or simple acceptance of the stressful situation.

▪ **Symptom minimization.** A psychological response to a stressful situation may also be appropriate, in which the employee attempts to *minimize* the stress *symptoms* experienced. This can be done through activities such as sleeping, daydreaming, alcohol consumption, and/or denial. In this quadrant there is no change in the actual problem situation itself, but only an attempt to physically or psychologically avoid the stress-induced pain.

▪ **Problem minimization.** A psychological response to a stressful situation wherein the employee attempts to change his/her perception of the stressor is termed *problem minimization.* An employee *minimizes problems* by reducing any possible negative consequences, increasing his/her ability to deal with the stressful environment, or redefining the stressful situation to make it feel less threatening.

- Minimizing the negative personal costs suffered by employees who identify such problem areas
- Providing resources such as counseling or social networks for employees experiencing excessive stress in situations that cannot be easily changed
- Acting as a role model in constructively coping with stressful circumstances

You should also recognize that an individual's choice of a coping strategy is influenced by what has proved successful in the past for him/her. Thus, in an organizational climate that rewards individuals for "not rocking the boat" and "being part of the team," it will be difficult to move quickly to a climate where more openness in voicing problems is expected.

Managers who expect stressful situations to occur in the workplace should clearly tell employees that such problems can be openly discussed and will be changed if possible. This leads employees toward *problem solving,* because they perceive a stressful situation as a standard occurrence and not necessarily a problem to be hidden from others. This type of open atmosphere leads to fewer of the negative consequences that often occur if a less overt coping strategy is chosen.

The specificity of stress factors may influence the choice of coping responses by employees. For example, if the problem area can be pinpointed (i.e., one individual's management style, one particular project or job function) there is a greater likelihood that an individual may feel that a solution is possible and be able to articulate the problem. If the stress is coming from a variety of sources that prevail across the entire organization, the coping response may be less overt. Therefore, one task for you involves helping employees isolate specific stressors in their work (and even nonwork) environments.

When to Use the Window. This grid can be useful when you wish to:

- *Predict* how an employee will behave under stress. Knowledge of prior behavioral responses in similar situations can help immensely.
- Examine an employee's reaction to stress and explore the *reasons* for an employee's choice of a particular response pattern.
- Become more adept at managing your *own* reactions to stress. Here, the window can provide a framework for classifying the nature of your typical response and pointing out more viable alternatives.
- Discuss with an employee the dysfunctional effects (on both employee and on others) of various reactions to stress. Often, employees are unaware that there are any external impacts, and open discussion combined with a meaningful framework may help them gain some useful insight.

The Grid in Action. Joe Campbell is worried about his future with the company. He is employed as foreman of a night-shift production line in a pharmaceutical firm. Productivity on his shift is 12 percent below that of the day shift, even though historically productivity at night has always outpaced that of the day group. Joe knows that something is drastically wrong. He has already spoken with Bill Cartwright, a senior member of the crew and the informal leader of the line employees, but has gotten little help in identifying the problem.

Joe decides he will have to speak individually to each of the eight people he supervises to determine the nature of the problem, or even his job may be in jeopardy. The division manager has often mentioned eliminating the night shift entirely, and only the previously high productivity levels have prevented such drastic action in the past.

As Marie Blake enters Joe's office later that evening, he is already discouraged. None of the three previous employees he talked to have been able (or willing) to identify any problems that could be affecting production levels. Marie is visibly shaking as she enters the office and almost immediately begins to cry. She blurts out, "I'll tell, but please don't say it was me!" Then she proceeds to describe how three of the eight line employees are using cocaine regularly. She identifies Bill Cartwright as one of the individuals and says the problem escalated when rumors of the night shift phaseout spread throughout the plant. The five other crew members tried to be more productive to make up for the lack of performance by the other three, but it was not possible. Marie feels that if the others could just improve on the faster pace, the problem would go away.

Although Joe is shocked at this news, he is also somewhat relieved to discover the cause of the low productivity levels. The company has a drug-testing policy in place and Joe can implement a random test for each of the individuals on the line quickly. He can also meet with the whole group to reassure them about their job security after speaking with the division manager in regard to the rumor. If in fact Bill Cartwright and the other two employees are found to be using narcotics, they will be given a chance to rehabilitate themselves through the company's Employee Assistance Program. If they do not succeed, they will be terminated. Joe feels that productivity levels will soon return to their previous high levels.

Bill Cartwright's drug use is an example of *symptom minimization*. The fear of losing his job is so stressful that he chooses to avoid it through this psychological response. Marie Blake uses *problem minimization* by trying to compensate for loss of productivity on the line while hoping the drug use will cease. Joe's response to this situation is an illustration of the use of *problem solving,* since Joe feels he can reduce the stress level for both himself and his employees by directly confronting both the drug use problem and by defusing the "phaseout" rumor. The employees on the line who are not involved in drug use but are not as brave as Marie in coming forward are exhibiting a *problem toleration* response to the situation.

Reference

Davidson, M. J., and C. L. Cooper. "A Model of Occupational Stress." *Journal of Occupational Medicine,* Vol. 23 (1981), pp. 564–574.

Chapter 19

Training and Human Resource Development

Training and human resource development represents a large part of most human resource management budgets and consumes a major amount of direct and indirect supervisory time. Since training also reflects an organization's willingness to invest in its human resources, decisions in this area must be made with good information and sound decision-making practices. You (and trainers) require tools for improving your ability to train and develop employees.

The windows in this chapter help you pinpoint the types of information necessary to make sound training and development decisions. In addition, these windows also provide you and trainers with an understanding of the training and development process, enabling you to see how specific decisions (e.g., what employee characteristics to consider in the design of a training program) fit into the overall objective (e.g., to build and maintain a competitive work force).

The windows presented here focus on specific attributes of trainees (Learning Styles and Trainee Socialization) as well as on the entire development process (Employee Development Plans). They emphasize fulfilling the needs of the organization to have a competent and competitive work force by performing careful needs analysis and trainee assessments. Furthermore, different people have different learning styles (preferences for learning process) that must be considered in the design of any training or development experience. People also respond differently to organizational norms (both pivotal and peripheral), and this affects the ability of you or a trainer to utilize specific training and development methods.

Besides assessing specific characteristics of trainees in order to tailor or fit an appropriate training and development approach to employees, you must also determine what is an appropriate investment in your individual human resources. Analyzing the past performance levels and future potential of employees is a useful aid in making these decisions.

All managers are, in effect, human resource managers. People are resources that must be managed well for an organization to remain competitive and survive. Through training and development, you can have a major impact on the effectiveness of people in your organization. The windows in this chapter will help you improve your decision making in this vital area.

19-1. Learning Styles

Learning involves bringing about a change of behavior. Effective learning is a process that follows a four-stage cycle: (1) concrete experience, followed by (2) observation and reflection, which leads to (3) the formation of abstract concepts and generalizations, which leads to (4) assumptions (hypotheses) to be tested in future action. The cycle can then be repeated by testing the hypotheses through new concrete experiences (see Window 19-1). Recognition of employee learning styles (preferences for one or more of the four stages) is important because it determines how they will learn most effectively.

Applying the Learning Styles Window

This window can be used to group individuals with similar learning styles in a training environment. After trainees complete the Learning Style Inventory,[1] they can be grouped by

---

1. The Learning Style Inventory is copyrighted by David A. Kolb (1976) and distributed by McBer and Co., 137 Newbury St., Boston, MA 02116. Further information on theory, construction, reliability, and validity of the inventory is reported in *The Learning Style Inventory: Technical Manual*, available from McBer and Co.

Window 19-1. Learning Styles.

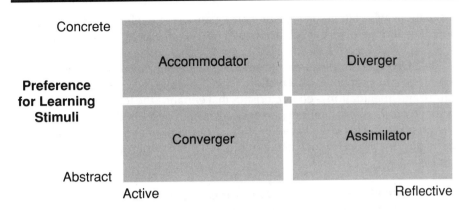

Preference for Learning Process

Source: Donald Wolfe and David Kolb, "Career Development, Personal Growth, and Experiential Learning," in *Organizational Psychology: Readings on Human Behavior in Organizations* (4th ed.), Copyright © 1984, pp. 124–152. Adapted by permission of Prentice-Hall, Inc., Englewood Cliffs, New Jersey.

Dimensions

Preference for learning process. This represents an individual's relative *preference* for a reflective or an active approach to learning. A *reflective* approach implies learning by thinking about your observations and prior experiences or thinking through the implications of a hypothetical situation. An *active* approach, on the other hand, often implies learning by doing, consciously thinking about experiences as they occur (and trying to make sense of them), or experiential learning.

Preference for learning stimuli. This describes an individual's *preferences* for thinking about stimuli that are *abstract* (e.g., working with mathematical variables in a calculus problem) or *concrete* (e.g., examining a work-related tool). A *preference for abstract stimuli* is associated with quantitative analysis and theory building. A *preference for concrete stimuli* is associated with feelings, intuition, and artistic creation.

Four Learning Styles

Converger. A person with a *convergent learning style* prefers abstract conceptualization and active experimentation. This learning style relies on unemotional and objective scientific logic and deductive reasoning. It fits well

Window19-1. (*Continued*)

in situations where there is a single correct answer. People who do well in engineering and the physical sciences often have *convergent* learning styles.

■ **Diverger.** Employees with a *divergent learning style* prefer concrete experiences and reflective observation. This learning style relies on emotion, values, and imagination—characteristics that enhance the learner's ability to see a situation from many different perspectives. Often described as "touchy-feely," these people tend to do well academically in humanities and the liberal arts. Professionally, they excel in such occupations as human resources management and counseling.

■ **Assimilator.** An *assimilation learning style* is characteristic of people who prefer abstract concepts and reflective observation. This learning style relies on inductive reasoning and integration, characteristics that allow the learner to piece together unrelated and abstract ideas into logically consistent theories. *Assimilators* do well in the basic sciences, where understanding how and why is more important than practical applications. They succeed in professions where they have freedom to pursue their ideas (e.g., a researcher in a large, flexibly run organization).

■ **Accommodator.** A person with an *accommodative learning style* prefers concrete experience and active experimentation. *Accommodators* rely on intuition and adaptation, characteristics that allow them to jump into a situation and modify theories as the need arises. These people often have the ability to think quickly on their feet. *Accommodators* do well in professional schools, such as business schools, and succeed in many areas of business (e.g., salespeople, entrepreneurs).

category *(accommodators, assimilators, convergers, divergers)* to work on case analyses, group discussions, or other *similar* tasks. This is an effective way of using the strengths inherent in similar styles to enhance learning.

Alternatively, trainers could wish to use Learning Style Inventory data to group people with *different* learning styles together, so group members are exposed to different approaches. This could enhance understanding both the process of learning as well as the content of learning.

A problem can occur when there is more than one learning style represented in a group of trainees and it is not possible to use homogeneous groups. What are your options? First, you may choose the most common (modal) learning style in the group of trainees and adapt your training program to it. Employees who have difficulty adapting to the dominant class mode can be given personal attention.

Second, the Learning Style Inventory scores for a group could be averaged, yielding an "average learning style" for the group. Training approaches could then follow this group average learning style. However, you may risk neglecting some important subgroups.

You might also choose to alternate the training approaches so that for some sessions one learning style is emphasized, while for other sessions the trainer emphasizes a different learning style. This could be accomplished by following the recommended sequence from concrete experience to observation and reflection leading to the formation of abstract concepts and generalizations resulting in hypothesis testing. This is an effective way to use variety and provide an opportunity for trainees with different learning styles to display their strengths.

Preferences for learning styles can also be used as a part of a comprehensive career management system. If jobs can be identified (through job analysis) that require a dominant learning style, individual employees can be provided information about potentially good fits based on their learning style preferences.

Group averages on the Learning Style Inventory can also be used to characterize departmental or unit learning styles. This in turn could be used to describe different styles between units, providing useful information to the human resource planners. Furthermore, to the extent that conflict is caused by the inability of people with different learning styles to communicate, this model may provide insight into the cause of a difficult problem.

A final word of caution is suggested. Because learning style inventories tend to measure different attributes, it is wise to use more than one of them. This provides additional information about preferred learning styles of your trainees.

There are several other learning style inventories frequently used by trainers for assessing trainees. These are described in greater detail in the Info-Line issue on training and learning styles (see References).

1. The *Productivity Environmental Preference Survey* (PEPS) (developed by Rita Dunn) assesses a person's preferred physical environment, emotionality, sociological needs, and physical needs for learning.

2. The *Grasha-Reichmann Learning Style Inventory* (developed by Anthony F. Grasha and Sheryl Riechmann-Hruska) is most appropriate for college-age employees. It measures how students prefer to deal with data and information.

3. The *Canfield Instructional Style Inventory and Canfield Learning Style Inventory* (developed by Albert Canfield) assesses preferences for conditions, content, mode of learning, and expectation for success.

4. Gregorc's Style Delineator (developed by Anthony Gregorc) categorizes learners into four categories: abstract random (nonlinear) learners, abstract sequential (well-organized) learners, concrete sequential (step-by-step) learners, and concrete random (trial-and-error) learners.

5. The *4MAT Survey Battery* (developed by Bernice McCarthy) categorizes learners as innovative ("Give me a reason"), analytic ("Teach it to me"), commonsense ("How does this work?"), and dynamic ("What can become of this?")

6. Malcolm Knowles provided a general model for describing how people learn. He proposed that adults have learning styles that are different from children and that training methods for adults must be based on different principles. He described *pedagogy* as an approach where trainers assume full responsibility for making all decisions about what should be learned, how it should be learned, when it should be learned, and whether it should be learned. In contrast, *andragogy* actively involves trainees in the learning process, determining what, how, and when learning takes place. Knowles argued that adults should be taught using the principles of andragogy and not pedagogy.

When to Use the Window. Managers, human resource departments, seminars, training and development laboratories (centers), and university-sponsored executive development programs are just a few examples of vehicles through which training is conducted. In each case there is a need to identify the learning styles of the trainees. Specifically, this window into organizations can be used when you are:

- Trying to recognize the type of learning experiences to design for a particular individual (employee)
- Selecting trainees (participants) for a particular training experience
- Engaged in career counseling as a part of the human resources development program
- Grouping individuals for participation in a training environment while attempting to construct a homogeneous (or heterogeneous) class

The Grid in Action. Janice gets a call from Chuck requesting that she help him get started on his new personal computer. She tells Chuck that she is tied up for the rest of the afternoon with meetings, but that she can meet him tomorrow at 10 A.M. in his office. Chuck says he will just wait until then before he starts using the new system. After all, Chuck has never used a personal computer before, and he is afraid that he will damage it if he tries to learn it on his own. He thinks it will be best if he does not read the numerous technical manuals that accompany the new computer until after he has talked with Janice. That way, he can "see it first" and then learn how it works afterwards.

Janice realizes that Chuck is a *diverger,* someone who prefers concrete experience and reflective observation. Thus, if she can "walk him through" some of the basics in using his new computer, Chuck will be able to understand the detailed technical manuals that accompany most personal computers. Furthermore, he will probably be able to generalize from his experience and quickly become proficient on his new computer. In fact, the "Read Me First" part of Chuck's computer instructions suggests just such a method. The instructions urge the new owner to read the introductory chapter and then get started using "your new, powerful work aid."

Janice types into her computer notepad a brief outline of what she will go over with Chuck the following day. She tries to identify the fundamental tasks, such as creating and saving files, in order to give Chuck an overview of the more important skills he will need to learn. Then, she searches her own files for one that will provide a good demonstration for Chuck. She finds a file that contains some typical information used at the company, copies it, and puts it on a disk to give Chuck the following day during their discussion.

The next day Janice spends two hours with Chuck answering his numerous questions as she tells him what to type on his keyboard. Chuck even persuades her to come back for an hour after lunch (which he pays for, at an elegant restaurant!) to continue their session. Janice leaves the demonstration disk with Chuck and tells him that he can give her a call "almost anytime" he runs across a problem he cannot solve. Chuck thanks her and spends the remainder of the day practicing the skills Janice has taught him. That night, after dinner, Chuck stays up late reading his new computer manuals, periodically waking his sleeping wife with such phrases as "Oh, now I get it!" Six months later Chuck becomes his department's "computer jock," routinely answering detailed questions about personal computers. This occurs because the learning style of the trainee (Chuck) was accurately assessed as being *divergent* and the teaching approach of the trainer (Janice) was effectively matched to optimize the learning environment.

Reference

Training and Learning Styles. Info-Line, Issue 804, American Society for Training and Development, 1988.

19-2. Trainee Socialization

Norms of group behavior are major factors in determining how well both groups and individuals within groups perform. Norms are the expected or accepted ways of behaving within a group. While norms are often elusive and difficult to measure, they can have tremendous influence within an organization.

If managed effectively, norms can contribute to organizational performance. If managed ineffectively, they can drastically undermine even the most carefully designed management programs. Because of the effect of group norms on organizational performance, they should be carefully considered in the design and implementation phases of training and development programs.

Window 19-2 encourages you to assess the degree of employee acceptance of group norms (or trainee socialization). They can be defined at any level (e.g., department, plant, company), providing different possibilities for levels of analysis. In addition to determining trainees' socialization to learn, this window can also be used to assess whether employees conform to organizational norms, which is important for any manager to understand.

Applying the Trainee Socialization Window

Trainee socialization to learn is a part of *organizational socialization*, which refers to the teaching of the organization's goals, norms, values, and preferred ways of doing things. "This is the way we do things around here" or "Here are the ropes to skip and the ropes to know" are common phrases heard by new employees in corporate hallways.

Socialization is usually viewed as a gradual process that begins at the time a new employee enters an organization and continues throughout his/her career. In terms of this window, new employees may start their careers with a "conservative" approach by accepting both pivotal and peripheral norms *(conformists)*. Over time, as they learn more about the organization and their roles in it, employees may choose to become *game players, rebels,* or *creative individualists.* Some people believe that organizations should create conditions that make it possible for members to be *creative individualists* rather than *conformists* or *rebels.*

Training norms are also related to *organizational (or corporate) culture,* which is comprised of the beliefs and assumptions shared by members of an organization. A company may have a dominant culture, but this is probably more accurately described as many subcultures in different units and levels. Norms are but one of the many means by which organizational culture is communicated to employees.

There are two types of norms you must consider. First, what are the *pivotal* and *peripheral norms* of the *work group* (department, plant, or whole company)? Does the training program's design take advantage of current norms to facilitate learning?

(Text continues on page 360)

Window 19-2. Trainee Socialization.

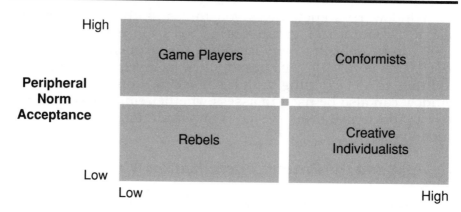

Pivotal Norm Acceptance

Source: Edgar H. Schein, *Organizational Psychology* (2nd ed.), Copyright 1970, pp. 78–79. Adapted by permission of Prentice-Hall, Inc., Englewood Cliffs, New Jersey.

Dimensions

Pivotal norm acceptance. *Pivotal norms* are central and necessary for learning and development to occur. Without *acceptance* of *pivotal norms*, it is unlikely that learning and development will take place. *Pivotal norms* may stem from trainer preferences, the organizational culture, or the nature of the training content. For traditional (academic) training they may include regular attendance, punctuality, and handed-in typed assignments. In an experiential classroom they may include sharing learning responsibility between trainer and trainee, and active trainee participation. A low rating on this dimension would indicate a *rejection of pivotal norms*, while a high evaluation would indicate *acceptance of them.*

Peripheral norm acceptance. These are "hoped for" behaviors that are important, but not absolutely necessary, for learning and development to occur in a specific training program. These behaviors might enhance or facilitate learning and development. However, lack of *peripheral norm acceptance* will not *prevent* learning and development from taking place. Examples in a traditional setting may include additional reading outside of class and discussing personal examples of class concepts. Examples in an experiential setting may include submitting papers on time and in the desired format and maintaining a formal relationship between trainer and trainee. A trainee who rates low on this dimension *rejects peripheral norms,* while a trainee rating high on this dimension readily *accepts* them.

Window 19-2. (*Continued*)

Types of Trainees

■ **Game players**. Trainees who *reject pivotal norms* but *accept peripheral norms* are *game players*. These trainees may provide personal insights in a discussion or read an "optional" reading assignment (*peripheral norm acceptance*). However, they may hand in their required papers late and the papers may not be in compliance with the required format (*rejection of pivotal norms*). While they may be ready to learn and make significant contributions to the learning experience of others, *game players* are difficult to evaluate because they don't adhere to *pivotal norms*. *The trainer's dilemma* is whether to reward *game players* for their contribution or withhold rewards because of their lack of acceptance of *pivotal norms*. *Game players* create the same dilemma in their daily jobs. They make contributions (e.g., occasional good ideas) that positively affect the organization, yet they don't meet critical deadlines, or conform to standards.

■ **Conformists.** Employees who *accept* both *pivotal and peripheral* norms are *conformists*. *Conformists* in their everyday job performance are often called "organization men/women." They are loyal but not very creative. In a learning environment, however, conformists outwardly look like the ideal trainees. For example, they do all of the required and optional work. Thus, they are receptive to the entire training and development effort. A *conformist's* performance in a training program would be affected by his/her ability. A high-ability conformist would perform well on training outcome measures. On the other hand, a low-ability conformist would not perform well on training outcome measures (the stereotypical hard worker whose efforts don't result in effective performance).

■ **Rebels.** A person who rejects both *pivotal and peripheral norms* is a *rebel*. These people create problems both from a human resources management and a training perspective. At the organizational level, they are misfits, selection errors, or problem employees. Eventually, they will leave the organization (either through voluntary or involuntary termination). As trainees, *rebels* are unwilling to go along with even the minimum norms of behavior (e.g., regular attendance). They may disrupt the training or pose serious management problems for the trainer or manager.

■ **Creative individualists.** These trainees accept pivotal norms but reject peripheral norms. Creative individualists work on behalf of the *pivotal* norms of the organization (e.g., create new products), but they retain their own sense of identity and express themselves through creative solutions that may bend a few rules. In a training environment *creative individualists* will accept the primary goals of the training program. They may, however, use unorthodox means for accomplishing those goals (e.g., trying a completely different method for making a class presentation).

Do current work group norms need to be changed? Can the training program be used to identify and reinforce new work group norms? These are all issues that you should consider before designing and implementing a training program.

Second, what are the *pivotal* and *peripheral norms* of the *learning environment?* There are clear differences between formal classroom learning and on-the-job learning. *Pivotal norms* for classroom learning may be *peripheral norms* for on-the-job learning.

Trainers should identify what expectations they have for the trainees (e.g., the expectation that trainees will actively participate in discussions). What are the minimum expectations that must be met for a program to be successful? What would you really like to see in an ideal seminar (i.e., things you might hope for but wouldn't expect)? These expectations should be clearly stated at the beginning of the training program to help create the optimal learning environment. Trainers should carefully identify two lists of norms *(pivotal and peripheral)* before confronting a room full of trainees or approaching an on-the-job learning situation. Data could be gathered from the trainees by placing the various norms on scales for response by trainees (e.g., $1 =$ strongly agree; $7 =$ strong disagree). Median scores (half of the respondents scoring above and half below) can be computed for groups of trainees by examining the *pivotal norm items* and the *peripheral norm items* separately. In this way scores on each type of norm *(pivotal and peripheral)* can then be characterized as high or low, allowing the trainer to locate trainees in the appropriate cell in the window.

This instrument to measure trainee socialization should be administered either before a training program is designed (have prospective trainees respond to the instrument) or at the beginning of the training program itself. In the latter case it could be used as a basis for group feedback and consensus building for necessary classroom norms and expectations. Either way, attention to work group norms and training norms can lead to more successful training and development programs.

When to Use the Window. As employees enter a new organization, job, or department, a socialization process unfolds. As a part of any training program, socialization also takes place.

This window can aid the training and development function in several ways. Employ this window when:

- Assessing an employee's acceptance (rejection) of a group's (department's, organization's) *pivotal* and/or *peripheral norms*
- Assessing the degree to which employees conform to organizational norms
- Preparing for an individual training program, because it enables the labeling of trainees in terms of the likelihood of their acceptance of the content of the training program
- Facilitating the design and implementation of a training program that will fit the type of trainees

The Grid in Action. Abby Kaufman is a difficult employee to describe. He has flashes of brilliance, makes undeniable contributions to the corporation, and yet he sometimes causes the older managers to shake their heads because of his behaviors. Abby just does not play the corporate game correctly. He drives a beat-up old Volkswagen Beetle and he dresses as if he were stranded in the 1960s (faded denims and work shirts decorated with "Save the whale" patches). He can always be counted on to be late for staff meetings, and he always insists on herb teas rather than the decaffeinated coffee that others prefer.

Despite his unorthodox behavior and his lack of acceptance of *peripheral norms,* he produces some of the best advertising campaigns in the business. His advertisements are always amusing and a bit off-centered, but they really sell the products. As the president of the company says, "Abby gets the job done and his ideas make money!" The most difficult problem created by Abby occurs when a formal presentation has to be made to a client. Abby's idea of dressing up is wearing a corduroy jacket over his decorated work shirt. Since most of the company's clients have more traditional expectations of business presentations, Abby's appearance often affects his credibility (at least initially). Over time, the company deals with Abby's presentations in a number of ways. They send a team of well-dressed junior executives along with Abby to maintain the image of the company. Occasionally, they even warn their clients to expect something unusual from Abby, so the client will not be caught off guard during the presentation.

Abby is, after all, a *creative individualist*—one of those people who accepts the *pivotal norms* of the organization (in this case, creates advertising campaigns that clients like and that sell products and services) while retaining a sense of personal identity and self-expression.

A new employee is hired who initially seems to be a lot like Abby Kaufman. Younger and even more brash than Abby, Joan Diaz makes a reputation for herself as a rule breaker. However, unlike Abby, Joan wants to produce advertising campaigns that always include a message of world peace, regardless of whether it is appropriate for the particular product or service being marketed. Clients dislike her self-righteous approach, and the few who do allow her to create a campaign for them end up losing market share. Eventually, Joan is terminated for inadequate job performance.

Joan is a *rebel,* a problem employee for any organization. Her lack of *acceptance of peripheral norms,* like Abby, might be tolerated if she, too, could produce winning advertising campaigns for her clients. Unfortunately she accepts neither the *pivotal* nor the *peripheral norms* of the company. This results in a poor match between her and the organization. The difficulty in recognizing employee types *(game players, conformists, rebels,* and *creative individualists)* is apparent from the preceding example. Employees with the same overt behaviors may, in fact, be quite different in how they embrace the mission of the organization. Therefore, it is vital for you to assess your employees along the dimensions of this window in order to determine which behaviors are dysfunctional and need to be changed or managed differently, and which behaviors are functional and need to be left alone, despite their appearance of breaking the rules.

References

Nahavandi, A., and A. R. Malekzadeh. "Acculturation in Mergers and Acquisitions." *Academy of Management Review,* No. 13 (1988), pp. 79–90.

Organ, D. W., and T. Bateman. *Organizational Behavior: An Applied Psychological Approach,* 3rd ed. Plano, Tex.: Business Publications, Inc., 1986.

Schein, E. H. *Organizational Psychology,* 2d ed. Englewood Cliffs, N.J.: Prentice-Hall, 1970.

19-3. Employee Development Plans

Training and development dollars are limited in most organizations, and yet the demands for training programs never cease. Trainers need guidance in allocating their resources to achieve the greatest organizational benefit. Window 19-3 provides a classification scheme for helping organizations decide among employee development programs (including training, job design, and compensation) for particular employees. It is based on an analysis of employees' past level of job performance and their future organizational potential.

Applying the Employee Development Window

It is important to see that the Employee Development Plans Window offers a much broader perspective along with action prescriptions. Entire human resource programs can be linked to specific employees within each type (DAP/MAP/RAP/TAP). That is, human resource programs can be individually tailored to meet individual needs and capabilities.

Assessment centers have been developed that use multiple measures of *potential* to assess job candidates by multiple raters. These measures of potential have shown high validity for predicting future managerial potential. The purpose of an assessment center is to collect data on how people would behave in a job by using various measures. However, they are expensive to create and operate and are rarely used except in larger corporations and for higher-level managers.

A *human resource development (HRD) philosophy* describes a company's overall perspective on employee development. HRD philosophies can range from advocating little or no training and development to fostering ongoing training and development by the organization. These philosophies, whether explicitly or implicit, may have a powerful impact on the company's DAP/MAP/RAP/TAP emphasis.

HRD philosophies are also closely linked with the overall corporate culture and business strategy pursued by the company. In a highly turbulent competitive environment, an organization may choose a "buy" skills versus a "make" skills human resources strategy. That is, it may choose to select employees

(Text continues on page 366)

Window 19-3. Employee Development Plans.

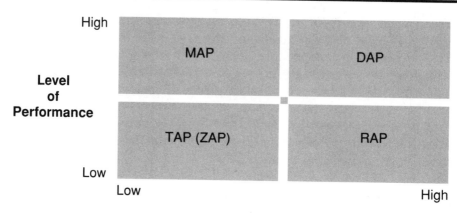

Source: L.L. Cummings and D.P. Schwab, *Performance in Organizations: Determinants and Appraisal*, Glenview, Ill.: Scott, Foresman, 1973.

Dimensions

Level of performance. Employees vary in the degree to which they have successfully performed their jobs in the past. Their performance may be assessed as high (they have proved able to meet or exceed the organization's standards for performance) or low (they are unable to meet the organization's standards for performance). The rating represents the typical *level of job performance* (averaged across multiple job factors) of the person being appraised.

Employee potential. Some employees have the potential for vertical growth (promotion to higher-level jobs), while others show more possibility of lateral growth (transfer to other jobs at the same level) in an organization. Other employees may already have reached a plateau. An employee may be assessed as high (much potential growth in both current and future job assignments) or low (little potential growth in either current or future job assignments).

Employee Development Plans

Development action program (DAP). A *DAP* focuses on preparing employees with high past *performance* and high *potential* for greater responsibilities within the organization. A successfully implemented DAP provides employees an incentive for realizing their potential (either monetary or other types of rewards) and allows them to have considerable discretion in the way job goals are accomplished. Management By Objectives can be an especially appropriate

Window 19-3. (*Continued*)

performance planning/appraisal process for these employees. Other developmental programs include promotion (assigning the employee greater job responsibilities in a higher-level job), job enlargement (assigning the employee more related things to do in the current job), or job enrichment (giving the employee more autonomy, responsibility, and control).

Maintenance action program (MAP). Employees with acceptable past job *performance* but little *potential* for growth because of either ability or motivational constraints might receive the *MAP* approach. This development program tries to maintain present *performance* at an acceptable level through fairly close direction and evaluation. These employees should be given specific examples of effective and ineffective *performance* on each of their job dimensions. Then *performance* discrepancies can be pinpointed and corrected to maintain an acceptable *performance* level. Competitive compensation and ongoing training to prevent skill obsolescence are also appropriate.

Remedial action program (RAP). A *RAP* could be used for those employees with low past *performance* levels but high *potential*. RAPs focus on immediate *performance* improvement through closer evaluation and progressively tighter controls. An employee who fails to respond to a RAP will often be terminated. Specific goals, frequent *performance* evaluation, and clear feedback need to be provided by the employee's superior. Employees must be aware of their clearly substandard *performance* (both verbally and in writing). This message may be reinforced by giving the employee no increase when merit pay raises are allocated.

Termination action program (TAP). Employees with low past *performance* levels and low *potential* have little future with the company and are candidates for *termination*. These employees are either selection errors (they passed through employment screening but could not perform the job) or were previously in the RAP category and failed to respond. A termination action program includes, at a minimum, a frank discussion with the employee about why the action is necessary, careful documentation of past *performance* problems, and other administrative activities necessary for the separation process. Additionally, some organizations may choose to provide outplacement help to employees in this category to smooth the transition period between jobs. (TAP programs are often called ZAP, for zero action program.)

from outside the company who have the needed knowledge, skills, and abilities rather than developing and modifying current employees to prepare for an uncertain future. Companies following this philosophy would be less likely to follow the developmental action planning (DAP) path in this window. Alternatively, these companies would focus on "weeding out" the low and even marginal employees rather than spending organizational resources on them.

On the other hand, in a more stable, less volatile competitive environment, an organization may choose to pursue a "make" skills rather than a "buy" skills human resources strategy. Loyalty and commitment, along with a stable, experienced work force, fit well with this approach. Companies like this would be very likely to follow the human resource development philosophy outlined in this window. Rather than "weeding out," they may focus more on the development and rehabilitation of even the most marginal employee. Selecting the appropriate development program for an individual employee is like choosing a financial investment strategy. Rational investors put their money where it will pay the greatest dividends. Human resources are investments as well. Assuming a 1.5 percent annual cost-of-living increase, an employee with a starting salary of 30,000 dollars will have cost an organization a half-million dollars in salary alone after only fifteen years! The investment is even greater when you add in direct and indirect training expenditures (e.g., funding a graduate business degree). You should calculate the amount of money you have invested in your employees and compare your human resource investments against other investments (e.g., machinery). This establishes the need for careful human resource management.

You should carefully monitor employees over time to ensure proper investment management. Ask questions such as "Are there a significant number of employees who were originally classified as DAP employees who have become MAP employees?" This may signal a need to examine existing human resource management policies and practices with the objective of maximizing a return on the human resources investment.

The Employee Development Plans model assists an organization in making wise human resource investments or disinvestments (as in the case of TAP employees). However, you must accurately measure both past performance as well as future potential. A few suggestions to improve assessment accuracy follows: (1) Use multiple raters (or evaluators) whenever possible. Include more than just the immediate supervisor in the assessment process. (2) Use *performance* appraisal instruments that assess several dimensions (i.e., more than "overall, how would you rate this employee's performance?"). Also, use instruments that define dimensions specifically (e.g., What is meant by "quality of work"?) and specify what is meant by "good," "average," and "poor." It is best to have specific job examples for raters to refer to when they are making their evaluations. (3) Use multiple measures of *potential*. For example, in addition to a supervisor's assessment of an employee's *potential*, use the employee's score on a validated ability test.

Careful use of this model can help an organization make better human resource investment decisions. At the very least, use of this model forces you to consider important factors you might otherwise neglect.

When to Use the Window. This grid can be useful when you wish to:

- Draw the maximum possible from an employee's *potential for performance*
- Improve a poorly *performing* employee up to a satisfactory or even stellar level of achievement
- Minimize the additional development costs allocated to an employee who does not wish to change or is incapable of changing
- Design a specific developmental plan for a particular employee
- Decide which developmental approach to use for which types of employee, based on past levels of performance
- Introduce and explain the organization's various programs to employees in advance, so they will know what approaches are available to be used with each of them

The Grid in Action. Betty is an excellent electronic components inspector. As a longtime employee of FASTEK Corporation, she has consistently met and frequently exceeded organizational standards for job performance. Her job as inspector, an exempt position, has a pay range from $9.55 to $13.55 per hour. Over time, Betty has received merit pay increases that have moved her to the top of her pay grade (i.e., $13.55 per hour). At FASTEK Betty has "topped-out" in her pay grade, posing a supervisory dilemma: What do you do with a "topped-out" employee who continues to make valuable contributions to the organization?

Betty's supervisor, Carl, sits at his desk pondering the problem. It is mid-March, and Carl has to make decisions about this year's merit increases. Once again, Betty has performed exceptionally well for the entire performance period. In fact, Carl is unsure how he can get along without Betty in his department. Frustrated by his limited options and fearing that Betty might leave the organization if her pay is not increased, he decides to call the personnel administrator, Frank, and ask for "special merit increase" (one that will move her base wage above the $13.55 pay grade ceiling) for Betty. After all, Betty has been with the corporation for many years, and FASTEK cannot afford to lose such a valuable employee.

Frank sympathizes with Carl's frustration over his dilemma, but is uncomfortable about Carl's suggestion to violate the pay system policy of keeping merit increases within the pay grades. He asks Carl to come by his office for further discussion of the issue.

By the time Carl arrives, Frank has had enough time to think about how he will deal with Carl. After asking Carl to get comfortable, Frank asks a few pointed questions about Betty. "Has Betty's performance been consistently good or excellent over time (i.e., has she met or exceeded the organization's standards for performance)?" Carl explains that Betty is the best inspector in his department and has been the best since she began her employment with FASTEK. Frank follows up with the next question "Does Betty have potential for growth in current or future job assignments?" Carl rubs his forehead and replies, "I really don't know. She's been great in her current job. She is careful and has a great eye for detail, but I don't know whether she has potential for other jobs besides the one she is currently performing." Frank smiles, recognizing that he has just diagnosed the problem. "Carl," he says, "you need to find out what kind of potential Betty has for further growth here at FASTEK before I can tell you specifically how you should deal with her. Until then, let me explain our programs a bit.

"If you decide that Betty has little or no potential for future growth at FASTEK, then she should receive a *Maintenance Action Program.* Maybe you can't give her more money, but you can sure give her more autonomy in her current job. Let her decide her schedule, allow her to make more decisions, but do something that will make her current job more intrinsically rewarding to her. You know, of course, that we pay the highest wages in town, and Betty could not make more money doing the same thing for another employer. She probably knows that, too, but it might be wise to gently remind her of that.

"If you decide that Betty has potential for growth in current or future job assignments at FASTEK, then a *Developmental Action Program* is warranted. This might involve enrolling Betty in one of our training programs to become a supervisor, letting her try out other jobs in the department, or even promoting her now to a new and high-level position.

"As you can see, knowing Betty's past job performance is only part of the analysis. You need to go back, get more information, and carefully think through what the appropriate action is for Betty."

"I see what you mean," Carl responds, "but how do I find out what Betty's potential is?" "It's not easy," Frank says, "but I would begin by having a discussion with Betty. Pull out her personnel file and see if there is any information that might suggest Betty has some unused talents. See if there is a test score in the file that might indicate a high level of mental ability that is not being tapped in her current job. Whatever you do, don't rely on just one piece of information or what you think her potential is, without getting some supporting data."

"OK," Carl says and he adds, "Of course, you will be available if I run into any problems, won't you?" "That's what I get paid for," Frank says.

Chapter 20

Transitions and Change

The management literature, both popular and academic, frequently prescribes what *ought* to be. It also provides methods to determine where the organization and its employees *presently* are. When the question arises, "How do we get there from here?" (i.e., from where we are to where we ought to be) recommendations become more tentative. Approaches are available, but they frequently do not encompass the scope of what is involved in making transitions and changing individuals and organizations.

The three models provided here consider several very interesting aspects of the change process. As a group, they contribute to a better understanding of the challenges presented to you when confronting change issues.

The first two models focus primarily on organizational change, and the last one addresses the reaction of employees caught in major system change. Those that focus on organizational change alert you to three essential issues:

1. The system will change even if you do nothing, so it is important to pay attention to maintaining the present system if it is working.
2. Managerial strategies should be matched to situational considerations.
3. Nonrational or political strategies have an important role to play in change.

The models focus on individual responses, provide ways of surviving transitions, and offer important insights into employee reactions to major change. Some are negative, and you need to minimize these while capitalizing on the constructive responses that emerge.

20-1. Situational Change

The primary objectives of this model are to help you characterize the change situation facing you and match your management style to its characteristics. Many managers believe that regardless of the change situation it is best to involve those who will be affected by the change in the development of change strategy. By contrast, Window 20-1 proposes that you examine the change conditions confronting you and your organization and then adopt a strategy that matches that situation. In some instances the strategy may be participatory in nature; in other instances a more directed approach will be most effective.

Applying the Situational Change Window

Change efforts will often be more effective when people affected by any change are allowed to *participate* in its development and implementation. Participation ensures that basic value systems are not threatened and a sense of security is fostered. This model, however, argues that additional factors must be considered before change is attempted. Sensitivity to *technical and interpersonal competence* issues suggests the use of a more situational approach to change. You should, therefore, match situational considerations and change strategies.

This window also has direct implications for managerial behavior in the change process. Managers tend to engage in those activities in which they are most proficient and avoid those where they perceive they lack competence. It is equally important, according to Reddin (see References), to match your style with the situational conditions confronting you. More specifically:

- *Natural* change is facilitated by a *separated* managerial style in which you provide consistent rules and procedures and operate "by the book."

Window 20-1. Situational Change.

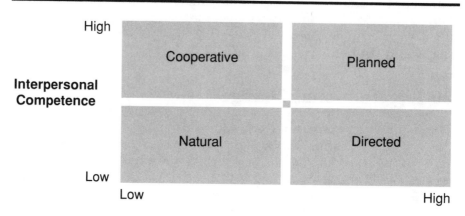

Source: Robin Stuart-Kotze, "A Situational Change Typology," © 1972 *Training and Development Journal*, American Society for Training and Development, Vol. 26, No. 1, January 1972, pp. 56–60. Reprinted with permission. All rights reserved.

Dimensions

Technical competence. This dimension assesses your *degree of competence* available in such areas as planning, controlling, designing, and producing. In the absence of strong *technical competence*, managers typically focus their change efforts on short-term issues. When you have strong *technical competence*, change efforts are more likely to involve long-term activities that achieve leverage from present potential and focus on future growth.

Interpersonal competence. This dimension characterizes the degree of sensitivity that the individuals involved have toward each other. To what extent are they *aware* of the influence that each has on the other? *Low interpersonal competence* is evidenced by low communication levels, minimal trust, and destructive confrontation. *High interpersonal competence* is present when trust among individuals is high and there is a spirit of mutual problem solving.

Situational Change Processes

Natural change. When both *technical* and *interpersonal competence* are lacking, *natural change* is the most effective approach to pursue. Change focuses on the present challenges of the company and tends to be reactive to existing problems. Tactical, rather than strategic change, is likely.

Window 20-1. (*Continued*)

■ **Directed change.** When *technical competence* is available but *interpersonal competence* is lacking, *directed change* is preferred. The preferred change is determined and then implemented "all at once." Because low *interpersonal competence* prevents substantial consensus building, it is important that other appropriate inducements are provided to gain initial compliance with the change.

■ **Cooperative change.** *Cooperative change* is employed when *interpersonal competence* is high but *technical competence* is lacking. Given high levels of trust, tight control is unnecessary and even avoided when attempts are made to implement it. Change in this instance requires supporting activities that permit individuals to gain additional *technical competence* through training or coaching.

■ **Planned change.** *Planned change* will be most effective when both *technical* and *interpersonal competence* are high. Significant effort can be devoted to long-term organizational development. A wide range of alternatives are considered in a climate of open trust and support.

- *Directed* change is enhanced by a *dedicated* managerial style in which you focus on the *technical* concerns confronting the organization, pay little concern to the individual welfare of the subordinates, and rely on your own judgment to determine the appropriate course of action.
- *Cooperative* change is improved by employing a *related* managerial style in which you focus on providing open and free communication in all directions. Primary concern is given to maintaining individual welfare.
- *Planned* change calls for an *integrated* managerial style in which you address short- and long-term *technical* issues while developing strong commitment to the organization on the part of all members. Individual and organizational needs become integrated.

Considerations to Make When Using the Window. Managers sometimes get "locked into" a preferred pattern for introducing changes within their organizations. This rigidity can be ineffective. By contrast, this model suggests that you:

- Examine your own degree of *technical competence* to assess your capacity for effectively steering an innovation through the organization
- Assess the status of interpersonal relationships within the work group to determine whether or not there are conflicts and competence inadequacies that may prevent the successful implementation of change
- Commit yourself to consciously use a wide variety of change strategies over an extended period of time, not allowing yourself to become emotionally attached to a single approach without a sound rationale for its pervasive use
- Help prepare yourself and your employees for greater use of the *planned* change approach, by upgrading both your technical and interpersonal competencies across time

The Grid in Action. Peter Rolfe, the business manager for a small manufacturing firm, has been giving serious consideration to the value that computerization would have for the company in general. Accounting, inventory control, and payroll activities are but a few of the many activities that could be streamlined if a computer system were installed. Accounting already does a substantial amount of its work on microcomputers, while payroll activities are still done by hand. Peter envisions introducing a computer system that would be more "integrated."

Typical to this type of situation, some employees welcome the suggestion with open arms while others view the computer as "some dumb machine that 'beeps' at me and will eventually take my job." To complicate matters, the level of trust and camaraderie among employees in some departments has deteriorated, because those who are computer literate look down on those who "can't find the on/off button."

The personnel department employees know little about computers and do not seem to care to learn, either. Computers represent a threat to their self-esteem and their job security. In this instance Peter will want to use *natural change*. He will have to make the decision, but should start with a task that is easy to computerize. As the employees gain familiarity with the system, their involvement in future system developments will be sought.

The manufacturing department is technically competent in inventory control and the use of computers for this purpose, but recent reductions in force make additional change very risky. *Directed change*, well thought-out but implemented in a very defined period of time, makes sense in this instance.

The purchasing department has historically done its work manually. The clerical employees in this department represent one of the largest groups of long-term employees in the company. While lacking in-depth technical competence in computers, there exists a strong "can-do" attitude if appropriate time and training are made available. In this instance Peter will want to utilize *cooperative change* to provide strong support and facilitate the change in procedures.

The accounting department is very technically competent and has experienced little, if any, dissension among the employees. Teamwork is good and the employees are always attempting to improve the work procedures for the good of all. In this instance Peter will want to employ *planned change*. Both technical and interpersonal competence provide a unique opportunity for the departmental employees to develop both short- and long-term programs that provide for needed quick fixes but also provide the capacity to grow as the situation warrants.

Reference

Reddin, W. J. *Managerial Effectiveness*. New York: McGraw-Hill, 1970.

20-2. Responses to Downsizing

Window 20-2 sensitizes you to the typical responses exhibited by survivors of an organizational downsizing—a dramatic and substantial decrease in size and scope of operations. Some responses support organizational objectives and should be rewarded. Others are detrimental to the organization and the employee and need to be addressed.

Applying the Downsizing Window

This model provides a very important message for management. Most of the attention during downsizing focuses on em-

Window 20-2. Responses to Downsizing.

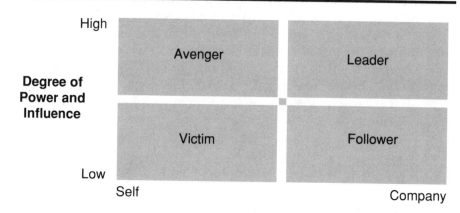

Focus of Employee Attention

Source: Joan Alevras and Arnold Frigeri, "Picking Up the Pieces After Downsizing," © 1987 *Training and Development Journal,* American Society for Training and Development, September 1987, pp. 29–31. Reprinted with permission. All rights reserved.

Dimensions

Focus of employee attention. This dimension identifies the primary *focus of the employee's concern* after a downsizing has occurred. For some employees, the concern is purely for themselves. Self-pity and anger are frequent responses. For others, concern focuses on the organization and how they can make it productive in the future.

Degree of power and influence. As an aftermath of the downsizing, some employees feel they have little control over their job or events that surround them. Others view the situation as an opportunity to positively affect their position in the organization. Their perceived *power and influence,* then, can range from low to high.

Types of Reactions

Leader. The most positive response occurs when employees are able to *focus attention* on how to improve the organization *and* feel that they possess the *power and influence* to contribute to future success. These individuals are *leaders,* and the organization will want to capitalize on their response. In fact, if opportunities are not provided to participate, these individuals may soon react negatively.

Window 20-2. (*Continued*)

▓ **Follower.** Another constructive response is exhibited by those whose concern focuses on improving the organization, but who do not perceive themselves as major players in determining its future direction. These individuals are *followers.* They will decide that the best way out of the present situation is to follow and contribute by supporting and implementing the directions initiated by the *leaders.*

▓ **Victim.** Some people respond to change by focusing primarily on their own plight. They also may feel that they have little influence on events surrounding them. Persecuted by their surroundings and powerless to change anything, these individuals are *victims.* Typically, they respond by withdrawing into their own "mental foxholes." Orders received from upper management are passed on down the line. Self-initiative and risk-taking behaviors are avoided.

▓ **Avenger**. The most negative response comes from those who focus on their own welfare and consequently use their power to support their own concerns. These are the *avengers.* Their objective is to get even for the pain they have suffered. They may work to enhance their position relative to others or they may wait in "ambush." Their response is frequently destructive to all concerned.

---

ployees who will no longer be employed. How do we decide who goes and who stays? What will be the impact on the professional and personal lives of those who go? What can the organization do to cushion the blow? Will the organization provide "outplacement" activities and who will receive them? The probable (but very simplistic) assumption during these times is that those who remain will be happy to have a job and will work constructively to maintain it. This model provides a balanced view that identifies *several* possible responses. Each of these will require direct action by management to build on the constructive responses and modify or eliminate the inappropriate responses.

The model also suggests that appropriate interventions can modify employee response patterns. It is possible to move *avengers* to the *victim* or even the *leader* category. Relatively creative leadership roles may permit the *avengers* to channel their efforts to more constructive ends. Similarly, *victims* can be moved into *follower* roles through additional coaching and clear role definitions. Given this type of assistance, individuals become more capable of making contributions to the organization and gaining some increased self-esteem and confidence in the process.

Considerations to Make When Using the Window. Although truly significant downsizing only infrequently affects any one company, its effects can be so traumatic that advance anticipation and preparation are highly appropriate. In addition, however, even minor cutbacks or losses of expected contract extensions can have the same internal effects. Therefore, you should:

- Try to predict which of your employees will focus inwardly vs. externally (on the organization), in response to a projected or actual downsizing.
- Assess which employees are basically optimistic about their futures with a down-scaled organization, and which ones are pessimistic.
- Develop four general plans for dealing with each major type of employee (*leader, follower, victim,* and *avenger*).
- Insist on providing honest and current information to all employees throughout the downsizing process, so they have the best information available at all times about their actual future with the organization.
- Recognize that even minor setbacks (e.g., the failure to win a budget increase for a pet project or the failure to be awarded a merit increase commensurate with an employee's expectations) can bring about similar types of employee responses. Consequently, you cannot insulate yourself from the predicted effects of this window simply because your organization has not officially engaged in downsizing.

The Grid in Action. Downsizing generally provides negative outcomes for those who go and even those who remain. Our concern in this instance is with the survivors. Bill Stevenson, the division manager, was recently instructed to implement a 10 percent reduction in force within his division, which employed 150 employees. The tasks exercised by the work force are relatively simple, so the retention of "critical skills" was not an issue. As a matter of fact, the directive from the human resource management department essentially dictates a "last in, first to go" policy. The real challenge for Bill is to redirect and motivate the survivors.

Some individuals "when given lemons, make lemonade." Downsizing creates tension, ambiguity, shifting power structures, and even the opportunity for change. Bill must identify this group because its members will become the next generation of *leaders*. They will seize the opportunity to change with the situation and, hopefully, improve it. Failure to provide the opportunity will probably force this group to leave in the relatively near future. Bill's challenge will be to focus the efforts of these individuals constructively.

The second group to emerge are the *followers*. They are happy to still be around but they are not risk takers. They see their role as implementing and following through. They will act in support of the new changes. Bill must recognize that this group is equally essential to meeting the challenges ahead. All chiefs and no *followers* makes life extremely unpleasant. They will require encouragement and appropriate rewards for implementing the new plans.

The next two groups, *victims* and *avengers*, provide special problems for Bill. *Victims* will hide out. They will do what they are told and little else. If this pattern of behavior continues, they become a drag on the division and potentially increase the likelihood of more cutbacks. Specific expectations, frequent reviews, and substantial positive reinforcement will be required to rebuild the motivation and productivity of this group. In essence, they have two choices: They become part of the solution or remain part of the problem and will be treated as such.

Avengers will probably seek revenge and become very destructive to all concerned. Frequent and specific documentation of their behavior is required due to the strong likelihood that termination may eventually be required if their behavior patterns do not improve. Bill sees a mixed task before him— working constructively with the *leaders* and *followers* while trying to convert (or minimize damage done by) the other two groups. Fortunately, he believes that the last two groups are rather small.

20-3. Ways of Surviving Transitions

Major organizational changes—mergers, acquisitions, takeovers, and deregulation—substantially affect the lives of thousands of employees daily. These changes also create situations in which productive employees are sometime no longer capable of replicating their past performance. Window 20-3 provides an overview of the process by which an employee copes with the uncertainty and eventually returns to the previous level of performance. It also suggests strategies that organizations can employ to assist the employee in this period of transition.

Applying the Surviving Transitions Window

The most important message for management is that it cannot expect "business as usual" during times of major change. Employees will typically exhibit, and move through, the four sequential stages from *denial* to *commitment*. What management can do is to *facilitate the passage*. For example, the introduction of word processing equipment and computers has been traumatic for many. One company helped employees through this period by bronzing one of the old typewriters and displaying it in a prominent place. Grieving the passage of the "good old days" was facilitated through this ceremony, and the subsequent introduction of the new technology went smoothly.

It should also be noted that the four phases require different managerial responses. The *resistance* stage requires frequent meetings, good listening, and accurate information from management concerning the change. *Exploration* and *commitment* will require the availability of additional resources to accomplish these constructive responses to major change.

Some employees respond better to the stress caused by a major change than do others. They frequently possess the following characteristics: 1) *commitment* to and a sense of purpose in their work, 2) *control* over their work, 3) *challenge* created by the opportunity to learn new things, and 4) *connection*, or a feeling of belonging among fellow workers. *Denial* and *resistance* do not enhance the feeling of control and therefore preclude commitment and challenge.

Finally, the model is not limited to individual responses. You can use the same model to predict both group and organizational responses to major change. The model also notes the possibility that not everyone will be in the same phase at the same time. Therefore, the astute manager will need to be sensitive to the individual differences.

Window 20-3. Ways of Surviving Transitions.

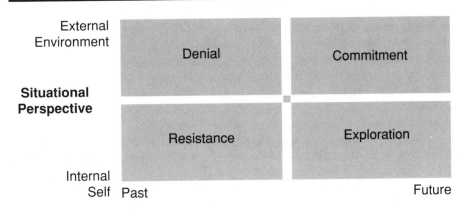

External Environment

Situational Perspective

Internal Self

Denial | Commitment

Resistance | Exploration

Past | Future

Time Perspective

Source: Cynthia D. Scott and Dennis T. Jaffe, "Survive and Thrive in Time of Change," © 1988 *Training and Development Journal,* American Society for Training and Development, April 1988, pp. 25–27. Reprinted with permission. All rights reserved.

Dimensions

Time perspective. This dimension identifies the focus of employee attention during the transition period. In the early stages of the transition, the employee typically focuses on the *past* and is unwilling to give up previous ways of doing things. Eventually the employee's attention turns to the *future* and what must be done to be successful under new conditions.

Situational perspective. This dimension examines the situational aspects that receive attention during the transition process. At one extreme, attention is focused on the *external* environment. Eventually, the focus of concern shifts to the *individual* and his/her feelings and thoughts concerning the upheaval.

Responses to Change

Denial. Just as a patient reacts to a physician's prognosis of terminal illness, *denial* is typically the employee's first response to a major change. Predictably, the employee does not want to believe that his/her work environment will be different. The employee may ignore the message and continue work as normal. Management may even foster this belief through communicating a "business as usual" posture and not allowing employees to vent their feelings about the change. Productivity frequently decreases during this period.

Window 20-3. (*Continued*)

Resistance. *Resistance* occurs in the second stage. During this period the employee experiences a wide range of inner-directed feelings that center around self-doubt, anxiety, frustration, and the general uncertainty experienced during a major change. Many complaints are heard, sickness increases, and résumés are updated. The company can minimize the negative outcomes of the *resistance* by facilitating the expression of feelings, but few managers react appropriately in this situation.

Exploration. Eventually, feelings are worked through and the employee begins to exhibit more positive behaviors. Renewed interest in the job emerges and the employee begins to *explore* personal options and behaviors. Creativity and innovation begin to increase and the workplace becomes enlivened again. Potential risks remain, because everything is now "up for evaluation" and the lack of structure can still be threatening for some.

Commitment. The exploration of the third period eventually settles on new patterns that will be employed to move the company forward. The employee is now ready to *commit* new energies to the organization. Goals and future directions are identified, new groups are formed, and roles and expectations are set.

Considerations to Make When Using the Window. Any manager interested in helping employees not only survive, but grow stronger from, a major organizational change could fruitfully apply this window in the following ways:

- Recognize that a fairly predictable response pattern exists as employees move from *denial* to *resistance* to *exploration* to *commitment* (although the length of time any one employee stays in a particular phase may vary broadly).
- Try to encourage employees involved in change to look forward rather than backward (this by itself, if successful, would result in an emphasis on *exploration* and *commitment* stages).
- Be wary of employees who *too* easily jump to the advanced (and more productive) response stages, because they may later regress back toward the earlier ones just when other employees are emerging from *denial* and *resistance*.

- Prepare employees for life/work changes in *general*, by alerting them to the predictable phases they might fall into. By intellectually discussing the more negative phases and their implications before ever getting emotionally involved, employees may be more ready to either bypass, or move quickly past, the earlier stages.

The Grid in Action. Bill Massina, Vice-President of Sales and Marketing, is a key member of the senior management team. This group has invested substantial thought into the strategic decision to market the company's line of chemicals for the petroleum industry on a "specialty" as opposed to "commodity" basis. Research and Development has historically provided product improvements and innovations that make this strategy feasible. What it will require, however, is a qualitative shift in the manner in which the sales force conducts its business. Most, if not all, of the present sales force are believed *capable* of making the changes if the appropriate motivation and resources are provided. Bill is responsible for ensuring the effective changeover among the sales force.

Bill's initial actions are critical, because many salespersons will *deny* that a need exists for the change in the first place. Even if Bill can show that the "old way" no longer works, *denial* will result because of the fear of change and the increased ambiguity. Bill will have to act aggressively to establish the "new order" and consistently reward individual people for implementing the desired changes. Substantial training will most probably be required at this time to ensure that the sales force understands the new strategy and what it means for them.

New programs typically take time to produce outcomes. The company may even note an initial decrease in sales as the new methods are brought "up to speed." The typical response of the sales force will be that the competition is taking their market share due to better pricing and that they had better return to the previous methods. *Resistance* becomes the order of the day. Bill's response needs to focus on getting these feelings on the table and addressed. The decrease in productivity may be due to individual concern about "measuring up to the new set of expectations."

If these first two phases are effectively addressed and Bill sticks with his plan and objectives, then the change effort will begin to assume an internal momentum. The sales force will now be more comfortable with the program and may begin to *explore* ways in which the program might be improved. Sharing among the sales force and with management will become an important way to further enhance methods that prove successful and modify those that may be less effective. Once this *exploration* and refinement stage is completed, *commitment* to the new program will be internalized and the need for substantial involvement by Bill will be reduced.

About the Contributors

Richard S. Blackburn received his Ph.D. in organizational behavior from the University of Wisconsin-Madison. Currently, he is on the faculty of the School of Business at the University of North Carolina at Chapel Hill. Professor Blackburn is the co-author of *Managing Organizational Behavior* (Irwin, 1989).

Kim Boal is an associate professor at Texas Tech University. He has conducted research and has written on a wide variety of management topics including motivation, employee attitudes, and leadership. His work has appeared in several leading academic journals, including *Academy of Management Journal, Journal of Management, Strategic Management Journal*, and *Organizational Behavior and Human Performance.*

David Cherrington is a professor of organizational behavior at Brigham Young University. He is the author of several articles and books, including two introductory textbooks, *Personnel Management* and *Organizational Behavior.* He completed a doctorate of business administration at Indiana University and has taught at the University of Illinois, the University of Wisconsin-Madison, Brigham Young University-Hawaii Campus, and Brigham Young University-Provo.

Robert C. Ford is a professor of management and former chair of the Department of Management at the University of Alabama at Birmingham. Prior to joining UAB, he was a faculty member at the University of North Florida. He holds a Ph.D. in management from Arizona State University. In addition to publishing texts on principles of management and organization theory, he has written articles on applied management practices, human resource management, and social responsibility.

Jane R. Goodson is an assistant professor of management at Auburn University-Montgomery. She received her M.A. in human resource management and her Ph.D. in organizational behavior from the University of Alabama. Her professional presentations and publications cover topics such as situational leadership, influence and power, organizational commitment, organizational effectiveness, stress, performance appraisal, career planning and development, and the strategic use of compensation and appraisal systems.

David B. Greenberger is an associate professor of management and human resources in the College of Administrative Sciences at Ohio State University. Professor Greenberger holds a Ph.D. in social psychology from the University of Wisconsin-Madison. His primary research interests are concerned with the employee's need for and exercise of control in organizations.

Ronald E. Gribbins is president of Gribbins & Associates, Inc., a St. Louis-based consulting firm specializing in human resource management and organizational change issues.

Jack D. Kartez is an associate professor of environmental science and regional planning at Washington State University. His research on planning for crises has been supported by the National Science Foundation and the Federal Emergency Management Agency. He has served as a training consultant to the National Emergency Training Center, state governments, and professional associations.

Cynthia A. Lengnick-Hall is an associate professor of strategic management at the University of Minnesota-Duluth. Her research interests center on the management of technology, human resources, organization structure, and innovation to develop distinct organizational competencies that can lead to competitive advantage. Her articles have appeared in journals such as *Academy of Management Review, Journal of Management, Organization Studies,* and *Organizational Development Journal.* Dr. Lengnick-Hall has actively worked with public and private organizations and with government agencies to improve strategic management practices.

Mark L. Lengnick-Hall is an assistant professor of human resources management at the University of Minnesota-Duluth. He has published articles in *Personnel Psychology, Academy of Management Review,* and *Personnel Journal.* His research interests include staffing, compensation, and strategic human resources management. Along with his co-author, Cynthia A. Lengnick-Hall, Mark is currently working on a book which will deal with the topic of strategic human resources management.

Jean M. Lundin is an instructor in the Management Studies Department at the University of Minnesota-Duluth, where she teaches business policy and finance. She previously taught at Northern Michigan University and Marquette University. She received her Ph.D. from

Southwest University in New Orleans, Louisiana. She was employed twelve years at Abbott Laboratories in a variety of positions, including manager of payroll. Her research interests include strategic planning in declining industries, and the assessment of stockout situation in industrial settings.

Gail McGee is an associate professor in the Department of Management at the University of Alabama at Birmingham. She received her Ph.D. in organizational behavior from the University of Alabama-Tuscaloosa in 1983, and has taught at UAB since then. Dr. McGee has published articles in *Personnel Administrator, Academy of Management Journal,* and *Journal of Applied Psychology.* She has also conducted management training seminars for a number of different types of organizations.

Robert Marx is an associate professor of management at the University of Massachusetts-Amherst. He received his doctorate in clinical psychology from the University of Illinois. His research efforts have focused on the problem of skill retention following management development programs. He has published on the topic of relapse prevention in *Academy of Management Review, Journal of Management Development,* and *Training and Development Journal.* He is on the board of directors of the Organizational Behavior Teaching Society.

Sara A. Morris is an assistant professor of management at Old Dominion University in Norfolk, Virginia. She received her Ph.D. from the University of Texas at Austin in the areas of business policy and strategy. While on the faculty of Marquette University in Milwaukee, she developed an interest in business ethics and corporate social responsibility. Her current research focuses on competitive corporate espionage and on attitudes toward corporate social responsibility.

Ann Wiggins Noe received her B.A. and M.B.A. in personnel/human resource management from Michigan State University. She taught and conducted human resource management research for several years. She has served as an independent consultant in the areas of training and employment law. Currently, she is completing work on her Ph.D. in industrial relations at the University of Minnesota-Minneapolis.

Stephen Rubenfeld is an associate professor of human resource management, and department head in management studies at the University of Minnesota-Duluth. His articles have appeared in *Psychological Reports, Personnel, Compensation Review, Industrial Relations Law Journal, Educational and Psychological Measurement,* and *Employee Relations Law Journal.* His current interests include personnel problems and practices of small business organizations, the future role of unions, employee retirement behavior, the effects of employee stock ownership, and the measurement of human resource climate.

Dr. Rubenfeld earned his Ph.D. at the University of Wisconsin-Madison.

John R. Schermerhorn is the Charles G. O'Bleness Professor of Management in the College of Business Administration at Ohio University in Athens. He earned a Ph.D. in organizational behavior from Northwestern University. He has worked in, and as a consultant to, a number of business and health care organizations. He is the author of two major books and a large number of articles on various topics in management.

David Vollrath is an assistant professor in the Division of Business and Economics at Indiana University-South Bend. He received his Ph.D. in social psychology from the University of Illinois at Urbana-Champaign. His research interests focus on group decision making.

William B. Werther, Jr., is the Samuel N. Friedland Professor of Executive Management in the School of Business Administration at the University of Miami. He is an active advisor to major North American corporations, assisting them to achieve higher employee productivity through greater employee participation. He is the author or coauthor of *Productivity Through People, Human Resources and Personnel Management,* 3rd ed., and *Dear Boss.*

Index

HD
38
N558
1990

DATE DUE

APR 28 1997			
AUG 2 3 1999			

Ireton Library
Marymount University
Arlington, VA 22207

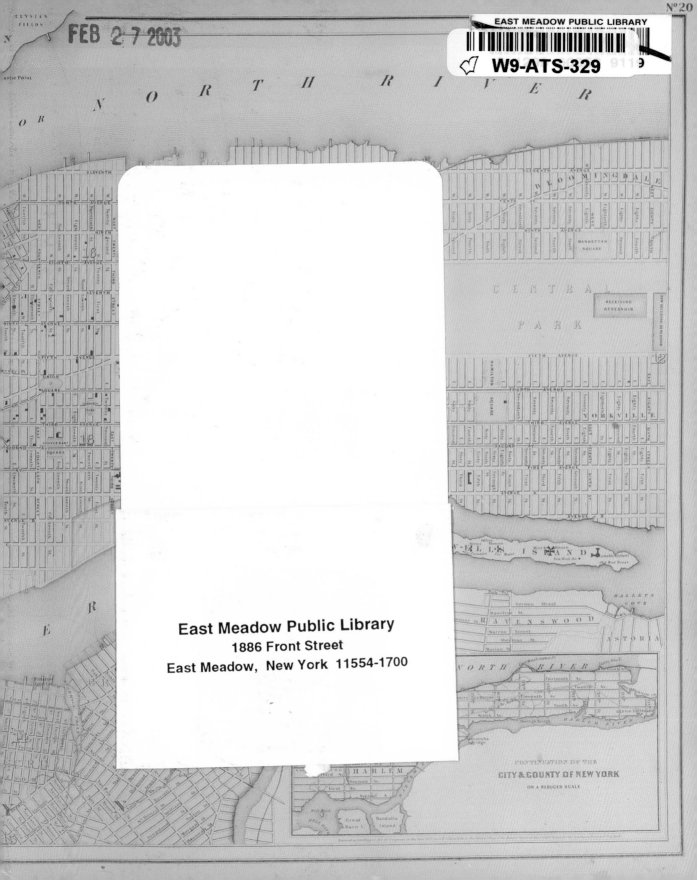

Mrs. Astor's New York

Also by Eric Homberger

New York City: A Cultural and Literary Companion

The Penguin Historical Atlas of North America

The Historical Atlas of New York City

Scenes from the Life of a City: Corruption and Conscience in Old New York

John Reed and the Russian Revolution: Uncollected Articles, Letters, and Speeches on Russia, 1917–1920 (edited with John Biggart)

John Reed

The Troubled Face of Biography (edited with John Charmley)

American Writers and Radical Politics, 1900–39: Equivocal Commitments

John le Carré

The Second World War in Fiction (edited with Holger Klein and John Flower)

The Art of the Real: Poetry in England and America since 1939

Ezra Pound: The Critical Heritage (edited)

The Cambridge Mind: Ninety Years of the Cambridge Review 1879–1969 (edited with William Janeway and Simon Schama)

Mrs. Astor's New York

Money and Social Power in a Gilded Age

Eric Homberger

Yale University Press
New Haven and London

Copyright © 2002 by Eric Homberger

For information about this and other Yale University Press publications, please contact:
U.S. Office: sales.press@yale.edu   www.yale.edu/yup
Europe Office: sales@yaleup.co.uk   www.yaleup.co.uk

Set in Minion by Northern Phototypesetting, Bolton, Lancashire
Printed in China through Worldprint

Library of Congress Cataloging-in-Publication Data

Homberger, Eric.
    Mrs. Astor's New York / Eric Homberger.
       p.   cm.
    Includes bibliographical references and index.
       1. New York (N.Y.)—Social life and customs—19th century.   2. New York (N.Y.)—History—1865–1898.   3. Aristocracy (Social class)—New York (State)—New York—History—19th century.   4. Rich people—New York (State)—New York—Social life and customs—19th century.   5. Astor, Caroline Schermerhorn, 1830–1908.   6. Rich people—New York (State)—New York—Biography.   7. New York (N.Y.)—Biography.   8. Wealth—Social aspects—New York (State)—New York—History—19th century.   I. Title.
       F128.47 .H69 2002
       974.7′1041—dc21   2002002034

ISBN 0-300-09501-5 (hbk.)

A catalogue record for this book is available from the British Library.

10 9 8 7 6 5 4 3 2 1

Endpapers: Map of New York and adjacent cities, published by J.H. Colton & Co., 1855.

For Margaret, Christian and Lara Judith Teresa Taylor

Contents

ILLUSTRATIONS

Plates

All illustrations are from the collection of the author unless otherwise stated.

PREFACE

While writing this book, obituaries of two Vanderbilts, a Fish, Whitney, Goelet, Rhinelander, Gerry, and a Roosevelt appeared in the *New York Times*. Two Astors—a Viscount and an Earl—won an election to remain in the House of Lords. A penthouse duplex on Park Avenue was put on the market for fifteen million dollars. Arthur and Will Zeckendorf, developers of the apartment building, expect that the net worth of purchasers will be $100 million. Patricia Duff, clearly a major contender in the world of excess, demanded $132,000 a month from her soon-to-be-divorced husband, Ronald Perelman, for the expenses of raising their four-year-old daughter Caleigh in Manhattan. ('This has never been about money,' said Ms. Duff, after a judge scathingly rejected the demand.) Nice reminders, in other words, that for anyone interested in the Gilded Age, the New York of the great bull market has a certain familiar air about it.[1] So too does the New York after September 11, a city of growing unemployment, tightening of belts, half-empty restaurants. It was in response to the economic hard times in the late 1890s that the Bradley Martins decided to stage a lavish masquerade ball at the Waldorf Hotel, assuming that the city would appreciate the cascade (that is, trickledown) of expenditure benefiting seamstresses, florists, jewelers, and caterers in the city. The ball was greeted with a torrent of criticism and the Bradley Martins removed themselves to England; there was much clucking of tongues in the society pages and sermons about foolish ostentation. Getting it spectacularly wrong was a skill possessed in abundance in the world of the New York rich.

The social milieu of the rich has changed in many ways. There is a lot more wealth about, and fewer plausible claims to the status of 'old New York families.' From the perspective of figures who attended the Patriarchs' balls in the late nineteenth century, or who were listed in the 'Four Hundred,' the division between 'new' money and 'old' money had a direct and practical meaning. The sharp struggles to resist the incursions of the new, and the social institutions (like the Patriarchs, the 'Four Hundred,' and such listings as the *Social Register*) were ways to strengthen the coherence and solidarity of the upper class. The leading figures in the world of the Patriarchs rejected the idea that wealth alone could form the basis of society. There were other values, other criteria, which they invoked, and which a century later have largely been lost in our understanding of the world of the late nineteenth-century rich. It was the pursuit of those other values that led me to write *Mrs. Astor's New York*.

The primary sources for the study of the aristocracy of New York are elusive, varied, fugitive. A detailed and unique portrait of the life of the wealthy appears in New York's newspapers. The *World, Sun, Times, Herald, Tribune,* and other New York papers act for us as both eyes and ears upon a complex social order. The difficulty of working through roll after roll of microfilm, often poorly indexed, or not indexed at all, has meant that newspapers have largely been an underused resource for students of nineteenth-century American social history. Obituaries (often requiring much decoding of nineteenth-century euphemisms), coverage of balls and other charitable and social events, and stories about places in the city provide a rich panorama of life in the upper reaches of society. Newspapers are scarcely founts of unadulterated truth, but their silences carry meaning.

My argument is that in the 1880s the 'society page' invented 'society,' and that the uneasy relations—the Faustian bargain—between New York's upper class and its journalists produced a dramatic change in the nature of upper-class life—an acceptance of the idea that aristocracy was 'conspicuous,' that of necessity it existed in the full glare of press publicity, and that the aristocrats were what a later generation would call celebrities.

Most of what is written about the nineteenth-century New York aristocracy seldom threatens to probe too deeply into the aristocracy and its values.[2] Among the contemporary sources, the diaries of Philip Hone (despite the editing of Allan Nevins) and George Templeton Strong are unrivaled. The Gansevoort-Lansing, Ward, Duer, Belmont, and Vanderbilt family papers, the manuscript diaries of E.N. Tailer, the archives of Trinity Church and Grace Church, and the manuscripts on society journalism by George Wotherspoon at the New-York Historical Society, are of primary value. The discovery of the manuscript of *The Fancy Ball Given by Mrs. S***********. A Description of the Characters, Dresses, &c. &c. Assumed on the Occasion* (1829), made it possible to reconstruct a missing moment in the history of the ball in New York City. The sardonic columns of 'The Saunterer' in *Town Topics* opened many windows for me on the malicious functions of gossip in New York society. Novels, paintings, short stories, cartoons, gossip columns, satires, and contemporary discussions of fashion provide considerable indirect social information. The way women dressed at Newport, why dentists were unwelcome neighbors, the passion in high society for the quadrille—if we want to understand the meaning people gave to these things, we have to observe their social rituals and listen unobtrusively but closely to their chatter. We have to take a seat among the chaperoning Mammas.

I would particularly like to thank Robert Hamburger and Ilene Sunshine, and also Don Wallace, for making it possible for me to spend the time in New York which this book needed; the Gilder Lehrman Institute of American History, New York City, for a fellowship which enabled me to work in the rich archives of Columbia University and Barnard College; and the University of East Anglia for granting me study leave and for continuing financial support. Thanks are also due to Mike Egan for a visit to Newport; and Mr. Scott Steward, formerly of the New England Historic Genealogical Society, for letting me see his work on the Vanderbilt Ball. The opportunity to work with Robert Baldock, Candida Brazil, Kevin Brown, Diana Yeh and Beth Humphries, their sharp-eyed copy editor at Yale University Press in London made this a better book. Thanks, also, to Barbara C. G. Wood at the National Gallery of Art, Michelle Bien at the Biltmore Estate, Mr. Nicholas Bruen and Morrison H. Heckscher, Lawrence A. Fleischman chair of the American Wing at the Metropolitan Museum, Melissa Carr and Nicole Wells at the New-York Historical Scoiety, Thomas Lisanti at the New York Public Library, and Anne Guernsey and Marguerite Lavin at the Museum of the City of New York. I am very pleased to thank Mr. Robert Tuggle, archivist of the Metropolitan Opera, Ms. Julia Silver, archivist of Trinity Church, and Mrs. Lynn Hoke who introduced me to the well-organized archives of Grace Church. Mark Krupnick, Robert Hamburger, Amy Farrell, and Kate Campbell read parts of the manuscript. Bill Albert has read the manuscript with his usual vigilance. I feel fortunate having such good readers and good friends.

This book could not have been written without Judy.

Eric Homberger
July 4, 2002, Norwich

New York Wisdom on Wealth and Social Position[1]

A man worth fifty thousand dollars is as well off as though he was rich.
John Jacob Astor

The only hard step in building up my fortune was the first thousand dollars.
After that it was easy.   John Jacob Astor

Money brings me nothing but a certain dull anxiety.
John Jacob Astor III

Money making he did not consider in his line.
Obituary of William Astor

A fortune of a million dollars is only respectable poverty.
Ward McAllister

We are only moderately well off; we have but a few million dollars.
Mrs. Stuyvesant Fish

We are all slaves, and the man who has one million dollars is the
greatest slave of all, except it be he who has two million.
Jay Gould

I have wealth, beauty and intellect:
what more could I wish?
James Hazen Hyde

The class of wealthy people are, in aggregate, such a mob of gilded dunces,
that, not to be wealthy carries with it a certain distinction and nobility.
Herman Melville

They had much better accept me. I am on their side. I believe in wealth.
I belong to their class. Theodore Roosevelt, on the Robber Barons

My life was never destined to be happy. Inherited wealth is a real handicap
to happiness. It is as certain death to ambition as cocaine is to morality.
William K. Vanderbilt

And to think he was not a rich man. Andrew Carnegie,
on learning that J.P. Morgan's estate was worth $68,300,000

I owe the public nothing. J.P. Morgan

After Mrs. Astor there was chaos. Frederick Townsend Martin

1
LOOKING AT ARISTOCRACY

There are, indeed, unmistakable signs everywhere of the growth of
aristocratic feelings, tastes, habits, and even prejudices among us.
—(1861)[1]

In this book I have sought to portray the aristocracy of an American city in the
nineteenth century, considering the entertainments, rituals, values, houses,
marriages, divorces, snobbishness, infidelities, and cultural horizons—as well
as the neighborhoods where these aristocrats lived. For obvious reasons I have
concentrated on New York City: 'All American society is modeled on that of
New York,' observed Louis Simonin in the *Revue des deux mondes*. 'The imperial city regulates American customs and fashions, as Paris regulates those of
France . . . no American city can dispute with New York in population, extent,
and magnificence, nor contest with her in the amount of business transactions, the riches of the nabobs, the elegance of the feminine toilets, the luxury
and splendor of the *fêtes* and receptions.'[2] What happened in New York mattered. The aristocracy of Philadelphia and Savannah moved on a local or
regional stage; the aristocrats of New York could confidently assume that their
houses, wealth, and entertainments would be subjects of interest whenever
and wherever Americans thought about money and class. From Henry
Brevoort's fancy dress ball at his home on lower Fifth Avenue in 1840, until the
death of Mrs. Astor at her home on Fifth Avenue in 1908, New York experienced an age of aristocracy.

As recent scholarship has shown, the aristocracy of New York was something of a hybrid. It was 'newer' than the equivalent groups in Charleston,
Philadelphia, or Boston, and less stable. Although the word 'aristocrat' has a
long and venerable history as a term of political abuse, it was widely used in a
descriptive and sometimes sardonic way, and without too much anxiety over
the differing nuances of 'aristocracy' and 'upper class.' Nathaniel Parker Willis,
littérateur and sharp-eyed observer of the *bon ton*, remarked on the prolifera-
tion of aristocracies in New York within the 'upperdom' or the 'upper ten,' the
10,000 New Yorkers constituting the city's social leaders.

There are all manner of standards for 'the best people.' The ten thousand
who live in the biggest houses would define New York upperdom with

1. N.P. Willis.

Nathaniel Parker Willis was a poet, dandy, editor, and aesthete. Until the visit of Oscar Wilde in 1882, New York had seen nothing quite like the flamboyant Willis. For all his foppishness, Willis was an acute observer of the passing Broadway scene, and had a clear grasp of the new role luxury was playing in the life of the city's aristocracy.

satisfactory clearness, to some. The ten thousand 'safest' men would satisfy others. The educated ten thousand—the religious ten thousand—the ten thousand who had grandfathers—the ten thousand who go to Saratoga and Newport—the liberal ten thousand who ride in carriages—the ten thousand who spend over a certain sum—the ten thousand 'above Bleecker'—the ten thousand 'ever heard of'—are aristocracies as others estimated them. And till the *really upper ten thousand* are indubitably defined, there are ninety thousand, more or less, who are in the enjoyment of a most desirable illusion.[3]

Aristocracy in America was not an established position in a comprehensible social hierarchy, as in Britain. Rather, it was a meaning attached to certain individuals, families, 'sets,' and locations by themselves and by others. In the nineteenth century the idea of aristocracy in America was at best a metaphor for high social status or prestige in a nation which had unequivocally rejected the basic mechanisms needed to create and sustain an aristocracy on the European model. Entail and primogeniture, which had ensured the transmission of wealth and property to a single heir in Europe, were abolished soon after the American revolution. But in practice inheritance remained the principal vehicle for maintaining aristocratic status in New York. The Astors with considerable success continued the rule of primogeniture over three generations following the death of John Jacob Astor in 1848. Under the Articles of Confederation and the Constitution of 1787, the states and the Federal Government were denied the right to grant titles of nobility. The Constitution also forbade American officeholders from accepting titles from a foreign ruler or nation without the consent of Congress.[4]

As I use the term here, 'aristocracy' signifies a group of high status possessing a conscious sense of shared rituals, identity, and organization. The term 'upper class' is a more functional term for the leading citizens—who may share nothing more than being wealthy, being prominent, and being New Yorkers. The element of consciousness is worth underlining. Willis argued that there was a Romantic aristocracy within the Upper Ten, consisting of a small class of those unappreciated by society at large, and 'unconscious of their own degree from nature,' who could only be recognized by those aware of the very highest standards. In New York society, as it will be described here, there were no natural or 'unconscious' aristocrats. A position in the aristocracy of New York, a small sub-group within the city's upper class, was largely self-defined. Aristocrats knew that they belonged, and had an acute sense of their entitlement to a position in 'society.' (The letters of Maria and Allan Melvill written in the 1820s, and discussed in Chapter 2, are perhaps the strongest example we have of the indignation caused when that entitlement was ignored.) The designation 'aristocrat' was a very knowing transaction between inner conviction and external confirmation.

The pretensions of aristocrats in a democracy would clearly have been intolerable. Yet, in the nineteenth century, a remarkably self-confident and powerful aristocracy emerged within American society, a great lumbering elephant of a social presence which historians have largely been happy to ignore. Other than in the work of Edward Pessen, Frederic Cople Jaher, and E. Digby Baltzell, and writers such as Cleveland Amory, Jerry Patterson, and Stephen Birmingham who have addressed a broader readership, little attention has been paid to the system of aristocratic society itself, its institutions, forms of amusement, and thirst for exclusivity. Despite our enduring interest in the Gilded Age, and its swashbuckling Wall Street predators, the refined social world of Bond Street and the inner life of Fifth Avenue mansions are more the terrain of novelists than social historians. The fate of the nineteenth-century aristocrats is to be remembered as stereotype and cliché, for their bad taste, heavy furniture, ostentatious mansions, and fondness for jeweled tiaras. ('I do mourn over this foolish, wasteful ostentation . . . ,' wrote William Ellery

Channing to Harriet Martineau in 1836, 'because it stands in the way of the particular social progress which belongs to us as a people.')[5]

In the 1870s, society in Britain was estimated to be composed of 500 families, expanding by the time of the First World War to some 4,000. Comparisons with English society were often made by social leaders in New York, who felt that their society had to be even more exclusive. As Mrs. Astor suggested, New York had to be more particular because 'in America there is no authority in society, and Americans in general are not inclined to admit its possibility. Each woman is for herself and trying to outdo the others in lavish display and mad extravagance, with little thought of any ultimate good or any ideal.'[6] In the late nineteenth century the New York aristocracy, under the leadership of Ward McAllister and Mrs. Astor, consisted notionally of 400 individuals marked by wealth, refinement, and family standing. The 'Four Hundred,' coined in a newspaper interview by McAllister, is perhaps the greatest single American contribution to the idea of aristocracy. The success of the label reflected a heightened self-awareness among the aristocrats that they constituted a narrowly defined and highly select inner circle of the New York upper class.

This book is an invitation to reconsider the 'Age of Aristocracy,' and the customs and rituals of the social elite as they evolved in the nation's most boisterous democracy. In that paradox is to be found the source of the anxieties which plagued aristocratic life. Social observers were convinced that by the 1840s there was a distinct aristocracy in the city. There were signs in every drawing room of aristocratic tones. Good manners seemed to require an ever narrower 'correctness' in social intercourse. An aristocratic frigidity of demeanor was believed to express social refinement. Ladies were advised to go through the formalities of an introduction 'with the most bland expression . . . yet insensibly convey to the introduced an impression that a further intimacy would not be agreeable.'[7] A contributor to a ladies' magazine remarked that 'It has apparently struck some women in the society of our new country . . . that they appear to stand well by being disagreeable—that an air of hauteur and rudeness is becoming and aristocratic.'[8] The coolness and hauteur of New York women were a social accomplishment necessary to social success. 'A faint smile and a formal bow,' wrote Abby Buchanan Longstreet,

are all that the most refined lady accords to the visitor of her family when she passes him in her walks or drives. If a gentleman lifts his hat and stops after she has recognized him, he may ask her permission to turn and accompany her for a little, or even a long distance. Under no circumstances will he stand still in the street to converse with her, or be offended if she excuse herself and pass on.[9]

But aristocratic hauteur could be learned, and was not an unquestionable sign of aristocratic lineage. There was in fact little common agreement about who was in the aristocracy, and who was excluded. William Armstrong's *The Aristocracy of New York* (1848) was little more than an annotated list of the city's wealthiest businessmen, with Hiram Anderson, a Bowery carpet dealer, and Dr. D.M. Reese, resident physician at Bellevue Hospital and author of *Humbugs in New York*, jostling for space with somewhat more august figures like John Jacob Astor.[10] In such a compilation, wealth was no guide to social position. The perimeter of the aristocracy was unstable, and the flood of 'new money' meant that membership of the aristocratic world seemed, to insiders, alarmingly fluid. Assurance of social superiority went hand in hand with a nagging concern that the wrong types were gaining admission to the right circles. Social leaders sought to make the aristocrats of New York, Newport, and elsewhere more conscious of their corporate existence, and more willing to organize and defend aristocratic life.

First, the idea of aristocracy had to be made acceptable. The mechanism for rehabilitating aristocracy came from a growing American interest in English taste and style. By the 1820s and 1830s, as the revolutionary generation passed from the scene, wealthy people in New York once again bought English goods, and looked to London (and Paris) for fashions in dance, music, dress, culture, and social life. The American love affair with the novels of Sir Walter Scott led to a cult of the Highlander. Dandies, in passable imitations of Regency bucks, strolled Broadway, affecting English accents (among the favorite Englishisms were 'dawnce,' 'cawn't,' 'pawth,' 'chawnce,' 'rathaw,' 'fathaw,' 'aw,' and 'demmit.')[11] When Dickens visited New York in the 1840s, the city was awash with Anglophilia. Reflecting on the visit of the Prince of Wales in 1860, the diarist George Templeton Strong expressed what was a commonplace belief in his social circle: there was a 'deep and almost universal feeling of respect and regard for Great Britain and for Her Britannic Majesty. The old anti-British patriotism of twenty years ago is nearly extinct.' Alice Duer Miller's grandfather loved English books, particularly enjoying *Peregrine Pickle*, Trollope, and Mrs. Inchbald's collection *The British Theatre*. 'And every year he re-read the *Lives of the Lord Chancellors*, bound in black cloth with a gold mace and woolsack on the cover.' The young Henry James recalled in the 1840s poring over the steel engravings in Joseph Nash's *Mansions of England in the Olden Time* at the James family's fashionable 'uptown' home at 58 West 14th Street.[12]

Wealthy New Yorkers, many of whom had visited England, told their architects to recreate the features of English stately homes in rural New Jersey or along the eastern bank of the Hudson River. The precise architectural styles, which tended towards the eclectic, mattered less than the feel of the estates, and the lives which their owners imagined were lived by aristocrats. Wealthy

Americans learned to drive fancy coaches, play polo, hunt with hounds, breed racehorses and pedigree livestock and took up yachting. They collected Old Masters, oriental carpets, heirloom silver, and precious jewels.[13] Americans began to describe themselves as 'sportsmen.' English taste and style, suggesting refinement, social position, and wealth, were professedly aristocratic in the eyes of New Yorkers. They still are. In so attractive a guise, the *idea* of aristocracy no longer seemed quite so repulsive to Americans, or at least to those with money. Noting the publication of such works as the handsomely illustrated *Republican Court, or, American Society in the Days of Washington* by Rufus Wilmot Griswold in 1855, recent scholarship has suggested a revival of interest in aristocracy in mid-century America. It was more like a tidal wave than a mere shift in fashion.[14]

The tone of social life in New York was shaped by a distinctive passion for aristocracy. Working girls were adopting names (Georgiana Trevelyan, Goldy Courtleigh, Gladys Carringford, Angelina Lancaster) from romantic stories about upper-class heroines. Social aspiration in the nineteenth-century city was an active agency. The misses Trevelyan, Courtleigh, Carringford, and Lancaster were not *passive* receptors of upper-class style, but enthusiastic collectors of every detail of aristocratic life. The décor, clothes, dances, and tones of the imputed aristocrats, and ultimately their names, were avidly scrutinized in New York. The hunger for emulation, and its utility, which Thorstein Veblen so persuasively identified in his *Theory of the Leisure Class* in 1899, was a central element in the commerce and culture of luxury in the nineteenth century city. Copying the aristocrats was *the* New York style.[15]

Debates among historians about the adequacy of a 'trickle-down' or 'filtering-down' model of American culture have clear bearings upon our understanding of this passion for aristocratic style. We are all wearing Nikes now, and find 'trickle-up' arguments more acceptable, and more useful, to explain contemporary style. A century and more ago when the social distance between rich and poor seemed vastly wider (see the discussion of Jacob Riis and Ward McAllister, pp. 27–34ff. below), there were few signs that social elites were emulating the accents or styles of the poor. When there was a vogue for Hungarian bonnets and Greek shawls, it was not because Hungarian or Greek immigrants were seen wearing them on the streets of New York. But there were many examples of 'aristocratic' tastes and styles finding widespread acceptance, and being emulated, far beneath the thin veneer of the city's wealthy and old families.

Scholars in the 1970s and 1980s offered metaphors for alternative patterns of upward cultural influence: Michael Kammen cites *straddling, permeability,* and *symbiosis*.[16] Even in the radically divided culture of a city like New York, there were terrains, places of popular entertainment, socialization, and culture where the New Yorks met, and where the traffic upwards encountered the flood of aristocratic notions and images filtering downward into the wider culture. Brothels in the better neighborhoods, like the jocularly named 'Seven Sisters' on West 25th Street, the 'Rialto' near 14th Street and Union Square, and those near Washington Square North, occupied handsome brownstone houses with parlors furnished to ensure that residents of the fashionable mansions on Fifth Avenue would feel at home. When John Morrissey opened his gambling establishment in Saratoga in 1869, a red-brick club house adjacent to the Congress Spring, patrons encountered richly carpeted rooms, and a chandeliered dining salon. It was by emulating the style of an elegant private club that Morrissey's fortune was built. The abortionist Madame Restell moved into a new home on Fifth Avenue at 52nd Street in 1865. The splendor of her domestic setting, with marble floors, gilded French mirrors, and solid silver service, reflected the same aspiration towards aristocratic luxury. It was also a good marketing strategy.[17]

With its crowded sidewalks, sharp class divisions, distinctive immigrant and working-class subcultures, New York virtually defined the nineteenth-century metropolis. Cutting across the ethnic diversity and multiplicity of languages was a strong sense in the city of social equality: 'The full *equality* that reigns in the country, is one of the greatest comforts of society there. *Nobody* looks up to anybody. An evening party is made up of *the neighbors*, and none are excluded because they are not good enough society!' Servants seemed to their employers to be particularly susceptible to the virus of equality. 'White servant girls have 6 Dollars or 27/—Sterling pr. month [lamented John Johnston Taylor, a Scottish emigrant who had prospered in New York,] and are nearly as proud as Lucifer; if you ask them to do the most trifling piece of service beyond what they choose to prescribe as the limits of their obligations it is ten to one if you do not get a flat refusal, at any rate saucy language. They go just about as fine on holidays as *your demi Gentry*.' Visitors from England and France were among the most sensitive to this pervading spirit of equality: 'Every body here,' wrote the English editor George Augustus Sala of New York, 'is as good as every body else, and will let you know it most unmistakably. If yonder shopkeeper sits on the counter with one leg on the ground and swinging the other, and picks his teeth with a nonchalant air, or whistles the waltz from *Faust*, while you mention the articles you require, it is to let you know that he is as good as you, and better.'[18]

In the midst of such aggressive sentiments, commentators were surprised to find that there was a widespread enthusiasm in New York for aristocratic values. There were many signs of a growing demand for exclusivity. 'A stranger visiting our city cannot well help being struck with the tenacious air of exclusiveness that pervades every clique of every class.' 'Ik Marvel' observed that New Yorkers 'invite more freely than the European caste-men, but we maintain our castes under the invitation. In word only, we are democratic; and in spirit, full of aristocratic cravings.' The Reverend E.H. Chapin, pastor of Fourth Universalist Church in New York, commented that 'here, where everybody says that all men are equal, and everybody is afraid they *will* be; where there are no adamantine barriers of birth and caste; people are anxiously exclusive. And though the forms of aristocracy flourish more gorgeously in their native soil, the genuine *virus* can be found in New York almost as readily as in London, or Vienna.'[19]

For those seeking to maintain the old powers of social exclusion, the parvenu became a troublesome problem. There was a rich vocabulary for the phenomenon: social climber, men of new money, arriviste, bouncer (as in the Yiddish *Luftmensch*, air man, someone who has arrived apparently from nowhere). The parvenus, objects of fierce social mockery, were assumed to be rich, crude, half-educated, and were seen as embodying the raw hunger for social distinction. From the formation of the Patriarchs' balls in the 1870s, to the publication of the *Social Register*, the *List* and the naming of the 'Four Hundred' in the 1880s, repeated attempts were made to establish the border separating the aristocrat from the parvenu. There was, inevitably, much drawing up of lists, in private as well as in the press, to establish who was in society. Such lists were an attempt to impose coherence and discipline upon a world which was not a coherent entity. Decisions about social acceptability thus expressed a form of social power. For all A.T. Stewart's or Commodore Vanderbilt's millions, they could not secure an invitation to one of Mrs. Astor's balls. (In the case of the Vanderbilts, the exclusion continued only until 1883.) The size of society, and its uncertain and constantly changing boundaries, was an enduring source of anxiety in nineteenth-century New York.

Consider the case of John G. Wendel. With the Astors and Goelets, he was among the largest owners of New York real estate. He lived with two sisters in a small brownstone house on Fifth Avenue which was valued on his death at $5,000. The lot on which the house stood, and the adjoining garden, were assessed at $1,902,000. When an offer was made to buy the garden, he politely declined, saying that his sister needed a place to walk her dog. Wendel's grandfather had worked as a porter for John Jacob Astor, and married Astor's half-sister Elizabeth. In late November 1914 Wendel died in New York City. When his will was probated the following year, his estate was worth eighty million dollars. His son John Gottlieb II with equal tenacity held on to their property. There was a sign at the Wendel estate office which informed callers: 'No Real Estate for Sale.' On Wendel's death in 1914, the *New York Times* remarked that 'No one ever saw the windows open to let in the sunshine and fresh air; the shades were invariably drawn, and even when occupied by the owner and his two elderly sisters, its appearance always suggested that the place had been closed for the season and left in charge of a caretaker.' Fearful of the adventurers who prowled the city looking for marriageable women with great fortunes, Wendel persuaded his sisters never to marry. Even at the depth of the Depression, when his last surviving sister died in 1931, the Wendel estate was worth seventy-five million dollars.

Dickens and the romancers of an earlier generation prepared New Yorkers for the association of great wealth with social isolation. New York had more than its fair share of eccentric millionaires living in closed, dark houses, without contact with the community. James Lenox (1800–80), who inherited a farm of 300 acres in Manhattan, lived on Fifth Avenue and 11th Street with his two maiden sisters. Rooms were packed from floor to ceiling with crates of uncatalogued books, including some of the greatest bibliographic treasures of western civilization. 'He tolerated no interviews or curiosity hunters, and his own door was seldom opened to visitors except by appointment.' Another example was Edmund Schermerhorn, who suggested to New Yorkers a similar moral about great wealth and personal isolation. A member of one of the city's oldest Knickerbocker families (the term 'Knickerbocker,' referring to the descendants of the original Dutch settlers of New York, and thus of people enjoying high social status, was given an ironic twist in Washington Irving's *Knickerbocker's History of New York* in 1809 and in 'Rip Van Winkle' and 'The Legend of Sleepy Hollow'), on his death in 1891 Schermerhorn left an estate of ten million dollars. Disappointed in love as a young man (the lady in question, Ruth Baylies, married Maturin Livingston and became a leading socialite), he spent the rest of his life as a recluse, attended by servants, seeing no one except visiting singers and opera stars, who would perform alone for him at his home on 23rd Street. The physical isolation of such millionaires was, in symbolic terms, a sign of their emotional and spiritual isolation from humanity, and served as a warning against the worship of money.[20]

Wendel, Lenox, and Schermerhorn chose not to belong to society. But the 'Four Hundred,' the people who attended Mrs. Astor's balls and who were seen at the Waldorf Hotel 'Peacock Alley,' wished to occupy a position of enhanced social visibility. Given the money, which is a large *given*, it was a matter of choice whether you attended the Metropolitan Opera or took oysters and champagne at Delmonico's. That was no guarantee that you would be able to rent a box at the opera or receive an invitation to Mrs. Astor's ball, but at least it clears away the oldest and falsest idea we have about an American aristocracy: that merely being rich made you an aristocrat. There were many aristocrats who had full-time jobs, and were not ashamed to work for a living; and those men of great wealth like Wendel and the others, who turned their back upon society. Belonging to the aristocracy in New York was, up to a point, a matter of choice.

At the center of the social mechanism which admitted or excluded individuals from society was Mrs. William Astor, the woman who, 'for the last twenty years, has been the acknowledged leader of society, with almost absolute power to make or mar the social destiny of those who sought her patronage. Her visiting list was the index of the socially elect. She ruled with a strong hand.'[21] Mrs. Astor enjoyed social precedence of a remarkable kind. She would regularly be invited by the social arbiter Ward McAllister to lead guests at dinner parties into the dining room. When Consuelo Vanderbilt married the Duke of Marlborough in 1895, Mrs. Astor stood immediately behind the British Ambassador in the church procession, and was seated at the head table at the wedding breakfast. Such courtesies were acknowledgments of her eminence. Someone of course had to follow the ambassador, and the chair next to Willie Vanderbilt had to be occupied. The power she wielded was bestowed upon her by others, expressing a collective judgment upon Mrs. Astor, and what she represented.

The power such a person enjoyed was complex and mediated, rooted in a network of family, class, and personal relations. The possession of wealth was no guarantee of that kind of social authority. The judgment made by Mrs. Astor and other society leaders upon who was socially acceptable was erected on a complex system of regulations, informal controls, and social rituals which sought, in the terminology of Norbert Elias, to impose constraints. The aim behind such acts of exclusion was to set standards of behavior in public and private places, as well as establishing the appropriate dress, forms of entertainment, domestic décor, and dozens of other aspects of the daily lives of those who were in society, and those who hoped to secure their admission. The people who believed it *was* simply a matter of money power were those like the railroad magnate Collis P. Huntington who tried to buy their way into Mrs. Astor's salon.

The tone of New York social life, its particular flavor of local snootiness, was rooted in an ethos of exclusion. New York had more gentlemen's clubs than any other American city, and they were defiantly aristocratic in tone. Membership was restricted by club rules, and the exclusion of undesirables was central to the social values of the club. There were to be no more than 2,000 members of the University Club; 1,000 members of the Union League and the Union Club. An observer in 1887 noted that 'membership in the Union implies social recognition and the highest respectability.'[22] The Manhattan Club, created for the social leadership of the Democratic Party, closed its membership roll when it reached 600. There were only fifty Patriarchs, thirty-five parterre boxes at the Metropolitan Opera, fourteen members of the Goosebury Island Fishing Club, the all-male social epitome of the private association which owned Bailey's Beach at Newport, and (from an earlier era) no more than twelve members of the Hone Club. Everywhere in the world of New York society there was a demand for stricter admission to the dancing classes, clubs, and the drawing rooms of society. The federal census of 1900 recorded more than three million inhabitants in New York, but perhaps no more than a tenth of 1 percent were felt suitable for inclusion in society.

The cry for exclusivity was at its most strident at the moment when public interest in the rich was intense and growing. Everyone seemed to want to read about the behavior, dress, marriages, divorces, and expensive homes of the American aristocracy. The first publication solely about society, Andrews' *American Queen* (1879), was aimed primarily at those in society itself, and at the commercial enterprises—hotels, shops, carriage-makers, importers of luxury goods—which hoped to do business with the wealthy. But interest was increasing so sharply that publications like Maurice M. Minton's *The List: A Visiting and Shopping Directory for the Season* (1880), Charles H. Crandall's *The Season: An Annual Record of Society in New York, Brooklyn, and Vicinity* (1883), *Town Topics* (1885), *The Social Register* (1887), and *Club Men of New York* (annually from 1893), served a broader readership. The display of such publications on a parlor table was an undoubted expression of social aspiration.

The growth of interest in society was something of a Faustian bargain for the wealthy. The pure of heart and the eccentrics like Wendel might turn away from publicity, but the rest, and one assumes them to have been the majority, colluded unashamedly in their heightened visibility. What inevitably followed was the discovery that once journalists had been admitted to a society ball, socialites were captives of the machinery of publicity. Even the wealthiest and most socially eminent, like the Astors and Vanderbilts in the 1890s, were unable to control the press's voracious hunger for stories about their world. A division was emerging in aristocratic life: on one side were activities like going to the opera, holding a ball, and the mansions on Fifth Avenue, which belonged to the public life. But when they traveled, the strong preference was to maintain social distance by the use of private railway cars and private yachts. The enthusiasm for country estates in part lay in the privacy such homes made possible. Most newspapers were content to print columns of inconsequential social chit-chat, but malicious gossip columnists soon found informants with inside knowledge of aristocratic misbehavior. The intrusiveness of the media had behind it a public no longer prepared to accept the old barriers which (in somewhat faded memory) had preserved private life from public scrutiny. Henry James regarded this as 'a very illustrative piece of contemporary life':

One sketches one's age but imperfectly if one doesn't touch on that particular matter: the invasion, the impudence and shamelessness, of the newspaper and the interviewer, the devouring *publicity* of life, the extinction of all sense between public and private. It is the highest expression of the note of "familiarity," the sinking of manners, in so many ways, which the democratization of the world brings with it.[23]

The structure of the American home, with its clear division between the parlor and dining room where guests were entertained, and the rear of the house, where domestic life was conducted in near-total privacy, reinforced the significance of the divide between public and private. Etiquette manuals vigorously defended the sacredness of privacy, and warned against eavesdropping, or asking personal questions of acquaintances. Yet there was a hunger to see the aristocrats and read about them. In this, the story of the 'Age of Aristocracy' has a strikingly contemporary feel. Unable to control the press, and unwilling to consider life without heightened visibility, the late nineteenth-century aristocrats were America's first celebrity-martyrs.

There were too many observers, too much prying curiosity, for the private lives of the socially prominent to remain truly private. 'Nineteenth-century candles are not hidden under bushels,' noted the *Cosmopolitan*. 'All that society does—eats, drinks and wears; the cost of its belongings, its charities, its churches; everything except its bons mots and jeux d'esprit—is chronicled by the daily papers.'[24] By the 1880s, an ambitious hostess could expect virtually every aspect of her life, from her dress and marriage to her home, children, and social relations, to be 'covered.' The management of publicity was a skill needed by a hostess with social ambitions. In the new age of social visibility, society leaders had to become professionals at their own publicity, or hire someone to do it for them. To deal with the press a social secretary became a practical necessity, whether a figure like Augusta Talltowers in David Graham Phillips' novelette *The Social Secretary* (1905), or Mrs. Carrie Fisher in Edith Wharton's *The House of Mirth* (1905) who becomes a paid companion, adviser, and secretary to the socially ambitious Wellington Brys.

The hunger for information about aristocratic circles contained an implied threat. Scandals became harder to hide. The costs of discovery could be high. Of all the scandals that gripped Americans after the Civil War, none came close to rivaling the public response to accusations of hypocrisy and infidelity made against the most eminent Protestant clergyman of the age, Henry Ward Beecher. In the 'scandal summer' of 1874, the press reprinted verbatim detailed testimony heard before a Church Investigating Committee. Theodore Tilton's lawsuit against Beecher for 'criminal conversation' with his wife Elizabeth dominated the newspapers in 1875, and a further church investigation in Brooklyn followed in 1876. The exoneration of Beecher left him a diminished figure. Tilton, ostracized in New York, fled to Paris. It would be misleading to think that the Brooklyn scandal crossed an older border between respectable private behavior and public life. Any such borderline had been thoroughly overturned by James Gordon Bennett and the *Morning Herald* as far back as the 1840s. After Richard Kyle Fox—described as a 'good hater' who detested Negroes, Jews, the Chinese, clergymen, doctors, foreigners, politicians, and the

2. James Gordon Bennett, Jr.

Son of the founder and publisher of the *New York Herald* (see p. 136), James Gordon Bennett, Jr. took control of the paper in 1867. His riotous personal life, and passionate devotion to yachting and horse racing, distracted attention from his highly successful tenure as an editor of one of the best newspapers in the United States.

upper class—took control of the *Police Gazette* in 1876, the public's appetite for titillation seemed insatiable. However earnestly social leaders tried to keep the slightest hint of scandal from the public prints, they were no more than intermittently successful. We only know about the failures.[25] For most of those in society the avoidance of bad publicity was a necessary survival skill. Keeping the indiscretions of one's family out of the pages of *Town Topics* could cost thousands of dollars in shakedown 'loans' to the proprietor, and the purchase of vanity publications, like Colonel Mann's *Fads and Fancies of Representative Americans of the Twentieth Century, being a Portrayal of their Tastes, Diversions and Achievements* (1905) which sold by subscription at $1,500 per copy.[26]

A society scandal, along the lines of the assault by Frederick May upon James Gordon Bennett, Jr., in front of the Union Club in 1877, opened a new window upon the activities of the wealthy. While engaged to May's sister, Bennett urinated on the fireplace in his fiancée's parlor. When the actor

3. Mrs. William K. Vanderbilt.

The strong-willed and socially ambitious Alva Smith was twenty-two when she married 'Willie' Vanderbilt in 1875. The Vanderbilt Ball in 1883, a topic of much interest across the nation, placed the Vanderbilt clan at the apogee of New York social life. Her costume, made in Paris, was that of a Venetian princess, in white and yellow brocade. She wore a strand of pearls which had once belonged to Catherine the Great to the ball.

William Florence was blackballed from the Union Club a decade later, the story was all over the newspapers. But something of a gentlemanly code still prevailed into the 1890s, which ensured that certain details of the behavior of participants were heavily wrapped in euphemisms. The friends and relations of Bennett and May knew exactly what Bennett had done in the May parlor, and how a duel between the two men had petered out in farce, but it remained still a matter of hints. Readers of the press could only guess the full awfulness. Bennett took refuge in Paris—in effect banned by New York society for his boorishness—but his social disgrace was short lived, and he was soon welcomed back.[27] Two decades later the euphemisms had gone. The divorce in 1895 of Alva Smith Vanderbilt from William K. Vanderbilt ('Willie' to his friends, and enemies) was splashed across eight columns in Pulitzer's *World*. Vanderbilt, who picked up Nellie Neustretter at the races in Paris, crossed a certain tangible social line (so far as New York was concerned) by installing her in a house at Deauville and provided her with a *pied-à-terre* in Paris. When his wife sued for divorce, the whole tawdry business came spilling out. Neustretter, an American 'adventuress' from Eureka, Nevada, had become a kept woman, 'one of the brilliant members of the demi-monde' in Paris. Vanderbilt gave her an allowance of $200,000 a year, and a carriage rather more splendid than that enjoyed by his wife. The Vanderbilt divorce was hardly the first in New York society, but its vulgar visibility—like the Vanderbilt fortune and the Vanderbilt mansions—takes us into a new and decidedly modern relationship between private life and public curiosity.[28]

The appointment of the first gossip columnists in the 1880s reflected a judgment that the persons who attended society events, as well as the decoration of public rooms and private homes, the dress of fashionable ladies and the music played in society, no longer belonged exclusively to the private sphere. Newspaper editors assumed that there were tens of thousands of Mrs. Penistons and Grace Stepneys, living in boarding houses, scanning the papers every day for society gossip. Edith Wharton described the dreary life of the two ladies in *The House of Mirth*.[29]

The crowds walking along Broadway and Fifth Avenue wanted to take a good look at the mansions of the rich. Tourists traveled the length of Fifth Avenue, eagerly making the journey from Mrs. Astor's old house at 34th Street to the French château Richard Morris Hunt built for her at 840 Fifth Avenue.

4. William K. Vanderbilt.

The easy-going 'Willie' Vanderbilt was the son of 'Billy' Vanderbilt and the grandson of the Commodore (see pp. 17 and 272). His marriage to Alva Smith ended with the first of the 'society' divorces in New York. At the 1883 ball he appeared as the Duc de Guise. Leader of the Catholic League and in alliance with the Spanish, Guise was assassinated at the Château de Blois in 1588 by order of Henri III. Vanderbilt's townhouse on Fifth Avenue was modeled on the Château de Blois.

5. Home of Mrs. Astor.

The gray limestone double-residence at 840 Fifth Avenue at 61st Street, which Richard Morris Hunt designed for Mrs. William Astor and her son Col. John Jacob Astor IV, was built between 1893 and 1895. Hunt drew upon the architecture of the mid-sixteenth century for inspiration, and was responsible for the interior decoration and choice of furniture. Mrs. Astor lived in the northern half of the mansion. On her death in 1908, her son employed Carrère & Hastings to remodel the house. He wanted larger rooms for even grander entertaining. The building was sold in 1926 and razed, to make way for Temple Emanu-El.

'Whenever they fancied they recognized anyone, they cried aloud in innocent delight: "There's Mrs. Jack Birdseye! I knew her the minute I seen her!" "If that ain't Waddy Sorreltop that give the milk-and-catnip dinner to the tomcats down in Lakewood two years ago!"'[30] (Fearing that she would be looked at by rubbernecking crowds, Mrs. Astor would not go near the windows of her new home on Fifth Avenue.) Society events were magnets: curious spectators lined the sidewalk on Broadway on gala nights at the Metropolitan Opera, hoping for a glimpse of well-dressed opera-goers. The more knowledgeable waited at the exclusive box-holders' entrances on 39th and 40th Streets for the carriages bearing the ultra-fashionables. There was always a crowd outside Delmonico's hoping to get a glimpse of society belles and bejeweled matrons. When Mary Paul Astor was buried at Trinity Cemetery in 1894, a crowd trampled over graves and climbed tombstones for a better view of her husband, William Waldorf Astor, and the other mourners. The sidewalk in front of May Goelet's Fifth Avenue home was mobbed when her engagement to the Duke of Roxburghe was announced in 1903. 'The highest luxury of all,' wrote Henry James in *The American Scene*, 'the supremely expensive thing, is constituted privacy. . . .'[31]

Photography played an important role in the enhanced visibility of the aristocracy.[32] The enthusiasm for camera-made portraits of eminent people dated back to the 1840s, when eminence was defined in ways which were traditional in terms of gender and social position. Matthew Brady's *Gallery of Illustrious Americans* (1850), an album of lithographs from Brady's daguerreotypes of men in public life (Presidents, politicians, military figures, and a few others, such as the ornithologist Audubon and the historian Prescott), drew upon a Roman ideal of disinterested public service. Such images had a distinct commercial value. Publishers did a mail order business in engraved likenesses. Framed lithographs made from photographs were displayed for sale in shop windows. Even during the height of the Civil War, remarked Thomas Wentworth Higginson, there were no millionaires among the 'illustrious,' and 'scarcely a man eminent in mere business pursuits; scarcely a man whose fame is based on his income.' A decade later, the Titans of finance and commerce enjoyed a visibility which the wealthy had never previously known in the United States. Two weeks after the death of Cornelius Vanderbilt, in January 1877, *Harper's Weekly* devoted the whole of its front page to an engraving of the Commodore.[33]

America's love affair with the super-rich was born in the decade after the Civil War, when there was a strong American commerce in images of celebrity. In the 1870s José Maria Mora's studio at 707 Broadway had a large display of 'Publics,' cabinet photographs of celebrities, selling at $12 a dozen. Actresses, popular performers, and operatic stars like Etelka Gerster were enticed to pose by the

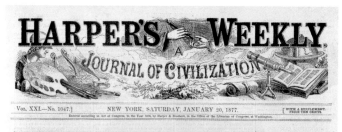

HARPER'S WEEKLY.
JOURNAL OF CIVILIZATION.

Vol. XXI.—No. 1047.]   NEW YORK, SATURDAY, JANUARY 20, 1877.   [WITH A SUPPLEMENT. PRICE TEN CENTS.

6. Cornelius Vanderbilt.

The Vanderbilts, an old Dutch family, had farmed in a small way in Brooklyn and Staten Island. Born in 1794, Cornelius Vanderbilt was a restless, energetic teenager, determined to compete with the older ferryboatmen on the New York waterfront. They mockingly called him 'Commodore,' but the mockery ceased as Vanderbilt proved himself a tenacious and clever rival. After the Civil War he dropped his steamboat business and obtained control of the New York and Harlem Railroad. At the age of seventy-three he took charge of the New York Central, consolidated it with his other lines, and operated the greatest railroad network in the world. His last words to his son 'Billy' in 1877 were: 'Keep the money together, hey. Keep the Central our road.'

promise of a commission for each portrait sold. Mora sold 35,000 copies of his portrait of the actress Maud Branscombe. Innovations in posing (the 'Rembrandt' portrait, with tasteful use of shadow, was introduced by William Kurtz at his Broadway studio in the 1870s), shorter exposure times (allowing more natural facial expressions), and improving skills in the touching-up of negatives made studio portraits increasingly 'life-like' and commercially popular. Napoleon Sarony had a stock of 40,000 photographs of actors, actresses, dancers, and operatic performers available at his gallery at Broadway near Bond Street.

There was a distinct market for images of women at the highest level of American society. Mrs. Frances Burke Roche (*née* Fanny Work) and Lady Randolph Churchill (*née* Jennie Jerome), two celebrated New York 'beauties,' were among the bestsellers. These were not the stolen images of paparazzi, but

7. Mrs. Francis Burke Roche (Fanny Work).

Against the wishes of her father, the railroad magnate Frank Work (who regarded European aristocrats as little more than fortune-hunters), Fanny Work married the brother of Baron Fermoy. Her son Edmund later inherited the (Irish) title. Through Edmund's daughter Fanny Work became the great-grandmother of Diana, Princess of Wales. Her luck in the marrying business was about as poor as Diana's, and she was later disinherited after divorcing her husband in 1891 and marrying a Hungarian horse-trainer—a marriage which lasted only four years.

fully posed professional portraits, taken with the cooperation of the subjects. A photographer remarked: 'The daughters and wives of Fifth Avenue and Murray Hill possess wealth, social position and beauty. They cannot very easily divide the former among the *hoi polloi*—the common people—but they can let the public share, in a certain limited way, in their beauty. And doing this I think they deserve praise.' Photographers, now advertising themselves as 'Society photographers,' were a necessary presence at social events. Mora took portraits of the costumed guests at the Vanderbilt ball in 1883. Joseph Byron set up a studio at Sherry's to photograph the guests at the James Hazen Hyde Ball in 1905. Participants in a tableau presented at the Bradley Martin Ball reassembled after the event to be photographed for charity.[34] Events were beginning to be planned in terms of the way they would be photographed.

Byron, Sarony, and Mora were defining aristocratic life for the wider community. The Prince of Wales was reported to have ordered a large number of photographs from Mora after an assembly ball in New York in 1872. Such patronage counted in aristocratic New York every bit as much as in London. When the half-tone process was introduced in late 1896, allowing photographs to be printed in the daily press, among the most popular innovations was an illustrated supplement printed on quality paper with the regular Sunday edition of the *New York Times*. The illustrated Sunday sections specialized in photographs of entertainers and figures in society. Hostesses were not slow to realize that getting their pictures, and especially their daughters' pictures, in the papers was an important thing. It was a very important thing indeed.[35]

The press presented a story about society to the public. It was a story with a strong, recurrent narrative form, building towards seasonal high points (the opening of the opera, Mrs. Astor's ball, and the exclusive balls held during the Winter season by the Patriarchs, the association created by Ward McAllister in 1872 to strengthen the aristocratic tone of society). In the eyes of the city editor of a New York daily, it was a story with wealth, color, power, and fancy clothes. From the early 1880s the *Times, Herald, World, Sun*, and other New York papers devoted increasing space to the doings of society leaders. Although no American newspaper sought to become a journal of record for court life, like *The Times* in London, with its daily listing of the sovereign's activities ('The Queen . . . gave a dinner Party this evening at Balmoral Castle . . .' and the deadpan list of other royal comings and goings, such as the doubtless long anticipated visit of the Duke of York to the Gdansk University Seal Institute),[36] the society pages of New York newspapers maintained a record of daily events, and reinforced what was perceived as the established hierarchy. A column of society coverage in a New York paper began invariably with news of the Astors or Vanderbilts. They were the royal families in New York.

Ward McAllister, whose career in society is discussed in the fifth chapter, led the recognition that the intense press interest had to be accepted and managed. At his small cottage on LeRoy Avenue in Newport, McAllister kept an office where he was normally available to reporters from nine until ten o'clock in the morning. 'I was often there at the stated hour,' recalled a reporter for the *Herald*, 'to find him very cordial and willing to tell of his plans. He loved publicity and he knew how to obtain it.' An active socialite, McAllister also provided pungent commentaries upon the activities of the leaders. He could quickly alert a reporter to new faces in town, the rising figures, the ones who were coasting. He was an invaluable tipster of current social form.[37]

Nonetheless the idea of 'professional' management of publicity stuck in the throat of the New York elite. There was much sneering talk of 'professional beautifiers,' 'professional agents,' 'professional ball-givers,' and 'professional beauties,'[38] of which Eleanora Winslow and Sallie Hargous were exceptionally polished examples. (A journalist played a role in the nationwide interest in Sallie Hargous, 'the prize beauty of the day.' 'The fact is, our universally beloved Sallie never was the most beautiful of the society girls, but there was a touch of professionalism about her loveliness that tempted me to take the liberty of selecting her as the symbol of society beauty and grace in the abstract.')[39] The path to social acceptance was itself professionalized. A hostess of established position, such as Mrs. J. Townsend Burden or Mrs. Paran Stevens, would 'take up' a beautiful débutante, preferably from out of town, and 'push her' at the opera and at private balls, and make sure she was invited to the right dinner parties. Being seen in the right places, and in the right company, would attract the attention of the press, and repeated mentions in the papers would in turn secure a flood of invitations for country weekends. That was the way it was worked.[40]

To achieve social success in New York, it occasionally became necessary to kick-start the process in London. 'The Saunterer' in *Town Topics* described how Eleanora Winslow was launched, and how she and her mother successfully pursued the Prince of Wales. When his attention was at last secured by 'a curtsey which would put an inexperienced person to the blush,' news that the Prince of Wales had 'made Miss Winslow the object of marked regard' was immediately telegraphed to Boston and New York. Winslow's prestige was assured. American Mammas knew well that the Prince of Wales was an easy mark for good-looking heiresses, and that free-spending Americans found the business of making a social splash sometimes easier in London than in New York.[41]

Other kinds of professionalism were looked upon with sharp disapproval. It was acceptable for society beauties to appear in drawing room recitations, amateur theatrical performances and (like Wharton's Lily Bart) in tableaux vivants. Cora Potter, a 'professional beauty' with a flowing mass of red hair, set audiences alight in New York at Amateur Dramatic Comedy Club performances. She had similar success with the Prince of Wales in England. But when she formed a professional company, her husband sought a divorce, and she was excluded from society. Her young protégée Elsie de Wolfe appeared in benefits staged by Mrs. Cornelius Vanderbilt and other society matrons, and was taken up (the euphemism of choice) by Pierre Lorillard, one of the noted sugar-daddies of the age. In 1886 Lorillard obtained a ticket to a Patriarchs' ball for de Wolfe. Unfortunately, her presence was noted, and angry questions were asked. *Town Topics* and the daily press carried full and humiliating details of the investigation into how an 'amateur actress' obtained a ticket to the most exclusive event of the New York season. It was a social disaster for the ambitious young woman.[42]

Newspapers were voracious for news of aristocratic life. Preparations for an elaborate ball were recorded in society gossip columns, with no skimping on adjectives. The host's statuary, paintings, and gilt-edged mirrors were described in respectful tones, as were the evening's flowers, the hostess's jewels, and the dresses of the guests. As social events rivaled each other in luxury and extravagance, a process egged on by the press, the public were turned into bystanders at the excitements in high circles. Columnists relished the feuds among the leading hostesses. The weighty thoughts of clergymen on the dangers of ostentation were sought out and reported at length. Provincial newspapers copied choice bits of society news from New York and other cosmopolitan centers.

Marriages at the very highest social level (involving Astors, Vanderbilts, or the betrothals of wealthy New York belles, like Jay Gould's daughter Anna, to European aristocrats), were coyly hinted, anticipated, weighed, doubted, officially denied, and warmly praised by intimates of the couple who, though remaining anonymous, spoke with the relish of all purveyors of court gossip: 'Personal friends of the lovely Miss White remarked . . .' and 'It is assumed in society that the engagement will soon be announced. . . .' The marriage itself (page one coverage in the *New York Times*), the guests, their dress, the travel plans of the happy couple, provided material for press coverage for days afterwards. Later, stories appeared about the rapid resumption of a 'gay' social round after a 'confinement' and the birth of an heir or heiress. Then, inevitably, paragraphs in *Town Topics* containing coded references to the husband's frequent absence, followed by reports—strongly denied—of gossip in the gentlemen's clubs, and hints of the existence of an unnamed third party. The daily press extensively covered the allegations, denials, negotiations, and final dissolution of the marriage, 'which everyone in society had known was in deep trouble.' The funerals of society leaders were reported in reverent detail. Then, the anticipation of the will, and the obligatory interpretation of winners and losers after the bequests, which in turn gave an opportunity for editorials deploring the inadequacy of the wealthy man's benevolence ('Compared with ordinary men, his [William Backhouse Astor's] public benefactions were large, it must be admitted; but when his vast opportunities are remembered his returns to the public from whom his wealth was derived seem very small'), or the celebration of a lifetime of Christian benevolence and generosity. The management of visibility, ensuring that wealth served the overriding purpose of maintaining social position, had come to be as much a part of being rich as possessing a fine carriage or a great mansion.[43]

8. Sallie Hargous.

There was a 'touch of professionalism about her loveliness,' and Sallie Hargous was received with open arms into New York society. By 1890 she was a regular at Mrs. Astor's dancing parties at Newport, and had been listed in the 'Four Hundred.' Being a celebrated débutante did not prepare her for the long littleness of married life. Her second marriage with the socialite Woodbury Kane, great-grandchild of John Jacob Astor, at least forged a connection with the Astors.

This expectation of social visibility was resisted by some individuals, but by definition they are hard to identify. A female reporter accosted President Chester Alan Arthur at Saratoga, demanding to know his attitude towards alcohol. He replied that he might be President of the United States, but his private life was nobody's damned business. When William Backhouse Astor died in 1875, an editorial in the *New York Herald* argued that 'Mr. Astor's social relations are not a proper topic of public comment. . . .'[44] However assiduously Mrs. Astor fed the press's hunger for information about her entertainments, she remained personally aloof. In the heyday of her social ascendancy (she 'reigned' from the 1880s to the end of the century) she gave not a single interview to the press. As a measure of the changes which followed Mrs. Astor's death, interviews with society leaders such as Mrs. Stuyvesant Fish appeared in the Sunday editions of the *New York Times*. The opinions of society hostesses on suffrage and higher education for women, wages in the rag trade, and the decline of contemporary manners, were reported and analyzed.[45]

In this complex transition towards heightened visibility, the ball was a social weathervane. Charity balls and assemblies were public events, and were treated as such in the press. But when 'private' balls began to be held on a newly lavish scale, the newspapers began to take notice. We can trace the beginnings of this view to the 1840s. Chapter 4 contains an account of a ball held at the Fifth Avenue home of Henry Brevoort, Jr. Or rather, the account begins with the presence at the ball of a reporter from the senior James Gordon Bennett's *Morning Herald*. A sharp-tongued enemy of the hypocrites, snobs, and aristocrats who infested New York, Bennett persuaded the host to admit a reporter to cover the ball, and splashed it across the front page of his paper. What made the Brevoort Ball a landmark was the change it indicated in the line separating private and public life. It was a change demanded, and embraced, by the public and welcomed at least by a segment of the aristocrats. By the 1880s private balls held in public places, such as the Patriarchs' at Delmonico's, had lost whatever remained of their private nature.

'Aristocracy' as a system offered valuable ways to deal with uncertainties about social identity and social trust which were becoming more pressing in American cities. In the rapid urban growth between 1820 and 1860, cities were a 'world of strangers,' inhabited by people who knew little about each other. Maintaining the boundaries of society mattered because it was an essential fortification against the outsider, the adventurer, and those who would prey on the respectable. There was a vast body of advice manuals in nineteenth-century America offering instruction on correct forms of behavior, and how to detect a respectable person from a 'light' woman or confidence trickster.[46] As N.P. Willis noted, external signs of class difference were sometimes less pronounced in New York than elsewhere. 'There are five or ten thousand young men who dress as well as the millionaire's son,' he wrote:

> five or ten thousand ladies for whom milliners and mantua-makers do their best; ten or twenty thousand who can show as well on foot, and walk as well without heart-burnings, in Broadway—one as another. New York is . . . the largest republic of "first quality" people that the world ever saw. . . . There is no telling, by any difference in dress, whether the youth going by has, probably, a sister who is an heiress, or a sister who is a sempstress. There is no telling the merchant from his bookkeeper—no guessing which is the diner

on eighteen pence, and which the *gourmet* of Delmonico's—no judging whether the man in the omnibus, whom you vaguely remember to have seen somewhere, was the tailor who tried on your coat, or your *vis-à-vis* last night at the ball.[47]

In the home, where wives and daughters might be assailed by strangers of uncertain motives, the need to ensure rigorous social scrutiny deepened. John G. Wendel's dread of adventurers and the pact he made with his sisters was perhaps an extreme expression of such fears, but it was a pervasive fact in the lives of anyone in New York with money. After an evening at the Century Association in October 1847, George Templeton Strong noted in his diary: 'Johnny H. Parish tells me that his sister's engaged to Robert J. Dillon. He's a humbug, and probably a wooer of the lady's expectations.'[48] Such gossip quietly made the rounds of the gentlemen's clubs, and might be heard in the more intimate drawing rooms. Few families with money were untouched by such predators. The scheming suitor, the 'thoughtless' heiress, and the mixed responses of the girl's family had all the makings of a distinctive narrative of social boundaries and their transgression.

One can imagine Henry James plucking with heightened interest at an invisible piece of lint on his trousers as he heard a curious story from Fanny Kemble in 1879 about her younger brother Henry. Her tale was quickly told. For the sake of the £4,000 fortune which a plain young woman was to inherit, her brother had paid a very disingenuous courtship. Discovering that the girl's father, Master of King's College, Cambridge, was opposed to the relationship and threatened to disinherit his daughter, Henry Kemble broke off the engagement. 'It was only in her money that H. was interested,' James wrote. '[H]e wanted a rich wife who would enable him to live at his ease and pursue his pleasures.' Some years later, after the death of the doctor, Kemble returned ('still a handsome, selfish, impecunious soldier') and proposed once again. 'She refused him—it was too late.' However much the heiress cared for Henry Kemble, his bad faith and hypocrisy had destroyed his hopes.[49]

As James re-imagined Fanny Kemble's tale in *Washington Square* (1881), he shifted the narrative perspective from the heiress and her suitor to the girl's father, Dr. Sloper, making *his* suspicions the driving force in the story. He set the narrative in the late 1830s or early 1840s, after a young man had paid a social call upon the physician's daughter. A second call soon followed, during which the gentleman, Morris Townsend, showed an excess of familiarity, lounging in his chair and casually slapping a cushion with his walking stick. It was natural to take offense at such behavior. Townsend's visit itself was socially troubling. It was inappropriate for a young lady to invite a gentleman to call. Even with an invitation, etiquette insisted that he might not make a call upon the young lady herself, but was expected to call upon her family. Dr. Sloper was naturally a concerned parent, and wanted to know who this young man was and why he had called upon his daughter Catherine. An etiquette manual written by a lady at the highest reaches of New York society was unequivocal on this point: 'no man is permitted to enter the household until his character has undergone the closest scrutiny.'[50]

Dr. Sloper consulted his sister, Mrs. Almond, to learn something of Townsend's background. It was not biographical information Dr. Sloper sought, but social knowledge. He wishes to *place* Morris Townsend, to locate the young man not only in the worldly sense of where he lives and how he earns his living, but in the informal but precise and complex social geography which a gentleman possessed of the city's families and their interlocking hierarchies. Mrs. Almond tells Dr. Sloper that Morris was not of the 'reigning' line of Townsends, and recalls that there was a 'vague story' circulating that he had once been 'wild.' Having inherited a small property, he spent it on traveling: 'I believe it was a kind of system, a theory he had,' remarked Mrs. Almond. That is, the young man was restless, unstable, and financially unsound. After Townsend called once more upon Catherine, Dr. Sloper satisfied himself about the young man's character and intentions. Catherine may have fallen in love, but the doctor was adamant:

> "She must get over it. He is not a gentleman."
>
> "Ah, take care! Remember that he is a branch of the Townsends."
>
> "He is not what I call a gentleman. He has not the soul of one. He is extremely insinuating; but it's a vulgar nature. I saw through it in a minute. He is altogether too familiar—I hate familiarity. He is a plausible coxcombe."[51]

By outward appearance Townsend was a handsome, presentable fellow, but a man in Dr. Sloper's position, with a substantial fortune and an unmarried daughter, had to be highly skilled at detecting impostors, even insinuating ones. The city was filled with 'plausible coxcombes' who preyed on credulous young women with private incomes. Two years before the publication of James's novel, there was a highly publicized annulment in New York of the marriage of Georgiana Morison to an adventurer, Joseph Lopez, who was subsequently indicted for perjury.[52] A man with means could not be too careful.

To describe the transaction between the social elite and the parvenu, between the suspicious Dr. Sloper and the enigmatic Morris Townsend, the press used quasi-military metaphors (of struggle and encroachment, all-out assault, breaches of the lines of defense). It flattered both old money and new to think of themselves as pursuing an objective and of sharing corporate discipline and coherence. But they were living in a community undergoing rapid social change, in which older values, taste, decorum, and social standards were dissolving. 'Overturn, overturn, overturn! is the maxim of New York,' wrote Philip Hone in his often-quoted diary.[53] The rush and confusion of the streets of the city, and the numerous anonymous, glancing social contacts, showed that the city was filled with people who were hard to place, hard to read. Was that Southern widow what she claimed to be? The young man who called upon Dr. Sloper's daughter—was he a gentleman? There were ambiguities and uncertainty dressed as a gentleman sitting properly in the parlor. Uncertainty threatened the very stability of society.[54]

Part of the appeal of aristocracy lay in its self-image of corporate solidarity. We have tended to see aristocratic life as a milieu more coherent and also perhaps more at ease with itself than actually was the case. 'The world of the Knickerbockers,' writes August Belmont's biographer,

> was small and safe. The children grew up together, went to school together, married each other, grew old together, and were buried in the same cemeteries. They shopped at the same stores, went to the same churches, followed the same routines, admired the same virtues (thrift, sobriety, industry, and modesty), condemned the same vices (idleness, luxury, recklessness, and ostentation), and shared the same opinions.[55]

Every part of this sentence may be accurate, yet the inner 'world of the Knickerbockers' is defined less by its stability than by its precariousness. It is easy enough to think of the elite as constituting a large extended family, a cousinage, in which everyone knows everyone else. Susan A. Ostrander, in a study of women in the upper class, writes of 'families . . . at the top of the social class hierarchy [who] . . . are brought up together, are friends, and are intermarried one with another; and, [who] finally, . . . maintain a distinctive style of life and a kind of primary group solidarity which sets them apart from the rest of the population.' This was the theme of May King Van Rensselaer's *The Social Ladder*: 'Families [in Old New York] knew the history of the families with which they had associated for generations, and these histories were vital parts of the record of the city in which they lived. The segments of the social circle were held together by intimate ties, and this intimacy made of the social organization a clan into which few might expect to force their way except by marriage with one of its members.' In a study of high society in Washington, DC, by Kathryn Jacob, this familiar view of a socially cohesive nineteenth-century elite serves as a touchstone: 'These social elites and the upper classes of which they were a part were marked by members with shared origins and common ancestors, and by cohesion, solidarity, continuity, and the hegemony they exercised over all of the major aspects of their city's life.'[56]

While much of what we know about upper-class life supports this view, the actual relations within society and the relations between new money and the aristocrats with old money and even older families were seldom so tidy. Kathryn Jacobs' terms—cohesion, solidarity, and continuity—may have been cherished values, but the activities of all too many expressed little more than a polite nod towards 'primary group solidarity.' 'The inward genius of the Fifth-avenue,' argued Greeley's *Tribune*, 'is as essentially pugilistic as that of Church and Mercer Streets; only the fist in the former case is so skillfully disguised under Paris bonbons and Strasbourg *patés*, that we who receive the weight of it seldom feel the blow, and indeed are apt to covet the muffled insult as an honor.' Competitive individualism was the defining characteristic of aristocratic life in New York City. Much of the institutional life created by the aristocrats was designed not only to exclude the parvenu but to tame the aristocrats themselves.[57]

The way to make sense of 'society' is to look at it as an attempt to establish and maintain, amidst the chaotic social milieu of the city, a stable community. Feeling that their world was under attack on all sides, many of the upper class felt the need for an enhanced rigidity and exclusivity. Frederick Cople Jaher, author of influential studies of high society in late nineteenth-century America, argued that upper-class life in New York, unlike Philadelphia or Boston, was composed of largely autonomous elites defined by profession and source of wealth, in trade, medicine, law, manufactures, politics, and culture. Lacking the continuity of elite families in other Eastern seaboard cities, upper-class life in New York was in a constant state of dissolution and reconstruction; in Jaher's term, it was 'amorphous.' It is striking that Louis Auchincloss uses the same word to describe the character of the 'Four Hundred.'[58] Jaher and Auchincloss agree that no single group in the nineteenth century possessed the authority to exercise hegemony over the whole of upper-class life. What people in society meant by 'society' was as much a process as an institution. 'Society' was an attempt to reconstruct the social order. Looking at the remorseless instability of New York, rigidity and exclusivity were but a small price to pay for a little island of coherence and a counterweight to the aggression and competitiveness of the world around them and within their parlors.

Jacob Riis, Ward McAllister and the 'other New York' in 1890

> Tenement houses have no aesthetic resources.
> —Jacob Riis (1890)[59]

For those in society and those seeking admission, there was a vast, bristling community everywhere around them. A fifteen-minute walk west from Fifth

Avenue would have brought the clubman and socialite to Hell's Kitchen. Walking east from A.T. Stewart's store on 10th Street, and then heading downtown, an aristocratic stroller would have plunged into the Bowery and the Seventh, Tenth and Thirteenth Wards. No ward in the city was a stranger place than the Tenth, formerly an area of predominantly German settlement, which had been occupied by immigrants from Russia and Poland: people with two American-born parents made up only 4 percent of its population.[60] What did our aristocrats make of that *other* New York?

Jacob Riis' pictures of the 'other half,' the tenements and sweatshops of immigrant New York, in lantern lecture, articles, photographs, and books, made an enduring claim upon the attention of everyone concerned with the city and its place in American civilization. *How the Other Half Lives*, published in 1890, is a disturbing text. It was *meant* to disturb the complacency of comfortable people. His earnestness, writerly gifts, and the pioneering use he made of visual materials persuaded a generation of Americans to look at the tenement world. Riis framed the tenements, and made the conditions of the immigrants and the poor a touchstone of the moral condition of the city.

In the same year, Ward McAllister published *Society As I Have Found It*. Both books were reviewed in November and December 1890. McAllister, a socialite, had made himself spokesman of the city's wealthy. He was the inventor of the 'Four Hundred' and organizer of the Patriarchs, the exclusive ball-giving society to which only the wealthiest and those from the oldest and most distinguished families might become subscribers. Riis hoped to speak for (or at least about) the Lower East Side; McAllister was the voice of Fifth Avenue. The two men, and their books, never quite make contact with each other. The geographical separation of their subjects (McAllister's world was to be found on the spine of Manhattan, on Fifth Avenue from Washington Square to the southern edge of Central Park; Riis' 'other half' was located on the outer rim of Manhattan, along both river-sides, and below 14th Street), and the sharp class divisions within the late nineteenth-century city was a moral and social fact of the greatest importance. It was universally assumed that the world of the poor and that of the rich existed in near-complete isolation from each other. These were the 'separate spheres' which so disturbed commentators on life in the city. The poor were educated in different schools from the rich, they attended different churches, voted for different political parties, lived in different parts of the city. Or perhaps the social distance was itself a product more of perception and culture than of empirical reality. For each complaint that the rich and poor were drawing apart, there was another observer ready and willing to point out that in the crowded conditions of life on Manhattan, and especially on the city streets, it was 'but a step from the merchant's mansion to the pauper's hovel. Wealth is everywhere elbowed by poverty, and being sternly told that social equality is not among the theories yet realized.'[61]

Riis' text is larded with facts garnered from the bureaucracies of administration and benevolence which in 1890 had achieved an unprecedented place in civic life. Early in that year, the city government reported a string of imposing statistics about life in the city, from the 157,358 square yards of paving laid to open new uptown streets to the number of passengers arriving at Castle Garden (315,228). In this proud display of numbers, the Coroner's Department contributed its share: there were 51 murders or homicides in 1889 in a city with a population of 1,575,406. There were 189 suicides, and 39,583 reported deaths. The deaths per 1,000 living persons in the population were 25.12, a figure reflecting the immense strides in sanitation and public health since the creation of the Metropolitan Board of Health in the aftermath of the Civil War. At the bottom of the tabulation of mortality were the deaths of children under one year (10,678) and deaths of children under five (17,051). A novelist like Stephen Crane put the tragedy of those child deaths a different way in *Maggie: A Girl of the Streets* (1893): 'The babe, Tommie, died.' The unsentimental novelist's offhand remark turns away from the task which Riis sets himself: moving the public, propelling conscience into action. An unfair world, he wrote, must be made to see its unfairness.[62]

Riis combed the city's newspapers, and talked to Health Department inspectors. Many of the figures suggested that there had been improvement in measurable aspects of city life. But the further he went into what the *New York Times* described as an 'Unhealthy District,' the more the picture darkened. In June 1890 a brief report appeared in the paper about a three-block stretch of Elizabeth Street, between Broome and Houston Streets. It was an area of tenements, largely occupied by Italians. In the first six months of the year, the tenement at 161 Elizabeth had reported six deaths. There were eight deaths at 167, seven at 197 and six at 199. In total 122 deaths had been reported on Elizabeth Street, 'an unusual mortality,' meriting further investigation. Many of the dead were children, victims of measles, pneumonia, bronchitis, and other respiratory illnesses.[63] Riis, who had covered crime in the slums, knew about such places. He had visited the tenements, and wrote about conditions in the sweatshops. (He describes a raid he accompanied on stale beer joints from a police station on Elizabeth Street.) As well, he read the reports of legislative investigations, and drew ammunition from the files of the leading civic charitable and benevolent bodies such as the Association for the Improvement of the Condition of the Poor, Charity Organization Society, Children's Aid Society, and Elbridge T. Gerry's Society for the Prevention of Cruelty to Children. The manager of the Fresh Air Fund, and officers at the Five Points Mission, Five Points House of Industry, and the Sisters of Charity told Riis about the deteriorating conditions in the tenements. Chief Inspector Byrnes, a high-profile member of the Police Department, was happy to use Riis to feed his arguments into the public domain. Riis was, in other words, a highly useful man. He admired honest civic-minded gentlemen like Theodore Roosevelt senior, and was an unabashed partisan of energetic reform politicians like the younger Theodore Roosevelt. Clergymen like the Reverend William S. Rainsford, who from the pulpit of St. George's Church summoned the wealthy to a heightened sense of their social responsibility, embodied precisely the social message in Riis' many books.[64]

Riis wanted to convey to the public that the tenements were the heart of the social problem. 'In the tenements,' he wrote, 'all the influences make for evil'. Since the 1840s reformers had by successive legislative measures tried to bring about improvements in the sanitary condition of the city. The rising number of immigrants crammed into tenements undermined each attempted reform. Writing in 1890, Riis insisted that there were more tenements, housing more of the population, than at any time in the city's history. The problem was getting worse. Riis believed that the facts cited in *How the Other Half Lives* were allies in his struggle. 'The figures speak for themselves . . .,' he wrote. 'I have aimed to set down a few dry facts merely. They carry their own comment.' Riis' naïve faith in 'facts' served as an antidote to what he believed to be pervasive ignorance, in the community as well as in the tenement-dwellers. Belief that there was wholesale ignorance of the causes of disease, of basic sanitary precautions, and a widespread public indifference to conditions in the tenements, made Riis exasperated. Impatience made him insensitive and sometimes insulting. He did not write as though he supposed his books would be read by the 'ignorant' masses. Rather, his audience was sought in the middle and upper ranks of society, among readers who might respond to his appeals to conscience and rejection of governmental activism.[65]

He supplemented 'facts' with acts of personal witness, inviting his readers to share an experience of visiting 'unknown New York,' far from Central Park, the Brooklyn Bridge, and the Statue of Liberty. Riis took his readers into Blind Man's Alley, Cherry Street, Bayard Street, Bottle Alley, and Bandit's Roost, describing the evening when he accompanied an aggressive police raid on a stale-beer dive in 'the Bend.' What he found below 14th Street was not the New York of 'sunlight,' of enterprise, and the straight streets of the city's grid plan, but a world of degradation, moral complexity, shadowy threat; the 'other half' lived in an urban world of twisting alleys and passageways hemmed in by dirty brick walls.[66]

From the middle of the century social observers had employed a language of 'sunlight' and 'gaslight' or 'shadow' to present what they felt was a deepening divide between rich and poor in the city. The readers of Riis' book would very likely know works in a popular genre of contemporary journalistic portrayals of the city, like Matthew Hale Smith's *Sunshine and Shadow in New York* (1868) or James D. McCabe's *Lights and Shadows of New York Life* (1872). Tenements, shantytown life, squatters, paupers, the Italians on Mulberry Street, the cellar haunts—such topics were in truth scarcely news.

For Riis, there were whole districts below 14th Street which were 'a maze of narrow, often unsuspected passage-ways.' In that world of low dives in cellars and basements, a whole community existed in 'an atmosphere of actual darkness, moral and physical.' For abandoned infants of the poor, left at Sister Irene's Asylum on 68th Street, 'no ray of light penetrates the gloom, and no effort is made to probe the mystery of sin and sorrow.' Darkness is the organizing figure through which Riis tries to help his readers understand the 'other half.' There were 'dark' rooms and unlit staircases in tenements—stale, grimy, unventilated, and untouched by cleansing sunlight. The 'rear' tenements were hidden from view, festering and threatening the health of the community. 'Take a look [Riis writes] into this Roosevelt Street alley; just about one step wide, with a five-story house on one side that gets its air—God help us for pitiful mockery!—from this slit between brick walls. There are no windows in the wall on either side; it is perfectly blank. The fire escapes of the long tenement fairly touch it; but the rays of the sun, rising, setting, or at high noon, never do. It never shone into the alley from the day the devil planned and man built it.' Untouched by sunlight, in the eyes of sanitary reformers such a building was above all a source of infection and breeding ground for disease, immorality, and criminality. Health inspectors and the experience of conscientious men, such as the managers of the Duane Street lodging-house for newsboys, concluded that light was an essential ingredient in health and an agent for morality, every bit as much as soap and water. To the reformers such an environment was degraded, and contrary to the values of civilized life. They could not see a tenement as a 'home.' The views of the poor mattered not at all to the reformers when they were making such a judgment.[67]

For Riis, the rich were no less at the heart of the problem of the tenements than the poor. They were the owners of tenements, the speculators in slum real estate who distanced themselves from the day to day management of their properties by the employment of agents. If the poor lived in the 'dark,' the owners were happy to be invisible. The identities of the owners were often unknown to their tenants, and were protected by the silence of the agent, whose sole task was to screw the highest income possible from the property. Every penny spent on improvements was a lowering of the income produced for both agent and owner. Agents had abundant reasons to collude in the degraded conditions in the slums. Riis found that both the poor and the owners resisted any attempt by housing reformers to interfere with the freedom of contract. The account he offers of the role of the rich begins with their abandonment of the antebellum Lower East Side, and the transformation of their homes into tenements. By the 1890s, rents were 25 percent to 35 percent higher than for similar properties uptown. Riis intemperately blames the Jews for their 'instinct of dollars and cents' and 'constitutional greed' but the 'honored family' who Riis discovered owned one of the worst slums in 'the Bend' needed no lessons in avarice. Riis was indignant at the Jews for their greed, but in *How the Other Half Lives* there is a comprehensive indictment of respectable New Yorkers who were ultimately responsible for the poorest and most insanitary housing in North America.[68]

On balance, Riis was harsher on the ignorance and degraded condition of the poor than on the role of the wealthy. For this reason, the legacy of Riis as a social reformer is curiously ambivalent. The wealthy owners of slum property were not named and shamed, but permitted by Riis to remain invisible. If he had, for example, chosen to raise once again the notorious record of Trinity Church as a landlord, or taken the list of the Patriarchs of 1872 provided in McAllister's *Society As I Have Known It*, and asked what role such men were playing in the real estate market in the Lower East Side, there might have been an interesting engagement of Fifth Avenue and Delancey Street, at the heart of the slum world. But that was far from Riis' intentions.

Where he does 'name' the rich, it is to praise them as friends of the homeless, or as supporters of model tenements. The rich were to serve for Riis as exemplars of social concern, or not at all. Charlotte Augusta Gibbes, wife of John Jacob Astor III (see below pp. 247–9, for a more detailed consideration of her role in the Astor family), seemed such an exemplary figure. With the manners of a duchess, and the fabled riches of the Astors at her command, it was her support for Charles Loring Brace's Children's Aid Society, and the orphan trains which the society sponsored, which made her a true 'friend' of the poor and the homeless. In the 1870s she generously paid for nearly 700 New York street children (orphaned, homeless, abandoned) to be transported to the Midwest and placed with farm families.[69]

There is occasionally a comic side to the charitable efforts of the Astors, such as the gift of a dozen volumes of the *Illustrated London News* which Mrs. John Jacob Astor III presented when an appeal went out for reading matter for the Newsboys' Lodging-House. The charitable gusto of Theodore Roosevelt senior was no less memorable. He invited his wealthiest friends for a reception at his home on behalf of the Orthopedic Hospital. At the height of the reception, Roosevelt ordered the sliding doors to the dining room drawn aside, revealing a group of crippled children, all wearing the kind of heavy braces which only generous charity could provide. The guests gathered round for his demonstration of how the braces were fitted. It so impressed Mrs. Astor that she agreed to support the hospital.[70]

But a closer look at the Astor Estate Office would have shown that the Astors, with their fabulous riches, strenuously opposed any attempt by politicians or the courts to require landlords to make 'uneconomic' improvements. Better housing conditions for the poor meant higher tax assessments for the rich, and that was self-evidently intolerable. A biographer of the family summarizes the ambiguous legacy of the Astors as landlords: 'For twenty years the Astors stood in the way of tenement reform and they also opposed municipal plans for rapid development of the still-green acres in the northern part of Manhattan. The more congested the lower portion of the island, the greater the demand for tenements and the better the returns for them.'[71]

Riis was a profound believer in the need for the many problems of the tenements to be addressed by the private sector. Legal reform, in the form of strengthened building codes and sanitary regulations, was not enough. Social justice, he argued, could only be built on the sympathy of the human heart. Mrs. John Jacob Astor III was the most important example cited in *How the Other Half Lives* of that generosity of spirit upon which social reform could be based. Riis of course saw the urgency of the crisis ('The gap between the classes . . . is widening day by day,') but for an abundance of reasons he ignored the responsibility of the rich for tenement problems. Riis at one point noted that in New York there was no tradition of personal benevolence across class lines: the rich did not adopt the orphans of the poor. There were to be no fairy-tale endings for the poor orphans like those told by Horatio Alger in his 'Ragged Dick' stories.[72]

A small number of clergyman of the muscular Christian persuasion, like Rainsford of St. George's Church, became sharp critics of New York society. 'In the early '90s,' he wrote, 'I was practically alone among the clergy in the Protestant Episcopal Church in attacking the social conditions among the poor—and the rich—in New York.' To Rainsford, the rich were self-regarding and indifferent to the conditions experienced by the poor. Only a minority of the wealthy gave thought to the slums, and the same—so Rainsford believed—was true of the clergy, who went about their placid daily tasks without disturbing their well-heeled parishes by talking about poverty and hardship in the city and the larger responsibilities which properly fell to the wealthy. A preoccupation with trivia and the media obscured graver concerns: 'The question on Murray Hill and Park Row alike is: Will the Pulitzers be invited to the Patriarchs'?[73] Factory workers and tenement dwellers did not loom large in the social chit-chat of Fifth Avenue. Even their domestic servants were, with the exception of French chefs and English butlers, interchangeable, highly replaceable, and invisible.

The social invisibility of the rich for Riis and the poor for McAllister united the strategies of the two writers: they were content to ignore inconvenient presences. Despite his flash-lit photographs and skilled social reportage, Riis allowed the role of the rich to remain in the dark. McAllister, with his careful mastery of publicity, was equally content to ignore the poor. Both were engaged in a highly selective management of social visibility. But neither the rich, nor the poor, could remain unscrutinized.

2

THE ART OF SOCIAL CLIMBING

The departure of the British Army from New York City in 1783 was an event viewed with anxiety by the new state's governor, George Clinton. When the British departed on November 25, he feared there would be a collapse of law and order. The arrival of the Continental Army, tattered and weather-beaten in contrast to the immaculate scarlet coats of the British Army, was choreographed to leave no dangerous vacuum in the city. A mob, principally led by women, managed to seize the notorious British Provost Marshal William Cunningham and hauled him back to the Provost's Guard in City Hall Park, where he had treated American patriots with such harshness. He would have been lynched if word had not reached General Washington, who personally intervened to persuade the mob to release Cunningham. Hatred of the British ran with passion through the streets of New York. Cunningham later confessed to having been responsible for the deaths of as many as 2,000 Americans who were hanged at midnight on a gallows in a silent and empty Barrack Street, or who through neglect and overcrowding starved to death in Cunningham's prison, or died of disease.

Former residents had begun returning to the city, seeking to recover houses and other property, demanding immediate compensation for damages. Terrified by the threat of revenge attacks and fearful of anti-Tory legislation when the new government was established, Loyalists and Tories, friends of the British crown, were grateful when they were offered free passage away from New York with the Royal Navy. They departed, perhaps 30,000 in the second half of 1783, with servants, slaves, frantic tradesmen, clerks, officials, and clergymen. Three-quarters settled in Canada.[1] With the departure of the Loyalists, one aristocratic New York elite was dispersed, and the way was opened for the emergence of another—scarcely less aristocratic, but one that existed in a culture which was professedly democratic, and for a generation and more was deeply suspicious about all things British. The term 'aristocracy' did not fall out of use; rather, it was increasingly used to describe a mechanism to channel and control power through social means. By regulation of entrée into the drawing rooms, parlors, clubs, assemblies, and other institutions, the new masters of New York sought to maintain power through social exclusion.

In the experience of the daughters of Governor Trumbull of Connecticut visiting New York in 1800–1, there are materials for a light-hearted social comedy of provincials being trained for a place in the sophisticated life of the metropolis. In the struggle of Allan Melvill and his wife Maria to gain and maintain social recognition in the 1820s there is a darker-tinged narrative of the anguish experienced by those who were simply not rich enough. We begin with arrivals in, and departures from, the city's aristocracy.

The Trumbull sisters spend a season in New York

Maria and Harriet, daughters of Jonathan Trumbull, Jr., Governor of Connecticut, reported the 'melancholly news' to their father that supporters of the newly elected President Thomas Jefferson and Vice-President Aaron Burr had been aggressively celebrating their political triumph in the presidential election of 1800. 'There was quite a rejoicing about and the cannons at the Battery were going as brisk as need be—and when we came home in the evening there was a large mob in the broad way made up of the very dregs of the town, and they to besure were fighting at a most terrible rate, however we got safe home at last—tho' we were not a *little* frightened.'[2] The idea that their parents might be so alarmed at the dangers of disorder and rapine in New York as to summon home Maria, who was fifteen, and Harriet, seventeen, caused a rapid toning down of their subsequent letters. 'People here seem quiet and peaceable enough' (March 2, 1801).

Governor Trumbull, an aide to General Washington during the war for independence, had emerged as a considerable figure on the national stage. He served in the first Federal Congress which met in New York from 1789 to 1791, and was elected Speaker of the House in the second Congress in 1795. Trumbull was appointed to the Senate and two years later was elected Governor of Connecticut. He had been a conspicuous Federalist, and a loyal supporter of the administrations of Washington and John Adams. Washington described him as one of those 'disinterested and respectable characters' upon whom the integrity of the new nation's legislature depended.[3] Not long after his daughters arrived in New York, Trumbull's address to the Connecticut Legislature appeared in the press. His Federalism was more than a political doctrine. It expressed the ancient virtues of the people. Convulsions and 'internal agitations' in the United States, wars and revolutions in Europe, 'may endanger our national quiet, harmony, and order;—I know no better course for this State to pursue, than to adhere steadily to her long-tried stability of religious, moral, and political virtues, and to attend cautiously to her ancient habits of internal order; to her quiet submission to established regulations, and tranquil observance of her present institutions of moral and civil administration.'4 The doctrines of hierarchy and discipline which Trumbull believed should form the basis of civil governance applied no less to the family, and to the regulation of daughters, particularly teenage daughters, busy with shopping and music lessons in New York. The Trumbull sisters could scarcely forget that they were by birth and upbringing members of the Federalist aristocracy in post-revolutionary America.

Despite their domination of the political institutions of New York State, and secure position bolstered by the handsomely endowed Episcopal Church and Columbia College, as well as control over New York banks, the stock exchange and the courts, the political revolution of 1800 filled Federalist hearts with dread. Paid Federalist wits turned upon the insurgent Republicans, sarcastically prophesying that if the Republicans won, '—the lamb will lie down with the lion—every hungry office seeker will be gratified—brambles will cast their thorns and bear apples of gold—the clouds will pour down fat turkies and canvasback ducks—and our land shall overflow with liberty and the rights of man!!!'5 Rhymesters in Connecticut, anticipating the likely Republican joy at Jefferson's victory, make the association with the British interest and the aristocracy:

The *Federalists* are down at last,
The *Monarchists* completely cast,
The *Aristocrats* are stripped of power,
Storms on the *British-faction* lour.
Soon we *Republicans* shall see,
Columbia's slaves from bondage free. . . .
What glorious times! when great men wait,
And *little ones* direct the state;
When *Tom*, and *Dick*, and *Harry* rise
Two feet above their common size . . .'6

The Trumbull family repeatedly expressed concern for the well-being of their daughters, but the girls patiently reassured them that the long-term benefits of a stay in New York outweighed any dangers. Harriet and Maria had come to New York to be schooled in urban manners.7 The drawing master at the Columbian Academy of Painting at 79 Liberty Street (as the victors of 1783 renamed Crown Street) seemed quite pleased at their advancing skills. Their music master James Hewitt, who held regular concerts at the Mount Vernon Garden on Leonard Street, praised the girls' 'considerable progress' on the pianoforte—the instrument which since the late 1790s had begun to displace the spinet in cultured circles. Family friends were positively insistent that the girls remain in New York through the winter. 'Cockloft Pindar,' poet laureate of the city's fashionables, celebrated the social rounds of such young provincial ladies in the fifth number of *Salmagundi*:

> . . . t'other day,
> I went a morning call to pay,
> On two young nieces, just come down
> To take the *polish* of the town;
> By which I mean no more nor less
> Than *a la française* to *undress*;
> To whirl the modest waltz's rounds,
> Taught by Duport for *snug ten pounds*.
> To thump and thunder through a song,
> Play *fortes* soft and *dolce's* strong . . .[8]

The Trumbull sisters soon proved adept at managing a busy round of lessons, concerts, dinners, balls, and evenings at the theater. Taking tea was itself a central rite of gentility for women in the early nineteenth century. Easily prepared at home, tea was served to the mixed company of the family parlor (the coffee-houses were exclusively a male preserve), and the implements of the occasion (teapot, strainer, cream pitcher, sugar bowl, teaspoons, cups, saucers), preferably made of the best china and silver, themselves became objects of conspicuous consumption. The tea table possessed a reputation for gossip, and hence for young girls there was a danger of receiving the wrong lessons about coquetry and fashionableness.[9]

Both sisters pursued instruction and amusement with a determined earnestness. Repeated references in their letters to shopping and discussion of the various merits of neatly trimmed bonnets suggest that few days went by without expeditions downtown to merchants and vendues. It did not occur to either of the Trumbull sisters that they were doing anything new in the amount of time they devoted to the arts of consumption, or that their interests set them apart from their family's world in Connecticut. The Trumbulls were not among the wealthiest in fashionable New York, and they clearly wished their parents to understand that they were conducting themselves, and managing their purses, accordingly. Simplicity of manners and taste was appropriate, because it reflected a disciplined character. To dress as was fitting for women of their age and the position of their family in society was an expensive necessity. 'I will enclose my account of my expenses since Brother left us,' Harriet wrote to Governor Trumbull on January 10, 1801, 'and of the money we have received from Mr. Sebor; I hope you will think it moderate, tho

I was almost freightened at it: we have purchased us some new dresses today, as we thought they were quite necessary—we dont wish to appear as some young ladies we meet with [do, but] to dress handsomely and so as your friends would not be asha[med of us].'

Harriet and Maria were acquiring other kinds of useful knowledge in New York: of manners, and conduct in accordance with their social position. Contrary to the fears of a more puritanical older generation, they did not believe that such knowledge endangered their character or morals. The ability to distinguish between the fashionable and the unfashionable was not merely a frivolous thing. It was a way to protect themselves from the smooth talk and beguilements of merchants and artisans, the false attentions of the *nouveaux riches* and the glittering charms of the seducer or adventurer. To be able to read the social standing of someone to whom they were introduced was knowledge of considerable value, particularly in New York.

In addition to executing an occasional commission for their mother (for a ring or a bonnet), they assumed the role of fashion advisers for the family. They sent a requested wig to their mother with a letter pointing out that fashionable ladies in New York 'wear white *hair* altogather now, and there can be nothing *less tonish* than a black wig' (April 24, 1801). Fashion news reached New York much earlier than Connecticut, and style news reached into Connecticut by the hallowed route of letters home. Stylish young ladies like the Trumbull sisters eagerly sought the latest London and Paris looks. At Longworth's Gallery, a few doors down from the Park Theater, elegant colored prints from the latest issue of the *Gallery of Fashion* just arrived from London were framed and placed on display. The knowledge that the young fashionable ladies in London wore their hair cut short, with 'loose curls round the face' was news, and a kind of currency with appreciable exchange value at the next soirée. Equally, the details accompanying the *Gallery of Fashion* plates contained valuable hints on fabrics, bonnets, feathers, ribbons, jewelry, and cloaks. Black and white chip bonnets were being worn with morning dress in London in the summer of 1801 with a 'black feather placed on the left side; a wreath of black fancy flowers across the crown. Round dress of black and white striped muslin; short close sleeves. Grey-coloured gloves and shoes. Black bear muff.'[10]

New York had a considerable reputation for fashionableness. 'The women wear silk and gauze dresses, hats, and even elaborate hairdos,' noted Brissot de Warville.[11] The latest fashions in morning and evening wear were becoming obsolescent altogether more quickly than provincial Mammas realized. Their correspondence was a small part of that circulation of gentility outward from the aristocratic centers of Europe to the New World. The basic mechanism, in Richard Bushman's poetic trope, was of gentility 'spreading across the land, from focal points in the cities down long, elegant avenues, into more modest side streets, through space to smaller country towns, out to prosperous farm-houses and estates in the countryside.'[12] Knowledge of London and Paris style was part of the larger education young women of social position sought to acquire in New York. A mastery of the art of shopping, and knowledge of the various craftsmen in the city, prepared them for the position such young ladies were likely to occupy in the future. When the Trumbull girls found a mantua-maker who would make up gowns from the dark muslin they had bought in New York, it was an event to report to their mother (December 2, 1800).

Both sisters attended the dancing school of M. Lalliet, one of seven such dancing academies in New York in 1800.

> ### Mr. Lalliet
>
> Respectfully informs his friends and the inhabitants of New-York, that his Dancing School, at Mr. Little's Hotel, Broad-street, will be opened every day after the first of November next, for the convenience of young ladies who attend the drawing and other schools, who wish to favour him.—Terms as before.
>
> The School-ball will be held on every Tuesday night during the winter, and on an improved plan, to which any gentleman may subscribe.[13]

French refugees from the revolution in Santo Domingo in 1791 and aristocratic exiles from the Terror included skilled tutors in polite languages, fashion, dance, music, and cuisine. Among their number were instructors in other European niceties such as the *code duello*. They, too, were instrumental in diffusing European genteel culture in America. Dancing classes were normally held four times a week. Each *maître* organized balls at New York hotels, which gentlemen were invited to attend. Dancing was a passion in New York, and as with fashion, the possibilities of elegant tuition, and school balls, attracted young men.

In addition, Maria had three drawing classes a week and Harriet three music lessons. They attended amateur musical concerts, such as that given by the Columbian Anacreontic Society at the City Hotel, important social events in the city's winter season:[14]

> . . . the concert was in the city assembly room, it is a *very* large elegant room, and full of Ladies and Gentlemen all splendidly drest, I believe there were certainly 6 hundred Ladies, and a number very handsome and beautifully drest, we had some fine music and singing, a great many good things to eat, as cakes grapes almonds &c a great deal of mirth and noise, and came home between eleven and twelve O Clock. (January 7, 1801)

9. City Hotel.

The City Hotel was erected on the west side of Broadway, in the block north of Trinity Church, in 1794. With 137 rooms, a bar, coffee room, concert hall, and the City Assembly room, it was the most celebrated house of entertainment in New York. John Jacob Astor bought the City Hotel in 1828 for $101,000. It was torn down in 1847 to make room for an even grander establishment, the Astor House (see p. 71). The City Hotel was the location of the famous dinner in honor of Charles Dickens held in 1842.

Life in New York for the Trumbull sisters was a round of shopping, dancing, drawing, and playing music. Only the frequently wet weather and the poor condition of the city streets persuaded the sisters to remain at home. 'Today,' Maria wrote to her mother, 'we have been sitting as I told you before quite alone and not in very good spirit—here sits Harriet gapeing away like everything and I must stop a minute and laugh at her' (March 18, 1801). They proudly informed their family that of late they had walked as much as four or five miles a day, in a constant round of visits and amusements. Clearly they were not the New York belles whose complexion seemed so 'pallid & unhealthy' to the visiting Richard Cobden in 1835. Rather, the Trumbull sisters embodied an emerging ideal of the New York belle who, claimed 'Jonathan Oldstyle' in the *Morning Chronicle* in 1802, 'trips along with the greatest vivacity. Her laughing eye, her countenance enlivened with affability and good humor, inspire with kindred animation every beholder. . . .'[15]

The city offered distractions that Lebanon, Connecticut, could not begin to rival. There was, above all, the flood of things from all over the world pouring into the city's shops and auctions. The sales were advertised in the New York newspapers: Italian lute string, Jamaica rum, Coleraine linen, 'Havannah' sugar, Dutch vermillion, Ceylon cinnamon, and fancy dry goods of every description: 'coatings, serges, plains, baizes and flannels; Wildbores, camblets, jeans, calimancoes, and durants.' The latest London and Paris novels and romances were available at H. Caritat's bookstore and circulating library, 153 Broadway. (Caritat was another of the émigrés from France who made such a powerful impact on the cultural life of New York.) Peale's portraits of American patriots were exhibited at 126 Broadway, at the corner of Cedar Street (admission for adults 25¢, half price for children). Jeremiah Vanderbilt operated the stage line to Far Rockaway, and Peter B. Goelet sold fancy hats and bonnets from a shop at 63 Water Street: humble origins of great fortunes.[16]

The city itself seemed something to write home about.[17] 'All the principal streets are now handsomely paved,' wrote 'Sertorius,' 'and what is yet better, kept clean and respectable. In 1790, few beside old houses were to be seen; they are now almost obscured by new ones.' Beyond Chambers Street lay the Fifth and Sixth Wards, where mechanics lived in small wood houses on muddy lanes. Above Duane Street west of Broadway lay Lispenard's Meadow, extending down to the North River, but scarcely the place for a midwinter walk by young ladies of fashion. 'It was a wild and marshy spot of no inconsiderable extent,' recalled an elderly historian of Trinity Church, 'surrounded with bushes and bulrushes, which in winter was a favorite place for skaters, and at certain seasons for gunners, and where in my boyhood I have seen snakes which were killed on its borders. Indeed, even so late as 1808 it was only . . . partially filled up and reclaimed by the elevation of the grounds for the course of streets . . .'[18] The taverns, small farms, and country estates which ran along the course of the Boston High Road (beginning on the Bowery) and the Bloomingdale Road (which continued north from the end of Broadway) offered little incentive to walkers. To the south of Chambers Street lay the solidly Federalist Third Ward, with its paved sidewalks, neat brick houses and busy traffic on Broadway. The west side of the street was the more fashionable, and the modest wooden frame houses on the east side remained the combined residences and place of business for tavern keepers, shopkeepers, tallow chandlers, shoemakers, painters, glaziers, drapers, tailors, grocers, and carpenters. On Sundays the sisters attended church twice, usually at Trinity Church and St. Paul's Chapel, and did not even complain at hearing a sermon twice—the pastors normally delivered the same sermon as they rotated between churches. Out of curiosity, they several times attended Roman Catholic services at St. Peter's Chapel in Barclay Street.

They had come to New York to partake of the genteel world, not to look at picturesque slums or muddy streets. The one New Yorker in ten who was either a free black or a slave makes no appearance in the Trumbull sisters' letters.[19] The city in their eyes possessed a geography principally marked by places of refinement, pleasure, and culture. The gardens, parlors, fashionable walks, and assembly rooms were the setting for an elite. Lower Broadway, Bowling Green, and the Battery offered ladies an opportunity to show themselves which was not so attractively available elsewhere in the bustling city. The letters of the Trumbull sisters reveal no interest in what, for most of the inhabitants of New York, was the actual city, with its decayed wharves, common taverns, warehouses, and shabby artisans' dwellings. The threatening presence of ugly mobs on the streets, and drunken tavern carousers, could not quite be ignored, but with circumspection might be avoided.

That is precisely what the gracefully dressed ladies and gentlemen merchants are doing in Francis Guy's painting of the Tontine Coffee House at the intersection of Wall and Water Streets (1798 or 1799): they ignore the workers, and the black workers, slaves or freemen, ignore them. The foreground of the painting is dominated by the Meal Market, where bending workmen attend to

10. Guy's Tontine Coffee House.

The Tontine Coffee House stood on the corner of Wall and Water Streets. Financed by the sale of 203 shares at $200 each, sub-scribers placed their investment in the name of another person. When death reduced their number to seven, the assets were divided. The original building, painted by Francis Guy in 1797, was razed in 1855. When the tontine was finally divided in 1876, the names of the surviving nominees were a rollcall of Old New York families: Bayard, Kemble, Benson, Hoffman, Stevens, King, and Campbell.

barrels, crates, lumber and the packing and uncrating of the goods upon which the city's prosperity depended. The workmen scarcely cast a glance up at the raised balcony of the Coffee House where four groups of merchants, twelve men in all, stand chatting among themselves, casually ignoring the busy street scene. Their dress tells us they are gentlemen. Groups of ladies stand on the sidewalk, waiting an opportunity to cross the street. They too find nothing of interest in the workmen or in the commercial confusion which dominates the street. The ladies and gentlemen are doing what people of their class are expected to do, what it is natural to assume they would do. Their class roles in the economy of Guy's painting are as distinctive as their dress. The busiest commercial intersection of the city offers to the painter a scene of bustle and social distance.[20]

The Trumbull sisters knew that the etiquette of paying calls and leaving cards, the correct dress and demeanor at a ball or concert, was meticulously observed in the world in which they moved in New York. Social skills were proof of their refinement, and thus of their rightful claim to a place in a recognizable social hierarchy. But the detailed operation of etiquette, its finer and more arcane points, was a continuing source of social anxiety for the Connecticut teenagers. Calls made, or ignored, nuances misunderstood, left them vulnerable to snubs and slights. They were assiduous in returning the calls of those who had returned their initial calls. Even Virginia grandees were sometimes in need of such advice: Alexander Hamilton drafted a code of etiquette for the new President in 1789, which asserted that 'the dignity of the office' of President precluded the possibility of returning calls. For young ladies of the Trumbull sisters' social position, knowledge of etiquette was hard-learned and necessary.

So simple a matter as paying a morning call was hedged around with complications. A male escort or female companion was not needed if a lady went in a carriage, but a gentleman was expected to accompany a lady walking on foot. It was permissible (much to the relief of the Trumbull sisters) for two ladies walking together to make a call without male escort. When paying a call, female guests were expected to remain seated in chairs or benches lining the perimeter of the room, waiting for servants to pass refreshments in sequence. (These were the dreaded 'handed teas.') A hostess alone had the freedom to stand and cross the room. Larger social events, variously termed 'routs,' 'conversaziones,' and 'squeezes,' were less rigid in the assignation of gender roles, and the provision of tables for chess and cards, or music for dancing, greatly increased the variety of the entertainment.[21]

The Trumbull sisters' first social calls—that initial overture which expressed the wish for an acquaintanceship—were made upon Connecticut friends and political associates of the family. While it was assumed that an 'inferior' did not

11. Richard Varick.

Varick had a distinguished record in the revolutionary war, serving as George Washington's secretary. After the war he held a number of important political offices, and served as president of the New York chapter of the Society of the Cincinnati. From 1789 to 1801 Richard Varick was mayor of New York. He was the last Federalist to hold that office.

call upon a social 'superior,' at least without invitation, where social equality prevailed, it fell to a younger woman to pay a call upon an elder woman. The flood of New Englanders who had settled in New York after the Revolution, and who in time assumed a dominant place in the commercial life of the city, formed the primary social circle of the visitors.[22] They called at the home of Colonel Richard Varick and his wife Maria Roosevelt. Varick was a tall figure, austere and lofty, who had served as aide-de-camp to General Benedict Arnold. After a court of inquiry cleared him of any involvement in Arnold's treason, he served as recording secretary on General Washington's staff during the Revolutionary War. Varick had a distinguished career in New York politics, serving as Speaker of the New York State Assembly, State Attorney General and mayor of New York from 1789 until 1801. Varick's political career ended with the defeat of the Federalists in the election of 1800, but he remained, in the estimation of the Trumbull sisters, an example of the city's finest men.[23] The Trumbull sisters also called on James Watson, a merchant and Federalist politician from Hartford who was Naval Officer of New York City. From the balcony of his home at number 7 State Street they would have had an incomparable view of the Battery and New York Harbor. They also called upon Weltha, the sixteen-year-old daughter of the Hartford banker John Jordan Morgan. Former residents of Lebanon and friends of the family paid calls upon the girls. Each call carried with it a specific obligation to make a return call.

Invited to dine at the home of John Barker Church at 52 Broadway, the girls accepted—and wrote to their parents how much they regretted the attention. When later they were ignored by the Churches, they were even more upset at the slight. Mrs. Church, *née* Angelica Schuyler, was the sister of Sarah and Elizabeth Jay, and while the Jays were abroad in England she had assumed a position of leadership in New York society. Mrs. Church's entertainments were noted for their lavishness, and her flirtations with her brother-in-law Alexander Hamilton were the subject of many rumors in the city.[24] The Churches were wealthy people who lived in a grand house on Broadway, but Maria and Harriet shared the family reserve towards them.

The painter John Trumbull, Governor Trumbull's brother and the girls' uncle, had borrowed money from Church to speculate in French loans, and buy Old Master paintings for re-sale in America. Heavy debts soured relations between the Trumbulls and the Churches. Nonetheless, politeness required that they make a social call. When in reply 'Mrs. Church and Mrs. Hamilton condescended to call' the girls were out and they returned the visit. Finding no one at home, they left cards (December 25, 1800). That no further call was made gave justified offense. 'You need not fear Mama,' Harriet wrote, 'that we shall be troubled with civilities from the Churches, the young ladies have never call'd to see us, they have parties every week to which young ladies of our age and acquaintance are invited, but we have never received invitations, to our great joy' (January 18, 1801).

They wrote home in midwinter that they had been cordially received at the Churches,' where, although Mrs. Church was out, their daughter Betsey had been 'very polite indeed, and quite friendly' (February 21, 1801). Several weeks later, at a ball given by the Murray family in their home on Pearl Street, they simply noted that 'the Miss Churches and Miss Barclays were there' (March 2 and 6, 1801). Despite a friendly greeting in the Churches' home, which signified their social equality and acceptability, Harriet soon revealed that they had been harshly cut by that very same Betsey Church: 'at Miss Murray's ball, she told her [Miss Murray] that she was not acquainted with us' [March 11, 1801]). This was not the only occasion during their stay in New York when they admitted to their mother that they had been snubbed. Failure to receive an invitation to a party held by their hostess Lady Kitty's sister, Lady Mary Watts in March was no less hurtful. Occasional bouts of homesickness, and Maria's admission that 'I don't think people are very happy here' (April 2, 1801), punctuate the normal reports of shopping and entertainments.

The social judgments recorded in the Trumbull sisters' letters are rooted in the gentility of their class. On Monday, Harriet wrote, 'we went to Mr. Murray's to spend the day, and a charming day it was, Mr. & Mrs. Murray are very plain good people[.] Mrs. Murray's mother who is an old quaker lady lives with them, and her brother, the young ladies are very amiable and accomplished, they all appear to wish to have us feel happy and at home there' (March 11, 1801). Their reception by Mayor Varick at his home at 108 Broadway was equally warm. 'Mr. Varick is I think a most charming man—he seemed to love us so—and treated us with so much kindness I declare I almost felt as if I was by Papa. Mrs. Varick too is a dear little woman—and they both begged of us to come very often to see them, indeed they were almost angry that we had been in town so long and had been there so seldom' (January 17, 1801). The contrast with the Church family was plain enough.

There was no expectation in their world that there should be a general abolition of distinctions and gradations of rank. The post-revolutionary Governor of New York was given his own pew in St. Paul's Chapel, across the aisle from the President's pew. The pew at St. Paul's which had been the property of the proscribed De Lanceys, punished for their unstinting Loyalism, was acquired, along with substantial De Lancey properties in New York City, by Robert R. Livingston and his family. For all the changes brought about by the Revolution, great men still sat in their own pews and owned choice stretches of the city's real estate.

If the Trumbull sisters' sensitivity to social nuances was acute, they were no less sharply observant of political distinctions. Their world was radically divided between respectable people and the mob, between Federalists and Jeffersonians, and there were no Jeffersonians among their visitors. On the afternoon of March 4, 1801, to celebrate the inauguration of Thomas Jefferson, a political procession down Chambers Street, led by an ox destined for the almshouse nearby, was scornfully described in a letter from Maria to her mother: 'there was a monstrous large ox all dressed with ribbons and flowers—and followed by such a *despicable rabble* as you never saw in *our* state . . . wednesday was a day of great rejoicing among the wicked ones' (March 5, 1801). The presence of so many 'disorderly creatures in the streets' persuaded the girls' host, Mrs. Sebor, to advise them not to risk the journey home in the dark. They spent the evening with the Watsons, who had been among their most welcoming friends. Chambers Street was, in their eyes, almost enemy territory: 'there were such rejoicings in honour of Jefferson, that we were afraid to be at home, as at our part of the town they are chiefly Democrats, and not very *reputable* people' (March 6 and 11, 1801).

The streets on New York seemed always to be filled with parades and politics, unlike home, and public fervor often seemed capable of exploding into violence. Dr. John W. Francis recalled the wild enthusiasm for France in the city: '[t]he tricolor was in every hand or affixed to every watch-chain, while from every lip was vociferated the carmagnole.' Federalists in Philadelphia feared a massacre of all honest citizens had been planned for the Fast Day proclaimed by President Adams in May 1798. (The President had a chest of arms secretly brought to his residence when a mob of forty young men wearing French cockades fought a pitched battle with his supporters on Market Street.) There were dangers from Federalist as well as Republican mobs. After a 'liberty pole' had been erected in Warren Street by New York Democratic Republicans, two-fisted petty officers from the United States fleet, sympathizers with the Federalists, formed a carousing-and-disturbing-the-peace organization, the Knights of the Dagger, and assaulted the Republicans, and tore down the liberty pole. Twenty-five years earlier, it was British sailors and soldiers who had assaulted patriots and dragged down their liberty poles. One of the Knights was the son of the disgraced financier William Duer and his wife Lady Kitty. His tales of politics and warfare in the streets may have been a welcome escape from the longueurs of polite society for the Trumbull sisters while they were staying at Lady Kitty's home on Chambers Street.[25]

Admission to the homes of the Varicks, Morgans, Churches, and Murrays was on the basis of kinship, family friendship, and political association, but also upon Maria and Harriet Trumbull's mastery of the social skills required by society. Money, polite manners, and fancy clothes did not alone establish social position. When Uncle John Trumbull brought his English wife Sarah back to New York in 1804, establishing himself in a large house at the corner of Pine Street and Broadway, the family judged her domestic education and lack of a desirable background so harshly that she felt criticized and rejected. Her drinking and outlandish behavior further alienated the Trumbulls. The wife of a financier of doubtful probity, such as Mrs. Church, who entertained lavishly and lived in a handsome mansion, was welcome in the best society. As the Trumbull sisters discovered, their host in New York, Lady Kitty Duer, who lived in an unfashionable street on the edge of the city, and was the widow of a disgraced but equally freebooting financier, retained a social position guaranteed by family associations. That she, along with her sister Lady Mary Watts and their mother Lady Stirling, had been among a select body of ladies to call upon Mrs. Washington when she arrived in New York in May 1789, was a social credential of the highest order.[26]

Of all the complexities of New York etiquette and social relations, the fact that the sisters were paying guests of 'Lady Kitty,' Catherine Alexander Duer, shaped their experience of New York society. Through her grandfather Philip Livingston, Lady Kitty belonged to the clan which had played a distinguished part in the colonial history of New York, and who in 1800 were social leaders.

12. 'Lady Kitty' Duer.

Catherine Alexander was the second daughter of General William Alexander who bore the courtesy title of 'Lord Stirling.' She was known as 'Lady Catherine' or 'Lady Kitty.' After her husband William Duer's financial disgrace, she settled in Chambers Street, where she took genteel boarders, like the Trumbull sisters.

Perhaps more than a dozen families of the large Livingston clan, descendants of Robert Livingston of Clermont, maintained winter residences in New York. Until her death in the summer of 1800, the matriarch of the clan, Margaret Beekman Livingston, would gather the clan on winter evenings at her Pearl Street home. The Chancellor, Robert R. Livingston, and his two brothers, John R. and Henry, spent winters in New York, as did their younger brother Edward, known as 'Beau Ned,' whose wife Mary's ostrich-feather headdress caught fire at a reception given by Mrs. Washington. Their sister Janet was the widow of General Montgomery, the military hero of the assault on Quebec in 1775. Sister Gertrude was the wife of Governor Morgan Lewis, and Sister Alida had married General John Armstrong. All had homes in New York. Lady Kitty's mother, Lady Stirling, *née* Sarah Livingston, was the daughter of Philip Livingston, older brother of the Chancellor.[27]

In the closely knit circle of patrician families who provided the political and social leadership of New York, Lady Kitty's credentials were gilt-edged. Her title derived from the claim of her father William Alexander to a Scottish earldom. Although his claim was rejected by the House of Lords, throughout the Revolution he was known as 'Lord Stirling' and his wife and daughters enjoyed the distinction of a courtesy title. Lady Kitty's older sister, 'Lady Mary,' married Robert Watts, who sided with the British in the revolutionary struggle. She remained in New York, while Lord Sterling and the rest of the family fled the city. Letters between the two sisters continued to be exchanged throughout the war.

An Englishman who had emigrated to New York before the Revolution, Duer served in the Continental Congress, and was a signer of the Articles of Confederation. He built up a reputation as a shrewd money man and as a patriot. 'It would be difficult to find a man who better combines a good head for figures, broad vision, and quick penetration in dealing with the most complicated problems. To these qualities,' noted Brissot de Warville of Duer, 'add goodness of heart.' He enjoyed connections with the Schuylers, and through their influence he came into contact with Alexander Hamilton, who had married General Philip Schuyler's daughter Elizabeth. Through his wife's relations, and his own commercial and political interests, Duer met the Trumbull family in Connecticut, and it was to his widow Lady Kitty that Governor Trumbull turned when they wished to send their daughters to New York.

Colonel Duer was a founder of the Bank of New York and was assistant secretary of the Treasury under Hamilton. 'To these subjects he devoted his whole attention,' wrote his son, 'and by his calculations and counsels aided and diminished the labors of his chief.'[28] While virtuously serving the public interest, Duer engaged in speculation in public securities which involved men from the most distinguished families in the city. His speculations ended in tears in 1792 when bankruptcy precipitated the new nation's first financial panic. Real estate prices fell, credit tightened, and bitter accusations continued for months. Duer and Lady Kitty had lived in grand style in New York, and were believed to be the first in the city openly to defy democratic opinion and dress their servants in livery. Their fall was sudden and highly visible. At the insistence of creditors, their property was sold at a sheriff's sale and Duer clapped into prison for debt. Angry screams of the mob filled the Park, demanding 'We will have Mr. Duer, he has gotten our money.' He died in prison in 1799, a scorned and disgraced man, abandoned by Hamilton and his former allies. But her husband's misfortunes did not disturb the ties which linked Lady Kitty to the best families in New York. Before her husband's disgrace she had lived grandly on Broadway. Now she and her children resided in Chambers Street, on the northern edge of the city, in 'a very comfortable small brick house with two rooms which are furnished very pretily' (December 2, 1800).[29]

Instructed by their mother, no doubt many times, to be *very* particular' in New York, the Trumbull sisters reported home on the behavior of Lady Kitty's children and the dowager Lady Stirling. They were pleased to say that 'the whole family treat one another with a *great deal of affection*'. At first their hostess impressed them as 'a very fine woman' who treated them 'with great kindness' (December 2 and 7, 1800). Lady Kitty was 'really a lovely good woman' (February 4, 1801), but they ended their stay at her crowded home with little regret. There were eight children in the house from her marriage with Colonel Duer, between the ages of twenty and seven. (When Lady Kitty married the merchant William Neilson, several additional children were brought into the household.) Lady Kitty, wrote Maria, 'has I think lived too much in the *fashionable world* to have much of a *heart*—she has always treated us with extreme politeness but no affection—tho we have often felt *affectionately disposed towards her*' (May 20, 1801). There was no sign of the fashionable invitations they may have expected from the relations of Lady Kitty. This was probably the most visible consequence of their position as paying guests.

The complexities of that position were perhaps too much for teenagers fully to grasp. They would have been quite familiar with the idea that young ladies made extended stays in distant households, often those of married siblings or cousins. Their friends and schoolmates in Connecticut would likely have made such visits as part of a system of informal training in domesticity, rooted in the large and far-flung families of that age. Maria and Harriet were not expected to do chores in Lady Kitty's home. The necessary domestic skills, from cooking to sewing and domestic management, were things young ladies learned at their mother's apron. What set them apart from other relatives who might have stayed at Lady Kitty's home was the payment she received for providing their room and board. 'I paid Lady Kitty several days ago 15 dollars,' Harriet wrote to her mother, 'she has received in all 125 dollars, just her terms for three months, expired the 1st March, she desires not to be paid till the 1st May' (March 11, 1801). As far as Lady Kitty was concerned, circumstances forced her to welcome the Trumbull sisters to Chambers Street; they were a significant part of her system of domestic economy. Their position was clearly distinguished from that of the young girls who assisted with household chores or other domestic servants, and was no less clearly different from that of family members and the daughters of friends, who would have been welcome in Lady Kitty's home on terms of complete social equality and inclusion. However highly placed and distinguished, despite their manifest gentility and social distinction, Harriet and Maria were *paying guests* and though politely welcomed into the Duer family's home, there could be no forgetting the social trans-action implied by the fees paid by Governor Trumbull. It subtly altered the meaning of their stay in New York.

Unable to re-settle in Lebanon, Maria went to live with a married sister in Hartford. In 1804 she married a Connecticut businessman, and as Mrs. Henry Hudson she briefly lived in New York before setting up housekeeping in Hartford. Within a year she died after giving birth to a son. Her sister Harriet returned to New York in 1802, staying with the Sebors. She married the chemist Professor Benjamin Silliman of Yale University in 1809, had twelve children, one of whom, another Benjamin, succeeded his father as professor of science at Yale. In time the memory of the pleasures of a season in New York faded before the serious and respectable business of being a professor's wife and mother of a large family. Harriet was buried in 1850 in the Grove Street Cemetery in New Haven.

'Wealth is their reigning God': the Melvill family in New York

The life of a merchant in New York was ever a roller-coaster journey of hard work, elation, hope, disappointment, retrenchment, and contemplation of the blackest abyss of financial failure and disgrace. 'In this City,' Henry Brevoort wrote to Washington Irving, 'fortune is resolved to let no one escape her caprices.' Frequent voyages to Europe gave Allan Melvill a metaphor for the changeableness of man's condition: the sea 'is at best a most capricious & deceitful element, one moment decked in smiles & the next foaming with rage.' On hearing of an unexpected commercial failure in Boston, he observed that 'Commerce, like the Winds which waft her treasures, is subject to constant fluctuations—.' The sudden death due to cholera of the wife of their minister prompted similar thoughts in Maria Melvill: 'the longer we live the more we are convinced of the unsettled state of all things earthly.'[30]

It was Michael Paul Rogin's claim that 'family connections' located the work of Herman Melville, son of Allan and Maria Melvill, at the center of the dominant public issues of his time. Thinking of slavery, Manifest Destiny and capitalist expansion, Rogin drew upon the rich Gansevoort-Lansing archive at the New York Public Library.[31] I found in that archive a different story of social aspiration and financial failure which shed considerable light on the experience of a young couple who sought to enter antebellum New York society. The commercial fortunes of Allan Melvill, bolstered by frequent loans from his family and in-laws, lurched repeatedly from one failure to another, punctuated by periods of buoyant good fortune.

The esteemed position of the prosperous Gansevoort family in Albany, with whom he lived for four years after his marriage to Maria Gansevoort in 1814, was matched by Melvill's intense pride in his own family. His father, Major Thomas Melvill, Collector of the Port of Boston, had taken part in the Boston Tea Party. A vial of tea was cherished within the family as a relic of that celebrated act of symbolic political terrorism and vandalism.[32] In nineteenth-century America, a family's most valuable possession was its 'name,' its honor, to be protected like a symbolic form of capital. But Allan and Maria were alone in New York, and their name was a faded asset in the bustling city. Like so many Albanians who migrated down the Hudson, they lacked the broad network of family and friends to sustain a position in society. As he struggled with commercial uncertainty, the discrepancy between their names and justifiable family pride, and the social isolation and commercial precariousness of a merchant newly established in a large city, made him uncomfortable, indignant, even rather self-righteous. They were staying at a boarding house; such places were hotbeds of gossip and social life for the large transient population in the city:

> . . . for myself I care not a fig for the selfish civilities of the little vulgar & the great, [for I am] sprung from a noble stock through a long line of paternal ancestry, who have lived in the annals of old Scotland for more than eight good centuries, & come of gentle blood through my mother also which can be traced back full many a year uncontaminated to its parent source in the Orkneys. I have that within me, without boasting . . . that soars above the frippery & *dandyism* of the age & region we inhabit.

It was for his wife's sake that Melvill resented the inattention and contemptible frivolity of New York society: Maria possessed 'honest exultation' in the distinction of her 'parental origin' and had 'a mind capable of justly estimating her relative rank in the scale of society.' For such a person to have 'attracted so little attention in the very Temple of Fashion & chief City of her native state, where *she is known to many, & ought to have been known to more*,' was an indignity beyond bearing. In New York outsiders like the 'imported Coxcombe' and Southern belles are fêted; even 'my landlady's Daughters bedecked in white topazes [are now] flashing upon the Town.' All this, he writes, is 'ridiculous' and 'contemptible,'

> but the Devil help me if it does not make me frit[33] when I think of it, which is seldom & by the life, thanks to better employment, while Maria laughs it off, says she is perfectly contented, *wishes* no attention at heart for the present, & if serious as I trust she is, as far as the accomplishment of wishes go, she must indeed be happy—for myself I could blow them all sky high, if they would alight safe [?] & receive their appropriate station among honest people—but enough I have blown my blast & you will hear no more of it—[34]

13. Maria Gansevoort Melvill.

Maria Gansevoort Melvill was painted *c*.1815 by Ezra Ames. There is a quasi-fictionalized portrait of her in Herman Melville's novel *Pierre, or, The Ambiguities* (1852): 'Pierre [Glendinning] was the only son of an affluent and haughty widow; a lady who externally furnished a singular example of the preservative and beautifying influences of unfluctuating rank, health and wealth, when joined to a fine mind of medium culture, uncankered by any inconsolable grief, and never worn by sordid cares. In mature age, the rose still miraculously clung to her cheek . . .'.

Coxcombs were 'imported,' that is, they were dandies after the European mold. That it was their landlady's daughter who was 'flashing upon the Town' gave a xenophobic flavor and class basis to Melvill's indignation.

Maria described the slights of boarding house life in a letter to her brother, written at the same time (December 1818), which laid a bill of specifics before the general court of respectable Albany. New Yorkers were ungrateful. Having accepted her hospitality, they 'feign not to know me.' The Melvills encountered daily slights in their boarding house. Other guests failed to include them in their 'talk of Parties' and they were ignored while all the others went out. The wife of the mayor, Mrs. Cadwallader Colden, made courtesy calls upon every newly arrived lady of consequence in the city, and gave large parties attended by everyone—except the Melvills. Even actresses received solicitous attention.

Mrs. Bartley an actress is . . . visited, visited, invited, to the first houses in this City, while I am worse than forgotten, shunned. It is next to improper that people, should not enquire and know who we are, altogether this is a selfish hateful Place & when Mr. M—— complains of their want of common civility, as respects myself, I say it is for the best, & when we commence housekeeping, we shall be perfectly independent of the whole city except about 10, & those we shall be able to entertain with great ease. I have too much pride to allow to Mr. M— but really the inhabitants of this Place will not [see merit], they shut their Eyes against every thing but wealth, wealth is their reigning God. If you have not wealth, you must have patience to put up with every slight, & many mortifications.[35]

Maria was responsible for the day to day civilities which came with their place in society. She particularly resented personal slights (the failure to return hospitality; the unkindness of their exclusion from the boarding house 'talk of Parties'), but seemed to be less concerned at the social success of their landlady's daughter and 'Coxcombes'. She primly noted the extent and quality of the actress Mrs. Bartley's invitations. Maria felt isolated, 'forgotten, shunned.'

Success in commerce would heal the wounds inflicted by an uncaring society. In a world where wealth alone seemed to afford protection against slights and mortifications, she looked forward to setting up housekeeping on their own. At the end of December, 1819, Maria wrote to Albany that the mayor's wife had at last paid a gracious call, and afterwards the Rapelyes and Miss Eliza Cruger had visited. She proudly noted that she had attended a party at which she had been singled out for special attention by 'Mrs. Vice President & Daughter.' Hannah Minthorne Tompkins, an old friend of Maria Melvill's mother in Albany, was the daughter of Mangle Minthorne, a prominent New York City Republican. Her husband Daniel D. Tompkins, who served three terms as Governor of New York State, had been Vice-President during the administrations of James Monroe, 1817–25. In the same letter Maria confirmed their intention to move to their own house, and asked for a loan of $1,000 for furnishings. Eight dining chairs had been purchased at auction, she wrote, and they planned to order four additional matching chairs. In New York,

all the Carpets are Brussels & the Curtains of the Dining room Damask . . . of the same color. Now in Boston scotch carpets were much used & did not appear singular, & *curtains* were singular—I have been over several houses that were offer'd to be lett & had an opportunity of seeing furniture.

It is impossible to furnish a house less than $3,000, in this Place, to appear at all Genteel. However, I shall do my utmost to economise, & get nothing unnecessary.[36]

Maria's understanding of a hierarchy of consumption values (led by the choice of Brussels carpet and damask cloth) was not 'singular'—it was, she assured her brother, shared by respectable New Yorkers. What she saw in other comparable households confirmed her sense of how people of their social standing lived in the city. Increasingly sensitive to the slightest appearance of failure or hint of discourtesy, and no doubt keeping in mind the embarrassment of his brother Thomas' financial misfortunes and then imprisonment for debt in 1821, Allan Melvill sensed the need to create and sustain an *appearance* of high status and social position, whatever the vagaries of the market. In 1820 the Melvills hired a cook and a nurse, and looked forward to the hiring of a waiter. Six months later he appealed once more to his father for an additional loan of $2,000 to support his business. In their domestic arrangements, and in commercial life, New York was a financial black hole for the Melvills.

In 1823, Allan reported that 'Business continued depressed beyond example at this season.' He feared yet another 'dull & unprofitable year.' More level-headed than her husband, Maria soon contemplated the prospect of a 'reduction of the establishment' and 'the closest economy.' The precariousness of a merchant's life was summed up by Jonathan Sturges in a comment to his wife: 'If things do not soon take a turn, we will break up housekeeping in a little while, and board.' A house in Brooklyn might indeed be rented more cheaply than on Cortlandt Street, and had the additional advantage for the Melvills of being less likely to be repeatedly disrupted by summer epidemics. 'You have kept all communications on this subject confined to your own breast. Mr.——[Melvill's] delicacy on this subject is greater than you can imagine.'[37]

Ten months later there was no more talk of retrenchment. Allan Melvill moved his family from Cortlandt Street to a new house at 33 Bleecker Street, some twenty-five blocks further up Broadway. The famous Depau Row of brick houses on Bleecker Street, noted for their lavish interiors, had become an object of considerable interest for house hunters in the 1820s. 'These were the first houses ever seen in New York with porte-cochères,' wrote Harriet Duer.[38]

Melvill's hope was at full flow when he wrote to his brother-in-law of the proud advantages of the family's new home. It was a new brick two-story house leased for four years at a rent of $300 per annum. It will be 'handsomely furnished in the modern style under our directions, & a vacant lot of equal size [is] attached to it, which will be invaluable as play ground for the Children, it is situate in Bleecker ... [in] an open, dry & elevated location equidistant from Broadway to the Bowery, in plain sight of both & almost uniting the advantages of town & country, but its distance from my Store [at 162 Pearl Street], nearly two miles, will compel me to dine [apart] from my family most of the time . . .'[39] The house was decorated in a stylish manner. 'We have had our Parlour painted, a pretty Fancy color between French Grey & a Lilac. Painted walls are more to be preferred where their [*sic*] are Children than paper, being so easily washed when accidentally touched with dirty fingers, which it is next to impossible to prevent when so many are together.'[40]

Living uptown obliged Allan to ride the Broadway stage to his business office downtown. That he did so with estimable brokers, bankers, and merchants like James Gore King (son of Rufus King, Federalist politician who served twice as American minister to Great Britain) and John Aspinwall was an item of news to be conveyed to Albany. An earlier generation of the city's merchants lived in the same building as his place of business, but the recurrent outbreaks of yellow fever had made living uptown the norm. 'Our principal merchants,' wrote John Pintard in 1826, 'are all resorting up B^{d}way.' The Broadway stagecoach at 8¢ per ride passed every five minutes. The ease of travel, noted Pintard, 'raised the value of Lots in the upper districts of our city & the number will increase with its growth.'[41]

The pleasant sociability of their new Bleecker Street neighbors impressed Maria. They were from distinguished old Knickerbocker families like the Roosevelts, and Yankees like the Aspinwalls, whose dry-goods firm, Gilbert & John Aspinwall on Pearl Street had a solid and respectable downtown reputation. Mr. and Mrs. John Aspinwall paid a call on their new neighbors. Unable to receive callers due to her frequent indispositions, Maria asked her husband to give the Aspinwalls some choice plums which had recently arrived from her brother in Albany. Plums were also given to Mrs. Roosevelt, who kindly reciprocated by sending a bunch of flowers to Maria 'on a rich silver service,' asking after her health.[42] It was out of such moments that Sarah Orne Jewett made a career as a novelist. The domestic ties which united the wives and children of the city's leading merchants enabled other kinds of information to be shared. Around Gramercy Park information about servants, repairmen, and other matters circulated, helping middle-class households avoid the dangers of inattentive or dishonest servants. Caroline Pine remembered such a moment in her brief memoir of growing up in Gramercy Park. Their neighbor Bamie Roosevelt come by to ask for a cook's reference. 'My mother was not well and sent me down, although I was still a young school girl, to give the information to Mrs. Roosevelt. In those days the matter of references was a serious thing, and I was also sent to inquire of Mrs. Wm. Vanderbilt something about the cook whom Mrs. Atterbury thought of engaging. Mrs. Vanderbilt very graciously came to her drawing room to answer my inquiries, but it was decided that the Vanderbilt's standard was much too grand for us.'[43]

As the family fortunes improved, Allan Melvill was determined to wring every potential advantage for his wife and children. They had not come to New York to set down roots, for Albany and Boston provided their emotional touchstones and truest sense of home. In 1828, the Melvill family moved from Bleecker Street to another rented house at 675 Broadway, between Bond and Great Jones Streets. Theirs was a New York kind of success story. What seems a frenetic restlessness in their repeated moves from one rented property to another was actually, in the context of the city, an intelligent response to the swiftly changing real estate market. It also reflected their sharp sense of the social geography of city life. By settling in the area 'above Bleecker' they placed themselves in the vicinity of Washington Square, Bond Street, and Lafayette Place: over the next two decades this was to be *the* fashionable upper-class residential district in the city. The residents in this area (see pp. 83–111) were precisely those whose social approval was necessary if they were to enter the city's upper class. We can see in the topsy-turvy lives of the Melvills what New York was actually like for people of their social position in the 1820s. They were not wealthy enough to adopt an aristocratic indifference to commerce, but they were sufficiently well-to-do to move out of the deteriorating residential conditions downtown. Lacking the social credentials to ensure their automatic admission to the upper reaches of New York society, they hoped to situate themselves so that, if financial conditions improved, they might gain a secure position. They were classic social climbers.

As Jan Cohn has argued, the house was a visible and potent symbol for Americans of material success.[44] Even a rented home, and not one of the grandest, was still a sign of the progress the Melvills were making in their social ascent in New York. Made of brick, 675 Broadway had four bedrooms on the second floor and two small garret bedrooms. On a standard New York lot of 25 feet frontage, and 200 feet depth, there was 'a fine Garden prettily laid out with fruit trees shrubbery bulbous roots & fine grass Plot.' Maria wrote that there 'is not a more healthful or agreeable situation in the City.'

The move to Broadway settled a long-established tension between Allan and Maria (or perhaps an ongoing family joke) about a fashionable residence: 'Mr Melvill playfully says I have at last gained my point which has always been a House on Broadway—My Spirits are better & I am a more agreeable companion than I have been for some time past.' Success in the worldly sense undeniably did make one feel better about a marriage, about children, and about the city itself. The Melvill family rapidly assumed the trappings of their new place in society. Four of the children attended Mrs. Plucknett's dancing school 'kept in one of the Marble Houses in Broadway,' Maria noted, where they joined the children of the most respectable local families, the Kings, Tompkins, Thompsons, Aspinwalls. Maria proudly reported that her daughter

Augusta, who 'moves her body gracefully & with lightness,' was anticipating a ball and 'is trying very hard to dance a Cotillon at it.' (In dancing academies the most popular cotillon figures were practiced for weeks before a ball.) When it became appropriate to hold children's' parties—with great quantities of lemonade, cakes, and sugared plums—the children at dancing school formed their first choice of guests.[45]

At last their lives in New York were coming into accord with the expectations of a Gansevoort and a Melvill. The friendship of Mrs. Tompkins was a welcome addition to Maria's society, and a delicious rebuke to those who had paid insufficient attention to the Melvill family. 'She has become a member of Doctor Broadhead's [Dutch Reformed] Church [and] I frequently ride home with her, when [the] weather is at all unpleasant, the footman steps up & says Mrs. Melvill Miss Tompkins begs you will ride with her, it is too unpleasant to walk.' Mrs. Tompkins' kindness meant something very special to Maria Melvill. The knowledge they shared of their husbands' dread of financial failure and disgrace formed a sympathetic bond between the two women. For the moment, things were well, and a ride in Mrs. Tompkins' coach was graciously accepted. Accusations of financial improprieties against the Vice-President in the 1820s blighted the family's life. Despite a Congressional vindication, Tompkins' health was broken before his death in 1825.

But soon enough Mrs. Dash's request, in Halleck's poem 'Domestic Happiness,' was Mrs. Melvill's refrain:

'I want a little money, dear,
    For Vandervoort and Flandin,
Their bill, which now has run a year,
    To-morrow mean to hand in.'[46]

For merchants like Melvill there were, as Halleck wrote, dreams 'of nothing else all night/But brokers, banks and ruin.' Within two years Allan Melvill's business had collapsed. In August 1830 his creditors began legal proceedings. After a humiliating move back to Albany, and writing begging letters to his father to repay the loans from his brother-in-law, and vice versa, he suffered a mental collapse, followed swiftly in 1832 by death. He was forty-nine. It was later discovered that he owed his father $22,000, and his brother-in-law $4,000.[47] Dancing lessons for the children were at an end. The Melvill family changed the spelling of their name to Melville. Their son Herman at thirteen left the Albany Academy to take a clerkship at the New York State Bank. Across the century, the society bankrupts of New York (Colonel William Duer, Allan Melvill, John Ward, and William Butler Duncan) extend a sympathetic hand to each other, united in the fellowship of commercial failure.

The experiences of the Trumbull sisters and the Melvill family enable us to see with the eyes of social climbers. Their concerns were those of any persons of good birth who sought entry into New York society. Establishing and maintaining a place within society became more complicated as the importance of family perceptibly declined—but was far from being irrelevant. The Trumbulls and Melvills shared with many old, established families a sense of pride in their family's roles in the making of the nation. They passionately believed that past services, and the civic values which they embodied, deserved the notice of society and its respect. The Trumbulls and Melvills were raised as members of an elite in which money, while central to the cultivation of social position, was not, of itself, sufficient to secure social prominence. Maria Melvill's denunciation of the worship of wealth in New York, like a similar sentiment expressed by Henry Brevoort in 1827, quoted in Chapter 2, was based on a belief that the values of an aristocracy were higher and finer than the mere worship of money. In reality, throughout the century the relationship between wealth and social position was deeply complex, and growing more so as society became wealthier.

The traditional routes of emulation and, in Veblen's phrase, conspicuous consumption, by which wealthy individuals sought to gain admission into society surprised no one. However necessary wealth was for a position in the structure of aristocracy, the comforting belief persisted that money alone could not secure social entrée. Without financial security the Trumbull sisters could not receive the social polish of a season in New York, and the Melvills could not remain at 675 Broadway. In the face of adversity Lady Kitty Duer was able to move to a smaller house on Chambers Street, where she retained the social esteem which her birth as a Livingston had assured. The collapse of the Melvill fortunes removed the family from New York. However they denounced the crude ostentation of new money, the reality was stark: without money there was no place for them in fashionable society.

3

ARISTOCRATIC NEIGHBORHOODS

In 1800, commercial interests in New York were creating a more divided community out of the economically mixed wards of the colonial city. Corlaer's Hook was being developed by shipbuilders and the many businesses which serviced maritime commerce. Banks, lawyers, and financial interests were transforming Wall Street. Pearl Street became synonymous with the dry-goods trade. Brewers, tanners, and tallow-makers found space in the Sixth Ward where their smelly trades would be least objectionable. In addition to areas defined by commerce, the city's first neighborhood based on class was forming at the southernmost tip of Manhattan around lower Broadway, Bowling Green, and the Battery.

The key characteristic of New York neighborhoods was their fluidity, and not only in physical terms. Borders regularly expanded and contracted. The social identities of neighborhoods had not been permanently established in colonial New York, but were continually under construction. The idea of what constituted an 'aristocratic neighborhood' changed rapidly in the antebellum period, as did their location.[1] The emergence, and then the social and economic decline of neighborhoods defined by class is a striking fact of the nineteenth-century city. St. John's Park, thriving in 1830, and Bond Street, at the height of its fashionableness in the 1840s, had largely disappeared off the map of elite residential areas by the 1870s. The causes of such decline are heavily over-determined: the real estate market, housing needs, economic forces, fashion, architectural taste, and transportation were factors pressing upon every neighborhood. Above all, wealth itself was a powerful solvent of community. As individuals became wealthier, expectations rose, as did the demand for increased personal space and modern conveniences.

An intangible element in the decline of such neighborhoods lay in a certain weakness of sentimental attachments in the city. New York was regarded by many contemporaries as the least sentimental of communities, where the ties of memory and affection mattered less than in less avidly commercial cities.[2]

to dabble, no sudden fortunes to be made. There was but little commerce between the colony and the mother-country, and men who embarked in this business were contented to spend their lives in acquiring competence. They never aspired to rival the landed families.'[6]

The sense of displacement touched many of those in society, though a sentimental attachment to the past seldom proved a sufficient motive to resist change. The home of Levi P. Morton at 503 Fifth Avenue, where Edith Wharton's débutante ball was held, was transformed into 'French flats' in 1879. Following the death of August Belmont in 1890, the banker's double house on Fifth Avenue at 18th Street, with a frontage of 100 feet, was sold by his sons for $650,000 to Arnold, Constable & Co. After his brother's death in 1893, William C. Schermerhorn unsentimentally had pulled down the house where his brother Edmund had lived so long in isolation on West 23rd Street.[7] George William Curtis argued that the fatal enemy of picturesqueness in New York was the constant demolition and erection of new buildings. 'No house remains long enough to become hallowed and interesting from association,' he argued:

> Half of the charm of the great cities of the world is the identification of famous persons with famous places. In this house Milton lived. Here was Shakespeare born. This was Mozart's home, or Dante's, or Goethe's. To see what they saw, to surround ourselves with the outward influences to which they were subject, is to come as near to them as possible, and to have new light thrown on what they did. But it is doubtful if there is any building in New York, except perhaps some church, more than fifty years old. It is constantly a new city with new inhabitants.[8]

In the midst of such incessant change James Stokes went downtown for a walk on the Battery, recollecting the time over a half-century before when he had lived at the Atlantic Hotel. 'I tried to compare the scenes and surroundings,' he wrote to his wife. 'The houses that were then the first-class private residences are now emigrant boarding houses, and all the occupants are passed away,— not so much as a trace of them. . . . Everything is changed beyond belief of any but an old resident. If the aristocracy that once lived around the Battery and Bowling Green should be permitted to see the change, they would be horrified at it.'[9]

Such narratives of displacement were often rooted in the memory of a time when classes and races (the Bishop's 'sable retainers') happily acknowledged their rightful place in the social hierarchy. Nostalgia for rural innocence could bring a tear to sardonic New York theater-goers, but the nostalgia for an aristocratic past and subordination to the rich was largely greeted with hostility in nineteenth-century New York. That iconoclasm is perhaps one of the greatest strengths of the city. The ruins which Hone, Bishop Kip, and James Stokes contemplated were the Knickerbocker world itself, increasingly regarded as a disposable relic.

My subject is not so much the process of change, of rise and fall, but the process by which neighborhoods acquired social meaning and the nature of the social ties which held such neighborhoods together. Edward Pessen and others have argued (unsurprisingly) that the rich preferred to live exclusively in neighborhoods inhabited by those like themselves.[10] What seems rather more interesting is that when the pace of social change increased, the social ties in such elite residential enclaves could prove alarmingly weak. The identity of the neighborhood itself was highly unstable. A larger district, like Greenwich Village, might be sufficiently established over time to create and then retain a distinctive ethnic or commercial character, and thus acquire a more permanent identity.[11] By and large, my concerns here are with the small, early proto-neighborhoods, and the ties which failed to hold these impermanent communities together.

The rich had more resources at their command than artisans, cartmen, and laborers, but were only fitfully more successful than the poor in opposing commercial incursions. Neighborhoods were not self-contained economic units, and individuals were free to move uptown, but as individuals they seemed incapable of collective mobilization to stay. It was easier to keep social climbers from a Patriarchs' ball, or blackball an inappropriate someone from the Union Club, than to prevent an abortionist with money from building a mansion on Fifth Avenue.

With the greatest array of mansions ever seen in an American city, Fifth Avenue had been a street of placid luxury in the center of the bustling city. Nonetheless when the city began to keep records of building in 1866–7, the first application to turn a Fifth Avenue mansion into a boarding house came in 1869. By the 1870s, from 14th to 23rd Streets, Fifth Avenue had become a first-class shopping district occupied by clothiers, piano salesrooms, and suppliers of decorative goods. The obituary of Fifth Avenue as place for aristocratic residence was being written as early as the 1880s. 'Even the parts of the avenue that are apparently still devoted to residences are the prey of the boarding-house keeper, a sure precursor of the store and of business.' The new 'social landscape' in New York, with its high levels of mobility, tenancy, and new social institutions such as the apartment house, was the product of commercial pressures on the housing market.[12] Even the strongest community associations, the churches, were seldom able to resist the pressure of social change.[13]

The idea of neighborhood, so seductive in the midst of urban disintegration and anomie, seldom decisively shaped the mental boundaries of inhabitants.

There were strong family ties which linked the inhabitants of St. John's Park to relatives elsewhere in the metropolitan area. Equally, class, ethnic, gender, religious affiliations, education, employment, as well the national and international concerns of finance and business, connected the inhabitants of every neighborhood to the larger city. The 'meaning' of neighborhood, and the kinds of sociability and community which neighborhood life makes possible, must be seen as a part, and not always a decisive part, of the experience of individuals and families in the urban community.

Samuel Ward, one of the leading figures in the early years of Bond Street, had interests which linked him to the highest banking circles in London (Baring Brothers were the corresponding partners of Prime, Ward & King). John Jacob Astor's interests were worldwide. The polite civilities maintained between a Ward and an Astor did not ultimately depend upon the norms of Bond Street and Lafayette Place. Yet the traditional New Year's Day calls which Astor made to Ward's Corner House in the 1830s, and the calls which the Wards made to Astor's home in Colonnade Row, should not be relegated to the mere ephemera of social life. New Year's Day calls, and the neighborliness they expressed, reflected something more meaningful than an old custom, already in decline by mid-century, and which seemed to have disappeared altogether by the 1870s. 'Of course,' wrote George Templeton Strong in his diary on January 3, 1859, 'a very large percentage of this aggregate of radiance and hospitality is social sham. But there is still a certain very valuable residuum or balance of sincere good feeling which is brought out by this much reviled institution of New Year's Day. And this kind of *sham* hurts no one; social usage that requires everybody to receive everybody else with the shew [*sic*] of kindness and cordiality one day in the year does no harm. Perhaps we should be the gainers if the anniversary came *twice* a year.' The social norms which underlay the old Dutch custom of New Year's Day calls were those which men like Ward and Astor believed *should* govern the social and civic relations of gentlemen.[14]

Working-class areas, as opposed to the aristocratic locations discussed elsewhere in this chapter, suggest a different role for neighborhoods in urban life. Gender seemed to work in a different way. Women in working-class neighborhoods could benefit from the presence of other women nearby. Offers of help and gestures of solidarity in a domestic dispute, or in the face of domestic violence, might transform the social isolation of a working-class woman. 'Neighbors intervened in family fights and, on occasion,' as Christine Stansell has shown, 'made their own judgments about the justice of men's demands on women. They pleaded with angry men, sought to temper their violence and often called the watch or the police when their efforts failed.'[15] There were customary rules by which neighbors might intervene in domestic disputes; the neighborhood was thus an 'alternative court, judge and jury,' offering redress and support for the victim. The 'court' administered a sometimes harsh and vengeful local justice. But there was also a range of other behaviors, from gossip to snooping, which might leave neighborly relations charged with tension. And the working class and poor were subject to the intervention of charities and bodies such as the Children's Aid Society in ways unknown to middle-class families. Of course aristocratic neighborhoods had no observable shortage of gossip and snooping, but they were more successful in maintaining boundaries between the family and the community. The strength of the 'separate spheres' ideology established the primacy of married women in the family home and served to insulate 'respectable' women at the higher social levels from the interventions of neighborhood 'courts.'[16] (The bland façade of family approval, and whether it should be extended to Ellen Olenska in Edith Wharton's novel, *The Age of Innocence*, would protect her from the socially disastrous consequences of a divorce from Count Olenski. The denial of that support would have left her exposed and vulnerable.)

The period discussed in this chapter begins in 1800, about the time the Trumbull sisters arrived in New York, when lower Broadway, Bowling Green, and the Battery were at the peak of their social ascendancy, and ends in the 1850s when the social decline of Bond Street and Lafayette Place had begun. By 1803 work had started on St. John's Chapel. Bond Street was still farmland. The three areas did not tidily succeed one another, but rather overlapped, making any account of aristocratic neighborhoods one which, of necessity, scurries back and forth geographically and in time across the half-century. For New Yorkers, the three neighborhoods possessed specific social meaning as urban symbols of an aristocratic way of life. The people who lived there occupied a privileged place in the community. The men were often leaders in professional and mercantile life. Nonetheless, wealth was an ethically 'difficult' fact, as the experience of the banker Samuel Ward, one of the great money men of the city, suggests. When Ward warned his profligate son Sam against luxury and Parisian frippery, he was not simply a rich hypocrite, expressing nostalgia for the Republican simplicity of an America receding into the past. Rather, he was a man made deeply uncomfortable by the ambiguities of great wealth. New Yorkers, no less than those like the Trumbull sisters who came to the city in search of the distinctive finish which a metropolis alone afforded, had to *learn* to be comfortable with wealth.

'Aristocratic' locations after the 1830s were the places where the leading gentlemen's clubs were to be found, and the restaurants like Delmonico's which the clubmen patronized. Social bodies which the aristocrats created and supported, like the Stuyvesant Institute and the New-York Historical Society, were integral constituents of such districts. By far the most visible sign of an ascendant neighborhood was a new aristocratic church—the model would be

Grace Church, opened on a prominent site on Broadway above 10th Street in 1846—or a handsome park nearby.

Bowling Green

> . . . the Governor has made a Very Pretty bowlling greens with a handsome Walk of trees Raild and Painted Just before the fort in t[ha]t Large Durty Place it Reaches three doers beyond.
> —Abigail Franks, 1734[17]

When the Federal Congress voted in 1784 to move the government to New York, plans to remake the old City Hall at the head of Broad Street into a Federal Hall symbolized the reconstruction of the city, liberated from British occupation only the year before. The remains of Fort George, on the site of the first Dutch fortifications, were razed in 1788 to make way for a mansion intended for use as the President's House—part of an unsuccessful strategy to retain the federal capital in New York. The four-columned structure was occupied briefly by Governor Jay, but when the state capital moved to Albany in 1797 the Government House served as a boarding house before being torn down in 1815. Cass Gilbert's lavish Custom House was erected on this site in 1907. The streets around Fort George, site of the Colonial Government-house, had long been considered the 'Court-end' of the town; the substantial homes of the great colonial families, the Van Dams, De Lanceys, Livingstons, Bayards, Morrises, Crugers, and De Peysters, gave the southern tip of Manhattan a distinctively aristocratic tone. A new patriot aristocracy, Whiggish in sympathy, and strongly inclined to defend the popular legislative prerogative, was determined to reside where so recently the vanquished Tories had lived.

New York was not the largest city in the new nation in the 1780s, but already it had begun to think of itself as offering cultural and financial leadership. 'The people here presumptuously call their town the Capital,' remarked a Pennsylvania representative to the Federal Congress in 1789. 'I don't suppose this folly will be suffered to last very long.'[18] New Yorkers did not disguise their belief that political pre-eminence would surely follow their city's emerging economic fortunes. The first elite neighborhood in the city was located in the streets facing the site of Fort George, and around Bowling Green, with its decorative iron railing. Nearby streets—Greenwich, Whitehall, Beaver, Broad, Water, and Pearl—were lined with handsome brick and stone buildings. There was a fine row of houses on State Street facing the Battery (the colonnaded James Watson House at number 7, erected 1794–1806, is the lone survivor in our time of the mansions which once dominated this area).[19] Bowling Green was a highly desirable residential enclave, for its proximity to the commercial

and social center of New York life, and because it (briefly) promised a place as near as possible to the future home of the President. The Patriot grandees and leading New York merchants, led by Abraham Kennedy, John Watts, Chancellor Livingston, and John Stevens, constructed residences facing Bowling Green and similar structures lined the lower part of Broadway.

The most fashionable homes and most important churches, taverns, and hotels were to be found on Broadway, described by the Duke of La Rochefoucauld-Liancourt as one of the great wonders of the world. 'There is not in any city in the world a finer street than Broadway; it is near a mile in length, and is meant to be farther extended: it is more than a hundred feet wide from one end to the other.' The leading residence was the Kennedy Mansion, with an imposing 56-foot frontage at 1 Broadway (on the left of ill. 14). Chancellor Robert R. Livingston lived at number 5, and Alexander Hamilton at 26. George Washington occupied the Macomb Mansion at 39 Broadway. John R. Livingston lived at 67. The home of John Jay and his wife Sarah was at 133. In the 1790s, John Jacob Astor's residence and fur business were located at 149 Broadway, at the corner with Vesey Street. (In the next decade, while renting a commercial store on Liberty Street, Astor bought the house at 223 Broadway, which had been built by Rufus King and then sold upon his appointment as Ambassador to the Court of St. James in 1796.) He later erected the Astor House on this site.[20]

14. Bowling Green.

The wealthy merchants and bankers who built fine homes on Bowling Green, and on the nearby streets, made it the leading residential neighborhood in the city. In the early years of the republic, Bowling Green remained at the heart of fashionable life. By the 1820s the movement uptown was well underway, and Bowling Green became a gateway to the commercial life of lower Broadway.

The milieu they inhabited on Broadway and Bowling Green was in crucial respects unlike other neighborhoods in New York. The presence of individuals of such distinction on Broadway reflected their leadership in public life. Broadway was a stage in a career rather than a place to make a home. All knew that they might, like Rufus King, find themselves suddenly sent abroad to serve their nation. Washington and the Livingstons had great country estates elsewhere which were more truly 'home' than a rented house in New York. Their attachment to a Mount Vernon or Clermont was an assurance that public service was not being conducted for low motives or ambitions, but out of disinterested commitment to the public good. These were men who scorned the limitations of petty 'local attachments' every bit as much as they disdained faction or party spirit. Nor did they see themselves as playing principally upon a local stage, and they urged locally oriented associates to think more broadly about the role of government and its ability to shape the dispositions of the people. As gentlemen, they were loyal to universal concepts of character and standards of honor. The removal of the government to Philadelphia, and then its relocation to the banks of the Potomac, while part of a low political compromise engineered between the Virginians and Hamilton to ensure the federal assumption of state debt from the revolutionary struggle, meant little to high-minded men devoted more to the ideal of national independence than to the parochial interests of any city.[21]

The appeal of Bowling Green and the Battery as an exclusive and fashionable district was based upon its proximity to commerce, government, and its charms as a place to go for a pleasant stroll and view of the harbor. 'In the summer and early fall,' recalled the merchant William E. Dodge, 'a band of music in the evening enlivened the scene, and the grounds were crowded with the élite of the city; it was as polite and marked a compliment for a young lady to be invited by a gentleman to take a walk on the Battery as now to be invited to a drive in the park.' We see the Trumbull sisters at the Battery after attending drawing school on January 14, 1801. Elizabeth DeHart Bleecker noted in her diary on June 11, 1801: 'Mr. Macdonald and I went round the Battery, went to the Columbia Gardens, there join'd by Miss Sally McComb and her Brother and we made a little party en Bosc to eat Ice Creams—.' With the population stretching further up the island, it was a longer walk to reach Bowling Green and the Battery, and the absence of benches was greatly regretted. Short of inelegantly sitting on the grass, a lady could find no place to rest.[22]

If we listen to what was being said, in letters, articles, and books about the Battery at this time, we can observe with great clarity the way the meaning of a social space changed, and did so within a few years. The increasing popularity of all public spaces on Manhattan, and particularly the Battery, attracted the 'wrong' sort of person. The construction between 1807 and 1811 of the

15. Astor House.

Astor spent $400,000 on the Astor House. With 300 rooms and accommodation for 600 guests, it filled the entire block on the west side of Broadway between Barclay and Vesey Streets. For nearly two decades the Astor House was the most important hotel in New York. It was something of a sensation that there were toilets and provision for baths on each floor. It was razed in 1913.

Southwest Battery (later Castle Clinton and then Castle Garden), some hundred yards off the shingle beach at the edge of the Battery, and the fierce armament (twenty-eight 32-pound cannons) it displayed to the commerce in New York Bay, made the Battery a site of public curiosity. The firing of blank cartridges attracted crowds, who lined the wooden fence along the waterside. Where there were soldiers and a flagpole, and regular performances of military marches, the men of New York paraded, enjoying cool drinks. For the Knickerbocker novelist James Kirke Paulding the changing meaning of the Battery was a product of the increasing diversity of the crowds enjoying the city's finest summer amenity: 'About three hours ago,' he wrote,

> I was in the midst of a crowd assembled on the Battery, to hear a Band of music which played from the Flag Staff. Gentlemen, Boys, Negroes, wenches, Ladies, all jumbled together in the true spirit of sublime Equality, presented a Scene of confusion which Baffles the powers of my Pen, and I was ready to exclaim, as I surveyed the Scene at a distance, "Chaos is come again"!—I did not dare to mix with this moving Sea of Living Animals, for I have a strange custom of getting angry when People Elbow and jostle me about, and I sometimes actually Knock them down, by which means I get into *Scrapes*, and get Knocked down myself in return; a thing by no means pleasant. The Band was exactly calculated for the organs of this motley collection.[23]

During Jeremy Cockloft's visit to Broadway he observed a changed attitude among the *ton*: 'Battery a very pleasant place to walk on a Sunday evening—not quite genteel though—every body walks there, and a pleasure, however genuine, is spoiled by general participation—the fashionable ladies of New-York turn up their noses if you ask them to walk on the Battery on Sunday—quere, have they scruples of conscience, or scruples of delicacy?—neither—they have only scruples of gentility, which are quite different things.' In 1808 John Lambert noted that the Battery was no longer much enjoyed by the fashionables. The area had become much too common. 'The genteel lounge is in the Broadway, from eleven to three o'clock, during which time it is as much crowded as the Bond-street of London: and the carriages, though not so numerous, are driven to and fro with as much velocity. The foot paths are planted with poplars, and afford an agreeable shade from the sun in summer.'[24] '"I am in the habit,"' noted the narrator in Francis Grund's satirical exploration of *Aristocracy in America*,

> "of taking a stroll here [the Battery] every evening; but have not, for the space of two months, met with a single individual known in the higher circles. Foreigners are the only persons who enjoy this spot."
>
> "And do you know why?" interrupted one of my friends: "it is because our fashionable Americans do not wish to be seen with the people; they dread that more than the tempest; and it is for this reason all that is really beautiful in the United States is considered *vulgar*."[25]

On Sundays in the 1830s, noted N.P. Willis, the Battery was crowded with foreigners, and not of the 'better class.' 'They are the newly-arrived, the artisans, the German toymakers and the French bootmakers—people who still wear the spacious-hipped trousers and scant coats, the gold rings in the ears, and the ruffled shirts of the lands of undandyfied poverty.'[26] The changing attitude towards the Battery which was recorded by Paulding, Lambert, Willis and others, and mocked by Grund, had become, after the opening of the attractive pleasure grounds of the Elysian Fields in Hoboken in 1831, a confirmed social prejudice. The Battery was dead, finished, so far as fashionable New York was concerned.

The regular disruptions caused by fires and disease (including recurrent yellow fever epidemics) turned the fashionables away from the Battery, Bowling Green, and eventually from lower Broadway. In October 1801 the Bleecker family moved to a rented house on the Bowery to escape that season's yellow fever. The epidemic in 1803 drove away those merchants who had continued to reside near Old Slip, whose marshy soil and damp, decaying warehouses had been among the first places where outbreaks of yellow fever occurred. Front, Water, and Pearl Streets were increasingly regarded by merchants as dangerous places to live. Within a few days of the first outbreak on Rector Street at the end of July, 1803, the Custom House, the Post Office, the banks, insurance offices, and printers relocated to temporary quarters in Greenwich Village or to addresses on upper Broadway. The return of the epidemic in 1819 found a merchant class well drilled in urban relocation: 'there was but *one* case of Fever yesterday, & *none* today, although the alarm has so much increased, that most of the Merchants in Water, Front & South Streets & many in my immediate Neighborhood in Pearl Street, between old Slip & Wall Street, *the proscribed District*, have removed.' On September 10, Allan Melvill sent his wife and children, including their infant son Herman, to live with her family in Albany. They did not return until November. The sudden death from yellow fever on September 18 of the merchant Gilbert Aspinwall (whose brother John became Allan Melvill's neighbor on Bleecker Street) had a strong impact on the mercantile community. John Pintard, manager of the Savings Bank, wrote to his daughter of the rapid spread of anxiety across the city. 'Stores are shutting up & goods removing to the upper parts of Greenwich & B^{d}way. The Banks have not yet started, but several of the Insurance Offices remove this day, on the principle that they must follow their customers. I presume that the same rule must guide us, altho' I absolutely declare that I think the city is panick struck.' The streets were jammed with carts carrying merchandise and household effects. To John Pintard, it seemed as though '[w]e are like a city in a siege, the inhabitants fleeing they knew not whither. . . .' The threat of epidemic in succeeding summers saw a similar removal. In 1822, Melvill wrote to his brother-in-law that 'New York is in a most deplorable condition, the Inhabitants south of Courtlandt St. & Maiden Lane are flying in all directions, & no one can anticipate the consequences of such a calamity.'[27]

The forms of social decline were varied, though the old stand-by, commercial encroachment, steadily challenged the remaining residents' hopes that their homes might be left in their ancient state of gentility. Old buildings were demolished, or reconstructed for other uses, like the Macomb mansion, which was turned into a hotel in 1821.[28] The Southwest Battery, ceded by the Federal Government to the city in 1822, was turned into a place of amusement. Boarding houses, hotels, and commercial premises had largely displaced the private residences below Wall Street by the 1830s. The 'spacious dwelling house' on Franklin Street formerly owned by the commission merchant James Brown and the 28-foot-wide home of the coffee and tea merchant Jonathan Sturges on 45 Murray Street were let as boarding houses in the 1840s. In 1845, A.T. Stewart purchased land on the southeast corner of Broadway and Reade Street from the Coster Estate. Until a recent fire, this had been the site of Washington Hall, erected in 1809 as the home of the Washington Benevolent Society. The former headquarters of the Federalists in New York, and meeting-place of James Fenimore Cooper's

Bread and Cheese Club in the 1820s, became a dry-goods store. (Dandies criticized Stewart for defying fashion and opening his store, the new temple of taste and fashion, on the less prestigious east side of Broadway: 'As a general rule, the finest buildings are on the west side of the street, called the dollar side, in contradistinction to the eastern, which is called the shilling side.')[29]

Efforts by residents to revitalize the environment downtown were seldom successful. Hone records in his diary in 1843 a brutal encounter with the reality of political power. A group of residents in the area of Bowling Green petitioned the Board of Aldermen for permission to erect a fountain at their own expense, under the direction of the Croton Water Commissioners. The president of the Board of Aldermen, Elijah Purdy, dismissed the petition 'on the ground that the petitioners were rich men, Aristocrats, and lived in large houses.' Mob violence and rowdy scenes in public life dismayed men like Hone, and Purdy's response seemed to confirm that public life in New York was now a form of class warfare. 'To be rich,' Hone wrote with mounting bitterness,

> however honestly Riches may have been acquired, and however liberally expended is a reproach in the eyes of the vile faction who rule this ill-fated city, although they have to depend upon that class of men to furnish the means of extending and perpetuating their power. Munificence and public spirit are denounced as qualities too exclusive for general use. Good manners are anti-republican. Religion is a reproach to those who are conscious of the want of it, and a Gentleman belongs to a Genus so nearly extinct that he will be compelled ere long to become re-naturalized and assimilate with the Mob, if he would preserve his municipal rights.[30]

The deterioration of the quality of life in Lower Manhattan took many shapes. Though 'quality of life' issues were not normally part of political discourse in the 1830s, such concerns were among the strongest forces behind the pace of change in the city. George Templeton Strong, living in 110 Greenwich Street in the 1840s, complained (in his diary) of an 'average choir of cats, a pulmonary horse (stabled within twenty-five feet of this room) afflicted with a periodic cough of great severity at regular intervals of about fifteen minutes, and a few drunken Dutch emigrants singing what I've no doubt's a highly indecent Low Dutch canticle.' The 'cracked clarinet,' piano, and two trumpets of two Dutch 'lust-houses' in Washington Street disrupted the 'Sabbath stillness' of the neighborhood.[31]

St. John's Park

In October 1869 the unveiling took place of one of the most extraordinary pieces of self-assertion of nineteenth-century New York: a large bas-relief

depicting Commodore Vanderbilt was erected on the summit of the western wall of the depot of the Hudson River Railroad. On either side of the figure of the Commodore were the vessels which represented the stages in his marine career, and the railroads upon which his fortune was based after the Civil War. It seemed a monument, noted E.L. Godkin's *Nation*, to those peculiarly American virtues of 'audacity, push, unscrupulousness, and brazen disregard of others' rights or others' good opinion.'[32]

Vanderbilt's monument adorned a large railroad freight depot built on the site of what had formerly been St. John's Park, bordered by Varick, Beach, Hudson, and Laight Streets. The park, the surrounding square, and the elegant St. John's Chapel which looked out over the scene from Varick Street, had once been among the most handsome neighborhoods in New York. 'St. John's Park was a gay, beautiful sight on a Sabbath morning,' recalled Mary Sturges, 'with its grand old trees, and the beautifully dressed people of all ages trooping along to St. John's church, which still stands (1885) on the east side, and the Laight Street church, which has long since been torn down. The houses around this square were at that time occupied by some of the best and most substantial

16. St. John's Chapel and Park.

St. John's Chapel, facing St. John's Park in lower Manhattan, was a house of Episcopal worship between 1807 and 1908. During that century the district where the park and its handsome church stood transformed from a rural location into an immigrant neighborhood of saloons, factories, and sweatshops.

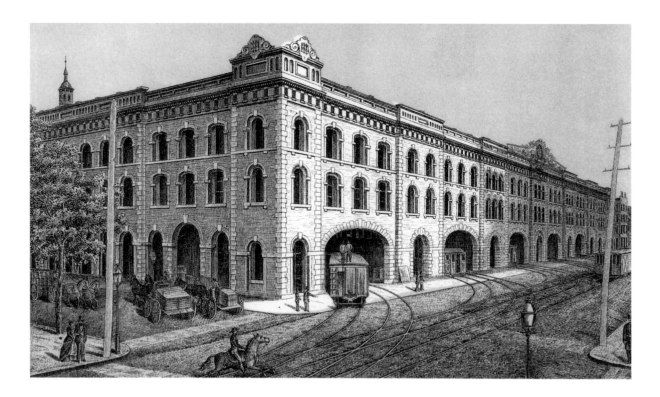

17. Hudson River Rail Road Depot.

In the 1860s the struggle over control of the Hudson River Rail Road pitted Cornelius Vanderbilt against a motley assortment of speculators and political schemers. If they could have blocked Vanderbilt from operating the Harlem Line in downtown Manhattan, they might have been able to drive the stock price down and make a killing at Vanderbilt's expense. The purchase of St. John's Park, and the depot he erected with its flamboyant memorial to the Hudson River's largest stockholder, told the world who won that struggle.

families in New York.' Like Gramercy Park (whose creator, Samuel B. Ruggles, made repeated visits downtown to examine every feature of St. John's Park and the surrounding neighborhood),[33] St. John's was a small development, somewhat off the mainstream of traffic and commerce, which had been planned from the outset to be an aristocratic enclave.

A few minutes north of St. John's Park was Richmond Hill, at one time Aaron Burr's country seat, located at what became the corner of Varick and Charlton Streets. The conversion of the Richmond Hill mansion into an opera house in 1831 was a turning point for the whole neighborhood. Success would have greatly strengthened the appeal of the area west of Broadway. Likewise, failure of the opera undermined the willingness of the city's wealthy to remain downtown. The Richmond Hill Theater was greeted with warm enthusiasm in St. John's Park. The 1832 season of grand opera, presented by the company of Giacomo Montresor, and with the energetic sponsorship of the eighty-five-year-old Lorenzo Da Ponte, began with a performance of *La Cenerentola*. Wealthy men like Philip Hone, Samuel Shaw Howland, and Peter Schermerhorn joined together at the sale of private boxes to buy the largest available, which had thirteen seats, for the princely sum of $750 for a season of thirty-five nights. For the second season Hone enthusiastically acquired box number 8 with Peter Schermerhorn, James Jones, and William Moon. The city's leading theater, the Park, had fallen upon evil times. Under the proprietorship of John Jacob Astor, the Park had become little more than a 'dingy abode of dreariness.' Pervaded by evil smells, infested with rats, patronized by 'howling roughs' in the gallery and prostitutes in the upper tier, it was regarded by New Yorkers of gentility (the *bon ton*, or the *tong*, as N.P. Willis satirically called them, adding a nasal element to the favored term for fashionable society) as a disgrace and what was worse, an embarrassment.

The Richmond Hill Theater was created to rival the Park, and its management openly sought the patronage of the rich. Tickets at $1.50 for parterre and box, and $1.00 for the gallery were higher than was usual in New York. Boxes at the Richmond Hill were furnished as though they were an extension of the elegant parlors of St. John's Park, with 'light blue hangings, gilded panels and cornice, arm-chairs, and a sofa. Some of the others have rich silk ornaments; some are painted in fresco, and each proprietor seems to have tried to outdo the rest in comfort and magnificence.' The décor conveyed an unmistakable social meaning that the opera did not belong to the world of the Bowery and Broadway, where entertainments were offered to the whole community. Rather, it was performed in isolation, and aimed solely at a homogeneous audience drawn from 'the better class,' like those living at St. John's Park.

Despite the beauty of the house, Hone wondered about the prospects for such a form of entertainment in New York City: 'Will this splendid and refined amusement be supported in New York? I am doubtful.' As it lurched from one theatrical manager to another, and from closure to closure, the history of the Richmond Hill Theater answered Hone's doubt in the negative. (With the commercial failure of the Montresor company Da Ponte turned to the building of a dedicated structure for opera, and opened the Italian Opera House

18. Richmond Hill Theater.

The Richmond Hill Theater had once been the home of Vice-President John Adams. Aaron Burr acquired the estate in 1797. The hill, which provided spectacular views across the Hudson River, was leveled by the Commissioner's Plan of 1811. Burr's handsome Greek Revival wooden dwelling, originally built in 1767, was enlarged to serve as a theater. After one unsuccessful season after another, it was turned into a ballroom, and then a saloon, before it was demolished in 1849.

at Church and Leonard Streets, under the management of the Chevalier Rivafinoli, in 1833.) For a time the Richmond Hill Theater lingered on as a ballroom under the name of the Tivoli Saloon. With the failure of the theater the idea of an extended aristocratic development west of Broadway vanished. In the absence of a cultural infrastructure like that represented by the Stuyvesant Institute, or amenities like Delmonico's and the leading clubs, St. John's never achieved the scale needed to fend off other and unwelcome changes nearby.[34]

At the first night of the Richmond Hill Theater in 1831, Fitz-Greene Halleck read a dedicatory poem:

> . . . To you the hour that consecrates this dome,
> Will call up dreams of prouder hours to come,
> When some creating poet, born your own,
> May waken here the drama's loftiest tone . . .[35]

The victory of Halleck in a competition for the best dedicatory poem was one of those ironies which poets have had to endure in New York. Halleck later entered the office of John Jacob Astor, who in 1804 had acquired Burr's interest in the Richmond Hill leases for $82,500. The leases had passed to Burr through several hands, but ultimately descended from Trinity Corporation's original lessee, Abraham Mortier, Paymaster General to the British forces in North America. Mortier's lease, issued in 1767, ran for a ninety-nine-year term, at an annual rent of $269. Astor, as Halleck knew very well, had no interest in 'dreams of prouder hours to come.' He specialized in short-term leases, and regarded real estate as nothing more than an investment. He was content to let others like Ruggles donate valuable plots for civilized amenities like Gramercy Park.[36]

After the war of 1812 St. John's Park and the surrounding streets enjoyed the reputation of a prime residential district. Worthy lawyers, merchants, and clergymen lived in the neighborhood, whose social tone was set by families like the Lydigs, principal flour merchants in the city. David Lydig erected a mill near West Point, and operated sloops which carried flour to the warehouse in the city where his wholesale business thrived. He also acquired the much-admired West Farm in Westchester County, the pre-revolutionary country estate of the De Lanceys. Anticipating the consequences of the Erie Canal, which opened the Hudson River farms to harsh competition from farmers in the west, Lydig sold his business, and then sold the family home at 225 Broadway, to his neighbor John Jacob Astor who planned to build a hotel (the Astor House) on the site. In 1830 Lydig moved to 34 Laight Street, facing St. John's Park, and lived the life of a quiet, respectable old New York man, dividing his time between Laight Street and West Farm. After his death in 1842, the house was inherited by his son Philip, who married the eldest daughter of John

19. Fitz-Greene Halleck.

Of all the great literary figures of nineteenth-century New York, Fitz-Greene Halleck flew highest (there is a statue of him in Central Park, the first in the city to commemorate a poet) and fell into near-total obscurity. Bayard Taylor's novel, *Joseph and His Friend* (1903), the first openly gay novel in American literature, gave a thinly disguised portrayal of Halleck's relationship with the poet Joseph Rodman Drake. It is his sexuality, not his poetry, which interests contemporary critics.

Suydam, and lived an equally agreeable life on the accumulated wealth of two prominent families. The Lydigs and Suydams were joint holders of pew 66 at Grace Church. Family ties among the Lydigs, Suydams, Hamiltons, Aymars, Colts, Schuylers, Gibbes, and Lords knitted together the community around St. John's Park. When Charlotte Augusta Gibbes married John Jacob Astor III, it was as much a neighborhood alliance as the Bond Street and Lafayette Place marriages of William Astor and Caroline Schermerhorn, and Sam Ward and Emily Astor. The Astors married well, and in the right neighborhoods.

The little social institutions like day schools, scarcely visible to the larger community, strengthened the sense of community. Many residents sent their daughters to a select school for young ladies on the corner of Varick and Beach Streets run by Miss Maria Forbes, where the girls were taught spelling, grammar, needlework, and embroidery. Regular visits by a writing master, an instructor in French, and a dancing master (who taught the cotillon and the three-step waltz) added the desired St. John's Park polish. The better neighborhoods had similar establishments: at Washington Square and lower Fifth Avenue the Misses Lucy and Mary Green ran a highly regarded school; at Clinton Place Mrs. Okill had a particularly select academy for young ladies; and at Gramercy Park the market leader was a Miss Haines. Such academies were part of the social infrastructure of districts inhabited by the wealthy.[37]

The origins of the neighborhood lay in the city's population growth, and rapid expansion above Wall Street. Faced with a growing Episcopal community, the Bishop of New York, the Reverend Benjamin Moore, looked for a site for a new chapel. 'The many respectable applicants for pews, who could not be furnished with them in the existing [Episcopal] churches, made it expedient that another one should be built, and a committee was therefore appointed in reference to it, and authorized to inquire and select a suitable site for the same.'[38] In 1803 a site on Hudson Street was purchased, along with a burying ground at the corner of Clarkson and Hudson Streets. The anchor of the development was John McComb's St. John's Chapel, erected in 1807, which stood on Varick Street facing the square. The total cost of the structure was $172,833, with an additional $8,000 for the organ. These were quite fabulous sums for a development virtually out of town. The vestry of Trinity Church planned an ornamental development to ensure that the chapel was supported by a sufficiently prosperous parish. Ninety-nine-year leases, with restrictions on the kind of houses which could be built, were offered to builders. In exchange, lease-holders were given access to the private locked park—an aristocratic precedent followed by Ruggles when he created Gramercy Park.

The houses facing St. John's Park were designed for handsome entertaining. (Kenneth Scherzer points out that 'we often know more about the buildings [of New York] than the people who inhabited them.')[39] The entrance hall, done in the New York fashion with alternating squares of black and white marble on the floor, ran the length of the house. At the far end of the hall, stairs led to the servants' quarters in the basement. In the middle of the hall there was an oval opening which rose two stories to the roof. A circular staircase ascended from the oval to the open gallery of the first and then the second floor. (They were the first things to be boarded up when the St. John's Park houses were converted into tenements.) Graceful Ionic columns in the gallery supported the floors above. The parlors were usually 50 feet long, and 18 feet wide—sufficient for a double quadrille, and leaving enough space for a small orchestra. The back parlor was separated from the larger room by mahogany sliding doors.

In the early 1830s, the park was among the finest in the city. The view from a parlor looking out over the park was charming, in contrast to the usual cramped perspectives which characterized the commercial city. The mature trees and tasteful Federal row houses gave St. John's Park a European aura of elegance. Gravel paths and an ornate iron railing ('as high and as handsome as that of the Tuileries,' thought Fanny Trollope) were admired design features. In the unusually cold winters in the 1860s, when ice-skating at Central Park had become fashionable, the trustees of St. John's Park agreed to the flooding of the park, creating the largest downtown ice-skating space. The park's keeper

admitted the general public, for the democratic sum of 10¢. Sleighs lined the Hudson Street side of the park for a good view of the wintry entertainment.[40]

Commercial development pressing northward along Greenwich Street, bustling with warehouses and commercial traffic in the 1840s, began the process of gradual decline. The Hudson River waterfront was inevitably a disruption to tranquil residential life. Workmen streamed through the streets around the park at all hours, causing the mayor in 1848 to order the area to be lit with gas. The horse-drawn carriages of the Hudson River Railroad ran noisily along Hudson Street, on the western edge of the park. In the 1840s St. John's Park became a target for radical discontent aimed at Trinity Church, owner of some of the worst tenements in the city. The journalist and all-round labor agitator Mike Walsh regarded the park as an affront to the citizens of New York. 'A more exclusive concern than this park does not exist on earth. Its gates are all locked, and keys for it are sold, by the church which *claims* it, for ten dollars a year, to none however, but the upper ten thousand, who reside in the surrounding palaces.—Can anything be more insultingly aristocratic than

20. Skating at St. John's Park.

The first organized ice-skating rink in the United States was opened in Central Park in 1858. Ice-skating (as this scene from St. John's Park suggests) became one of the great passions of New Yorkers. The attempt to segregate male and female skaters was abandoned, by popular demand, in 1870. Public and private rinks, including the outdoor rink at Rockefeller Center, opened in 1936, have helped this enthusiasm to survive into contemporary New York.

this?' He made a democrat's protest by climbing over the ornate railing of St. John's Park and strolling on the forbidden gravel paths. The private character of the park helped shape attitudes towards the neighborhood as a whole, and not always favorably. 'St. John's Park,' noted Lydia Maria Child in her second 'Letter from New York,' 'though not without pretensions to beauty, never strikes my eye agreeably because it is shut up from the people; the key being kept by a few genteel families in the vicinity.'[41]

The ownership of St. John's Park was divided between the householders and Trinity Church, and as the neighborhood declined, there were repeated approaches to buy the park. Agreement to sell it to Cornelius Vanderbilt's Hudson River Railroad for a freight depot was finally reached in 1866. As George Templeton Strong feared, the $400,000 which Trinity Church received stirred up 'a perilous storm of abuse and misrepresentation' against the 'bloated corporation.' The lot-owners shared the princely sum of $600,000. The press unsentimentally reported in November 1867 that the 200 trees which had formerly adorned St. John's Park had been cut down. It was expected that there would now be a rapid conversion of private residences on the square into tenements and places of trade, which would add substantially to the value of each lot. 'This increase in the value of their holdings, with the $13,000 bonus for the cession of the little bit of landscape opposite, ought to satisfy the good people, not only as to the wisdom of the original investment, but with the progress of things generally, even when it entails the necessity of moving up town for a fine prospect and good air.'[42]

The area surrounding St. John's Park had become a slum by the 1890s, and for those who retained any recollection of what the neighborhood had once been, the comparisons between then and now were painful. 'Lines of dripping, soap-smelling washtubs are stretched along hallways, through which one might drive a coach and four; stovepipes are run into fire places in which one might set a dining table, and cot beds stand thick around parlors that look like ballrooms turned into rag shops.'[43] Thomas A. Janvier noted 'the aggressive presence of several distinctively Neapolitan smells. The stately houses, swarming with this unwashed humanity, are sunk in such squalor that upon them rests ever an air of melancholy devoid of hope. They are tragedies in mellow-toned brick and carved wood-work that once was very beautiful.'[44]

Attendance at the chapel fell steadily, and the vestry of Trinity Church, confronted by declining income from the church's real estate holdings and unable to keep the congregation alive, concluded that the building had to be sold. Turning his face against sentimental considerations, Bishop Potter gave his assent to the closure in 1894. When finally confirmed in 1908, the decision was greeted with a storm of high-placed Episcopalian indignation. The chapel itself was a fine architectural landmark ('one of the most beloved, most beautiful and historically most precious edifices in the city') and had energetic defenders.[45] An injunction was obtained in the Supreme Court blocking the closure, but the rights of Trinity Church were maintained in the subsequent trial.

To improve the flow of traffic in the West Village and on Seventh Avenue, the city proposed the widening of Varick Street in 1912. In the absence of public opposition to the plan, defenders of the chapel, who had launched a public campaign to save the structure, found the politics of the issue impenetrable. The widening would force the removal of the chapel's portico, and probably the belfry as well. The vestry of Trinity Church was prepared to sell the structure at a reasonable cost, but would not agree to maintain religious services. Weighty voices in the community opposed the vestry. Anna Gould, a strong supporter of benevolent causes in the city, published a letter imploring the vestry to draw back at the last minute from closure. The editor of the *Century*, R.W. Gilder, wrote a bitter poem, 'Lines on the Proposed Demolition of St. John's Chapel', denouncing the sale as an act of vandalism. A group of the most powerful men in America signed a letter imploring the vestry to consider again the responsibility they had to the neighborhood, the larger community and its architectural heritage: those who signed included the former Vice-President Levi P. Morton, J. Pierpont Morgan, William Dean Howells, former President Theodore Roosevelt, and many other worthies. Even these powerful men could not shake the resolve of the vestry, and contracts were signed in August 1918. The demolition was completed in 1919.[46]

The sale of the park in 1866 drew a line under what had once been an adornment of the antebellum city. The small number of decayed houses from that era surviving in St. John's today look out upon an entrance rotary of the Holland Tunnel—the most anonymous location in Lower Manhattan. For a few decades St. John's Square was insulated from commercial pressures by its symbolic identity. In the end, there was only a monument to Vanderbilt's commercial power, 'an air of melancholy,' and a recollection of what St. John's Park had once represented. The destruction of the park and the decline of the surrounding neighborhood may have been remembered, and with bitterness, by a few of the older residents, now dispersed across the city, when the Vanderbilts urged their uncertain claims to social acceptability in the 1870s.

Bond Street

> Tell the merchant you live on Bond street
> and there will be no question as to receiving credit.
> —New York proverb, 1840s

Above Bleecker, between Broadway and the Bowery, lay neighborhood of quiet streets, each no more than 1,000 feet long. It was a location well suited for an urban enclave; from the 1830s it was the site of a small experiment in aristocratic residential life. Bond Street and the adjacent neighborhood formed a 'tranquil stronghold of caste and exclusiveness. Its births, marriages and deaths were all touched with a modest distinction. Extravagance was its horror and ostentation its antipathy.' By the middle of the nineteenth century, to live on Bond Street 'conferred a certain patent of respectability.'[47] The Seabury Tredwell House, erected in 1830 on East 4th Street between Lafayette Place and the Bowery, is one of the very few surviving structures from the period when this was an unruffled center of fashionable life.

The peculiar charm of houses on Bond Street, and those on the surrounding streets, came from the knowledge that hereabouts resided some of the best families of the city. Jonas Minturn's row house at 22 Bond Street, with its elaborate marble front, was the first to be erected on the street. By the mid-1830s there were more than sixty houses on Bond Street. Dr. Gardiner Spring, pastor of the Brick Presbyterian Church, and the clergyman who had led the city's Sabbatarians in an unsuccessful and widely mocked petition in 1821 demanding police action against the Sunday opening of pleasure gardens, moved to the politer environment of 3 Bond Street in 1826, where he remained for three decades. Nathaniel Weed, a Pearl Street dry-goods merchant and president of the North River Bank, lived at number 4. His next-door neighbor at 5 was Albert Gallatin, who remained on Bond until his death in 1849. Gallatin had been secretary of the Treasury for twelve years, and served as Minister to France, and American Minister at the Court of St. James. He was also John Jacob Astor's oldest and closest friend. Number 5 Bond Street was later occupied by Major-General Winfield Scott, and then by Judge William Kent, son of Chancellor Kent.

Bond Street was the home of naval officers, brokers, lawyers, and judges. Jonathan Prescott Hall, later United States District Attorney for the Southern District, lived at 24 Bond Street for twenty-five years; Samuel B. Ruggles, lawyer and developer of Gramercy Park, lived at 36 for five years from 1834. John Duer, who lived at 20 Bond Street in the 1830s, was the son of Lady Kitty and Colonel William Duer, and was a brother of the president of Columbia College. He successfully defended Alexander Slidell Mackenzie in the *Somers* case in the 1840s (one of the central figures in the trial was Lieutenant Guert Gansevoort, a nephew of Maria Melvill) and later became Chief Justice of the New York State Supreme Court. Bond Street accommodated some of the city's leading merchants and importers, such as Henry Grinnell, partner with his brother Moses in the mercantile firm of Fish and Grinnell. Abraham Schermerhorn lived at 36 Bond Street from 1839 until his death in 1850. His daughter Caroline spent her early years in Bond Street before marrying William Astor, the grandson of John Jacob Astor, in 1853.[48]

The residents of Bond Street formed a natural clientele for American painters, sculptors, and architects.[49] Judgments on the work of an artist were passed from parlor to parlor, generating commissions and establishing reputations in the broader community. Philip Hone—who moved to a house on Broadway and Great Jones Street in October 1837—was often at the center of Bond Street aesthetic taste, as the early career of Samuel F.B. Morse makes clear. When Morse opened a studio in New York in 1823, among his first commissions was a portrait of Chancellor James Kent. (Kent's son later lived on Bond Street.) A copy of this painting was bought by Hone, who recommended Morse to his brother Isaac, who commissioned a portrait of his daughter (*Little Miss Hone*) in 1824. Philip Hone purchased one of Morse's original sketches of Lafayette, and owned a portrait of DeWitt Clinton by Ingham. Morse was thus launched upon a meteoric career, becoming president of the National Academy of Design and receiving commissions from the common council for a full-length heroic portrait of Lafayette, a portrait of Columbus and a traditional mayor's portrait of William Paulding for the Governor's Room in City Hall. (John Vanderlyn was chosen to do a portrait of Hone on the conclusion of the latter's term as mayor in 1826.)

Other painters followed the same trail in search of commissions. When Thomas Cole first arrived in New York from Philadelphia in 1825, his work attracted the interest of John Trumbull, who arranged for an exhibition for him at the American Academy. Trumbull alerted leading figures in the Federalist world to the merits of Cole's work, and they seem scarcely to have been deterred by the young painter's lack of formal training. Cole's patrons included lawyers and merchants in Hartford and New Haven, and leading figures in New York commercial life. Two of his Catskill scenes were purchased by Hone, who remained an enthusiastic and discriminating admirer. The large commission from Samuel Ward (see below, p. 97) reflected Bond Street's verdict upon Cole's work.[50] Ward's enthusiasm for the sculptor John Frazee, who exhibited a bust of John Jay at the Merchants' Exchange in 1832, led the remaining partners of Prime, Ward & King to commission a bust of their retiring partner, Samuel Prime. In 1837 the sculptor Thomas Crawford executed figures for the mantel at Samuel Ward's home on Bond Street, and a small bust of Mrs. John James Schermerhorn (Mary Hone), but large-scale commissions eluded him in New York. Crawford courted Louisa Ward at the home of her uncle John Ward at 8 Bond Street, and married her in 1844. Their son was the novelist Francis Marion Crawford. Although Crawford enjoyed the support of Philip Hone, who commissioned a statue of Henry Clay intended for the new Merchants' Exchange, the $10,000 needed for the work could not be raised in the wake of Clay's defeat in the 1844 presidential election.

At the heart of the social glue which kept Bond Street a community was the entertaining led by the Howlands and Schermerhorns. There was on Bond Street a complex world of gentlemen's clubs, civic societies, cultural associations, and dining clubs.[51] Rooted in neighborhood relations and professional and intellectual interests, such bodies served as a gathering point for political and economic intelligence. We might single out three such institutions, all created in the 1830s, as bearing the unmistakable stamp of the Bond Street ethos: the St. Nicholas Society, the Union Club, and the Stuyvesant Institute, as well as the small dining societies named after Chancellor Kent and Philip Hone.

Membership of the St. Nicholas Society, established in 1835, was confined to the Knickerbocker elite and was restricted to 500 members drawn from those of 'respectable standing in society.' A proposed member had to be able to demonstrate that his family had lived in New York before 1785. John Jacob Astor, who came to New York in 1784, barely qualified for this pinnacle of Knickerbocker society in the 1830s.

The Union Club, founded in 1836 at a meeting held at the home of John McCrackan at 1 Bond Street, was the most thoroughly aristocratic private institution in the city. The addresses of nine of the thirteen signatories to the founding document can be traced. Six lived in the immediate vicinity on Bleecker, Broadway, Bond Street, and Lafayette Place; only two lived downtown on lower Broadway or Bowling Green. In the 1850s the Union Club occupied premises at 691 Broadway, between Great Jones and East 4th Streets, literally around the corner for the gentlemen of Lafayette Place and Bond Street. Founded purely for social reasons, the Union Club had from the first an 'older' membership dominated by conservative merchants and lawyers. Younger men found the atmosphere of the club house hide-bound and stuffy. Those with cultural and literary interests found the Arcadian Club, the Lotos Club, and the Century Association with Verplanck, Bancroft, and Bryant serving as successive presidents, far more to their taste; for Democrats there was the Manhattan Club; the Union League Club was founded during the Civil War to strengthen support for Lincoln, the Republican party and the Northern cause. Younger socialites founded the Knickerbocker Club as a refuge from the tedium of the Union Club, dominated by men of their parents' generation. Within a year or two of its foundation the Union Club decided not to hold dances or balls. No games were allowed in the club house, except whist, écarté, euchre, bezique, and cribbage, and the stakes could not exceed $20. By mid-century evening dress was worn by members taking dinner in the club house. Membership of the Union carried with it the highest cachet. Though there were several newspaper proprietors (Charles King of the *New York American* and James Watson Webb of the *Courier*) among the members of the Union, there was a settled prejudice against journalists and actors—often targets of blackballs in the balloting on membership nominations. Membership was closed at 1,000 (throughout the nineteenth century there were seldom fewer than 500 applicants awaiting election), with an entrance fee of $100 and yearly dues of $20.[52]

21. Philip Hone.

Philip Hone may have been an undistinguished politician, serving one term as mayor of New York in 1826, and his career as a businessman was scarcely more impressive. But his diary, kept faithfully between 1828 and 1851, comprising twenty-eight quarto volumes containing some two million words, is one of the most remarkable private documents of nineteenth-century urban life. First published in 1889, with an introduction by Bayard Tuckerman, and in an edition by Allan Nevins in 1927, Hone's memoir has been an invaluable source for historians, and a delight to readers who have come to appreciate this solemn, worldly, curious observer of New York life.

The Stuyvesant Institute moved into a 'fine building' at 659 Broadway in 1837. Dedicated to 'the diffusion of knowledge by means of popular lectures,' and offering rooms to the New-York Historical Society with its rich collection of manuscripts and historical works, it enjoyed the generous support of prominent men like Peter G. Stuyvesant and the banker Samuel Ward, whose 'Corner House' was located across the street. Ward's son Sam was invited to deliver the inaugural discourse before the Society.[53] The Stuyvesant Institute was the benevolent face of the Bond Street world of the St. Nicholas Society, drawing upon a narrow, well-heeled membership, and offering to the public lectures on topics of little general interest. The insistence upon exclusivity of membership, and a distaste for popular entertainment, left to others—the showman P.T. Barnum and the Institute for the Advancement of Science and Art which Peter Cooper donated to the city in 1857—a role in the community which Bond Street might have played, but did not. While rejecting anything smacking of commercialism, the funding of such high-minded civic bodies as the Stuyvesant Institute and the New-York Historical Society was always insecure. In the absence of a mass membership capable of sustaining their activities, the struggle to balance the books became impossible as one private benefactor after another succumbed to the banking panic in the late 1830s. The Stuyvesant Institute was declared bankrupt in 1839, and its building on Broadway was sold. Homeless again, the Historical Society was offered a lease on rooms at New York University on Washington Square.

In 1838 two representative institutions of Bond Street met for the first time: the Kent Club of judges and lawyers, and the dining club named in honor of Philip Hone, consisting of twelve convivial men of Whig persuasion. Hone, whose diaries are filled with the guest lists of many all-male dinners, was the club's president, and members included the auctioneer Simeon Draper, Moses G. Grinnell, William Ward (brother of the builder of the Corner House), and Jonathan Prescott Hall. Hone's ode embodied the ideals of the club:

> Shall innocent mirth and good humour abound,
> And our bosoms beat high as each Monday comes round?
> Gentlemen of the Jury, are you all agreed?
> Pres^t: Agreed.
> Chorus: Agreed, agreed, we are all of one mind.
> For truth, love and friendship our verdict we find.

When the worthies of Bond Street entertained there was always 'a good Dinner, good singing and plenty of wine'—and a careful attentiveness to the suitability of guests invited to such occasions.[54]

Houses on Bond Street occupied lots 25 or 26 feet wide, with a depth of 125 to 200 feet. They were three- and four-story residences (counting the cellars), largely made of brick. The rear of the lot might contain stables. The amount of marble or granite on the house was a fairly reliable indicator of the cost of the dwelling—and perhaps the social aspiration of the owner. Marble was used in the better row houses for decorative framing of doorways and in some cases for the stoops, and for mantels in the principal rooms. (Mary Sturges recalled with some pleasure a 'good' landlord in the 1830s who took out the wooden mantels and put in marble ones with grates, and installed folding doors between the parlors.) A guidebook to the city published in 1837 noted the change in taste when brick gave way to stone:

> Most of the houses in New York are built of brick. . . . A few of the old wooden buildings remain; and a few of the more new and elegant structures are of stone. . . . Granite pillars in front of the stores are of recent introduction. Five or six years ago there were scarcely a dozen of such fronts in all New York. Now every new store is built with granite columns, as high as the first story, and some of them higher. But the new stores are not the only recipients of these improvements. The brick walls are knocked away from the fronts of many of the old homes, and granite pillars are inserted.

The first use of Greek Orders for doorways executed in New York City appeared on Bleecker Street and Lafayette Place in 1829. It did not take long before side- and fanlights were stripped out, and Doric doorways installed.[55]

The real estate market and the high cost of rented property conspired to produce generic New York interiors. A home which appeared 'singular,' in either layout or architecture, was less likely to command a premium rent. 'Good taste' as defined by the real estate market proved a determined enemy to 'singularity.' George William Curtis, writing on 'Our Best Society,' in the 1850s, set out an angry indictment of the 'insipid uniformity' seen everywhere in fashionable urban residences. 'Every new house is the counterpart of every other, with the exception of more gilt, if the owner can afford it. The interior arrangement, instead of being characteristic, instead of revealing something of the tastes and feelings of the owner, is rigorously conformed to every other interior. The same hollow and tame complaisance rules in the intercourse of society.'[56] The tradition of annual leases, ending on the frantic May 1st moving day, kept most owners and tenants of rented property attuned to the small features which might define a comfortable and up-to-date New York home.

Bells were installed to summon servants from the kitchen in the basement. Wrought-iron railings descending to the sidewalk became increasingly ornate. There were fancy cast-iron balconies on the LeRoy Place row houses, and wood shutters for all front-facing rooms. The builder Isaac G. Pearson's row houses in LeRoy Place sold for the princely sum of $11,000 or $12,000 in the 1830s, but that was less than half the price obtained for houses in nearby Colonnade Row.[57] Interior sliding doors made of mahogany separated the principal rooms on the first floor (less expensive folding doors were used on the second floor). The dining room normally faced the rear and the drawing room or parlor looked out on the street. Proper domestic management decreed that everything in the household be covered. The dinner table was usually covered with a fancy oilcloth, then a sheet of green baize, and only then a spotless tablecloth would be laid. Fearful that the cloth might be soiled, every dish and plate stood on a separate mat. After each meal the tablecloth was folded up and put away. A careful household manager would insist that the lines of the main creases were scrupulously followed. Every item of furniture, including the cabinet piano, had its cover sewn out of Holland cotton.[58]

As families grew larger, the garret in smaller homes was usually divided to make two small sleeping rooms, each with a dormer window, used by servants or children. Houses with deeper lots could have small additional structures in the rear to be used as a summer tea room. Bond Street was lined with trees, two in front of each house. By mid-century they had grown so tall that in the evening the lamps in front of the houses cast a fitful light through the leaves, giving the impression that Bond Street belonged more to Paris than to New

York. It is perhaps less important to notice when trees were planted in New York streets, than when, as a sign of the increasing pressure of traffic and commercial activity, they were cut down. In Bond Street that day came in the 1860s.

The interior décor of the finer antebellum New York houses was becoming darker and ever more ornate. Satin, and exceptionally silk, was used in preference to chintz on furniture. Mirrors were large, with elaborately carved frames. Deftly cut silhouettes of the family adorned drawing-room walls. (By mid-century the silhouettes had largely been replaced by elegant maroon-cased daguerreotypes displayed in cabinets on shelves.) Everywhere there was a feeling of abundance, of select possessions arrayed for display. On side tables in the most proper parlors there were thick albums holding cartes-de-visite, the latest number of the *North American Review* or the *Home Journal*, perhaps the dark red morocco edition of Mrs. Rowson's *Charlotte Temple*, with a faded flower found one day at the gravestone of the tragic fictional heroine in Trinity Churchyard, or an album containing autographs of the Episcopal bishops of New York. 'Little tables, looking and smelling like flower beds, portfolios, nicknacks, bronzes, busts, cameos, and alabaster vases, illustrated copies of lady-like rhymes bound in silk, and, in short, all the cox-comalities of the drawing room scattered about with the same profuse and studied negligence as with us,' wrote Mrs. Trollope in her *Domestic Manners of the Americans*.[59]

There is a striking painting by Francis Heinrich of a Bond Street parlor in 1850 which gives us several hints at the inner life of Bond Street.[60] It is a scene far from work. ('America is the home of work,' wrote William Dean Howells.)[61] In a culture in which manhood was defined by work, Heinrich's scene assumes the spatial division between 'home' and 'work' upon which the development of New York in the preceding three or four decades was based. In 1823–4, when Allan Melvill moved from Cortlandt Street uptown to a new house on Bleecker Street, and Samuel Ward moved from Bowling Green to Bond street, work was exiled from the domestic sphere. To his daughter Julia, Ward's day-by-day activities at the bank are unknown and unmentioned. The commercial affairs of Allan Melvill were too precarious to be ignored by his wife; there were too many imploring letters which had to be written to her brother asking for money. But such matters were never discussed in front of the children. The parlor on Bond Street is a theater in which members of the family enact roles which carried meaning for contemporary New Yorkers. The five children of the Fiedler family enact carefully gendered sex roles, with the daughters arranged in graceful and affectionate poses, looking after the baby of the family ("It is a beautiful sight to see sisters willing to devote their talents and industry to the education of brothers," wrote Lydia Maria Child in *The Mother's Book*),[62] while the son has transformed the parlor floor into a construction site for his play with a deck of cards.

Mr. Fiedler stands impassively at his wife's shoulder, evidently concerned with things outside the family circle. In the painting he is of the same height as his wife, and is far from the dominating visual or domestic presence demanded by the conservative proponents of the patriarchal family. In this he is a modern husband, preoccupied and distant. Mrs. Fiedler lifts her hands towards the infant, who has reached out for her. In an age in which radical critiques of the domestic household were made by communitarian thinkers (Albert Brisbane's presentation of the Utopian socialist ideas of Charles Fourier were published in Horace Greeley's *Tribune* in the 1840s) and the sentimental cult of domesticity was coming under attack from feminists, she embodies a direct reaffirmation of domestic and sentimental ideology. She is a woman who has made children the center of her life, and prefers to be seen in this role.

The parlor curtains are tied back, admitting a pale daylight from the front of the house. A warm, strong light comes from the garden, suggesting that the orientation of domestic life is away from Bond Street, and expands in the private spaces at the rear of the family home and garden. But it is a curiously

22. Heinrich's Fiedler family.

The Ernest Fiedler family lived in a Greek Revival townhouse at 38 Bond Street, probably built in the 1830s. Francis H. Heinrich's family portrait, executed *c.*1850, is regarded as 'probably the most faithful contemporary illustration' of the parlors in that decade.

austere private space. There are expanses of bare walls and the trappings of classic revival architecture, from half-relief caryatids supporting the (unlit) fireplace, a classical bust on a pedestal, and substantial Ionic columns at either end of the opening between front and rear parlors, which give the scene a rather old-fashioned elegance. (When Bond Street lost its fashionableness, and houses like that of the Fiedlers were occupied by sweatshops and small commercial enterprises, the handsome marble fireplaces remained, a reminder of former elegance.) The piano, paintings, and statuary establish the parlor as, in Bushman's phrase, a place 'dedicated to leisure and to higher pleasures of the mind.' Concessions to current taste are seen in the fringed fabric thrown over the piano, a heavy crystal and gilt chandelier, and the figured wall-to-wall carpet. To hang this substantial painting in the very room it depicts would have offered the Fiedler family a version of itself, and the values with which its members wished to be identified. It is a scene at once modern and yet thoroughly traditional, eschewing the patriarchal rigidity of an older age while suggesting, in the differentiation of the children's poses and the gestures of Mrs. Fiedler, that this was a family respectful of the enlightened domestic values of mid-century.

A quarter of a century later the William Astor family was painted by Lucius Rossi. Where the Fiedlers were enacting the roles of a loving family, the ethos of the Astors is cool to the point of frigidity. The Fiedlers appear in their own parlor, with their young son playing on the floor; that informality has no place in the self-representation of the Astors in 1878. Everyone carefully avoids eye contact. William Astor pauses from the reading of a newspaper to glance across the room at his wife (a very idealized portrait) and daughter Carrie, seated on a cushion. His daughter Emily, who had married two years earlier in the face of stern opposition from her father, turns away from the family to pet a dog. Her husband James J. Van Alen's absence from this portrait is notable. Helen Astor stands in the center of the picture, while young John Jacob IV leans against the rear of the couch, and looks at his sister's hand, placed upon his mother's lap. The figures of the family are small in relationship to the room where they sit, drawing attention to the rich (and expensive) décor. The sterling silver tea set, and the cushions upon which the slippered feet of Emily and Mrs. Astor rest, call attention to the social position occupied by the Astors. It is a portrait without warmth or charm, but which makes a forceful display of wealth.

By 1878 the Astors were no longer the wealthiest family in New York—a distinction which had passed to A.T. Stewart, and then to Cornelius Vanderbilt, but their display was impressive. We can imagine the Rossi painting as in some sense a riposte to Seymour J. Guy's domestic portrait of the William H. Vanderbilt family, executed in 1873, which is presently at the Biltmore House

in Asheville, North Carolina. The Astors, dressed by Worth in Paris, inhabit a larger and more gracious space, hung with important pictures, but leaving clearly in view an expanse of polished floor. The thirteen Vanderbilts in Guy's painting crowd into the library of a Manhattan house. The elder Vanderbilts are at one side of the scene, retaining their preferred sober dress. It is their narrow library where the family have assembled. The crowdedness of the scene, and the confinement of the family, strikingly differentiates it from the Rossi portrait of the Astors. Every inch of the mantel is piled with *objets d'art*, small statues, ceramic figures, and candelabra. Paintings crowd the walls. A gas chandelier with glass globes bathes the lavish ball gowns of the Vanderbilt women in a strong yellow light. Guy's painting captures a family before its impressive social emergence in the 1880s. Released from the confines of William Henry Vanderbilt, they marked their ascent to the highest levels of worldwide wealth by building the largest and most luxurious mansions ever known on Fifth Avenue, Newport, and across the nation. None of the persons in the Guy portrait ever again inhabit a room as poky as 'Billy' Vanderbilt's library. The family of William Astor in 1878 had no such dramatic story in their future.[63]

The social tone of Bond Street was set by the house on the northeast corner of Broadway and Bond Street. Built for Samuel Ward, partner of the banking house of Prime, Ward & King, in 1831, the Corner House was by common consent the finest mansion in the city. It stood on valuable lots Ward had purchased for $11,000 in 1826, with an extended frontage along Broadway to Great Jones Street on a lot bought for $40,000 in the early 1830s. The increasing value of real estate 'above Bleecker' was meteoric, and the Corner House contributed to the growing perception that the Bond Street area was the coming elite neighborhood.

The position Ward occupied in New York in the 1830s enhanced the social distinction which his family had enjoyed in Rhode Island for a century. The banker's grandfather, another Samuel Ward, had been Chief Justice of the Rhode Island Supreme Court before serving two terms as Governor in the 1760s. His grandson Samuel Ward (1786–1839) came to New York at the age of fourteen, to live in the home of Nathaniel Prime, and work as a clerk in Prime's stock and exchange offices on Wall Street. Ward rose to junior partner, and on Prime's retirement became head of one of the leading banking houses in New York. Prime & Ward was a large, powerful bank with extensive business in Europe and across the United States.

He married Julia Cutler from Jamaica Plain, near Boston, in 1812, and during the couple's early married life they resided at 1 Marketfield Street. When serious prosperity beckoned, Ward moved downtown, purchasing a house at 5

23. *Going to the Opera*: the William H. Vanderbilt family.

Seymour Guy's conversation piece, *Going to the Opera*, was executed in 1873. 'Billy' Vanderbilt and his wife Maria Louisa Kissam preside over a cluttered room filled with four sons, four daughters, and three in-laws, awaiting their departure for the opera. When his father the Commodore died in 1877, 'Billy' inherited $90 million.

Bowling Green. On the other side of the Green was the considerably grander home of his partner, Nathaniel Prime, at 1 Broadway. A survey of *The Rich Men of 1822* valued Ward's new home at $18,000, and his personal property at $30,000. 'A liberal and elegant hospitality presided over his household, while the domestic hearth was gladdened with merry voices of the children of their marriage.' One of the earliest childhood memories of Julia Ward Howe was a ball held at her parents' house at Bowling Green:

> Quite late in the evening [about 1823], I was taken out of bed and arrayed in an embroidered cambric slip . . . I was brought into our drawing-rooms, which had undergone a surprising transformation. The floors were bare, and from the ceiling of either room was suspended a circle of wax lights and artificial flowers. The orchestra included a double bass. I surveyed the company of the dancers, but soon curled myself up on a sofa, where one of the dowagers fed me ice-cream.[64]

After giving birth to six children (five survived infancy), Julia Cutler Ward died at twenty-seven in 1824.

For fifteen years, until his own death in 1839, the loss of his wife cast a grim shadow over Samuel Ward.[65] He could not bear the sight of the home he had bought for his family, so he sold 5 Bowling Green and moved with his six children uptown to 16 Bond Street. Jonathan Sturges, no less cautious than Samuel Ward, considered Bond Street too remote from the center of business

in New York. 'There was a fine block of houses built on the north side of Bond Street, east of Broadway. He took a carriage and drove uptown to look at a home there,—calculated the time it would take to go to and from business, and decided it would not answer.' But for Ward the distance from Bowling Green was exactly what he needed.

While Ward was living at a rented house at number 16, a new family home, eventually known as 'The Corner' or the 'Corner House,' was built for him by Isaac G. Pearson, with a façade reputedly designed by Alexander Jackson Davis. Despite a household overflowing with children, Ward withdrew from social life, and became an ever more ardent evangelical. Prayers were regularly said with meals. He gave up cigars, and abandoned the consumption of wines and spirituous liquors. (To the horror of his worldly neighbor Philip Hone, Ward disposed of a highly regarded wine cellar.) He became a stalwart of the City Temperance Society, and a generous supporter of missionary work around the world. 'My father's views of religious duty became much more stringent after my mother's death,' recalled his daughter Julia, who as Mrs. Samuel Gridley Howe was herself a leading American social and cultural figure in the late nineteenth century. She felt her father had kept her away from the world. 'I seemed to myself like a young damsel of olden time, shut up within an enchanted castle. And I must say that my dear father, with all his noble generosity and overweening affection, sometimes appeared to me as my jailer.'[66]

The austerity of the new Ward mansion built in 1831 was an expression of the piety and rigidity of Samuel Ward's Calvinism. An unadorned three-story

24. The Corner House.

'Mr. Ward lived in a noble house, which he built a few years ago on the corner of Broadway and Bond Street— the corner below my house —where he had a picture gallery and one of the finest libraries in the city. He was a rich man, and made good use of his money; and such men are not easily spared at this time.'—From the diary of Philip Hone, November 27, 1839, recording the death of Samuel Ward.

brick structure with contrasting stone lintels, the house was surrounded by a cast-iron fence. Four Ionic columns supported the entablature above the front entrance on Bond Street. The look of the Corner House suggested an aloofness and simplicity, a temple to the holy family. Jutting above the flat roof was a cupola, which offered a unique vantage point for observing the neighborhood. When his daughter Julia was frightened by lightning and thunder, Samuel Ward would take her to the cupola to observe the beauty of the storm.

There was a careful gradation of public and private space within the Corner House, and an educational regime imposed by Ward to make sure his children understood the behavior appropriate for each room. The second floor contained the family's private rooms, principally bedrooms. Small rooms with tiny windows for servants were found on the third story. In addition to the entrance hall and stairway, the Corner House had a library and three large rooms on the first floor, each named after the color of the silk curtains hung in the room. Dinner was taken in the Red Room, looking out upon the rear garden. The Blue Room was an everyday drawing room for visits. The Yellow Room was reserved strictly for public occasions, however infrequently these occurred. The library was generally off limits to the children, whose behavior in the Red Room was carefully regulated. The Blue Room, for family use in the evening, was the one space in the house in which the children were able to freely enjoy themselves. Both front drawing rooms had sculptured mantelpieces executed by Thomas Crawford.[67]

Later generations of wealthy New Yorkers might regard the building of a great home as a gesture of social aggrandizement. The antebellum public would have seen such a handsome structure more as a symbol of the banker's worldly success. Ward's art gallery and library were promising signs of the progress of the arts and letters in a city scarcely renowned for its cultural leadership. Housed in a colonnaded extension at the rear of the house, it was the first such private gallery in the city. Its primary purpose was for the enjoyment and education of his children. There was no separate entrance to allow the public to enter the gallery from the street. Unlike Luman Reed, who converted the third floor of his home on Greenwich Street into an art gallery which he opened to the public one day a week, there is no record of Ward ever having provided public access to his collection. A New York gentleman believed in his childhood that all of the money of New York was kept at 'The Corner,' because there were no doors or windows for robbers to gain entry.[68]

A friend, Jonathan Prescott Hall, purchased a collection of paintings for Ward in Europe, said to include a Poussin, a Rembrandt, and a reputed Velázquez. The attribution of Old Masters in the Ward collection was doubtful; good quality copies were more likely. Ward had ordered copies of other masterpieces from the great European galleries. When invited to view

Ward's gallery, the English writer Anna Jameson expressed her doubts at the attribution to Van Dyck of two portraits of Charles I and his queen. He had less interest in American painting than his contemporary Luman Reed, but commissioned four paintings by Thomas Cole, *The Voyage of Life*, which embodied the growing religious sentiments of both the patron and painter. Ward died before completion of the $2,500 commission—as had Luman Reed before the completion of Cole's *The Course of Empire*. The four canvases of Cole's *Voyage of Life* might have been understood by Samuel Ward as a last, urgent letter to his son, warning of the passage of time, the dangers of each successive stage in life, and, in the last canvas (*The Voyage of Life: Old Age*), with its high, black storm clouds and absence of light except in the far reaches of the uneasy sky, the certainty of our knowledge that personal salvation may only be found through grace.[69] To the very eve of his father's death in 1839, Sam Ward received letters from him urging greater economy and caution in financial matters.

The simplicity of the design of the Corner House seemed to acknowledge the uncomfortableness felt by antebellum America about ostentation and display. 'When the rich are hard-hearted and luxurious,' advised Francis Wayland in his *Elements of Political Economy* (1837), 'the poor are disaffected, anti-social and destructive.' Luxury, as Ward knew, was a looming threat to his family as well as to the community. He believed that luxury undermined self-restraint, and feared the effects of unbridled wealth on his children's moral character. The rising wealth of the city, and the frenzied pursuit of luxury, led ineluctably to selfishness, materialism, and the undermining of the traditional institutions of society. ('Wherever luxury abounds,' wrote Abigail Adams, 'there you will find corruption and degeneracy of manners.') For Ward, then, the Corner House and what it stood for in New York life did not have an uncomplicated meaning. To the public the house expressed the prosperity of the family. The Corner House emphatically asserted the place Ward occupied in the social order, but at the same time the cast-iron fence and severe exterior embodied his fear of 'society' and its seductive wiles. For Ward, the house was a refuge against the fallen world, and a shrine to the sanctity of the Christian home. (The house survived until 1873 when it was razed and a building to house the gentlemen's outfitters Brooks Brothers was erected on the site. Ten years later the nimble Brooks Brothers moved further uptown to 22nd Street.)[70]

Ward's relationship with his children embodied the same concern about luxury and society. He deplored his son Sam's lavish ways, and the growing taste in New York for 'Paris frippery and froideur.' 'I sent you to France to study,' he sternly wrote, 'not to play the gentleman by becoming a genteel vagabond.' Ward was the leading banker in the city, and numbered among his clients even the aged John Jacob Astor. As a banker Ward was instrumental in wealth creation in New York—and was a fierce opponent of President Jackson's attack on the Bank of the United States, 'an act so lawless, violent, and fraught with disaster, that it would and must eventually overthrow the men and the party that resorted to it.'

As the owner of the Corner House, he possessed one of the great mansions in the antebellum city; but as a wealthy man amidst a sea of poor immigrants, laborers, domestic servants, and factory workers, and at a time when inequalities of wealth were sharply increasing, Samuel Ward believed in self-restraint, industry, temperance, and usefulness. He sought to instill values that would defend his young family from 'Paris frippery' and the insidious temptations of luxury which were the great threat to salvation. 'The early years of my youth,' wrote Julia Ward Howe, 'were passed in the seclusion not only of home life, but of a home most carefully and jealously guarded from all that might be represented in the orthodox trinity of evil, the world, the flesh and the devil. My father had become deeply imbued with the religious ideas of the time. He dreaded for his children the dissipations of fashionable society, and even the risks of general intercourse with the unsanctified many.' Julia Ward Howe's daughters summarize their mother's experience: 'Mr. Ward had money and sympathy to spare for every benevolent enterprise, but he disliked and distrusted "society"; he would neither entertain it nor be entertained by it.'[71]

Every rich family in the city had anxieties about the dangerous effects of money. In the large Roosevelt clan, when James Roosevelt expressed a wish to return from the pastoral exile of Mr. Alexander Hyde's school at Lee, Massachusetts, an uncle, the Yankee merchant Gardner G. Howland, warned that 'he will become a Dandy & will walk Broadway with his cane.' There were thousands of dandies in New York in the 1830s. 'They abound more or less in every part of the city, from Corlaer's Hook to the Battery, and from Blooming Dale to White Hall. But they are mostly to be seen in public places—at the corners of streets, on the door-steps of hotels, and in the various public walks.' Anti-abolitionists in the 1830s feared that African-Americans, carrying canes and emulating the city's dandies, were assuming 'airs,' and strolling up and down Broadway in search of white wives. Dandies were flamboyant figures, expressing a new spirit in the city, far from the earnest piety of men like Ward and Howland. To appear on Broadway wearing spotless, tight-fitting pantaloons, a white Marseilles vest, faultless necktie, white shirt with tiny gold studs and fine, primrose-colored gloves was to make a very large social assertion. Howland's mention of the dandy's cane carried quite specific meaning, for the dandies were differentiated by prominent items of display: the watch chain, the 'quizzing glass' (lorgnette), and the cane: 'The switched, or caned, dandy is so denominated from a slender cane, or switch, about the size of a pipe-stem, made of whale-bone, or of steel . . . of a shining black, neatly polished, with an ivory head, a brass foot, a golden eye, and a tassel of silk; which cane or switch, he constantly carries and switches about him . . .'[72] Men like Ward and Howland, encountering such figures on their daily progress down Broadway to their counting houses, saw in the dandy a threat to morality and civic virtue. The prospect of young Sam Ward joining their number and swaggering up and down Broadway wearing plaid trousers which (as was the fashion) measured sixty inches around the bottom of the leg filled his father with deep horror.

The Ward family gave Bond Street its distinctive tone. Like so many other New York clans, they sought to live as close to each other as possible.[73] Ward's father, the family patriarch Lieutenant-Colonel Samuel Ward, had moved from Long Island to 7 Bond Street in 1829, and provided a home for his bachelor sons Richard, John, and William. Richard and John moved to 32 Bond Street in 1840, where they in turn provided a home for two of their nieces after the banker's death. Both girls were married from their uncles' home. Despite financial setbacks and the personal bankruptcy of John Ward (which resulted in the humiliating sale of the family furniture at a public auction), a last surviving brother Henry, remained on Bond Street until 1873.

Samuel Ward's partner, James Gore King, lived with a large family at 12 Bond Street. The society physician Dr. John W. Francis (who had been Julia Cutler Ward's obstetrician, and who joined the Ward household soon after the children were orphaned) married Samuel Ward's sister-in-law Eliza Cutler. 'Auntie Francis' continued to look after the children. Francis was a stalwart of the Stuyvesant Institute, and was the moving force behind a literary salon regularly attended by Dr. Valentine Mott, President Charles A. King of Columbia College, the essayist Henry T. Tuckerman, the brothers Duyckinck and, on rare occasions, Edgar Allan Poe.[74]

On the young Sam Ward's return from Europe in 1836, he found himself welcomed at every rout, soirée, and conversazione on Bond Street, Lafayette Place, and Great Jones Street. Now a distinctively cosmopolitan figure, he brought back a spectacular mathematical library, as well as a notable taste for good food and wines. His time abroad detached him from the strait-laced values of his father, and the older commercial world which Ward symbolized. The America that Sam Ward encountered in the late 1830s seemed all too familiar in outward ways. New Yorkers, when not Calvinists like his father, seemed to be outright money-grubbers. 'Yes, dear friend,' he wrote in 1837, 'everything here is greed, everything is arid, like the great desert of Africa for me, poor Sybarite, accustomed to tread with light and care free step the paths of soft indulgence.' He aspired to be a bon viveur, and to live a more gracious and higher life. Ward kept a diary in French while working at the bank. There

25. 1 Bond Street.

Dr. John W. Francis lived at 1 Bond Street. Running between Broadway and the Bowery, one block north of Bleecker, Bond Street was developed in the 1820s. Elegant three- and four-story row houses, erected in the 1830s and 1840s, made Bond Street one of the most attractive uptown residential addresses. Dr. Francis was a man of letters, and author of a chatty recollection of *Old New York* (1857), who presided over a literary salon which was attended by the Duyckinck brothers and Edgar Allan Poe.

was occasional business to conduct with France, but the diary was a way to pretend that he was not, day after day, up to his neck in the city's commerce. His niece Maud recalled 'Uncle Sam' as being 'rather French than American in appearance and manner, sparkling, effervescent, full of laughter, motion, gesture. His dress was striking. He wore handsome rings and scarfpins, checked trousers, superb waistcoats, an overcoat of pale gray box cloth with large white pearl buttons, unmistakably from London.'[75]

In 1838 the dandified son married William B. Astor's daughter Emily ('Emmie'). With the Wards living at 1 Bond Street, and William B. Astor and his formidable wife Margaret living on Lafayette Place, across the street from the Colonnade Row, it was a powerful marriage of New York fortunes and one which was firmly rooted in the neighborhood. The couple lived at the Corner House. Along with trunks and crates filled with her bridal trousseau, she came with a trust worth $200,000, carefully designed to preserve the principal for Emily and her 'issue.' Sam was obliged to sign a waiver, abandoning any future claims against the Astor estate. The couple, thus hog-tied by Astor trusts, moved into the Corner House while their new home on Bond Street was being built.

At last Samuel Ward's ban on entertaining was lifted. Early in their married life the bills flooded in: the services of a coachman amounted to $198.25, which included thirty-two visits to the Astors on Broadway, Lafayette Place, or Hell Gate, a black Brussels lace veil (a present for Mrs. Astor) cost $6, miscellaneous hats, veils, and taffeta were $151, eighteen polished rosewood chairs were made to order, at $242, a dozen bottles of Lafitte claret cost $18, 40 yards of printed calico at $17.50, cravats from a Parisian tailor for 139 francs, waterproof boots $12, house fixings $1,218.07, and $1,000 for marble mantelpieces. Every day the merchants' bills for sperm candles, flock mattresses, books, milk, tubs of butter, bread, Madeira (with added freight, duty, and 'cartages'), strawberries, and a Sèvres tea service ($100), arrived, were paid, and were dutifully fixed in the receipt book. Even for a Ward, marriage to an Astor was exhilarating.[76]

Samuel Ward bought the lot adjacent to the Corner House where he erected 'a lovely little house' for the couple. Testimony given years later in an angry lawsuit brought by the Astors against Sam Ward shed interesting light on the house, and the relations between the two families. After the marriage William Backhouse Astor offered to give a house to Sam and Emily Ward, inviting Ward to select a suitable site, build the residence to suit himself, and send the bills to his father-in-law. But there was a sensible need to retain a rough balance of contribution from the two families, and with no doubt heartfelt expressions of gratitude, Ward preferred to buy a house with money furnished by his father. The marriage settlement from the Astors included City of New York Water stock worth $27,000 and an $8,000 contribution from the Astors towards furnishing the young couple's house.

With both families falling over themselves to express approval of the Ward-Astor wedding, Sam Ward could but smile. The stylish house was expensively furnished. A door was cut through, connecting the two dwellings, which allowed direct access from the Blue Room into Sam Ward's library. After his sister Julia, Sam was the most literary of the Ward children. He had earned a reputation for thoughtful if sometimes impenetrable discourses on intellectual subjects published in the *American Quarterly Review*. He collected several papers into a small volume of *Essays* (1834), which he dedicated to his old friend John W. Francis, MD. He delivered lectures before the Stuyvesant Institute on topics like the rise of science, the defeat of the Americans by the British at the battle of Brooklyn Heights, and the disastrous march on Quebec in 1775. There was much more to Sam Ward than the dandy so feared by his father.[77]

As part of the marriage settlement, the house which Samuel Ward had paid for was given to his daughter-in-law Emily. A daughter, Margaret ('Maddie') was born to the young couple in 1840. A year later Emily died suddenly along with an infant son. The house on Bond Street reverted to Sam Ward upon his wife's death. Sam watched his uncle John, executor and guardian of the younger Ward children, sell off the family real estate (including the Corner

House), and at a time when prices were down. The great Ward wealth vanished. And in the end it was money, property, and the strong feelings aroused by *things*, which brought Sam Ward down. When he gave the house to his second wife, Medora Grymes, on their marriage in 1843, the Astors were outraged.

To the Astors, the reversion of the property from their daughter to Sam Ward seemed unfair, a trick, a kind of outwitting. When property was involved, the Astors became even more drearily humorless. Grymes' parents were divorced, and Margaret Astor made her feelings clear about that social impropriety by declining to offer her hospitality to Miss Grymes. The Astors successfully demanded that Maddie be sent to live with Mrs. Astor at Rokeby, her parents' Hudson River estate which William Backhouse had purchased, and did their best to sever all contact between their granddaughter and her father. However unsatisfactory relations were, the fate of the thirty-two lots on 14th Street, adjoining the Hudson River, which were conveyed to Emily Astor by her grandfather as part of her marriage settlement, stuck in the throat of the Astors well into the 1860s. Sam Ward inherited the lots upon Emily's death. When a lawsuit brought by Maddie's trustees sought to detach her father from any interest in the real estate, many embarrassing details of the private lives of the Astors and Wards were revealed in the press. The dissolution of Prime, Ward & King in 1846, and the failure of the successor firm, Prime, Ward & Co., in 1847 marked the erasure of the former owner of the Corner House from civic memory.[78]

The sordid conflict between the Astors and Sam Ward over lots on 14th Street obscures the issue which obsessed Samuel Ward, and so blighted his children's lives: that 'society' was an enduring threat to their well-being. He wanted to preserve his family in a sphere set apart from the dangerous influences of the city around them. While the Melvill family living nearby on Broadway in the 1820s sought to improve the social opportunities of their children by cultivating neighborly relations, Ward's dislike of society casts him in a mold apart. He had the elevated social position which the Melvills coveted, and lived in a great mansion, yet chose to draw tight the shutters of the Corner House against such influences. His rejection of society, tempered somewhat after the marriage of his son to Emily Astor, makes Ward of a piece with figures like the eccentric J.G. Wendel, possessed of a vast fortune yet living in little more than a modest house with his sisters. With his religious fervor, Ward was a type of aristocrat which later generations of New Yorkers neither understood nor admired. The sociability of a Bond Street figure like Philip Hone or Abraham Schermerhorn was the preferred model of how a gentleman should live in society.

The 'decline' of Bond Street took several forms. The increase in multiple occupancy and of commercial premises, the cutting down of trees, increase in traffic—above all, social change in the residents—made clear that broader changes were taking place in the neighborhood. By the 1850s the commercial pressure on Bond Street was unmistakable. The Opera House at Astor Place was now occupied by a library, and there were large, new buildings under construction (the American Bible Society opened in 1853 and was followed by the Cooper Institute, 1854–9). The elegant brownstone where Judge David S. Jones had lived at 2 Bond Street was turned into a fashionable boarding house after his departure. When 16 Bond Street, home of Mayor Gideon Lee during his term of office in 1833–4, fell vacant, new tenants from families of social distinction were hard to find. The building was eventually rented as a boarding house. The days of Bond Street as a place of family residence were ending. The more vigorous of the 'better sort' on Lafayette Place and Bond Street began to look northwards, to Fifth Avenue, for a quieter, more exclusive residential environment, where there were fewer homes with lodgers, and a safer distance from the Bowery and its riotous inhabitants.

There was intense demand for boarding accommodation in good neighborhoods, and where boarding houses thrived, others, like dentists, were soon to follow. In the 1820s and 1830s dentists were, in terms of social status, a notch or two above a common barber, but well below a surgeon. Without recognized courses of study or even a professional body, dentistry was not a 'learned profession.' (Inhalation anesthesia—the use of ether—was not introduced until the 1840s.) In New York, patients were not expected to recognize their dentists in the street, any more than they would have greeted a butcher or tradesman.

In the early 1820s when Eliza Astor fell in love with Eleazer Parmly, a handsome young dentist, her father flatly rejected the match. The cautious attentions of James Gallatin, son of the diplomat Albert Gallatin and his wife Hannah, were more warmly received, for the Astors and Gallatins had been friends for some time. Despite Eliza's dowry of $100,000, Mrs. Gallatin shared the prejudice against Astor's ruthless business methods, and nothing came of the relationship. Hoping she would forget Parmly, Astor took his daughter to Paris, where he pushed her into a marriage with Count Vincent Rumpff. The rejected suitor had a place in the sentimental history of antebellum New York, and Parmly's subsequent success (he went on to become a wealthy practitioner of dentistry, and was rumored to have a fortune of three million dollars on his death) and the poems he circulated describing his poignant visits to Eliza Astor's grave in a Swiss churchyard brought an element of pathos to the otherwise unsentimental story of the Astors.[79]

The murder in January 1857 of Harvey Burdell, a dentist living at 31 Bond Street, signaled the kinds of change which had caught up with the neighborhood. Burdell rented rooms to lodgers. A widow named Mrs. Cunningham was the dentist's housekeeper. Four grown children lived with her. When

Burdell was found murdered, public opinion blamed the luxury-loving widow and her life came under close scrutiny. That she 'passed her summers among the gay and fashionable at Newport and Saratoga' inevitably put her among women of doubtful morals. Respectable women were not supposed to lead lives of unashamed luxury. She was arrested, tried, and acquitted of the crime. After the trial she appeared before the Surrogate, claiming to be Burdell's widow. With a child in her arms, she boldly demanded a widow's share of Burdell's estate. It later emerged that she had faked the pregnancy, and that through an attendant at Bellevue Hospital she had bought an infant which she later claimed was Burdell's. (In the 1840s a young woman named Mary Applegate accused Madam Restell of selling the infant she had borne in the abortionist's Greenwich Street establishment. Baby-farming and the trade in infants was among the city's most degraded forms of commerce.) The fraud was uncovered, and Mrs. Cunningham fled the city, leaving in her wake the sense that the other New York—of vice and crime—had swallowed Bond Street, entire.[80]

The *New York Times* noted the transformed standing of the street as early as 1860: 'Bond-street, once the head-quarters of fashionable society, and only a few years ago filled exclusively with private residences, is yielding to the irresistible tide of business. Two or three business establishments have already invaded its precincts, and it is the first step which tells in such a movement, they will have followers and imitators rapidly.' In any event, the cachet of an address in Bond Street, once fondly remembered for its 'quietude and dignity' and as a 'tranquil stronghold,' was something of an illusion: it had always been a restless neighborhood, like everywhere else in the city, with a substantial proportion of the houses changing hands in each decade after the 1820s. The older residents felt no inclination to remain when boarding houses and dentists' offices lined the street. By the 1880s nearby Bleecker Street and East 4th Street were familiar haunts for streetwalkers. 'Brazen women' on the sidewalk screamed rude abuse to respectable women, and lewd invitations to passing men. A visitor to Bond Street in 1905 noted that the elegant houses were now 'shabby and prosaic,' and were occupied by artificial-flower makers. 'We only pay a dollar and a half to learners,' remarked a boss with large yellow teeth and an unpleasant smile. Bond Street was now a street of sweatshops.[81]

Lafayette Place

The development of Bond Street in the late 1820s was accompanied by many other signs that the streets 'above Bleecker' were going to be a particularly desirable residential area. There was, at first, the decision to jettison the name 'Bowery,' with its well-established and largely negative associations, and to

rename the street which linked Astor Place with Union Square as the more neutral and thus commercially attractive Fourth Avenue. (In 1898 there was an attempt to change the name of the entire Bowery, but residents pessimistically doubted whether the reputation of the street could be improved even by a new name.)[82] Lafayette Place was cut through from Art Street (Astor Place) south to Great Jones Street in 1826, reducing the size of the Vauxhall Gardens by one half. Development began in the 1830s when Seth Geer commissioned Alexander Jackson Davis to erect a row of nine town houses on the west side of the street which shared a single bold façade of marble columns. It was named La Grange Terrace, after the country estate of the Marquis de Lafayette. New Yorkers termed it 'Colonnade Row.' The houses were entered from the sidewalk, with a dramatic staircase leading up to the main floor. Lafayette Place was no more than two blocks long, but the Colonnade Row and the presence of the Astors made the street very special. Four of the original nine properties survive, though heavily altered, and in a poor physical condition.[83]

The elderly John Jacob Astor resided at 37 La Grange Terrace. His immediate neighbor was E.D. Morgan, grocer, banker, and millionaire broker, who served two terms as a strikingly popular Governor of New York State (1858–62). Two Delanos, Warren and Franklin, lived at 39 and 45. On marrying William Backhouse Astor's daughter Laura, Franklin Delano 'retired' at the age of thirty-one from the firm of Grinnell, Minturn & Co. to live in the Colonnade Row house which John Jacob Astor bought for a favorite granddaughter. Warren Delano, who made his fortune selling opium to the Chinese, had to buy his

26. Colonnade Row, Lafayette Place.

From 1830, when La Grange Terrace was opened, until 1915, when the last of the private residents departed, the marble terrace of elegant houses built by Seth Geer retained a distinctive place in the history of housing in New York. Built of marble quarried by convict labor from Sing Sing prison, and occupied by the wealthiest families in New York, 'Colonnade Row' was the grandest of all the nineteenth-century attempts to reproduce the upper-class townhouses and aristocratic neighborhoods of London and Paris.

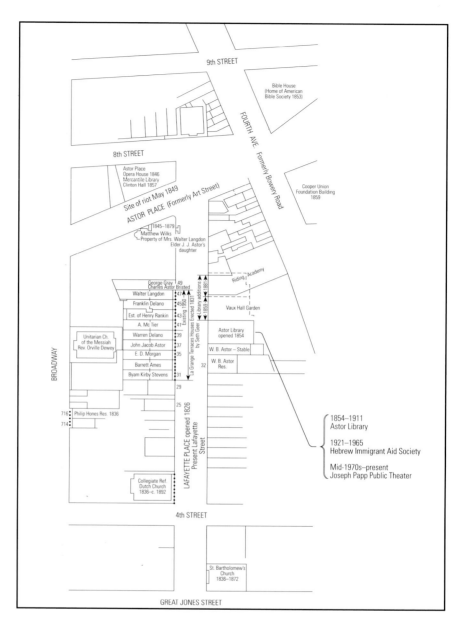

Fig. 1. Lafayette Place, as it was in 1852.

own house. His daughter Sara (known in the family as 'Sallie') married James Roosevelt—the man, Delano later remarked, who convinced him of the hitherto foreign idea that a Democrat might also be a gentleman. The son of Sallie Delano and James Roosevelt, born in 1882, was named after both his father's and mother's side of the family: Franklin Delano Roosevelt.

Astor's son-in-law Colonel Walter Langdon, who had eloped with Dorothea Astor during the war of 1812, and survived the patriarch's outrage to become a loyal part of the Astor circle, had a magnificent house which occupied four city lots at the northern end of the street at number 47. 'One don't see spending money on one's self in its true light,' noted George Templeton Strong in his diary after a New Year's call at the Langdons in 1846, 'till he sees it done on a large scale in luxuries of this sort. Langdon's arrangements are said to have cost not much less than eighty thousand dollars.'[84] Across the street at 32 was the residence John Jacob had erected for his son and intended heir, William Backhouse. Adjacent to the stables was the site upon which the Astor Library was built in 1854; it expanded in 1859 and again in 1881, when another portion of Vauxhall Garden was closed, and the site of a riding academy halved.

Few other streets in the city could compare with Lafayette Place in the moneybags sweepstakes. In addition to the Astors, the other residents were drawn from the city's wealthiest and most successful merchants. Thomas W. Pearsall, estimated to be worth $200,000, lived at 16. The Pine Street merchant David Hadden, whose worth was also set at $200,000, lived at 20 Lafayette Place. The banker David Thompson lived at 25. Jacob LeRoy lived at 26. At number 29 lived Benjamin Swan, a Boston dry-goods importer who had done so well that when his firm relocated to New York he was able to retire while still a young man with a fortune of $750,000. At 33 resided Barret Ames, a merchant who had retired with a fortune ($100,000), and whose firm, Ames & Witherill, were iron dealers in the Southern trade. Richard Haight, whose worth was also estimated at $100,000, lived at 37 Lafayette. The estate of Henry Rankin, valued at $250,000, owned 43.[85]

On March 8, 1836, the day after he sold his house at 235 Broadway for $60,000, Philip Hone reflected on the common experience of New Yorkers. 'We are tempted with prices so exorbitantly high that none can resist,' he wrote. Even the oldest and most traditional residents, with a deep loyalty to the old way of life downtown, and who had lived at the same address all of their lives, were now to be seen 'marching reluctantly north to pitch their tents in places which, in their time, were orchards, cornfields, or morasses a pretty smart distance from town.' The most fashionable quarter of New York was formerly a location which required a journey of some moment. But of all the newly fashionable locations, thought Hone, '[w]e did not see any lots which appeared to us so desirable as some on Lafayette Place.'[86]

Within a few minutes' walk of Colonnade Row were the leading social, cultural, and spiritual institutions of antebellum New York: the Astor Place Opera and Grace Church to the north, Washington Square and the Union Club, at 691 Broadway, lay immediately to the west. Clinton Place and St. Mark's Place, both residential streets of considerable charm and respectability, crossed Fourth Avenue at the intersection with Astor Place. The center of the elite world 'above Bleecker' lay in the streets on either side of Broadway, 'thronged' on January 1st by gentlemen paying traditional New Year's calls. At every fashionable house 'a grinning domestic was seen ushering in the visitors to the well-furnished saloon in which the fair inmates were ready to receive with smiles their homage and good wishes.'[87]

As the Richmond Hill opera symbolized the milieu of St. John's Park, the Astor Place Opera House was the most important symbol of aristocratic Lafayette Place. Designed by Isaiah Rogers, it was a severe neo-classical box with Doric piers and pilasters at the top of Lafayette Place, looking out upon the homes of the Astors and Delanos. It was a demonstration of the wealth and power of the city's richest inhabitants, and it was precisely the privileges arrogated by the wealthy which were a cause of the hostility expressed by the public. 'The monopoly of the best seats by certain subscribers and stockholders,' noted an observer,

> has been the great objection and drawback to that establishment. To the masses of the rest of the community, it has an appearance of exclusiveness and monopoly which will not be tolerated by them. The stockholders in the new opera house must place themselves on the same level with the rest of the community, and not arrogate any particular rights to themselves, merely because they may have subscribed to, or been stockholders in the speculation.[88]

A small matter, the decision to exclude non-paying newspapermen from the opera house, although soon reversed, was precisely the kind of act of exclusion that stuck in the throat of the city. The denizens of Bowery saloons knew very well that opera on Astor Place was not meant for them. Seats in the amphitheater cost 50¢, but had a badly obstructed view of the stage. The press referred to it as seating reserved for the *canaille*. Rabble-rousing, Nativist periodicals, their authors enraged at the growing number of immigrants in New York, had savagely attacked the opera as an 'abomination' foisted upon the Republic by a conspiracy of rich men and their foreign friends. The lessees, Antonio Sanquirico and Salvatore Patti, brought a company back from Italy which included several relations of Patti. His fifteen-year-old daughter Amalia, was billed as the *prima donna assoluta* of the company. Opera in the 1840s was emphatically perceived as a non-American cultural activity, heavily dependent upon imported European singers.[89]

The first season in 1843 of Ferdinand Palmo's opera house, located on Chambers Street, was admired by the city's fashionables. N.P. Willis noted the widespread approval of the *ton* for Palmo's 'small and beautiful edifice,' which was admirably well suited for 'white kid and cashmere.' 'The opera gets more crowded, more dressy, and more fashionable nightly.' The city's immigrant population would of course have nothing to do with such an aggressively upper-class institution, and Palmo's commercial failure impelled the forma-

27. Astor Place Riot, 1849.

May 10, 1849. An opera house at Astor Place, created by the city elite; a rivalry between two actors, the American Forrest and the Englishman Macready; a bristling patriotism; hostility towards opera as a foreign conspiracy against American culture; class tensions between Lafayette Place and the Bowery; and a mayor (Caleb S. Woodhull) prepared to suppress public disorder by military force—these were the ingredients which led to the riot. The outcome: twenty-two dead on the spot or mortally wounded, and thirty more seriously injured.

tion of the Astor Place Opera Association in 1845, with the support of fifty gentlemen, each purchasing a share in the company for a fee of $1,000 per year. Shareholders received one free ticket for each of seventy-five performances once the opera house opened on Astor Place in November 1847. The successive impresarios, buoyed by strong upper-class support, failed to see the need for well-known European performers. Nor did they seek an audience in the city's middle class, or among immigrants. That miscalculation, which had destroyed the Richmond Hill Opera, the Stuyvesant Institute, and other elite bodies, resulted in many empty seats for the first season, which was devoted exclusively to Verdi, Donizetti, and Bellini.

A second season beginning in November 1848, devoted almost exclusively to Donizetti, was abandoned by the upper class and ended in commercial failure. 'The Italian opera,' wrote Park Benjamin,

has closed its first season with considerable loss to its urbane and competent manager [Edward Fry]. The successive failures of two winters must have at length convinced a set of people, whom Mr. Willis exaggeratingly called "The Upper Ten Thousand," but who would be more than comprised in Hundreds, that they cannot sustain an establishment of this sort. . . . They cannot monopolize all the best boxes and turn up their noses at the commonalty in the pit and upper tiers. No theater or opera can be sustained here unless all parts of the house are free to all comers. *Exclusivism* must confine itself to private edifices. It is an exotic that dies in the open, strong air of democracy.[90]

Opera at Astor Place became the object of a form of class struggle, in which the Lafayette Place upper class, the families who created and patronized the opera as a form of amusement and cultural stimulation, were confronted by the 'Bowery B'hoy' supporters of the actor Edwin Forrest. The Nativist protests at the opera house in May 1849, designed to drive the English tragedian Macready off the stage, were violently suppressed. It was the first occasion since the Revolution when the militia were used in the city to suppress a rioting mob. There was a particularly good view of the riot from outside the window of Dorothea Astor Langdon's home on the southwest corner of Lafayette Place and Astor Place. Sylvester L. Wiley, standing on the sidewalk, sought assistance at the Langdon home for a bystander who had been shot in the first volley by the infantry:

> We tried to get into Mrs. Langdon's house, as we did not know how much he was hurt. We knocked at the door, which was opened by a gentleman, who repulsed us as soon as he saw what we wanted; he closed the door as far as he could but the crowd pressed so he could not get it quite closed, he sang out for assistance, when three or four men came from the back door, one of whom—a policeman, I knew him by his star—struck me over the head and knocked my hat off, so that it fell in the hall. I called on the crowd to give way, that we could not get in there. . . .[91]

'The beautiful opera-house is half dismantled,' Lydia Maria Child wrote to friends in New England, 'and the paving-stones all round it are torn up by the mob.' Calling to bid farewell to a friend, Mrs. Silsbee, at the New York Hotel, Child found an 'infuriated mob' screaming for Macready. 'Volleys of musketry were being discharged in quick succession, in the opera-house street near by.' 'Oh what a frightful city N. York is!' exclaimed the shaken Mrs. Silsbee.[92]

There were twenty-two dead, many wounded and even more arrested after the Astor Place riot. The feelings of the wealthy men living on Lafayette Place and Bond Street about the riot were expressed by the signatures of William Kent, Jonathan Prescott Hall, and Dr. John Francis on a 'card' on behalf of Macready which was published in the *Herald* on May 9. The card was signed by a broad range of journalists, writers—including Washington Irving, Cornelius Mathews, Evert Duyckinck, and the young Herman Melville— lawyers, city brokers, traders, and merchants, but Macready abandoned the struggle and fled New York. The whole affair left a bitter feeling in the clubs and better parlors. 'I walked up this morning to the field of battle in Astor Place,' noted Philip Hone on May 11. 'The Opera-House presents a shocking spectacle, and the adjacent buildings are marked with bullet holes. Mrs. Langdon's house looks as if it had withstood a siege.'[93] The 1849 riot was a moment when the charms of Lafayette Place began to fade and when the illusion that it could sustain itself as an aristocratic enclave ended. The mob which attacked the Opera House was not an *imaginary* threat to life and property.

The wealthy increasingly felt alarmed at the deepening levels of social disorder in the city. After three further and unsuccessful seasons, the Opera House was sold to the Mercantile Library Association. The Astor Library remained. A public bath house was erected on an adjacent lot. When Lafayette Place was cut through from Great Jones Street to City Hall in the 1880s, the thundering uptown traffic drove away the remaining memories of what had been the city's most fashionable area before the Civil War. 'Lafayette Place,' wrote F. Marion Crawford in 1894, 'is an unfashionable nook, rather quiet and . . . remote from civilisation.'[94]

Grace Church

The churches 'above Bleecker' occupied a commanding position in the city's social hierarchy. Much admired for its rusticated Gothic design, St. Thomas' Episcopal Church, on the corner of Houston Street and Broadway, was consecrated in 1826. In the 1840s it was the church where a Whig grandee like Luther Bradish might be married, and a funeral service for a millionaire like John Jacob Astor held.[95] Other churches flocked to the area. St. Bartholomew's Episcopal Church was built in 1835–6 at the northeast corner of Lafayette Place and Great Jones Street. The Collegiate Dutch Church was erected in 1839 on the northwest corner of East 4th Street and Lafayette Place.

The Reverend Orville Dewey's Church of the Messiah (Unitarian) was on the east side of Broadway, immediately behind John Jacob Astor's house on Lafayette Place. Consecrated in 1839, by the early 1840s Dewey's church was, 'all the fashion. The crowds which attend it on Sunday mornings makes our neighborhood exceedingly gay. The Ladies in particular pass by in great numbers, attracted by a handsome new church, and doctrines somewhat out of the regular track of Orthodoxy.' Figures like Dewey and his protégé, Henry W. Bellows, who became pastor of the First Congregational Church in New York in 1839, moved comfortably in the fashionable world and brought a new liberal Christianity to New York. They joined clubs, bought handsome houses, and attended meetings of exclusive bodies such as the Kent Club. Bellows, as president of the United States Sanitary Commission during the Civil War, urged his fellow-countrymen to make a religion of patriotism.[96]

The churches 'above Bleecker' were handsome structures, and well supported by the wealthy who had come to live nearby. Their success sent a shiver down the spine of the vestries of the older downtown churches. George Templeton Strong, elected a vestryman of Trinity Church in 1847, was soon discussing the need for Trinity to move with the times, 'for the tide of uptown emigration has left the church and its present chapels almost bare of parishioners.'

28. Grace Church.

Located at 800 Broadway, James Renwick's Grace Church (Episcopal) was dedicated in 1846. Norval White and Elliot Willensky regard it as 'magnificent' and one of the city's great architectural treasures. In the nineteenth century it was the most fashionable church in New York. Ferdinand Joachim Richardt's portrait of the church, and the fashionable churchgoers, was painted in 1858.

In 1843 the vestry of Grace Church, which since 1809 had occupied a plain, box-like building at the corner of Broadway and Rector Street, facing the rather grander structure of the second Trinity Church, decided that it, too, must follow the procession uptown. Henry Brevoort was approached about a plot of land with 125 feet frontage on Broadway at the intersection with 10th Street. It was a move of about two miles, along the route of the heavily traveled Broadway omnibus. The stolid Dutch Brevoort family, who had farmed on Manhattan for some 200 years, owned a large tract between Fourth and Sixth Avenues, from 8th to 13th Street. It was Elias Brevoort's vigorous protest which forced the city to relocate the line of Broadway to the west. His son Henry accepted $35,000 for the land sought by the vestry, and made a firm Brevoortian refusal to guarantee the vestry against any assessment if 11th Street was cut through to the Bowery. The Gothic structure, topped by a wooden steeple, was located at the corner of Broadway and East 10th Street, and was consecrated in 1846.[97]

A 'fashionable' church was self-evidently a church patronized by fashionable people. From the moment of its consecration, Hone observed, Grace Church was to be 'the fashionable church, and already its aisles are filled (especially on Sundays after the morning service in other churches) with gay parties of Ladies in Feathers and Mousseline de Laine dresses, and Dandies with mustaches and high-heeled boots, and the lofty arches resound with astute criticisms upon *gothic architecture . . .'*[98] This was not a neutral environment where the intense spiritual experience of Protestant revivals could be sought. Rather, it was a handsome venue for a collective social display of the city's most privileged citizens, and a place dedicated to secular affirmations of class solidarity. Radicals regarded institutions such as Grace Church as expressing the increasing demand by the rich to insulate themselves from the poor. On the dedication of Grace Church in 1846, the leading radical paper in New York, Mike Walsh's *Subterranean,* argued that '[t]he church in its many denominations is the instrument which wealth is employing to divide the community into two distinct classes—the *select few,* who can pay hundreds of dollars to build and sustain the church, and the *unprivileged masses,* who are as effectually excluded from places of public worship . . . unless they pay for admission the money which, in homely honesty, belongs to their families or their creditors.'[99]

The prices paid for pews in New York churches was one way in which a 'market' solution to social distance was established. The price of a pew was an index not only of the wealth of the parishioners, but of the social standing of the neighborhood of the church itself. The sale of pews was a device to provide financial support for churches, and the sums raised at the most fashionable churches could be substantial.[100] The Church of the Messiah raised $70,000 in 1839 from its pew auction. In 1872 a well-attended sale of some 200 pews at St. Bartholomew's realized $321,900. The pew was a form of real property, for which there was a market, and there is much anecdotal evidence in the diaries of the social elite about the way the market worked. Fortunately some churches have maintained highly detailed records of pew ownership.

The sale of a pew was a civil contract between the vestry and the purchaser, but the subsequent disposal of the pew to a third party was ultimately controlled by the vestry, which retained the right of approval of a new purchaser. The restricted supply of pews in the best churches kept the prices rising, and they were regarded as a particularly safe form of investment. John Pintard, who paid $300 for pew 127 in Grace Church (the annual rent was $12) when it was still located downtown at Broadway and Rector Street, sold the same pew for $400 in 1826. A pew in Calvary Church cost $550 in 1848. The relative standing of St. Ann's Roman Catholic Church on East 12th Street, and the new St. Bartholomew's Church, opened in 1872 at Madison and 44th Street, is neatly suggested by the costs of pews: Lorenzo Delmonico paid $575 for a pew at St. Ann's. Cornelius Vanderbilt paid $1,509 for a pew at St. Bartholomew's. And pew-holders held a position of considerable importance in the eyes of the management of even the most financially solid churches. Annual rental charges of 6 percent or 8 percent of the purchase price provided an essential source of funds for the maintenance of the institution. A church with a poor parish, or one declining in numbers, or in a neighborhood in the midst of rapid social change, would have its difficulties compounded by financial woes. The decision to close a church was often taken because the income was inadequate. It was to the pew-holders that the rector turned when a church showed an annual deficit, and that gave the pew holders leverage which could be used against rectors who had annoyed them, or who had taken the wrong side on issues of church governance or theology.[101]

James Renwick's Grace Church—the 'new church' to distinguish it from its downtown predecessor—contained 206 pews which were sold by auction in 1846. (The nine pews in the gallery were rented.) The location and size of a pew had a powerful influence on the sum paid, and on the annual rental—which is why random comparisons of sums paid for pews from one church to another are of limited usefulness. Most of the pews at Grace Church are 8 feet wide. Pew 17, acquired by Luther Bradish in 1846 for $650, was 10 feet 7 inches wide. Pews 21 and 22, acquired by Benjamin W. Rogers and the proprietor of the *New York Times*, George F. Jones, were only 6 feet 7 inches wide, with restricted visibility, and were bought for $400 each. Pew 44, on the rear of the right transept, was 13 feet 2 inches wide and acquired by James Foster, Jr., for $900. David Austen bought pew 98 ($712.50) and 55 ($237) and had a carpenter consolidate the two, forming the largest pew in the church at 16 feet.

The 1846 auction at Grace Church produced an interesting distribution of value. The surviving records indicate that only six pews failed to reach the valuation price. Nearly half of the pews sold were valued at more than $500. And of those 97 individuals, holding 103 pews, more than a third were to be found on Edward Pessen's list of the 1,000 wealthiest New Yorkers in 1845.[102] This is almost certainly an underestimate of the presence of great wealth among the pew-holders, for fifteen of the 103 most expensive pews were purchased by women, who for obvious reasons do not figure very largely in the upper ranks of Pessen's list, those assessed at $250,000 or more. But consider the case of Elizabeth Jones, purchaser of pew 38 for $800. She was the sister of Peter and Abraham Schermerhorn and later became the grandmother of Edith Wharton. And of Adeline Schermerhorn, *née* Coster, the wife of Peter A. Schermerhorn, who bought pew 115 in his own name. Neither woman figured in Pessen's list, yet by any reckoning the marriage of a Jones to a Schermerhorn and a Coster to a Schermerhorn meant wealth, great cascades of wealth, yet nothing easily measured by tax assessors or directly counted by historians.

Pews and shares in pews were a form of real property in an estate, and were left by will to benefactors. A decision to sell or transfer a pew was often made by executors, and in sizable families the disposal of shares in pews took on a byzantine complexity. Pew 106, which was at the front of the main aisle, opposite the rector's pew, and therefore the most 'eminent' in Grace Church, was purchased by Abraham Schermerhorn for $800 in the 1846 auction. The annual rental was $64. On his death in 1850, the pew was divided into six shares which passed to each of his children. It took thirty years after the death of Abraham Schermerhorn before pew 106 at Grace Church was again owned by an individual member of the Schermerhorn family.[103] In addition to being pew-holders, the Schermerhorns were generous supporters of the church fabric. They presented the north transept doorway, a marble cross, and the stained glass windows in both the north and south transepts.

The *tone* of the pew-holders was very much set by the presence of old Yankee and Knickerbocker families, and that was a mixed blessing. Four pews at Grace Church were owned by Suydams, two by Roosevelts, and three by Livingstons. There were Crugers, Howlands, Keteltas, Van Rensselaers, Cuttings, Van Burens, and Rhinelanders among the original pew-holders. Their presence would have attracted the socially ambitious, but—as all elite enterprises were to learn—repelled and excluded the city's artisans and working class, the very group who seemed, to Protestant clergymen and social commentators, discouragingly indifferent to religion in any form. Nonetheless, one out of three New Yorkers attended church, though that figure was probably much higher on days of special Christian worship.[104]

Most pews changed hands five, six, or seven times; very few, like pew 196, remained in the hands of a single family for ninety years from the 1840s. A changed attitude towards pew holding within the vestry (and considerable hardship caused by the Depression) led to a gentle pressure on all pew-holders to transfer their interests to the church. By the 1930s that process was largely complete. The brass plates bearing the pew-holders' names, rather worn and in need of a good polish, are still to be found on the dark brown wooden doors of the pews: Remsen, Kountze, Kernochan, Stewart, Bronson, Townsend, Schermerhorn. No longer pew-holders, perhaps no longer New

York families, and a lifetime away; a small reminder of the old forgotten life of an Episcopal church stranded below Union Square, on the now heavily traveled route between the Strand Bookstore and Tower Records.

It was the 'beadle-faced' Isaac Hull Brown, sexton of Grace Church from 1845 to 1880, a vast figure of a man who joked that his usual weight was the same number as his Masonic lodge (he was first master of Puritan Lodge, No. 399), who imprinted his memorable visage upon the whole institution. To the old families of New York—the Stuyvesants, Van Rensselaers, and Livingstons—he was a devoted servant, a model of respect and deference. On the north wall of Grace Church a bronze plaque bears an inscription:

To the memory of
Isaac Hull Brown
Born Dec. 4, 1812 Died Aug. 21, 1880
For thirty five years the faithful Sexton of Grace Church.
This tablet is erected by members of the Congregation who gladly recall
his Fidelity, his Generosity, and his Stainless Integrity.

N.P Willis, editor of the *Home Journal*, once remarked that Brown served society with a 'courteous manner and polite word that would well become the nobleman who is Gold Stick in Waiting at the Court of Her Majesty, Queen Victoria of England.'[105] To those without heritage or family, Brown's majestic air of condescension put nonentities sharply in their place.

Brown came from a humble background and upbringing. Born on Duane Street, two blocks north of City Hall, in 1812, he grew up in a working-class family. During the boom in residential construction and public works in the 1830s (the Great Fire of 1835 was a boon to the construction trade), he worked as a journeyman carpenter. Carpenters were the largest group of building workmen in the city, and with the printers were among the best-paid craft workers. A journeyman might reasonably aspire to the state of master carpenter, and the widespread subcontracting and use of sweated labor in the trade turned the eyes of an ambitious young man like Isaac Brown to grander things. If he joined any of the journeymen's societies, or felt craft sentiment and trade solidarity, there is no trace in accounts of Brown's career.[106]

He was a lifelong Democrat, and rose high in the ranks of New York masonry. But it was his practical skills and a general handiness with repairs which earned him appointment as sexton when Grace Church was consecrated in 1846. Brown intensely observed the congregation which included families of distinction and great wealth. What Grace Church represented to Brown was 'quality,' wealth, old families, breeding, and tradition, and he allied himself unreservedly with their values and social perspectives. The social parvenus and 'shoddyites' filled him with scorn and indignation. Brown sought to turn what he had seen, and what he learned about the families at Grace Church, into wealth for himself, and a distinct kind of social power.

Brown established himself as the leading clerical factotum for the city's rich and famous Episcopalians. As sexton his duties were concerned with the management of the physical plant of the church. He collected rents from the pew-holders, and made sure that the furnaces were lit, the aisles kept clean. Brown energetically expanded the role of sexton, showing entrepreneurial skills by becoming undertaker for Grace Church and for other Episcopal parishes in the city. He cultivated the cooks, domestic servants, and butlers of the wealthy, and learned what services were needed by the residents of Washington Square, Bond Street, and Fifth Avenue. The normal run of domestic servants in America in the 1840s and 1850s had little knowledge of the demands of high society entertainments. Brown's efficiency and authoritative manner lent plausibility when he offered to greet guests at the front of the home for a distracted hostess, and make sure the carriages were ready when guests departed. Brown knew just the right merchants from whom tables, chairs, and the appropriate linen could be rented. He also ran a carriage-hire business, and those in society knew that there was no reason to wait for the return of their own carriage when one of Brown's fleet was at hand.

Mastery of detail and reliability made Brown wealthy and powerful, but it was his visibility at Grace Church, and the fact that everyone knew his name, which made his services indispensable. Stories and anecdotes about him went the rounds of society. As 'Pink' he was celebrated in verse by the lawyer William Allen Butler:

> . . . his sextonship rose, by means he invented,
> To a post of importance quite unprecedented.
> No mere undertaker was he, . . .
> There was nothing at all he did *not* undertake;
> Discharging at once such a complex variety
> Of functions pertaining to genteel society,
> As gave him with every one great notoriety;
> Blending his care of the church and the cloisters
> With funerals, fancy balls, suppers and oysters . . .
> Dinners for aldermen, parties for brides,
> And a hundred and fifty arrangements besides;
> Great as he was at a funeral, greater
> As master of feasts, purveyor, *gustator*,
> Little less than the host, but far more than the waiter.[107]

Herman Melville wrote a satiric sketch of Sexton Brown and Grace Church,

'The Two Temples,' which he submitted to *Putnam's Magazine* in 1854. The editor, Charles F. Briggs gently advised Melville that satirical jabs at Grace Church were unwise, however 'exquisitely fine' and 'pungent' the execution: 'my editorial experience compels me to be very cautious in offending the religious sensibilities of the public, and the moral of the Two Temples would array against us the whole power of the pulpit, to say nothing of Brown, and the congregation of Grace Church.'[108] A society jest like Peter Marié's apostrophe to the sexton carried fewer risks:

> O Glorious Brown! Thou medly strange,
>   of church-yard, ball-room, saint and sinner
> Flying by morn through Fashion's range,
>   And burying mortals after dinner—
> Walking one day with invitations,
> Passing the next at consecrations.
> Tossing the sod at eve on coffins,
> With one hand drying the tears of orphans,
> And one unclasping ball-room carriage,
> Or cutting plum cake up for marriage—
> Dusting by day the pew and missal—
> Sounding by night the ball-room whistle—
> Admitting free through Fashion's wicket,
> And skilled at psalms, at punch, and cricket . . .'[109]

By 1860, Brown had become quite an intimidating figure in society. He supervised that year the arrangements for the reception and ball given in honor of the Prince of Wales at the Academy of Music, and took charge when a corner of the dancing floor collapsed. He managed large social events with such authority that he was in heavy demand to plan and organize private dinners, parties, and balls—on the condition that he be given control of the invitation list and responsibility for all arrangements. He was an expert on the nuances of the invitation list, knowing 'who will come, who will not come, and whom to omit.'[110] He could also be relied upon to provide a list of eligible young men (known as 'Brown's Brigade' or 'Brown's 100') who would arrive correctly dressed in evening clothes, whose manners were good, and who were skilled at the waltz. Brown's young men were also expected—at the risk of social banishment—to know their place, which was not at the side of wealthy society belles strolling on Broadway. (Etiquette stipulated that an introduction made at a public assembly room was provisional, and ended at the conclusion of the evening. It was improper for a gentleman subsequently to acknowledge a lady met in such circumstances.) He seemed to know the names of socially eligible strangers who were staying in New York hotels. Brown had a sharp sense of everyone who was anyone, and it was widely believed that he could make or break the legions of those seeking entrance to society. He took on the 'task of deciding who among social aspirants justified his aspirations and was presentable, not being rich, or, being rich, was not too unpresentable.' Knowledge of this kind gave Brown a kind of power which he wielded with malice. Unfriendly gossip repeatedly linked the application or withholding of the sexton's social favor to the payment of bribes, but in the nature of such things there was little evidence of his less savory dealings. But everyone knew that Brown's services were available for hire.[111]

He had firm views on all forms of social pretense. The sexton's supreme accolade was the description of a social occasion as 'thoroughbred.' To Mrs. Sherwood, novelist and author of etiquette books, he remarked after a ball at the Goelets' or Gerrys', 'Ah, Madame, this has been an aristocratic assemblage; no *mixture here*.' He prided himself in his ability to recall family relationships and the complex cousinage which underlay the city's elite. Edgar Fawcett recalled Brown in his satire of social climbing, *The Buntling Ball*:

Poor Brown (peace rest him!) knew with searching ken
The grades of difference in all families
Whose carriages for half a century
He had called at weddings, funerals, and balls.[112]

'His memory was something remarkable,' noted Ward McAllister. 'He knew all and everything about everybody.'[113] In this he was a corpulent model for Sillerton Jackson, Edith Wharton's expert on 'family' connections and remembrancer of scandals and mysteries, in *The Age of Innocence*. Brown occasionally remarked to parishioners at Grace Church 'that if he was so minded he could write a book exposing the shams of New-York society which would shake the town to its center.' His sharp-tongued complaints at the decline of contemporary manners and 'breaches of etiquette' were unforgettable. To the public, Brown embodied the inner doctrine of the world of Grace Church: that correct form was in all things next to Holy Scripture. Newspapers like Greeley's *Tribune* had rich opportunities to mock the sexton for the way his concern for form seemed to represent the real 'values' of Fifth Avenue and its inhabitants. But he *believed* in 'quality' and no such exposé was ever written. 'He must have possessed a Christian name,' recalled Marian Gouverneur, 'but if so I never heard it for he was only plain Brown, and Brown he was called.'[114] To the people he served, the pew-holders and vestrymen of Grace Church, he remained 'Brown,' not 'Mr. Brown.'

4

Going to the Ball

Dancing was the one great article in the code of the fashionables to which all other amusements or occupations were subordinate.
—Charles Astor Bristed, 1852[1]

The ball structured the social calendar of nineteenth-century New York as no other social event. The dances inevitably changed over time, as did the music, dress, food, and venues, yet the institution of the ball remained one of the most important fixtures in the social season. Someone in society might attend two or three balls a week at the height of the season. When we think about upper-class New Yorkers in the nineteenth century, an enduring image of the city and its most genteel pleasures is a person in formal evening dress at a ball. It was by no means permitted simply to be a hedonistic enjoyment, for the ball was among the most complexly regulated and coded forms of social interaction. The etiquette of the ballroom was designed to ensure that social decorum was maintained. As the only place where a gentleman might actually be permitted to touch the person of a lady to whom he had not been fully introduced, the ball was a minefield of social dangers, to be treated with the strictest vigilance.[2] The preparations for a ball set seamstresses in motion, musicians were engaged, decorations planned, food ordered and served. Dances had to be learned. No young person whose parents had social ambitions could escape long hours at dancing-school and its demanding dancing-master. The ball was one of the most important cultural forms through which society regulated pleasure.

The age of the ball begins

If you have good sense, you will never attempt to dance in a quadrille, with the figures of which you are unacquainted.
—Ballroom advice, 1873[3]

In 1807–8 an English traveler, James Lambert, spent the winter in New York, and was present at a moment when the ball ceased to be a simple amusement and revealed itself as a social battlefield. Young American ladies, he found, were particularly accomplished in music and drawing, but this was nothing compared to their wild enthusiasm for dancing. 'Dancing is an amusement that the New York ladies are passionately fond of, and they are said to excel those of every city in the Union.' Lambert attended the City Assembly, a subscription dance usually held at the City Hotel or in other substantial hotels or taverns, and was pleased to note that the evening was conducted entirely in the manner of an English assembly.[4]

The spirit of the City Assembly in New York was thoroughly exclusive. 'None but the first class of society can become subscribers to this assembly.' The decision to raise the price of tickets, which would restrict admission, and to impose a strict limit on the number of tickets offered for sale, was angrily resented. In response, a New Assembly was organized. It was an act of insurrection. This rebellious event opened the assemblies to 'the genteel part of the second class' who had been excluded from the City Assembly. 'A spirit of jealousy and pride has caused the subscribers of the *new assembly* to make their subscription three dollars, and to have their balls also at the City Hotel. It was so well conducted that many of the subscribers of the City Assembly seceded, and joined the opposition one, or subscribed to both.'[5] Lambert's account of the rival assemblies is a parable of the difficulty of maintaining social barriers in New York. Excluded from one body, those with social ambitions created a new, hybrid institution which proved a considerable success. The city assemblies had become a terrain where social supremacy was contested.

Assemblies need have little organizational structure behind them, though the rules for their organization and conduct appeared as early as the 1790s. A group of families or perhaps a number of young unmarried men (the evening might then be referred to as a 'Bachelors' Ball'), would form a society and seek subscribers for a ball. The cost of arrangements would be shared, and they hoped subscriptions would repay their outlay. A small committee of 'managers' would take responsibility for the sale of tickets, see to the music and refreshments, and superintend the conduct of the assembly itself. In New York, the City Assemblies usually had four managers, only one of which, the acting manager or Master of Ceremonies, would officiate on the evening of the ball itself. An Assembly Ball with a broader basis for support would have a much longer list of managers, and invitations would be issued in their names.[6]

An assembly would normally begin at eight o'clock (fashionables would usually not appear until nine) with a grand entrée into the ballroom, a promenade in which the company would march around the room to musical accompaniment. At the conclusion of the promenade the company was seated in chairs lining the walls of the room, leaving space for the dancers. Bystanders were not always politely prepared to retreat from the dancing, and the manager might be confronted by enthusiastic observers arranged in tight rings around a particularly attractive or deft dancer.[7] The dance would be called by the fiddler in the balcony above: 'Right and left!—four hands round!—chassez!—ballancez!' They usually began with country dances (the 'Devil among the Tailors' and 'Sir Roger de Coverley' were traditional favorites) and progressed to 'cotillons', and then returned to country dances. The 'longways' formation of the *contredanse*, in which men and women faced each other in the traditional extended pattern, survived in provincial America in the eighteenth century long after it had been replaced in London by the four-couple square pattern of the cotillon.

The first quadrilles were danced in 1815 at Almack's in London by eight specially picked couples. The quadrille was composed of four of the most popular French *contredanses* and for some time the terms 'contredanse' and 'quadrille' were used interchangeably. (The terminology used to describe social dance in the nineteenth century was highly unstable.) The sets of the quadrille were composed of figures, each with prescribed motions, such as the *tour des deux mains* (two-hand turn, in which a couple would turn while holding hands), or *la chaîne continue des dames* (ladies' chain, requiring a woman to pass her female opposite number by the right hand, and then extend her left hand to the opposite man, who received her into position beside himself; the movement was completed with the repeat of the motion, returning the lady to her partner).

Other popular figures enacted playful social transactions. In one, a gentleman and the opposite lady advance towards each other, making a menacing gesture with an extended forefinger, and then retire, clapping their hands three times, then turn to their original partners to make a grand round to conclude the figure. In 'The Ladies Deceived,' a gentleman and his partner promenaded around a circle, and approached several ladies in succession, pretending to invite each to dance. 'The moment a lady rises, he turns quickly to another; after deceiving a number, he at last makes a choice. The lady of the conductor dances with the partner of the lady chosen.' As the 'German cotillion' grew in popularity in mid-century the word 'cotillion' was dropped, leaving the dance simply to be known informally as the german (see description above, pp. 19f). With the great popularity of the waltz and polka in the 1840s, the quadrille step was reduced to a simple glide-walk or *marche*. Not the least of the appeal of the quadrille for older dancers was the way it allowed polite conversation, something quite impossible with energetic waltzes and polkas.[8]

As the *cotillon*, a figure dance for four couples, passed out of fashion, it was replaced by the *cotillion*, a court dance taken up by aristocratic circles in Vienna, Paris, London, and New York. The graceful pattern of pairing, division, and then recombination offered a visual representation of the court as a collective entity. From the stately procession entering the ballroom to the final figure of the last quadrille, the dance asserted not the thrilling physical exuberance of the polka, the romantic elegance of the waltz, or national character (the mazurka and polonaise), but the graceful manifestation of the pattern and demeanor of a court of the *ancien régime*. Long after the polka and waltz had swept all before them, the stately quadrille, and its symbolic assertion of aristocratic values, remained the centerpiece of 'society' in New York city.

Although quadrilles were complex and needed leadership and experience (for the most important balls later in the century, intricate quadrilles might be rehearsed for weeks beforehand), little emphasis was placed upon high levels of individual skill. The constantly changing pattern of the quadrille was the objective, but within the formation the old serpent of competitiveness and personal ambition struggled to find expression. Being chosen for a dance, and how often, was inevitably regarded as a measure of social success. The award of favors to participants in the quadrille gave an edge to an evening's competitiveness. Beginning as modest mementos—a corsage or a rosette—favors became more expensive: fans, cigarette cases, enameled watches, jeweled stickpins. At Newport the favors were pinned on a belle's shoulder, or a beau's lapel. At the end of ball 'success' meant hauling away an array of favors. By the end of the century, the presentation of lavish favors had become intrinsic to the aristocratic private ball. At a ball hosted by Mrs. John Jacob Astor IV in 1897, favors for ladies included wands of roses with little bells attached, and tartan plaid silk sashes with Mrs. Astor's monogram in gold. Men received leather tobacco pouches with silver tops, and gold and silver trimmed golf sticks and golf balls.[9]

The competition for favors was a microcosm of larger social rivalries. Ralph Pulitzer, son of the proprietor of the *World*, argued that the men and women in the cotillion were not 'frivolous idlers' but ambitious people, working doggedly to achieve their goals: invitations to future dinners, weekends in the country, yachting parties.

Nor are the majority of the ladies crude enough to welcome these gentlemen for their pretty looks, for their polished dancing, for their wise brains, their witty tongues, or their loving hearts. All that each yearns for is to have more partners and more favors than any of her friends. To her wide perspective these partners have no more individuality than does each grouse that falls to the sportsman's gun. They are merely partners, and every new one but adds to the number of brace that she can finally count as her evening's "bag."[10]

A young lady attending a dancing class was being tutored in more than simply how to stand, walk, move her limbs and feet. There were social values embedded in every gesture and step. 'In the ball-room all the steps should be performed in an easy, graceful manner,' advised a writer on the dance in 1830, 'no noise of stamping should, on any account be made; the steps should be performed with minute neatness, and in as small a compass as possible; the feet should never be violently tossed about, or lifted high from the ground; the young lady should rather seem to glide with easy elegance, than strive to astonish by agility; or, by violent action, make it appear, that to her dancing is a boisterous and difficult exercise.'[11] The cotillion, in Allen Dodworth's opinion, was 'the representative dance of modern civilization,' because it inculcated values in the young upon which a civilization depended:

1st. *Alertness*, each dancer being at all times awake to the duties required of him or her.

2d. *Promptness* in taking places for the execution of a figure.

3d. *Silence* and attention during the explanation of any novelty.

4th. *Obedience* at all times to the conductor during the management of the dance.

5th. *Willingness* to sacrifice momentary personal pleasure, so that others may gain.[12]

The etiquette of the ball was designed to regulate relations between men and women. Introductions, for example, were only to be made when it was agreeable to both parties. An introduction was needed for a gentleman to ask a lady to dance, and without a proper introduction a lady was expected to refuse the invitation. An unwelcome partner could in practice be fended off by various means, but it was a breach of good manners for a lady arbitrarily to reject a gentleman to whom she had been introduced. Later in the century ladies carried dance cards, provided to formalize the procedure, and a request for a sight of the card was a customary form of polite overture. Gentlemen were to be introduced to ladies, and not vice versa. But at a private ball, introductions were normally assumed to be unnecessary; the host vouchsafed the respectability of his or her guests.[13]

Satirists were quick to appreciate the comic possibilities of country bumpkins come to the city for some urban polish, and won an appreciative readership for portraits of maladroit partners at City Assemblies. Washington Irving's Will Wizard, a paragon of unfashionable dress, tedious stories, and general social ineptitude, makes a memorable appearance at a City Assembly, with his hair tufted at the top, frizzed out at the ears, and with 'a profusion of powder puffed over the whole, and a long plaited club swung gracefully from shoulder to shoulder, describing a pleasing semicircle of powder and pomatum. His claret colored coat was decorated with a profusion of gilt buttons, and reached to his calves'.

Women were warned against any demonstration of 'preference' for one partner over another, and so Will Wizard had no shortage of dancing partners. The rules of etiquette enforced a fictional world of correct behavior, and obliged men and women to conduct themselves at a ball as though they were actors in 'a large family where universal urbanity and cheerfulness prevail.' Young ladies were admonished to behave as though their every gesture was under surveillance: a lady 'is ever observed by all eyes, and therefore cannot comport herself too strictly. . . . It is better to be deemed prudish than to be incautious and indiscreet. In walking up and down the room, the lady should always be accompanied by a gentleman, it being very improper for her to do so alone.' One of the guests at Mrs. Houston's ball in Cooper's *Home as Found* (1838), remarked that there was something 'excessively indelicate in a young lady's moving about a room without having a gentleman's arm to lean on!' Etiquette thus insisted that those in society ignore the ostentation and competitiveness around them, and act as though the ball expressed the higher and more amicable values of a community. The ball as an organized form of polite hypocrisy occupied a unique place in the hearts of the city's aristocracy.[14]

Costumes, roles, and narratives of the ball

> To tell the truth, my dear friend, I think we are all too fond of dress
> and display in this city . . .
> —Clara Foster, 1828[15]

Assemblies were public events, and as such were occasionally described in the press. Masquerade balls at the Park and Bowery Theaters in New York, large popular events, were written up in James Watson Webb's *Morning Courier* as occasions for an amusing kind of public performance. A fiddler observed at the Bowery masquerade 'executed his part to the life, and so did the overgrown boy with the trumpet. He did it to a T. The Ethiop was a masterly performance—he put on and off his *invisibility* with the easy dignity of a magician.' Private balls, on the other hand, passed largely without benefit of public scrutiny, though there was an old tradition of private memorials of balls and social events. An account of a 'Fancy Ball' in Boston in Webb's paper, and the publication of two private accounts of English balls in Louis Godey's *Lady's Book* in 1830 were invitations to American ladies to become the recorders of their own experiences.[16]

Accounts of New York balls were made in private diaries, or were prepared for limited circulation as letters or manuscripts for the pleasure of hosts, guests, and absent friends. A few of these manuscripts have survived. Abigail Adams attended a ball given in 1786 by the comte d'Adhémer, French Ambassador to the Court of St. James. In a letter to her niece Lucy Cranch, Mrs. Adams spared no one, not least herself, in a marvelously sharp-eyed description of manners, appearance, and dress. After reassuring her niece that nothing to be seen at St. James' or 'set off with Parisian rouge' could compare to the 'blooming health, the sparkling eye, and modest deportment of the dear girls of my native land,' she described her dress for the ball:

> a full-dress court cap without the lappets, in which was a wreath of white flowers, and blue sheafs, two black and blue flat feathers (which cost her half a guinea a-piece, but that you need not tell of), three pearl pins, bought for Court, and a pair of pearl earrings, the cost of them—no matter what; less than diamonds, however. A sapphire blue *demi-saison* with a satin stripe, sack and petticoat trimmed with a broad black lace; crape flounce, &c.; leaves made of blue ribbon, and trimmed with white floss; wreaths of black velvet ribbon spotted with steel beads, which are much in fashion, and brought to such perfection as to resemble diamonds; white ribbon also in the Vandyke style, made up of the triming, which looked very elegant; a full dress handkerchief, and a bouquet of roses. "Full gay, I think, for my *aunt*." That is true, Lucy, but nobody is old in Europe.[17]

Few accounts of balls were as deftly crafted as Mrs. Adams', but the literary resources brought to the task suggested no weakening of aspiration to give an adequate account of the occasion. After a ball at the home of Mrs. George Douglas at 55 Broadway in 1815, Anne Macmaster sent a 'poetic epistle' to Mrs. Grant, a widow in Edinburgh with numerous children who, like Lady Kitty Duer, took in young ladies with the object of giving them an introduction to the mind and manners of the metropolis:

> And pray who were there? is the question you'll ask.
> To name the one half would be no easy task—
> There were Bayards and Clarksons, Van Hornes and Le Roys,
> All famous, you well know, for making a noise.
> There were Livingstons, Lenoxes, Henrys and Hoffmans,
> And Crugers and Carys, Barnewells and Bronsons,
> Delanceys and Dyckmans and little De Veaux,
> Gouverneurs and Goelets and Mr. Picot . . .

The evening was a success, and there was no shortage of dancing partners:

> Of *Beaux* there were plenty, some new ones 'tis true,
> But I won't mention names, no, not even to you.
> I was lucky in getting good partners, however,
> Above all, the two Emmetts, so lively and clever.

With Morris and Maitland I danced; and with Sedgwick,
Martin Wilkins, young Armstrong and droll William Renwick . . .[18]

Such a verse epistle might be transcribed into a diary, or copied into a letter and carefully saved, to reach the hands of a biographer more than a century later. Facility at polite verse was a skill which a young lady who was a persistent 'lionizer' in the literary salons of Europe, and who numbered Scott and Wordsworth among her sometimes reluctant counselors and correspondents, might have been proud to display. Such materials give us a glimpse of the New York ball at the last moment when such events were still private occasions.

Other manuscript sources exist in an intermediate space between the private and the public. When Mrs. Basil Hall wrote a letter to her sister Jane in England about a ball in 1827 at the Broadway home of Philip Hone, the self-consciousness of her quasi-public communication was palpable. (Her letters were *aides-mémoire* for her husband Basil, grandson of Lord Selkirk, who published *Travels in North America in the Years 1827 and 1828* in 1829.) In her comments on American social insecurities, the incurably third-, fourth-, or fifth-rate quality of the evening's singer (Madame Maria Garcia Malibran), and the deplorable appearance of American women, lay a determination to trash the Republic and its pretensions. Yet we get a valuable sense from Mrs. Basil Hall's letter of the awkward and uncomfortable atmosphere of a New York ball at the very highest social level: 'We went at half past nine and found a terribly formal circle of ladies and a group of gentlemen in the middle of the room. There were two large rooms open, communicating by folding doors and handsomely furnished and lighted. Quadrilles were danced in both rooms, the same set with very slight variation that is danced in Edinburgh.'[19]

Of the manuscript sources from this period, two found their way into print (of a kind), but were not written consciously for 'the public.' They are shaped by the expectations and tone of an audience which was small and intimate. Yet they each present the fancy ball as a public performance of a 'character,' to be judged by the quality and appropriateness of the 'portrayal' or 'personation.' In addition to Anne Macmaster's poem, the principal manuscript sources are *The Fancy Ball Given by Mrs. S************ which was copied from a manuscript source and published in James Watson Webb's *Morning Courier* on February 16, 1829; two manuscript notebooks, *A Hasty Sketch of the Late Fancy Ball at G.G. Howland's*, which describes a ball held on State Street in Lower Manhattan on March 3, 1830; and a lengthy description in the diaries of Philip Hone of a fancy ball held at the Hotel Sans Souci at Ballston spa on August 13, 1830.[20]

The name of Mrs. S***********, the hostess, is a perfect type of the dual forms of concealment and expression which society demanded in antebellum

29. Fashion.

'The lovely ladies who had bowling costumes this morning, have driving costumes to-night. They smile and bow. The ribbons flutter, the gloves glisten. The air is soft, the band plays pleasantly; over all shines the summer sun. But Newport lies beyond, imperturbable, and has other belles and beauties to remember.'
Harper's Monthly Magazine, 1854.

New York. In the absence of internal evidence of either the location of Mrs. S***********'s home or of her name, we may find hints in a family genealogy of the Schermerhorns: 'He [Abraham Schermerhorn] was a wealthy merchant and was also prominent in social affairs. . . . Many were the delightful social gatherings held at the Schermerhorn residence, one worthy of particular notice being a fancy dress ball given by Mrs. Abraham Schermerhorn, Feb. 6, 1829. This was attended by all the representative families of New York City of that day.' In her family history Margaret Armstrong printed a letter from the wife of James Fenimore Cooper in 1829, expressing dismay at the 'want of delicacy' of young ladies 'who appeared in breeches at Mrs. Schermerhorn's fancy ball.' Further confirmation appears in the manuscript diary of Philip Hone. On February 6 Hone wrote: 'I dined with Isaac L. Hone. In the evening attended a fancy ball at Mr. Abraham Schermerhorn's, a very splendid and delightful affair.'[21] *The Fancy Ball Given by Mrs. S********** was, as the discussion of the

Schermerhorn family in Chapter 6 will suggest, a society event at the upper reaches of New York life.

The three manuscripts (Schermerhorn, Howland, and Hone) seek within differing conventions to make visible the identities of participants within the coterie to which they belong, while at the same time shielding these identities from outsiders. The use of initials (Mr. LeR . . . , Miss McE . . .) acknowledged the guests' right to privacy while sharing their identity with those who had been present, and who were within the inner circle. 'Mr. LeR . . . ,' 'an oldtime gentleman, dressed to perfection,' was no doubt Jacob LeRoy, a prominent New York merchant. 'Miss McE . . .' was a daughter of Charles McEvers, partner in the firm of LeRoy, Bayard & McEvers of 66 Broadway, in whose counting office G.G. Howland rose to become head clerk. The use of initials and a certain coyness of tone betrays a self-consciousness in these manuscripts. The narrators observe the convention which demanded secrecy, while colluding in an act of exposure. At the center of this curious form of exposure is the social knowledge common both to the author and readers of the manuscripts. The narrators are *of* this world and share its values, yet by writing the manuscript they transgress (in the most delicate and respectful manner possible) the very conventions of society itself.

Samuel Shaw Howland and his brother Gardner Greene Howland owned a prosperous shipping firm. Their father Joseph, a Connecticut Yankee who had migrated down to New York around the turn of the century, had been a ship owner and merchant. The Howland brothers formed S.S. and G.G. Howland in 1816, and were among the leading merchants in the South American trade. (After they had retired from business in 1834, the successor firm of Howland & Aspinwall was among the great shipping firms on the Panama and California route.) The manuscripts produced after the 1830 ball at the home of G.G. Howland follow two conventions. The first notebook provides the last names of guests. The second, in a rather more playful spirit, adopts the convention 'Ogxxn' with the omitted letters (for Ogden) usually provided in superscript. Duplication between the two Howland manuscripts usually allows identifications to be confirmed, and are cited without the xxxs. The substantial entry in the Hone diary for the Ballston fancy dress ball was followed by a table listing by name thirty-two participants and the 'character' they had represented. Hone's account was first published in the *Crumb Basket*, a little 'newspaper' he and other guests put together for the party at the Sans Souci Hotel in August 1830, and was copied into Hone's diary. It was the most ephemeral form of 'publication' imaginable. Because Hone's was the most private, it was the clearest at identifying individuals.

The 'fancy balls,' that is, costume balls, obliged guests to wear elaborate costumes inspired by a broad range of allegorical, historical, and literary figures.

The evening was crowded with an amusing muddle of costumes, nationality, period, and rank. Within the chaos, there was a form of internal order shaped by the need for recognizability. All kinds of costumes—peasants, gypsies, figures in court or military dress—depended upon the existence of a common fund of social knowledge or stereotypes, whether of peasantness or gypsiness, which circulated in society. To be successful, a character had not only to be in a costume which was handsome and made of fine fabrics; self-evidently it had to convey a recognizable referent, and items of clothing (for a later generation, the cowboy hat, beret, top hat, cloth cap, bowler) functioned as signifiers of historical and cultural types. Choice of a costume was a collective recognition of the role of cultural memory itself. The general fund of historical and cultural knowledge was not something existing in an abstract or universal realm. Rather, it was commonly shared by people at such-and-such a ball, at a particular time, and the way those images and stereotypes changed over time tells us something about the common culture of that class.

In the case of a fancy ball in New York in 1829 and 1830, it was the English historical, cultural, and literary tradition upon which ball-goers relied. Few identifiably American characters appeared at Mrs. Schermerhorn's ball (a plainly clad diplomat, a Quaker, and an elderly Knickerbocker lady), a phenomenon which Henry Adams observed: 'Without heroes, the national character of the United States had few charms of imagination [in 1815,] even to Americans.'[22] The British figures, from Queen Elizabeth and Mary Queen of Scots, to Sir Walter Raleigh, the Earls of Leicester and Suffolk, Lord Douglas and Lady Ellen Douglas, Robin Hood, and generic figures in court dress or in the professional garb of an English barrister, far outnumbered the single French Marquise, Mexican cavaliers, Venetian nobleman, Lady Abbess or Capuchin Monk. The Howlands' ball was chock-full of Swiss peasants, Catalonian señoritas, Highland chiefs, dashing French lancers, 'Turbaned Turks,' and a Napoleon.

In the aftermath of the war of 1812 England had begun to seem less of an enemy. Much irritation was felt at the supercilious tone of English travelers' accounts of American manners, but even when planning modest things like a costume for a fancy dress ball, wealthy New Yorkers showed a distinct Anglophile bias. They looked to Britain for a model of civilized life. Despite the revolutionary struggle against the crown, and the more recent conflict of 1812–14, for Americans of British descent, British history and institutions were far more a living part of their heritage than were those of any other European country. Shakespeare and Scott were central to that sense of a common culture.[23] (There were five ladies at the Howland's ball dressed as characters from Scott's novels.) The enthusiasm for Scott and the cult of the Highlanders was easily accommodated in most upper-class American hearts side by side with a growing passion for English dress, fashions, and literature. 'Throughout the country,' wrote Washington Irving,

> there was something of enthusiasm connected with the idea of England. We looked to it with a hallowed feeling of tenderness and veneration as the land of our forefathers—the august repository of the monuments and antiquities of our race—the birth place and mausoleum of the sages and heroes of our paternal history. After our own country there was none in whose glory we more delighted—none whose good opinion we were more anxious to possess—none towards which our hearts yearned with such throbbings of warm consanguinity.[24]

The manuscripts are far more than simple lists of participants and their costumes. All three are in the form of anonymous first-person narratives. *The Fancy Ball* has an elaborate framing device explaining how the manuscript came to the newspaper. 'Mrs. A. had sent it to Miss B., and Miss B. to Mrs. C., Mrs. C to Miss D., and so on through half the city till we absolutely despaired of getting possession of it.' An overheard comment at the Park Theater gave the journalist a lead:

> Miss L: Fancy Ball?
> Miss Q: Yes. How do you like the description of Miss T.'s dress?
> Miss L: Oh, 'tis done to the life, as is the whole of it. Miss T. is now reading it, and so much did she enter into the feelings of the writer, that she refused to accompany me here, but ordered the carriage for eight o'clock, when she will certainly join us.

The authors of such manuscripts assumed that their readers were not simply in search of information, but as Miss L. suggests, the manuscript offered a way to 'enter into the feelings of the writer' and thus participate in the intimate world of the event. What the authors and readers shared was far from the distant and abstract bond between author and readers of commercially published texts. Such manuscripts belong to an earlier cultural moment. The act of sharing accounts of balls, parties, and similar social events was an affirmation of the essentially private nature of the antebellum New York City social world.

In retrospect, the Howland ball possessed a distinctive meaning for some of those present. To Philip Hone, who was a close friend of Gardner Howland, the event was one of the most glittering and successful in living memory. It set an ever higher standard for entertaining in the city. Hone, his wife and two daughters (he wrote in his diary) 'went in the Evening to a fancy Ball at Mrs Howland's, State Street, their large house was entirely thrown open to the Company. The Characters were generally splendidly and appropriately dressed & well supported. The whole affair went off well, and has never been surpassed in this city.'[25] For his daughter Mary, who made her social début at the ball, memories of the evening were even more highly charged. She attended in the costume of a shepherdess, and about her (the Howland manuscript noted) 'Many a hopeful *swain* sighed for the green hills and fertile plains to tend their *flocks* with so interesting and lovely a *partner*—This was her début & she has already enslaved her thousands—.' Also present at the Howland ball was the handsome eldest son of the ship chandler Peter Schermerhorn: 'Mr. *John Schermerhorn* as *a Turk*. Some questioned his sex & a bystander swore it was a *pretty gay deceiver.*' Two years later the marriage of Mary Hone and Jones Schermerhorn (as he was known) became a leading society event. The alliance between the two families and the young man's 'amiable disposition, good morals, [and] agreeable deportment' greatly pleased Hone.[26]

The manuscript narratives draw upon a repertoire of strategies to portray social events which by their nature are highly repetitive and formulaic. Each begins with the announcement of the ball, and its impact on the city. Mrs. S***********, 'one of the leading fashionables in this goodly city,' issued a hundred invitations to her fancy ball, giving her guests a month's advance notice. The city's 'operatives' (seamstresses, tailors, mantuamakers), or at least those with 'talent or taste,' were quickly put to work. At Ballston, the process of transformation was no less dramatic. The 'spacious hotel of Sans Souci' was, at a moment's order, transformed into 'the House of Industry' or a casbah of commerce. 'Little feet were heard tripping from door to door in search of the various trappings which the scanty wardrobe of some could not supply, and a general interchange of commodities took place, unrestricted by Tariff or Custom House regulation.' The village shops, the epitome of rural somnolence, were 'ransacked' to furnish 'coloured cambrics, flannels of varied hues, ribbons, buckles, counterfeit Jewels and gaudy chintzes.' In the hotel's galleries 'the hoarse cries of Brigadier Generals' were heard, 'calling for pillows to swell their tummies; while soft female voices were heard soliciting the loan of Pistols and Daggers, to impart an unnatural air of Ferocity to feminine grace.' The note of gender fluidity, of men dressed in the costumes of women (at the Howlands' ball, William Emmet was so successful in the role of Miss Primrose that even his closest friends failed to discover the lady's true identity), and women equipping themselves for lethal mayhem, underlies the way the fancy ball became a carnivalesque opportunity for reversals and loosening of the daylight perimeters of gender.

The evening of the ball itself is related as it would have been experienced by a guest, beginning at Mrs. Schermerhorn's with sight of eight brilliantly illuminated rooms, and five supper tables laden with 'viands' and wines. Carriages arrived from all over the city. (Within two or three decades cross-town travel to society balls was at an end, and the 'fashionables' would have been coming from a far narrower strip of the city—from Washington Square to the entrance of Central Park on Fifth Avenue.) By ten o'clock 250 guests had arrived. 'The first hour was passed in mutual greetings and recognitions' (Ballston). 'As they entered the rooms, the exclamations of pleasure and delight which escaped them, must have fallen most agreeably on the ear of our hostess.' The narrator groans under his great responsibility ('Oh! it is impossible to give but a faint description of this enchanting scene') and then proceeds to do so. In a fit of mock-heroic aspiration, the Ballston narrator, no less than Philip Hone, conjured up the spirit of Homer to help him portray the 'shock of arms' as the ball began.

At the fancy ball participants were not only wearing costumes, they were performing roles: the terms *personate*, *personation*, *personated* and *habited* frequently recur. Thus, at Mrs. Schermerhorn's ball, Mr. C.M.E. . . . sustained 'an admirable personation' of a Suabian peasant. Mr. C. . . . , in Knickerbocker dress as Mrs. Van Bruntsen, 'was habited to the life, and sustained with tact and judgment.' Mrs. J. . . . 'successfully supported' the character of Queen Elizabeth by her dignified, affable and condescending' manner. Similarly, at the Howlands' ball, Mrs. E. Jones as a Quakeress 'looked the character to life.' Mr. Hoffman appeared as a Winnebago chief and 'sustained his character with astonishing accuracy.' Success at personation was more than a felicitous coincidence. It was something to be worked at. When Philip Hone commented on his own costume at Ballston in 1830, he remarked: 'He exerted himself to "play well his part" for not withstanding the gold Chains, Laces & snuff Box "there all the honour lies."'

The enthusiasm in society for tableaux vivants built upon the skills in personation demonstrated at the fancy ball. The tableau, along with parlor games like charades, became fashionable in the 1830s and was a favored entertainment of country-house parties. A frame made out of canvas was erected in the parlor, enabling a curtain to be drawn aside to reveal an individual or a small group posed as a familiar historical figure or a work of art. Painters had long used such acts of personation, as in Sir Joshua Reynolds' *Miss Mary Meyer in the Character of Hebe* (1772) and John Singleton Copley's *The Red Cross Knight* (1793), the latter using his three children posed as figures from *The Faerie Queen*, book I, canto 10. At the Bradley Martins' Scottish estate at Balmacaan on Loch Ness, 'Morning and Evening,' 'The Seasons,' and 'The Huguenots' were popular subjects. Bradley Martin had purchased a half-length Sir Joshua Reynolds portrait at the Cavendish-Bentinck sale, and the 'brilliant success' of the 1891 tableau vivant may have owed much to the inspiration of Reynolds. In the course of 'a general entertainment' by the social-climbing Bry family in *The House of Mirth*, Lily Bart personates Reynolds' *Mrs. Lloyd*, wearing a loose fancy vest tied about her waist with a fringed sash. In the fashion of the day, her hair was piled to an extravagant height. Reynolds' painting, first exhibited at the Royal Academy in 1776, celebrated the engagement of Joanna Leigh to Richard Bennett Lloyd, and so the tableau may be taken as Wharton's ironic commentary on Bart's failure to secure the pompous, wealthy Percy Gryce. When the curtain was drawn, the audience gasped an 'Oh!' of appreciation (Wharton tells us) for Lily's beauty. 'She had shown her artistic intelligence in selecting a type so like her own that she could embody the person represented without ceasing to be herself. It was as though she had stepped, not out of, but into, Reynolds's canvas . . .'. The subtle skill of being Mrs. Lloyd and at the same time being Lily Bart was a model of the personation which the tableau and fancy ball asked of society.[27]

American newspapers in 1829 seldom commented on the appearance, dress, and behavior of private persons, and the amused cosmopolitanism found in *The Fancy Ball* was rarer still. The manuscript descriptions were written in an arch style, well suited to an occasional light undertone of innuendo: 'Miss T. . . . , in the dress of an interesting, modest, Piedmontese peasant girl, attracted the marked attention of several of the handsome pages, who seemed jealous of the notice she took of a grateful peer, who ever and anon left the royal train, to renew his admiration of this little sylph.' Each descriptive paragraph was an attempt to construct a 'character' for an individual. Physical features, gestures, and facial expressions were described, and the interaction with other guests indicated. Of course the costume worn was reported in some detail:

> The Messrs. D. . . . , as heavy whiskered Mamalukes, paraded round the spacious rooms with folded arms and scrutinizing eyes, examining the peasant girls with marked attention, and ever and anon saying agreeable things to the Sultana, who seemed to receive their soft whisperings with marked kindness of manner, which left little doubt of the interest she felt in the gallant attention of these dignified mussulmen.
>
> Mr. W. . . . appeared as the dashing Goldfinch, in a scarlet hunting jacket, sky-blue vest, top boots, cap and whip—he was in good spirits, and had no doubt just left the fascinating widow Warren, and might have been for all we know, on the way to procure the marriage license.

There is about the manuscripts a worldly recognition that the fancy ball provided many opportunities for contact with the opposite sex. The narrator's presentation of the 'marked attention' exhibited by Messrs. D., and the 'marked kindness of manner' exhibited in return by the Sultana, as well as the welcoming 'good spirits' of Mr. W., linked to 'the fascinating widow Warren,' is far removed from the proscriptions of the etiquette books, and a reminder that balls were events uniquely charged with erotic possibilities.

James Gordon Bennett and the Brevoort Ball, 1840

> There is no doing anything in this city, without *eating & dancing.* . . .
> —John Pintard, 1827[28]

Edgar Allan Poe published 'The Masque of the Red Death' in *Graham's Magazine* in May 1842, and it was reprinted in the *Broadway Journal* three years later. Following the arrival of the 'Red Death,' Prince Prospero summoned 'a thousand hale and light-hearted friends' for a ball, ordering the gates of his abbey closed and welded. The outside world was to be excluded. Employing the emerging conventions in the press for the covering of society balls, Poe describes the multicolored rooms of the imperial suite, noting the sliding doors, windows, tapestries, décor. 'There were much glare and glitter and piquancy and phantasm . . .'. Marie Bonaparte has noticed the absence of lasciviousness from this 'voluptuous scene': that, too, was characteristic of the newspaper coverage of such events. Drawing upon the great cholera epidemic in New York in 1832, Poe described the onset of the disease: 'There were sharp pains, and sudden dizziness, and then profuse bleeding at the pores, with dissolution.' The densely crowded apartments and the 'gay and magnificent revel' set the scene for the appearance of a ghastly 'spectral image' walking slowly and solemnly through the apartments. Like the other guests, it, too, was to be judged by the quality of the personation: the 'spectral image' seemed to be performing a character, 'as if more fully to sustain its rôle.' 'The Masque of the Red Death' transforms the New York ball into a Gothic horror—a reminder that the idea of the ball itself possessed a symbolic resonance not simply reducible to frivolous social entertainment.[29]

The New York tradition of costume balls was reinvented in the 1840s—not by the 'new' families, determined to spend their way into society, but by old Knickerbocker families like the Howlands, Schermerhorns, and Brevoorts, asserting their social pre-eminence. The Brevoort family had been among the earliest settlers in New Amsterdam, and had accumulated wealth and real estate in the two centuries in which they had respectably lived in Manhattan. A man of considerable personal charm and cultivation, Henry Brevoort Jr. was a close friend of Verplanck, Hosack, Irving, and Cooper and other worthies of the city's cultural life. A *bal costumé*—that is, costumes but no masks—was held in 1840 at Brevoort's home at 24 Fifth Avenue.

By universal consent, the Brevoort Ball was one of the defining social events of antebellum New York. The press, not yet accustomed to public scrutiny of the private lives of eminent citizens, struggled to find the right tone to describe the event. James Gordon Bennett's *Herald* veered between sober coverage and comic hyperbole, confident that '[i]t will beat the Eglinton Tournament all to

30. James Gordon Bennett, Sr.

James Gordon Bennett, editor of the *Herald*, managed to offend every respectable and self-righteous person in New York. Though he was a 'notorious scoffer, liar and poltroon,' his paper made a great deal of money.

atoms.'[30] The event itself did not disappoint the high-flying expectations: 'This ball has created a greater sensation in the fashionable world than any thing of the kind since the creation of the world, or the fall of beauteous woman, or the first frolic of old Noah, after he left the ark and took to wine drinking.' Straightforward news coverage proved highly popular. The issue of the *Weekly Herald* which covered the ball had surprisingly good sales in rural areas. The public's taste for detailed reports of life high and low in the metropolis had been whetted by sensational coverage in the *Herald* of the axe murder of the prostitute Helen Jewett in 1836, and the mystifying case of the murder of Mary Rogers two years later, which occasioned a scathing attack on the courts and the police in Bennett's pages. The *Herald*, founded in 1835 as a penny paper, proudly catered to the new taste for lurid scandal and stories about crime.

The aggressive tone and scurrilous iconoclasm of the *Herald* made Bennett a reviled man, hated by the Knickerbockers. Bennett repaid their scorn with bold mockery. He may have been a great newspaper editor, but, in the verdict of Henry J. Raymond, Bennett was '[o]ne of the slimiest scoundrels in existence.'[31] The great 'moral war' against Bennett and his paper, launched in May 1840 by the city's leading editors, was accompanied by a call for advertisers to boycott his pages. The assault on Bennett produced some magnificent abuse. Park Benjamin in the *Evening Signal* described Bennett as a 'notorious scoffer, liar and poltroon,' who deserved to be 'scourged, kicked, cuffed, tweaked by the nose, trodden on and spit upon in the open street, times without number.' Others, in disgust, blamed Bennett for corrupting morals and degrading public taste.[32] The 'Moral War' or the 'War of the Holy Alliance' was not without effect. When the *Morning Herald* was renamed the *New York Herald* in September 1840 the paper became more circumspect about religion and the social proprieties. But Bennett's interest in the city's aristocracy continued unabated, and on March 6, 1840 the *Herald* was the first New York paper to print a gossip column. (The *Herald* also continued to carry loquacious advertisements for the services of Madame Restell, the city's most notorious abortionist, until the middle of the decade.) Bennett declined to be respectful of the privacy of the rich, and printed, across the six columns of the front page of the *Herald* on April 5, 1848, the full text of the will of John Jacob Astor. It was a spectacular invasion of the private affairs of an ordinary citizen, though Bennett might have argued that a man who had accumulated twenty million dollars was far from being a private citizen in any antebellum city in America. Joseph Pulitzer came to a similar conclusion about William H. Vanderbilt in 1883.[33]

Bennett requested Brevoort's permission for a reporter (the crime reporter William H. 'Oily' Attree, one of the profession's least savory types) to attend the forthcoming ball. By agreeing to admit Attree, and thus accepting that his ball could be written about in Bennett's paper, Brevoort tacitly imposed an obligation on Bennett to refrain from abusing his family, their home, and their guests. Brevoort assumed that if he refused, he would become a target for the *Herald.* Those who learned of this arrangement found it hard to accept. 'This kind of surveillance is getting to be intolerable,' grumbled Hone, 'and nothing but the force of public opinion will correct the insolence.'[34]

It is a delicate matter to decide who was manipulating whom in this transaction. Bennett achieved his goal of detailed coverage and Brevoort managed to keep a lid on the tone of the *Herald*'s reporting (when Hone saw the *Herald* after the ball, he found the coverage 'tame, flat and tasteless'). The decision to sup with the devil, made in earnest naïveté by Brevoort, was no doubt repented in much greater earnestness by the host. For two decades, others in a similar position tried to keep (in Hone's words) the 'insolence' of the press at bay, and figures like Attree as far as possible from their homes. As a reporter for the *Transcript* in 1836, Attree's letters were found in the dead prostitute Helen

31. O'Dogherty Ball.

James Gordon Bennett's *Herald* relished the opportunity afforded by the Brevoort Ball to mock the wealthy as fools and hypocrites.

Jewett's room after her death, revealing that she had been his informant, lover, and close friend.[35]

After the ball was over, Bennett seems to have felt that the *Herald* was released from whatever implied commitment he had made to Brevoort. He turned upon the whole affair with characteristically 'tasteless' savagery with a satire in the *Herald* on March 5, 1840, of a *bal costumé* given at O'Dogherty House, whose 'cabbage grounds, potato patch, and pigsty were all thrown open upon this interesting occasion.' There was a list of the 'celebrated company,' including Mr. Philip 'Bone' (Hone) who was in costume as a pie baker. Among the tableaux staged at the O'Dogherty's was a mock trial of Bone for putting dead dog's meat into his pies. (He was declared guilty and fined $15 with costs.) The evening's entertainment commenced with an elegant Irish jig, led off by four of the O'Dohertys. There was a scene from a Donnybrook fair in the second tableau. The older of the two O'Dogherty girls sang an 'exquisitely sentimental song' with lyrics by George Pope Morris (co-editor of the *New York Mirror*) and music by Rossini, with the stirring chorus: 'Thump, thump, scold, scold, thump, thump away,/For the devil a bit of comfort is there on a washing day.'[36] A three-column drawing by Elton accompanying the story made the satiric point most unmistakably, with the foregrounded lewd expressions, drunken joviality, and carousing. Interest in the activities of the rich, and scorn for their ostentation and snobbishness, went hand in hand.

Bennett's paper stirred widespread interest in the Brevoort Ball by covering other events, even quite grand affairs like a fancy dress ball given by Charles King at Cherry Lawn, his mansion in Elizabethtown, New Jersey, as rehearsals for the Brevoort Ball. Stories appeared describing the urgent preparations across the city: 'All the tailors, and costumers, and milliners, and dress makers in the city, are at work night and day to complete the costumes . . . .'[37] So enthusiastically did New York take to masquerades and fancy dress balls that requests were made to the leading theaters, the Park and the Bowery, to borrow costumes and props for authentic Hamlets, Othellos, Romeos, and Rob Roys. Mr. Amerman, the former costumer of the Park Theater, responded to the demand for fancy outfits by taking a room at Morse's Coffee House at 31 Park Place, where he accepted orders 'for Dominos, Masks, fancy and character Dresses, of every description at the shortest notice and on the most reasonable terms.'[38] A list of planned costumes appeared in the papers, using the convention of first and last initials to protect (and reveal) the guest's names:

Miss M———n J———s.....as.....Queen Victoria
Mrs. H———t.....as.....Grand Sultana
Mr. H———t.....as.....Smike

Mary Mason Jones, one of the leading society belles of the 1840s, married Régis Denis de Kererdern, Baron de Trobriand, in Paris in 1843 and remained a leading figure in the aristocratic American expatriate community. Henry Hoyt, and his wife Frances Duer Hoyt, were prominent figures in the large Duer clan, and socially belonged to the world which reached from Columbia College (Frances Duer's father was president of the college) to the Ward family at the Corner House, the King family on Bond Street (her sister Elizabeth married Archibald Gracie King), and the Brevoorts on lower Fifth Avenue.[39]

Brevoort's mother was the sister of the widow Sarah Todd, wife of John Jacob Astor, and the Brevoorts belonged to the extended social circle which marriages had created around the Astors. (His daughter Laura married Charles Astor Bristed, grandson of the Astor patriarch.) He worked for a time for Astor's fur empire. After withdrawing from business he resided in London and Paris where he had a broad friendship among writers and politicians. Back in New York in the 1820s, Brevoort bought a house at 15 Broadway, and was sustained, he wrote to Irving, by 'a little club of intelligent individuals who are in the habit of meeting at each others houses for social & conversational purposes.' He looked upon the avarice rampant in New York with the same gentlemanly misgivings expressed by Sam Ward. 'Money getting [he wrote], which may be called the besetting sin of this community has never absorbed my attention; but in avoiding the infection I have sometimes thought myself an unwise exception, judging from the keen excitement which its pursuit seems to

32. Henry Brevoort.

An old knickerbocker family of Dutch origin, the Brevoorts were connected by marriage to the Astors. Henry Brevoort, Jr., lamented the decline of his home town ('this our native land is degenerate & corrupt to the very core'), but lived in high style and in 1843 sold land for the building of Grace Church on Broadway.

impart to its votaries.' His cultured retirement was so complete that his old friend Philip Hone, after attending a musical party at the Brevoorts' in 1838, noted in his diary: 'This is the first time all this has been shown to the *bon-ton*, and the capriciousness of the master and mistress is so great that it may remain a sealed book for half a dozen years, unless the present freak should continue.' For all his gentlemanly protestations of distaste for money-grubbing, Brevoort had investments in Fifth Avenue real estate, and had plans to build a hotel a block or two north of his home. The decision to allow a reporter from Bennett's *Herald* to attend the affair—in costume—was, despite being a certain breach of propriety, an early instance of the mixture of high society, real estate speculation, and public relations which became a commonplace in the latter part of the century.[40]

Brevoort's home, built in 1834 on the corner of Fifth Avenue and 9th Street was far in advance of the great development on that street. It was a freestanding Georgian mansion designed by Ithiel Town and A.J. Davis. There is not a house in the city, thought Hone, 'so well calculated to entertain . . . an assemblage.' It had five large rooms on the ground floor, a hall, and a 'noble' staircase. William Cullen Bryant described Brevoort's home as 'a kind of palace in a Garden.' (It survived on Fifth Avenue until it was torn down in 1925.) His social prestige was sufficient to alert other wealthy New Yorkers to the possible appeal of the farm land and pasture which lay north of

Washington Square. Each of the rooms was enthusiastically described in the press, as were the décor, paintings, and statuary.[41]

The dry-goods merchant and banker Henry De Rham, who later purchased Brevoort's house, came to the ball 'as a magnificent modern Greek' and several other guests appeared in similar costumes. None, so far as is known, had quite the right to wear such a costume as did Samuel Gridley Howe, who in the 1820s spent six years in the cause of the Greek struggle for independence from the Ottoman empire. But costumes offered socialites a way to make a modest gesture of solidarity with socially approved causes. (By the 1850s, enthusiasm for all things Hungarian had swept Greek costumes out of fashion at *bals costumés*.) Other guests drew upon the usual panoply of historical and mythological figures. Gentlemen strutted around the Brevoort mansion as Charles II and Richard III, pirates, Highland chieftains, polar bears, Indian chiefs, and Bedouin Arabs. Other guests appeared as Jeanne d'Arc, Lady Rowena, Catherine of Aragon, Diana, and Queen Esther. Philip Hone came dressed as Cardinal Wolsey with a (borrowed) cape of real ermine. Two of his daughters came as Day and Night, and his third daughter Margaret came as a character from 'The Legend of Montrose.' The Hones were so delighted by the effect of their costumes that they held a 'preparatory gathering' of friends before the ball so that everyone could see their striking costumes.[42]

33. Brevoort's home.

Brevoort's fancy dress ball in 1840, given at his mansion on Fifth Avenue and 9th Street, was universally regarded as the most luxurious social affair of antebellum New York. After Brevoort's death in 1848, the mansion was sold to Henry C. de Rham for $57,000. It was demolished in 1925 to make way for the Fifth Avenue Hotel.

If the Howland Ball in 1830 was overwhelmingly Anglophile, the guests at the Brevoort Ball a decade later were considerably less so. The vogue for Scott and the Highlander had passed, and in the aftermath of the United States' war with Mexico there were nine guests in one form or another of 'Spanish' costume, and the same number of modern Greeks. Peasants, as ever, had an enduring appeal for upper-class New Yorkers. Ten ladies and gentlemen spent the evening as picturesque European peasants. The George Barclays were in the costume of a fox hunter and a peasant woman; their daughter, the fashionable belle Matilda Barclay, 'Miss B———y,' came as Lalla-Rookh. Her gown was made by Madame Harche, and was reputed to have cost $300—'a thin slice,' the *Herald* reported, 'from a fortune of $150,000 which, with her excellent heart and beautiful self, she intends to bestow on one of the gallant young gentlemen whom she meets at the ball.' (The aftermath of the ball for the Barclay family would be a subject of hushed discussion in the city for years afterwards.)

The guest list of 500 was drawn from the old New York families, selected friends from nearby cities, and a number of foreign visitors, including a captain of the Grenadier Guards, and the Neapolitan and Swiss consuls. Brevoort's old friend Washington Irving attended, in the dress of a Chargee. Brevoort's former business associate, John Jacob Astor, departed early. The press failed to note if he was wearing a costume. Those excluded from the guest list tell us something of where the proverbial line was drawn in New York society in the 1840s. Before the ball, the *Herald* reported that the city's parvenus were 'moving heaven and earth to get an introduction to this highly respectable Dutch family, and hence an invitation.'[43] While merchants and representatives of the city's commercial elite were present, few Wall Street brokers received invitations to attend the ball. That may have reflected Brevoort's highly jaundiced attitude towards financial speculators; it also reflected a discrimination between the socially acceptable gentlemanly entrepreneurs, who played such a visible role in the city's life, and the upstart money manipulators.

One guest, August Belmont, who will be discussed in greater detail in Chapter 5, certainly raised eyebrows in Knickerbocker New York. In 1840, Belmont had been in the city only three years and had made himself a personal fortune of $100,000 as the representative of the Rothschilds in the New York financial markets. A quintessential New Man in the 1840s, Belmont's personal charm overcame distaste for his Jewish origins.[44] The most highly visible among the excluded was Prince John Van Buren—so titled in the affectionately mocking New York fashion because he had once danced with Queen Victoria before her ascent to the throne. He was the son of ex-President Van Buren, and a mighty power in New York State politics. The Van Burens were an ancient and respected Dutch family. Van Buren senior was a Jacksonian, and his son Prince John—

'exceptionally brilliant and witty, with attractive manners and marked ability as a speaker and *raconteur*'—was a lawyer and a leading figure in Tammany Hall.[45] (He was briefly engaged to the daughter of the president of Columbia College, William Alexander Duer.) A hint of the future may be observed in the fact that Van Buren's embarrassing exclusion was recorded in a sentence in the *Herald*. A generation later, social leaders looked enviously back to the 1840s as a golden age when Wall Street speculators and Democratic Party politicians could comfortably be excluded from society.

The evening ended in a scandal, when one of the guests, Matilda Barclay, eloped with the improbably named T. Pollock Burgwyne of South Carolina, causing much discussion about the propriety and acceptability of masked balls. Eloped may not be precisely the right term: the young lady, as the *Herald* ironically noted, was seen with her new husband the following day 'playing the fancy dress character of a married lady at the Astor House.'[46]

The Barclay elopement brought to the fancy ball the opprobrium which since the 1820s had been attached to the masked ball in New York. The public outcry following a shooting at a masquerade ball at the old Park Theater in December 1828, in which the assailant escaped wearing a mask, led the Legislature the next year to ban masquerade balls from any place of public entertainment. (Masked balls in private homes, like the Brevoorts', remained unaffected by this law.)[47] In 1848–9, in an attempt to suppress Anti-Rent mobs, a law was passed to prevent assemblages of more than three persons with their faces painted or concealed in public houses *or other places*. Further legislation in the city in 1850 made the holding of a masked ball a misdemeanor, punishable with a fine of $2,500 and nine months' imprisonment. The attack on masked balls was part of a campaign by evangelicals in New York to impose temperance and the 'Puritan Sabbath.' The anti-liquor, anti-immigrant evangelicals succeeded in banning the sale of beer and liquor on Sundays, but enforcement was sabotaged by Mayor Fernando Wood. Evangelicals had more success in banning masked balls.

By the late 1850s, when the masked balls made a return in New York, they were at first regarded as an open invitation for drunken routs and sexual license. Fearing a further onslaught from evangelicals and the police, organizers tried to control the enthusiasms of dancing New York. The German *Sängerbunde* or choral societies, like the Leiderkranz and the Arion (where Leopold Damrosch was the choral director) led the way in staging vastly popular masked balls. The Leiderkranz was a leading institution of the city's German-American upper class, and the society's balls were among New York's most popular social events.[48] Other bodies followed their example. The Arion Gesangverein and the Cercle Français de l'Harmonie held balls which were popular in the German and French immigrant communities. What was striking about such balls was their appeal to New Yorkers from diverse communities. Such events became civic institutions which, in practice, encouraged the crossing of national and ethnic borders—but not racial ones, or at least not until the twentieth century. These 'ethnic' balls conveyed to New York unfamiliar and vivid new cultural forms, such as the can-can which was a highly popular feature at Cercle balls. Other groups in the city's rich ethnic mix responded to the success of the Liederkranz, Arion, and Cercle balls, by staging their own occasions. The Purim Ball, held under Jewish auspices, soon became one of the most popular *bals masqués*. In multicultural New York at mid-century, you could go to a ball virtually every week in the year.

Citing the law of 1829, the Police Board threatened to increase the legal pressure on the organizers of masked balls. The organizers in turn tried to evade the law by telling guests to substitute veils for masks. Lawyers explained that *any* attempt to disguise the face was apparently against the law. One alternative, pursued by the Cercle, was to make their ball a fancy dress affair: costumes aplenty, but no masks. Changing the law was an alternative, but only a large and powerful immigrant community like the Germans, who were the most sophisticated and radical in the matter of social organization, could pursue such a secular goal. The Liederkranz Gesangverein formed a committee to seek changes in the law in Albany. Warmly supported by the major institutions of German New York, and funded by the numerous German owners of ballrooms, a lobbying campaign, led by ex-Mayor C. Godfrey Gunther, took up the cause. The politics of the issue were clear: as long as the Police Board in New York tried to suppress masked balls, Albany alone could and did provide relief. The city's Irish police and politicians were rather less popular in Albany than Germans who drank beer, liked to dance wearing masks, and might be persuaded to vote for Republicans.[49]

Accounts of masked balls, fancy dress balls, routs, and soirées appear in the burgeoning American literature of social climbing. For satirists the figures of Mrs. Megrim (from a poem in the *Knickerbocker* in February 1833), Mrs. Jarvis in James Fenimore Cooper's *Home as Found* (1838), who had 'an itching desire to figure in the world of fashion,'[50] Mrs. Tiffany in Anna Cora Mowatt's popular play *Fashion, or Life in New York* (1849), Mrs. Musky and Mrs. Blowhard in *New York Aristocracy* by 'Joseph' (1851), Mrs. Potiphar in George William Curtis' *The Potiphar Papers* (1853), and Edgar Fawcett's Anastasia Buntling, exemplify the types of ambitious and misguided women, for whom the giving of a ball was a way to an elevated social status:

> . . . Anastasia's heart ambitious grew
> She fain would ape the airs of folk she saw
> In street or theatre; we must change our life;

Dry-goods of costly kind must clothe her form;
She thought our basement no fit dining-room;
She thought our upper dining-room too small . . .
She wanted servants, footmen, carriages;
And last of all she clamored stubbornly
That we should go abroad and marry Jane
To some great duke or prince . . .[51]

Of the authors of such social satires, Mowatt alone was of 'good' New York lineage. Her mother's family included a 'signer' of the Declaration of Independence, and her father, Samuel Gouverneur Ogden, a merchant of repute, had played a part in society (he was one of the guests of the Howland ball in 1830). Mowatt held up for ridicule Mrs. Tiffany's taste for the aristocratic, her malapropisms (calling her armchair a 'fow-tool,' her coach a 'voyture'), and her worship of the false gods of fashion. When Adam Trueman stormed on to the stage in Act I and denounced Mrs. Tiffany's pretensions, New York audiences cheered and cheered:

Mrs. Tiffany: Let me tell you, sir, that liveries are all the fashion!

Trueman: The fashion, are they? To make men wear the *badge of servitude* in a free land,—that's the fashion, it is? Hurray, for republican simplicity! I will venture to say now, that you have your coat of arms too!

Mrs. Tiffany: Certainly, sir; you can see it on the panels of my *voyture*.

Trueman: Oh! No need of that. I know what your escutcheon must be! A bandbox *rampant* with a bonnet *couchant*, and a pedler's pack *passant*! Ha, ha, ha! That shows both houses united![52]

The figure of the social climber had become among the most easily mocked character-types in the popular culture of New York, along with the grasping merchant, the hypocritical banker, and the virtuous workman or Bowery b'hoy. The parvenu came to occupy such a place in the popular imagination principally because the ground under the mansions of the Howlands, Hones, and Brevoorts had begun to waver. The expanded commerce made possible by the Erie Canal, the railroads, gold in California, and the rise of industrial manufacturing created new wealth, and new demands were articulated by those like Mrs. Megrim and Mrs. Tiffany for a place among the ball-goers. Along with Maria Melvill, they thirsted for invitations to the homes of those who gave the balls. The fortunes of 'old money' families, rooted in the established mercantile firms, commission merchants, and ship chandlers, did not grow as fast, or failed to survive the crisis of 1837.

Through the 1840s the diaries of Hone and Strong, both fully paid-up members of 'the soirée-suffering aristocracy,' were filled with the hardships of life among the upper crust.[53] In their diaries they adopted the comic pose of socialite St. Sebastians, suffering for their position in society. Often in low spirits and seldom at ease at large social events, Strong loathed the wildly fashionable polka as 'disagreeable music of an uncivilized character' and found that endless discussions about parties and balls afterwards made social life even more oppressive. Typically Strong made sarcastic comments in his diary about his host and the other guests, and portrayed himself as anxious to be home. Of the ball at the home of Baron de Trobriand and his socialite wife Mary Mason Jones, he wrote: 'Everybody was there and I loafed about in a most independent manner and found it less of a bore than I expected.' After another ball held two nights later, Strong vowed to give up balls altogether. 'Rational speech there is none, and none is expected; people leave their common sense in the dressing rooms with their cloaks and hats, and one finds himself the next day unfit for business and wholly stupified [*sic*] and done up without having had anything in the way of amusements or edification to show for it.'[54]

Despite the great difference in their ages (Hone was born in 1780, Strong in 1820), Hone seems to have endured the hardship of a lifetime of parties and increasingly lavish entertainments with greater gusto. Having retired from business with a generous fortune in 1820, Hone was left a poor man by the panic of May 1837. He sought the New York postmastership, and became president of the American Mutual Insurance Company. But the fire of July 1845 drove that company into receivership, and forced Hone to seek a public position. A life spent in elegance, in the highest strata of society, which had been interrupted by periods of financial embarrassment and a need for unaccustomed economies, made Hone particularly sensitive to the growing signs of great wealth and luxury around him. The home of Robert Ray, a partner in the banking house of Prime, Ward & King, had become a touchstone of domestic luxury. Hone's account of a party at the home of the Rays in 1834 emphasized the 'utmost magnificence' of the banker's establishment. 'Mr. Ray has the finest house in New York, and it is furnished and fitted up in a style of the utmost magnificence—painted ceilings, gilded moldings, rich satin ottomans, curtains in the last Parisian taste, and splendid mirrors, which reflect and multiply all the *rays*, great and small.' The labors of decorators, cooks, and confectioners produced what Hone regarded as the *ne plus ultra* of entertainment. (When Ellen Duer, the eighteen-year-old daughter of William Alexander Duer, president of Columbia University, was invited to a ball at the home of Robert Ray in 1832, it was an occasion of sufficient importance for her parents to buy her, for the first time, a new ball gown. For lesser social events she was expected, as a third daughter, to make do with hand-me-downs.)[55] Strong was also impressed by the size and style of the Ray establishment, writing with vivacity in praise of 'the uncommonly good dancing, music, and so on, [which] made it one of the most successful affairs I ever attended'. Nevertheless, Strong retreated to the library that evening, where he sat talking with a friend as he desultorily glanced at the latest prints by Audubon, 'and then came home, supperless, with a headache.'

After the Civil War, the city was riotous with celebrations and balls of every description. As we have seen with the Leiderkranz, Arion, and Cercle balls, in New York such events crossed social boundaries and ethnic divides. Newspapers listed the 'Balls of the Season' and were often able to fill two columns of dense type with the annual entertainments of the New York regimental associations, guilds, societies, and fraternal bodies, high and low, from the Letter-Carriers and the Western Union Telegraph operators, to the John F. Kelly Association, the Young Men's Roman Catholic Benevolent Association, the Hoboken Turtle Club, and the St. John Baptist Society. At the height of the winter season, the Academy of Music was heavily booked:

Jan. 13—The Infant Asylum Ball
Jan. 17—The Roman Catholic Orphan Asylum Ball
Jan. 20—The Cercle Français de l'Harmonie Ball
Feb. 1—The Charity Ball
Feb. 22—The Lady Washington Tea Party in aid of St. John's Guild
Feb. 24—The Leiderkranz Ball.[56]

During the winter season of 1865–6, 600 balls were held in New York. The number of German balls, with three assembly rooms largely devoted to the social activities of German societies, astonished New Yorkers: between mid-December and early March, 1875, there were 112 balls planned for the Germania Assembly Rooms, the Beethoven Maennercher Hall, and the Turn Hall. It was estimated that seven million dollars were spent on jewelry and ball gowns alone.

These balls were an expression of the city's hedonistic pluralism. The promoters were also, as Mary P. Ryan has argued, engaged in a competitive struggle which infused every aspect of the ceremonies of a civic culture. A larger and more lavish ball was a sign of the health of a society and a community. Balls, outings—often beginning with a public meeting followed by a procession led by brass bands, with military companies in uniform, Tammany men wearing the headgear of braves, Orangemen wearing their sashes, and the eye-catching banners of trades unions and fraternal lodges—were frankly staged with one eye towards securing competitive advantage in a struggle with rival societies. The balls were also infused with political concerns, whether to denounce the latest Russian pogrom, oppose Sabbatarianism, or call for Home Rule for Ireland. Others, like the Pickwick Ball, attended by guests in the dress of characters from Dickens' novel, celebrated with oysters, champagne, and dance the greatest literary enthusiasm of the day. Hone attended the 'Young Guard' ball in 1844 held in honor of Henry Clay, the defeated Whig candidate in the 1844 presidential election. The Eighth Ward Calhoun Association held annual balls at Tammany Hall from 1846, attended, according to Mike Walsh, by 'good men—honest, intelligent and independent, and they have espoused the cause of the purest and brightest statesman living.' There were balls held by political clubs, from Tweed's Americus Club to the Richard B. Connolly Association. They became a regular feature of democratic political life in the city. Candidates used balls to commemorate anniversaries, launch a campaign, raise funds, and hearten their supporters. It is possible that more people attended balls than all the other sorts of political activity in the city put together. A device for political mobilization and propaganda, the ball was also a distinctive expression of the civic culture of New York, and one of the pleasures of city life.[57]

The upper-class assemblies patronized by McAllister and his friends stood at an apex of enthusiastic polkas, elegant cotillions, romantic waltzes, and determined gaiety which spread across the community. Puritans, evangelicals, and other enemies of frivolity saw in the craze for dancing proof of the city's imminent damnation. 'The dance is destructive to Christian life,' warned a preacher. 'Many excellent people who are examples of the common virtues may dance but the prayerful Christian soul finds that he must choose between the dance and his religious life; he cannot maintain both.' As well, Lutheran pastors in Kansas argued that dancing was hostile to proper intellectual and social development. The need to warn the public of the dangers caused by dancing was clear: it not only destroyed the love of study, of intelligent conversation, it also discredited 'straightforward living,' and stimulated a taste for display. 'The people of fashionable society do not read, they are not capable of sustaining an interesting conversation, and there is no way of entertaining them but by letting them dance. . . .' New Yorkers certainly had among their number men like Samuel Ward and James Lenox, who regarded balls and parties with distaste. But it was the party-going Philip Hone who was closer to the spirit of the city. In the decade after the Civil War, with the creation of the Patriarch Society (see Chapter 5), the ball entered its most aristocratic era.[58]

5

WARD MCALLISTER

Everyone realizes that the one end and aim of life here
[in New York] is to accumulate money.
—Ward McAllister (1890)[1]

For three decades until his death in 1895, the portly Ward McAllister was a man of consequence. For most Americans he stood for the principle of social exclusivity. As the organizer and leader of the Patriarchs, the most prestigious social institution of the age, McAllister articulated the ideals upon which the aristocratic idea in America took its stand. A flamboyant and outspoken figure, McAllister deserves closer scrutiny.[2]

The possessor of independent means, from the age of thirty-five McAllister lived the life of a gentleman, a man in society. 'He devoted himself,' noted Pulitzer's *World*, 'to the task of social discrimination.' In this he was strictly a professional. He was regarded by his contemporaries as an authority on entertaining, wines, and food. 'He can detect the different brands of Madeira, and knows the effect of age in producing the subtle Cobweb, Sealing Wax and Dry flavors, as contrasted with the too-sweet and thick Madeira of a modern vintage.'[3] Proud of his expertise on the preparation and service of quality food, he was a dogmatist on the correct alternation between white and brown sauces. Boasting that he knew the secrets of the great chefs of Europe, from the 1860s he won the respect of the old families and proud possessors of wealth in Newport and New York. He aimed to raise standards of entertaining in the highest reaches of American society, and McAllister's word was gospel for the planning of a successful dinner or a ball, and his judgment was sufficient to damn a sauce, or blight an aspiring millionaire.

In a society dominated by some of the wealthiest people in the United States, McAllister enjoyed a distinctive kind of social power. Why he possessed that power, how he used it, and what practical limitations hedged its use, will be explored in this chapter. The power a figure like McAllister enjoyed was not the power of a Jay Gould or Cornelius Vanderbilt, built upon hard cash, nor that of Mrs. Astor, who brought together wealth and social position. We can best think of McAllister as an ambitious outsider who set out, in the name of exclusivity, to make the nation's richest families more aware that they had a shared sense of corporate identity. To do this, he had to invent a 'Ward McAllister' who was something more than the son of a Georgia lawyer and politician, yet another Southerner with good manners and not quite enough money.

Feeding a carefully polished version of family genealogy to the press, he tried to prove, by reaching far back to his mother's family, that he belonged by birth and standing to the old New England and New York families which exercised social leadership early in the Republic. One genealogical inquiry traced the McAllister lineage to Isabella, sister of King Robert the Bruce, and thence to a king of Norway.[4] He did not particularly look like an aristocrat. Undistinguished in dress, and resembling a slightly out-of-focus Napoleon III, his affectations were regularly mocked in the press. Nonetheless, through force of will and an undoubted skill at flattery, he became a social leader after the Civil War. As far as a certain stratum of wealthy New Yorkers were concerned, it was hardly an irresistible rise, but with the patronage of Mrs. William Astor, McAllister did much to transform society in New York.

In 1890 McAllister told his own story in *Society As I Have Found It*. He coyly named no names, and revealed few secrets, and the book should have been quickly forgotten as a light-hearted inconsequential society memoir. That it was greeted with scorn and mockery, is less surprising than the revelation the book makes of McAllister's 'dirty little secret'. This great spokesman for exclusivity and renowned gastronomical expert was himself a social climber of studied and comical determination. McAllister's interest for us, then, is as someone who, having devoted much of his adult life to keeping 'parvenuism' at bay, was himself an ambitious schemer, determined through flattery and emulation to win the acceptance of those who, in his own judgment, truly belonged to the city's aristocracy. *Society As I Have Found It* warned New York against people like himself.[5]

A society funeral

> Wal, I've rid fifteen miles a-purpos to see that dude McAlister
> an' I don't begrutch it, not a mite
> —farmer in Cumberland Gap, Tennessee, 1892[6]

The funeral service for Ward McAllister, dead at the age of sixty-eight, was held at James Renwick's Grace Church on Broadway at East 10th Street on February 5, 1895. Sexton Partridge, successor to Isaac Brown, and his assistants stood alertly in the vestibule to ensure that only persons they recognized were to be admitted to the center aisle. The sidewalk in front of the church was crowded with bystanders, and a photographer from Byron's studio was present to

record the scene. A squad of police from the Mercer Street Station was in attendance to prevent disorder. The new mayor, William Strong, who led the new Republican administration, had been in power barely a month. Nothing yet had been done to purge the police department of its reputation for corruption and violence. But someone in the police force was mindful that a death reported on the front pages of the *Herald*, *World*, and the *New York Times* and a funeral at Grace Church required careful attention from a police force that had long ignored the sensitivities of rich Republicans. There were rumors that Theodore Roosevelt was going to be appointed to the Police Board; he may have been a silk-stocking like the congregation at Grace Church, but even his enemies granted that Roosevelt was no fop or dilettante. There were good reasons why the Mercer Street contingent were smartly turned out, and on their best behavior.

34. McAllister funeral, 1895.

Grace Church, February 5, 1895, the day of Ward McAllister's funeral.

The funeral cortège, led by a hearse and five carriages, proceeded down Fifth Avenue from McAllister's home at 16 West 36th Street, arriving at Grace Church at 10 a.m. The coffin was carried into the church by pall-bearers, followed by distinguished honorary pall-bearers, led by the rector, Dr. Huntington. The New York Central lawyer Chauncey M. Depew, De Lancey Astor Kane, Cornelius Vanderbilt II, Bradley Martin, and James Abercrombie Burden, followed the coffin into the church. These were men of social standing and wealth. Kane was best known to his contemporaries for importing the celebrated English coach *Tally Ho* in 1876 and for being one of the most important whips in the New York coaching world. His family connections were impeccable, with his mother Louisa a granddaughter of John Jacob Astor. Kane married a daughter of the banker and socialite Adrian Iselin. Vanderbilt, the grandson of the Commodore, had inherited the immense fortune of William Henry Vanderbilt. Martin was a New York lawyer and clubman, noted mainly for his lavish entertainments and admiration of rich capitalists. Burden was the president of the Burden Iron Works in Troy. His son Jay was engaged to marry Florence Adele Sloane,[7] daughter of William Douglas Sloane and Emily (Vanderbilt) Sloane, who was the daughter of William Henry Vanderbilt. McAllister's send-off was quality, pure quality.

The funeral was predominantly a 'Vanderbilt' occasion, yet the Vanderbilts, the richest of the 'new families,' had perhaps little obvious reason to be fond of McAllister. The social system he sought to create had effectively kept them and people like them frozen out of New York society from the creation of the Patriarchs in 1872 to the end of the decade. But McAllister had been something of an easy acquaintance of the Commodore's, and his greatest enemies were often those who had scorned the Vanderbilt millions, and yearned for an even more exclusive society. In the end, McAllister's fate was to have the Vanderbilts remain loyal, while his great patroness, Mrs. Astor, acquiesced in his social downfall. On the evening of his funeral she declined to cancel a dinner party. It was something of a commemorative event, the last to be held before the house was demolished to make way for the Astoria Hotel. And, as Louis Auchincloss noted, 'McAllister was not a relative.'[8]

The city's newspapers reported that McAllister's pew, number 113, was filled to the brim with floral tributes and his coffin was heavily laden with wreaths and flowers. The somber 'Dead March' from *Saul* was played from the organ loft by John M. Lander and his orchestra. It was a nice touch that Lander, who had been such a fixture at society balls organized by McAllister over the past two decades, should play his patron's funeral. As the coffin was carried out of the church on to Broadway where the hearse waited for the slow journey across the Brooklyn Bridge to Greenwood Cemetery, there was a sudden scramble by ladies for flowers from the McAllister pew. Caught unprepared for the rush,

WARD McALLISTER
FROM HIS LAST PHOTOGRAPH,
BY PRINCE OF UNION SQUARE

35. McAllister.

Joseph Pulitzer took up Ward McAllister, and printed his weekly columns in the *World*. When McAllister died, the paper covered the funeral as an important civic story.

the sexton had to threaten one woman with arrest before she would release the wreath she had seized. In the unseemly scuffle other ladies successfully carried away trophies from the season's most fashionable funeral.[9]

While the grab for souvenirs was taking place, reporters were scribbling down names of those who filed out of the church. The sexton might later be prevailed upon, or politely bribed, to allow reporters to have a look at the guest book for the funeral, but the evening editions of the papers could not wait. The society turnout for McAllister was glittering enough to fill a column or two in the papers. The Astors were principally represented by John Jacob IV, the only son of the late William Astor. Mrs. William Astor had completed the customary two-year period of mourning, and in 1893 had resumed her normal pace of entertaining; but the lady had a perfect horror of being photographed, and seldom attended social events where there was a risk of lurking photographers.

Other prominent hostesses exiting the church, such as Mrs. Paran Stevens, society 'swells' (Lispenard Stewart, Elisha Dyer, Matthew Astor Wilks),[10] and prominent Wall Street brokers (Henry Clews) were more comfortable with the persistent attentions of the press. A blur of dark-coated Beekmans, Fishes, Rhinelanders, Van Cortlandts, Delafields, Crugers, Cuttings, and Jays looked for their near-identical carriages lining both sides of East 10th Street, or turned uptown hoping to reach the Union Club or the Knickerbocker in time for lunch. Mrs. William D. Sloane and Mrs. W. Seward Webb, both daughters of the late William Henry Vanderbilt, had further to travel, for the Vanderbilt 'mile' along Fifth Avenue was far uptown.

Only the most knowledgeable student of the society pages, perhaps someone like Mrs. Peniston in Edith Wharton's *The House of Mirth*, who interrogated Lily about every detail of the Gryce/Van Osburgh wedding, might have raised a knowing eyebrow at the list of those who attended McAllister's funeral, and those who stayed away. It was the height of the New York season, and all of the leading figures were in town. Some of course had prior commitments, or were unwell; others were in mourning or unavailable for one reason or another, but there were many in New York society who stayed away because they detested McAllister, and declined to play the hypocrite at his funeral. There were no Morgans or Whitneys at Grace Church, nor did the Goelets (Robert and Ogden), Schermerhorns, Costers, or Roosevelts make an appearance. Mrs. Stuyvesant Fish—the florid, willful Mamie Fish who clashed so fiercely with McAllister[11]—was positively incandescent in her absence. August Belmont, Jr., and his brothers Perry and Oliver stayed away, as did Edward Cooper, Lloyd Bryce, and James P. Kernochan. The Patriarchs, created by McAllister in 1872, the 'close corporation' which embodied the idea of society in New York, and which he had served with great enthusiasm, turned their back upon his funeral.[12]

Whole categories of people in society had quite good reasons to stay away from the funeral. Families excluded from the 'Four Hundred,' and thereby tacitly deemed unworthy of admission into society, formed an indignant phalanx of hostility to McAllister and all he stood for. A young actress like Elsie de Wolfe, humiliated by McAllister when she was caught attending a Patriarchs' ball on someone else's ticket, also had reasons to boycott the funeral. Some had been outraged by McAllister's gossipy memoir, *Society As I Have Found It*, and had dropped him from their visiting list. (After the funeral a Patriarch was heard to remark: 'Poor McAllister! What a pity it is he wrote a book!')[13]

It was McAllister's growing presence in the newspapers in the decade before his death which had begun to turn society opinion against him. His interviews and columns in the *World* were capable of giving offense to those who detested the wrong kind of publicity. Pulitzer was a man deeply loathed in

36. McAllister.

In Chicago, McAllister was described as the 'Head Butler,' a 'New York Flunky' and the 'Premier of Cadsville'—all of which he accepted with equanimity. The Arbiter of Fashionable Life, as this photograph suggests, need not concern himself with little people in provincial cities.

New York society, and the appearance of McAllister in *that* paper was a boundless irritation. Interviews with McAllister had begun to appear regularly in the New York press in the late 1880s. By 1893 he was sending Pulitzer's paper daily telegraphic 'bulletins' of society news from Newport and Bar Harbor.[14] (*Town Topics* had a parallel, covert intelligence apparatus at work at the fashionable summer resorts.) McAllister's lesser sins included his verbal affectations, not least his London aristo-cockney 'y'know' at the end of sentence after sentence. His activities as a marriage broker, and his suspected willingness to accept payment from wealthy outsiders like Collis P. Huntington for invitations to the 'right' parties, made McAllister a figure who had become objectionable in some of the best homes in the city. He was also detested by the rivals of Mrs. Astor for his role as her chamberlain, adviser, and effusive admirer.

Others among the old Knickerbocker families had reason to remember McAllister with affection. McAllister had championed and defended the old families. At the Patriarchs in February, 1896, the guest list prominently featured Duers, Delafields, Jays, Winthrops, Cuttings, Rhinelanders, Gouverneurs, Livingstons, Beekmans, Lydigs, and Van Rensselaers—families which the

Trumbull sisters had encountered in 1800.[15] The guest list at his funeral was a reminder of what McAllister had sought to do on their behalf. The young 'smart' set, led by Mamie Fish, Mrs. Ogden Mills (herself a Livingston who presided over a Stanford White mansion overlooking the Hudson at Staatsburg, and was unflatteringly portrayed as Judy Trenor in Wharton's *The House of Mirth*), the Belmonts, Bryce and Harry Payne Whitney, had found the social leadership of McAllister increasingly irksome. The New York season, dominated by the same elderly dandies dancing the same cotillions as they had while young beaux in the 1860s, seemed to the 'swells' to be increasingly dreary. 'Who speaks of society in terms and tones of real enjoyment?' asked Richard Grant White. 'The nearly unanimous verdict of those who are most competent to pass upon it, men who are past thirty, and women who are past twenty-five—pronounces society dreary, barren, hopeless.'[16] Perhaps they felt that Mrs. Astor, with her famous jewels trotted out each season for the opening night at the Metropolitan Opera, was rich and equally dreary.

There was also an undercurrent of sentiment that McAllister, spokesman for the Patriarchs and leading national symbol of snobbish exclusivity, had opened the portals of society too widely. There were repeated stories in the press that cabals led by leading figures of the 'old money' families were about to wage merciless war against the parvenus. As a well-informed (but anonymous) informant revealed in the *World*, family and tradition, not wealth, were to form the standards for society in the future: 'Grandfathers, great-grandfathers and genealogy will be made the tests. Those who can only show bank accounts, railroad bonds and coupons will be refused recognition. There will be no parleying. The refusal will be absolute.'[17]

As a sign of the seriousness of the intended counter-revolution, or of the deepening anxiety of old families in a New York they no longer recognized, the dozen years following 1885 saw the founding of the Holland Society, Daughters of the Cincinnati, Sons of the Revolution, Daughters of the American Revolution, Colonial Dames, Colonial Order of the Acorn, Society of Mayflower Descendants, the Baronial Order of Runnymede, and the Aryan Order of St. George of the Holy Roman Empire in the Colonies of America, as well as the New York Society of the Order of the Founders and Patriots of America. The members of these societies were against democracy, immigration, crime, racial degeneration, and parvenus—New York, in brief. New York in the new republic was already bristling with social and fraternal bodies which served the cause of fellowship, but which also asserted a claim to social position for those with a common heritage. Membership of the St. Andrews Society (1756, revived 1784), German Society (1784), St. George's Society (1786), St. Patrick's Society (1789), and the Society of the Cincinnati (1795) were early established. The New-York Historical Society, whose president in 1828 urged the society 'to elevate the pride of ancestry,' followed in 1804. There were dozens of other bodies which celebrated the distinction of one's ancestors.

The ancestor-pride of McAllister's generation was nothing new in New York, though the importance he placed on lineage can scarcely be overstated. Genealogical research confirmed the most snobbish of prejudices about the superiority of family lineage in a democracy. Although McAllister had never been fully accepted by the Old Guard, members of those old families were present at his funeral, but so too, with great visibility, were the Vanderbilts. McAllister represented the muddled compromise between new and old money, between genealogy and railroad bonds, which gave New York society its distinctive coloration. Leaving the church that afternoon, Frederick Townsend Martin, socialite brother of Bradley Martin, was struck by the irony of McAllister's funeral. A person to be placated during his lifetime, in death he was ignored by the Patriarchs as a dead lion. Martin struggled to come to terms with how little McAllister's memory seemed to be appreciated. '"Man and his littleness perish, erased like an error and canceled."' At that moment for Martin, society in New York was no longer a community.[18]

Families

> In New York Society the older families never allow the turmoil of outside life to enter their social scheme.
> —Henry Cabot Lodge, 1913[19]

New York was quite literally a city of nobodies. The immigrants brought brass candlesticks and goose-down quilts with them, along with their guttural languages and folk traditions. However many relatives they had back in the Old Country, or already settled in the new, in the eyes of Ward McAllister and his world, they did not possess the single indispensable qualification: they had no *family*. For McAllister the family was not simply the sum of the connections created by a large, extended set of relations. A family in McAllister's sense was a name, a material and symbolic patrimony, and a form of stakeholding in America. Family in this sense may have been an eighteenth-century and specifically an upper-class usage, as Lawrence Stone has suggested, describing a 'total lineage, past, present, and future.' Genealogy for such families was a certificate of authenticity. 'I am by the Fathers side *pure* Dutch,' wrote the novelist James Kirke Paulding. '[B]oth my Grandfather & Grandmother, whom I remember, were Dutch—spoke Dutch—and read Dutch out of an Old Dutch Bible with Silver Corners & Silver clasps. By my mother, I am adulterated with some French & English blood—but I am so far a Dutchman yet, that I hate all interlopers, and reverence Old customs . . . though a little sophisticated, I am a

Dutchman all over, and . . . have a great respect for the name of DeWitt—I don't mean DeWitt Clinton.' As Mrs. Potiphar confides to a friend in George William Curtis' satire of the New York parvenu, *The Potiphar Papers*:

> Starr Mole, who interests himself in genealogies, and knows the family name and crest of all the English nobility, has 'climbed our family tree,' as Staggers says, and finds that I am lineally descended from one of those two brothers who came over in some of those old times, in some of those old ships, and settled in some of those old places somewhere. So you see, dear Caroline, if birth gives any one a right to coats of arms and liveries, and all those things, I feel myself sufficiently entitled to have them.[20]

In an age of 'new money' to have a family set a person apart from the other hungry claimants for social position. Julia, Louisa, and Eliza Cutler of Jamaica Plain, who were to marry into the Ward, McAllister, and Francis families, were distinctly not nobodies. Their maternal grandmother was a niece of a great revolutionary hero, the 'Swamp Fox,' General Francis Marion. That was a game which everyone in society played, and New York society was positively crawling with people anxious to let everyone know how distinguished their family had been. However tenuous, New Yorkers cherished their descent from the nation's founders. The large and highly visible Winthrop clan claimed direct descent from Governor John Winthrop of Massachusetts.[21] Samuel Denison Babcock claimed lineal descent from one of the important group of Puritans who emigrated from Leyden before arriving at the Plymouth colony. The father of the novelist Mrs. Burton Harrison was a nephew of Thomas Jefferson. The Wall Street broker Henry Clews was married to Lucy Madison Worthington of Kentucky, a grandniece of President James Madison. Elbridge Gerry was the grandson and namesake of a signer of the Declaration of Independence who also served as Vice-President of the United States. Walter Langdon, the grandson of Judge John Langdon who had served twelve years in the United States Senate, and was President *pro tempore* at the inauguration of Washington, eloped with John Jacob Astor's daughter Dorothea, unkindly known as 'Fat Dolly' in the Astor family. The millionaire was not impressed, and disinherited his daughter. (They were later reconciled.) When Astor's granddaughter Emily married Sam Ward in 1838, the young couple's grandparents were heavily but unequally burdened with military distinction from the revolutionary struggle. *Her* maternal grandfather was General John Armstrong; *his* paternal grandfather was Lieutenant-Colonel Samuel Ward. All this distinction paled to nothing before the Willings of Philadelphia, whose daughter Ava married John Jacob Astor IV in 1890. They were a prominent family, with a Willing elected to the Continental

Congress and another serving as mayor of Philadelphia. The family proudly claimed descent from Alfred the Great, Henry I of France, and a run of English monarchs from Henry I to Henry IV.

McAllister entertained his oldest chums with tales of the admiration George Washington had felt for his grandmother, Sarah Mitchell Cutler. Had things gone slightly differently, McAllister intimated with an attractive modesty, perhaps he might have been the grandson of the first President. The passion for colonial ancestry had its impact on the look of New York homes, where space was set aside to display sacred family heirlooms. 'No house is now completely fashionable,' a society columnist in the *World* ironically noted, 'without its little museum of old china, silver ware and antique cutlery, a dirty picture or two and some faded and extremely uncomfortable pieces of furniture coming in as incidental but important accessories.'[22]

The Cutler sisters were the quintessence of handsome society belles. Sent to Mrs. Graham's girls' boarding school in New York in 1802, a decade later, in 1812, Julia was placed with her sister Eliza in a respectable New York boarding house, where she first met Samuel Ward. She was then fifteen, the same age as Maria Trumbull when she spent the season in New York in 1800–1. Ward was twenty-six, but their marriage swiftly won family approval. They began housekeeping on Marketfield Street, where their first child, named after Ward's father, was born in 1814. Samuel and Julia Ward introduced her sister Louisa Cutler into New York society. Her first conquest was a handsome young beau named Matthew Hall McAllister from a prominent Savannah family, who had studied law at Princeton. Marriage to McAllister took Louisa far from her sister in New York, but even after the early death of Julia in 1828, the McAllisters and Wards remained as close as any family could be, separated by 900 miles of poor American roads. Julia visited her sister Louisa in 1821, and was greeted with outpourings of Southern courtesy and versifying in Savannah, Charleston, and Augusta. She brought with her on that trip a leather-bound keepsake album, preserved in the Beinecke Library, in which original compositions, translations, and transcriptions from well-known poets were written as a sentimental record of the visit. The tone of the inscriptions veers from witty turns of phrase to flowery effusiveness by A.E.M., dated Charleston, October 31, 1821.

> Sweet jessamine! Thou fragrant Flower
> Let me transplant thee to my bower . . .

For years Julia Ward had kept an album of favorite poetical passages transcribed from her reading. An ideal husband is described in a poem entitled 'Day Dreams':

He must have mind whom I could love
Of noble generous cast;
He must be good, & virtues friend
Or love would never last.

Julia Ward Howe, who remembered so little about her mother, cherished these poetical keepsakes. The McAllister family in Georgia connected Samuel Ward to the sacred memory of his wife. 'Mr. Ward felt a special tenderness for his wife's people,' recalled his granddaughter, 'and kept up a correspondence with her sisters as long as they lived.' The closeness between the families survived into the 1870s, when Julia Ward Howe and her daughter Maud were joined by Julia McAllister for a grand tour of Europe. Louisa's son was the godson and namesake of his uncle Samuel Ward. Though he was baptized Samuel Ward McAllister, he did not use his uncle Samuel Ward's first name. (Four generations of male Wards were *Samuel*, and that may have been quite enough.) His cousin Louisa, Julia Ward's second daughter, was named after Louisa McAllister in Savannah. The Ward children paid visits to the McAllisters in Savannah, and the McAllisters joined the Wards at Newport, when the summers in South Carolina became unbearable.[23]

Matthew Hall McAllister began a legal career on his return home which led to his becoming a leading figure in the Savannah bar. He also served as an officer of the Georgia Hussars, and was elected Democratic mayor of Savannah for several terms. McAllister was, like every other lawyer, banker, and leading citizen of Savannah, a slave owner, but he remained a staunch Union man, and an opponent of nullification. (The attempt by South Carolina to nullify the tariff of 1832 was aggressively rejected by President Andrew Jackson.)

Ward McAllister later recalled that in the eyes of her husband's family in Savannah, his mother Louisa was always a New Englander. For many Northerners the adjustment to Southern conditions, and Southern attitudes, was a difficult one. Describing a visit to Savannah in 1854, N.P. Willis was surprised to find the streets empty, and everywhere there was a 'shut-up look of families absent.' The trees were so large as to prevent an unobstructed look at the stars. Willis was puzzled to find no 'dress' street, no Broadway in Savannah, which in his eyes was 'one of the general human necessities'. The sanded streets, which enabled wheeled vehicles to pass silently through the city, did not make for pleasant journeys. With a population of 20,000, the city was 'ready-cloistered and hushed.' When asked her opinion of 'our blackies' on her first visit to Savannah in 1838, Fanny Kemble declined to reply. There were, she felt, 'some small prejudices in favor of freedom and justice' yet to overcome before joining the universal praise in South Carolina of the 'beneficent' system' which condemned so many to 'perpetual degradation.' On the subject of slavery (which Willis ignored) there were many reasons why a New Englander like Louisa McAllister, married into a prominent Savannah family, would choose to keep her opinions to herself. In addition to his legal work, her husband owned several plantations, an abundance of slaves, and the family's fortunes depended upon their management. In one of Louisa McAllister's letters to her relatives in New York, she made an indignant complaint at the rigidity of legal controls on black seamen, forbidden to come ashore in Charleston. It is a hint, no more, of what may have been her own feelings about the operation of the slave code in the South.[24]

Of their three sons, one received an appointment to West Point, served in the Mexican War, and later joined the Confederate army. Another, Hall, studied at Yale and followed his father to enter the Georgia bar. He moved to California after word reached the South of the discovery of gold at Sutter's Mill. In 1848–9, at the age of twenty-one, Ward McAllister was sent to New York to live with his father's cousin, Miss Mary Telford, at her house on 10th Street. The Ward family in New York no longer held its position of exalted social eminence: the Corner House had been sold, Prime, Ward & King had failed and the second marriage of Sam Ward was a social disaster. McAllister, who had spent summers in Newport, and visited his family in New York, did not dwell on the misfortunes of the Wards. His stay in New York was the beginning of a long career in society.

His relationship to the Wards gave McAllister a remembered identity in New York. With a legacy of $1,000, McAllister equipped himself for the ardors of the New York season, buying the finest available fancy dress for the winter's festivities. He remembered that first stay in New York in 1849 not in terms of his studies (he was desultorily learning bookkeeping), or the great public events of the day, such as the Astor Place riots (which go unmentioned in his memoirs). Rather, his was a débutante's New York, a whirl of invitations to vivid balls and parties. He attended a ball on February 3, 1849, at the 'Palace' at College Place, the home Alexander Jackson Davis designed for John C. Stevens. Philip Hone was also a guest at this ball, and wrote an account of the evening in his diary. Hone was deeply impressed by the Greek-style mansion, located on a large lot adjacent to the campus of Columbia College. The Stevenses' table was magnificent, and the host performed his duties with the utmost good breeding and unobtrusive hospitality. The company, judging by the spirited conversation, were highly pleased with their entertainment. In Hone's world the 'agreeableness' of a host, and not their sheer wealth was a powerful factor in maintaining social relations. Happily for Hone, being rich and being agreeable often coincided. The vast majority of the people he entertained, and who played roles in his dedicated social life, were drawn from the very wealthiest 1 percent

37. Stevens' mansion, College Place.

'A glimpse of aristocracy': the 'Palace' on College Place, designed by Alexander Jackson Davis for John C. Stevens. 'Saturday, February 3. I was a guest at a splendid dinner to-day in Mr. John C. Stevens's palace, College Place. The house is, indeed, a palace. The Palais Bourbon in Paris, Buckingham Palace in London, and Sans-Souci at Berlin, are little grander than this residence of a simple citizen of our republican city, a steamboat builder and proprietor . . .'—From the diary of Philip Hone, February 3, 1849.

of the city's population. In less than a decade after the completion of the Stevenses' mansion, Columbia College moved uptown to East 49th Street and the 'Palace' was demolished, making way for commercial buildings.[25]

The second major event in McAllister's stay in New York was a fancy dress ball at the home of Peter and Sarah Schermerhorn, 6 Great Jones Street (see Chapter 6 on the family and their place in the Knickerbocker elite). The Schermerhorn guests were requested to attend in costumes from the time of Louis XV. Even the domestic servants were in correct period costume, and the guests (he recalled) threw themselves into the spirit of the occasion, competing for the honor of having the handsomest costume.

The Stevenses' and Schermerhorns' gave McAllister a glimpse of aristocracy in New York. Theirs was a social order rooted in a small number of wealthy, powerful families. What he saw was a world of refinement and civility, without the slightest hint of raw personal ostentatiousness. Such families set a standard against which newer wealth would be measured. When he came back to live in New York two decades later, the Stevenses had moved to New Jersey, and the Schermerhorns had partitioned their large estates, and in the process had lost much of the eminence they had enjoyed in the antebellum Knickerbocker aristocracy. Nonetheless, there was a Schermerhorn among the original Patriarchs, and Mrs. Astor, daughter of Abraham Schermerhorn, was on the verge of her unique social triumph. McAllister remembered their world, and later tried to reconstruct society as they understood it.

McAllister seemed energized in 1849 by his glimpse of cultivated New York. He promptly abandoned any thoughts of bookkeeping, and returned to Savannah where he studied Blackstone and passed the Georgia bar exam. A legal career in the footsteps of his father and brother loomed. But brother Hall's letters from San Francisco contained intriguing, hardly to be credited, stories of immense wealth to be made from practicing law in the eye of the storm of gold which was overwhelming California. Judge Matthew Hall McAllister's doubts were silenced when bags of gold dust arrived from San Francisco, along with a reiterated plea from his son that they all join him. Ward McAllister sailed for California on the *Panama* on February 20, 1849, with his cousin Sam Ward as companion. The journey around the Straits of Magellan took 116 days. The McAllister brothers began to practice law in San Francisco in 1850. Ward McAllister's legal work is scarcely mentioned in his memoir, and he may have played more of a social role, wining and dining clients rather than providing them with high-powered legal advice. (A letter in the *Tribune* in 1891 discussing the legal position of the city's waterfront is a solitary glimpse of McAllister's legal expertise.)[26]

The prospect of great wealth attracted Americans of every class and background, and held out the promise of changed fortunes, changed identities. San Francisco was filled with newly rich, self-invented men, and their ostentatious world was the very antithesis of the planter's aristocracy in which McAllister had been raised in Savannah, and the settled upper class of old families he encountered in New York. But the McAllisters made lots of money in San Francisco, and earned the respect of the local legal community. By 1855 Ward McAllister, yearning (he tells us) for a more gentlemanly life, had already returned to New York. He courted Sarah T. Gibbons, the daughter of a Georgia millionaire who was living in northern New Jersey. The rental on a New Jersey harbor property which Mrs. McAllister brought to the marriage underpinned their affairs. But after bearing several children, she became a recluse, and was never known to go into society. She did not attend her husband's funeral in 1895. Having married money, McAllister bought Bayside, a farm on Narragansett Bay at Newport and looked around for a gentleman's occupation.

An attempt to obtain appointment as Secretary of the United States Legation in London was thwarted because James Buchanan, appointed minister by President Pierce, had promised to support the appointment of McAllister *père* as the first United States circuit judge in California. His diplomatic hopes come to nothing, McAllister spent the rest of the 1850s in leisurely travel between London, Florence, Rome, and Baden-Baden, before settling in Pau, in southwestern France, for two congenial winters, where he learned about the wines of Bordeaux. McAllister found life in Europe much cheaper than in the United States, and befriended numerous American merchants who were similarly touring European capitals and leading resorts. For such men McAllister was a valuable source of advice, whether about the intricacies of

European etiquette or the correct choice of wines. His wide acquaintanceship among freeloading European aristocrats made him doubly welcome in the eyes of wealthy American merchants and their socially ambitious wives.

Newport

'How do people live in Newport?' 'In the morning they bathe; in the afternoon they dine; and in the evening they drive.'
—(1873)[27]

McAllister returned to the United States in 1859. After a visit to Savannah, he settled permanently in Newport where he began a new phase, a pastoral idyll, in the cultivation of society. Newport, and other seaside resorts like Bar Harbor, were rivals of a rather snooty kind to the two leading New York resorts, Ballston Spring and Saratoga. The great rise in the popularity of Saratoga began with the opening of the rail link between Albany and Schenectady in 1833. In a resort dominated by large hotels, and with a sharply defined season which began on the first day of July, the clientele of the leading Saratoga hotels marked out a distinctive topography of class and wealth. Congress Hall, opened in 1802, was patronized by the old Yankee families of New England. With its large courtyard and cottages, Elias Benedict's United States Hotel, built in 1824, was favored by the Saratoga smart set and *nouveaux riches*. The 'middling sort' preferred the Pavilion and the Columbian. The more devout and elderly patronized Union Hall, which by mid-century had a commanding 400-foot frontage on Broadway. By the 1840s the luxury hotels at Saratoga had taken on a partisan political coloration, with Congress Hall being heavily patronized by Whigs, while Democrats preferred the Grand Union and the United States Hotel. Saratoga remained the nation's premier summer resort. Among the newly arrived guests at Congress Hall in July 1873 were the president of Yale, the proprietor of the *New York Times*, Commodore Vanderbilt, his son William Henry, and George Opdyke, Republican ex-mayor of New York City. Tammany and Mozart Hall stalwarts included ex-mayor Fernando Wood, his brother Ben, and their families, who were staying at the Grand Union.[28]

Despite the universal belief in the medicinal benefit of taking the waters (which tasted very salty and nasty to a correspondent from the *New York Times* in 1875, 'and the chemical analysis sounds very alarming'), a holiday spirit prevailed. Guests at Saratoga dressed well, and passionately enjoyed the polka. No direct social barriers were at work to insulate the wealthy and the socially eminent from those anxious to be seen in their company. The daily routine of checking the hotel register each morning for new arrivals was normally followed by taking the waters. In the essentially democratic ethos of Saratoga, guests did not hesitate to seek the acquaintance of other guests. A traveling Englishman, Captain Marryat, wrote sourly of Saratoga and its mania for introductions: 'Mr. A introduced Mr. B and C, Mr. B and C introduce Mr. D, E, F and G. Messrs. D, E, F, and G introduce Messrs. H, I, J, K, L, M, N, O, and so it goes, *ad infinitum* during the whole of the day . . .'. Each introduction was accompanied by an expectation, repellent to Marryat, that the English visitor would shake hands with each of his new acquaintances. The entrenched familiarity of social relations in the young democracy struck many observers as a defining quality of American life. Aristabulus in James Fenimore Cooper's *Home as Found* (1838) 'fancied he had a right, under the Constitution of the United States of America, to be introduced to every human being with whom he came in contact.'

Saratoga was a resort with a distinctly national feel, where people discussed politics and the great affairs of the day. 'Saratoga belongs to the world of men,' wrote Mary Gay Humphreys. 'Nowhere do women seem so much like appendages.' The hotels at Saratoga were filled with 'Western land speculators, Southern planters, [and] New Orleans cotton kings.' The guests who lined the hotel piazzas or verandahs suggested to Henry James 'the swarming vastness—of our young civilization. They come from the uttermost ends of the Union—from San Francisco, from New Orleans, from Alaska. As they sit with their white hats tilted forward, and their chairs tilted back, and the feet tilted up, and their cigars and toothpicks forming various angles with these various lines, I seem to see in their faces a tacit reference to the affairs of a continent.'[29]

Politics was one of the main topics of interest at Saratoga. President Martin Van Buren had a cottage in the grounds of the United States Hotel, 'where he spent much of the summer and where the business of the Chief Executive of the nation was conveniently transacted.' And it was in the large parlor of the hotel that the widow of DeWitt Clinton administered one of the most widely discussed snubs of the decade, turning her back upon President Van Buren as he extended his hand to her companion, the Portuguese *chargé d'affaires*. Cutting a man of Van Buren's stature was an extreme expression of disapproval. The subtle art of the 'cut' was one of the most striking forms of social power in the hands of a woman of Mrs. Clinton's social position.[30]

James Gordon Bennett's *Herald* led the way in changing the public attitude towards Saratoga. Bennett's paper delighted in reporting sinful goings on at the spa. The old respectable guests increasingly found themselves surrounded by new money, gamblers, and fast women. The trotting season in July, followed by flat racing in August, attracted a raffish element. 'Dashing women and bedizened new-rich ones jostle each other on the crowded side-walks,' wrote one visitor to Saratoga in 1866, 'or vie with each other in the vulgarity of the most flashing turn-outs. . . . Vice lifts her head unblushingly, and Sensuality holds "high revel." [31]

The growing popularity of Saratoga had cost the resort its claim to exclusivity. A pre-emptive move to exclude Jews from the hotels in Saratoga in 1877 was a response to the growing perception that the resort had become too 'general.' The protagonist of this move against Jews was Judge Henry Hilton, who had taken control of A.T. Stewart's estate in 1876. On the basis of Stewart's two million dollar investment in the Grand Union, Hilton assumed the management of the world's largest hotel. Among his first acts as manager was to bar the Jewish banker Joseph Seligman from the Grand Union Hotel in 1877. Hilton presided over a meeting, also at the Grand Union, of a short-lived American Society for the Suppression of the Jews. The society called for widespread boycotts to counter the growing influence of Jews in American life. Hilton wanted organized opposition to Jewish candidates for political office, plays in which Jews performed, all books by Jewish authors, and a boycott of Jewish-owned businesses. The American Society for the Suppression of the Jews demanded that the 'Jews must be excluded from all first class society.' The nationwide response to the humiliation of Seligman brought the rising spirit of anti-Semitism in the Gilded Age into the open. (It was from this time that Anna Morton decided that she could no longer bear referring to her banker husband by his Old Testament Hebrew name, Levi, and insisted he be referred to as 'L.P.') There were letters and advertisements in the press taking sides, and an anti-Hilton boycott was organized against A.T. Stewart's store. Henry Ward Beecher made a sermon denouncing the exclusion of Seligman. The decline of Saratoga was if anything accelerated by the scandal. [32]

By the 1850s there were deepening tensions between Northern and Southern guests at Saratoga. When the stage adaptation of Mrs. Stowe's *Uncle Tom's Cabin* was performed at the Springs in 1856, to the great indignation of Southerners there was not a dry eye in the audience. [33] It was an environment in which Southerners felt increasingly unwelcome. They began to look for a more congenial summer environment. As early as the 1830s the first Southern families built 'cottages'—a preferred local euphemism for the substantial mansions designed for summer occupancy—at Newport. Rhode Island offered a notably more comfortable political environment to Southerners than the unpredictable radicalism of New York state. At Newport planters from Savannah like George Noble Jones, Hugh Ball, Henry Middleton, and Ralph Izard from Charleston encountered grandees of the China trade, New York brokers and bankers, Boston merchants, and the best New England families. Such men, many of whose interests were tied to the cotton trade, had much to lose by wild talk of abolition or Southern secession, and the so-called 'Silver Gray' Whigs of Fifth Avenue and Madison Square were leading proponents

38. Anna Morton.

Anna Morton preferred to call her husband Levi Parsons Morton by his initials, L.P.

of compromise and conciliation in the 1850s. They had every reason to wish their Southern brethren to feel welcome at Newport. McAllister, with his Southern family, was well placed to ease relations between Southerners and Northerners.

With its daily steamship links with Boston and New York from 1847, and its rich stock of picturesque colonial buildings, Newport had little of the piney rawness of Saratoga. If Saratoga was a masculine resort, Newport was distinctly feminine, even matronly, in its ethos. The ban on business, politics, and religion as topics of polite conversation was rigorously insisted upon. A guidebook in 1852 noted: 'In the business streets are many excellent and some really elegant stores. An air of prosperity seems to pervade the place generally—but in "the season" all is hurry and drive. Then in the shop windows are displayed the most attractive wares. Fashion rattles by in gorgeous equipages; and from balcony and verandah beauty looks forth.'[34] 'Nowhere else in this country,' wrote Henry James, 'nowhere, of course, within the range of our better civilization—does business seem so remote, so vague, and unreal.' To a sharp-eyed English diplomat visiting Newport in 1890, the prevailing note was a stylish affectation of boredom: 'They [the cottagers] don't seem to care for anything in the world. They have nothing to talk about, except each other, and nothing to do except to talk.' Living in their own (or rented) homes, accompanied by their servants and all domestic comforts, the cottagers dominated society at Newport.

For many hostesses there was a 'court' of handsome, fashionable younger swells who danced elegantly, and knew better than to bore débutantes with talk of stocks and bonds. The respectableness and quiet were a considerable source of snobbish pride. The cottagers preferred to think that Newport possessed a moral elevation as well as a higher social tone. Everyone was quite sure that there were no adventurers or ladies of questionable virtue at the Rhode Island resort. There was, self-evidently, no shortage of *male* adventurers paying attention to wives and daughters in Newport for the season. Families had many reasons to hide the attempted seduction by unprincipled men of 'foolish ill regulated girls, muddled by French novels and by a life of idleness.' One such attempted seduction at Newport by the journalist W.H. Hurlbert of the wife of the lawyer Charley Strong was recorded in outraged detail in the diaries of Strong's brother George in 1857.[35]

Until the building of the casino on Bellevue Avenue in 1879–80 (it was the first major commission of the architect Charles McKim, and contained a gold-trimmed theater designed by Stanford White), the 'gay season' had been confined to August. The resort was noted for its daily rituals: at nine o'clock in the morning, when the white flag fluttered over Easton's Beach,

> from every hotel, boarding house and private dwelling, may be seen issuing numberless groups of gentlemen and countless bevies of beauties. Every horse's head is turned in the direction of the beach. All along the Bath road is a rush of vehicles, laden with loveliness and fashion. Gaily sparkle the bright portions of the harness of each well-appointed team, and brilliant are the liveries of the "Jeames Yellow-plushes" who direct and control them.[36]

At noon, the throng made even hastier retreat from the beach, for when the red banner was raised, the beach was reserved for male use and nude swimming.

In the evenings, there was a procession of carriages on Bellevue Avenue. Barouches, landaus, victorias, dog-carts, pony phaetons, four-in-hands,

tandems—and, sometimes, a spike team of three horses, two abreast and one in advance, 'drove up and down that short stretch of road, passing and repassing each other.' Accompanied by their footmen, elderly ladies were driven every day the length of Bellevue Avenue, and then along Ocean Drive from Narragansett Bay to the Atlantic Ocean. 'For this drive,' recalled Edith Wharton, 'it was customary to dress as elegantly as for a race-meeting at Auteuil or Ascot. A brocaded or satin-striped dress, powerfully whale-boned, a small flower-trimmed bonnet tied with a large tulle bow under the chin, a dotted tulle veil and a fringed silk or velvet sunshade, sometimes with a jointed handle of elaborately carved ivory, composed what was thought a suitable toilet for this daily circuit between wilderness and waves.'[37]

Newport matrons created a society in which meticulous attention was paid to clothes and social rituals. Bostonian ladies regarded the New York belles at Newport as too rich and too inclined to flaunt their expensive clothes. 'Some of the New Yorkers are very rich,' wrote the Appleton sisters of Boston in 1834, 'and dress too much for good taste, at least in a place like this. A gay widow appears every morning at breakfast with a fresh pair of white kid gloves.'[38] Newport fashion demanded that a lady change her outfits about nine times a day. 'First, we put on a dress to dress in. Then we are ready for breakfast. After that we dress for the beach, then for the bath, then for dinner, then for the drive, then for the ball, and then for the bed. If that isn't being put through a regular course of dimity and diamonds, then I am no judge of such performances.' It was estimated that a lady needed at least twenty gowns for the Newport season, costing no less than $500 apiece.[39]

The ritual began with a loose-fitting calf-length chemise, followed by a corset with back lacing, and a light corset cover. The best corsets were French and were available in a wide range of materials and fittings. There was a short corset for wear with evening dresses or riding, and models designed for stout figures with extra abdominal support. Prices at Lord & Taylor's in the 1880s, varying by weight of bone, quality of the materials, stitching and embroidery, ran from $1.25 for Thompson's 'glove-fitting' model to $10 for a made-to-measure 'Imperial.' The under petticoat, fastened at the waist, was worn above the corset cover, with as many as six being worn at any given time. The introduction of the hoop petticoat relieved the need for multiple petticoats. By the mid-1850s the cage crinoline, with the use of lightweight steel bands, had largely supplanted the use of buckram, whalebone, and horsehair to hold a skirt at a fashionable distance from the legs, without adding weight or bulk. The over petticoat with its neatly embroided hem, followed. Then the dress itself, worn with gloves and a hat fastened beneath the ear with a colored ribbon. A cloak or mantle would have been worn in foul weather, and a color-coordinated umbrella completed the outfit of a fashionably dressed lady.

39. Edith Wharton.

Fernand Paillet's miniature of Edith Wharton (Marié collection) was painted in 1890, when Wharton was twenty-eight. She had been married to Edward Wharton for five years, and moved in the highest social circles in Newport and New York. Her first book, *The Decoration of Houses*, written with Ogden Codman, Jr., appeared in 1897.

At Bailey's Beach, Mrs. James Kernochan, sister of Pierre Lorillard, wore bathing shoes, a black blouse, black pantaloons, a full black skirt, a jacket with billowing sleeves, and a large Mother Hubbard bonnet. She was an apparition, suggested Richard O'Connor, 'to frighten off any cruising sharks.' (The concluding scene of Kate Chopin's *The Awakening* [1899], when a naked Edna Pontellier enters the sea, embraced by its sensuous touch, would have seemed particularly scandalous in an age when women bathed in outfits like Mrs. Kernochan's.)

Other aspects of social life were regulated with equally sharp attention. The paying of a call was expected after every social visit. For Wharton the 'onerous

and endless' business of calling scarcely left time for other activities. In her mother's day, a footman would inquire if the hostess was at home. If she was, the customary visit lasted precisely a half-hour. Her own generation tried to emancipate themselves from this tedious ritual by depositing cards with the upper left-hand corner turned down (which indicated that no personal visit had been possible) and departing without asking for the hostess. Unseemly acts, like the presentation by the Prince de Joinville of gold chains to every lady he danced with at Newport in 1838, were noted and deplored. Even the daily round of shopping was infused with formality: when Mrs. Thomas Hitchcock, wife of a New York lawyer and newspaper proprietor, called at a florist's shop, accompanied by her maid and her footman, she would sit primly in the coupé while her servants bought the desired flowers. William Dean Howells, who enjoyed his summer vacations as long as he and his wife Elinor did not have to go to Newport, felt that formality was itself gendered. Women sought it out. American men, Howells argued, 'are everywhere impatient of form. It burdens and bothers them, and they like to throw it off whenever they can.' An extreme formality was the social expression of the resort's matronly ethos.[40]

Among the cottagers there were undoubted social leaders, such as Julia Ward Howe, Ward McAllister's cousin, who was the head of the resort's Town and Country Club. With a membership restricted to fifty families, including Professor Alexander Agassiz, the architect R.M. Hunt, Mrs. John LaFarge, the novelist Dr. S. Weir Mitchell, the writer Thomas W. Higginson—and the daughters of Moses Lazarus, the Jewish sugar merchant from New York who built a cottage on Bellevue Avenue in 1870—the Town and Country met once a week in the season for scientific, cultural, and educational entertainments. Mrs. Howe, ever the do-gooder, organized readings at Hunt's studio in Newport for charitable purposes. A public reading of her 'Battle Hymn of the Republic' seldom failed to sell tickets and stir the assembled cottagers. The historian George Bancroft, who summered in Newport, occasionally could be prevailed upon to chair a meeting, or introduce a notable guest speaker. Visits from distinguished foreigners, such as Lord and Lady Amberley and writers like Dicey and James Bryce, provided occasions for hospitable entertaining. The venerable Redwood Library on Touro Street, established in 1730, was 'remarkably rich in classical and theological works' but by the 1830s and 1840s lack of interest in that kind of institution led to a decline. The 'culture' which thrived at Newport combined entertainment with self-improvement.[41]

The 1880s saw an important social transition at Newport. Summer dances open to 'general society,' rather in the spirit of the old City Assemblies, had traditionally been held at the Ocean Hotel, which with 600 beds was the largest in Newport. Private entertaining largely took the form of smaller lunches and

dinners. By the late 1880s the wealthier cottagers brought to the resort an expectation of private balls and 'state' dinners on a lavish scale as regular features of Newport social life. When the custom of eight o'clock dinners arrived, any little remaining informality was lost, and the strict decorum which prevailed on Beacon Hill and Fifth Avenue was confirmed at the cottages. The 'ball-giving mania' had so taken hold in Newport that one commentator humorously noted the plight of socially ambitious hostesses: 'there is hardly room for all the postulants who desire to entertain their guests in this troublous and very expensive manner. It is said that certain ladies are waiting patiently for a little break in the steady downpour of festivities, in the hope that they may secure a clear evening. Even in crowded Newport, there is not room for two full-fledged balls on the same night.'[42]

McAllister cherished the 'select little community' at Newport which 'the most charming people in the country' had formed. The resort's tone was becoming increasingly aristocratic. 'Newport has been basking in the sunshine of nobility and aristocracy this last fortnight,' wrote Charles Eliot Norton, '—and (whisper it not) this sunshine has produced an unusual growth of snobbishness,—for we take after our ancestors on the other side in this . . .'.[43]

Julia Ward Howe gave a distinct tone of Boston and its earnestness to Newport life. 'We do not like idle inheritors here,' she wrote. 'Our seriousness is sometimes complained of, usually by people whose jests and pleasantries fail to amuse us. Let us not apologize for this, nor envy any nation its power of trifling and of *persiflage*. We have mighty problems to solve; great questions to answer. The fate of the world's future is concerned in what we shall do or leave undone.'[44] Her cousin McAllister's entertainments came largely without improving lectures. He attended to the quality of the food, the choice of wines, and to the sybaritic pleasures of *alfresco* champagne picnics which became immensely popular. 'My dear friend,' he recalled Mrs. Maturin Livingston imploring, 'we are all dying for a picnic. Can't you get one up for us?' The guests each contributed a dish and brought a bottle of chilled champagne. McAllister bustled around, arranging everything. He would rent a nearby farmhouse, and send carpenters in advance to put up a dancing floor. Servants were hired and musicians booked. Men were placed along the route to direct the guests arriving in a procession of carriages from a central meeting point on Narragansett Avenue. The local florists were ransacked for the most attractive seasonal flowers. When McAllister entertained at his own farm to the north of Newport, he engagingly admitted in his memoirs that he rented a picturesque selection of sheep and cows for the occasion. (Yet more good advice on ways to please his wealthy guests.) Everyone enjoyed a waltz while the wine chilled and food was prepared, and then he would invite 'our Society queen' to lead the procession to the banquet which followed.

The Belmont problem

> . . . the city is distressed by prosperity
> —Dr. Samuel Osgood (1866)[45]

McAllister's choice of a 'society queen,' a little ritual at his picnics, placed him in the gracious position of acknowledging the social pre-eminence of Mrs. August Belmont, the former Caroline Perry, daughter of Commodore Matthew Calbraith Perry, and niece of Commodore Oliver Hazard Perry. A naval hero of the opening of Japan in the previous decade, Commodore Perry was a native of Newport, where for years the Belmonts had returned to take their summer holidays. It was in New York that the ambiguities of the social position of August Belmont were most intricate.

40. Caroline Perry (Mrs. August Belmont).

Mrs. August Belmont, *née* Caroline Perry, was photographed by Mora in costume for a *bal masqué*. She was the undoubted 'Queen of High Life' in the 1860s and 1870s.

41. August Belmont.

August Belmont was a leading financier, politician, and prominent figure in the 'fast set.' 'He is small in stature,' remarked a contemporary, 'with a typical German face, and more than the typical German geniality of temperament and manner.'

It was as a representative man of new money in the metropolis that the career of Belmont seemed most problematic.[46] There was about him one contradiction after another: he married into the old Yankee aristocracy, but was a power in the Democratic Party. Marriage made him welcome in society; politics cast him into the outer darkness. His entertaining was sophisticated and worldly, and his house, designed by the English architect Frederick Draper, was a highly admired example of Italianesque domestic architecture, carried out with quiet and gracious dignity.[47] On the other hand, Belmont, whose real name was Schönberg, and who came from a one-horse village in the Rhenish Palatinate, was a non-observant Jew, who had converted to Christianity (it was assumed) for social reasons. Raised in the Jewish quarter of Frankfurt when he was orphaned at the age of eight, Belmont was apprenticed to the Rothschilds' bank at fifteen. Known in New York as the financial representative of the Rothschilds, his status was actually highly ambiguous, not least in the eyes of the Rothschilds. They had sent him across the Atlantic in 1837 to take stock of the American situation and then proceed to Havana.

While the London and Paris branches of the Rothschilds' bank debated somewhat testily the future place, if any, of America in their financial plans, Belmont installed himself in an office at 78 Wall Street, and announced his determination to remain where he was. Denounced as 'stupid' and an 'ass' in letters from James de Rothschild, and regarded as thoroughly unreliable, nonetheless Belmont persuaded the family to pay him a salary of £500, and grant him a credit facility of £10,000 on the family's London bank. When they tried to rein him in, Belmont threatened to commence business with other banking houses. Rothschilds never trusted Belmont, though nervously agreed, on his recommendation, to loan the United States government fifteen million dollars to pay compensation to Mexico under the Treaty of Guadalupe Hidalgo.

To New Yorkers, Belmont seemed a mysteriously powerful figure, with untold resources at his command. In the Rothschild banks in London and Paris, he was altogether a more exasperating figure, regularly accused of exceeding his powers. His was a 'singular' position, wrote Alphonse de Rothschild in 1848, 'which is at once semi-dependent and semi-independent, simultaneously that of an agent and a correspondent.' Belmont's frustration with the Rothschilds poured out in letters to his younger sister Babette: 'What provokes them more than my independent manners,' he wrote in 1849, 'is that I have made a fortune for myself with which I can live comfortably and happily anywhere I like. These gentlemen want me to be dependent on them and they want to profit from my services and experience as long as it is convenient for them and then they'll show me the door as soon as it suits them.'[48]

In every court in Europe there were such money men seeking to rise from the mere possession of great wealth to yet higher rungs of honor and prestige. A small number, like the Jewish banker Gerson Bleichröder at the Prussian court in Berlin, might achieve a patent of hereditary nobility. But there was no one faintly comparable to Bleichröder's patron, Bismarck, in the democratic and intensely commercial culture of New York. Other financiers of modest social background found, for a time, the front doors of New York hostesses firmly closed against them. If there was no Bismarck in New York, nor was there a Prince of Wales, hobnobbing with Jewish capitalists and reveling in the company of London's *nouveaux riches*. Lady Paget, daughter of Mrs. Paran Stevens, complained that the Prince shared 'the same taste as the Semites, the same love of pleasure and comfort.' For all the pride in which certain elements in society delighted in all-out resistance to the parvenu, and an undercurrent of anti-Semitism, the British experience suggested that the old aristocracy could not, in any coherent sense, resist new money. Belmont's wealth and eminence were a very large and very complicated statement that in New York, no less than in London, it was money, and not family or tradition, which was in the ascendant.[49]

McAllister sententiously wrote in his memoir that at the end of the Civil War European tastes and fashions were warmly welcomed in New York. 'The French *chef* then literally, for the first time, made his appearance, and artistic dinners replaced the old-fashioned, solid repasts of the earlier period.' In his coded way, McAllister was referring to Belmont. After resigning from his diplomatic position at The Hague in 1857, Belmont returned to New York bringing with him the first French chef to be employed in a private home. There were, McAllister noted, not more than a half-dozen men in the city who spent as much $60,000 each year in entertaining. Belmont was unquestionably at the head of those who were prepared to spend and spend and spend. The rich were proudly flaunting their wealth:

> Our dresses and our diamonds were as rich and costly as any aristocrat's; our equipages as splendid; our residences as palatial; our servants as gayly liveried. Here in New York we have been giving dinners, soirees, receptions and fetes champetre which princes could not outrival, and which princes attended. We have been flashing about in coaches and carriages drawn by blooded horses. We have been dining, and wineing and pampering ourselves.[50]

It was Belmont and his crowd who led the way in 'dining and wineing.'

Thanks to his example, the fast set around Belmont which included William Travers and Leonard Jerome egged each other on in competitive display. Entertainments at Jerome's new house at Madison Square were marvels of luxury and elaborate decoration. On one evening, guests were greeted by the Roman extravagance of a fountain of champagne, and one of eau-de-Cologne. Jerome, Travers, and Belmont boldly competed to host the most elaborate dinner parties. When Jerome placed a gold bracelet with a jeweled pendant in every lady's napkin, Belmont topped this extravagance with a platinum bracelet. Those with less money than Belmont and his friends deplored such vulgar excesses, but their example worked its way insidiously into the central nervous system of the aristocracy. From Belmont New York learned that aristocrats entertained largely, and were generous in their hospitality. Few could resist following their example.

Belmont's mansion on Fifth Avenue struck visitors as 'the most splendid and showy in the city.'[51] To William Howard Russell, corespondent of *The Times* who arrived in New York in March 1861 to cover the unfolding secession crisis, theirs was

> an elegant house—I use the word in its real meaning—with pretty statues, rich carpets, handsome furniture, and a gallery of charming Meissoniers and genre pieces; the saloons admirably lighted—a fair fine large suite, filled

with the prettiest women in the most delightful toilettes, with a proper fringe of young men, orderly, neat, and well turned-out, fretting against the usual advanced posts of turbaned and jeweled dowagers, and provided with every accessory to make the whole good society; for there was wit, sense, intelligence, vivacity . . ..[52]

The Belmonts knew how to live well. Mrs. Belmont's undated photo album, in the New York Public Library, is worth perusing. Beneath each of the ninety photos carefully mounted in the album was the subject's name, beginning with 'S.M. L'empereur des Français' and 'L'imperatrice Eugénie,' including composers (Rossini, Verdi), painters (Horace Vernet), generals (Maréchal Pelissier, Le General de Chasseloup Laubat), politicians (Lord Palmerston, Garibaldi, Thiers, Lord John Russell), Pope Pius IX, dozens of French aristocrats, members of the Bonaparte family, and, at the end, August Belmont standing with a cane and a hat, and Mrs. Belmont, in a conventional pose by Disdéri, sitting reading a book. How grand the Belmonts were! No one casually examining their handsome photo album, on display on a parlor table, could have any doubt that they, too, were aristocrats. The fact that such cartes-de-visite could be bought from photographic studios in Paris convicts the Belmonts of nothing more than presumption—a condition which was reaching epidemic proportions in New York. The album was a class symbol, designed to maintain solidarity with the aristocracy, and influence the judgment others made of the Belmonts.[53]

Their entertaining in New York made a stunning assertion of wealth. At each telling the luxury grew more extravagant, the numbers of guests swelled, the servants' livery became more princely. New York soberly believed that the Belmonts could sit 200 guests at table, each attended by a footman in maroon and scarlet Belmont livery, with dinner served on gold plates. 'Twenty years ago we saw an English servant hooted in the streets of New York, because he wore the badge of his master;' wrote an observer in 1861, 'now liveried flunkies, natives of these states, are as common here as pretty girls and women are.'[54] By personal example, Belmont was leading society towards an aristocratic future. His 'demi-d'Aumont,' a calèche pulled by four horses, two of which had postillions, was reputed to be the first carriage of its kind in America. His landau and broughams, his T carts and coaches, were always the last word in English build. Belmont's fine horses and elegant carriages first made New Yorkers envious, and then anxious to emulate. Red carpets were rolled out when guests arrived at the great Belmont mansion on Fifth Avenue.

McAllister felt that such men exercised a malignant influence over society. Critics, whether of Belmont's wealth, his visibility, his politics, or his (ancestral) Jewishness, feared that such men, if unchecked, would debauch public

42. Belmont's mansion, 109 Fifth Avenue, on the north-east corner of Fifth Avenue and 18th Street.

The Belmont mansion at contained the first private ballroom in the city. There was a picture gallery with a skylight (to the right of the picture). The entertaining of the Belmonts set new standards for lavish expenditure.

virtue, and mark the final loss of Republican simplicity. So much had his reputation come to embody the negative aspect of great wealth, that in 1858, when George Templeton Strong first met Belmont, he was surprised to find the man 'pleasant and free from any offensive millionaire-isms.'[55]

Nowhere was Belmont's reputation more problematic for New Yorkers than in relation to his highly visible role in the Democratic Party. The 'Tweed Ring,' the Tammany Hall political machine, and its boss William Tweed, which was in control of the city's finances from 1866, had managed to steal everything that wasn't nailed down. Driven from office after the great frauds were exposed in 1871, the instrument of that large act of political cleansing was a tough-minded Committee of Seventy, led by insurgent Democrats, Republican lawyers, and city merchants. Belmont was not, politically or any other way, in sympathy with such reformers, and saw them as little more than a vehicle for his party's enemies.

In theory, the fall of Tweed left Belmont among the victors in the city's political warfare. Tweed had been his enemy within the party, and had repeatedly tried to unseat Belmont from his position as chairman of the Democratic National Committee. With Tweed expelled from Tammany Hall, Belmont was in a position to win election as a Sachem, the title reserved for leading 'braves' in the Democratic organization. But in the previous decade Belmont had worked closely with Tweed, and was tainted by his association with the Ring. On October 27, 1870, Belmont appeared on the platform at a great rally at Tammany Hall, defending Tweed against attacks which had been appearing in the *New York Times*. One of the members of the Ring, the mayor, A. Oakey Hall, was standing for re-election in November. As a personal friend

Belmont would not desert him. It was the kind of thing which political enemies remembered. Belmont provided respectable cover for Tweed's Viaduct Railway Company, which secured legislative approval to build an enormous stone viaduct or arcade across the city to carry an elevated railway. It was one of Tweed's most outrageous schemes. Belmont had even invited Tweed to his home. 'My dear Tweed,' he wrote on January 31, 1871, 'I sent you a note last week, asking you to do me the honor of dining with me next Thursday at seven o'clock. Not having received your reply permit me to ask you whether I can count upon having the pleasure of your company. Yours very truly, August Belmont.'[56] Pleasure? Honor! What malicious delight this letter would have given to those who regarded Belmont as much an enemy of civic virtue as Tweed himself.

However useful Tweed found the city's wealthy men, it was widely recognized on Wall Street that the public finances of New York to some extent depended on Belmont. Much of the revenue for the city's activities (and the Tweed thefts) was funded by the sale of city bonds. New York's credit was sustained on the European exchanges by the Rothschilds. The Seligman family underwrote a successful sale of two million dollars' worth of New York City bonds in 1869. When the Seligmans declined a further issue of two million in April 1870, the London and Frankfurt branches of the Rothschild Bank and the Discounts Gesellschaft underwrote the issue. The judgment of their representative, Belmont, on Tweed's conduct of the city's affairs was decisive. The Astor Committee and Belmont shielded Tweed from the serious claim that the city's debt was out of control.[57] During the Tweed years the dividing line which society had long insisted upon between crooks, parvenus, and gentlemen grew more problematic. Tainted by his association with Tweed, Belmont's social position remained ambiguous. His wife, however, known by her nickname 'Tiny,' enjoyed the highest status in New York society.

The hauteur and grandness of company manners might, however briefly, be put aside for McAllister's little fêtes and moonlight farmhouse dances at Newport, where men and women enjoyed an idyll of rural freedom. McAllister's guests 'frisked about' like 'lambs gamboling in the fields.'[58] He could take such risks because he possessed a strong sense of being part of a privileged 'inner circle' surrounded by 'newcomers' seeking invitations to such entertainments. He wanted his guests to feel that they were all engaged upon a mutual enterprise. Secure within the elite, everyone was placed on the same footing. Etiquette required guests to regard every other guest with a presumption of social equality. When guests meet at a party, wrote Mrs. Longstreet, '[i]ntroductions should be considered wholly unnecessary to a pleasant conversation. . . . A lady or gentleman must conduct himself or herself, while remaining in the house, as if there were no more exalted society than that which is present.' There might be rivalry over whose house was finer, whose carriage was more elegant, or whose servants wore the handsomest livery; McAllister wanted to strengthen the sense that they shared common values and recognized the need, growing more urgent with each passing year, to maintain the strictest exclusivity. If you were not of the inner circle, and were a newcomer, McAllister wrote, 'it took the combined efforts of all your friends' backing and pushing to procure an invitation for you. For years, whole families sat on the stool of probation, awaiting trial and acceptance, and many were then rejected, but once received, you were put on an intimate footing with all.'[59]

In defense of exclusivity McAllister articulated a *raison d'être* for society. By enhancing the sense of a corporate identity within the 'inner circle,' McAllister sought to protect society from the unwelcome attentions of newcomers. The great perennial anxiety about the parvenu, which provided the plot of numerous popular plays and serious novels, suggests that McAllister's objective was simple, and circumspect: he sought to raise the consciousness of the class to which he devoted himself, and to make that heightened consciousness the inner principle of a reorganization of society itself. He accepted the notion that he would serve that reorganization, and guide it. But only in Newport did he occupy such an advantageous position. When the Prince of Wales visited New York in 1860, McAllister secured an invitation to the reception and dinner, but was not invited to join Hamilton Fish, Luther Bradish, Robert B. Minturn, and George Templeton Strong and others on the reception committee. At one point in the evening when McAllister sought to gain early entry to the supper room, he encountered John Jacob Astor III who was guarding the door near the royal dais. 'He bid me wait my turn.' At that moment, humiliated and rebuffed, McAllister's true relationship to the 'inner circle' stood revealed.[60]

He began to spend more time in New York after the Civil War. Underlying the bland sense in McAllister's memoir that the city seemed a different place was a torrent of social and economic change. There were forces at work which were turning upside down the aristocratic world he had encountered in the 1840s. The gentlemanly milieu of the aristocrats had now to venture upon a world in which all the old navigational aids had vanished. At the Union League Club just over a month after the assassination of President Lincoln, George Templeton Strong spent an hour looking over scrapbooks of newspaper articles illustrating the course of the war. He felt that the impassioned words of 1861, now read in faded newspaper clippings, seemed strange, like 'the records of some remote age and of a people wholly unlike our own.'[61]

The change which had the greatest immediate consequence for the aristocracy was money. New York was literally swirling with cash. Prices rocketed, but even inflated costs seemed to have no effect upon the *ton*. 'Ladies now sweep along Broadway with dresses which cost hundreds of dollars,' noted the *Herald*, 'their bonnets alone represent a price which a few years since would more than have paid for an entire outfit. Silks, satins and laces have risen in price to an extent which would seem beyond the means of any save millionaires, and yet the sale of these articles is greater than ever.'[62] The holdings of the New York banks had risen from $80 million in the early 1860s to $225 million in 1865. When the Open Board of Stock Brokers merged in 1869 with the New York Stock & Exchange Board, forming the New York Stock Exchange, membership increased from 533 to 1,060. There were many more millionaires in the city than there had ever been before. The visible signs of this rapidly expanding wealth lay in the explosion of luxury consumption. In 1865 the British stock promoter Sir Morton Peto, MP, hosted a dinner for 100 tea and coffee merchants at Delmonico's. The city's press carried a full description of the feast: in addition to the meal and drinks, there were rare flowers, embroidered cushions for the guests, and select arias sung by the reigning prima donna at the Academy of Music. The evening cost Sir Morton $20,000. On his return to England, he published *The Resources and Prospects of America* (1866), an enthusiastic and heavily documented account of the economic prospects of the Union at the end of the Civil War. Social life had never seemed more frantic. 'At no time in many years,' wrote an editorial pen in the *New York Times*, 'have the houses of entertainment been so thronged, at no time have the various public resorts been so gay as at present. Wallacks Theater, the New-York Theater, the Olympic, Winter Garden, the Minstrels, the Concert Halls and the Brooklyn Academy of Music, are literally packed with the residents of our city, and the strangers who fill our hotels and overcrowd our boarding houses.'[63]

That year the Wall Street speculator Leonard Jerome bought hundreds of acres in Fordham for a race track, and built a grandstand with seats for 8,000. He leased the racecourse to the newly formed American Jockey Club, and agreed to underwrite an annual loss of $25,000. In response to press attacks on the very idea of horse racing, Jerome banned the sale of liquor at the track. The public well understood that the racecourse was for their pleasure, and acted accordingly. Enterprising speculators

> got up vehicles of all kinds to convey jovial parties thither. Farmer wagons, market wagons, butcher carts, express wagons, &c., &c., *ad libitum*, were fitted up with temporary seats, and passengers taken at so much per head. In contrast with these, were the stylish turn-outs of the moneyed men: phaetons, four-in-hands, barouches, tandem teams, carriages, drays, dog carts, sulkies, light wagons, &c., &c., were spinning past each other on the Bloomingdale road. Many of them were freighted with bevies of beauties,

and the male friends and relatives. The occupants of all the vehicles seemed imbued with the spirit of the occasion, and even the ladies entered into the subject with spirit and animation.[64]

General Grant was the guest of honor in the 'royal box' on the first race meeting in September 1866, and prominently seen among the throng were Boss Tweed, Jim Fisk, the pugilist and gambler John Morrissey, and Josie Woods, keeper of the city's most expensive bordello. (The city's 'shadow' or 'gaslight' life had never been more brazen, or more visible.) The enthusiasm for horse racing in New York brought the world of 'gaslight' and 'sunlight' out upon the roads, turning Central Park and the road to Jerome Park 'into race-courses for the Fifth Avenue "silk-slingers" and the *demi monde* fashionables. Where you find one, you will invariably find the other. Fashionable gamblers nudge fashionable pulpit beaters, and literary celebrities "turn out" for thieves and aldermen. . . . The city generally seems crazy with excitement, and is evidently bent on a spree of vast dimensions.'[65] Those who recalled an older New York, and who cherished its social niceties and refinement, found 1865 a difficult year to endure. New York never again seemed *their* city. Mrs. John King Van Rensselaer feared and detested the new world which these immense fortunes were making, and despised the newcomers who boldly set up 'a standard of their own and a society of their own making.'[66]

The Patriarchs

> The Patriarchs—they are myself.
> —Ward McAllister (1897)[67]

Studies of the wealthiest Americans by Frederic Cople Jaher have shown that from mid-century the possessors of 'old' fortunes in New York were 'engulfed by a massive tide of newcomers.' The figure of engulfment was true: New York was by the standards of an earlier age a 'Foreign City,' with increasing numbers of newcomers, from elsewhere in America as well as from Ireland, Germany, and other European countries. In the state census of 1845, 36 percent of New Yorkers were foreign-born. By 1865, that proportion had risen to 43 percent. In addition to feeling threatened economically by new money, the New York wealthy struggled to make a coherent response to the threats they perceived to their established social position. Unlike the world over which the Brahmins of Boston and the aristocracy of Philadelphia and Charleston presided, New York was a larger and richer community, but its wealthy had weaker roots in the city. The millionaires of Boston were far more likely to have been born in Massachusetts than the wealthy of New York were to have roots in New York

City or State. The proportion of 'outsiders' was higher in New York than in other settled genteel communities, and newcomers found New York less insular, and more porous, if not noticeably more welcoming. In addition to being more geographically diverse, fortunes in New York seemed more fluid and far less stable. There were fewer rich men in New York in 1892 whose fortunes went back even three generations than there had been half a century earlier. The picture Jaher paints of the situation at the end of the Gilded Age is one of disintegration and decline, of diminished commercial power, vanished social leadership, and the inevitable consequences for great fortunes of divorce and fast living. The perspective of Jaher's argument is Spenglerian: new sources of wealth, and men more determined and fecund, made inevitable the decline of the antebellum aristocracy.[68]

Might another outcome have been possible for the group described by Jaher as the 'Old Guard'? Can we imagine a counter-factual narrative of nineteenth-century New York society, in which the aristocracy did not decline, but throughout the Gilded Age enjoyed heightened national and local prominence?[69] Such an account would have seemed plausible to many contemporaries. However conscious the possessors of old money were of challenges to their position, the idea that theirs was to be the generation of New York wealthy to witness the final dissolution of 'Old New York' would have been greeted with incredulity.

Although the city was crawling with new wealth, the continuing vigor of the old Knickerbocker leadership of the St. Nicholas Society, the long waiting list for membership in the Union Club and the Knickerbocker, the wealth and prestige of Grace Church and crowds at the Horse Show, were all signs of an elite which was both confident and thriving. The world of New York and Newport which Edith Wharton portrayed in her memoir *A Backward Glance* (1934), was 'safe, monotonous, and rigidly circumscribed, with scarcely a word about literature or music or art', and was inhabited by men like her old friend Egerton Winthrop ('never, I believe, have an intelligence so distinguished and a character so admirable been combined with interests for the most part so trivial'). Her biographers, and the critics following in their wake, have largely accepted Wharton's portrait of New York society. In reality, it was not quite such a cultural desert. Jaher dismisses the crowd around Mrs. Astor and Mrs. Stuyvesant Fish as 'intellectually barren', but he has not, in this particular case, looked at the evidence.[70] In the generation after the Civil War there was an aristocratic vein of authorship in New York. Novels, plays and short stories appeared by William Waldorf Astor, John Jacob Astor IV, Lloyd Stevens Bryce, Hobart Chatfield Chatfield-Taylor, F. Marion Crawford, Mrs. Schuyler Crowninshield, Mrs. Van Rensselaer Cruger, Caroline King Duer, Mrs. Burton Harrison, Amélie Rives, and Mrs. M.E.W. Sherwood. There were distinguished

THE PATRIARCHS, 1872

John Jacob Astor III
Royal Phelps
William Astor
Edwin A. Post
De Lancey Kane
Archibald Gracie King
Ward McAllister
Lewis Morris Rutherfurd
George Henry Warren
Robert G. Remsen
Eugene A. Livingston
William C. Schermerhorn
William Butler Duncan
Francis R. Rives
Edward Templeton Snelling
Maturin Livingston
Lewis Colford Jones
Alexander Van Rensselaer
John W. Hamersley
Walter Langdon
Benjamin S. Welles
Frederick G. d'Hauteville
Frederick Sheldon
C.C. Goodhue
William R. Travers

writings on architecture and New York history by Mariana Griswold Van Rensselaer. Wharton's point needs to be reconsidered. The literary career of Theodore Roosevelt belongs to this world. Wharton comes late, and sardonically, to this world of aristocratic authorship.

Similarly, rather than Theodore Roosevelt being a maverick aristocrat, dirtying his hands in New York politics, in the political careers of William Waldorf Astor, Cortlandt Schuyler Van Rensselaer, Perry Belmont, Levi Parsons Morton, Hamilton Fish, and W.C. Whitney there were signs that the studied posture of indifference to public life was only part of the truth. Despite the near-universal belief, in the words of Howard Crosby, that politics in New York was 'run by rowdies and criminals, with whom decent men cannot associate, except to be defiled,' the career of Theodore Roosevelt suggests that the box-holders at the opera, members of the elite clubs, and the 'Four Hundred' itself, were far from turning their collective back on public life. Under the leadership of such men and women, civic cultural institutions which have permanently shaped the city, such as the Metropolitan Opera and Metropolitan Museum of Art, were founded. In this they were at one with the elites in Boston and Chicago for whom the opera houses, Art Institute, Museum of Fine Arts and the symphony orchestras were expressions of cultural values, and an assertion of the cultural leadership, of a native-born Protestant elite. High culture was *their* culture, and was in every case surrounded by rituals of suitable dress and behavior, and situated in large, impressive civic structures, which emphasized the ability of the benefactors to control 'high culture' on their own terms.[71]

The influence of the aristocrats extended to many aspects of New York life, from architecture and interior decoration to entertaining and fashion. Their benevolence sent orphans to new homes in the Midwest, established libraries and hospitals, and built churches. The influence of the city's aristocrats shaped the tone of social relations. Good manners seemed increasingly to require an ever narrower 'correctness' in social intercourse. Frigidity of demeanor was recommended as an expression of social refinement. Ladies were advised to go through the formalities of an introduction 'with the most bland expression . . . yet insensibly [to] convey to the introduced an impression that a further intimacy would not be agreeable.' A contributor to a lady's magazine in 1871 remarked that 'It has apparently struck some women in the society of our new country . . . that they appear to stand well by being disagreeable—that an air of hauteur and rudeness is becoming and aristocratic.'[72]

In that aristocratic counter-history of New York, the Patriarchs would receive a close examination. They represented the pinnacle of the city's aristocracy. The Patriarchs gave social expression to the determination to repel unwanted change. Railroad millionaires, freebooting stock speculators, and proprietors of powerful newspapers were all building mansions on Fifth Avenue; their wives and daughters shopped at Tiffany's and A.T. Stewart's. Such forceful men could not be chased away by setting ever higher standards of conspicuous expenditure. They demanded admission into the exclusive clubs, boxes at the opera, and invitations to the most prestigious balls, and only the idea of society as represented by the Patriarchs, and its expectation of refined manners and breeding, could act as a minimal restraint. If wealthy men like Gould and Vanderbilt were indifferent to society, their wives and children had far more at stake.

The irony is that the Patriarchs became a device by which changing relations within the upper strata of New York society were managed and accommodated. Virtually forgotten by historians like Pessen and Jaher in their discussion of the nineteenth-century elites, the Patriarchs embodied the aristocrats' confident assertion of leadership; the society also soberly registered the realities of wealth which were undermining the ability of the Old Guard to keep new money at bay.

There is a need for an interpretive distinction about appearances. Outwardly, the association preserved a highly ritualized and repetitive life, and much of what follows in this section is an attempt to explain how things were done at the Patriarchs, and why they were done in the same way, at the same time, and seemingly by the same people. Over three decades, McAllister's Patriarchs appeared to be a rock of tradition and continuity. In reality, the admission of Belmont, William Butler Duncan, the Vanderbilts and the like represented, in its purest form, graceful accommodation to the financial reality of the city's *nouveaux riches*. Much fuss was made about maintaining standards, while a cool realism prevailed when membership decisions were taken in the autumn at the start of the New York season. The trick was to maintain that placid outward appearance of continuity, while in practice accepting change. If the Patriarchs pretended to remain unchallengeably the same, the parvenu joined them in the maintenance of the illusion by building Fifth Avenue mansions, shopping at A.T. Stewart's and Tiffany's, worshiping at Grace Church, sending their children to Dodworth's Dancing Academy, dressing their wives in Worth gowns and enjoying the canvasback ducks at Delmonico's. When they entered a Patriarchs ball, they were, to outward appearances, indistinguishable from the other members.

Initiated and organized in the immediate aftermath of the overthrow of the Tweed Ring in 1871–2, the Patriarchs was explicitly an instrument of resistance to the bearers of new wealth. McAllister presents the society as a collective attempt to resist the handful of men with 'royal fortunes' who claimed a sovereign's prerogative 'to say whom society shall receive, and whom society shall shut out.' With Belmont's hospitality to Tweed in mind, the 'Belmont problem' was a nagging issue for McAllister's aristocratic project. A wealthy man in society could with impunity invite a Tweed or a gambler like John Morrissey into his home, and society was powerless to prevent it. 'All this,' McAllister wrote, 'many of us saw, and saw how it worked, and we resolved to band together the respectable element of the city, and by this union make such strength that no individual could withstand us.'[73] Further, as the discussion of the Belmont problem suggests, Tweed had compromised an extraordinary range of prominent capitalists from the city's upper crust. In social terms it was time, thought McAllister, to cleanse the stables. The origin of the Patriarchs thus ultimately lay in the ambiguous relations between the Tweed Ring and the city's wealthiest men.

Despite all the furious entertaining in the city in the decade after the Civil War, McAllister believed that there was no order, no central intelligence, to establish and maintain the values of heightened exclusivity upon which aristocratic society depended. He sensed that an individual, or even a small group such as that led by Belmont, could not possess the full authority of society. What was needed was a body small enough to be highly selective, and yet sufficiently representative of the leading families to be accepted as a social arbiter. What was needed, he argued in parlors and tea parties up and down Fifth Avenue, was for men of wealth and good family to take more seriously the responsibilities of their social position.

The need for an attitude of responsibility, of *noblesse oblige*, strongly appealed to reformers like Charles Loring Brace, founder of the Children's Aid Society, who lamented the fragmentation of city life, and the growing divisions which kept the rich apart from the poor. He wanted to develop philanthropic organizations to provide a 'link of sympathy' between the classes, and found in John Jacob Astor III and his wife Augusta high-minded and wealthy benefactors. For all too many New Yorkers, Brace argued, society called for nothing more than an annual bout of entertaining, a grand ball once a year, or a party in the evening, where the crush of the crowd inevitably prevented anything like conversation. For the rest of the year the magnificent drawing rooms were shut up, cold and dark, and chance callers were received in a library, or a small closet off the hall. Brace wrote that New York commercial life had made social life nearly impossible. Despite having 'an abundance of intelligent, lively, agreeable men and women of the world,' there was great difficulty in getting them together. They were scattered, busy, distrait. 'After a while, having abjured balls and forsworn party suppers, they drop out of society, and one hardly knows where they are. We see them, indeed, at occasional meetings of a more important kind, and now and then at clubs, but to fairly pin them down to a table and "have a chat" with them, we seldom succeed. The consequence is, New York society exists, like her up-town districts, in a most broken and chaotic condition.'[74]

After the war McAllister held a series of subscription dinners and assemblies, with a committee of management of matrons of established social position. However successful, they were merely an addition to the social maelstrom of New York. Such ad hoc entertainments could not change the way society saw itself. In 1870 Archibald Gracie King, son and partner of the banker James Gore King, broke with precedent to give a private ball at Delmonico's. The success of the ball created a fashion for the use of public venues for private entertaining which McAllister rapidly seized upon. In the following year he abandoned hope that Newport, with its leading hostesses in control, might provide a corrective to the disorder of New York. His relationship with Mrs. Astor had deepened from admiration to a gushing adulation, and he continued to believe that women could provide the social basis for a redirection of society. But it may have been Mrs. Astor who helped McAllister see that a list of men, drawn not from the 'fast' set around Belmont and Jerome, but from the 'quiet representative men of this city,' would do far more to establish an institution to reconstruct the city's aristocracy.

McAllister shaped the Patriarchs' balls on two institutions which offered models for New York society. Almack's Assembly Rooms on King Street, St. James', London, was the strongest influence on his thinking. Founded by a Scot, William MacCall, in 1765, Almack's was a large, handsomely decorated ballroom where subscription balls and concerts were held. At the peak of its exclusiveness in the early nineteenth century, a committee of great ladies, a 'feminine oligarchy' of hostesses led by Lady Jersey, Lady Castlereagh, and the Princess Lieven, with the influential support of the Duke of Wellington, took control of the subscription list with the specific intention of excluding the mere possessors of wealth. Lady Jersey's fastidiousness and taste for luxury were proverbial, as was her insistence upon the meticulous observance of social rituals. 'Knowing that the eyes of all female exquisites were turned upon her, she changed every article of clothing from head to foot four times a day.' Her other accomplishments were of a modest nature. 'The Countess,' remarked an observer, 'did not excel in music; nor, if the truth must be told, did she excel in any accomplishment. Hers was an active but restless mind, which did not incline towards study.' Certain that a 'shadow' of mere wealth, the dreaded parvenus, was creeping over the aristocracy, she managed Almack's with an iron determination to keep out 'those sort of people!' She would distribute her vouchers for Almack's only to 'those who knew each other, and who suited each other, [who] enjoyed themselves in those far-famed rooms with a cordon of exclusion around the doors.' N.P. Willis, who had visited Almack's in 1839, came away persuaded that rumors of decline in the old exclusivity were untrue. In McAllister's family, attending Almack's was a cherished tradition.[75]

Another potential model for the Patriarchs was that of the Leiderkranz Balls in New York. The Leiderkranz was an 'expensive and exclusive' voluntary association of German-Americans, dominated by Oswald Ottendorfer, publisher of the *Staats-Zeitung*, and the piano manufacturer William Steinway. With its own *Halle* on East 4th Street, and a membership of 1,000 by 1869, the Leiderkranz expressed the emerging power of aristocratic clubs in the immigrant world. McAllister adopted the organization of the Leiderkranz, whose General Committee consisted of twenty-five members formed into subcommittees with responsibility for the masquerade, floor, reception, music, and the press. The Almack's idea of 'powerful women of influence' banding together for the purpose of getting up exclusive subscription balls, combined with the structure of the Leiderkranz, suggested a form of organization for the Patriarchs. Similar ideas for upper-class social control had been in circulation early in the 1860s, when George Templeton Strong was approached with an invitation to join twenty 'men about town' in a synod 'to take charge of polite society, regulate its interests, keep it pure, and decide who shall be admitted hereafter to "Bachelors' Balls" and other annual entertainments.'[76]

His first step was to draw together an executive committee of three, who would compile a list of twenty-five Patriarchs who would be invited to become subscribers for the season. The aim behind the selection was set out in McAllister's memoir. With a strong committee behind him, and control of arrangements in his own hands, McAllister hoped to exert a counter-pressure against the raw ostentation of the Belmont set. As the *New York Times* explained, the decision to hold the balls at Delmonico's would serve in some measure to restrain the excesses of the rich: 'It was also thought that the balls should be held in a public place in order that persons of moderate means could enjoy themselves and enjoy social privileges on the same footing as the richer element in New-York society.' The choice of the Patriarchs also suggested that McAllister had worked out something of a strategy. He sought to 'embrace' the old Colonial New Yorkers, and to welcome 'our adopted citizens' (by which he of course did not mean Irish or German immigrants, but rather the New Englanders and Southerners, like himself, men of good breeding who had settled in the city). In addition, there was room for 'men whose ability and integrity had won the esteem of the community.'

'We wanted money power,' McAllister wrote, 'but not in any way to be controlled by it.' Patriarchs were chosen not simply for their fitness; but according to an ideal of exclusivity. It was a firm but unwritten law that 'a Patriarch must be a married man and have a certain well-defined social position.' 'We knew then,' McAllister stated, 'that the whole secret of the success of these Patriarch Balls lay in making them select; in making them the most brilliant balls of each winter; in making it extremely difficult to obtain an invitation, and to make such invitations of great value; to make them the stepping-stone to the best New York society . . .'.[77]

The twenty-five Patriarchs (later raised to fifty) occupied the summit of New York society, yet, paradoxically, many of them were unknown to the wider community. The organization of the Patriarchs was that of a close corporation, complete with a seal featuring an old man with an unkempt beard. Each year the members were invited to renew their subscriptions. There were usually some who planned to be in Europe, or for whom there had been a bereavement or change in family circumstance (such as bankruptcy), which meant there was a small annual turnover of membership. The Patriarchs elected their own successors, and by the mid-1890s membership was strongly evolving towards hereditary tenure. A solid core of the Patriarchs in 1894—Hamersley, King, Astor, Fish, and Belmont—were the sons of Patriarchs from the 1870s. With a waiting list of 100 to join, it was easier to marry a Patriarch's daughter than to win election independently. The St. Cecilia Society in Charleston, which traced its origins back to a musical society founded in 1737, retained its exclusivity by allowing membership to be passed only from fathers to sons. Had it survived, it is quite possible that the Patriarchs would have become an hereditary association.[78]

The lines of intimacy and relationships between these men is suggestive. They were not, in 1872, among the richest men in New York, nor were they actively involved in cultural or political life, nor were they in any strict sense leading figures in the city's clubs. It would be understandable to assume that leaders of society would also be those who had taken leadership positions in the creation of important New York cultural institutions, like the Metropolitan Museum of Art when it was founded in 1870. Curiously, none of the Patriarchs in 1872 had been among the founding officers, trustees, or members of the executive committee of the museum. John Jacob Astor III was the only Patriarch to have been a member of the Committee of Seventy, which had so recently triumphed over the Tweed Ring. (Five of the Museum's twenty-four leaders joined the Committee of Seventy.) None of the presidents of the Union Club between 1872 and 1897, and only one of the vice-presidents, Frederick Sheldon, was a Patriarch. Of the sixty-six founding members of the Union League Club in 1863, only one man, Van Rensselaer, was a Patriarch in 1872. Eight of the original Patriarchs were members of the Century Association (John Jacob Astor, Duncan, Hamersley, Sheldon, Phelps, Rutherfurd, Schermerhorn, and Rives). By 1880, when the number of Patriarchs had increased to 47, the complete domination of club membership was clearer. They may not have been high officials in the clubs, but of the 47 Patriarchs, 27 were members of the Union Club, 18 were members of the Knickerbocker, nine of the Century, five of the University, four of the St.

Nicholas. The Calumet and Lotos clubs claimed one member each.[79] They constituted a curious and perhaps unprecedented kind of social leadership, contributing to the community only the example of their exclusivity.

The Patriarchs reflected the continuing importance of family connections in New York society. The Astors, led by John Jacob III and his younger brother William, sons of William Backhouse Astor, were the leading family group, which included Walter Langdon (the son of Dorothea Astor Langdon) and De Lancey Kane (great-grandson of the first John Jacob Astor, and one of McAllister's pall-bearers). At a stretch, Benjamin S. Welles belonged to the Astor mishpoche, having married Catherine Schermerhorn, Mrs. Astor's older sister. Close personal friends of the Astors included Duncan, a conservative Democratic banker and railroad tycoon, and Sheldon.

Family, friendships, and business connections largely determined membership of the Patriarchs for the two and a half decades of its existence. Duncan was a partner in the firm of Duncan & Sherman, at whose offices at 11 Pine Street the young J.P. Morgan began his career on Wall Street in 1857. John Jacob Astor III, Sheldon, and Rives were social friends of William C. Schermerhorn. Rutherfurd and Schermerhorn were trustees of Columbia College. D'Hauteville's father was a Swiss baron who had married a lady of some fortune from Boston. He had done equally well in a worldly sense, marrying Bessy Fish, the daughter of a Patriarch, Hamilton Fish, Secretary of State in the Grant administration. Knickerbocker families were represented by the two Livingstons, the Van Rensselaers, Schermerhorns, Remsens, and Rutherfurds. Of the 1880 Patriarchs, thirteen lived on Fifth Avenue and an additional seventeen lived on the blocks immediately east and west of Fifth. Three Patriarchs lived on Madison Avenue, two on Lexington Avenue, and two lived on Gramercy Park. Only two continued to live on Washington Square. The departure from the Bond Street area was complete. None lived below Washington Square. Geographically, the Patriarchs were a Fifth Avenue outfit.[80]

Within four years of the formation of the Patriarchs, the firm of Duncan, Sherman & Co. failed. (More precisely, the firm stopped payment of $227,857, and on the next day the partners transferred all of their property to an assignee. The resulting lawsuits dragged on for several years.) As part of the winding up of the partnership and sale of the remaining assets, 100 oil paintings and pieces of statuary belonging to William Butler Duncan (1830–1912) from his double mansion at numbers 12 and 13 Washington Square North were auctioned at the Leavitt Art Rooms. The list of items to be sold, and the prices they fetched, gives us a sense of the domestic décor of a Patriarch, not perhaps the wealthiest, but one who was certainly a figure of political presence. He was a man with social connections at the highest level in New York.

43. Mrs. William Butler Duncan.

Mrs. William Butler Duncan was the wife of a wealthy merchant (partner in Duncan, Sherman & Co.), an active Democratic Party politician, a founding member of the Manhattan Club, a supporter of the Bartholdi Memorial Fund, attender of Mrs. Astor's balls, member of the Patriarchs—and a bankrupt whose personal effects were sold at a public auction.

A long-standing Democrat, Duncan had been rumored as a possible Tammany nominee for mayor in September 1874. Duncan was principally a collector of French paintings, though none were regarded at the auction as being 'of very great merit.' The keynote of the sale was a pair of life-size paintings by Edouard Dubuffe, *The Departure* and *The Return*, portraying a peasant woman and the soldier she sends off to war, and joyously welcomes home ($1,525 each). Antoine Emile Plassen's *Taking a Nap* (a young lady asleep in a chair in her boudoir, with a poodle playing at her feet, $235), Lasalle's *The Wood Gatherers* (peasant children collecting faggots, $185), and Reynaud's *The Peasants* and *Beggar Boys* ($125 for both), reflected Duncan's largely sentimental taste and preference for pictures that told a story, with cheerful rural subjects which might appeal to the imagination of an ordinary person.[81]

Men of the Patriarchs did not think of themselves as rakes, and generally preferred that their homes were adorned with paintings which conformed to conventional standards. A comment about the taste of William Henry Vanderbilt, who refused to purchase any painting of a nude subject, suggests a widespread attitude. '[H]e had a natural delicacy which made him dislike anything bordering on the doubtful or prurient, hence there are no such pictures in his gallery.' The Brahmin aristocrat Edward W. Hooper, trustee of the Museum of Fine Arts in Boston, argued that nudes by Gustav Boulanger seemed to gratify 'a vicious taste for the display of mere nakedness. I am quite in favor of exhibiting *clean* nudes, and even some less clean if painted by very great men, or having a classical reputation.'[82]

The Duncan sale realized more than $15,000. It was, of course, a profound humiliation, but not an unfamiliar one in the lives of brokers and merchants in New York. In less than a year Duncan had bounced back. He was elected treasurer of the Manhattan Club, and later became president of the Mobile and Ohio Railroad. He was noted on Fifth Avenue for being the only American member of the Travellers Club in London. The Patriarchs did not hold ancient political grudges, but the memory of his attempt to effect a fusion of candidates in the presidential election of 1860 to defeat Lincoln, Duncan's (later repented) role during the Civil War as a leading Democratic friend of the South, left a bitterness among the city's hard-line Republicans. To George Templeton Strong, 'Willy' Duncan was 'vermin' like his fellow Democrats Ben and Fernando Wood and August Belmont. Duncan's name had surfaced in 1863 when the Union League Club was being formed. For Strong he was precisely the type of man 'against whom we are organizing ourselves.' 'I fear he is a snob and a "squirt,"' wrote Strong, who described Duncan as 'the dining partner of his banking house, and the toady of British aristocracy when they condescended to visit New York.' (Duncan entertained the Prince of Wales at his home on Fifth Avenue in 1860.) Being a snob, squirt, socialite, or toady was apparently insufficient reason to exclude Duncan from the Patriarchs. With all his faults, Duncan was rich, a party-giver and a man of affairs. He represented precisely the kind of compromised figure whom McAllister welcomed into the Patriarchs. When hostesses later denounced McAllister for the absence of true exclusivity at Patriarchs' balls, they may have been thinking of a figure like William Butler Duncan.[83]

The Patriarchs of 1872 did not enjoy 'royal fortunes.' With the inevitable exception of the Astors, they were possessors of independent means, but were not among the city's super-rich. In the 1880s, when J.P. Morgan, Bradley Martin, Cornelius Vanderbilt II, and Robert Goelet were elected to membership of the Patriarchs, sheer wealth was far more in evidence. The tax rolls for 1866–7 constructed quite a different aristocracy:

William B. Astor	$16,114,000
Wm. C. Rhinelander	$7,745,000

A.T. Stewart	$6,091,500
Peter and Robert Goelet	$4,417,000
James Lenox	$4,260,000
Peter Lorillard	$4,424,000
John David Wolfe	$3,997,000
M.M. Hendricks	$1,690,000
Rufus L. Lord	$1,500,000
C.V.S. Roosevelt	$1,346,000
TOTAL	$51,405,500 [84]

Such a list was heavily slanted towards land-owning wealth, but even among the city's great landlords the figures were misleading. The real value of the property owned by these men may have been double the ratable value, and the estimates wholly ignore income. William B. Astor's income in 1869 was $1,079,212. The great merchant prince, Alexander T. Stewart, reported an income of $3,019,218.[85]

The ten richest men, who between them owned a tenth of the city's entire taxable property, included no one who was a Patriarch in 1872, and several men, such as the bachelor recluse James Lenox, who had a perfect abhorrence of any form of social life. There were other factors which complicated the social position of wealthy men. Important judgments were still being made about the source of their wealth. Stewart's social ambitions had been blighted by a deep-seated contempt for shopkeepers among the city's social leaders. 'I buy my carpets from them,' remarked Mrs. Astor when planning the guest list for a ball, 'but then is that any reason why I should invite them to walk on them?' Mrs. Astor may have been thinking of the carpet merchant William Sloane, who emigrated to New York from Scotland in 1834, and whose son advantageously married a daughter of William Henry Vanderbilt. Similar sentiments served to exclude A.T. Stewart from society. 'No retail dealer, no matter how palatial his shop-front or how tempting his millions,' wrote Edith Wharton with some relish, 'was received in New York society until long after I was grown up.'[86] Similarly, exclusions were made upon other grounds, such as a reputation for social unconventionality or too close a proximity to people regarded as 'fast'—or worse. Travers alone from the 'fast' set was a Patriarch; leaving his great rivals Belmont and Jerome in the shadow. Jim Fisk had been killed before the first of the Patriarchs' balls, but other figures like Jay Gould and the son of the proprietor of the *Herald*, James Gordon Bennett Jr., were far from receiving the imprimatur of social acceptability. The directors of Western Union would not have Gould on their board; the New York Yacht Club would not admit him as a member; Mrs. Astor never invited the Goulds to her entertainments—he was a fully paid-up member (the yearly dues were $200)

44. The Gould Mansion on Fifth Avenue.

The Jay Gould mansion (579 Fifth Avenue) was the site of the reception in 1891 in honor of Anna Gould, which announced the arrival of the family to social prominence in New York. On his death in 1892, Gould left an estate valued at $72,224,547.08.

of Boss Tweed's Americus Club in Greenwich, Connecticut, but that was more in the way of a business expense for a money man in New York.[87] Gould in fact had no taste for socializing, rich foods, small talk, or flattery; outside his family he was regarded as antisocial, a loner. It was his family who wished to remember a more 'social' Jay Gould; it was his sons Howard and George, and their wives, whose social aspirations were aggressively aristocratic.

Two among the excluded positively defined what the Patriarchs sought to do: until later in the decade there was no place for Belmont and Cornelius Vanderbilt. It no doubt seemed a self-evident proposition that there should be no place for Belmont among the Patriarchs. But there were those like Duncan who were equally committed Democrats (when Belmont was elected president of the Manhattan Club in 1874, Duncan became treasurer), whose status as a Patriarch was secure. The exclusion of Belmont was a measured rebuke, but one which was not sustainable. The exclusion of Commodore Vanderbilt from the Patriarchs was an easier call. Monarch of the nation's railroad system, despoiler of St. John's Park, Vanderbilt rivaled John Jacob Astor as the greatest of the city's *nouveaux riches*. Like Astor, no one had ever accused him of polished manners or social refinement. He was a hard-driving railroad man, who didn't give a damn about the Patriarchs. For Vanderbilt, playing cards, smoking cigars, and going to the races constituted an ideal evening's entertainment. McAllister's attempt to draw a social line between the Patriarchs and men like Belmont and the Vanderbilts, rich, ostentatious, and 'new,' was largely a symbolic gesture. The *idea* of exclusivity was the point of the Patriarchs, not its practical application.[88]

In 1872–3, the Patriarchs were something of an innovation in social life. At the resorts of Saratoga and Newport, as Charles Astor Bristed observed, 'the Papas and Mammas were absolutely set aside, and became mere formulas and appendages. The old people were nowhere; no one looked after their comfort in a crowd, or consulted them about any arrangement till after the arrangement was made. They had no influence and no authority.'[89] Unlike the city's assemblies and débutante balls, where match-making and the social needs of the younger set were the primary concern and where the Mammas fussed in the background, the Patriarchs was an institution of married couples, where married women played a more prominent role than had been customary in New York.

In return for their subscriptions of $125, Patriarchs would each receive the right to invite four women guests and five gentlemen to each ball. The names and addresses of intended guests were sent to McAllister, who forwarded the invitations. As requests for tickets were unending, there was strong pressure to expand the Patriarchs. The scarcity of tickets, and the careful surveillance of all guests by McAllister, was designed to placate the clamor to exclude 'any objectionable element.' Each Patriarch was held responsible not only for the behavior of his own guests, but for their general social acceptability.

By the 1880s, there was an undercurrent of alarm that the Patriarchs would become too 'general,' and thus would be abandoned by the smart set. New York socialites knew how things were done in London, or at least some did, and for those who had no first-hand knowledge there were the well-informed reports on London high society by George Washburne Smalley in the New York *Tribune*. Smalley reported the bold requests made by social climbers in London: '"Can you get me a card for Lady Pimlico's dance?" is a question you may hear openly put, time after time, in crowded rooms. There is no pretense of concealment or sense of shame in these appeals. They are made and repeated with unblushing pertinacity.'[90] In New York there was a determination to squash that impudence, and to ensure that tickets for the Patriarchs could not be begged or wheedled from harried socialites. Repeatedly, McAllister was pressed to take even stricter control of the procedure. In response to simmering discontent that he had been overly generous in handing out invitations (in the 1890s attendance fluctuated between 350 and 400), he sought in 1895 to restrict the number of guests at Patriarchs to 275. That left important people unable to extend as many invitations as they wished. To deflect criticisms of his own position, McAllister said he was merely a simple servant of 'the powers that be' in denying entry.[91]

The organization of the balls, and rituals which marked their conduct, emphasized the hierarchical values of the Patriarchs. When a cotillion was to be danced at Delmonico's, chairs were arranged in a square, with the front seats

45. Delmonico's.

The Delmonico family, of French-speaking Swiss origin, established themselves in the New York restaurant business in the 1820s. In 1862 they leased the residence of Moses H. Grinnell on the corner of Fifth Avenue and 14th Street. This was the location of the first Patriarchs' Ball in 1872. The restaurant moved uptown in 1876 to Fifth Avenue and 26th Street.

reserved for Patriarchs and their families. At the late-evening supper there would be fifty tables, one for each of the Patriarchs and his family and guests. At precisely 12.45 a.m. McAllister (or in his absence, De Lancey Kane) would give the signal for the supper march, and began the procession by escorting Mrs. Astor (or a lady of comparable status if Mrs. Astor was absent) downstairs. Behind them, there was a crush as hundreds of guests sought to get on the small lift at Delmonico's, or join the crowd slowly filing downstairs. Invitations to a Patriarchs' ball acquired the usefulness of a private currency. The arrival of the engraved invitation, with its list of the Patriarchs, sufficed to wipe out any number of pressing social obligations. 'The greatest compliment that can be paid to visiting strangers of distinction or position in this city by their hosts is to extend to them an invitation to a Patriarch's ball.'[92] 'Distinguished strangers' at the Patriarchs included several presidents (Hayes, Grant), generals (McClellan), commodores, admirals, statesmen, titled Europeans (from the Duke and Duchess of Marlborough down to the holders of minor French and Italian baronetcies), various bankers, Saltonstalls, Everetts, Higginsons, and Lees from

Boston, the Leiter family from Washington, state governors, a minuscule number of cultural lions, including 'Mr. and Mrs. Matthew Arnold', whose daughter had married a New Yorker, and the physician-novelist Dr. Weir Mitchell of Philadelphia—but not a single figure active in the government of New York City. The Vanderbilts became regular guests at Patriarchs in the two years before their much-discussed ball in March 1883. By 1888 Cornelius Vanderbilt II had been elected to membership in the society.[93]

The Family Circle Dancing Class (FCDC), later renamed the Junior Patriarchs, was founded by McAllister in 1872 for younger members of New York society. He recalled being 'assailed on all sides' for invitations, as Smalley had described the situation in London, and saw at once that opening the door even a little threatened to destroy what was most valuable about the FCDC balls. 'My mornings were given up to being interviewed of and about them; mothers would call at my house, entirely unknown to me, the sole words of introduction being, "Kind sir, I have a daughter." ' When asked about the daughter, and the family's lineage, he would regularly be told that the family went back to King John; 'all were Huguenots, Pilgrims, or Puritans'; if Southerners, their families were near relatives of Washington. The comedy and tragedy of social aspiration were written across the humorous pages on the FCDC in his memoirs.[94]

Held at first in the homes of Patriarchs, and conceived to be less formal in organization, as they grew in popularity FCDC balls were held at Allen Dodworth's Dancing Academy, an elegant brownstone at 681 Fifth Avenue, and then at Delmonico's, where the entire second floor was thrown open to dancers and guests. The débutantes dressed in identical white tulle costumes, creating a striking visual pattern in the subdued light of Delmonico's, where the gas jets were surrounded by yellow shades imported from Paris. There were fancy dress FCDC balls, at which powdered hair was *de rigueur*. At another FCDC the 'Mother Goose' Quadrille was followed by the singing of nursery rhymes. The Pinafore Quadrille, with music from the Gilbert and Sullivan operetta, was a popular success. (Everyone said the young men looked *adorable* in their sailors' uniforms.) With a subscription of $12 for three balls a season, the social life of FCDC was at first more light-hearted and lively than the Patriarchs. But when the number of subscribers reached between 300 and 400, the evenings soon lost whatever had distinguished them from the other balls in the city, whether charity events, Patriarchs, assemblies, or Bachelors' balls. Delmonico's was perhaps not quite so lavishly decorated for FCDC evenings, and there were generally no favors for participants, but the guests included the same seasonal débutantes, eligible beaux, and matrons in furs.[95]

Ritual and formality characterized the senior and Junior Patriarchs, and press accounts—McAllister was lavish with interviews—stress the importance of continuity and tradition in organization. Year after year the ballroom was supplied with flowers and greenery by the leading upper-class florist, Klunder. There were always two orchestras playing in the rooms set aside for dancing, with opportunities for promenades between dances. The evening began punctually at 10 p.m. with waltzes, and the ever-popular lancer, in which each couple in the square would perform a short solo at the center. At 11 o'clock the upper supper room was thrown open for ices and light refreshments, followed by a more elaborate supper at 12.30. After the late supper the german was danced, with as many as fifty couples. Taking up to two hours to complete, it was akin to a musical dance game. The german would begin with couples seated around the sides of the ballroom. The leader (chosen by the hostess or, at a Patriarchs, selected by McAllister) would signal the musicians to strike up a waltz or gallop, and would designate certain couples to dance. They were then said to be 'up.' At an interval the leader would instruct the couples who were dancing to select other partners. The new partners would then be conducted in the execution of a figure. At a further signal, the figure broke up and a general waltz followed. The leader then signaled for everyone to return to their seats. (Ladies would be escorted by the dancing partners back to their original partner.) Another set of couples would then be 'up' and a new set of figures and dances completed. And so forth, until every couple had been 'up' and had a chance to take part in any of the myriad figures which an imaginative leader might design. The best leaders were those who could bring about an intermingling of participants in an amusing and playful manner. With figures often rehearsed, and sometimes conducted in costume, the german was perhaps the most heavily ritualized and unspontaneous dance in the nineteenth-century ballroom. It perfectly suited the taste of the New York aristocracy for control, formality, and pronounced leadership. Ninety-two couples participated in a german at a Patriarchs in 1881.[96]

The press delighted in stories about 'rivals' to the FCDC and the Patriarchs, but such competing events were usually held at Delmonico's, and attended by many of the same persons. The Astors, Kanes, Winthrops, and Iselins were present with some 250 other guests at an FCDC in 1884, as well as Mrs. Paran Stevens, the Ogden Goelets and J. Pierpont Morgan. The cotillions were led by the same figures: H. Le Grand Cannon, Thomas Howard, Lispenard Stewart, Worthington Whitehouse, Ridgway Moore, Elisha Dyer, and Harry Lehr, who had all been leading quadrilles and germans for as long as anyone could remember, and whose notorious rivalries provided entertaining copy for gossip in *Town Topics*. (Fawcett in *The Buntling Ball* suggests that a socially ambitious woman might pay figures like these to lead a german at her ball.)[97] The qualities needed for superior management of a german, as exemplified by Cannon, Howard, Dyer, and the leading New York figures, were debated in ballroom manuals. A cool head, an even temper, energy, and self-confidence were among the essentials. The first of these qualities, a cool head, reappears as a necessity across the professional literature. Leaders were advised to maintain a demeanor which established a tone of authority. 'The Leader is for the time an autocrat, but it is scarcely necessary to say that he must exercise his power with judgment and discretion; he must avoid all appearance of pretension, and direct with tact and moderation.' Dancers should not be able to read meaning in the leader's disposition, emotions, or facial expression. 'Moral: keep your temper perfectly and always. When pleased, smile; when provoked, if you cannot smile, at least come as near it as you can.' Such matters as tone of voice must be carefully regulated. 'When you must speak, do so in as low a tone of voice as can be heard by those to whom your remarks are addressed.'[98]

The nomenclature for balls—assemblies, bouncers' ball, bachelors' ball—carried sometimes intangible social meanings. There was a tacit generational line in the 1880s between balls principally for older couples (the Patriarchs was familiarly and rather scornfully referred to as a Dowagers' Ball) and those organized by groups of younger men, 'young bloods' often from the Knickerbocker Club. When the invitation list extended much beyond the families who were regularly seen at the Patriarchs, the occasions might be referred to as a 'bouncers' ball,' 'bouncer' being the slang term used for those who had made a sudden fortune in the Civil War and afterwards. The term carried a powerful association of fast, new people and the dreaded parvenu. William Dean Howells summoned a great reserve of human sympathy for Silas Lapham in 1885 in his fictional portrait of a 'bouncer' in Boston in *The Rise of Silas Lapham*. In New York society scorn, not sympathetic understanding, seems to have been the prevailing response. But when we look at accounts of events labeled 'bouncers' balls,' such as a subscription ball held in New York in 1874, we find it under the management of an impeccable group of young bluebloods led by Charles Post, William Jay, and Peter Marié. Dowagers, or at least a narrow section of elderly and conservative opinion, regarded 'bouncers' balls' as threatening the triumph of money over breeding. Another ball, held at the Metropolitan Opera in 1884, was given by a consortium of fifty-six younger men, and was attended by 150 couples drawn from the city's social elite. There was no sign in 1874 or in 1884 that a 'new' and alternative elite had emerged. The six patronesses of the 1884 ball were Mrs. Astor, Mrs. Maturin Livingston, Mrs. Francis Rives, Mrs. W.C. Schermerhorn, Mrs. Adrian Iselin, and Mrs. Alexander Van Rensselaer—wives, one and all, of Patriarchs.[99] The upper-class young seemed determined to reproduce the social whirl of their elders.

By the 1890s, there was an increasing number of social occasions of a more 'cultural' bent, and which seemed scarcely to lessen the New York passion for exclusivity. 'The tendency of great wealth to segregate itself more and more, and to flock by itself, as it were, has been so clearly evidenced at Newport and in New York,' noted a society column in the *New York Times*. Events which mixed cultural and social pleasures gained in appeal in New York. The Tuesday Evening Club, restricted to twenty members, each permitted to invite five guests outside their immediate household, met at the homes of members for a musical evening or recitation, followed by a light supper. Membership was largely drawn from the box-holders of the Metropolitan Opera, and the club enjoyed the patronage of Mrs. John Jacob Astor III. A much larger body, the Thursday Evening Club, had over 200 members, had an ambitious cultural program which included musical performances, recitations, amateur dramatic evenings, and talks on travel and matters of civic interest. Members of the Thursday Evening Club were proud of their seriousness, and made a point of what differentiated them from the Tuesday Evening Club: the relative absence of fashionables and the decision to skip the champagne supper which customarily ended such entertainments.

What distinguished the Tuesday from the Thursday club was largely a matter of taste and inclination. The former was more 'social,' the latter more 'cultural.' Membership of both clubs was drawn largely from the same stratum of New York upper-class life. They differed radically from the membership of Sorosis, founded in 1868 by female writers, journalists, and editors in New York. The members of Sorosis were, in the phrase of Karen J. Blair, 'adventurous women.' The members of the Tuesday and Thursday clubs were, by the norms of New York society, scarcely that. In the upper class the pursuit of culture had less of the potential for self-liberation than it possessed for the middle-class membership of Sorosis. Ironically, it was four of the founding members of the 'social' Tuesday Evening Club who were on the organizing committee which founded the Colony Club in 1903, the first women's club in New York.[100]

Women who had sponsored the Thursday Evening Club were also involved in the ultra-fashionable dances of the 'howling swells' on Tuesday evenings. 'These dances are really small Patriarchs, and membership in them is very carefully guarded and highly prized when once obtained.' Held at the pink room at Sherry's on Fifth Avenue and 37th Street, the 'howling swells' catered for the set who found the FCDCs a little too family centered, and the Patriarchs too elderly. The name 'howling swells' conveyed an attractive mixture of style and outrageousness, and the familiar name identified an inner elite of youthful fashionableness: But the patronesses led by the indefatigable Mrs. Astor, who received, the subscribers and the guests were all drawn from those who attended the other society balls in New York. The 'howling swells'— and an even more elite group, the 'howling, howling swells' who held dances at the Metropolitan Club Annex—acted as a lightning rod for those who had been critical of McAllister's self-promotion, convinced the Patriarchs had become too 'general,' and who were quite sure that Mrs. Astor was ready to retire from her position of social leadership. Mr. and Mrs. Elliot Roosevelt, parents of Eleanor Roosevelt, were among those who felt that the Patriarchs under McAllister had become too democratic and who supported the 'howling swells' at Sherry's on Tuesdays.[101]

Society journalists were expected to give readers a sense of how the evening *felt* and the costumes of the best-dressed and most beautiful guests. There was emerging a distinctive lushness in the descriptions of ladies' dresses. In 1883, Mrs. Henry Clews appeared in a 'Worth dress of white tulle, embroidered in silver, and with pearl colored satin, brocaded in pansies falling over the train. The drapery was looped up with clusters of begonia leaves and grasses, and in which were nestled gayly plumaged birds. The bodice was décolleté, and her ornaments were magnificent diamonds.' In 1888, the débutantes came in for special praise: Sally Hargous was a flamboyant spectacle, looking 'radiantly beautiful in white satin and tulle, cut décolleté and without sleeves and flecked all over with silver. She wore a diamond crescent in her dark hair, just above the crown, and carried three big bouquets of roses.' Amy Bend's dress was described with a cloying condescension: her 'delicate blonde loveliness was brought out by a nice green tulle dress, décolleté, with a little zouave jacket of the same, all edged with silver, and a little blue bird in the hair.' Amy Bend's father George, head of the New York Stock Exchange, died in 1900, when the market was low, leaving his widow and daughter Amy, like Wharton's Lily Bart, dependent upon old family friends for their Zouave jackets and tulle dresses. The descriptions of acknowledged social leaders by society columnists suggested a quick list rather than the more engaged tone used for débutantes. They were women who knew how to put on a show for the public, but their frequent appearance at important social events, and thus on society pages, created problems for writers which could best be dealt with by a shorthand. In 1888 Mrs. John Jacob Astor IV, *née* Ava Lowle Willing, appeared at a ball dressed in 'violet velvet, diamonds and emeralds on the corsage; feather aigrette.' And, in 1898, Mrs. William Astor dressed in 'white satin, embroidered in silver; necklace, tiara and stomacher of diamonds and sapphire.'[102]

Season after season, a place in society required that new clothes be worn. Gowns from Worth in Paris had to be ordered months in advance (and the duty paid at the rate of 50 percent on arrival at the New York Customs House). Dresses made by New York seamstresses had to be ordered in time for busy-season delays to be avoided. Every season there would be so many assemblies, bachelors', charity balls, 'howling swells,' and Patriarchs, as well as private balls, given by the likes of Mrs. Astor, Mrs. Marshall O. Roberts, Mrs. Paran Stevens, and the Vanderbilts. The repetitiousness of the New York season was in part a function of the long-term planning needed for the hand-manufacture of ball gowns, and also of the annoying ability of gossips to notice if a certain gown had been worn earlier in the season. Although women in society seemed uniquely privileged in their luxury, looked at another way, they were prisoners of a system of entertaining and fashion which demanded continued high levels of expenditure and left little room for spontaneity. The system of ball-giving and ball-going was deadening. It is hard not to feel that going to the ball was characterized by a reassuring sameness, season after season. Innovation might appear in details of dance, dress, or menu, but there was little hunger for variety or stimulating innovations. The 'Idler' in *Town Topics* put his finger on the issue: 'The second Patriarchs' ball was about as stupid an affair as I have ever attended. There was the usual gathering of fossils, wall flowers and simpering buds, the latter adding to the dreariness of the occasion by continuous complaint of the extreme juvenility of their partners.'[103] Amidst a sycophantic daily press, *Town Topics* was a breath of fresh air.

The press and society

> I can scarcely pick up a weekly paper that has any illustrations in it at all that does not contain the portraits and accompanying print that is full in its praise of some of the chosen few.
> —'The Saunterer', 1891[104]

Until the early 1880s, the Patriarchs were 'invisible.' The New York press paid little attention to the emerging social 'season,' and McAllister's role as the organizer of the Patriarchs was largely unknown to the newspaper-reading public. 'Society news' remained 'small town stuff' in the opinion of metropolitan editors. Yet, by the end of the decade, every newspaper in the city was devoting increasing space to covering high society. This was a remarkable change of visibility which was to have important consequences for society and its role in New York life.[105]

There were two audiences for society journalism, of sharply unequal size and with somewhat differing interests. The broad audience was made up of women like Wharton's Mrs. Peniston who stands for the large number of readers, assumed to be female, who were basically passive consumers of society news, fashions, and gossip. News of the wonders of Fifth Avenue penetrated into every tenement in the city: 'My imagination began to stir,' wrote Marie Ganz, who left school at thirteen for a job in a button factory. Her day went from 7 a.m. to 7 p.m., with an hour for lunch, for $2.50 per week.

> What tales I had heard of that street [Fifth Avenue]—of its splendid homes, its great hotels, its stores where one could spend a fortune on a bit of jewelry, on a tiny vase that the squeeze of a rough hand might shatter into dust, on

a dress that might be spoiled in a night; what tales of its endless procession of carriages and automobiles, its myriads of sparkling electric lights that turned the darkness into day! Of course I had never been there. . . . We children of the ghetto's poor never, unless through some miracle, strayed so far from our own neighborhood as that. Indeed, very few of the grown folks among us ever went beyond the bounds of the lower East Side.[106]

The problem with that passive model is that the readers of society journalism were anything but passive. As was noted in the first chapter, the dress, dances, and mannerisms of the aristocrats were studied and emulated. A striking look at a ball would re-emerge promptly in the fashions worn by a far wider constituency. 'Aristocratic' names and tones of voice were adopted by women far from the inner circles of society. What seems at first to be a 'trickle-down' model of class emulation on further inspection turns out to be an expression of American social aspiration: this is what success looks like, this is what you do.

As society journalism spread outwards to every American city and many small towns, being aristocratic was demystified. Social exclusivity was far from being a phenomenon solely of the metropolis. Virtually every community in the country contained an inner circle of old, wealthy families, and a large, socially ambitious, discontented penumbra of those with unsatisfied aspirations. Every reader could find in accounts of rich, badly behaved New York socialites a version of leading figures in their home town. Reports of jewels positively dripping from the dresses of the women in New York society fed many social envies and aggressions elsewhere.

And then there was a smaller readership, consisting of the participants themselves, engaged in competitive display, and concerned to ensure that their entertainments, dress, and presence at important occasions were covered. They colluded in the growing attention to society by feeding news of their activities and detailed descriptions of dress and décor to the press. An anonymous novel about New York society, *The Money-Makers*, published in 1885, offers a sardonic insight into the inner mechanism of society journalism. A character in the novel complains in amazement that 'a frivolous gathering of a few hundred idle people' is given ten times the coverage of a scientific convention. A more worldly colleague explains the system: '"It all means money—money, my boy."' *Modistes*, jewelers, and merchants found their business enhanced by being identified in the press with a particularly beautiful society belle, and provided a steady stream of information to journalists. Press coverage of society entertainments encouraged them to take advertisements. Decorators and florists were similarly more likely to advertise in papers which described their contribution to the event. The names of guests were of considerable interest to the retail trade. '"There is, I'll venture,"' remarks a character in *The Money-Makers*, '"not a line in all these reports except in rare instances, that is not paid for, directly or indirectly, three or four times over. Nearly every line of the matter has been in type in the various newspaper offices for days, and in many cases proofs have been submitted to those paying most largely. Even the reporters receive *douceurs*, such of them as will accept them."' Social leaders proclaimed higher values, but everyone except Mrs. Peniston seemed to know that ' "It all means money—money, my boy." '[107]

Publishers and journalists searched for ways to make society a subject on which people were prepared to spend good money. Several strategies were tried, and which survived decade after decade of ironic mockery: the overtly respectful, sycophantic, and flattering attempt to portray society as a vision of elegance and luxury. We rightly ask what was the *purpose* of such a description appearing in the *Tribune* on January 18, 1881: 'The ball-room presented a dazzling spectacle, the costumes of the ladies were elegant, and hundreds of diamonds glistened and sparkled in the flood of light.' More than a description, it was an invitation to enter a fairyland where there were no angry polemics on hard money, the tariff, immigration, strikes, poverty, abortion, crime, or unemployment; where there was no exploitation of labor, and no politics. And where no connection was hinted at between the wealth of some, and the poverty of many others.

The first modest attempt to create a society journalism came in 1879, with the publication of W.H. Andrews' *American Queen*, conceived as an up-market rival to the venerable *Godey's Lady's Book*. Devoted to the publication of social reports from American cities, and long lists of invited guests, *American Queen* provided a dry account of current fashions being worn across the nation. Andrews' venture failed to attract either circulation or advertising, and was abandoned to the journal's creditors in 1883. Two years later James B. Townsend and Louis Keller (who launched the *Social Register* in 1887) were appointed editors of the revived publication. Keller changed the magazine's name to *The American Queen and Town Topics*, and within two months it was once again in bankruptcy. The failed magazine was bought by Eugene D. Mann, and his older brother, William D'Alton Mann (1839–1920) in 1885, and relaunched with its title slimmed down to *Town Topics*.

The advent of the Manns transformed society journalism in America. Colonel Mann was a colorful scamp and blackmailer. A former cavalry officer, he claimed, perhaps truthfully, to have led the Union cavalry against Mosby in northern Virginia. He had prospered after the war with a series of hypothetical petroleum fields, non-existent oil refineries, elaborate unrealized schemes to establish iron mines, and railroads which were never built. A restless genius of vaporous promotion, Mann was a real-life Colonel Beriah Sellers, protagonist of Twain and Warner's *The Gilded Age* (1873). After serving in Congress from Alabama for one term as an anti-Reconstruction Democrat, he published a paper in Mobile which became a rallying point for Southern racism. He went on to patent a railroad refrigerator car, and developed a 'boudoir car' meant to rival the success of Pullman's sleeping car. The 'boudoir car' was successfully manufactured, and rights to the design were leased to railway lines in the 1870s. Mann was bought out in 1882 for two million dollars, and the brothers Mann turned up in New York three years later. Bursting with money, they purchased the bankrupt *Town Topics* from its creditors.[108] Colonel Mann became chief owner and editor in 1891.

Promoters and editors seemed to feel that providing society information was the principal task of society journalism. Among the earliest ventures was *The List*, a directory of social information aimed explicitly at the several thousand families who made up society in New York. An unexpected success in 1880, it was published annually by Maurice M. Minton, a sign that interest in high society was increasing. There was no editorial content in Minton's publication, simply the names, addresses, and club memberships of between 3,000 and 4,000 persons in society. *The List* also provided a directory of clubs and their officers, a shopping list, seating plans of the city's major theaters and paid advertisements from purveyors of luxury goods. Anyone doing business with that world would want a copy of *The List*. From 1884 Minton included more than 1,000 Brooklynites. The process of selection was not explained, and the openly commercial nature of the venture probably meant that inclusion or exclusion was not important enough to cause a fuss. Later lists of those within society would be far more contentious.

There were other signs of changing interest in society. In June 1880 Charles A. Dana's *Sun* began to carry a column of society chat, largely written for the amusement of the 'smart set.' There was much speculation about the identity of the well-informed columnist. Paul Dana, the editor's son, was a hotly tipped candidate. The New York lawyer Thomas Hitchcock was another plausible candidate. He had joined Dana in the purchase of the *Sun* in 1868. Under the pseudonym 'Matthew Marshall,' Hitchcock had written a weekly column on political and financial issues. A man with a decided literary bent, he was a member of the Century Association, and had written *Unhappy Loves of Men of Genius* (1891).

From the early 1880s every editor in New York was looking for society informants and columnists. The identity of the columnist in the *Sun* was never revealed, but the speculation attracted increasing attention to the topic. The *Tribune* followed with society coverage in the Sunday issues in 1882. Hurlbert hired 'Jenny June' in 1882 to contribute a column on the doings in society in the *World* while it was still owned by Jay Gould.[109] When Pulitzer bought the paper in May 1883, he aimed to settle accounts with the 'aristocracy of gaudy establishments and mountebank liveries' in his first editorials. His passion for social justice and scorn for the irresponsible rich gave the *World* an abiding interest in covering the activities of the city's social elite. In December Pulitzer began a six-part front-page series, 'Our Crested Nobility,' which was adorned by the armorial shields of the city's leading citizens.[110] Mattie Sheridan contributed a column titled 'A Few Words About Society' to the *Epoch*. James Gordon Bennett, Jr., appointed Nicholas Biddle as 'social advisor extraordinary' to the *Herald*, and installed William Bininger as editor of the paper's society page. In 1884 *The Times* hired George Wotherspoon, a contributor to *Town Topics*, to do society articles. When he was replaced by James Bliss Townsend (formerly one of the proprietors of *Town Topics*), Wotherspoon went to the *Mail and Express* to write an unsigned society column.

The position of this new breed of society journalists was complicated. Wotherspoon was able to maintain the life of an eligible society bachelor only so long as his authorship of columns in *The Times* remained hidden. Not a wealthy man, Wotherspoon needed the work (he later joined the theatrical agency run by Elisabeth Marbury). Society journalists faced the same hostility as Cora Potter encountered when she became a professional actress. The dangers of unwanted intrusions into private life, and distaste for anyone who would turn a position in society into a money-making career opportunity, reinforced a strong but ambivalent inhibition about professionalism. That particular line was not casually to be crossed. An editor had, naturally, a different perspective. Editors had to make sure their society informants were not using the press to further their own aims. An element of independence from factions was needed, but at the same time a society journalist was expected to have personal access to the most exclusive society events. Editors did not want contributions which would arouse hostility among the wealthiest families in the city. A kid-glove treatment was expected, and the tone of the society coverage in the early 1880s was extremely respectful. Wotherspoon found newspaper editors even more willful and arbitrary than society prima donnas. He was hired and fired by James Gordon Bennett, Jr., when the *Herald* expanded its society coverage.

Wotherspoon belonged to the first generation of dilettante society journalists. Like Louis Keller, who firmly believed that 'journalism can be clean and decent and yet thrive,' Wotherspoon wanted to import the values of a gentleman into a profession in which courteousness and discretion were not exactly prized.

> It was necessary [he wrote] to tell the sponsors [of *Town Topics*] that nothing in the nature of scandal would ever appear in the columns, or that those mentioned would be offended at any time by what was written about them. They were well aware that neither Townsend nor myself were so inclined.

46. Mrs. Bradley Martin.

Like Maria Gansevoort Melvill, Mrs. Bradley Martin, *née* Cornelia Sherman, originally came from Albany. Unlike Mrs. Melvill, she was very rich, and determined to put her money to good use—a cluster of diamond grapes once owned by Louis XIV, a ruby necklace made for Marie Antoinette. At a time of widespread unemployment in the city, the Bradley Martin's Louis XV costume ball, held at the Waldorf Hotel on February 10, 1897, was estimated to cost $180,000.

Like themselves we could not afford for social reasons, to be identified with a journal that was concerned in any way with exploiting the foibles and eccentricities of those who comprised society of the day. This policy was adhered to strictly.

The Mann brothers made no such assertions of gentlemanly decorum, and in the sharply honed paragraphs by 'The Saunterer' turned *Town Topics* into the most widely read society weekly in the country. Its circulation rose rapidly from 5,000 to 63,000 in the six years from 1885. At the turn of the century *Town Topics* claimed a subscription list of 140,000. However doubtful such a claim, it was read in the drawing rooms and clubs, and in tens of thousands of homes across the country by people who had never attended a Patriarchs' ball or known anyone in the 'Four Hundred.' Mann (and others) wrote the paper in the form of paragraphs on society events and figures. Mann cloaked his 'paragraphs' in the guise of reform, and supported sensible amendments to social customs. Excessively late balls drew his repeated condemnation. He provided a commentary on current fads in dress, décor, and food and was happy to point out when people in society were behaving foolishly. He also included inconsequential information deeply satisfying to those anxious to see their names in the newspapers: when Mrs. X planned to open her New York home, the postponement of a ball, a trip to Europe, a 'coming out' party for a débutante.

'The Saunterer' was seldom less than readable, and often seemed to possess an extraordinary kind of inside information:

A fair correspondent writes: "George Gould evidently allows himself to think of other things besides stocks, bond, and the market. Not only are there jolly good times on board the Hildegard but a pretty picture of domestic repose as well. George certainly thinks more of his personal appearance than his noted father ever did. On one of the recent rainy days I stopped for shelter in our most fashionable establishment devoted to gentlemen's outfitting. While there Mr. Gould was a customer, and I gazed with wrapt [*sic*] attention as he bought several suits of the finest silk underwear at $20 per set. He was particular as to color too, and selected some of pearl color, blue, pink and cream. He democratically marched off with the parcel under his arm." (July 28, 1887)

'The Saunterer' wrote descriptions of figures in society which could be harsher and with a greater sense of the ridiculous than any daily newspaper would permit: 'Mrs. Bradley Martin was so ablaze with diamonds from head to foot that she looked like a dumpy lighthouse' (January 7, 1897). The closest a newspaper got to that cruel witticism was to quote a remark that the scene at the Astor box at the opera resembled 'a walking jewelry store.'[111] Despite being an outsider in New York, he seemed to know which figures in society could be mocked, and in which way. Like a good con man, Mann had an insight into the hierarchy of contempt which established such things, and was adept at speaking for society, an entity to which he did not belong, and of playing one supremely self-confident faction off against another.

There were hundreds of figures who appeared in *Town Topics* who had no other claim to fame—other than their position in society. Mann was a deft portraitist, and could give readers a delicious sense of figures like Mrs. Paran Stevens, *née* Marietta Reed, daughter of a Lowell, Massachusetts, grocer and the second wife of a prominent Bostonian hotel owner. Remembered in an obituary as 'an ambitious woman, eager for social prestige, [who] stamped out everything that stood in the pathway of her ambition,' she was present at every social event.[112] 'The Saunterer' encountered her on a visit to Madison Square Garden: 'With her glasses raised to her eyes, her nose *en l'air*, and a lovely aspect of serene unconsciousness of the existence or propinquity of anybody else, Mrs. Stevens' look, bearing and movements made up a vision and a lesson. The prevailing hue of her dress and decoration was pink' (July 16, 1891).

Mann was rather less successful in parodic versions of the names of socialites (Mrs. Paraffine Stewpans, Jewsharp Polecatzer [Joseph Pulitzer], and so on).

Writing for society meant that 'The Saunterer' necessarily employed an elaborate and coded way to hint at topics without stooping to spell matters out for the entire country. He wanted to reveal, and to conceal at the same time. *Pas devant les enfants* seems to have been a guiding principle on certain topics. He assumed that his readership in the upper circles at Newport and New York would pick up references (say) to a disgraceful scene at the Union Club. Those who did not (which would invariably have constituted ninety-nine readers of *Town Topics* out of a hundred) might share the pleasure of coming so close to embarrassments in high places. It was also possible by a clever conjunction of stories to say what he preferred not say directly. Mann had an 'immune list' of people who, for various reasons, were only to be mentioned in a favorable light. Turning up at Delmonico's with his galleys, he was known to strike an awkward paragraph from the paper—for a consideration.

Town Topics included comment on Wall Street, theater, book reviews, literary topics (knowledgeable paragraphs on the death of Herman Melville in 1891, and regular warnings against French novels) and comic playlets and *vers de société*. But it was the society paragraphs which made the magazine. To keep the material flowing Mann operated a clever and sophisticated intelligence operation against society and its leading personages. The Western Union telegraph operator at Newport, Robert R. Rowe, was an unusually well-placed informant. In addition to passing on to Mann the choicest tid-bits from the day's telegrams, Rowe went up and down Bellevue Avenue, passing himself off as a bystander, snooping on the cottagers. Domestic staff knew that they might supplement their meager income by passing information on to Colonel Mann. Rowe recalled that all day long his female informants 'trooped into and out of his office.' They were reassured that confidentiality would be preserved. All of which encouraged those with a grudge, who had suffered a slight, or who had observed what George Gould might have preferred to keep hidden, to use *Town Topics* to take their revenge.

The flood of gossip, some arriving as anonymous tips, and occasional indiscreet gems of social news, soon gave Mann a reputation of someone to placate. It was a position of power which he ruthlessly abused. Mann's spies were feared, and disinformation about the source of a certain piece of information spread confusion and recrimination among the 'Four Hundred.' Men of wealth would do much to keep Mann's hints at extra-marital liaisons and reports of drunken sons or compromised daughters out of *Town Topics*. (One of Mann's favorite tactics was to print a paragraph commenting on a husband who was away from home for some reason or another, leaving readers to draw their own conclusion about the state of the marriage.) After a number of unflattering paragraphs about James

Hazen Hyde, Mann found the Equitable Life Assurance Company, of which Hyde was the leading shareholder, more than willing to advance $160,000 against unimproved property Mann owned on West 38th Street. There were no further paragraphs about the Hazen Hyde family, or unfriendly remarks about the Equitable in the columns of 'The Saunterer.' Perry Belmont, a Democratic member of Congress and leading New York socialite, purchased 100 shares in US Steel from Mann at twice their market value. When Belmont's brother Oliver was approached by Mann and asked to buy shares in *Town Topics* worth $5,000, he refused. After the refusal, fifty abusive items about Belmont were published in *Town Topics*. Mann, in other words, was a shakedown artist whose victims included some of the wealthiest men in America, from William K. Vanderbilt to the Secretary of the Navy, William C. Whitney.

Mann was also writing for society itself, and assumed the role of an inside tipster on society engagements and the prospects of débutantes; he was also a consoler of the bereaved, a supporter of virtue, a sharp tutor in matters of etiquette, a judge of social success, and a thorn in the side of social climbers. 'I have long been convinced,' he wrote on December 17, 1891,

> that the 400 of New York is an element so absolutely shallow and unhealthy that it deserves to be derided almost incessantly . . . there are a few conspicuous individuals who are constantly figuring as "leaders" of the fashionable lot, and there are others that are constantly pushing and clawing to get recognition and publicity, and to these I am merciless. I have iterated and reiterated that one inflated and preposterous man was a jackass, and that a vain and jealous old lady, who persists in being at the head of the court, is undeserving of the courtesy and tenderness that gentle and true womanhood commands from me, as from nearly all men.

An enemy of ostentation and pretension, 'The Saunterer' urged good sense and the correction of manners. The need for good citizenship and *noblesse oblige* was a constant theme. When in 1898 the supremely wealthy Robert Goelet tried to evade paying the 1 percent income tax levied by New York City by declaring Newport to be his legal residence, 'The Saunterer' poured scorn on such behavior: 'For a man owning a considerable portion of Manhattan island and deriving from the community an income surpassing that of the heir apparent to the richest empire in the world to "swear-off" his citizenship in order to evade a few thousands of taxes, is to disgrace his colors; He and his friends may pretend to think the act admirable for cunning, shrewdness and contempt of public opinion, but it is really a deed sinful to patriotism and disgusting to gentlehood' (February 3, 1898). His dislike of newspaper owners like Bennett and Pulitzer was boundless. Ward McAllister, that 'inflated and preposterous man,' and Mrs. Astor, 'a vain and jealous old lady,' were the repeated targets of his sharp pen.

Indiscretion

> If you want to be fashionable, be always in the company
> of fashionable people.
> —Ward McAllister (1890)[113]

McAllister occupied an important place in the demonology of *Town Topics*, and it was a sign of his expanded role in society that he should be such a target for Mann's scorn. In addition to the Patriarchs, McAllister was seen as a person who could manage a successful entertainment. He not only claimed to know what should be done, he also possessed great concern for the kind of details which most other men ignored. For all his affectations, in the area of his expertise few openly challenged his judgment. He was invited to be the manager of the Banner Ball in 1876, held in Chickering Hall in aid of the Centennial Union. He led the quadrille in which the ladies dressed in colonial costumes. When a ball was mooted in 1877 to raise funds for Christians suffering in the Russo-Turkish War, Mrs. John Jacob Astor III turned to McAllister to organize the event and left in his hands the socially sensitive choice of participants in the opening quadrille. The ball held to celebrate the centennial of the battle of Yorktown in 1881 saw McAllister in charge of the dancing.[114]

In the eyes of New York McAllister was principally the organizer of the Patriarchs and the FCDCs. In society, he had a monarch's power to grant invitations to some of the city's most exclusive social events. Such power, and his increasing visibility in the pages of *Town Topics* and elsewhere, made him an alluring figure for journalists hunting for a good story about society and its leaders. A reporter for the *Tribune* caught up with McAllister on an evening in March 1888. When asked about how he had risen to his present eminence, McAllister dated the beginning of his involvement with society to the late 1850s, and the picnics he gave at Newport. He claimed that from the outset there were two principles behind his activities: the need to 'enlist the leading men, fathers of families, who would stand by me and make failure impossible,' and the need for exclusivity. 'A ball that any one can gain admission to is never attractive, while one that is rigidly exclusive will make invitations sought for by everybody.'[115] He attributed the creation of the Patriarchs in the previous decade to the need felt by the leading families for 'an exclusive series of assemblies at which to bring out their daughters and introduce to them eligible young men of good character, as well as to entertain each other and foreigners or strangers in the city.' As for his own role, with characteristic modesty he suggested that he was merely an administrator, executing the wishes of 'society.' The social standing of the Patriarchs was the only guarantee of the suitability of the guests.

As he drawled on, it became clear that McAllister enjoyed considerable discretionary power. He claimed it was not his role to serve as gatekeeper, though his judgment about a potential guest was sometimes sought out. His power certainly lay in the regular requests he received to distribute tickets which Patriarchs were unable to send out themselves. Each of the Patriarchs would send a list of names to McAllister. If there was duplication of intended recipients, they would be returned with a request for substitutions. 'I have to keep, therefore, a record of all the guests invited and who invites them.' Once an invitation card was issued, it was against the rules for another name to be substituted on the card. But when he considered the 'bouncers,' social climbers seeking to enter society, he reflected that even with a good start, many were unable to 'float themselves': 'These people have not the poise, the aptitude, for polite conversation, the polished and deferential manner, the infinite capacity of good humor and ability to entertain or be entertained that society demands.' It would be no kindness to welcome such people into society's inner sanctum. 'Why,' he explained, 'there are only about four hundred people in fashionable New-York society. If you go outside that number you strike people who are either not at ease in a ball-room or else make other people not at ease. See the point?'

Journalists across the nation did, indeed, see the point, and demanded to know who was in the 'Four Hundred' and who was excluded. In 1890 the Melville Publishing Company issued *The 400 (Officially Supervised)*.[116] In practice, the large balls in New York with 800 and 1,000 guests drew upon 'cultivated and highly respectable, even distinguished people' from the ranks of professional men: doctors, lawyers, editors. The 'exclusive fashionable set' or the 'Four Hundred' consisted of a far smaller number, and entry could not simply be procured by the possession of great wealth. The day when great wealth admitted men to exclusive society has gone by, McAllister argued. 'Twenty or thirty years ago it was otherwise. But now with the rapid growth of riches, millionaires are too common to receive much deference; a fortune of a million is only respectable poverty. So we have to draw social boundaries on another basis: old connections, gentle breeding, perfection in all the requisite accomplishments of a gentleman, elegant leisure and an unstained private reputation count for more than newly gotten riches.'

The boundary which McAllister sought to impose with the 'Four Hundred' was the same project he had begun in the 1850s at Newport, and resumed in the 1870s with the Patriarchs: 'We wanted money power, but not in any way to be controlled by it.' McAllister stood by the belief that society could only be founded on gentlemen, not millionaires; on breeding, not ostentation. But by 1888 Belmont had been a Patriarch for a decade, and with the success of their ball in 1883 the Vanderbilts had fully entered society. It was not immediately

47. Mrs. Stuyvesant Fish.

'Mamie' Fish, Alva Belmont and 'Tessie' Oelrichs formed a troika of intensely competitive and wealthy hostesses at Newport. Of the three, the 'florid, willful Mamie Fish' had the sharpest tongue, and the most scorn for solemnity—which did not prevent her, in later years as Mrs. O.H.P. Belmont, from pontificating on everything under the sun in the *New York Times*.

clear, now that the children of Jay Gould had begun to make their way into society, who was worth excluding.

By the late 1880s McAllister saw himself as something of a public figure, increasingly sought out for interviews, and flattered by journalists. Their attention encouraged a tendency towards pontification on all issues concerning society. He thought it appropriate to offer advice to Chicago about the need for fine French chefs, the proper technique to serve *frappé* wine, and (his favorite theme) the need for exclusivity: in return, McAllister was addressed as Singular Personage, Head Butler, New York Flunky, A Popinjay, and The Premier of Cadsville in the Chicago newspapers.[117]

McAllister had a knack for making a fool of himself. Indiscreet words undermined his position, and aroused the contempt of those who took literally the notion that McAllister was merely a servant of society. Among these in 1889 was Stuyvesant Fish, banker and president of the Illinois Central Railroad. The tall, taciturn Fish was from an old Yankee family, with a lineage of public service and probity. His father Hamilton Fish had served in Congress, and had been elected Governor of New York. Stuyvesant Fish graduated from Columbia College, worked five years in the banking firm of Morton, Bliss & Co., and in 1877, at the age of twenty-six, was made a director of the Illinois Central. Fish had married Marion ('Mamie') Graves Anthon, and it was her intense social ambition which made The Crossways, their cottage at Newport (designed by McKim, Mead & White), and town house at Gramercy Park, rivals to the social power enjoyed by Mrs. Astor. Mamie Fish was a hostess with flair and a capacity for the unexpected, qualities notably lacking in Mrs. Astor's entertainments. Her wit was long cherished in society. She had a strong, domineering personality (remarking of her husband: 'Where would he be without me? I made him. I put him on the throne')[118] and prided herself on her mastery of the black arts of social strategy. Her campaign to dethrone Mrs. Astor began, in 1889, with a humiliating dismissal of McAllister by her husband.

The feud was begun when McAllister was heard to remark in the Union Club that there was not enough wine at one of the millionaire's dinners, and his chef should have served white wine sauce when he served brown. Considering himself a stickler in such matters, McAllister casually made powerful enemies in the Fishes, and revenge was not long in coming. Fish was chairman of the General Committee of a ball given in 1889 to celebrate the Centennial. McAllister was the inevitable choice for secretary of the Entertainments Committee and manager of the ball and banquet. As McAllister later explained, Fish's political ambitions drove him to insist that he dance in the quadrille opposite the President. 'I declined to give him this place because I considered him utterly unfit for participation in such a delicate social event.' When President Harrison withdrew from the quadrille, Fish blamed McAllister's mismanagement.

At the same time McAllister had incurred the anger of another powerful New Yorker, Elbridge T. Gerry, chairman of the Centennial Ball Executive Committee, when he refused Gerry's demanded to preside over the banquet attended by the President, Vice-President and distinguished guests. Gerry, whose mother was a Goelet and whose wife was a Livingston, was a very wealthy New York lawyer who had founded the Society for the Prevention of Cruelty to Children, and was Commodore of the New York Yacht Club. His grandfather had been one of the signers of the Declaration of Independence. 'My idea,' McAllister explained, 'was to make the ball purely democratic and therefore a purely American occasion.' Objections were raised to McAllister's plans for the banquet and ball within the Executive Committee and complaints were made at their extravagance. Indignant, McAllister resigned from the committee. Fish's parting shot threw doubt upon McAllister's fabled skills as the manager of the Patriarchs: 'while he is a good society man he is utterly incompetent to transact business affairs.' 'All this talk about McAllister's Four Hundred is the sheerest nonsense,' continued Stuyvesant Fish.

48. Gerry Mansion, Fifth Avenue at 61st Street.

Richard Morris Hunt drew upon the exuberant architecture of the early French Renaissance when he was commissioned by Elbridge Gerry to build a family home at 2 East 61st Street, on the corner of Fifth Avenue at 61st Street. It was built between 1892 and 1894. Two years after Gerry's death in 1927, his mansion was razed to make way for the Hotel Pierre.

McAllister didn't create any Four Hundred at all. It was Charley Delmonico who did it when he built a hall that would hold just that number of people. Why, there are two Four Hundreds. One of them is the Patriarch Four Hundred and the other the Assembly Four Hundred. One is just as good as the other, and McAllister has nothing to do with the Assembly faction, yet they manage to get along pretty well. To show that one is as good as the other, I will tell you that my brother [Hamilton] belongs to one and I to the other.[119]

The 'Fish-ball,' as McAllister described it, was an ill-managed affair which attracted much scorn in the press. McAllister was able to console himself at Fish's public humiliation, and had begun work on a book, *Society As I Have Found It*, which would make a general reply to Fish's aspersions, and set the record straight about his contribution to New York society. It was perhaps the worst decision of McAllister's career. It was rumored that he received $50,000 from Cassell for the book. Prosaically, as *Town Topics* reported (August 20, 1891), the sum he actually received was $3,500 against a guaranteed and generous royalty of 30¢ a copy. The sale of over 11,000 copies was no disgrace. It was a respectable success, disappointing only in the light of McAllister's engorged expectations.

In the book he rather coyly tried to disguise the identity of some of the persons he referred to, but after his death a copy of the book was deposited in the New York Society Library with tiny annotations in McAllister's red ink which identified some of the personages. The strategy was half-hearted in any event, and pleased neither those named nor those hinted at. McAllister's snobbishness, the self-flattering tone which runs throughout, and the author's obsequiousness towards his 'social superiors' were mocked in a notably hostile press reception. McAllister seemed to contemporaries a man of misplaced seriousness, and, worse, to lack a sense of irony—an unforgivable crime. 'No suspicion that he is making a continental laughing stock of himself must disturb his mind or interfere with the singleness of his devotion. It would be fatal to him. In this volume there is no trace of such a suspicion. The degree of fervor that the author puts into undertakings that adults commonly leave to adolescents is really wonderful.'[120]

Society As I Have Found It caused 'nausea' in New York society. Leading 'ultra-fashionables' such as Mrs. Willie Vanderbilt, Mrs. Ogden Mills, Mrs. Seward Webb, and Mrs. Twombly dropped McAllister from their visiting lists. Now that their own place in society was secure, the reaction against McAllister among the Vanderbilts was fierce. Mrs. Webb and Mrs. Twombly were daughters of William Henry Vanderbilt, and Mrs. Willie Vanderbilt was their sister-in-law. It was strongly felt that no *gentleman* could have written a book like McAllister's. 'He tells us, if he meets a friend wearing a shabby coat, that he crosses the street. We know he fawns before the rich; is forever scraping acquaintance with people he believes distinguished; is forever parading himself in the public prints; is forever struggling to puff up his little self like the toad in the fable. He soils with ignoble use the grand old name of gentleman.' Mrs. Astor indicated her own support for McAllister by allowing him to escort her into dinner at the Patriarchs in December 1890. But when there was a decline in attendance at the Patriarchs in January and February 1891, a 'slight indisposition' kept Mrs. Astor away. This was correctly interpreted as a further sign of the disapproval of McAllister which was sweeping society.[121]

Mocked in *Town Topics* as 'Mr. Ward M'Hustler,' and portrayed as 'Steward McGuzzler' in a lively parody entitled *Society As It Has Found Me Out*, McAllister insouciantly carried on. He ignored the fiasco of the Centennial Ball, said nothing about the hostile response to his book, and gave an impression that nothing had changed in his social standing. He agreed to give a dinner party to Collis P. Huntington, the large, bearded railway tycoon who had sought with increasing desperation to win a place in New York society. In 1892 Huntington commissioned George B. Post to design a Romanesque mansion on the southeast corner of Fifth Avenue and 57th Street. The other corners of this high-toned intersection were occupied by Cornelius Vanderbilt II, W.C. Whitney and Mrs. Herman Oelrichs. Huntington lacked the social cachet of his neighbors. McAllister's act of kindness backfired when the details of the financial arrangement between them appeared in the press. Huntington had agreed to pay McAllister $9,000 for being ushered into the 'Four Hundred.' But once invited to a Patriarchs' ball and introduced to Mrs. Astor, he refused to pay more than $1,000 for services rendered. McAllister threatened to sue, talked indiscreetly to a reporter, and both men were thoroughly humiliated when the story appeared in print. Huntington found other ways to curry social favor in New York. He gave a full-length portrait of Washington to the Metropolitan Museum in 1896, and in his will left Vermeer's *Woman with a Lute*, two Rembrandts, and a fine group of aristocratic portraits by Raeburn, Romney, Gainsborough, and Lawrence to the Met. These kinds of bequests were planned long in advance with the blue-blooded trustees of the museum.

Other figures close to McAllister were also benefiting financially from their standing in society. McAllister encouraged the social career of Harry Lehr, who received a secret commission from restaurants and the suppliers of luxury goods. Freddy Martin—Frederick Townsend Martin, brother of the ball-giving Bradley Martin—was paid a percentage by the Plaza Hotel for his services as 'social organizer and agent in general.' In other words, he received a commission for encouraging his friends to patronize the hotel. McAllister, and before him Sexton Isaac Brown, had learned how to make society pay.[122]

McAllister had a lucky knack for turning misfortune into marketing opportunities. Recognizing the great notoriety which now surrounded him, Pulitzer extended a welcoming hand, and a salary of $50 per week, for McAllister to write for the *World*. A weekly column, 'Ward McAllister's Letters,' appeared in October 1891. In *Town Topics* Colonel Mann wondered when the Pulitzers could expect their first invitation to a Patriarchs. McAllister found the opportunity to pontificate irresistible, and in the pages of Pulitzer's paper flattered and defended fashion, good manners, courtesy, and wealth, while deprecating ostentation, and carefully making sure to offend no one in particular. As a strategy, it seemed to work.[123]

The season of 1893 saw a vigorous restoration of McAllister's social position. A general thirst for publicity in society overcame the distaste in which McAllister was held by the Fishes, Mrs. Ogden Mills, and their chums. The Patriarchs held on December 13 was a great success, and McAllister used what had been a liability—his status as a 'society reporter'—to the hilt. At his insistence reporters from rival papers were excluded from Delmonico's while preparations for the ball were concluded. He provided the *World* with an exclusive account of the dresses worn by leading guests, and the most detailed and authoritative account of the ball. In 1894, with an unusually large number of débutantes to be introduced, McAllister positively crowed with delight at the success of his arrangements. Never before, noted a reporter, 'have his efforts on behalf of the great ball been so promising of bright results. He is jubilant over the prospect of a gay season.' The Stuyvesant Fishes absented themselves from the Patriarchs in the 1890s, as did the Seward Webbs, Mrs. Burke Roche, and Mr. and Mrs. Ogden Mills.[124] The Vanderbilts seemed to change their minds about McAllister, and turned out in numbers. When he died at the end of January, 1895, McAllister was clearly the rather bruised winner in the great social wars.

After McAllister's death, the Patriarchs were hurriedly reorganized, and a new committee formed. The last surviving member of the original society of 1872–3, Robert G. Remsen, was elected president. George Griswold Haven succeeded McAllister as secretary. A graduate of Columbia, at the age of fifty-eight Haven was a clubman of impeccable orthodoxy (he had memberships at the Tuxedo, Metropolitan, Knickerbocker, Union, Manhattan, and Union League). Until his retirement, he had a seat on the Stock Exchange, and had been president and managing director of the Metropolitan Opera and Real Estate Company. The new Executive Committee of the Patriarchs for 1895–6 consisted of the clubman and lawyer Buchanan Winthrop, the younger August Belmont, and Edmund T. Baylies (who was also on the board of the Metropolitan Opera). Baylies was singled out in *Town Topics* for having played a particularly objectionable role in the last phase of the Patriarchs: 'Mr. Edmund T. Baylies, who was given the management after Mr. McAllister's death, is said to have offended so many people by his lack of tact that, after much consultation, a new executive committee . . . was appointed to take charge of the balls' (April 15, 1897). Remsen died within a year, Baylies was dropped, and the committee was reorganized once again. James Powell Kernochan, William C. Whitney, and W. Watts Sherman formed the committee for 1896–7. Kernochan was among the blue-bloods of clubland. His wife Katherine was a daughter of Pierre Lorillard, and her sisters married into the Kip and Barbey families. Noted for a certain aggressiveness of temperament and gruffness of manner, he sought to return the Patriarchs to their original exclusivity. He drew up an 'index expurgatorius,' but succeeded in alienating as many people as he pleased. While heading towards a meeting of the Patriarchs at the Waldorf Hotel on Fifth Avenue on March 6, 1897 (that year the Patriarchs abandoned Delmonico's for the more modern and larger ballroom of the Waldorf), Kernochan was knocked down by a carriage driven by the daughter of George F. Baker, president of the First National Bank. His sudden death wholly upset plans for the Patriarchs' future.[125] Without McAllister's flamboyant presence and attention to detail, and after the death of the forceful Kernochan, the Patriarchs collapsed. The ball held on March 2, 1897, was not strongly attended. At a meeting of the Patriarchs' Society on April 9, attended by only eleven of the fifty members, it was clear that without a figure like McAllister there was no one who was prepared to assume energetic responsibility for the balls. By ten to one, the remaining Patriarchs voted to disband the society. Their first response seemed to be to forget what McAllister had taught society about the need to manage publicity. The Patriarchs wanted to treat the decision as though it was a purely private matter. But a moment's reflection reminded them of the strong press interest in the Patriarchs, and the prospect of facing inquisitive reporters on the steps of the Union Club was distasteful. A decision was made to announce the dissolution. A note in the distinctive handwriting of Miss Maria de Barril, assistant secretary of the Patriarchs, was sent to the *Herald.*

> It was resolved at a meeting of the Patriarchs, held at the Waldorf Friday, April 9, that the association be dissolved.
> New York, April 9, 1897.

With the demise of the Patriarchs, the last bastion of defense of the aristocratic principle in New York fell to a widow of sixty-seven, Mrs. William Astor—known simply as *the* Mrs. Astor.

6

BEING MRS. ASTOR

I resented the extravagances of this carnivore family.
—Poultney Bigelow on the Astors (1925)[1]

At the end, there remained little more than the boundless civility of a hostess. After a severe nervous breakdown in 1906, the usual daily rounds of a woman in the upper reaches of New York society were resumed. Each morning after breakfast the day's meals would be discussed with the staff, led by Thomas Hade, who had been with her since 1876, and her longtime companion, Miss Simrock. Correspondence was attended to. The day's other business might be transacted on the telephone. Regular shopping expeditions continued, but at the instructions of her family the goods were never delivered. Mrs. Astor's social secretary, Maria de Barril, whose ostrich-feathered hats and dramatic gowns made her something of a New York and Newport celebrity, prepared invitation lists, discussed menus and caterers, and addressed by hand the envelopes containing invitations to Mrs. Astor's entertainments.[2] But on the instruction of her physician the invitations were never sent out, the orders for flowers did not reach Klunder, and the menus for her entertainments, however closely planned, were quietly placed aside. In the afternoons Mrs. Astor went for her regular carriage drive through Central Park. At her side were attentive and smartly dressed medical assistants. She nodded to imaginary acquaintances on Fifth Avenue and on the carriage drives in the Park, and at her home at 840 Fifth Avenue a constant and agreeable flow of visitors, all old friends, all in Mrs. Astor's imagination, were received with her utmost graciousness.

On good days the old decidedness and clarity returned. After so many years at the top of society, she consented to give an interview to a reporter from the *Delineator*, and had some pungent things to say. Looking back at the experience of a half-century in society, she administered a sharp rebuke to her rivals:

> I hope my influence will be felt in one thing, and that is in discountenancing the undignified methods employed by certain New York women to attract a following. They have given entertainments that belonged under a circus tent rather than in a gentlewoman's home. Their sole object is notoriety, a thing that no lady ever seeks, but, rather, shrinks from. Women of this stamp are few in New York, but, alas! they are so appallingly active![3]

49. Mrs. Astor (Carolus-Duran).

To students in his Parisian *atelier*, who included John Singer Sargent, Carolus-Duran preached a simple message: 'Love glory more than money, art more than glory, nature more than art.' From the 1860s, Carolus-Duran was the king of fashionable portrait painters. His life-size portrait of Mrs. Astor, wearing a black Marie Antoinette gown, portrays the reigning monarch of New York society. With one glove removed, she stood patiently ready to greet her guests.

50. Central Park.

When Central Park opened in 1858, it offered the city elite an incomparable setting for display—of fine clothes, horses, and carriages. From a carriage at the top of the Terrace there was the most perfectly executed of all the Central Park vistas. Beyond Bethesda Fountain was the Lake and the heavily-wooded Ramble.

She might have been thinking of Tessie Oelrich's 'Bal Blanc' at Newport in 1904. Rosecliff, the cottage which McKim, Mead & White designed for the Oelrichs, was decorated wholly in white for the ball. Female guests were instructed to dress in white and to powder their hair; gentlemen were told to wear black. At the 'Servants' Ball' given by the Clewses at Newport, guests wore servants' outfits and were greeted by Clews holding a duster in one hand and a pail in the other, disguised as his own valet. Behind him in the entry hall Tessie Oelrichs, dressed as a maid, was mopping the floor, Oliver Belmont presided as chief attendant in the cloakroom while Harry Lehr carried off an impeccable performance as the butler. Mrs. Astor may have also been thinking of her old rival, Alva Belmont, who gave a breakfast in honor of Consul, a chimpanzee dressed in a frock coat. The event received prominent coverage in the *New York Times*. None of this seemed amusing to Mrs. Astor.[4]

For the interview in the *Delineator*, Mrs. Astor wore a plain black gown, a black hat and veil, and was described as being a little less than medium height, with firm shoulders, an erect posture and gray eyes. Her figure was youthful, and not in the least inclined towards *embonpoint*. Wishing to conclude the interview in the art gallery, Mrs. Astor found the door too difficult and summoned a servant. The gallery, which also served as a ballroom, housed Mrs.

Astor's large collection of Meissoniers.[5] The Astors had an expensive art collection, but one of extreme conventionality. Charles Astor Bristed referred to Meissonier as 'one of the most consummate painters of the modern French school.' But his family, and his class, did not share the heavily qualified judgments he went on to make, judgments which were to be ruthlessly confirmed in the next century. The Frenchman painted 'without a passion, without anything but a wonderfully-trained hand.' His canvases appealed to a public 'tired of emotions and ideas and revolts, but interested in every thing mechanical and laborious.' Meissonier's art 'has no inner meaning; it has no suggestion; it is *realisation*.' Meissonier, he wrote, 'is an example of a modern artist wholly independent of the actual life of his time—an artist who has given *no place to woman* in his works, no place to the ideal, no place to the disturbing facts of his own epoch.' A later age would feel that the taste for Meissonier in Gilded Age New York inadvertently opened a revealing window on the meager inner life of the city's wealthy art patrons.[6]

51. Mrs. Astor's art gallery.

The art gallery at Mrs. Astor's double-residence at 840 Fifth Avenue (see p. 15) also served as a ballroom. This view, published as a postcard by William Randolph Hearst's newspaper, reflected that paper's interest in high society. Where Pulitzer's *World* attacked the 'Four Hundred,' Hearst's *Sunday American & Journal* in 1903 was much friendlier to the rich and powerful.

In Mrs. Astor's home could be found a Beauvais tapestry, a Sèvres vase, fine Louis XIV furniture, and a signed portrait of the Duke and Duchess of Orléans. Did that make Mrs. Astor a supporter of the French royalist cause? Had she not been accused of having aristocratic pretensions, of treating the oversize red damask divan which stood on a raised platform in her drawing room as a throne? The interviewer's tactful euphemisms only hinted at the rich fund of venom directed towards the Astors and their pretensions. 'The livery of their footmen,' wrote Poultney Bigelow in his autobiography, 'was a close copy of that familiar at Windsor Castle, and their linen was marked with emblems of royalty. At the opera they wore tiaras, and when they dined the plates were in keeping with imperial pretensions, at least so far as money could buy the outward signs of sovereignty. Indeed, the daughter of Queen Victoria in her Potsdam palace could have made no such display of money as did the Astors of New York.'[7] Of course such sentiments were never expressed openly to Mrs. Astor's face, and in the best tradition of celebrity journalism the interviewer for the *Delineator* ducked the issue. Few in New York doubted that the Astors were envied, scorned, and hated in the city.

The implied invitation to reflect upon the politics and social values of the Astors was neatly deflected by Mrs. Astor. 'I believe in a republic,' she said,

> and I believe in a republic in which money has a great deal to say, as in ours. Money represents with us energy and character; it is acquired by brains and untiring effort; it is kept intact only by the same means. It were well if Europe were imbued more with the American ideas of money power—I do not say ideals—that is another thing . . . I have no sympathy with the establishment of a monarchy in France. In the first place, I am an American and a very sincere one, and opposed to the overthrow of any republic.

Reading between the lines, this comment too had a specific target. Her nephew William Waldorf Astor had left New York, bought the *Pall Mall Gazette* and the *Observer* in London and in 1903 became the owner of Hever Castle in Kent. His desire for a peerage was clear, though only after a flood of Astor benevolence in the first year of the war, amounting to £500,000, was he made a baron in 1916. She was not the only Astor with aristocratic pretensions.

At the opera

Lorgnettes were levelled in all directions.
—first night at the Metropolitan Opera (1883)[8]

Tradition required that she be late. And Mrs. Astor did not disappoint tradition. She arrived at parterre box 7 at the Metropolitan Opera House on

52. Mrs. Astor.

Mrs. Astor intensely disliked being photographed. For many years she would only appear in public wearing a hat and veil. Even in the evening she wore a veil. It helped, perhaps, to strengthen the Astor mystique. All of the photographs which were taken of her were formal portraits, carefully controlled, and posed.

November 30, 1898, after the first entr'acte of Wagner's *Tannhaüser*, which for more than a decade had been one of the most popular of the many Wagnerian operas regularly performed at the Met. Mrs. Astor's entrance caused quite a stir. 'Every lorgnette in the house and opera glasses as well were trained on the Astor box . . .'.[9]

The fall opera season of 1898 had been delayed by one night due to a heavy winter storm during the night of November 28–29 which deposited ten inches of snow on the city. The streets were blocked, ferries and trains were canceled. An editorial appeared in the *New York Times* on 'The Blockade of New York.' Political accusations added to the wintry scene, for snow was *political* in New York. The Street Cleaning Commissioner blamed the Board of Aldermen, the Aldermen attacked the Board of Estimate, and everyone blamed the Dock Board for the failure to clean the streets. The city's traditional arts of buck-passing were on glittering display. Reform administrations, which had won notable victories against Tammany Hall in the 1894 elections, had made clean streets a test of honesty and efficiency in municipal government. Colonel George Waring, appointed Street Commissioner in 1894, hired 1,400 men, dressed in white duck uniforms (they were called the 'White Angels'), to clean the city's streets. For the first time within living memory a street commissioner actually succeeded in cleaning the streets of New York.[10]

The victory of Tammany Hall in the 1898 elections returned the city to the political jobbery which made Tammany notorious. Judge Robert Van Wyck, the victorious candidate, was mayor during the snowstorm in November. The storm was a test of his administration, and it failed. The disruption of the city was of little consequence, because, as Richard Croker, the boss of Tammany, never tired of repeating, the 'cultured, leisured citizens' who led the reform movement were living in a city in which half the population was born abroad, did not speak English, and knew nothing of American laws or traditions. Tammany liked to think of itself as 'a great digestive apparatus' bringing the immigrants in, making them citizens. Croker's clinching point was that not a single upper-class reformer in the city 'would shake hands with them.' To Croker, men like Waring, Robert Fulton Cutting (president of the Charity Organization Society and leader of the Citizens' Union), and Theodore Roosevelt belonged to the silk-stocking milieu of gentlemen's clubs and Fifth Avenue mansions.

Roosevelt, though he did make occasional appearances at Patriarchs' balls, declined to be painted into that particular corner. Accompanied by Jacob Riis, he spent most of an evening in early 1897 at a labor union meeting at the Clarendon Hall talking as Police Commissioner to delegates. He offered his services as an arbitrator between laboring men and their employers. 'He said that the rich had no pull with him, but that the poor had his sympathy . . .'. After his talk, which was enthusiastically received, he drank beer with the delegates and enjoyed a music hall performance which burlesqued a recent society dinner. The object of the burlesque was the frantic preparations, widely publicized in the press, for the Bradley Martin *Bal Masqué* held at the Waldorf Hotel on February 10, 1897, which was among the most expensive, and most controversial, entertainments of the century. Widespread denunciations of the 'heartless extravagance' of the ball from pulpit and in the press weakened the political position of silk-stocking Republicans, and helped drive the Good Government coalition out of power. For taking part, however tangentially, in the baiting of the rich, and for a tendency towards political slumming, as well as for the near-universal belief in upper-class New York that he was guilty of 'class treason,' Roosevelt aroused a violent hostility in his own class.[11]

On the opening night of the opera in 1898 Mrs. Astor was every inch the embodiment of aristocratic New York. She was sixty-eight years old. Entering her box at the opera with a Louis XVI fan of duchesse lace in her hand, she was described as 'the most gorgeously gemmed of the older matrons.'[12] She observed around her in the parterre boxes that evening the corporation of upper-class life. The Metropolitan Opera House, perhaps more than any other civic institution, embodied the values of the city's late nineteenth-century aristocracy. The greatest and most distinguished families in the city were present.

53. Academy of Music.

'On a January evening in the early seventies, Christine Nilsson was singing in *Faust* at the Academy of Music in New York.' Thus begins Edith Wharton's *The Age of Innocence* (1925). In the 'remote metropolitan distances' there was talk of a new, grander opera house. But for the time being, the 'small and inconvenient' Academy on 14th Street, with its 'historic association' and excellent acoustics, still commanded the loyalty of opera goers. Much of Wharton's portrait is pure nostalgia. The Academy was huge, seating 4,000 in the auditorium; it was scarcely two decades old, having been founded in 1853; and by the 1870s the great European divas like Patti and Nilsson (see p. 229) charged more than the Academy could afford.

These were the men who controlled the banks and insurance companies, who dominated the boards of directors of the mining companies and railroads. Together, they made a great assertion of wealth, position, and apparent social solidarity. They shared a sense of possession: this was their world, around them were their relations, their opera house, their glittering gowns and jewels, and their mansions up and down Fifth Avenue. And, of course, these were clubmen. The majority of the male box-holders belonged to five New York clubs (the Union, Union League, Metropolitan, Knickerbocker, and the Century Association); many personally belonged to eight or ten different clubs. Darius Ogden Mills, J.P. Morgan, and Cornelius Vanderbilt were trustees of the Metropolitan Museum of Art, and were later joined on the board by Harris C. Fahnestock and George F. Baker. In 1897, sixteen of the box-holders were Patriarchs.[13] Such trophy memberships were a sign of who was who in the city's social hierarchy. Twelve box-holders had attended Columbia College, while only eight were Harvard and Yale graduates. The city's upper class in 1898 still at least possessed a nominal sense of having roots in New York.

The Met was the winner in the great struggle in nineteenth-century New York over control of the opera, or more precisely control of the box seats. Between the two institutions the struggle of old money and new was writ large. The Met triumphed over the Academy of Music, an institution which had floundered and struggled for decades, and after its final closure came to acquire the sentimental halo of a key institution of 'Old New York.' Located on the corner of 14th Street and Irving Place, next door to Tammany Hall, the Academy was founded in 1853, in the aftermath of the Astor Place Riot of 1849,[14] and the closure of the Astor Place Opera House three years later. The Academy of Music reflected the cultural ambitions of wealthy New Yorkers and their enthusiasm for Italian opera. The building was conceived on a scale which flattered their sense of self-importance. There were 4,000 seats in the auditorium.

For thirty years the Academy was at the center of the cultural map of the city.[15] It proved virtually impossible, however, to run it at a profit. The Academy was not an inexpensive institution, as the price list for the 1883–4 season makes clear:

subscription for 30 nights:
Parquette seats and balcony (first 4 rows) $125
Balcony (other rows) $80
Balcony boxes $800
Artists' boxes $800
Proscenium boxes (to hold 6 persons) $800
Proscenium boxes (to hold 4 persons) $500
Mezzanine boxes (to hold 6 persons) $600
Mezzanine boxes (to hold 4 persons) $400.[16]

Lacking a resident or permanent company, the Academy was normally rented each season to an impresario. In 1878, the deficit having reached the sum of $17,500, the stockholders sacked the old board and replaced them with a group led by August Belmont. Belmont's attempts to attract a top European singer, like Adelina Patti or Christine Nilsson, proved unavailing. The great *divas* distrusted the way Americans did business, and had reasons to view the Academy with suspicion. Having been bilked of her fee after an earlier performance at the Academy, Patti rejected outright Belmont's inquiries. (By the late 1870s she commanded the sum of $5,000 for one night's performance.)

There were other reasons why the Academy of Music struggled to attract the top European performers. One of the most intractable problems for the successful management of the Academy was the city's audience itself. Writing to his prospective agent, Levi P. Morton, in London, and then to Mapleson, Belmont tried to explain the difficulty with the taste of the Academy audience:

You know that our people will rush to pay liberally for celebrities & for real good artists. . . . The capacity of our Academy of Music is greater than that of Covent Garden or the Italian Opera House in Paris by far & with stars like Nilsson, Patti, Lucca &c, the impresarios have realized always very handsome profits while these 'Divas' themselves secured their own share, now represented in substantial Government Bonds.

54. Christine Nilsson.

On October 22, 1883, at the first night of the Metropolitan Opera House, Christine Nilsson sang the role of Marguerite in Gounod's *Faust*. Nilsson created the role of Marguerite in the Lyric Opera in Paris, and had been a favorite in New York since her debut in 1870. The 'old' Met, occupying the block bounded by Broadway, West 40th Street, Seventh Avenue and West 39th Street, survived until April 16, 1966, when it was demolished and the Met moved to Lincoln Center.

We have a very music loving & enthusiastic audience, but not yet of sufficient culture to do without the additional stimulant of some European Celebrity or some native phenomenon (a combination of both as in the case of Patti of course most desirable).[17]

The American love affair with celebrity was not born in the 1870s, but was already a constraint upon impresarios. Without the 'stimulant' of a 'European celebrity' the New York newspapers had nothing to write about, and the audience looked elsewhere for more lively entertainment. Belmont knew that there was no shortage of amusing and distracting things going on in New York, in direct competition with the Academy of Music.

Belmont's struggles with European artists were a frustrating annoyance; and he regularly subsidized the season's losses. But there were compensations for the managers: the person in control of the Academy decided who would be allowed to rent the prestigious boxes. At a time when Mrs. Astor and Ward McAllister were staking their claim through the Patriarchs to regulate New

York society, the man in charge of the boxes at the Academy was, in practical terms, a rival social Czar of the city.[18] The power which Belmont possessed was precariously balanced between the insistent demands of the new money and the die-hard resistance of the old.

The small number of boxes at the Academy was at the heart of the problem: Belmont could not satisfy the clamor of wealthy New Yorkers for additional boxes. Irving Kolodin identifies William H. Vanderbilt as the likely leader in the demand for new boxes, and as one of the few men wealthy enough to act upon his wish. Belmont saw wisdom in appeasing the new money set led by the Vanderbilts, and offered to build twenty-six new boxes at the Academy. The men around Vanderbilt demanded nothing less than access to the old box circle. The Knickerbockers led by the Barclays, Barlows, Beekmans, Livingstons, and Schuylers on the board of the Academy rejected any concessions to the *nouveaux riches*.[19] Sheer impatience led to the founding of the Metropolitan Opera-House Company in April 1880. (This was not long after Belmont had been elected to the Patriarchs, and while the Vanderbilts were still excluded.) The site was purchased for $600,000 in 1881, and when the building on Broadway was completed the stockholders and directors participated in a draw for the boxes. The successful box-holders at the Met included the Vanderbilts, John Jacob Astor III, William Rockefeller, and J.P. Morgan.[20] Vanderbilt spent the opening night at the Met in 'an unusual degree of sociability' chatting with various acquaintances as he passed through the lobby between the three boxes which he now owned. Virtually single-handedly, he had summoned the new opera house into existence.[21]

Carefully designed to rub the noses of the old money in their humiliation, the grand opening of the Metropolitan Opera in 1883 featured Christine Nilsson singing Marguerite in *Faust*. In *The Age of Innocence* Wharton's recollection of Nilsson as singing at the Academy was correct, but by the 1880s she belonged to another world of big money symbolized by the new Metropolitan Opera House. A reporter at the opening night on October 22, 1883, noted that 'All the nouveaux riches were there. The Goulds and Vanderbilts and people of that ilk perfumed the air with the odor of crisp greenbacks. The tiers of boxes looked like cages in a menagerie of monopolists. When somebody remarked that the house looked *as bright as a new dollar*, the appropriate character of the assemblage became apparent. To the refined eye, the decorations of the edifice seemed in particularly bad taste.'[22]

The audiences that night at the two opera houses revealed an old faultline in the aristocracy. Where you attended on the opening night told the world which side you were on. At the Academy, with Etelka Gerster singing Amina in Bellini's *La Sonnambula* were the senior and junior August Belmonts, Costers, Duers, Cuttings, Burdens, LeRoys, Beckwiths, Lorillards, Dixes, and Phelpses.

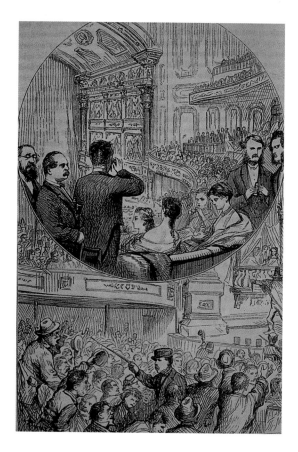

55. Academy of Music and the Bowery Theater.

The nature of New York as a community was debated through paired images, such as this representation of the Academy of Music (above), and the Bowery Theater. Aristocracy and democracy, refinement and social disorder, suggest the alternatives. The caped villain on the stage of the Bowery, dagger in hand, grips the audience. At the Academy the audience itself was the main attraction.

In five glittering boxes at the Met, as well as the Goulds and Vanderbilts, were John Jacob Astor III, Russell Sage, Henry Clews, Cyrus W. Field, William Rockefeller, Richard T. Wilson, Robert Hoe, D.O. Mills—and the socially-rehabilitated Patriarch William Butler Duncan. The Met boxes were also adorned by old money who were now moving with considerable style into the orbit of the new: the Ogden and Robert Goelets, Remsens, Babcocks, Roosevelts, and Rhinelanders.[23] Mrs. Paran Stevens spent the evening in her brougham shuttling her daughter Minnie, later Lady Paget, up and down between the two opera houses, in order to safeguard her status in both camps. Mrs. Astor, who declared her undying allegiance to the Academy, on the night remained in the country. Perhaps she wanted to know the outcome before entering the struggle. The October 31, 1883, issue of *Puck* featured a double-page cartoon of the battling impresarios, singers, and musicians.[24] For the first time in New York, opera had become the hottest show in town.

Outgunned in the competition for European *divas*, and seemingly abandoned by the wealthy, the Academy closed as an opera house in 1885. A Consolidated Edison building was eventually built on the site.

The first impression visitors had when entering the gaslit Met, a large building situated between Broadway and Seventh Avenue, between 39th and 40th Streets, was of overweening scale. 'Nobody ever entered that auditorium for the first time without a gasp at its grandeur.' Everything else—acoustics, décor, sightlines, the absence of rehearsal space—proved to be poorly thought out, and shoddily executed.[25] (After the end of the first season, the entire amphitheater was redecorated.) The horseshoe auditorium had five tiers and 122 boxes, later reduced to 74, plus a double-sized 'omnibus box.' By nineteenth-century standards, the ratio of boxes to the seating capacity of the auditorium was extraordinary. Even-numbered boxes on the right, looking towards the stage, faced the odd-numbered boxes.

There were eighty-three named box-holders in 1898, many of whom shared tenancy. Box 24 was jointly held by Robert Goelet (for performances on Mondays, Fridays, and matinées) and the painter Albert Bierstadt (Wednesdays). Box 28 had four holders: ex-Civil Service Commissioner Cutting (Mondays and matinées), W.S. Gurnee, Jr. (odd Wednesdays), Miss Annie Leary (even Wednesdays), and Clarence H. Mackey (Fridays). Only seven boxes were held by single individuals; nine of the box-holders were women and one box was held by an estate. Names of the box-holders were published by the Metropolitan Opera, and appeared in the press. At the level above the parterre boxes there were stall boxes, grand tier boxes and omnibus boxes, which attracted less interest than those on the more prestigious parterre level. Like pews, boxes at the Metropolitan Opera were a form of personal property. And as was the case with the transfer of pews at Grace Church, the Metropolitan's bylaws held that 'no transfer of stock shall be made except to a person or persons previously approved by the directorate.'[26]

Throughout the opera house the lines of relationship between box-holders were as thick and complex as the overhead telephone and telegraph wires which cluttered the streets. There were relationships which were commercial or financial, and many which came from marriage. The occupant of box 5, H.A.C. Taylor, son of the merchant Moses Taylor, was Stanford White's landlord on 21st Street (box 9). Samuel D. Babcock was a partner of George G. Haven, with whom he shared box 26. Augustus Juilliard (box 2) bought William Waldorf Astor's mansion at Tuxedo in 1894. But there were some commercial relations which were neither collegial or amicable, and which revealed the sharper edge of predatory capitalism. William Bayard Cutting (box 28) had been a director of the Illinois Central railroad with Stuyvesant Fish (box 6). But Fish's great nemesis, Edward H. Harriman, who later drove him off the board of directors of the Illinois Central in 1906, occupied nearby box 4. There were knots of personal and commercial interest which bound together men with money and the architect Stanford White, who designed Newport cottages

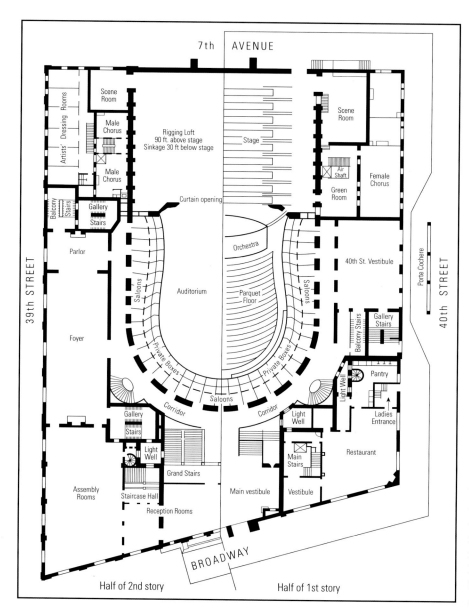

Fig. 2. Metropolitan Opera House.

The Metropolitan Opera in 1883 had 122 boxes, in four tiers, seating 750 persons. There were twelve huge boxes on the ground floor; above these a first tier of thirty-eight parterre boxes, which were the most prized, and reserved for stockholders only. The next tier had thirty-six boxes, also reserved for stockholders. Only the fourth tier of thirty-six boxes was available for yearly rent by non-stockholders. This arrangement deprived impresarios at the Met of the most valuable seats in the house. In compensation, the boxholders guaranteed a subsidy of the season's costs.

for the Oelrichs (box 5), Robert Goelet (box 24), an Interborough Rapid Transit Company power station for Charles Tracy Barney (box 9), and a mansion for the Stuyvesant Fishes on Madison Avenue. Fish had worked in Levi P. Morton's banking firm, Morton, Bliss & Co. (box 16). John Jacob Astor (box 7) served on Morton's staff in the US Volunteers in the successful Cuban campaign.

Marriage formed the most pervasive and strongest of the bonds among the box holders. Robert Goelet married a sister of George Henry Warren (box 14). Henry Dimock (box 19) and Charles Tracy Barney married sisters of

W.C. Whitney (box 30). W. Seward Webb (box 22), William D. Sloane, and Hamilton McK. Twombly (who shared box 17) married daughters of William Henry Vanderbilt, and were thus brothers-in-law of Willie and Cornelius Vanderbilt, who were also box-holders. In the marrying business, no one was more successful than Richard T. Wilson (box 3), whose son Orme married a daughter of Mrs. Astor (box 7). Wilson's daughter Mary married Ogden Goelet, brother of Robert Goelet (box 24), and another daughter married Cornelius Vanderbilt, II (box 31). Sometimes the marriage ties were through brothers or sisters, or children. The Sloanes' daughter Florence married James Abercrombie Burden (box 29). Eleanora Iselin, daughter of Adrian Iselin (box 15), married Colonel De Lancey Kane, a relation of Mrs. Astor. Perry Belmont (box 11) married a Sloane (boxes 17 and 25); his brother Oliver married the ex-wife of Willie Vanderbilt (box 6). We do not need to suggest a hierarchy for these ties, or to assert the primacy of club or church membership. The box-holders were bound together by intricate lines of relationship and interest. The air that night at the Metropolitan Opera was humming with what they knew about each other. An outsider, a figure like Morris Townsend in *Washington Square*, was someone with no place in the social geography of the city's families and their interlocking hierarchies.

To an old New Yorker like Mrs. Astor, the occupants of the parterre boxes were not alone, in couples or in small parties, but had around them an aura in which the spirits of parents, grandparents, and ancestors hovered.[27] Allowing herself for a moment to recall the world around Bowling Green where she had grown up, where some of the elderly residents had retained the dress and tastes of the colonial world, those who were present in the parterre boxes, and those who belonged to the greater 'family' of society, shared the sense of owning New York. Mrs. Astor's parents and grandparents had known that world of Old New York, and at the deepest level of her being she remained true to the memory of their city. At the opera, and among those on her large visiting list, were many who shared similar recollections. They were possessors in memory of a community which was no more. She knew these people, and knew why they were sitting comfortably around her in the parterre boxes at the opera. When she thought of them, it was not simply as people who shared her hospitality (or not), but as leading figures in a great historical procession uniting past and present. It gave her a feeling of strength and coherence, of something fortifying against the ugly chaos of New York City and its snow-piled streets.

Yet around her there were also rivals, sharp-eyed women who craved notoriety, and whose ostentation was a continuing source of annoyance. Mrs. Astor wanted to reign over a contented realm, and hoped that everyone would behave properly, dress well, enjoy her hospitality, and take pleasure in her

supremacy. Mrs. Stuyvesant Fish in box 9 posed a continuing dilemma. Though pug-faced and dumpy, Mamie Fish was quite regally dressed in an embroidered white satin gown, and a stunning sable-edged peacock blue moiré cape. Her diamond tiara was a little reminder—though Mrs. Astor did not need reminding—that the Fish family had more ancient claims to distinction than either the Schermerhorns or Astors. A tiara told the world that she regarded herself as a fit person to challenge Mrs. Astor for social leadership. Mamie Fish yielded to no one in sheer snobbishness: she instructed Stanford White to design a ballroom for their new home on 78th Street 'in which a person who was not well bred would feel uncomfortable.' This was yet another vehicle for the heightened passion for aristocratic exclusivity. As Samuel G. White has argued, by the 1880s the New York rich were beginning to demand an architecture 'that celebrated the differences between them and their countrymen.'[28]

A dignified attentiveness, rather as she imagined Queen Victoria had endured her loquacious prime ministers, was more congenial to Mrs. Astor. Contemporaries could rarely recall anything she actually said. It was Mamie Fish's wit and Harry Lehr's wounding remarks which traveled from mansion to mansion. Guests talked more about the wonderful display of flowers and jewels at an Astor entertainment than of the food or wine; even less was said of bright sayings or clever talk. 'As a spectacle to fill the eye and gratify every taste,' noted a reporter in the *Sun*, the Astor entertainments 'are unequaled in any country; but nothing is exacted or expected from the guests but to look their best and to enjoy the bountiful feast that is set before them.'[29] Where Mamie Fish delighted in shocking her guests, and openly expressed her scorn for social conventions, Mrs. Astor had about her a certain expensive incuriousness, and the gracious, boring skills of a monarch. Being Mrs. Astor was sufficient, and no further performance was on offer. She had no intimate friends. Service to her family, and to society, were obligations enough for any monarch. This meant that she gave the impression of someone who acted as though unpleasant things like snow piled in the streets or the infidelity of her husband did not exist. She simply turned away from anything that might trouble her. It was clear that Mamie Fish was a disruptive presence in society, but the most powerful of Mrs. Astor's instincts was the regal desire to reconcile her troublesome subjects. She sought to mend fences even after Mamie Fish had nearly managed the defenestration of Ward McAllister in 1891. Signaling to society that amicableness, not feuds, was the order of the day she held a dinner that summer for her daughter Charlotte and her miserable husband James Coleman Drayton, which was attended by the Willie Vanderbilts, Townsend Burdens, James Kernochans, and Mamie Fish.[30] The Fishes were, after all, Mrs. Astor's neighbors at Newport and the distance from 20 Gramercy Park to Fifth Avenue was in social terms small, and smaller still when the Fishes moved into a Stanford White mansion on Madison Avenue at the corner of 78th Street in 1900. The dinner for Charlotte, attended by the principal plotters against McAllister, was a sign that she, alone, had the power to transcend factions.

Mrs. Astor smiled vaguely in the direction of box 23, acknowledging the distinguished Elbridge Gerry, who, with his mutton-chop whiskers and love of yachting, so curiously resembled her late husband William. Levi P. Morton, Vice-President under Benjamin Harrison and then Republican Governor of New York in 1895–6, was on the other side of the horseshoe in box 16. Such men as Gerry and Morton, from the heart of the New York aristocracy, moved on the national stage. Two days before the opening night of the opera, after a month criss-crossing the state with a small troop of Rough Riders, a bugler, and enough American flags to stir the most blasé of New Yorkers, Theodore Roosevelt had been elected Republican Governor of the state. This was an even stronger reason to feel content with the world. One could overlook much about Roosevelt for he, too, was one of *ours*, one of the aristocrats.

Her guests began arriving at 842 Fifth Avenue after 10.30 p.m., many coming directly from the opera. The procession of carriages had in recent years been augmented by increasing numbers of automobiles. A van from the Church Temperance Society was always on hand, to provide the coachmen with sandwiches and coffee. (Mrs. Astor only once rode in an automobile, and then announced 'This is the last time.'[31]) It was a 'Small Dance,' with only 400 invitations issued, and 300 acceptances received. Guests entered a circular hall of cream-colored Caen stone, at the end of which was a marble staircase flanked by life-sized female figures sculpted by Carl Ritter. The hall rose to the roof of the building. Guests would proceed up the marble staircase to dressing rooms before descending to enter the drawing room of the north house where Mrs. Astor received alone, beneath her life-sized portrait by Carolus Duran. She was wearing a gown of black velvet, with a low-cut bodice trimmed with white appliqué, and a throat band of black velvet, edged with small diamond stars. The drawing room was smothered in the heavy fragrance of expensive flowers.[32]

The doors separating the north or upper house where Mrs. Astor lived, and the south house of her son Colonel John Jacob Astor IV, 840 Fifth Avenue, were thrown open for the evening. There was general dancing in the ballroom, lit now by a combination of electric lights and candles. Amidst so much luxury, she preferred simplicity in profusion, decorating her home with overflowing displays of Easter lilies and carnations. Her favorite flower was the American Beauty rose, a newly introduced flower which was first imported from France in the 1880s. 'It has so long a stem,' noted Paul Bourget after his first visit to Newport, 'it is so intensely red, so wide open, and so strongly perfumed, that it does not seem like a natural flower. It requires the greenhouse, the exposition, a public display.'[33] Lander's orchestra and the Hungarian Band provided the evening's music. Supper from Sherry's was served at 12.30 at forty small tables in the south house, and a cotillion, so large as to require two leaders (Harry Lehr and Elisha Dyer, Jr.) was danced afterwards. For each figure of the cotillion there were favors, including silver baskets, paper-cutters, canes, pipes, pin cushions, fans, gold and silver belt buckles, satin ribbons, and other attractive things. Once the evening's duty of greeting 300 guests was complete she quietly withdrew to her bedroom. Mrs. Astor cared little for dancing on such large public occasions, and was happy for her daughters to represent the family and enjoy the cotillion.

The evening went smoothly. It always did.

Schermerhorns

> When somebody objected that the Vanderbilts had no great grandmothers . . . somebody else replied that Mrs. William Astor was only a Schermerhorn, and the Schermerhorns used to be shipchandlers.
> —Gossip (1887)[34]

The woman who presided with such magisterial ease at the leading social events of the New York season belonged to an old New York family, the Schermerhorns. Pronounced *Skairmern*, with an emphatic growling Dutch *k*, the Schermerhorns were a family of Dutch origin who, in the spirit of an American success story, made their way in the New World as farmers, mechanics, small tradesmen, and merchants.[35] By the time Caroline Webster Schermerhorn—the 'Webster' was a tribute to the Massachusetts Whig politician, and his wife Caroline LeRoy, a New Yorker, just as another family named their son Alexander Jackson Davis or Thomas Jefferson Whitman—was born in 1830, the family had become quite grand as bankers, merchants, and substantial landowners. If not quite on a par with the property-owning Astors, Costers, Wendels, and Goelets, the name Schermerhorn was one which commanded respect in New York City.

Known for pride in their lineage and a dislike of public life, the Schermerhorns were cautious Dutch husbandmen, nurturing their fortunes and looking after their kinfolk. When the threat of war loomed in the 1770s, Peter Schermerhorn (in the family he was 'Peter the Elder') removed his small fleet from New York to Hyde Park, thus saving his vessels from seizure during the Revolutionary War. After the withdrawal of the British Army from New York, Peter the Elder relocated his shipping and ship chandlery business to Water Street on Manhattan, where he proved to be an industrious merchant. He was elected a director of the Bank of New York in 1796, a position he held until his death three decades later. Judicious investments in commercial real estate, and a large tract of land in Gowanus (a neighborhood in northwestern Brooklyn), on which he erected a summer cottage, as well as the construction of nine federal-style row houses on Fulton Street in 1811–12 (now known as 'Schermerhorn Row,' the heavily altered buildings form part of the South Street Seaport Museum), were the foundation of the family's fortune. He also bought four and a half acres along the East River at the foot of 84th Street where a handsome country home was erected. Peter the Elder began the transformation of the Schermerhorns from merchants and traders to land-owning gentry. The family lived in some style at 68 Broadway.

His sons were brought into the family business. Peter ('Peter the Younger') and then Abraham became partners in the firm of Peter Schermerhorn & Sons, Ship Chandlers. The two brothers engaged in a wide range of other commercial activities. In 1814 Peter the Younger joined his father as a director of the Bank of New York. On their father's death, the two brothers formed separate banks: Schermerhorn, Banker & Co., at 243 Water Street, and Schermerhorn, Willis & Co. at 53 South Street. Peter the Younger married one of the great heiresses of the day, Sarah Jones, and lived at 21 Park Place. Like his neighbor Samuel Ward, Peter Schermerhorn was one of the banking grandees of the city. On the death of her father John Jones, Sarah Schermerhorn received the southernmost division of Louvre Farm, a great estate of 132 acres lying between Third Avenue and the East River, from 66th Street to 75th Street. Acquiring an adjacent 20 acres, Peter Schermerhorn built a country home at the foot of 64th Street. A Schermerhorn musical soirée at their estate on 64th Street, with visiting opera stars performing, was regarded by Hone as the 'greatest party of the season' in 1845. An early and passionate supporter of Italian opera in New York, Peter the Younger joined Hone and Samuel Shaw Howland in the purchase of a box at the Richmond Hill Theater. He was a founder of the Knickerbocker Society. The social standing of the family is suggested by Peter the Younger's election as vestryman, and then senior warden, of Grace Church. When he died, Strong sarcastically commented that Peter Schermerhorn was 'reduced to destitution, deprived of all his property and estate real and personal, last Wednesday—having been so recklessly extravagant as to die on that day. He must be sadly bored in a world where there are no rents to collect and no investments to be made . . .'.[36]

Four of their six children—the cousins of Mrs. Astor—survived into adulthood. Jones Schermerhorn attended Columbia College and, as we have seen, married the daughter of Philip Hone. His brother Peter married the daughter of Henry Coster. Edmund, the third surviving brother, was the saddest and strangest of the sons of 'Peter the Younger,' spending much of his adult life as a recluse, having been cruelly disappointed in love. William Colford

Schermerhorn, born in 1821, was the youngest, liveliest, and most aristocratic of the Schermerhorn brothers. After graduating from Columbia College with honors in 1840, he was admitted to the bar, but preferred to devote himself to gentry cultural institutions in the city, serving on the boards of the American Museum of Natural History and the Metropolitan Museum of Art as well as becoming a trustee of Columbia College. He was also a convert to homeopathy, a dabbler in ouija, a patron of mediums, an enthusiastic participant of tableaux vivants, and a supporter of the opera and the amateur musical life in the city. Married to Annie Laight Cottenet, daughter of a Swiss merchant long based in New York, he lived on Lafayette Place. 'Everything the Schermerhorns undertake is carried out to the utmost perfection of detail,' noted an admiring Strong. William was the first of the Schermerhorns to enter the city's fashionable life.[37]

The other branch of the family was led by Abraham Schermerhorn. When his youngest daughter Caroline was born in 1830, he was forty-seven years old and estimated to be worth half a million dollars. A pew-holder at Grace Church, and a member of the Union Club, like his brother Peter the Younger, he was a prosperous merchant enjoying the respect of the community. '"Being a Schermerhorn,"' noted the family's genealogist, 'has always carried with it a most serious sense of honor and self respect.' Abraham had been buying New York and Brooklyn real estate for decades, and owned many valuable lots as well as 170 acres at Gowanus.[38] His wife, Helen White, was the daughter of Henry White and Ann Van Cortlandt.[39] Caroline Schermerhorn's grandfather, a die-hard Loyalist, fled New York with the departing British forces in 1783, and died not long after in London. His widow returned to New York with her children Helen, Peter, and Harry White, and lived comfortably and respectably on Broadway. Being a Van Cortlandt and a Schermerhorn gave the woman who became Mrs. Astor a strong claim to a place at the highest level of New York's oldest families.

Abraham and Helen Schermerhorn had a large family; with the arrival of her last child, she had given birth to nine children (eight were alive) by the age of thirty-eight. As the youngest, Caroline (always called 'Lina' in the family) was everyone's pet. In 1830 the Schermerhorns lived at the southwest corner of Greenwich Street, at the corner of Battery Place, and had a garden which extended down to the banks of the Hudson River. The fancy ball given by Mrs. S*********** in 1829 (see pp. 127–9) suggests the prosperity enjoyed by Abraham and Helen Schermerhorn: they could comfortably entertain 250 guests in eight brilliantly illuminated rooms. Memories of living near Bowling Green, of taking childhood walks on the Battery, and having a garden like those described in accounts of colonial New York, gave Caroline Schermerhorn a strong proprietary sense that the history of the city and its great growth in her lifetime was truly a living part of her family's history. A few representatives of the old Yankee and Knickerbocker families (Ferdinand Suydam, Stephen Whitney, Jonathan Sturges, Jonathan Goodhue) remained on lower Greenwich Street, Bowling Green, and Whitehall, but by the 1850s only a few elderly residents were left to remember the social prestige of the city's first aristocratic neighborhood.

On Bond Street in the 1840s and 1850s a young and cherished daughter of one of the city's leading merchants was surrounded by relations, looked after by nurses, tutors, nannies, and servants, entertained at parties at the homes of neighbors, and taken to Europe for all the reasons parents took their smartly dressed daughters to Europe. She was educated at a school conducted by a French émigré, Mrs. Bensee, in the things thought necessary for a young woman of the class and social position of the Schermerhorns: deportment, penmanship, needlework, and dancing. She became a fluent speaker of French, and a lifelong believer in the superiority of French institutions, painters, manners, cuisine, clothes, furniture, and jewelry. She was at home among the leading families in Paris, where she invariably spent several months each year and maintained an apartment at 146 Avenue des Champs-Elysées. (In an aggressively Anglophile New York upper class, she did not care for the English, and rarely visited England.)

The neighborhood was teeming with relations and family friends. Uncle 'Peter the Younger' and his family lived at the corner of Great Jones Street and Lafayette Place. The Hones, regular dinner guests, lived at the corner of Great Jones Street and Broadway. The Delanos, Morgans, Langdons, and Astors lived down the block.

The Schermerhorns were heavily involved during the 1850s in the debates over proposals to create a large park in New York. Nudged along by Andrew Jackson Downing, N.P. Willis, and William Cullen Bryant, enlightened opinion in New York had for several decades urged the creation of a large uptown public park. Attention turned to Jones Wood, on the East River, where the Jones family owned substantial property and where Peter the Younger had his handsome country estate. Peter and Abraham had by then retired from business, but their estates remained undivided, and the family's interests were closely entwined. It was their sons who took up the defense of the family's property. In June 1851 a committee of the common council recommended that the city acquire 90 acres of woodland owned by John Jones and an adjacent tract owned by 'Peter the Younger,' to form a public park running north from 66th to 75th Streets, from the East River to Third Avenue. At current property valuations, the land was probably worth over one million dollars. The Schermerhorns opposed the park, arguing that government had no legal right to take private property for a place of public amusement: 'a park is not

sufficient public necessity to justify its being taken by the state in opposition to the wishes of the owner and by the violent exercise of eminent domain.' 'The Schermerhorns don't like it a bit,' noted Strong in his diary, 'or pretend they don't, notwithstanding the $1,500,000 of which they'll get their share.' The first legislative attempts to acquire Jones Wood were blocked by the State Supreme Court in 1851, and by the time the legislative procedures had been re-started, a more central and larger site, at a significantly lower price per acre, was available. For the first time the name 'Central Park' began to appear in print, to the immense delight of the Schermerhorns, who promptly joined the ranks of those who supported the new proposal for the park.[40]

With the marriage of Anna to Charles Suydam in 1849, and Catherine to Benjamin Welles in June 1850, Caroline was the last of the Schermerhorn sisters to remain at home. It was not the family tradition for daughters to marry young. Her sisters Elizabeth and Catherine both married at 22, Anna at 31, Helen at 18. The death of her father Abraham in February 1850 and marriage of Catherine five months later may have delayed any thought on the topic. At 23, with little overt pressure to marry, she might look forward to remaining her mother's companion. But marriage was an unavoidable question, even in a

56. Schermerhorn house on the East River.

In the nineteenth century the banks of the East River, from mid-town to Harlem, was lined with the handsome clapboarded country homes of the great landowners of New York. One branch of the Schermerhorns had an estate on East 73rd Street. The other Schermerhorn estate, portrayed above, was on 84th Street. From the rear verandah you could see the picturesque shipping on the river, and beyond, Hell Gate and semi-rural Queens.

family as well established as the Schermerhorns. Of all the families in the city with whom an advantageous match might be imagined, the Astors, with their vast holdings of city real estate, were the top—providing that is, a genteel family were prepared to overlook the unappetizing aspects of the recently deceased John Jacob Astor. Marriage to the youngest son of William B. Astor, his father's namesake, appeared to be an answer to the plight of an unwed daughter acceptable to both Astors and Schermerhorns.

A rich man and his sons

> . . . a hard dreary looking old man and the richest in the world.
> —Lord Rosebery, on first seeing William Backhouse Astor $(1873)^{41}$

By the 1850s the Astors had made a successful transition from 'new money' to a respected and generally admired position in the city's social elite. The social success of the Astors was founded upon the substantial bedrock of wealth amassed by John Jacob; but it was the personal qualities of his heir, William Backhouse, and his formidable wife Margaret that established the social prominence which the Astor family enjoyed at mid-century. The old, humiliating stories about John Jacob long continued to circulate in the city. If contemporaries found Astor to be the ultimate American success story, rising from poverty to immense wealth, there was also a widespread scorn for his crudity, meanness, and absence of charitable benevolence. His ungrammatical English and the thick German accent which he never managed to lose were repeatedly mentioned in nineteenth-century accounts of the family, as were the inadequacies of his table manners. Albert Gallatin and his son James, who had many opportunities to observe Astor on informal occasions, were horrified by his crudeness at table. While having dinner one evening at the Gallatins' in 1820, he reached across to Frances Gallatin, James' sister, and casually wiped his fingers on the sleeve of her white jacket.^{42} In the moral double-entry bookkeeping which Americans kept, habits of thrift were praiseworthy; bad manners, tightfistedness, and meanness on the part of a man worth millions were regarded as contemptible.

In the first substantial biography of Astor, written within two decades of his death, James Parton spelled out a truth about Astor: he was not a useful role model. Astor was not generous, Parton argued, 'except to his own kindred. His liberality began and ended in his own family. Very seldom during his lifetime did he willingly do a generous act outside of the little circle of his relations and descendants. To get all he could, and to keep nearly all that he got—those were the laws of his being. He had a vast genius for making money, and that was all that he had.' Parton's Astor was constructed of American stereotypes. He was

57. John Jacob Astor.

John Jacob Astor was a complex emblem of antebellum America, and its values. His wealth fascinated and repelled his contemporaries. It was the former sentiment which proved the most enduring. John Jacob Astor, as the narrator of Herman Melville's story 'Bartleby the Scrivener' (1856) put it, was 'a name which I admit, I love to repeat, for it hath a rounded and orbicular sound to it, and rings like unto bullion.'

the young boy who, '[w]ith a small bundle of clothes hung over his shoulder upon a stick, with a crown or two in his pocket, . . . said the last farewell to his father and his friends, and set out on foot for the Rhine'. But he was also a miser in his counting-house, pawing his gold: 'The roll-book of his possessions was his Bible. He scanned it fondly, and saw with quiet but deep delight the catalogue of his property lengthening from month to month. The love of accumulation grew with his years until it ruled him like a tyrant.'[43]

Albert Gallatin had worked closely with Astor for years, but when Astor asked him to become a partner in the American Fur Company he politely declined. The entry in his son James' diary richly sets out the scorn and snobbishness with which Astor was regarded: 'His reasons for refusing were, although he respected Mr. Astor, he never could place himself on the same level with him. I am not surprised, as Astor was a butcher's son at Waldorf— came as an emigrant to this country with a pack on his back. He peddled furs, was very clever, and is, I believe, one of the kings of the fur trade, He dined here and ate his ice-cream and peas with a knife.' Those like Francis Lieber who sought Astor's patronage found him affable enough, but unreachable: 'If I could talk anything of interest with the old man, about his intended library &c I should like it,' he explained, 'but thus as it is, I might as well look at the out-side of a cask of ducats.' Others who encountered Astor socially found him to be 'one of the most wretched men,' displeased with his daughters, and obsessed with the granddaughter by his estranged daughter Mrs. Langdon. There was something about Astor which made New Yorkers uneasy, and it was not only his table manners or money that disturbed them.[44]

Parton made a judgment, congenial to later generations, that Astor represented wealth divorced from social responsibility or conscience: 'He probably never thought of the public good in connection with the bulk of his property'. The most heartfelt condemnation of Astor came from the Knickerbocker novelist James Kirke Paulding: 'I used to know him, when an ignoble dealer in Musk Rat Skins,' he wrote to Martin Van Buren in 1848, 'but cut his acquaintance when he became a Millionaire, for I found he grew mean faster than he grew rich, and that his avarice increased with his means of being generous. He lived miserably and died miserably; for in the latter Years of his life, he became ambitious to build up a great family by matching his Daughters to some of the European aristocracy. But they all ran-away, except one who matched with a little German or Swiss Baron, the tail of Diplomacy in Paris.'[45]

William Backhouse and Margaret Astor conducted their domestic lives in a befitting and simple manner. Even when they entertained at their home on Lafayette Place, as Marian Gouverneur recalled, Margaret did not wear jewels. (Her daughters-in-law were of another mind on the subject of jewels.) 'Yesterday, the twenty-seventh,' wrote Mrs. Basil Hall to her sister, 'we dressed for a dinner at the very fashionable hour of five at the house of Mr. and Mrs. William Astor.' Mrs. Hall, ever skilled at a backhanded compliment, was happy to find the elderly John Jacob Astor 'a good, honest, plain sort of a man himself, totally free of the affectation of pretending to be a gentleman.' Astor had tried to raise his son as a gentleman, and 'as far as I can judge upon a short acquaintance, he has succeeded, for he [William Backhouse Astor] is in appearance and first manner very gentleman-like. His wife [Margaret, *née* Armstrong] is a very pretty, nice-looking young woman, and the whole style of their house is good. We had dinner in much better taste than any I have before seen in New York, . . . and no mixing up of columns of ice along with pies and puddings.'[46]

John Jacob Astor died on March 29, 1848. His funeral took place on April 1st from his son's mansion on Lafayette Place. As a young man, the dry-goods merchant Edward N. Tailer, an inveterate diary keeper from his early years,

58. Astor Library on Lafayette Place.

The Astor Library was, from its earliest conception, a research library. Cogswell was dismayed when the reading room filled up with schoolboys reading 'trashy' books by Scott, Dickens and James Fenimore Cooper. He raised the minimum age for use of the library from fourteen to sixteen. Represented here is the original structure, erected 1853-4. The library was expanded to the north in 1859 and 1881.

attended the funeral. 'The upper part of the coffin was open, and within lay that which once was life, the solid massive features were there. . . . Alas, that was the corpse of the richest man in all this wide continent. See what throngs of gazers!' The coffin, 'covered with a rich velvet fall,' was raised on the shoulders of four pall-bearers, and was followed by a group of men led by Washington Irving, James Gallatin, William Backhouse Astor, and Charles Astor Bristed. A large number of followers—Tailer believed there were as many as 500—walked in procession to St. Thomas' Church on Broadway. William Backhouse, six feet tall with stooped shoulders, was by then fifty-six, and a man of independent wealth.[47]

No son of John Jacob Astor could have emerged into adulthood without bearing the harsh impression of his overbearing father. Magdalen Astor, a willful and spoiled woman, divorced her first husband and was abandoned by her second. Dorothea Astor fled the family home to elope with Colonel Walter Langdon. Eliza Astor, crushed by her father's unwillingness to let her marry a dentist, was pushed into an arranged marriage. She spent the remainder of her life consoled by evangelical religion and charitable good works. In her father's obituary in the *Herald*, the bleak life of a daughter of John Jacob Astor was summarized: 'Hers was a life of watchfulness, of self-distrust, of prayer. She read the Scriptures not only daily, but much [of] every day.' Her father had a memoir written of Eliza, and over 100 copies of this sickly and exculpatory document were among his possessions when his estate was inventoried in 1848. John Jacob Astor was no less determined to control his son's life. He sent William Backhouse to study at Heidelberg and then at Göttingen, in the company of a hired tutor and companion, and then summoned him back to New York in 1817 to enter the family business as a partner. At Heidelberg William Backhouse was remembered as an affable young man with literary interests. In New York he became silent and self-contained. 'The youth studied his father's methods and began to live his father's life.' For a decade while John Jacob spent long periods in Europe, William Backhouse proved himself to be a cautious businessman, meticulous in his stewardship of the Astor holdings.[48]

John Jacob was determined that his fortune should largely pass intact to his son's oldest male heir. As the residuary legatee of his father's estate, worth eighteen million dollars, for the rest of his life William Backhouse acted for the property. The torpid matter of leases and rents held him, bound hand and foot, to his father's fortune. William Backhouse doubled or trebled his father's great wealth. Lacking the aggressive, buccaneering spirit of a Vanderbilt or Gould, there was little about him that fit the 'Robber Baron' stereotype. He did not speculate, and seemed, in an age of vivid personalities on Wall Street and in mercantile New York, to be respectable but uninteresting. After interviewing William Backhouse, Matthew Hale Smith compared the small Astor office on Prince Street to a cell in a house of detention. Smith was impressed with his close knowledge of the estate ('He knows every inch of real estate that stands in his name, every bond, contract, and lease. He knows what is due when leases expire, and attends personally to all this matter') but regarded Astor himself as a paradoxical figure, living in considerable domestic luxury yet taking pleasure in nothing other than his family, perhaps not even in the details of his business affairs.[49] There was about him the heavy gloominess of a man shouldering great responsibilities. A diligent Episcopalian, like the Schermerhorns he was a pew-holder at Grace Church. The family into which Caroline Schermerhorn married held an annual family dinner on New Year's Day, a 'ponderous' event, recalled his grandson William Waldorf: 'We were two dozen at table, few of the party convivially gifted, several none too pleased to meet, the host and hostess too old to enjoy anything.'[50] A woman of fashion might have looked at the Astors with dismay. They were unpromising terrain for social leadership.

William Backhouse Astor married Margaret Armstrong in 1818, and over the next fourteen years they had seven children. Margaret Armstrong's mother was a Livingston, and her father, General Armstrong, had served as Secretary of War in the cabinet of James Madison. The domestic lives of William Backhouse and Margaret were regarded by their contemporaries as models of social decorum. His children were indeed seen and not heard. Brought up not to laugh aloud, or to speak during meals, they wore clothes of a somber color, and were expected to back respectfully from the room after bidding goodnight to their mother and father.[51] When their daughter Eliza Ward died, her surviving child Margaret ('Maddie') was raised at Rokeby, the Armstrong estate at Rhinebeck by the same servants who had been in domestic service with Maddie's grandmother, and given the same largely feudal upbringing. Margaret Astor's daughters and her granddaughter grew up in a world where social gradations, good manners, reserve, and decorum were enforced with an unblinking severity.

William Backhouse and Margaret lived in the city on lower Broadway, and then on Lafayette Place, a home which Hone regarded as 'noble' and 'magnificent.' As the diaries of Philip Hone and George Templeton Strong make clear, their entertaining was easily on a par with that of the Stevens, Hones, Howlands, Schermerhorns, Rays, and other leading antebellum New York families. The marriage of William Backhouse's oldest son, John Jacob Astor III, to Augusta Gibbes in 1846 brought forth Hone's ambivalent praise for the

> splendid crowd of charming women, pretty girls, and well-dressed beaux, some with smooth faces. And many whose mouths were closed and chins covered by filthy masses of black hair. The spacious mansion in Lafayette place was open from cellar to garret, blazing with a thousand lights. . . . The crowd was excessive; the ladies (such part of their exquisite forms as could be distinguished in the mêlée) elegantly and tastefully attired, with a display of rich jewelry, enough to pay one day's expense of the Mexican war.[52]

William Backhouse seemed determined to repeat the pattern of his childhood and education: John Jacob III (called 'Johann' within the family) lacked his father's academic abilities. After an unsuccessful term at Columbia College, he was sent to Göttingen in the company of Joseph Cogswell for two years' study far from the distractions of New York. A year at Harvard Law School gave a suitable gloss to a young man, before he was brought into the office of the Astor Estate and devoted himself, as his father had done, to the management of property. He was the oldest son, and the Astors fervently believed in primogeniture. Younger sons could expect less solicitous care. When William Backhouse's youngest son Henry married beneath his parents' expectations, and when he moved to a farmhouse in Columbia County with his bride, he was summarily cut off from the family.[53]

John Jacob III's wife Charlotte Augusta Gibbes was an extraordinary woman from a South Carolina family which had settled into the little community living around St. John's Park in New York. (Her father, Thomas Gibbes, was a founder member of the Union Club in 1836.) More of a socialite than her in-laws, she had cultural interests which were unknown in the Astor family.

59. Joseph Cogswell.

This is a face which ought to be better known, and more revered, in New York City. A merchant and former schoolteacher, Joseph Green Cogswell became the companion of and adviser to John Jacob Astor. He planted, and nourished, the idea that a public library would be a personal legacy to the city where he had made his wealth. Astor was surrounded by people who had interesting ideas about how he should spend his money. Most went away empty-handed. Cogswell persisted. When the Astor Library opened in 1854, Cogswell was the librarian.

Augusta (as she preferred to be called) hosted literary teas on Mondays, which were inevitably known as *causeries de lundi*, and gave a reception for the tragedienne Madame Ristori, which broke the New York society embargo on actresses. As she demonstrated to her nonplussed husband on their wedding journey, Augusta Astor was unconventional in other ways: she was a better shot than he with revolver or rifle and owned a personal collection of guns, which she would proudly show to her closest friends. She was fond not only of shooting but of open air amusements, and frequently played tennis and golf, and joined her husband sailing.

Augusta Astor was the first of that wealthy family to be so directly moved by evangelical religion as to turn their great wealth to the benefit of the community. She wore jewelry worth $300,000, but was a generous supporter of Charles Loring Brace's Children's Aid Society. Brace had a powerful impact upon society matrons with his accounts of 10,000 abandoned, orphaned, and runaway children on the streets of New York. Above all, Brace gave people like Augusta Astor a practical way to translate their religious faith into material help for the poor. 'We take it for granted,' Brace wrote, that every Christian man and every humane man would gladly do his share to reform such districts in our City. . . . It is a solemn duty, not to be avoided, in every one who professes to follow CHRIST to help these, his poorer and weaker brethren. But *how* to do it? Not all can rummage among the cellars, and lofts, and lanes of the poor—or preach, or teach, or personally help. We cannot expect it. Still, there is an immense deal which never has been done, and yet which ought to be done by the *laity*—when once the old idea is thoroughly and utterly driven out, that Religion belongs to one class or one day.[54]

Brace found in John Jacob III and Augusta an instinctive sympathy for the disadvantaged. The fact that in *Home-Life in Germany* (1856) Brace had written with evident sympathy about Germany and the German people did him no harm with the Astors. Such charitable benevolence seemed uncharacteristic of the Astors, and it was widely believed in New York that Augusta's charitable gifts were made out of her marriage portion. Surely the Astors were not *that* generous.[55]

For all her concern for the poor, and deserved reputation for being the most generous, independent, and likable of the Astor women, there was a vein of harsh piety that made family life oppressive. Her son William Waldorf recalled that 'Sundays were a day of penance. My Mother fixed the employment of the hours left free between morning and afternoon service. No exercise, nor game, nor merriment. To walk (except to Church) was Sabbath breaking, to whistle a tune was sin. To write a letter, or pay a visit, or read a newspaper, or listen to music was desecration. Apart from Church, it must be a day of idle vacuity. "I see no reason," she said, "why a Christian should not be cheerful," a phrase which now sounds ridiculous. She was proficient in the Christian doctrine of Hell.'[56] Augusta Astor was to be Caroline Schermerhorn's sister-in-law.

The fictions of a happy family

> Dear William is so good to me. I have been so fortunate in my marriage.
> —Mrs. Astor (1875)[57]

At the instigation of his wife, William Backhouse Astor, Jr., the second son, lost his *Backhouse* and abandoned his *Jr.*, becoming William Astor. It made little difference to his anonymity. News of his engagement came on June 13, 1853, with an ironic twist from George Templeton Strong, who was scarcely able to recall the name of the young man in question: '. . . Woodbury Langdon back from Europe. Kane engaged to Miss Edith Brevoort, and one of the junior Astors to Miss Caroline Schermerhorn. Trust the young couple will be able to live on their little incomes together . . .'[58]

60. William Astor.

William Astor, the intelligent, cultured younger son of William Backhouse Astor, was deprived of a meaningful role in the Astor family affairs because his father and grandfather, John Jacob Astor, believed in primogeniture, which meant that the family fortune passed virtually intact to his older brother John Jacob Astor III. His marriage to Caroline Schermerhorn was not a happy one—for either of them.

Born on July 12, 1830, William Astor was an undergraduate at Columbia College when his older brother married. Their first child was a son, securing the Astor line. While John Jacob III began work in the offices of the Astor Estate, the younger son, William Astor, graduated in 1849, nearly at the head of his class, and was allowed—perhaps encouraged would be a better term—to spend several years traveling in Egypt, the Holy Land, Turkey, and Greece, returning with an enthusiastic amateur interest in oriental art and literature. Regarded as cleverer than his older brother, and far more charming, terms like 'outgoing,' 'spirited,' and 'polished' were used about him as a young man.[59] Upon his return to New York he entered his father's office on 26th Street, where he remained, looking for something to do, until his father's death in

1875. There was no real place for a younger son in the family business, and he received no encouragement to involve himself in affairs which were controlled by his father and older brother.

Back in New York, he devoted himself to a 'love of ease and comfort'—and how dreadful the words 'ease' and 'comfort' were to maternal ears, with their associations of dandyism and dissipation. A good shot, a devotee of horse racing, yachting, and country pursuits, he was also inclined to drink. To his strait-laced parents, these were all ominous signs, and they would have urged, and in not too subtle a fashion, the benefits of marriage upon their twenty-three-year-old son. William Backhouse, who had little emotional investment in his relationship with his son, turned to the one source of control which he and his father had always relied upon: he decided to punish his younger son by leaving him one million dollars only—the identical sum he planned to leave to each of his daughters. 'He was dissatisfied with the young man's manner of living, and he did not believe that the son was fitted to care for a larger fortune.' John Jacob III objected to his father's decision. 'It is not right that my only brother should be put on a par with the girls of the family.'[60] In time, William Backhouse's decision was rescinded, and William Astor was left a great fortune, but it was only about one-fourth that which his older brother inherited. The emotional estrangement between the brothers, and between the father and younger son, was complete.

A marriage was soon arranged, though the small world of Lafayette Place and Bond Street knew nothing of the *what* and *how*, of the courting relationship, the testing of romantic bonds. Was there a sharing of the essential, private self, beyond the conventions of social expectation, between Caroline Schermerhorn and William Astor? Elsewhere in American society an emerging belief in the supremacy of romantic love enabled young couples largely to dispense with the old restraints of chaperonage. That would probably have been true for twenty-three-year-olds in the New York city upper class in 1853. But virtually every aspect of romantic intimacy is, in this relationship, missing. If there were highly charged rituals and secret feelings of doubt, we have no record of them. There is a chilling passage in the memoirs of Consuelo Vanderbilt Balsan, herself a victim of an even more notorious dynastic marriage, which suggests the otherwise invisible scene: 'It was in the comparative quiet of an evening at home that Marlborough proposed to me in the Gothic Room [in the Marble House at Newport], whose atmosphere was so propitious to sacrifice. There was no need for sentiment.'[61]

Tradition largely governed the way these things were done in New York. Once the couple had made a decision, William Astor would be expected to call upon Caroline's mother, seeking her permission for the marriage. That call would soon have been followed by a visit by William Backhouse and his wife

61. William Astor.

William Astor took his pleasures at Ferncliff on the Hudson, and on his yacht. New York held little for him other than humiliation at the hands of his brother and wife. There are no known photographs of William Astor with a smile on his face.

Margaret upon their old friend Helen Schermerhorn. Nothing so vulgar as a financial settlement would be discussed openly on such occasions, but an intermediary, perhaps a mutual friend or family lawyer, would iron out the details. The young bride was given a life interest in an annual income of $80,000 as part of the marriage settlement. To protect the Astor fortune, she would also have been required to sign a waiver, like Sam Ward in the previous decade, abandoning any future claims against the Astors. (She had already inherited a share of her father's estate, which made Caroline independently wealthy, and on the death of her older brother Bruce in 1861, she also inherited his estate.) William Astor married Caroline Schermerhorn at Grace Church on September 24, 1853.[62]

Historians of the Astor family have long puzzled over this relationship. Virginia Cowles has suggested that Caroline Schermerhorn did it for the money. Given the abundant wealth of her family, Cowles is deeply unpersuasive. 'There was no love in their marriage,' writes Derek Wilson, 'and the two

62. Mrs. Astor.

The Astor family photo album in the New York Public Library has this image from 1875, one of the very few pictures which Mrs. Astor allowed to be taken of herself.

young people had little in common.' Well, they had everything in common: age, wealth, social position, experience living abroad, Bond Street and Lafayette Place; they were both younger children of parents who were conservative in social values, and had been raised to accept the supremacy of their parents in all aspects of family life. To friends and family alike they seemed a handsome couple. Caroline Schermerhorn's black hair, olive complexion, and splendid carriage, by the side of the tall, gallant figure of her fiancé, already hinting at a respectable fullness of masculine figure, were not discordant or displeasing.[63]

Her looks have been discussed with a venomous relish. Caroline Astor was later described as an 'ugly, heavy woman' and as 'really homely.' Another recalled her as being 'dumpy, empty-headed, plain and [an] insufferably vain girl whose one aim in life was to acquire for herself the social status which she believed her lineage deserved.' In 1898, at her son's wedding in Philadelphia, she was described as 'a matronly-looking lady, tall and very pale, and wearing a long sealskin cape.' In 1908, she was said to have been as a girl 'attractive in feature and manner' and to be 'tall, of striking figure, and dignified demeanor. She possessed that sweet and kindly expression of face, which was further enhanced and softened as she grew older and remained one of her chief charms throughout life.' Frank Crowninshield noted that in her sixties she was tall, a little on the heavy side, and had a slight though not disfiguring cast in her eye—a detail he alone recorded.[64] The few images we possess of Mrs. Astor are certainly not that of a heavy, ugly woman. She looks dignified in the best image we have of her, taken in 1875.

The couple lived in a house on 22nd Street near Broadway, and then moved to 34 Lafayette Place. The roles they would perform were largely those well established by the domestic division of labor and the doctrine of separate spheres. William Astor would have expected his wife to be dutiful, complaisant, and socially presentable. She would naturally satisfy the family's need of a son and heir, and would assume responsibility for the management of family time, the organization and direction of servants (in their class, a minimum staff would have included a valet-coachman, cook, and chambermaid), the planning of meals, social visits, and all entertaining. Crucial decisions relating to the education of their children were jointly taken. To fulfill these obligations, in most American families of their class the husband would have provided his wife with a clothing and housekeeping budget, and expected her to keep records of expenditure, like Sam Ward's receipt book. We do not know if such mundane tasks were ever undertaken by Caroline Astor, and it is easy to conjecture that William was unlikely to bother with such things. On the other hand, his parents, William Backhouse and Margaret, did not care to live princely lives, and may have imposed a regime of surveillance and penny-pinching as a form of moral instruction.

Through their marriage William Astor assumed the place in society which his parents expected of him, and which his brother had already achieved. She had her responsibilities, and he had his own. Having money of her own, and a clear terrain of authority, Caroline was far less dependent on her husband than most American women in 1853; but the strict codes of married life required the independence which she possessed as a result of her own wealth to be carefully disguised. In public, she was never less than an obedient and dutiful wife. The values which Caroline Astor brought into her marriage did not include a yearning for any role other than the one she occupied. Mrs. Astor was no feminist. One may assume that she was content that her husband kept a respectful distance in most aspects of their marriage. Feminists in the 1850s advocated a marital ideal of openness, disclosure, and the absence of secrets, but it is doubtful that husband or wife expected the other to become a pal, a friend.

Caroline brought to the Astor family a preference for French décor, gowns by Worth, and jewelry with a French aristocratic lineage, all of which gave their home and public appearances a stylishness lacking in either the Schermerhorns or the older generation of Astors. Nonetheless, the differences in taste and temperament were striking. William Astor loathed fashionable society and could not abide the opera. The Schermerhorns had been patrons of the opera from its earliest appearance in New York. While she enjoyed the season in New York, he continued to go to the estate office. As to their duty to the Astor lineage, Caroline had four daughters in succession and then a son and heir, John Jacob IV, in the first eleven years after their marriage.

When it was time to contemplate the marriages of their daughters, the issue proved complicated for William and Caroline. Like his grandfather John Jacob, William Astor took angry exception to the marriage of his oldest daughter Emily (known as 'Rose' in the family) to the socialite Newport widower and millionaire, James J. Van Alen. Noted for his devotion to all things English, and for the fanaticism of his determination that the grooms' liveries of the Coaching Club should be perfect in every detail, Van Alen was a comic creature whose conversation was flavored with 'egads' and 'zounds.' He wore a monocle and took himself with terrible seriousness.[65] William Astor had not forgiven his daughter for this ridiculous marriage when she unexpectedly died in 1881. When their youngest daughter Carrie expressed a desire to marry Orme Wilson, it was Mrs. Astor's turn to mount a forceful campaign of objection and delay. Wilson's father Richard was an unsavory character, with a solid claim to be among the shoddiest of the 'shoddy millionaires.' During the Civil War he made a fortune selling cotton blankets to the Confederate army, and charging them for wool. In New York, he bought Tweed's Fifth Avenue mansion, and became a speculator in cotton and horse-car franchises. Wilson's other daughters had married into the Goelet and Vanderbilt families, successfully greasing the path of the Wilsons into high society. A marriage to an Astor didn't exactly hurt, either. The strong-willed daughters of Mrs. Astor stood firm, and insisted upon the marriages of their choice. However unhappy Mamma and Papa were at their choice of husbands, their marriage settlements were imposing. Each daughter received the income from a trust fund, and a house bought by their father. Mrs. Astor ordered a turkey and chicken dinner to be served to the patients at Bellevue Hospital to celebrate the marriage in turn of each of her daughters.

As a result of these parental defeats, Mrs. Astor intervened early and successfully to settle an arranged match between 'Miss Augusta,' her third daughter, and James Coleman Drayton. Number 372 Fifth Avenue, next door to the brownstone where her sister lived, was purchased for the couple. Their marriage was the most thoroughly disastrous relationship of the lot, ending

63. Emily Astor Van Alen.

'Damned if I want my family mixed in with the Van Alens,' exclaimed William Astor. His daughter Emily thought otherwise, and married James J. Van Alen in 1876.

with the humiliation of a divorce, the publication of her letters to a 'third party,' Hallett Alsop Borrowe, in the *Sun* on March 18, 1892, and the threatened loss of her children. A sentence in a letter from Drayton to Borrowe ('You have done me the greatest wrong that one man can do another') was universally assumed to refer to adultery, but Drayton insisted that it referred to the breaking up of their home by Borrowe. It was expected in society that Augusta would be cut off with a bequest of a shilling in her father's will. When it was published in 1892 she received 372 Fifth Avenue and the income from $850,000, the same sum which was left to her sisters Helen Roosevelt and Carrie Wilson. Her twenty-eight-year-old brother inherited $30–50 million. William Astor, no less than his father, believed in primogeniture. The Astors also believed in Augusta's innocence, and brought her back to New York and the family home.[66]

When William Astor bought an estate at Ferncliff, on the Hudson at Rhinebeck, where he could indulge his enthusiasms for horse breeding and

64. Charlotte Augusta Astor Drayton.

Of all the children of Caroline and William Astor, the marriage of Charlotte Augusta to James Coleman Drayton proved the most unhappy. After marrying in 1879, the Draytons settled in New Jersey where they lived quietly for ten years. Growing bored, she had an affair and abandoned her children to chase after her lover, a vice-president of the Equitable Life Insurance Company, who had fled to Europe. Drayton received $12,000 a year to look after their children, and $5,000 a year for his acquiescence in his wife's behavior. She was traced to the St. Pancras Hotel in London, long a favorite for respectable infidelity. After much legal turmoil and many trans-Atlantic journeys, the marriage was dissolved. In the meantime Charlotte Augusta lost interest in her lover, and returned to New York, bringing the coffin of her father who had died suddenly in Paris. 'I've got an awful pain,' he said, and then expired.

farming, no complaints were heard from Caroline. In winter he sailed to Florida on his yacht the *Ambassadress*, but talk of his yachts and cronies, his drinking and gambling friends and even rumors of the women he entertained on board ship, were kept far from the family drawing room. When asked by reporters about her husband William's prolonged absences, Mrs. Astor deftly constructed a wife's façade, confessing that she was a terrible sailor and had never been on board his ship—but sailing was so good for her dear husband's health, and how enthusiastically she anticipated his return to New York. The fact that she made annual voyages to France over many years was tactfully ignored.

Largely at the instigation of the wives of John Jacob III and William Astor, the two sons requested a portion of the Thompson Farm site from their father where they proposed to build mansions on Fifth Avenue in the block between 33rd and 34th Streets. (The Hegira uptown of the Astors marks the successive stages of fashionable residence in New York: lower Broadway before the 1830s,

65. Residence of William Astor on Fifth Avenue at 34th Street.

William and Caroline Astor lived in this understated house on Fifth Avenue at 34th Street. There is a glimpse of A.T. Stewart's mansion (see p. 264) on the right of this picture. The garden shared with her brother and sister-in-law is marked by the wall on the left. The erection of the Waldorf Hotel by her nephew, William Waldorf Astor, forced Mrs. Astor to move uptown to 65th Street (see p. 15). On this site the Empire State Building was erected in 1931.

Lafayette Place in the 1840s, Fifth Avenue around 34th Street in the 1860s, to Mrs. Astor's final residence overlooking Central Park at Fifth Avenue and 61st Street in the 1890s.)[67] William and Caroline Astor's home, a plain four-story town house on the southwest corner at 34th Street, was erected in 1856. Three years later John Jacob III and Augusta's brick house on the northwest corner of 33rd Street was completed. At 50 by 107 feet, and with Nova Scotia freestone used in window dressings, architraves, cornices, Corinthian columns, and a double stoop, the building certainly had an imposing air.[68] There was a fenced-in private garden between the two houses. The location was fashionable. Although the two brothers had little fondness for each other's company, a shared delight in fashion and society entertaining was a valuable bond between Caroline and Augusta. Caroline's third daughter was named after her sister-in-law. The two women were happy to make common cause against the Astor dullness, but Augusta's interest in golf, tennis, and other kinds of energetic physical activity had little appeal for her sister-in-law. She was also more cautious socially than Augusta, and less concerned with people who made a fuss about conscience and duty, like Charles Loring Brace. She preferred the old families, and their solid conservative ways.

When war broke out in 1861, John Jacob III was a strong supporter of Lincoln. His father tried to restrain him, fearing the consequences of a long and ruinous war on their fortunes. William Backhouse had supported Democratic mayor Fernando Wood, and may have felt some sympathy for Wood's proposal that New York secede from the Union. John Jacob III would have nothing to do with such schemes, and donated $3,000 to arm a tugboat to relieve the besieged garrison at Fort Sumter. He volunteered for military service during the first winter of the war. At the age of thirty-nine a front-line command was probably unavailable, but he was a strong supporter of 'Little Mac' and became General McClellan's aide-de-camp with the rank of colonel, and supervised the riverine supply columns of the Army of the Potomac. Astor resigned his commission when McClellan was sacked in late 1862. Unlike the senior Theodore Roosevelt's Southern wife Martha Bulloch, Augusta was no Copperhead. She vigorously supported the war effort, and helped raise funds for a Negro regiment. William Astor paid for the organization of a regiment at Rondout, which dutifully elected him colonel, and also funded the Astor Gun Squad raised at Rhinebeck. But William Backhouse intervened. One son in the army was quite sufficient, and a no doubt deeply frustrated younger son was

66. Departure of the 7th Regiment, New York State Militia, April 19, 1861.

The Astors feared the consequences of secession of the South. In the months before the outbreak of the rebellion in April 1861, William Backhouse Astor and other New York merchants attempted to find a compromise with the South. Once the war began, buoyed by the outpouring of patriotism which accompanied such scenes as the departure of the 7th Regiment, New York State Militia, on April 19, 1861, seen from Broadway at Cortlandt Street (below), fears were pushed aside. Both of William Backhouse's sons became energetic supporters of the Union cause.

forced to decline the proffered colonelcy, and resume civilian life. After the war, John Jacob III collaborated closely with the Tammany Hall machine which ran New York. His brother William was a strong supporter of the Republican party.

Although each year William and Caroline spent less and less time together, the proprieties, the fictions of a happy family, were strictly maintained. As the emotional ties—such as they were—between the two waned, they were replaced by a constrained, formal politeness. In their world couples addressed each other with a public decorousness; there were many things which could not be said between a husband and a wife. His drinking loomed increasingly large as an issue, and it was believed in society that William Astor's drunkenness and rudeness made him unwelcome at his wife's entertainments. There were rumors that when he threatened to appear at her balls, he would be intercepted by male friends who would spend the evening with him drinking at one or another of the New York clubs. In the place where a loving marriage might have been, there were formal feelings—of duty which she owed to her children, her mother, her extended family, and to the position in society which she occupied.

Challenges to that social order might take unexpected forms, like the building of a mansion across the street. At a sheriff's sale during the Civil War A.T. Stewart paid $73,400 for the mansion of 'Sarsaparilla' Townsend on the northwest corner of Fifth Avenue and 34th Street. He had it torn down and erected what the *New York Times* judged to be 'perhaps the most palatial private residence of the Continent.' As work progressed, details of the beauty and magnificence of the structure were breathlessly enumerated in the press: the stairways alone cost over $60,000, and the stucco work was an astounding $275,000. The façade is of 'the finest Parian marble.' The ceilings were over 18 feet high. The front entrance contained ghostly life-sized statues, including Hiram Powers' much-admired *The Greek Slave* and Harriet Hosmer's *Zenobia*. There was a commissioned Aubusson carpet in the reception room. The picture gallery, a windowless space 75 feet long, 30 feet wide and an impressive 50 feet high, was crammed full of French academic painting (canvases by Delaroche, Couture, and Vernet, three Gérômes, three Bouguereaus, and four Meissoniers, as well as Rosa Bonheur's 17-foot-wide *The Horse Fair* which Cornelius Vanderbilt II later gave to the Metropolitan Museum in 1887). The principal guest room was known as the 'General Grant Room.' Americans preferred to think of Stewart's post-war home as a vindication of endeavor and commercial success. Hence the praise it received in *Harper's Weekly* as 'a monument of individual enterprise.' Mariana Griswold Van Rensselaer regarded the Stewart mansion as a 'very showy house,' without good propor-

67. Residence of 'Sarsaparilla' Townsend razed by A.T. Stewart.

A contemporary account describes the residence of 'Sarsaparilla' Townsend on Fifth Avenue at 34th Street: it is '90 by 56 feet, and occupies five lots of ground, in an elevated position, which cost $42,000. Its general appearance is of the rich, massive character common to many first-class houses... The galleries, walls and columns are all decorated in the richest manner, with fresco-painting, gilding and elaborate mouldings. The ... effect of the whole, when first beheld, is to bewilder with a sense of magnificence.' A.T. Stewart had this edifice razed, and built a far more extravagant structure on this site (see p. 264).

tions and lacking in artistic knowledge of design. When the furniture in Stewart's mansion was sold at auction in 1890, it raised perhaps 10¢ on the dollar, being regarded as old-fashioned and too ponderous for contemporary taste. The suite from the Grant Room fetched $700, and was divided up for sale to different buyers. After his widow's death the house was rented to the Manhattan Club. The celebrated Stewart picture gallery, without the pictures, was used as a billiards room.[69]

In the imperious act of tearing down a mansion, reputed to have been the largest brownstone in the city, and building the most expensive private home ever erected to that date in the United States, Mrs. Astor sensed a challenge to the social order itself and her place within it. Every bit as much as John Jacob Astor, Stewart was held up as a model of the American success story. He was the owner of the greatest retail and wholesale operation in the country, and every family in New York who bought luxury goods—including the Astors—was his customer. Stewart's 'marble palace,' opened in 1846 on the east side of Broadway between Chambers and Reade Streets, was like Tiffany's on the corner of Warren Street and Broadway, a shrine to the consumption of luxury goods. N.P. Willis sang the praises of Stewart's establishments in the *Home Journal*. 'No need to go to Paris now for any indulgence of taste, any vagary of fancy. It is as well worth an artist's while as a purchaser's, however, to make the round of this museum of luxuries . . .' . When that location proved too small for his growing trade, in 1862 Stewart transferred his retail business to a 'business palace' on Broadway in the block below Grace Church. The white-painted five-story cast-iron structure, with large windows on all four sides, gave him a retail space of about two acres on each floor.

Civil War tax assessments listed Stewart as having a personal income, at $1,843,631, which was a million dollars more than the reported income of William Backhouse Astor. Stewart's wealth gave him the means to express a broad-ranging vulgarity: everything about his house was lavish, excessive, extreme. In this the comparison with the Astor homes on the block downtown was striking. The Lucius Rossi family portrait from 1878 suggests that the Astors lived in regal surroundings. Yet, by the standards now being set by figures like Stewart, the Astor residence could hardly be described as outstanding. A journalist in *Cosmopolitan* noted in 1888 that the Astors give

> elaborate entertainments, mainly dinner parties, but give them sparingly, and always see that they are fully and correctly advertised in the social columns of the newspapers. Even festivity is a business with the family, who are methodical and considerate of cost in everything. They are trained to be so from their infancy. Hence, impulse, sensibility, romance, sympathy, whatever belongs to the emotional or ideal, is, if it appear, sedulously repressed.

The Astors' tight-lipped disapproval of the Stewart establishment reflected one aspect of the Astors' relations to New York society. In the background was the attempt by Augusta and Caroline to raise the family to higher levels of social prominence than William Backhouse had ever contemplated. That was why they instigated the move to Fifth Avenue. But Stewart was raising the stakes, as the Vanderbilts and others would do in the 1870s, and in their response to his extravagance was their first great confrontation with new money in the city.[70]

Stewart was five feet tall, with fair, reddish hair, and spoke with the harsh accent of Belfast. He had received an academic education, graduating at the head of his class at Trinity College, Dublin. Possessing little of the polished manners of a gentleman, Stewart was closer to the hard-driving John Jacob Astor than to William Backhouse, and the Astors sensed this. He, too, like the first Astor, was not quite a self-made man, having inherited $5,000 which

68. A.T. Stewart.

Alexander T. Stewart was the most successful merchant the city had ever seen. At his death in 1876, he was worth $80 million. His wealth meant many things in New York. But the man who had accumulated so much money so quickly, and so single-mindedly, was an enigmatic figure. 'He has foregone all that many men value,' wrote a contemporary, 'all pleasures and ambitions. Friendships and hatreds, societies and philanthropies, theories and philosophies, have been . . . made quite subordinate to this main and only purpose in life.'

enabled him to purchase the Irish lace which he sold in his first small shop at 283 Broadway. Mrs. Astor would know that Stewart's wife Cornelia was the daughter of Jacob Clinch, of the firm of Jones and Clinch, ship chandlers at 84 Wall Street. The daughters of two ship chandlers who had married well: that was a comparison she did not wish made between herself and the mousy Mrs. Stewart. She kept the Astor door firmly closed to the Stewarts.

Newspapers made a fuss over Stewart's charitable benefactions, but he also had the reputation of a hard-faced employer, single-minded in his devotion to profit. Although he sold luxury goods, there was by New York standards nothing particularly refined or genteel about the way Stewart conducted his business. 'He could easily be taken for his book-keeper or porter. He meets you with the air of a man who is impatient from interruption; who wishes you to say your say and be done.' While greeting Peter Cooper at his 10th Street establishment, Stewart pointed out the 'great array of salesmen, cash boys and porters' and proudly noted that 'not one of them has discretion. They are simply machines, working in a system which determines all their actions.'[71]

69. Residence of A.T. Stewart.

Stewart's mansion was on the northeast corner of Fifth Avenue and 34th Street.

Stewart moved in the upper circles of New York life. He was a member of the Union Club, the Century Association, and the Union League, and owned a large portfolio of properties which included the Metropolitan Hotel in New York and the Grand Union Hotel in Saratoga. In total his real estate holdings were estimated at a value of more than ten million dollars. President Grant wanted to nominate Stewart as Secretary of the Treasury. But New York society never forgot another facet of Stewart. Mabel Osgood Wright recalled that he had never been regarded by Washington Square as anything other than a parvenu.[72]

Stewart moved into his mansion in 1869, and until his death in April 1876, the Astor and Stewart families lived on opposite sides of the corner of 34th Street and Fifth Avenue. Yet during the years in which they were neighbors Mrs. Astor acted as though Stewart and his wife did not exist. Stewart had been one of the pall-bearers at the 1872 funeral of Margaret Armstrong Astor, Caroline Astor's mother-in-law, but even the memory of that courtesy was insufficient to melt the barrier of icy exclusion emanating from across the street. When such a highly visible check was administered, and to a man who was so rich and prominent, it represented a very public drawing of the line between the acceptable and the unacceptable in society. In the weeks before Stewart died, he had offered to hold a grand reception in honor of the

Emperor of Brazil, who was coming to New York on a state visit. The offer was accepted with alacrity. Nonetheless, Mrs. Astor had decided that the Stewarts were to be excluded, and excluded they remained. The project of exclusion did not come from Ward McAllister, or from the Patriarchs, but in this case reflected one woman's determination to block the inroads being made into society by new money. It was a measure of Mrs. Astor's social independence that she could make such a judgment, and stick with it. It showed a steeliness which made her powerful.

Powerful women

> Human nature, maternal sentiments, have no place in the case; she must remember only the obligations of the throne and condemn without mercy or reprieve.
> —Julian Hawthorne on Mrs. Astor (1896)[73]

McAllister first met Mrs. Astor in 1872, at a time when she had daughters to introduce into society: Emily was eighteen, Helen seventeen. He recognized at once that this woman had the presence, money, birth, breeding, ambition, and the administrative ability to become society's leader. The only trouble was that the same might have been said for Mrs. Hamilton Fish, Mrs. Lewis Morris Rutherfurd, Mrs. Theodore Roosevelt, Mrs. August Belmont, or any of a handful of other wealthy and active matrons on the New York scene in the 1870s. 'Society was so defined in those days,' wrote Mrs. Sherwood, 'that every one knew where every one stood. There was an aristocracy. It was a smaller and less glittering society than it is now, but it was far more elegant, well bred, exclusive, and distinguished. It was a society to which it was an honor to be admitted.' There were many on Fifth Avenue for whom the circle around Mrs. Belmont was the most interesting. McAllister had done much to flatter her social pre-eminence in his Newport picnics, and Frederick Townsend Martin recalled that she surrounded herself with cultivated people. 'The first thing that anybody of note took care to do when they visited New York was to obtain letters of introduction to Mrs. Belmont.'[74] But, as we have seen, her husband August was a Large Problem, and McAllister may have felt that a society leader with a wealthy but absent husband was, all things considered, preferable. There was another factor, hard to measure as an element in McAllister's calculations, but meaningful nonetheless: there was about Mrs. Astor nothing of the aggression or maliciousness of a Mamie Fish. After the treatment of A.T. Stewart, did he suppose that she was biddable? To McAllister, she was a *grande dame* waiting to be crowned a constitutional monarch. He was ready to assume the role of adviser and *éminence grise*.

In *Society As I Have Found It* McAllister appears as the one who first recognized Mrs. Astor's calling, and anticipated her triumph. Such after-the-fact wisdom is self-inflated and misleading—yet historians will continue to take his account of their relationship at face value. 'He knew how to play upon the vanity of his patroness,' writes David Sinclair, 'how to inveigle her into spending more and more money, and there is no doubt that he was indispensable to her success.' It is hard in any social sense to see what particular need Mrs. Astor had for McAllister. She had long since moved from Lafayette Place to Fifth Avenue, where she began giving what George T. Strong described as 'state dinners.' Another diarist, Edward Tailer, wrote on February 17, 1871, 'upon Friday we went to Mrs. William Astor's—where we met many old New Yorkers including the Warrens, Jones, Winthrops, Posts.' Before meeting McAllister, she had a prominent place in the social milieu and had created a superior domestic establishment for her entertaining. There was in her social horizon a defined constituency of 'old New Yorkers' and a well-known hostility to 'parvenuism.' She had cut the Stewarts, and needed no lessons from McAllister on exclusivity.[75]

With the death of her stepmother Margaret in 1872, and William Backhouse three years later, there was an end to pressure from within the Astor family to inhibit or restrict her social life. By dressing her servants in livery, and serving dinner on a gold service, her mother-in-law brought a new refinement to the social world of the Astors. But William Backhouse took no pleasure in society, and with their preference for earlier dining times and simpler menus, the senior Astors belonged to the society of another age. Nor did William Astor exert much of an influence on his wife's socializing; as usual, he preferred to be elsewhere. After the death of William Backhouse only Augusta Astor, wife of the oldest son of the senior branch of the family, could occupy the position of social leadership. There was little tension between the sisters-in-law. Society was an enthusiasm for Augusta, but her benevolence, piety, and zeal for social reform were far more important. 'Not for me, thank you,' Augusta Astor remarked to her son when he urged her to claim the social supremacy which was Augusta's as of right.[76] In the early 1870s Caroline Astor was already in social terms the dominant figure in the wealthiest family in the city.

What then did McAllister have to offer? He had built a solid reputation in Newport as a provider of informal entertainments, and in New York he was principally known as an organizer of balls. He did not have the money to be a ball-giver in his own right, but his knowledge of the city's wine merchants and luxury grocers and firm grounding in European cuisine and social etiquette made him an ideal social organizer. Mrs. Astor had no need of help with wines, invitation lists, etiquette, the spending of money, or anything else. That is a preposterous idea, coming as it does spiraling out of McAllister's vanity into the accounts of society by credulous historians of the family. The fact that he was a cousin of Sam Ward, the man who had briefly been Margaret and William Backhouse's son-in-law, and whom they heartily detested, added a nuance to her interest in McAllister. By taking him up, Caroline was asserting her independence from the Astors and their ancestral bitternesses. Principally, what McAllister had to offer was a belief in society itself. He detested new money every bit as strongly as she did, and was utterly devoted to the notion that society could only be saved from the parvenus by cultivating the old New York families. He agreed with Mrs. Astor and said so in as flattering a way as possible. He may have seen her as someone who could fulfill *his* project. In her eyes, McAllister was a pompous, practical little man who might become an ally in *her* desire for a society of refinement rather than sheer wealth. Keeping the Stewarts out was something to which McAllister might make a contribution. He perhaps never grasped how truly dispensable he was. Few flatterers do.

We do not have an alternative account of Mrs. Astor in the 1870s, written either by a contemporary, or by anyone in a position to have inside knowledge of the early years of the Patriarchs. In the two years before he died, William Backhouse Astor ordered the destruction of fifteen packing cases of the papers of his father. Most of the remaining Astor Estate records were destroyed when the office was later moved. Personal papers from this period are virtually unknown.[77] Mrs. Astor was never more an Astor than when she kept silent about the years when her social leadership emerged. By the time the press had discovered society in the early 1880s, Mrs. Astor's social world, as we know it from the following decade, with its large receptions, gold service, glorious flowers, jewels, cotillions, lavish favors, and the experience of sending out 400 invitations to a 'small dance,' was already in place.

In portraying McAllister's role as founder of the Patriarchs in Chapter 5, it seemed sensible to suggest that Mrs. Astor may have encouraged him to see the benefit of placing social leadership in the hands of a small group of unimpeachable men, and to abandon the idea of leadership by women. With her husband as an example, if one was needed, it was clear that no force—certainly not wives, children, parents, or 'society' in an abstract sense—could have imposed social discipline upon a headstrong, irascible, arrogant, hard-drinking, and fabulously wealthy man. The opinions of his peers, at the Union Club, the Yacht Club, or in other elite associations, was one of the few forms of social control which might overcome the self-seeking of a willful and very rich man. In the terminology of Norbert Elias, who has forcefully argued the importance of aristocratic self-restraint in the making of civilization, William Astor perhaps thought of himself as a throwback, more akin to the free warriors of the Middle Ages than to the more refined products of courtly life.[78] His father, William Backhouse, had been constrained by religion, a strong-minded father, a determined wife who was his social equal, and a sense of responsibility to the vast fortune accumulated by his father. Once his father had died, and it was clear that William Astor was to have no role in the Astor Estate, there was little pressure to keep his nose to the grindstone. There was a nose, of decided forcefulness, but no grindstone, and a wife who did not particularly require his presence.

The choice of the first Patriarchs strongly reflected Mrs. Astor's family ties. (She was reported to be directly involved in the selection of members.) Her husband *in absentia* and brother-in-law were among the Patriarchs in 1872. In the absence of any records from that time, the best that can be said is that the membership of the Patriarchs flatteringly placed the Astors and Schermerhorns at the center of society. McAllister found other ways to emphasize the Astors' social supremacy, and to place the 'Mystic Rose' at the forefront of social esteem. His flattery was blatant, but also purposeful. Having so unimpeachable a leader enabled McAllister to remain even-handed between the claims of other women. Praising her was a way to defend himself.

The marriage of Emily Astor to James J. Van Alen in 1876 left a legacy of ill-will in the family. It was followed two years later by the far happier marriage of her daughter Helen to 'Rosy' Roosevelt. ('Rosy' was the son of James and Rebecca Howland Roosevelt, who lived on an estate of 1,000 acres at Hyde Park and had a town house at 15 Washington Square North. Rebecca Roosevelt was the daughter of Gardner G. Howland. The connections over several generations which united Schermerhorns, Roosevelts, and Howlands, encompassing Bond Street and Grace Church, made everything about this marriage seem *right*.)

Mrs. Astor was not yet *the* leader of society—there was no coronation, no public acclamation and there were others similarly determined to claim the role. But her home and family, the quality of her entertainments, earned her a formidable reputation. In the 1870s the existence of a society figurehead remained unknown to the general public. Even the idea that there was a confirmed leader had no particular place in the way people thought about society. The Patriarchs, and the emergence of Mrs. Astor as queen of New York society, were designed to bring an end to the 'social republic' and inaugurate a monarchic and aristocratic social order.

As she watched the Stewarts erect a palatial structure across the street from her home on Fifth Avenue, there were new cottages at Newport that made a no less bold assertion of the power of money. The purchase of Beaulieu on Bellevue Avenue in Newport by Augusta and John Jacob Astor III was followed by Mrs. Astor's Beechwood, bought in 1880, and extended in quick order by the addition of a ballroom. The Astors brought to Newport a taste for large, expensively catered balls which helped propel the resort towards its apotheosis

70. 'Rosecliff', Newport.

'Rosecliff,' the white terracotta showcase at Newport designed by Stanford White for Herman and Theresa ('Tessie') Oelrichs, was modeled after the Grand Trianon at Versailles. Oelrichs was the American agent of the North German Lloyd shipping line. 'Tessie' was the daughter of James Fair, an Irishman who went to California in the Gold Rush and made a great fortune in the Comstock silver lode in Nevada. 'Rosecliff' was completed in 1900.

in the 1890s as the summer home of the very, very rich. Gossip had it that the Vanderbilts only went to Newport because the Astors were there.[79] In the dozen years from 1888, much larger structures than Beaulieu and Beechwood were built at Newport: Ogden Goelet's Ochre Court, William K. Vanderbilt's Marble House, The Breakers built by Richard Morris Hunt for Cornelius Vanderbilt II, and the Oelrichs' Rosecliff, a bijou re-imagining of the Grand Trianon at Versailles. Ironically, by declining to compete, the Astors affirmed their social supremacy. Newport for decades had been a summer resort of the Astors (and before the Astors, it had been the resort of choice of the Schermerhorns), and their priority was a form of social defense against even the wealthiest of rivals. Being there first mattered. Nor did they feel the need to compete directly with the Vanderbilts when they began constructing the Fifth Avenue mansions which transformed the upper reaches of the avenue into the 'Vanderbilt Mile.'

When Mrs. Astor insisted at Newport in 1890, in a blaze of publicity, that she be addressed as 'Mrs. Astor' she was asserting a superiority over rival claimants, such as William Waldorf Astor's wife Mary Paul, and Mrs. Astor's daughter-in-law, Ava Willing. Insisting on her right to the name was taken as yet another sign of an aging matron's snobbishness. It is worth recalling, however, that J.P. Morgan had refused to put a nameplate upon 23 Wall Street where J.P. Morgan & Co. was located. The number of the building alone appeared on a discreet brass tablet. 'The absence of a shingle reflected that the banker was a regal figure, far more important than his visitors,' wrote Ron Chernow.[80] Similarly, to ask *which* Mrs. Astor was Mrs. Astor, was in her eyes to occupy a place in the outer darkness of society. She was not slow to insist upon the acknowledgment of her social pre-eminence. With certain exceptions, the New York press was an enthusiastic abettor of the aristocratic project. Under the spotlight of press interest, the story of the struggle for social supremacy was constructed. It required a leader of high-born, wealthy, and distinguished lineage; there had to be challengers, always fabulously wealthy and ambitious; scenes of high conflict in settings of unimaginable luxury; and then, an outcome, an allocation of laurels for the winners and humiliation for the defeated. Mrs. Astor was a superb symbol for the whole of society, repelling with a withering glance the challenges to her position.

By far the most dramatic of these conflicts turned upon the ambitions of Alva Vanderbilt, who in 1883 decided to celebrate the completion of the opulent mansion at 660 Fifth Avenue by holding a fancy dress ball. The story of the Vanderbilt has been repeatedly told. It signaled 'the beginning of a new era of extravagance in New York social life, and triumph of the nouveaux riches over the older Knickerbocker families.'[81] The key moment in this struggle came when Mrs. Astor, who had formerly ignored the Vanderbilts, was obliged to pay a call on Mrs. Vanderbilt. That she paid the call is certainly true. Etiquette obliged the 'older' and more 'senior' lady to call first. No loss of face was involved. (In 1901, when J.P. Morgan sought to acquire rights in the Mesabi iron range for United States Steel, John D. Rockefeller obliged the banker to call at his home at 4 West 54th Street. That was all about power, not etiquette, for Morgan and Rockefeller heartily disliked each other.)[82] Much of the surrounding story is misleading, not least the description of Alva Smith Vanderbilt as a socially ambitious arriviste. Originally from Mobile, Alabama, the Smiths settled in New York in the 1850s, and lived at 40 Fifth Avenue. After the Civil War they spent time in Paris, where Alva and her sister Armide were introduced to the highest levels of French society. Her father Murray F. Smith, a member of the Union Club, was one of many Wall Street dealers who suffered financial reversals in the 1873 depression, but her marriage to William K. Vanderbilt two years later was a leading society event, attended by Mrs. 'Tiny' Belmont and Augusta Astor.

71. Mr. and Mrs. Cornelius Vanderbilt II, 1883.

Cornelius Vanderbilt II, grandson of the 'Commodore,' married Alice Claypoole Gwynne in 1867. Despite their costumes for the famous Vanderbilt Ball of 1883, they were not by preference party animals. They lived in an aura of wealth, Christian piety and intense respectability. When he died in 1899 he left an estate of more than $72 million.

The death of Commodore Vanderbilt in 1877 cleared the way for the social arrival of his son, William Henry (universally known as 'Billy'), and the younger generation of Vanderbilts led by Cornelius II, aged thirty-four, and William Kissam, twenty-eight. Over the next six years the younger Vanderbilts attended the grandest parties and balls, and Mrs. Astor had frequently been in their company. They were guests at Patriarchs' balls in 1882 and early 1883. Mrs. W.K. Vanderbilt and Mrs. Astor were on the Executive Committee of the Bartholdi Pedestal Fund. The idea that they were excluded as A.T. Stewart had been in the 1870s is obviously incorrect, and much of the highly personal social

72. 'Billy' Vanderbilt.

'I am the richest man in the world,' remarked a smiling 'Billy' Vanderbilt in 1883. And who was to say he was not? He had investments worth $194 million, and an annual tax-free income of over $10 million.

rivalry between Alva Vanderbilt and Mrs. Astor was heightened and exaggerated by the press. (Hurlbert, who attended the Vanderbilt ball in the costume of a seventeenth-century Spanish knight, published a detailed account of the evening in the *World* on March 27, which was syndicated nationally through the Associated Press.) The ball did not *introduce* the Vanderbilts to society, but set them on a pinnacle of lavish expenditure. In her obituaries Mrs. Astor was said to be the first to recognize the right of the Vanderbilts to a place in fashionable New York society. 'We have no right,' she commented in 1883, 'to exclude those whom the growth of this great country has brought forward, provided they are not vulgar in speech and appearance. The time has come for the Vanderbilts.'[83] She may have believed that she played such a role, but the truth was otherwise.

With a reputation founded upon a highly visible commitment to exclusivity, in practice Mrs. Astor presided over a large social enterprise. By the turn of the century there were 600 names on her calling list, and 2,200 invitations were not uncommonly issued for a ball held in the week before Christmas. Her events were attended by as many as 800 or 1,000 guests, a number which did not attract comment. Such entertainments, so large as to require substantial trained staffs to plan and organize the evening, had the atmosphere of a court *levée*. A guest expected to stand in long slow-moving lines at an Astor occasion. Mrs. Astor in the late 1890s was simply a professional hostess. The idea that she maintained a restricted invitation list, whether set at 400 or another figure, has no meaning in relationship to her social activities. She invited on a grand scale, and although she was praised for always remembering old friends (the *Herald* recalled that 'no matter how fortune had treated those whom she considered had a right to enter her hospitable house, such were always included. . . .'),[84] there was little time to chat in the crush of guests.

If Mrs. Astor's ultra-exclusivity was more a matter of repute than actual practice, she also had a fierce reputation as an upholder of the sanctity of marriage and traditional morality. 'In that day,' wrote Mrs. John King Van Rensselaer, 'the woman who obtained a divorce was a Pariah. There was no appeal. By her action she became a social outcast.' Mrs. Astor was someone, reminded Pulitzer's *World*, who 'resolutely set herself against scandal and would not tolerate spitefulness in any of her friends toward one another.'[85] Nonetheless, she chose to turn a blind eye to her husband's infidelities and drunkenness. There were obvious reasons for sustaining the fiction of her marriage, and in this Mrs. Astor was, like so many women of her class, a clear-headed pragmatist. In Wharton's *The Age of Innocence*, the reaction in New York society to Ellen Olenska, returned to the city after fleeing from her husband, illustrates the social problems caused by a divorcée. On the night of Ellen's first appearance in New York, Newland Archer wants to appear publicly in Mrs. Mingott's box at the opera. It was the only act of family solidarity which was available to him to defend his fiancée.

When confronted with the breakdown of her daughter Charlotte's marriage, and the widespread belief that Charlotte's infidelity lay at the heart of the divorce, Mrs. Astor made a strong gesture of solidarity. Setting her immense social prestige against the assumption in New York that divorce meant social suicide, she stood loyally by her daughter, and did whatever was in her power to help the deeply unhappy young woman return to a place in society. The year after the divorce she gave a great entertainment in her daughter's honor at Newport. After so many years during which she had received alone, in 1898 she chose to stand by her daughter—quite literally, receiving guests by Charlotte's side—thus obliging every guest who attended personally to greet her disgraced daughter. Mrs. Astor proved in that moment that her will and personality were strong enough to command the loyalty of her doubtless uncomfortable guests. The presence of Bishop Potter at the reception sealed her victory, but not even Mrs. Astor could overcome the deep-seated social objection to the divorced, and Mrs. Drayton eventually settled in England where she later married George Ogilvie Haig, brother of the polo-playing cavalryman Douglas Haig, who became Field Marshal of the British Army.

When it came to other social taboos, Mrs. Astor proved to be equally pragmatic. Ellen Prince was reputedly one of the earliest women in society to go into trade, opening a tea room in the Knickerbocker Building. Mrs. Astor did not hesitate to bring a party to enjoy the Elizabethan-style decorations and waitresses in period costume. When the Jewish banker James Speyer proposed to Ellen Prince, she turned to Mrs. Astor for advice. 'Not a single Jew,' wrote Elizabeth Drexel Lehr, 'could boast of an invitation to any of the houses of the Four Hundred. Not a hostess in New York would be the first to open her salon to one.' This was not true, for there had been a handful of Jews in society, mostly Sephardim, who were members of the Knickerbocker and the Union Club. The three Seligman brothers, for example, had been members of the Union League—until 1893, when Jesse Seligman's son Theodore was blackballed on purely racial grounds. He never set foot in the Union League again. Nonetheless, when directly asked by Ellen Prince whether anyone in society would receive a Jew and a Jew's wife, Mrs. Astor confronted the issue with a modulated sympathy. 'I don't think we have any alternative, for we are all so fond of you. Marry him, my dear, if you want to. I for one will invite you both to my parties and I think everyone else will do the same.' Which is precisely what they did. For many years Speyer was the only Jewish member of the Racquet Club.[86]

After a long stay in Paris, Frederick Townsend Martin returned to New York in 1907. He found society greatly changed. It was more selfish, indifferent, bored, and discontented Due to a recurrence of her heart ailment, Mrs. Astor had largely withdrawn from entertaining in 1906. The pace of change and dissolution had taken on a frightening momentum. Without Mrs. Astor's 'restraining hand,' sets which had formerly seen themselves as elements of a whole became detached from society itself. 'Each set holds aloof from the others, and with the passing of the great Astor balls, the organization never assembles nowadays.' Martin thought that society had become disastrously enlarged and fragmented. 'There are the Meadowbrook set, the Tuxedo set, the Southampton set, the Westchester set, the Lenox set, the Aiken set. . . . These people are perfectly happy with a little, never changing circle of friends.' Martin concluded that there was no one capable of uniting the diverse sets, nor was there a shared boundary, or agreed membership list, to reflect society's sense of who belonged and who did not. 'There is no social leader in New York to-day,' Martin remarked. 'Perhaps there will never be another, because the requisite qualifications are rare. Each little set has its leader, who rules arbitrarily and is looked up to, even idolized.' Every attempt over the past four decades to draw up a definitive list, to define society, had been swamped by those demanding inclusion. It seemed as though *everyone* wanted to be an aristocrat, and to enjoy a place in New York society. Abandoning McAllister's 'Four Hundred,' Martin suggested that there were perhaps 1,100 persons in society, but no one's version of such a list, like McAllister's, could possess any real authority.[87]

McAllister's dream of 'general society,' or the 'Four Hundred,' expired in New York in 1908. McAllister believed in the power of collective judgment, and hoped that society could enforce its norms, and inculcate its values, through a directorate of leaders whose position was, in his favorite term, unchallengeable. Mrs. Astor was the embodiment of that kind of social authority. On her retirement from society the authority she once possessed seemed to have quietly and suddenly vanished.

'After Mrs. Astor,' he remarked, 'there was chaos.' Martin's view was that the day of the list had passed. 'It is now the individual, not the list, and hostesses ask the people whom they wish.' Mamie Fish, when asked about the successor to Mrs. Astor, remarked: 'There is no leader of society. It's too large to manage.' After Mrs. Astor's death, the famed Astor box at the Metropolitan Opera was sublet for the first time in the history of the organization. 'The traditional exclusiveness of the proud Diamond Horseshoe,' noted *Town Topics*, 'has been shattered.'[88]

A world of 'sets' was multivalent, competitive, fissiparous, incoherent. Martin was enough of a realist to see the way the world was going. The pressures in every sphere of American life towards increasing specialization and division of labor changed aristocratic life in New York. With his commercial relations with the Plaza Hotel, he was a ready participant in the professionalization of society. What was first seen in commercial life in the 1870s, with the provision of luxury services for the society market, was in the next decade enforced by the emergence of periodicals wholly devoted to society, and the arrival of 'professional' beauties, ball-givers, and hostesses. Specialization and professionalization contributed mightily to the destruction of the idea of general society. Being a serious hostess was, by the late 1890s, no longer an amateur job. Hostesses were expected to establish a position in a social 'market' which was differentiated from their rivals'. Mrs. Astor's role in this process is clearly central. She embodied the ideal of a general society while at the same time equipping herself for a career as a professional hostess. Her competitive advantage lay in her family origins as a Schermerhorn, with roots in the Knickerbocker world of Old New York; in being an Astor; and, in a city

73. Mrs. Henry Clews.

Lucy Madison Worthington's family were ruined by the Civil War. Her father died fighting in the Confederate army. Her sister married a general in the Union army who was later disgraced by a scandal in the Grant administration. Lucy married an Englishman, Henry Clews, who had made a fortune on Wall Street. His passion for making money nearly kept pace with her determination to spend it.

where the 'one aim in life,' as McAllister remarked, 'is to accumulate money,' she had the great advantage of not needing to feel overawed by anyone else's wealth.

The confusion Martin encountered in 1907 resembled the New York social world in the decades before Mrs. Astor's emergence as a hostess. It was perhaps the natural state of society in New York. N.P. Willis had repeatedly complained that society of his day lacked a crucial element of coherence and leadership. There was no one predominant 'set' in New York, 'whose combined superiority was definitely thought of—and there is no one or more whose acquaintance is indispensable—and this forms, of course . . . a social republic, without any recognized aristocracy.' Willis anticipated the need for a dynamic and autocratic leader to bring together 'the best elements.' Society awaited the emergence of 'some female Napoleon to concentrate and combine them.'[89]

In Mrs. Astor New York had found its Napoleon. But the social conditions in the Gilded Age which made possible the career of a Mrs. Astor were unrepeatable. Of the many social leaders and 'sets' which characterized aristocratic life in New York in the twentieth century, none enjoyed the widespread agreement that one hostess should, as of right, enjoy aristocratic power. There was too much money around, and too much ambition, for such a consensus. At a deeper level, contenders for social position exercised new kinds of social power. The educational and cultural opportunities open to children of the Patriarchs, like Elsie Clews Parsons, embodied the generational change which did so much to make the world of the Patriarchs seem old fashioned and irrelevant to the needs of the modern age. What Parsons found at Barnard College, and in her growing interest in anthropology (Franz Boas, Alfred Kroeber, Pliny Goddard and Robert Lowie became her friends and mentors), seemed richer and far more rewarding than anything her parents' world had to offer. 'When I wanted to go to college,' Parsons remarked of her mother Lucy Worthington Clews, 'I was called selfish. I should stay home, I was told, and be companionable to my mother. I had never noticed that my mother found me companionable. In those years we were not at all companionable.' Raised in the milieu of the FCDC and the Patriarchs by two socially prominent parents, she spent the summer of 1896 translating the French sociologist Gabriel Tarde's *Les Lois de l'imitation*, instead of enjoying Newport's many social pleasures. Her mother, who enjoyed balls and loved fine clothes, raised a daughter who was more concerned with the hardships of the poor than Worth gowns. It left Mrs. Clews indignant and mystified at the values which moved her daughter. Across that generational divide lay the fracture of New York society in the early twentieth century.[90] An influential minority of the women in society chose to lead another way of life.

Los Angeles and Washington became cultural and political capitals in the way that New York alone had been in the nineteenth century. As the financial interests of New York became global, its local society increasingly seemed parochial. New York no longer controlled the national system of image-making, and the Hollywood version of an aristocracy lacked the rather endearing New York obliviousness to the rest of the nation. With its face turned to London and Paris, the New York aristocracy ceased to command the social ambitions of the parvenu. There were better mountains to climb. For this reason the remarkable career of Mrs. Astor was only possible at the moment when there were fewer choices for women, and perhaps less irony altogether about the idea of a social aristocracy. The process of accommodation with new money which marked her career and that of McAllister may have prolonged the life of the aristocratic world she had known. But in the decade after her death New York and its press had found a spirit more truly attuned to the provisional and experimental character of the city. It was the new forms of rebellion and social experimentation in Greenwich Village which shaped values and culture, not Fifth Avenue.[91] Had she chosen, the passionately independent-minded and imperious Mrs. O.H.P. Belmont might have made herself queen of that Bohemia. But the Village was rightly suspicious of the rich and their presumptions. A Schermerhorn, however born to dignity and social leadership, would have been an interesting sight, calling for tea at the apartment in Greenwich Village which Crystal Eastman shared with Madeleine Doty in 1907. Ida Ruah and Inez Milholland would drop by. As conversation turned to gender injustice, Mrs. Astor would have had much to listen to, and perhaps much to contribute. It was another of those things, like the meeting between Riis and McAllister, which New York never managed to arrange. At Eastman's apartment there was a language she had never heard at Newport or on Fifth Avenue.

NOTES

Preface

1. *New York Times* obituaries: Alfred Gwynne Vanderbilt, 87, Nov. 13, 1999; Hamilton Fish, Jr., 70, July 24, 1996; Betsey Cushing Whitney, 89, March 26, 1998; Francis Goelet, 72, May 23, 1998; Phyllis Rhinelander, 77, Sept. 30, 1998, Elbridge T. Gerry, 90, March 6, 1999; Frederick Vanderbilt Field, Feb. 7, 2000; Theodore Roosevelt III, 86, May 5, 2001. The election to the House of Lords appeared in the *Independent*, Nov. 6, 1999, 3. David Rynecki, 'The House the Bull Built,' *USA Today*, Aug. 20, 1999, 1–2; Martin Kettle, 'Judge turns down £2,750-a-day plea for jet set child,' *Guardian*, Dec. 9, 1999. Students of such matters would have found in the 'Living' and 'New York Region' sections of the *New York Times* a regular stream of articles pointing out the way the 'newly' rich take after their predecessors: 'household managers' (i.e. butlers) offered salaries of $60,000 to $120,000 a year ('Molding Loyal Pamperers for the Newly Rich,' Oct. 24, 1999), and an article on the centenary of the Junior League (Jan. 28, 2001). See also the rich zeitgeist material in David Remnick's *The New Gilded Age: The New Yorker Looks at the Culture of Affluence* (New York: Random House, 2000), a compilation of *New Yorker* profiles and articles published principally in 1999 and 2000, which reads very strangely indeed in 2001.

2. Jerry E. Patterson has cornered the market in anecdotal accounts of the New York upper crust, plundering the back issues of *Town & Country* for *The Best Families: The "Town & Country" Social Directory 1846–1996* (New York: Harry N. Abrams, 1996). He has also written *The Vanderbilts* (New York: Harry N. Abrams, 1989), *Fifth Avenue: The Best Addresses* (New York: Rizzoli, 1998) and *The First Four Hundred: Mrs. Astor's New York in the Gilded Age* (New York: Rizzoli, 2000). Compared to Richard Bushman, *The Refinement of America: Persons, Houses, Cities* (New York: Knopf, 1992), the narrowness of Patterson's curiosity is striking. Mary Cable's abundantly illustrated *Top Drawer: American High Society from the Gilded Age to the Roaring Twenties* (New York: Atheneum, 1984), Marian Fowler's *In a Gilded Cage: From Heiress to Duchess* (New York: St. Martin's Press, 1993), telling the story of Consuelo Yznaga, May Goelet, and three other heiresses in a light style, and Alfred Allan Lewis, *Ladies and Not-so-Gentle Women* (New York: Viking, 2000), containing portraits of Elisabeth Marbury, Anne Morgan, Elsie de Wolfe, and Anne Vanderbilt, are Pattersonian in spirit. Maureen Montgomery, *"Gilded Prostitution": Status, Money and Transatlantic Marriages, 1870–1914* (London: Routledge, 1989), and *Displaying Women: Spectacles of Leisure in Edith Wharton's New York* (New York: Routledge, 1998), Kathryn Allamong Jacob, *Capital Elites: High Society in Washington, D.C., after the Civil War* (Washington: Smithsonian Institution Press, 1995) and M.H. Dunlop, *Gilded City: Scandal and Sensation in Turn-of-the-Century New York* (New York: William Morrow, 2000), based on solid research, have shown how to write seriously about the world of the rich. Sven Beckert's *The Monied Metropolis: New York City and the Consolidation of the American Bourgeoisie 1850–1896* (New York: Cambridge University Press, 2001), a study of the city's economic elite, adds important dimensions of class formation. Becker's 'bourgeoisie' includes many figures, such as August Belmont, who occupy distinctly 'aristocratic' positions in the New York I have written about.

New York Wisdom on Wealth and Social Position

1. John Jacob Astor: W. Frothingham, 'Astor and the Capitalists of New-York,' *Continental Monthly*, 2, (Aug. 1862), 208; Kenneth Wiggins Porter, *John Jacob Astor, Business Man*, 2 vols (Cambridge, MA: Harvard University Press, 1931), 1122; John Jacob Astor III: Lucy Kavaler, *The Astors: A Family Chronicle of Pomp and Power* (New York: Dodd, Mead, 1966), 90; William Astor: 'Death of William Astor,' *The Sun*, April 27, 1892, 7; Ward McAllister: 'Secrets of Ball-Giving,' *New York Daily Tribune*, March 25, 1888, 11; Mrs. Stuyvesant Fish: David Garrard Lowe, *Stanford White's New York*, rev. edn. (New York: Watson-Guptill, 1999), 65; Jay Gould: Robert Irving Warshow, *Jay Gould: The Story of a Fortune* (New York: Greenberg, 1928), 180; an alternative version of Gould's remark appears in 'Max O'Rell' and Jack Allyn, *Jonathan and His Continent*, trans. Madame Paul Blouët (New York: Cassell, 1889), 65: 'No man can own more than a million dollars. When his bank account outgrows that, he does not own it, it owns him, and he becomes its slave.' James Hazen Hyde: John A. Garraty, *Right-Hand Man: The Life of George W. Perkins* (New York: Harper & Brothers, 1960), 161–2; Herman Melville to Nathaniel Parker Willis, 1849, cited in Jay Leyda, *The Melville Log: A Documentary Life of Herman Melville 1819-1891*, 2 vols. (New York: Harcourt, Brace & Co., 1951), I, 347; Theodore Roosevelt: Owen Wister, *Roosevelt: The Story of a Friendship 1880–1919* (New York: Macmillan, 1930), 211; William K. Vanderbilt: Clarice Stasz, *The Vanderbilt Women: Dynasty of Wealth, Glamour, and Tragedy* (New York: St. Martin's Press, [1991]), 114; Andrew Carnegie: Ron Chernow, *The Death of the Banker: The Decline and Fall of the Great Financial Dynasties and the Triumph of the Small Investor* (London: Pimlico, 1997), 22. This remark has been attributed to John D. Rockefeller by Aline B. Saarinen, *The Proud Possessors* (London: Weidenfeld & Nicolson, 1959), 87; J.P Morgan: Andrew Sinclair, *Corsair: The Life of J. Pierpont Morgan* (London: Weidenfeld & Nicolson, 1981), 136; Frederick T. Martin: 'Mr. Martin's Analysis of New York Society: Chaos, He Declares, Followed the Retirement of Mrs. Astor, Resulting in More Marked Social Divisions and Greater Boredom,' *New York Times*, May 3, 1908, V, 6.

Chapter 1 Looking at Aristocracy

1. J.S., 'Class Distinctions a Social Necessity,' *New-York Illustrated*, June 1, 1861, 51.
2. 'A Frenchman in New York,' *Appleton's Journal*, 13 (April 3, 1875), 431–4. Simonin (1830–1886), a mining engineer, achieved considerable success in France with travel articles in the *Revue des deux mondes*, 1874–5, which were collected in *À travers les États-Unis de l'Atlantique au Pacifique* (1875) and *Le monde Amérique: souvenirs de mes voyages aux États-Unis* (1876).
3. N.P. Willis, *Dashes at Life with a Free Pencil. Part IV: Ephemera*, 3rd edn. (New York: J.S. Redfield, 1845), 196–7.
4. John R. Alden, *Pioneer America* (London: Hutchinson, 1966), 104.
5. *Memoir of William Ellery Channing, with Extracts from His Correspondence and Manuscripts*, 3 vols. (Boston: Crosby & Nichols, 1851), III, 112. Many stereotypes about nineteenth-century America were vividly overturned in Lewis Mumford's work, especially *The Brown Decades* (1931), although the title served unwittingly to perpetuate the modernist distaste for the art of Victorian America.
6. Estimates of the size of society: J. Mordaunt Crook, *The Rise of the "Nouveaux Riches": Style and Status in Victorian and Edwardian Architecture* (London: John Murray, 1999), 164. Leonore Davidoff, *The Best Circles: Society Etiquette and the Season* (London: Croom Helm, 1973), 61, suggests that by the end of the nineteenth century there were 4,000 families actively involved in society, which was a numerical limit 'for this kind of face to face community held together by gossip and information exchange.' Mrs. Astor quoted in Rebecca H. Insley, 'An Interview with Mrs. Astor,' *The Delineator*, 72 (Oct. 1908), 549–50, 638–9.
7. *Frank Leslie's Gazette of Fashion*, 1 (Jan., 1854), 16; see also Boni de Castellane's account of a visit to the Long Island home of George Gould in the 1890s, in *Confessions of the Marquis de Castellane* (London: Thornton Butterworth, 1924), 108–9.
8. 'Our Disregard of Good Breeding,' *Frank Leslie's Lady's Journal*, 1 (Dec. 2, 1871), 43. Articles on 'Frivolous Women,' 'Discourtesy,' 'Social Insincerities,' 'The Charm of Reserve,' and 'Evils of Gossip' enliven the first volumes of the magazine in the 1870s.
9. [Abby Buchanan Longstreet,] *Social Etiquette of New York* (New York: D. Appleton, 1879), 21–2.
10. [William Armstrong,] *The Aristocracy of New York: Who They Are and What They Were; Being a Social*

and Business History of the City for Many Years, by an Old Resident (New York: New York Publishing Co., 1848).

11. George Salisbury, 'The American Englishman,' *The Epoch*, 2, 33 (Sept. 23, 1887), 127.

12. Denning Duer, born in 1812, married the daughter of the banker James Gore King. See 'Alice's MS about the Family,' Alice Duer Miller Papers, Box 1, Barnard College Archives, New York City; Leon Edel, *Henry James: The Untried Years, 1843–1870* (London: Hart-Davis, 1953), 93.

13. Clive Aslet, *The American Country House* (New Haven: Yale University Press, 1990), 67–9.

14. Revival of interest in aristocracy: Bushman, *Refinement of America*, 416.

15. Adopting aristocratic names noted in Dorothy Richardson, *The Long Day: The Story of a New York Working Girl*, with an Introduction by Cindy Sondik Aron (Charlottesville: University Press of Virginia, 1990), 97. First published 1905.

16. Michael Kammen, *Selvages & Biases: The Fabric of History in American Culture* (Ithaca, NY: Cornell University Press, 1987), 143–7.

17. Marilyn Wood Hill, *Their Sisters' Keepers: Prostitution in New York City, 1830–1870* (Berkeley: University of California Press, 1993), 193–5, 220–1. On Morrissey, see Gustav Lening, *The Dark Side of New York Life and its Criminal Classes from Fifth Avenue down to the Five Points. A Complete Narrative of the Mysteries of New York* (New York: Fred'k. Gerhard, 1873), 288–9; 'Death of John Morrissey,' *New York Times*, May 2, 1878, 1; William Edgar Harding, compiler, *John Morrissey, His Life, Battles and Wrangles, from his Birth in Ireland until he Died a State Senator* (New York: R.K. Fox, 1881); George Waller, *Saratoga: Saga of an Impious Era* (Englewood Cliffs, NJ: Prentice-Hall, 1966), 119, 122,.132–4, 140–1. On Restell's move to Fifth Avenue and the décor of 'The Palace,' see Eric Homberger, *Scenes from the Life of a City: Corruption and Conscience in Old New York* (New Haven: Yale University Press, 1994), 119–23. See also Luc Sante, *Low Life: Lures and Snares of Old New York* (New York: Farrar, Straus, Giroux, 1991).

18. Gunther Barth, *City People: The Rise of Modern City Culture in Nineteenth-Century America* (New York: Oxford University Press, 1980), ch. 1, discusses the consequences of the divided city 'The full *equality*': [Samuel Irenaeus Prime,] *Life in New York* (New York: Robert Carter, 1847), 64; Emily Johnson De Forest, *John Johnston of New York: Merchant* (New York: Privately printed, 1909), 29; George Augustus Sala, 'The Streets of the World: New York: Broadway Itself,' *Temple Bar*, 14 (May 1865), 178; see also Simonin's 'A Frenchman in New York,' *Appleton's Journal*, 13 (April 3, 1875), 431–4.

19. A stranger's observations: 'Joseph,' *New York Aristocracy; or Gems of Japonica-dom* (New York: Charles B. Norton, 1851), 89; *The Lorgnette: or, Studies of the Town. By An Opera Goer* [Donald G. Mitchell ('Ik Marvell')], 2 vols. (New York: Charles Scribner, 1853) II, 9th edn., 62; Rev. E.H. Chapin, *Humanity in the City* (New York: De Witt & Davenport, [1854]), 71. See also Karen Halttunen, *Confidence Men and Painted Women: A Study in Middle-class Culture in America, 1830–1870* (New Haven and London: Yale University Press, 1982); John F. Kasson, *Rudeness & Civility: Manners in Nineteenth-Century Urban America* (New York: Hill & Wang, 1990); Montgomery, '*Gilded Prostitution*' and *Displaying Women*; Norbert Elias, *The Civilizing Process: The History of Manners and State Formation and Civilization*, trans. Edmund Jephcott (Oxford: Blackwell, 1994).

20. 'J.G. Wendel Dead, A Realty Croesus,' *New York Times*, Dec. 1, 1914, 1; the notion that the Wendel sisters lived in social isolation is probably exaggerated, as both attended Helen Gould's debutante reception in 1891. See Alice Northrop Snow with Henry Nicholas Snow, *The Story of Helen Gould, Daughter of Jay Gould, Great American* (New York: Fleming H. Revell, 1943), 190. For Lenox see *Recollections of Mr. James Lenox of New York and the Formation of His Library* (London: Henry Stevens & Son, 1886), and *Town Topics*, 18 (Sept. 29, 1887), 5. For Schermerhorn see 'He Died Sad, Rich, Alone,' *New York World*, Oct. 3, 1891, 3.

21. 'Mrs. Astor Is Critically Ill,' *New York Times*, Oct. 30, 1908, 1–2.

22. Arthur Charlton, 'A Fashionable Club,' *The Epoch*, 1, 22 (July 8, 1887), 514.

23. *The Notebooks of Henry James*, ed. F.O. Matthiessen and Kenneth B. Murdock (New York: Oxford University Press, 1947), 82. Entry for Nov. 17, 1887.

24. Mrs. Roger A. Pryor, 'American Society,' *Cosmopolitan*, 9 (July 1890), 309.

25. On the Beecher–Tilton scandal, see Altina L. Waller, *Reverend Beecher and Mrs. Tilton: Sex and Class in Victorian America* (Amherst: University of Massachusetts Press, [1982]). Edward Van Every, *Sins of New York as 'Exposed' by the Police Gazette* (New York: Frederick A. Stokes, 1930), and *The Police Gazette*, ed. Gene Smith and Jayne Barry Smith (New York: Simon & Schuster, 1972), suggest the rudeness and gaiety of the *Police Gazette*.

26. For *Town Topics*, see Andy Logan, *The Man Who Robbed the Robber Barons* (New York: W.W. Norton, 1965). Logan discusses *Fads and Fancies* and the use to which Mann put it in ch. 3. Aslet, *The American Country House*, 70–1, draws some interesting things from *Fads and Fancies*, without realizing its role in Colonel Mann's blackmails.

27. Coverage of the Bennett–May assault and subsequent duel in *New York Times*, Jan. 4, 1877; Stephen Fiske, *Off-Hand Portraits of Prominent New Yorkers* (New York: Geo. R. Lockwood & Son, 1884), 32–8; Charlton, 'A Fashionable Club,' 514.

28. 'Mrs. Vanderbilt Free,' *New York World*, March 6, 1895, 1–2. What made Pulitzer's paper so detested in society, and such entertaining reading outside society, may be seen in the front page of the issue of Jan. 29, 1895. Next to a story on the divorce of Mrs. Astor's daughter, which involved accusations of her infidelity, was a one-paragraph story: 'Nellie Neustretter a Mother.'

29. See Halttunen, *Confidence Men and Painted Women*, ch. 4; *A History of Private Life*, ed. Michelle Perrot. Vol. IV. *From the Fires of Revolution to the Great War*, trans. Arthur Goldhammer (Cambridge, MA: Belknap Press of Harvard University Press, 1990), ch. 3.

30. James L. Ford, 'Seeing the Real New York from the Deck of the Rubberneck Coach. Trip No. 2—At Society's Golden Portals,' *Cosmopolitan*, 40 (Dec. 1905), 218–26.

31. Henry James, *The American Scene* (1907) in *Collected Travel Writings: Great Britain and America*, ed. Richard Howard (New York: The Library of America, 1993), 365. Marvin Heiferman and Carole Kismaric's 'Fame after Photography' at the Museum of Modern Art, July–Oct. 1999, began with images of American aristocrats.

32. Leo Braudy's discussion of the 'democratization of fame,' and the role of photographers like Brady in the emergence of 'visual self-consciousness' in America appears in *The Frenzy of Renown: Fame & Its History* (New York: Oxford University Press, 1986), 450–505. Curiously, he says little about the role of the press in the construction of fame.

33. Brady's *Illustrious Americans* is discussed in Alan Trachtenberg, *Reading the American Photograph: Images as History, Matthew Brady to Walker Evans* (New York: Hill & Wang, 1989), 21–70. Higginson's remark on the lack of interest in rich men appears in 'A Plea for Culture,' *Atlantic Monthly*, 19 (Jan. 1867), 29–37. The engraving of Vanderbilt, from a photograph by Howell, appeared in *Harper's Weekly*, 21 (Jan. 20, 1877). Davidoff, *The Best Circles*, 62, notes the importance in Britain of society events being photographed

34. The Mora and Byron archives are at the Museum of the City of New York. Entries in Feb. 1897, Diary, Richard Ward Greene Welling Papers, New York Public Library (NYPL).

35. Robert Taft, *Photography and the American Scene: A Social History* (New York: Macmillan, 1938), *passim*. 'Our Beauties for Sale,' *New York World*, Oct. 28, 1883, 9. Prince of Wales: 'Fancy-Dress Balls of Other Days,' *The Season: An Annual Record of Society in New York, Brooklyn and Vicinity*, First year 1882–3, ed. Charles H. Crandall (New York: White, Stokes & Allen, 1883), 35. See *New York Interiors at the Turn of the Century in 131 Photographs by Joseph Byron*, text by Clay Lancaster (New York: Dover, [1976]). 'Society photographers' in New York were rather more like the city itself than their lucrative subjects. Sarony was born in Quebec of German parents, and came to New York at the age of ten. Mora, a Spaniard born in Cuba, was from a planter family who fled the island after an uprising in 1868. Byron, the leading New York society photographer of the day, emigrated from Nottingham in 1888.

36. *The Times*, Sept. 20, 2000, 22.

37. On Ward McAllister and the press, see Leander K. Carr, 'Gathering News in the Nineties,' *Bulletin of the Newport Historical Society*, 95 (July 1935), 3–8.

38. The 'professional beauty' is described in Paul Bourget, *Outre-Mer: Impressions of America* (London: T. Fisher Unwin, 1895), 86–8.

39. Winslow's campaign appears in *Town Topics*, 18 (Dec. 29, 1887), 5; for his comment on Hargous see *Town Topics*, 26 (Sept. 10, 1891), 1. Hargous married Duncan Elliott in 1891, and subsequently Woodbury Kane and then Captain Douglas Gill. In this case, the bride was the story so far as the New York press was concerned. 'Sally Hargous Married,' *New York Daily Tribune*, Sept. 16, 1891, 7.

40. The London 'Social Mentor' described by George W. Smalley in the New York *Tribune*, was closer to the role played by Isaac Brown of Grace Church than the private social enterprises of Mrs. Burden or Mrs. Stevens. See Smalley's *London Letters and Some Others*, 2 vols. (London: Macmillan, 1890), II, 24–30.

41. McAllister deplored the 'London strategy' of socially ambitious American matrons in 'Mr. McAllister on Society,' *New York Daily Tribune*, Dec. 7, 1890, 17. See Montgomery, 'Gilded Prostitution'.

42. The experience of de Wolfe as a 'professional' appears in Elsie de Wolfe (Lady Mendl), *After All* (London:

William Heinemann, 1935), Jane S. Smith, *Elsie de Wolfe: A Life in the High Style* (New York: Atheneum, 1982), and coverage in *Town Topics* in Nov. 1887 and Jan. 1888.

43. 'A Many-Millionaire,' *New York Independent*, Dec. 2, 1875, in a scrapbook containing obituary notices of W.B. Astor. NYPL.

44. President Arthur at Saratoga: Thomas Beer, *Hanna, Crane and the Mauve Decade*, with an Introduction by Leonard Bacon (New York: Knopf, 1941), 18, 206. 'William B. Astor,' *New York Herald*, Nov. 25, 1875, 6.

45. 'Mrs. Fish Drops Out of Garment Strike,' *New York Times*, Feb. 9, 1913, 3; 'Miss Morgan Tells of Women's Work,' *New York Times*, Jan. 15, 1915, 9; Edward Marshall, 'Mrs. Stuyvesant Fish Decries "Hard Up,"' *New York Times*, Jan. 17, 1915, V, 8. An even more visible figure was Mrs. O.H.P. Belmont, whose activities as a feminist were extensively reported in the press.

46. See A.M. Schlesinger, *Learning How to Behave* (New York: Macmillan, 1946); Gerald Carson, *The Polite American* (London: Macmillan, 1967); Halttunen, *Confidence Men and Painted Women*, ch. 2; Kasson, *Rudeness & Civility*; Bushman, *The Refinement of America*.

47. Willis, *Dashes at Life with a Free Pencil*, 161–2.

48. Oct. 10, 1847, *The Diary of George Templeton Strong, 1835–1875*, ed. Allan Nevins and Milton Halsey, 4 vols. (New York: Macmillan, 1952), I, 302. In the eyes of men like Strong, Dillon was a bounder and humbug. A lawyer and a Democrat closely allied with August Belmont and Peter B. Sweeny, Dillon was appointed to the first Central Park Board of Commissioners in 1858, where he proved to be a major critic of the Greensward design of the park's superintendent, Frederick Law Olmsted. With Belmont he proposed over a dozen amendments to Olmsted's plan, including the abandonment of the circuit drive and the sunken transverse roads. In 1860 he brought accusations of financial mismanagement against the Republican-dominated Commission, and when Tweed's new city charter was passed in 1870, Dillon joined the new park board led by Sweeny. Olmsted's struggle to block the Dillon and Belmont 'improvements' appears in *The Papers of Frederick Law Olmsted*, Vol. III. *Creating Central Park 1857–1861*, ed. Charles E. Beveridge and David Schuyler (Baltimore: Johns Hopkins University Press, 1983), *passim*.

49. Entry for Feb. 21, 1879, *The Notebooks of Henry James*, ed. Matthiessen and Murdock, 12–13; Leon Edel, *Henry James 1870–1881: The Conquest of London*

(Philadelphia: J.B. Lippincott, 1962), 398; Sheldon M. Novick, *Henry James: The Young Master* (New York: Random House, 1996), 407.

50. There is a very valuable discussion of 'calling' in Elsie Clews Parsons, *Fear and Conventionality*, with a new Introduction by Desley Deacon (1914; Chicago: University of Chicago Press, 1997), ch. 10; see also [Mrs. Abby Buchanan Longstreet,] *Cards: Their Significance and Proper Uses as Governed by the Usages of New York Society*, by the Author of 'Social Etiquette of New York' (New York: Frederick A. Stokes, 1889) and Mrs John Sherwood, *Manners and Social Usages* new and rev. edn. (New York: Harper & Brothers, 1897), 98.

51. Henry James, *Washington Square* (1881) in *Novels 1881–1886*, ed. William T. Stafford (New York: The Library of America, 1985), 34–7, 41. On Dr. Sloper's withering judgment ('He is not a gentleman'), see E. Digby Baltzell, *The Philadelphia Gentleman: The Making of a National Upper Class* (New York: The Free Press, 1958) and David Castronovo, *The American Gentleman: Social Prestige and the Modern Literary Mind* (New York: Continuum, 1991).

52. *New York Times*, March 12, 1878, 2; March 13, 8; March 14, 3; March 16, 3.

53. 'Newport Warfare: The Astor Feud and Here Is Still Another,' undated clipping, Astor Papers, Box 3, NYPL. Dated summer 1890. Entry for April 7, 1845, Hone Mss. diary, 28 vols., NYHS, XXII, 463; *The Diary of Philip Hone 1828–1851*, ed. Allan Nevins, 2 vols. (New York: Dodd, Mead, 1927), II, 730. The mistranscriptions, omissions, willful errors, and the silent addition of words and phrases not in the manuscript, makes Nevins' edition of the Hone diary highly unsatisfactory. It is also worth noting that Nevins actually marked the diary with instructions for his transcribers. All citations have been cross-checked against the microfilm of the diary in the NYHS. Hone is an irreplaceable observer of New York upper-class life and public affairs. There has been no complete edition of the diary, nor has he yet attracted a modern biographer. But see Herbert Kriedman, 'New York's Philip Hone' (Ph.D., NYU, 1965); Edward Pessen, 'Philip Hone's Set: The Social World of the New York City Elite in the "Age of Egalitarianism",' *New-York Historical Society Quarterly*, 56 (Oct. 1972), 285–308; and Peter G. Buckley, 'Culture, Class and Place in Antebellum New York,' in *Power, Culture and Place: Essays on New York City*, ed. John Hull Mollenkopf (New York: Russell Sage Foundation, 1988), 25–52.

54. See Mrs. John King Van Rensselaer, in Collaboration

with Frederic Van de Water, *The Social Ladder* (London: Eveleigh Nash & Grayson, 1925).

55. David Black, *The King of Fifth Avenue: The Fortunes of August Belmont* (New York: The Dial Press, 1981), 31.

56. Susan A. Ostrander, *Women of the Upper Class* (Philadelphia: Temple University Press, [1984]), 7; Mrs. John King Van Rensselaer, *The Social Ladder*, 22; see also Kathryn Allamong Jacob, *Capital Elites: High Society in Washington, D.C. after the Civil War* (Washington and London: Smithsonian Institution Press, 1995).

57. 'Our Best and Worst Society,' *New York Daily Tribune*, March 12, 1855, 4.

58. Frederic Cople Jaher, 'Style and Status in Late Nineteenth-Century New York,' in *The Rich, the Well Born, and the Powerful: Elites and Upper Classes in History*, ed. Jaher (Secaucus, NJ: The Citadel Press, 1975), 258–84; Louis Auchincloss, *The Vanderbilt Era: Profiles of a Gilded Age* (New York: Collier Books, 1989), 48.

59. Jacob Riis, *How the Other Half Lives: Studies among the Tenements of New York* (New York: Charles Scribner, 1890; Dover, 1971, with illustrations), 124.

60. Ira Rosenwaike, *Population History of New York City* (Syracuse, NY: Syracuse University Press, 1972), 84–5.

61. Lening, *The Dark Side of New York Life*, 7. See also Lydia Maria Child, *Letters from New-York*, ed. Bruce Mills (Athens: University of Georgia Press, 1998), 9.

62. Metropolitan Board of Health: Homberger, *Scenes from the Life of a City*, ch. 1. City statistics: 'The Year That Has Gone,' *New York Times*, Jan. 2, 1890, 8. *Maggie*: Stephen Crane, *Prose and Poetry*, ed. J.C. Levenson (New York: Library of America, 1984), 20. Unfair world: Riis, *How the Other Half Lives*, 189.

63. 'An Unhealthy District,' *New York Times*, June 18, 1890, 8.

64. See Jacob Riis, 'Theodore Roosevelt's Father,' *The Outlook*, 66 (Oct. 6, 1900), 305–9, *Theodore Roosevelt: The Man and the Citizen* (London: Hodder & Stoughton, 1904). On Rainsford, see Jacob A. Riis, 'Religion by Human Touch,' *The World's Work*, 1 (March 1901), 495–505. Riis paid a social cost for his highly visible criticism of the wealthy: see 'Morsel for New-York Clubmen,' *New York Times*, Feb. 24, 1894, 8, describing his being blackballed at the Metropolitan Club.

65. Riis, *How the Other Half Lives*, 2, 52, 186.

66. Riis, *How the Other Half Lives*, 28.

67. Riis, *How the Other Half Lives*, 49, 13, 146, 36, 156.

68. Riis, *How the Other Half Lives*, 13, 6, 91, 98.

69. 'A Generous Christmas Gift,' *New York Times*, Jan. 9, 1876, 4, and 'Mrs. J.J. Astor's Liberality,' *New York Times*, Jan. 14, 1880, 8. See also Marilyn Irvin Holt, *The Orphan Trains: Placing Out in America* (Lincoln: University of Nebraska Press, 1992) and Stephen

O'Connor, *Orphan Trains: The Story of Charles Loring Brace and the Children He Saved and Failed* (Boston: Houghton Mifflin, 2001). Neither author discusses Brace's supporters or how the Children's Aid Society (CAS) gained broad support in elite circles in New York. Under her influence John Jacob III, the first of the Astors to be born into regal wealth and splendor, endowed a lodging-house for street urchins, known as the 'Astor House.' He built the West Side Hostel for boys, and a trade school for German immigrant children. His largest donation was $250,000 for the Memorial Hospital for the Treatment of Cancer. As a memorial to his wife in 1889, Astor built the Fourteenth Ward Industrial School on Mott Street, which he presented to the Children's Aid Society.

70. Gary Scharnhorst with Jack Bales, *The Lost Life of Horatio Alger, Jr.* (Bloomington: Indiana University Press, 1985), 79; Orthopedic Hospital: David McCullough, *Mornings on Horseback* (New York: Simon & Schuster, 1981), 139. Fourteenth Ward Industrial School: 'A Fitting Memorial: Industrial School Monument to Mrs. John Jacob Astor,' *New York Times*, Feb. 8, 1889, 5.

71. David Sinclair, *Dynasty: The Astors and Their Times* (London: J.M. Dent, 1983), 178–9.

72. Michael Zuckerman, 'The Nursery Tales of Horatio Alger,' *American Quarterly*, 24, (May 1972), 191–209; Gary Scharnhorst with Jack Bales, *The Lost Life of Horatio Alger, Jr.* (Bloomington: Indiana University Press, 1985); Carol Nackenoff, *The Fictional Republic: Horatio Alger and American Political Discourse* (New York: Oxford University Press, 1994).

73. W.S. Rainsford, *The Story of a Varied Life: An Autobiography* (Garden City, NY: Doubleday, Page, 1922), 313; *Town Topics*, 26 (Nov. 19, 1891), 3.

Chapter 2 The Art of Social Climbing

1. Among their number was the Rev. Charles Inglis, rector of Trinity Church, who bested General Washington in a sharp-edged confrontation in 1776. On May 17, a day set aside by Congress for fasting and prayer, Inglis was asked by one of General Washington's officers to omit 'the violent prayers for the king and royal family.' Inglis 'paid no regard' to Washington's request, and later claimed to have received an 'awkward apology' for the impropriety of the request. Washington claimed he had not authorized the approach to Inglis. A boldly outspoken loyalist, Inglis settled in Nova Scotia in 1787, where he became Bishop. His successor as Rector, the Rev. Mr. Benjamin Moore, founded

St. John's Chapel. See Rev. William Berrian, DD, *An Historical Sketch of Trinity Church* (New York: Stanford & Sands, 1847), 139–61. Berrian was Moore's successor as rector of Trinity.

2. *A Season in New York 1801: Letters of Harriet and Maria Trumbull*, ed. with an Introduction by Helen M. Morgan (Pittsburgh: University of Pittsburgh Press, [1969]), 124. Letter of Feb. 21, 1801. Further references are cited in the text by date. The copious notes in this volume are particularly helpful in the reconstruction of the world of New York society in 1800–1. The Yale University Art Gallery possesses a drawing of Harriet Trumbull, reproduced in *A Season in New York 1801*.

3. Washington's letter welcoming Jonathan Trumbull to the first Congress is cited by Margaret C. S. Christman, *The First Federal Congress 1789–1791* (Washington, DC: The Smithsonian Institution Press for the National Portrait Gallery, 1989), 341.

4. 'Speech of His Excellency Governor Trumbull, to both houses of the Legislature of Connecticut . . . last Thursday,' *Commercial Advertiser*, Oct. 15, 1800, 3.

5. *Commercial Advertiser*, Dec. 22, 1800, 3.

6. 'The Triumph of Democracy,' *Commercial Advertiser*, Jan. 3, 1801, 3, reprinted from the *Courant* in Connecticut.

7. Jane C. Nylander, *Our Own Snug Fireside: Images of the New England Home 1760–1860* (New York: Knopf, 1993), 43–4; Nancy M. Theriot, *Mothers and Daughters in Nineteenth Century America: The Biosocial Construction of Femininity* (Lexington: University Press of Kentucky, 1996), 70–1.

8. Cockloft Pindar, 'To the Ladies,' *Salmagundi*, Letter V (March 7, 1807); Washington Irving, *History, Tales and Sketches*, ed. James W. Tuttleton (New York: The Library of America, 1983), 125.

9. David S. Shields, *Civil Tongues & Polite Letters in British America* (Chapel Hill: University of North Carolina Press, 1997), chs. 3–4. I would like to thank my colleague Simon Middleton for alerting me to Shields' interesting work.

10. 'Old New York Revived—Continued. 17. Longworth's Shakespeare Gallery. 1.—Description of the Gallery, 1800,' *Historical Magazine*, 11, 2nd. ser., 1 (Feb. 1867), 105–8; *Gallery of Fashion* (London), April 1801, unpaginated. The New York press was also an occasional source of reports on trends in fashionable life in England and the continent, which were among the rare items in the daily press specifically aimed at female readers. See 'Female Fashions in London,' *Commercial Advertiser*, Sept. 15, 1800, 3.

11. J.P. Brissot de Warville, *New Travels in the United States of America 1788*, trans. Mara Soceanu Vamos and Durand Echeverria, ed. Durand Echeverria (Cambridge, MA: Belknap Press of Harvard University Press, 1964), 142.

12. Bushman, *The Refinement of America*, 402.

13. *New-York Evening Post*, Jan. 5, 1802.

14. The annual membership fee was $10, *Commercial Advertiser*, Nov. 12, 1800, 2.

15. 'Sertorius,' letter to the editor, *Commercial Advertiser*, March 28, 1801, 3. *The American Diaries of Richard Cobden*, ed. Elizabeth Hoon Cawley (Princeton, NJ: Princeton University Press, 1952), 89; [Washington Irving,] Letter I, *Letters of Jonathan Oldstyle Gent.*, 1802–3, in Irving, *History, Tales and Sketches*, 6.

16. The *Commercial Advertiser* is a rich source of information on the city's life. Fancy dry goods for sale appear in every issue; see especially Dec. 27, 1800, 4; Caritat's library, Sept. 20, 1800, Vanderbilt and Goelet, June 9, 1800.

17. R.W.G. Vail's 'factual fantasy' of a walk taken by John Pintard through New York in 1804 amusingly suggests the sights. It was a route which the Trumbull sisters might easily have taken. See Vail's *Knickerbocker Birthday: A Sesqui-Centennial History of the New-York Historical Society 1804–1954* (New York: New-York Historical Society, 1954), 3–27.

18. The 'elderly historian' is Rev. William Berrian, DD, *Historical Sketch of Trinity Church*, 217. See *Manual of the Corporation of the City of New York* (New York: D.T. Valentine, 1865), 522–3, 583–4. When offered six acres of this wasteland, trustees of the Lutheran Church declined the gift, 'on the ground that it would not pay to fence it in.'

19. Shane White, *Somewhat More Independent: The End of Slavery in New York City, 1770–1810* (Athens: University of Georgia Press, 1991), 26.

20. Guy's large canvas at the New-York Historical Society is reproduced in John Kouwenhoven, *The Columbia Historical Portrait of New York: An Essay in Graphic History* (New York: Harper & Row, 1972), 107. Richard Bushman, *The Refinement of America*, 166–9, does not mention Francis Guy, but uses similar visual material to make a valuable distinction between the 'genteel city' and the 'actual city.'

21. Barbara G. Carson, *Ambitious Appetites: Dining Behavior, and Patterns of Consumption in Federal Washington* (Washington, DC: The American Institute of Architects Press, 1990), 104–30.

22. Dixon Ryan Fox, *Yankees and Yorkers* (New York: New York University Press, 1940), gracefully surveys the struggle, from the seventeenth century, between the New Englanders and the Dutch. Fox mentions the names of New Englanders such as the Griswolds,

Lows, Howlands, Aspinwalls, Goodhues, Fishes, Grinnells, Minturns, Sturges, and Phelpses who became leading figures in commercial life in New York.

23. Varick was succeeded as mayor in 1801 by Edward Livingston, from the clan with which he had feuded for two decades. Leo Hershkowitz, 'Federal New York: Mayors of the Nation's First Capital,' *World of the Founders: New York Communities in the Federal Period*, ed. Stephen L. Schechter and Wendell Tripp (Albany: New York State Commission on the Bicentennial of the United States Constitution, 1990), 25–56, and Graham Russell Hodges, *New York City Cartmen, 1667–1850* (New York: New York University Press, 1986), offer views of Varick as a public figure and Federalist partisan. The official document appointing Varick to his final term as mayor, dated Feb., 7, 1800, is in the Gilder Lehrman Collection, on loan in the Morgan Library.

24. Nathan Schachner, *Alexander Hamilton* (New York: D. Appleton-Century, 1946), 390.

25. John W. Francis, MD, *Old New York: or, Reminiscences of the Past Sixty Years, with a Memoir of the Author by Henry T. Tuckerman* (New York: W.J. Widdleton, 1866), 119. See also Simon P. Newman, *Parades and the Politics of the Street: Festive Culture in the Early American Republic* (Philadelphia: University of Pennsylvania Press, 1997), ch. 4. Street demonstrations and parades in support of France had largely vanished from American cities by the late 1790s. There was a pitched battle between Republicans and Federalists over a liberty pole in Dedham, Massachusetts, in 1799. For this, and the cockade riot in Philadelphia, see John C. Miller, *Crisis in Freedom: The Alien and Sedition Acts* (Boston: Little, Brown, 1951), 62, 114–16; Paul A. Gilje, *The Road to Mobocracy: Popular Disorder in New York City, 1763–1834* (Chapel Hill: Published for the Institute of Early American History and Culture by the University of North Carolina Press, 1987), 110–11. For recent research on Duer, see Robert E. Wright, 'Banking and Politics in New York, 1784–1829' (Ph.D., State University of New York at Buffalo, 1997).

26. *A Season in New York*, 87n. Rufus Wilmot Griswold, *The Republican Court; or, American Society in the Days of Washington*, new edn. (New York: D. Appleton, 1855), 164.

27. A transcription of Janet Montgomery's reminiscences, a cornucopia of extraordinary events, prophecies, uncanny visitations, and fortune-telling written late in life, is in the NYHS. Armstrong's daughter Margaret later married William B. Astor, and was the mother of John Jacob Astor III and

William Astor. On the Livingstons see Cynthia A. Kierner, *Traders and Gentlefolk: The Livingstons of New York, 1675–1790* (Ithaca, NY: Cornell University Press, 1992) and Clare Brandt, *An American Aristocracy: The Livingstons* (Garden City, NY: Doubleday, 1986); see also an account of a visit to Manhattan in 1806–7 by Helen, second daughter of Gilbert R. Livingston, in Helen Evertson Smith, 'A Group of American Girls: Early in the Century,' *Century*, 53, n.s. 31 (Dec. 1896), 163–80. Nancy Shippen, who married Colonel Henry Beekman Livingston (brother of the Chancellor), had a much darker experience of the Livingston family. See *Nancy Shippen Her Journal Book: The International Romance of a Young Lady of Fashion of Colonial Philadelphia with Letters to Her and About Her*, compiled and ed. Ethel Armes (Philadelphia: J.B. Lippincott, 1953).

28. William Alexander Duer, 'Colonel William Duer,' Duer Family Papers, Columbia University Library. Duer's heavily revised 21-page manuscript account of the life of his father, Colonel William Duer, offers an explanation, if not a full-blooded defense, of the financial conduct of his father.

29. Alan Valentine, *Lord Stirling* (New York: Oxford University Press, 1969); J.P. Brissot de Warville, *New Travels in the United States*, 149–50. Duer's servants' livery: Patterson, *The First Four Hundred*, 14. David L. Sterling, 'William Duer, John Pintard, and the Panic of 1792,' *Business Enterprise in Early New York*, ed. Joseph R. Frese, S.J. and Jacob Judd (Tarrytown: Sleepy Hollow Press and Rockefeller Archive Center, 1979), 99–132; Cathy Matson, 'Public Vices, Private Benefit: William Duer and His Circle, 1776–1792,' *New York and the Rise of American Capitalism*, ed. William Pencak and Conrad Edick Wright (New York: New-York Historical Society, 1989), 72–123, 107, citing the consequences of Duer's default; Schachner, *Alexander Hamilton*, 238–40, 280–7; Gilje, *The Road to Mobocracy*, 83–4. Valentine, *Lord Stirling*, 280, suggests that Lady Kitty 'was said to have spent her last years in near-poverty in a shabby boarding house.' The letters of the Trumbull sisters portray, in externals at least, a less straitened existence. On her death in 1826 John Pintard wrote warmly of Lady Kitty's many qualities: 'She was a very amiable lady dignified in her deportment & gentle in her manners.' *Letters from John Pintard to His Daughter Eliza Noel Pintard Davidson, 1816–1833*. ed. Dorothy C. Barck, 4 vols. (New York: Printed for the New-York Historical Society, 1940), II, 286–7. Some valuable details are filled in by May King Van Rensselaer's notes in 'Lady Catherine Alexander married William Duer,' Duer

Family Papers, Columbia University Library. When Lady's Kitty remarried, her daughter Catherine went to live with an aunt, Mrs. Lawrence. 'Aunt Kitty' lived to her nineties, and in later years was a rich source of family stories about Lady Kitty and the cruelties of her second husband, the merchant William Neilson. Neilson's estate was estimated at $200,000. See [Moses Y. Beach,] *Wealth and Biography of the Wealthy Citizens of New York City . . .* , 5th edn. enlarged (New York: Published at the Sun Office, 1845).

30. Brevoort to Irving, April 1820, *Letters of Henry Brevoort to Washington Irving*, ed. George S. Hellman (New York: G.P. Putnam's Sons, 1918), 122; Allan Melvill to Maria Melvill, May 12–15, June 28, 1818, and Maria Melvill to Peter Gansevoort, Aug. 25, 1825, Box 308, Gansevoort–Lansing Papers, NYPL.

31. Michael Paul Rogin, *Subversive Genealogy: The Politics and Art of Herman Melville* (Berkeley and Los Angeles: University of California Press, 1983). Jay Leyda, *The Melville Log: A Documentary Life of Herman Melville 1819–1891*, 2 vols. (New York: Harcourt, Brace, 1951) is the foundation upon which family study of the Melvills and Gansevoorts is based.

32. Edwin Havilland Miller, *Melville* (New York: George Braziller, 1975), 57. Maria's father, General Peter Gansevoort, had played a much more distinguished part in the revolutionary struggle. Allan Melvill's letters to Peter Gansevoort on the 'Hero of Fort Stanwix' (Feb. 28, 1823) and a letter occasioned by the visit of Lafayette to New York (Sep. 28, 1824) seem excessive, even to the point of hysteria, on this subject (Box 33, G–L, NYPL).

33. As famously used by Margaret Thatcher, a British dialect term meaning 'afraid'.

34. Allan Melvill to Peter Gansevoort, Dec. 11, 1818, Box 30, G–L, NYPL.

35. Maria Melvill to Peter Gansevoort, 'December Saturday morn,' 1818, ibid.

36. Maria Melvill to Peter Gansevoort, 'last day of December,' 1819, ibid.

37. Miller, *Melville*, 63; Allan Melvill to Peter Gansevoort, March 25, 1823, Box 33, G–L, NYPL; Maria Melvill to Peter Gansevoort, June 26, 1823, ibid. 'If things do not soon take a turn': recalled by Mrs. Jonathan Sturges [Mary Pemberton Sturges,] *Reminiscences of a Long Life* (New York: F.E. Parrish, 1894), 126–7. Later in the nineteenth century, as Halttunen, *Confidence Men and Painted Women*, 205, shows, the need to maintain a façade of success and prosperity had become a commonplace in behavior manuals.

38. 'Reminiscences of Miss Harriet Robinson Duer, youngest daughter of Judge John Duer and Anna Bunner,' 1891 in a binder of family papers collected and transcribed by May King Van Rensselaer, Duer Family Papers, Columbia University Library.

39. Allan Melvill to Peter Gansevoort April 1, 1824, Leyda, *Melville Log*, I, 17–18. In June 1997 this letter could not be found in the Gansevoort–Lansing Papers, NYPL, but the new house is enthusiastically referred to in letters sent on April 20 and June 12, 1824.

40. Maria Melvill to Peter Gansevoort, New York, Aug. 2, 1825, Box 38, G–L, NYPL.

41. Maria Melvill to Peter Gansevoort, Sept. 3, 1824, Box 34, G–L, NYPL; John Pintard, Jan. 25, 1826, *Letters*, II, 220; and March 1, 1833, *Letters*, IV, 130; Myron H. Luke, 'Some Characteristics of the New York Business Community, 1800–1810,' *New York History*, 34 (Oct. 1953), 393–405.

42. Maria Melvill to Peter Gansevoort, Sept. 3, 1824. Box 34, G–L, NYPL. The whole of this letter is a confirmation of the social standing which the Melvill family had achieved in their new home on Bleecker Street.

43. *Recollections of Mrs. John Pine (Caroline Pryor), 24–25 Gramercy Park, New York City: Sixties, Seventies and Eighties* (n.p., n.p., n.d.), 8. A copy is held in the NYPL.

44. Jan Cohn, *The Palace or the Poorhouse: The American House as a Cultural Symbol* (East Lansing: Michigan State University Press, 1979), 117.

45. Maria Melvill to Peter Gansevoort, Feb. 28, 1828, Box 37, G–L, NYPL; excerpt in Leyda, *Melville Log*, I, 33; Maria Melvill to Peter Gansevoort, Dec. 8, 1826, Box 308, G–L, NYPL; Maria Melvill to Peter Gansevoort, Feb. 20, 1827, ibid.

46. *The Poetical Writings of Fitz-Greene Halleck*, ed. James Grant Wilson (New York: D. Appleton, 1873), 55–6.

47. When Maria inquired about the rights of her children in the estate of Major Thomas Melvill, she was told that between 1818 and 1831 her husband had signed notes to the value of $21,268.74, which substantially exceeded what would have been his share of the estate. Lemuel Shaw to Maria Melvill, Feb. 12, 1834, Box 308, G–L, NYPL. See Miller, *Melville*, 65.

Chapter 3 Aristocratic Neighborhoods

1. See Kenneth E. Scherzer, 'Neighborhoods,' *The Encyclopedia of New York City*, ed. Kenneth T. Jackson (New Haven: Yale University Press, 1995), 804–5; and for a sample of the literature on New York neighborhoods, see Otho G. Cartwright, *The Middle*

West Side: A Historical Sketch, Russell Sage Foundation: West Side Studies (New York: Survey Associates, 1914); Caroline F. Ware, *Greenwich Village 1920–1930: A Comment on American Civilization in the Post-War Years* (Boston: Houghton Mifflin, 1935); Joseph Lyford, *The Airtight Cage: A Study of New York's West Side* (New York: Harper & Row, 1966); Carl Abbott, 'The Neighborhoods of New York, 1760–1775,' *New York History*, 45 (1974), 35–54; Bruce M. Wilkenfeld, 'New York City Neighborhoods, 1730,' *New York History*, 57 (April 1976), 165–182; Clay Lancaster, *Old Brooklyn Heights: New York's First Suburb*, 2nd edn. (New York: Dover, 1979); Charles R. Simpson, *SoHo: The Artist in the City* (Chicago: University of Chicago Press, 1981); Stanley Nadel, *Little Germany: Ethnicity, Religion, and Class in New York City, 1845–80* (Urbana: University of Illinois Press, 1990); Nan A. Rothschild, *New York City Neighborhoods: The 18th Century* (San Diego: Academic, 1990); Kenneth A. Scherzer, *The Unbounded Community: Neighborhood Life and Social Structure in New York City, 1830–1875* (Durham, NC: Duke University Press, 1992).

2. This is the theme of John A. Dix, 'Growth of New York City,' *Journal of Commerce*, Jan. 7, 1853, 2. The full text of Dix's address before the New-York Historical Society appears in Dix, *Speeches and Occasional Addresses*, 2 vols. (New York: D. Appleton, 1864), II, 337–59.

3. Entry for May 20, 1839, Hone Mss. Diary, XV, 342–3, silently omitted in Nevins.

4. Entry for May 24, 1844, Hone Mss. Diary, XXII, 59–60; slightly abridged in Nevins, II, 703.

5. William Allen Butler, *Two Millions* (New York: D. Appleton, 1858), 12.

6. [William Ingraham Kip], *The Olden Time in New York* (New York: G.P. Putnam's, 1872), 26–8. I.N. Phelps Stokes, *Iconography of Manhattan Island, 1498–1909*, 6 vols. (New York: 1915–28), V, 1831. See also 'Kip's House,' *The Subterranean*, 3 (June 25, 1845), 2.

7. 'The August Belmont Mansion Sold,' *New York Daily Tribune*, March 4, 1893, 7; Mosette Broderick, 'Fifth Avenue,' *The Grand American Avenue 1850–1920* (San Francisco: Pomegranate Art Books, 1994), 28, 340. 'The Old Schermerhorn House to be Razed,' *New York Daily Tribune*, May 18, 1893, 6.

8. G.W. Curtis, 'Editor's Easy Chair,' *Harper's Monthly*, 9 (July 1854), 260–1. From an Associated Press report: 'A judge has ruled that New York University can demolish a row of historic houses, including one where Edgar Allan Poe lived for about six months in

1845. State Supreme Court Justice Robert Lippmann said in his decision that nothing in the law authorizes him to block NYU's razing of the buildings in Greenwich Village.' 'Demolition [*sic*] of Poe's NYC House OK'd,' *New York Times*, Oct. 4, 2000.

9. James Stokes to Caroline Phelps Stokes, April 30, 1879, *Some Memories of James Stokes and Caroline Phelps Stokes, Arranged for their Children and Grandchildren* [ed. Anna B. Warner] (n.p.p.: Printed for the family, 1892), 258.

10. Pessen's *Riches, Class and Power before the Civil War* (Lexington, MA: D.C. Heath, 1973), ch. 9, compares the residential pattern of the wealthy in New York, Brooklyn, Philadelphia, and Boston.

11. See *Greenwich Village: Culture and Counterculture*, ed. Rick Beard and Leslie Cohen Berlowitz (New Brunswick, NJ: Rutgers University Press for the Museum of the City of New York, 1993).

12. 'Fifth Avenue's Doom,' *The Sun*, Jan. 1, 1888, 6; Broderick, 'Fifth Avenue,' 3–33, esp. 27–30; Patterson, *Fifth Avenue*. Burton Welles' 1911 photographic study of Fifth Avenue reveals how little of the 'old' Fifth Avenue had survived. (The Wendels still occupied 442, on the northwest corner of West 39th Street.) See *Fifth Avenue, 1911, From Start to Finish in Historic Block-by-Block Photographs*, ed. Christopher Gray (New York: Dover, 1994). See also Elizabeth Blackmar, *Manhattan for Rent, 1785–1850* (Ithaca, NY: Cornell University Press, 1989). A snapshot of the chaotic state of Fifth Avenue is in 'Fifth Ave. No Thing of Beauty,' *New York Daily Tribune*, Dec. 22, 1896, 12.

13. Pessen's *Riches, Class and Power*, ch. 9, discusses the residential patterns of the elite. For a study of neighborhood patterns, and the comment on neighborhoods not being self-contained economic units, see Scherzer, *The Unbounded Community*, 78 and ch. 6. See Edward Pessen, 'Philip Hone's Set'; Peter George Buckley, 'To the Opera House: Culture and Society in New York City, 1820–1860' Ph.D., SUNY-Stony Brook, 1984. On the attempted bribery of Restell, see Homberger, *Scenes from the Life of a City*, 118–23. An offer of $5,000—in truth, a piffling sum—was insufficient to persuade Madame Restell not to build on the ten lots she acquired on Fifth Avenue during the Civil War.

14. Ward–Astor calls in Julia Ward Howe, *Reminiscences 1819–1899* (Boston: Houghton Mifflin, 1899), 32. Strong, *Diary*, II, 430. See Barent Vanderlyn, *The Complete New Year's Visitor* (Albany: Staats & Fonda, 1833) on the establishment of the custom in New York.

15. Christine Stansell, *City of Women: Sex and Class in*

New York, 1789–1860 (New York: Knopf, 1986), 81–3.

16. Nancy Cott, *The Bonds of Womanhood: 'Women's Sphere' in New England, 1780–1835* (New Haven and London: Yale University Press, 1977).

17. Abigail Franks to Naphtali Franks, June 9, 1734, *Letters of the Franks Family (1733–1748)*, ed. Leo Hershkowitz and Isidore S. Meyer (Waltham: American Jewish Historical Society, 1968), 27.

18. Christman, *The First Federal Congress*, 110, quoting Representative George Clymer.

19. There is a photograph of 7 State Street (the James Watson house) as it was in the 1880s in Mary Black, *Old New York in Early Photographs 1853–1901*, rev. edn. (New York: Dover, 1976), plate 7.

20. 'Old Houses,' *New York Times*, Oct. 3, 1872, 1; Pauline Maier, *The Old Revolutionaries: Political Lives in the Age of Samuel Adams* (New York: Alfred A. Knopf, 1980), 91–2. The Duke of La Rochefoucauld-Liancourt, *Travels through the United States of North America . . .* , 2 vols. (London, 1799), II, 456; cited Bayrd Still, *Mirror for Gotham: New York as Seen by Contemporaries from Dutch Days to the Present* (New York: New York University Press, 1956), 67.

21. See the persuasive argument by Robert H. Wiebe, *The Opening of American Society from the Adoption of the Constitution to the Eve of Disunion* (New York: Random House, 1984), ch. 1.

22. William E. Dodge, *Old New York: A Lecture* (New York: Dodd, Mead, 1880), 21–2; 'New York Journal for the Year 1799 by Elizabeth DeHart Bleecker,' NYPL.

23. Paulding to Sally Hanlon, Aug. 27, 1802, *The Letters of James Kirke Paulding*, ed. Ralph M. Aderman (Madison: University of Wisconsin Press, 1962), 19. See also Thomas A. Janvier, *In Old New York* (New York: Harper & Brothers, 1894), 226–40.

24. Jeremy Cockloft: *Salmagundi*, 12 (June 27, 1807). Irving, *History, Tales and Sketches*, 225. Capitalization modernized. John Lambert, 'A Description of the City of New York, 1807–1808,' *Manual of the Corporation of the City of New York* (New York: John Hardy, Clerk of the Common Council, 1870), 847–67. Passage quoted, 849.

25. Francis J. Grund, *Aristocracy in America*, with an Introduction by George E. Probst (New York: Harper & Brothers, 1959), 10. First published in London, 1839.

26. Willis, *Dashes at Life with a Free Pencil*, 87.

27. The Bleecker relocation: entries for Oct. 6 and 13, 1801, 'New York Journal for the Year 1799 by Elizabeth DeHart Bleecker,' NYPL; John W. Barber and Henry Howe, *Historical Collections of the State of New York . . .* (New York: S. Tuttle, 1842), 313–15. Allan Melvill to his father, Major Thomas Melvill, Sept. 14, 1819,

quoted in Leyda, *Melville Log*, I, 4; Henry Brevoort to Washington Irving, Sept. 9, 1819, *Letters of Henry Brevoort*, 114. John Pintard, *Letters*, I, 220. Allan Melvill to his brother-in-law, Peter Gansevoort, Aug. 29, 1822, *Melville Log*, I, 11.

28. Chas. H. Haswell, *Reminiscences of an Octogenarian of the City of New York (1816 to 1860)* (New York: Harper & Brothers, 1897), 121.

29. Willis, *Dashes at Life with a Free Pencil*, 168; Chas. A. Dana, *The U.S. Illustrated* (New York, 1854), 156–7, cited I.N. Phelps Stokes, *Iconography*, V, 1856.

30. Entry for May 15, 1843. Hone Mss. Diary, XXI, 2–3. This intriguing entry was omitted by Nevins.

31. On the transformation of private residences downtown into boarding houses, see the sharply observant Mrs. Jonathan Sturges, *Reminiscences of a Long Life*, 182–3, 188–9. On Brown's residence see [Armstrong], *The Aristocracy of New York*, 13. Strong's complaint: entry for June 15, 1845, Strong, *Diary*, I, 262.

32. 'The Vanderbilt Memorial,' *The Nation*, 9 (Nov. 18, 1869), 432–3.

33. Mrs. Jonathan Sturges, *Reminiscences of a Long Life*, 98; Carole Klein, *Gramercy Park: An American Bloomsbury* (Boston: Houghton Mifflin, 1987), 15.

34. John Dizikes, *Opera in America: A Cultural History* (New Haven and London: Yale University Press, 1993), 74–9. Conditions at the Park Theater in the 1830s in Richard Grant White, 'Opera in New York,' *Century Magazine*, 23 (April, 1882), 869. Entry for Oct. 1, 1832, Hone Mss. Diary, V, 334–5; Nevins, I, 79. The distinctive problem of audience for opera is noted in Lawrence Levine, *Highbrow/Lowbrow: The Emergence of Cultural Hierarchy in America* (Cambridge, MA: Harvard University Press, 1988), 101. Hone described the décor of his box in his diary on Nov. 10, 1833. The price was calculated on a minimum fee of $1.50 per seat per performance, which in Hone's case saw a box valued at $622.50, pushed to $750 by competitive bidding. Among the other box-holders was Dominick Lynch.

35. Halleck, 'Address at the Opening of a New Theatre,' *Poetical Writings*, ed. Wilson, 201–2.

36. For Halleck's relations with Astor, see E.A. Duyckinck, 'Fitz-Greene Halleck,' *Putnam's Magazine*, 11, n.s. 1 (Feb. 1868), 231–47; Nelson Frederick Adkins, *Fitz-Greene Halleck: An Early Knickerbocker Wit and Poet* (New Haven and London: Yale University Press, 1930), and John W.M. Hallock, *The American Byron: Homosexuality and the Fall of Fitz-Greene Halleck* (Madison: University of Wisconsin Press, 2000). Astor's real estate practices are analyzed in Porter,

John Jacob Astor, Business Man, ch. 20; John Denis Haeger, *John Jacob Astor: Business and Finance in the Early Republic* (Detroit: Wayne State University Press, [1991]); and Derek Wilson, *The Astors 1763–1992: Landscape with Millionaires* (New York: St. Martin's Press, 1993). The comparison with Ruggles is irresistible: see D.G. Brinton Thompson, *Ruggles of New York: A Life of Samuel B. Ruggles* (New York: Columbia University Press, 1946), and Klein, *Gramercy Park.*

37. The history of the founding of St. John's Chapel appears in Dix, *History of Trinity Church*, Part II, 187–9. The social milieu and inhabitants are suggested in *Reminiscences of James A. Hamilton; or, Men and Events, at Home and Abroad, during Three Quarters of a Century* (New York: Charles Scribner, 1869), 46, 66. See also 'A list of the New Yorkers [1830] and their places of residence, compiled by Mrs Archibald Gracie King, February 1900,' among a volume of family papers assembled by May King Van Rensselaer in the Duer Family Papers, Columbia University Library. Lydig was an old friend of Philip Hone (entry for June 18, 1839, Hone Mss. Diary, XV, 384; Nevins, I, 402); see also 'Walter Barrett,' *The Old Merchants of New York City*, 3rd ser. (New York: Carleton, 1865), 9–16; for the arranged marriage of John Jacob III, see Kavaler, *The Astors*, 75. Local academies in Marian Gouverneur, *As I Remember: Recollections of American Society during the Nineteenth Century* (New York: D. Appleton, 1911), 22–30, and 'Alice's MS about the Family,' Alice Duer Miller Papers, Box 1, file 3, Barnard College Archives, New York City. A 'grand concert, soirée, musical melange, and ollapodrida' given by the pupils at Mrs. Okill's academy received extensive coverage in the press, where she was described as being 'at the head of one of the most fashionable establishments for the education and finishing of young ladies, that can be found in the United States.' See 'Grand Musical Soiree,' *Morning Herald*, Feb. 27, 1840, 2. Among the pupils attending Mrs. Okill's academy was Anna Cora Ogden, later the author of *Fashion.*

38. Berrian, *An Historical Sketch of Trinity Church*, 215. In the last days of the British occupation of the city, Moore was chosen to succeed the Rev. Charles Inglis as rector. He was a staunch supporter of the crown, and hostility towards Moore may have added fuel to the radical attack on Trinity that culminated in 1784 in the repeal of the Ministry Act of 1693, which thus disestablished the Anglican Church. Radicals also sought to expropriate the King's Farm, a valuable tract of Manhattan real estate, which had been

granted to Trinity in the reign of Queen Anne. Edwin G. Burrows and Mike Wallace, *Gotham: A History of New York City to 1898* (New York: Oxford University Press, 1999), 266–70.

39. Scherzer, *The Unbounded Community*, 29.

40. 'Homes of Fashion Once,' *The Sun*, Feb. 10, 1895, 6, gives an evocative description of the houses surrounding St. John's Park. Domestic interiors: Frances Trollope, *Domestic Manners of the Americans*, ed. Richard Mullen (Oxford: Oxford University Press, 1984), 299. First published 1832. 'Skating at St. John's Park,' *Frank Leslie's Illustrated Newspaper*, March 3, 1866, 380.

41. Edward K. Spann, *The New Metropolis: New York City, 1840–1857* (New York: Columbia University Press, 1981), 231, 233; 'St. John's Park,' *The Subterranean*, 3 (July 26, 1845), 2; Child, *Letters from New-York*, ed. Mills, 12. This letter was drawn from two letters published in the *National Anti-Slavery Standard* on Aug. 26, 1841 and April 21, 1842.

42. Entry [for Oct. 14.], 1866, Strong, *Diary*, IV, 108–9; trees cut down: *New York Commercial Advertiser*, Nov. 21, 1867, in I.N. Phelps Stokes, *Iconography*, V, 1929; 'Sale of St. John's Park,' Oct. 21, 1866, clipping from an unidentified newspaper in Edward Neufville Tailer, *Journal of Some of the Events Which Have Occured in my Life Time*, Vol. XV. NYHS.

43. 'Old New-York,' *New York Daily Tribune*, Feb. 10, 1890, 2; 'Homes of Fashion Once,' *The Sun*, Feb. 10, 1895, 6.

44. Thomas A. Janvier, 'Lispenard's Meadows,' *Harper's New Monthly Magazine*, 87 (Oct. 1893), 754. Reprinted in Janvier's *In Old New York*, 192–226. See Scherzer, *The Unbounded Community*, 148–9 and Charles Lockwood, *Manhattan Moves Uptown: An Illustrated History* (New York: Barnes & Noble, 1995), 326 and *passim* on St. John's Park.

45. Bishop Potter's assent: Trinity Church, Office of Parish Archives, Box 2, St. John's, 1804–1920, and scrapbook of clippings, 'The Struggle for Old St. John's.' There is extensive coverage in the city press through the end of Dec.: 'St. John's career Ended,' *Evening Post*, Nov. 21, 1908, 2. See also Nathan Silver, *Lost New York* (Boston: Houghton Mifflin, 1967), 151–3.

46. R.W. Gilder's poem: *Evening Post*, Dec. 14, 1908. Letter from powerful men to the vestry: *The Sun*, Dec. 17, 1908.

47. Edgar Fawcett, *Adventures of a Widow: A Novel* (Boston: James R. Osgood, 1884), 9–10.

48. Sturges S. Dunham, 'Bond Street,' *Valentine's Manual of the City of New York 1917–1918*, n.s., no. 2, ed. Henry

Collins Brown (New York: The Old Colony Press, 1918), 211. Charles Lockwood, 'The Bond Street Area,' *New-York Historical Society Quarterly*, 56 (Oct. 1972), 309–20, draws upon a wide range of contemporary descriptions of the street. Charles Lockwood, *Bricks & Brownstone: The New York Row House, 1783–1929* (New York: Abbeville Press, 1972), 40. There is a large literature on the *Somers* case. Among the most forceful and partisan is [James Fenimore Cooper,] *The Cruise of the Somers: Illustrative of the Despotism of the Quarterdeck; and of the Unmanly Conduct of Captain Mackenzie* (New York: J. Winchester, 1844). Gardiner Spring, DD, *Personal Reminiscences of the Life and Times of Gardiner Spring* (New York, 1866); Buckley, 'To the Opera House,' 138.

49. The 'Art and the Empire City: New York, 1825–1861' exhibition, at the Metropolitan Museum in New York, from Sept. 1999 to Jan. 2001, and the similarly titled catalog edited by Catherine Hoover Vorsanger and John K. Howat, published by the Museum and Yale University Press, 2000, contain much valuable material on antebellum taste, collectors, and art institutions in New York. See also *Rave Reviews: American Art and Its Critics, 1826–1925*, ed. David B. Dearinger (New York: National Academy of Design, 2000).

50. See Alan Wallach, 'Thomas Cole and the Aristocracy,' *Arts Magazine*, 56 (Nov. 1981), 94–106. Hone's diary traces his enthusiasm for Cole. Hone drew up a catalog of his art collection for William Dunlap, which is reprinted in *A History of the Rise and Progress of the Arts of Design in the United States*, 2 vols. (New York: George P. Scott, 1834; reprinted in 3 parts, New York: Dover, 1969), II, Part 2, 462–4. For Morse's career in New York (and his *Lafayette* and *Little Miss Hone*) see Oliver W. Larkin, *Samuel F.B. Morse and American Democratic Art* (Boston: Little, Brown, 1954), ch. 5, and William Kloss, *Samuel F. B. Morse* (New York: Harry N. Abrams in association with the National Museum of American Art, Smithsonian Institution, [1988]), 91–6.

51. Dr. John W. Francis, a luminary in New York society, gives an account of the city's clubs going back to the 1750s in *Old New York*, 288–96. See also Shields, *Civil Tongues & Polite Letters*, 312–13.

52. Reginald Townsend, *Mother of Clubs, Being the History of the First Hundred Years of the Union Club of the City of New York* (New York: [Union Club,] 1936); 'An Old New Yorker,' 'Clubs—Club Life—Some New York Clubs,' *The Galaxy*, 22 (Aug. 1876), 227–38; Arthur Charlton, 'A Fashionable Club,' *The Epoch*, 1,

22 (July 8, 1887), 514.

53. Hone noted the new home of the Stuyvesant Institute in an entry on Nov. 25, 1839, Mss. Diary, XVI, 108–9.

54. For the Hone Club, see entry for Dec. 25, 1838, ibid., XV, 79–81; Nevins, I, 376; and Pessen, 'Philip Hone's Set,' 308.

55. Mrs. Jonathan Sturges, *Reminiscences of a Long Life*, 123–4; *A Glance at New York* (New York: A. Greene, 1837), 7. Roger Hale Newton, *Town & Davis Architects* (New York: Columbia University Press, 1942), 61–4, 119–216; Talbot Hamlin, *Greek Revival Architecture in America* (New York: Oxford University Press, 1944; reprinted New York: Dover, 1964), 119–58.

56. [George William Curtis,] ' "Our Best Society",' *Putnam's Monthly*, 1 (Feb. 1853), 178. Collected as the first chapter of Curtis' *The Potiphar Papers* (1853).

57. Lockwood, *Manhattan Moves Uptown*, 52, 54.

58. 'The Particular Lady,' *Godey's Lady's Book*, 20 (April 1840), 277.

59. On the reverence in New York for Mrs. Rowson's sentimental story, see Mabel Osgood Wright, *My New York* (New York: Macmillan, 1926), 210–11; Frances Trollope, *Domestic Manners of the Americans*, 298–9. J.P. Morgan had a collection of the autographs of the Episcopal bishops which held pride of place in the youthful collections of stamps, coins, and shards of stained glass he brought home from Europe. His career as a great collector of antiquities was laid on this foundation. Herbert L. Satterlee, *J. Pierpont Morgan: An Intimate Portrait* (New York: Macmillan, 1939), 145.

60. Francis Heinrich's painting of the Fiedler family is reproduced in Catherine Hoover L. Voorsanger and John K. Hewat, eds., *Art and the Empire City: New York, 1825–1861* (New Haven and London: Yale University Press, 2000), 261. The survival of the elegant marble fireplaces is noted by Dorothy Richardson, *The Long Day*, 124. Bushman on the parlor in *The Refinement of America*, 411. I have found David Lubin's discussion of Lilly Martin Spencer's domestic genre paintings in *Picturing a Nation: Art and Social Change in Nineteenth-Century America* (New Haven: Yale University Press, 1994), 159–204, to be highly suggestive. Eastman Johnson's *The Hatch Family* (1871) in the Metropolitan Museum closely resembles Heinrich's portrait of the Fiedler family, down to the children at play in the parlor.

61. William Dean Howells, 'The Modern American Mood,' *Harper's New Monthly Magazine*, 566 (July 1897), 202.

62. Child, *The Mother's Book* (1831) excerpt in *A Lydia Maria Child Reader*, ed. Carolyn L. Karcher (Durham,

NC: Duke University Press, 1997), 112–22.

63. Lucius Rossi's 1878 painting is owned by Mrs. Vincent Astor, New York, and is reproduced in Lally Weymouth, *America in 1876: The Way We Were* (New York: Random House, 1976), 208–9. Guy's portrait of the Vanderbilts is reproduced in Peterson, *American Interiors from Colonial Times to the Late Victorians*, plate 144. See Edward Lucie-Smith and Celestine Dars, *How the Rich Lived: The Painter as Witness 1870–1914* (London: Paddington Press, 1976) for a selection of decidedly minor paintings of upper-class French life.

64. Prime's office in *Commercial Advertiser*, June 25, 1800, 2. [Charles King,] 'The Late Samuel Ward,' *Hunt's Merchants' Magazine*, 8 (June 1843), 551. This article provides a brief overview of Ward's public career. *The Rich Men of 1822* is cited in Louise Hall Tharp, *Three Saints and a Sinner: Julia Ward Howe, Louisa, Annie and Sam Ward* (Boston: Little, Brown, 1956), 377. The ball at Bowling Green appears in Julia Ward Howe, *Reminiscences*, 29–30.

65. Important passages from Hone's Mss. Diary entry on the death of Ward were omitted by Nevins. They appear at XVI, 109–11.

66. Mrs. Jonathan Sturges, *Reminiscences of a Long Life*, 182–3; Julia Ward Howe, *Reminiscences*, 15, 48–9.

67. John Kouwenhoven includes a drawing of the Corner House in *The Columbia Historical Portrait of New York*, 170; the house is described in Julia Ward Howe, *Reminiscences*, 44–5, and the visits to the cupola on 78; see also Thomas, *Sam Ward*, 72–3; Ward's art collection is briefly described in Ella M. Foshay, *Mr. Luman Reed's Picture Gallery: A Pioneer Collection of American Art* (New York: Harry N. Abrams in association with the New-York Historical Society, [1990]), 50, 54–5, 139.

68. Maud Howe Elliott, *Three Generations* (London: John Lane/The Bodley Head, [1925]), 65.

69. Purchases for Ward's gallery in Laura E. Richards and Maud Howe Elliott, *Julia Ward Howe*, 2 vols. (Boston and New York: Houghton Mifflin, 1915), I, 42. Anna Jameson's doubts about the Ward Van Dycks appear in Julia Ward Howe, *Reminiscences*, 41. Ward's relations with Cole are discussed in Alan Wallach, 'Thomas Cole and the Aristocracy,' *Arts Magazine*, 56 (Nov. 1981), 103. *The Voyage of Life* was exhibited at the Athenaeum Building on Broadway at Leonard Street in 1840, and received a glowing notice in the *Knickerbocker*, 16 (Dec. 1840), 543–4. The 'programme' printed in the *Knickerbocker* summarizes the fourth canvas: 'The world, to Old Age, is destitute of interest. There is no longer any green thing upon it.

The broken and drooping figures of the boat show that Time is nearly ended. The chains of corporeal existence are falling away; and already the mind has glimpses of Immortal Life.' In 1844 Cole's painting was made a prize in the annual Art Union draw. It had a dramatic impact on the public, raising subscribers to the Art Union from less than 800 to over 16,000. See Winifred E. Howe, *A History of the Metropolitan Museum of Art* (New York: Metropolitan Museum of Art, 1913), 60.

70. Abigail Adams to Miss Lucy Cranch, 2 April 1786, *Letters of Mrs. Adams . . . with an Introductory Memoir by Charles Francis Adams*, 2nd edn., 2 vols. (Boston: Charles C. Little & James Brown, 1840), II, 130. Wayland cited in Daniel Horowitz, *The Morality of Spending: Attitudes towards the Consumer Society in America, 1875–1940* (Baltimore: Johns Hopkins University Press, 1985), ch. 1. Strong noted the razing of the Ward house, 'a very venerable Broadwayian landmark,' in his diary on March 17, 1873, Strong, *Diary*, IV, 472.

71. Thomas, *Sam Ward*, 47–8, quotes Ward's complaint to his son Sam. For Ward's view of Jackson, see Charles King, 'The Late Samuel Ward,' *Hunt's Merchants' Magazine*, 8 (June 1843), 550–6. Inequalities of wealth: this argument had been forcibly pressed by Edward Pessen, 'The Egalitarian Myth and the American Social Reality: Wealth, Mobility, and Equality in the "Era of the Common Man",' *American Historical Review*, 76 (Oct. 1971), 989–1034. See also Jeffrey G. Williamson, 'American Prices and Urban Inequality since 1820,' *Journal of Economic History*, 36 (June 1976), 303–33, esp. the 'urban inequality index,' fig. 1. On the moral dilemmas of wealth: see Roger S. Mason, *Conspicuous Consumption: A Study of Exceptional Consumer Behaviour* (Farnborough: Gower, 1981) and Horowitz, *The Morality of Spending*, ch. 1. Julia Ward Howe, *Reminiscences*, 18; Richards and Elliott, *Julia Ward Howe*, I, 48.

72. African-American 'dandies': see Leonard L. Richards, *'Gentlemen of Property and Standing': Anti-Abolition Mobs in Jacksonian America* (New York: Oxford University Press, 1970), 115. Primrose gloves: 'Forcing the Season,' *Godey's Lady's Book*, 47 (July 1853), 30. Howland cited Geoffrey C. Ward, *Before the Trumpet: Young Franklin Roosevelt 1882–1905* (New York: Harper & Row, 1985), 26. [Anon.] *A Glance at New York . . .* (New York: A. Greene, 1837), 79–81. See also sarcastic sketches of the dandy under the title 'Police Office,' *Morning Courier*, Oct. 2, 1828, 2, and Oct. 8, 1828, 2; 'The Walking Dandy,' *The Corsair*, 1 (July 13, 1839), 282–3; [George G. Foster,] *New York in Slices;*

by An Experienced Carver (New York: William H. Graham, 1849), 76–9, and *Fresh Leaves from the Diary of a Broadway Dandy*, ed. John D. Vose (New York: Bunnel & Price, 1852).

73. Strong records in his diary in 1849 that after the completion of his move from Greenwich Street to a new house on 21st Street, his father moved into a house on the same block. See his *Diary*, I, 350. The Roosevelts were noted for their closeness, with Theodore Roosevelt Sr. living in the house adjoining that of his brother Robert on East 20th Street. In 1853 the Phelps brothers, Isaac, John, and George, built adjacent houses on Madison Avenue between 36th and 37th Streets. The adjacent houses of the Astors and Vanderbilts represented social norms of the wealthy in New York.

74. John W. Francis, MD, *Old New York*. Francis was Poe's physician, vainly warning the poet on numerous occasions of the dangers of excess. He was a friend and almost certainly the physician of Allan and Maria Melvill and in 1847 attended the marriage of their son Allan. Francis' 'Historical Discourse' was first delivered before the New-York Historical Society in 1857. See the obituary of Dr. Francis by Henry T. Tuckerman in the *New York Times*, Feb. 11, 1861, and the lengthy and adulatory obituary in the *Knickerbocker*, 57 (April 1861), 430–6; [Park Benjamin,], 'Letters from New York,' *Southern Literary Messenger*, 17, (March 1851), 180; and Maud Howe Elliott, *Three Generations*, 66. For Francis' literary salon, see Charles K. Tuckerman, 'Some Old New Yorkers,' *Magazine of American History*, 23 (June 1890), 433–49. Poe included a profile of Dr. Francis in a series of literary sketches of 'The Literati of New York City' in *Godey's Lady's Book* in 1846. See Edgar Allan Poe, *Essays and Reviews*, ed. G.R. Thompson (New York: The Library of America, 1984), 1135–6.

75. Diary for 1840, Box 4, Ward Papers, NYPL. Elliott, *Three Generations*, 69. Ward writing from New York on March 7, 1837, cited in Maud Howe Elliott, *Uncle Sam Ward and His Circle* (New York: Macmillan, 1938), 153.

76. Receipt book of household accounts of Samuel Ward (1814–84), Oct. 1838–June 1840, Ward Papers, NYPL; Elliott, *Uncle Sam Ward*, 171–2.

77. *Remarks on the Case of F. Morris v. Margaret Astor Ward, in the Supreme Court of the State of New York, and upon the rights of Mr. Samuel Ward, growing out of the settlement made by John Jacob Astor, Esq., upon the marriage of his grand-daughter, Miss Emily Astor, with the said Samuel Ward* (New York, March 3, 1862), 11. Ward Papers, NYPL. Elliott, *Uncle Sam Ward*, 153.

Rise of science: *New York American*, Nov. 10, 1839; battle of Flatbush: *New York American*, Feb. 9, 1839; march on Quebec: *National Gazette*, Feb. 23, 1838. Clippings pasted by date into the scrapbooks of Samuel Ward, NYPL.

78. Vanishing wealth: Julia Ward Howe, *Reminiscences*, 52; the Astors' reaction is described in a letter from Henry Brevoort to Washington Irving, Oct. 18, 1843, *Letters of Henry Brevoort*, 295–6. Ward's side of the case is set out in *Remarks on the Case of F. Morris v. Margaret Astor Ward* (1862).

79. The failed romance with Parmly appears in Arthur D. Howden Smith, *John Jacob Astor: Landlord of New York* (Philadelphia: J.B. Lippincott, 1929), 267–70; the notional interest of James Gallatin appears in Raymond Walters, Jr., *Albert Gallatin: Jeffersonian Financier and Diplomat* (New York: Macmillan, 1957), 327. In the 1850s Parmly commissioned Richard Morris Hunt to build a house at 17 West 38th Street for his daughter and son-in-law. It was Hunt's first major American commission, and it did not go well. The resulting lawsuit, which was won by Parmly, gave legal recognition to the fixed charges made by professional architects. See Paul R. Baker, *Richard Morris Hunt* (Cambridge, MA: MIT Press, 1980), ch. 6.

80. *Frank Leslie's Illustrated Newspaper*, 4 (Aug. 22, 1857), 565, quoted by Charles Lockwood, 'The Bond Street Area,' *New-York Historical Society Quarterly*, 56 (Oct. 1972), 318–19. The Applegate case appears in Homberger, *Scenes from the Life of a City*, 105–6. For the Burdell murder and subsequent trial, see Matthew Hale Smith, *Sunshine and Shadow in New York* (Hartford: J.B. Burr, 1868), 65–9, who was convinced of Mrs. Cunningham's innocence. The bloodstained carpet on which Burdell's corpse was found was later sold at auction. See 'The Auction Sale of Dr. Burdell's Furniture,' *New York Times*, April 11, 1857, 8. The case greatly interested William Waldorf Astor as a young man, and he sets out his own theory of the murder in [William Waldorf Astor, 1st Viscount Astor,] *Silhouettes 1855–1885* (London: Printed by Hazell & Viney, Ltd., [1917?]), 6–8.

81. Changing Bond Street in *New York Times*, Jan. 19, 1860. Timothy J. Gilfoyle, *City of Eros: New York City, Prostitution and the Commercialization of Sex 1790–1920* (New York: W.W. Norton, 1992), documents the social decline of nearby Bleecker Street. The flowermakers are noted in Dorothy Richardson, *The Long Day*, 49–50.

82. 'Will Still be the Bowery,' *New York Times*, Dec. 20, 1898, 8, reporting a hearing at the office of the

Manhattan Borough President.

83. 'Lafayette Place,' *The Knickerbocker*, 2 (July 1833), 71.

84. There is a vivid portrait of Warren Delano in Ward, *Before the Trumpet*. The gentleman Democrat witticism appears in Nathan Miller, *The Roosevelt Chronicles* (Garden City, NY: Doubleday, 1979), 172. Strong, *Diary*, I, 272–3. Dorothea Langdon received a life interest in her house on Lafayette Place in the 1848 will of John Jacob Astor, with the proviso that the rents were to be held in trust for her, a legal device to prevent her husband from benefiting from the property. Walter Langdon died in less than a year, 'in the odor of gentility,' according to Strong, *Diary*, I, 306–7.

85. Swan: [Armstrong], *The Aristocracy of New York*, 29; Ames: [Moses Y. Beach,] *Wealth and Biography of the Wealthy Citizens of New York City . . .*, 5th edn. enlarged (New York: Published at the Sun Office, 1845), 3; on Rankin see ibid., 25.

86. Entry for March 9, 1836, Hone, Mss. Diary, XI, 277; Nevins, I, 202.

87. Entry for Jan. 1, 1838, Hone, Mss. Diary, XIII, 397; Nevins, I, 295. The custom persisted into the 1870s, but declined in the following decade: 'New Years' Calls,' *New York Times*, Dec. 31, 1871, 4; 'New Years' Calls,' *New York Times*, Jan. 1, 1874, 4; 'The Season,' *New York Times*, Dec. 28, 1874, 4. There was a similar gradual decline in public interest in Evacuation Day in the 1870s, but see 'Evacuation Day,' *New York Times*, Nov. 26, 1890, 8. 'Decoration Day,' May 30, was made a national holiday in 1873.

88. 'New Opera House,' *Godey's Lady's Book*, 45 (Aug. 1852), 200.

89. The proprietors of the Astor Place Opera House included Luther Bradish, James W. Gerard, Thomas Addis Emmet, John Schermerhorn (son of Peter Schermerhorn, he was an older cousin of the children of Abraham Schermerhorn), and James M. Ray. See Vera Brodsky Lawrence, *Strong on Music, Vol. 1 Resonances 1836–1850* (New York: Oxford University Press, 1988), 454–60.

90. Willis, *Dashes at Life with a Free Pencil*, 89, 91. Dizikes, *Opera in America*, 153–63; [Park Benjamin,] 'Letters from New York,' *Southern Literary Messenger*, 15 (April 1849), 243.

91. Richard Moody, *The Astor Place Riot* (Bloomington: Indiana University Press, 1958), 158–9. See also Montrose J. Moses, *The Fabulous Forrest: The Record of an American Actor* (New York: Benjamin Blum, 1969), first published 1929; and Alan S. Downer, *The Eminent Tragedian William Charles Macready*

92. Lydia Maria Child to Ellis Gray and Louisa Loring, May 14, 1849, *Selected Letters, 1817–1880*, ed. Milton Meltzer and Patricia G. Holland (Amherst: University of Massachusetts Press, 1982), 246.

93. Entry for May 11, 1849, Hone Mss. Diary XXVII, 188; Nevins, II, 868–9. Nevins prints 'were smacked' for Hone's 'are marked.'

94. See Moody, *The Astor Place Riot*, 158–9, for Wiley's testimony of his experience at Mrs. Langdon's front door. F. Marion Crawford, *Katharine Lauderdale* (New York: Macmillan, 1894), 94–5. On the decline of Lafayette Place after 1850, see Alvin F. Harlow, *Old Bowery Days: The Chronicle of a Famous Street* (New York and London: D. Appleton, [1931]), 334.

95. St. Thomas' Church is described, and the sums paid for its construction, by Pintard on Feb. 23 and 27, 1826, *Letters*, II, 232–3, 234–5.

96. Entry for May 20, 1839, Hone Mss. Diary, XV, 342; Nevins, I, 398; *Autobiography and Letters of Orville Dewey, D.D.*, ed. Mary E. Dewey (Boston: Roberts Brothers, 1883), 79–89; Henry W. Bellows, DD, *Unconditional Loyalty* (New York: Anson D.F. Randolph, 1863), 15.

97. William Rhinelander Stewart, *Grace Church and Old New York* (New York: Dutton, 1924); *Letters of Henry Brevoort*, 395–7. The current marble-faced steeple was erected in 1883.

98. Entry for Feb. 5, 1846, Hone Mss. Diary, XXIII, 346; Nevins, II, 754.

99. 'Fashion in Churches,' *The Subterranean*, 3 (April 18, 1846), 1.

100. By the 1890s the issue of pew rents was hotly discussed in New York. Social Gospel reformers argued that pew rentals made it impossible to open a church to the masses. See 'Church of the Ascension Changes: A Lively Discussion over Making the Pews Free—Other Reforms,' *New York Daily Tribune*, May 12, 1893, 7. In that year the income from pew rentals at the Church of the Ascension, at Fifth Avenue and 10th Street, was $17,000.

101. Dewey, *Autobiography*, 80, expressed his great anxiety before word arrived of the successful sale of pews at the Church of the Messiah. The sale of pews at Grace Church in 1846: Name Index—Pews, Treasurer's Office, Archives of Grace Church in New York; Haswell, *Reminiscences*, 426–7. Strong, *Diary*, I, 310–11, 330, bought a Calvary Church pew in 1848. See also John Pintard, Feb. 20 and March 7, 1826, *Letters*, II, 231, 239–40. The 'Old Church' records for

Grace Church pew 127 give no purchase price. Hone's sarcastic comment in his Mss. Diary, Feb. 5, 1846, XXIII, 345; Nevins, II, 754. St. Ann's and St. Bartholomew's sale of pews: noted in E.N. Tailer, 'Journal,' Jan. 6, 1871 (vol. XVI) and Nov. 8, 1872, (vol. XVII), NYHS. Strong showed a willingness as a pew-holder of Calvary Church to keep his wallet firmly buttoned in protest at the 'egotism, vanity and indiscretion' of the rector, the Rev. Samuel L. Southard, Jr. Entry, June 4, 1849, Diary, I, 351–2, 355. Berrian, Historical Sketch of Trinity Church, 338–9, prints a list of patents for pews sold between 1724 and 1729.

102. Edward Pessen, 'The Wealthiest New Yorkers of the Jacksonian Era: A New List,' New-York Historical Society Quarterly, 54 (April 1970), 145–72. Pessen's list, based on a fresh examination of tax assessments of some 80,000 New Yorkers, came out of a debate among historians about the reliability of Moses Yale Beach's Biography of the Wealthy Citizens of New York City (New York, 1842; 13 editions by 1855). Pessen was much more skeptical about Beach than his principal academic disputant, Frank Otto Gatell, 'Money and Party in Jacksonian America: A Quantitative Look at New York City's Men of Quality,' Political Science Quarterly, 82 (June 1967), 235–52. The broader target target of Pessen's argument (that in the 'Jacksonian era cities were governed by the propertied for the propertied') was the long tradition of progressive historiography which had portrayed the Jacksonian era as one of a decline in aristocracy and the rise of the 'common man.'

103. The subsequent fate of these shares is recorded in the pew register. On the death of A. Bruce Schermerhorn his one-sixth share was left to his sister Caroline (Mrs. William Astor). Elizabeth Schermerhorn Jones left her one-sixth share to her three children. Other shares were inherited by Anne W. Suydam, Helen Irving, and Catherine Welles (whose one-sixth share was left to her husband Benjamin S. Welles, one of the original members of the Patriarchs). Mrs. Astor had her own one-sixth share plus the one-sixth share of her brother. In 1881, by family agreement, the pew came to be owned by one of Abraham Schermerhorn's children. Mrs. Astor transferred her one-third share to her sister, Helen Irving, who held a one-sixth share in her own right. Anne W. Suydam and Benjamin S. Welles sold their shares to Helen Irving for $1,800, and the three children of Elizabeth Schermerhorn Jones, who collectively held one-sixth share, completed the consolidation of the ownership by transferring their share to Helen Irving.

104. Scherzer, The Unbounded Community, 186–8, discusses church attendance, and the role of churches as voluntary associations. His picture of Protestants in New York worshiping in churches which were largely empty does not accord with a host of contemporary accounts and diaries.

105. There is a tablet commemorating Brown on the north aisle of the church. On Brown, see ' "Grace Church" Brown Dead,' New York World, Aug. 23, 1880; 'Burial of the Old Sexton,' New York World, Aug. 26, 1880; Lloyd Morris, Incredible New York (New York: Random House, 1951), 20–1, and Russell Edwards, 'From Carpenter to an Arbiter of Society,' New York Times, Sept. 11, 1966. Willis quoted Theodore James, Jr., Fifth Avenue (New York: Walker, [1971]), 127.

106. Sean Wilentz, Chants Democratic: New York City and the Rise of the American Working Class 1788–1850 (New York: Oxford University Press, 1984), 132–4 and 404 (table 14).

107. William Allen Butler, A Retrospect of Forty Years 1825–1865, ed. Harriet Allen Butler (New York: Charles Scribner's Sons, 1911), 204.

108. Charles F. Briggs to Herman Melville, May 12, 1854, Melville, Correspondence, ed. Lynn Horth (Evanston: Northwestern University Press and The Newberry Library, 1993), 636. Melville's reply to Briggs' letter is unlocated. 'The Two Temples' remained unpublished among Melville's papers on his death half a century later.

109. [Peter Marié,] A Midsummer Fete at Woodland Hall (New York: Henry Kernot, 1850), 8–9. There is an obituary of Marié in the New York Times, Jan. 14, 1903, 9, and a brief account in Patterson, The First Four Hundred, 28–9.

110. Hale Smith, Sunshine and Shadow, 38.

111. On the etiquette of introductions, see Thomas Hillgrove, A Complete Practical Guide to the Art of Dancing . . . (New York: Dick & Fitzgerald, 1868), 20; the assessment of Brown's social power in 'Ward McAllister,' New York Times, Feb. 2, 1895, 4.

112. M.E.W. Sherwood, An Epistle to Posterity: Being Rambling Recollections of Many Years of My Life (New York: Harper & Brothers, 1898), 179. Mrs. Burton Harrison recalled being warned away from a party at a 'new house' in New York. ' "Many people here, Brown?" asked my friend casually. "Too many," was the answer in a sepulchral tone tinged with melancholy. "If you ladies will take my advice, you'll go on to Mrs.——'s. This is mixed, very!" '—Mrs. Burton Harrison, Recollections Grave and Gay (New York, 1911; London: Smith, Elder, 1912), 315–16. A collection of anecdotes about Brown appears in Hale

Smith, *Sunshine and Shadow*, 38, and Stewart's *Grace Church and Old New York*, 177–9. Edgar Fawcett, *The Buntling Ball: A Graeco-American Play* (New York: Funk & Wagnall, 1884), 53. Whiteright Abendroth, in Fawcett's *A Demoralized Marriage* (Philadelphia: J.B. Lippincott, 1889), was another such society remembrancer: 'Nobody's affairs were too sacred, too august, or too disreputable, for his prying investigations. He had society at the ends of his fingers, and could have told you with an amazing glibness thousands of genealogical facts concerning it' (69–70). Brown appears in several of Fawcett's other society novels and stories, such as *The Adventures of a Widow: A Novel* (Boston: James R. Osgood, 1884), 45–6, and *Social Silhouettes (Being the Impressions of Mr. Mark Manhattan)*, ed. Edgar Fawcett (Boston: Ticknor, 1885), ch. 3.

113. Ward McAllister noted Brown's prodigious memory in *Society As I Have Found It* (New York: Cassell, 1890), 124. Before the emergence of Ward McAllister in New York society in the late 1870s, Brown's reign was unchallenged.

114. 'Burial of Sexton Brown,' undated press clipping, Grace Church Archives. See also 'Our Best and Worst Society,' *New York Daily Tribune*, March 12, 1855, 4; Gouverneur, *As I Remember*, 135.

Chapter 4 Going to the Ball

1. C[harles]. Astor Bristed, *The Upper Ten Thousand: Sketches of American Society*, 2nd edn., revised (New York: Stringer & Townsend, 1852), 128–9.

2. Erving Goffman's 'The Nature of Deference and Demeanor,' *Interaction Ritual* (London: Allen Lane The Penguin Press, 1972), 47–96, constructs a powerful argument about the rules governing personal distance.

3. *Assistant for A. Dodworth's Pupils* (New York: Nesbitt, 1873), 10.

4. Public assemblies in Britain became popular in the second quarter of the eighteenth century. Assembly rooms were often independent buildings of some stature. At first falling under suspicion by moralists, by mid-century assembly rooms were essential meeting places for society in towns of any social pretension. While the Quakers did not dance, the 'Dancing Assemblies' of Philadelphia, precursors of the Débutante Balls, were inaugurated in 1748 by a group of colonial families as devices for the presentation of young women into society.

5. John Lambert, 'A Description of the City of New York, 1807–1808,' *Manual of the Corporation of the City of New York* (John Hardy, Clerk of the Common Council, 1870), 847–67. See also 'Madame & Miss Deseze's Concert & Ball,' *The Town*, no. 1 (Jan. 1, 1807), 4; 'Roger de Coverley,' 'City Assembly,' *The Town*, no. 3 (Jan. 7, 1807), 1–2; 'Anthony Evergreen, Esq.,' 'New York Assembly,' *Salmagundi*, no. 1 (Jan. 24, 1807), and *Salmagundi*, no. 5 (March 7, 1807); Irving, *History, Tales and Sketches*.

6. Shields, *Civil Tongues & Polite Letters*, gives a valuable account of the variety of balls and assemblies in colonial society. One of the most popular events at the City Hotel was the annual ball on St. Valentine's Day held by the Young Bachelors' Association. Tickets were quite expensive at $10, and were printed on glazed cardboard from elaborately engraved plates. See Abram C. Dayton, *Last Days of Knickerbocker Life in New York*, illustrated edn. (New York: G.P. Putnam's Sons, 1897), 61. See the ball invitation reprinted in Marie Caroline Post, *The Life and Mémoirs of Comte Régis de Trobriand* (New York: E.P. Dutton, 1910), 178. There is a similar list for a New York assembly in 1841 in Gouverneur, *As I Remember*, 110–11.

7. *The Aristocratic Journey: Being the Outspoken Letters of Mrs. Basil Hall Written during a Fourteen Months' Sojourn in America 1827–1828*, ed. Una Pope-Hennessey (New York and London: G.P. Putnam's Sons, 1931), 23–4.

8. 'Historical Sketch of Dancing,' *The Lady's Book*, 2 (Jan. 1831), 53–5; Dodworth, *Dancing*, 168; Philip J.S. Richardson, *The Social Dances of the Nineteenth Century in England* (London: Herbert Jenkins, 1960), 136. Allen Dodworth, *Assistant for A. Dodworth's Pupils* (New York: Nesbitt, 1873), and *Dancing*, 145.

9. Emily Price 'was less concerned with the value of the cotillion favors she went home with than with the number of them. Four men were often required to carry the night's haul to her carriage.' Edwin Post, Jr., *Truly Emily Post* (New York: Funk & Wagnalls, 1961), 35.

10. 'A Ball at the Astors', *New York Times*, Jan. 19, 1897, 5; Ralph Pulitzer, *New York Society on Parade* (New York: Harper & Brothers, 1910), 128–9. The Newport cotillion is vividly described in Maud Howe Elliott, *This Was My Newport* (Cambridge, MA: The Mythology Co., 1944), 151.

11. 'Dancing,' *The Lady's Book*, 1 (Feb. 1830), 91–2.

12. Dodworth, *Dancing*, 147.

13. Thomas Hillgrove, *A Complete Practical Guide to the Art of Dancing . . .* (New York: Dick & Fitzgerald, 1868), 20. Allen Dodworth put this point slightly

differently: 'It [the cotillion] is peculiarly social, requiring a constant interchange of partners; all must, therefore, be upon terms of familiarity.'— *Dancing*, 145.

14. Washington Irving: *Salmagundi*, 5 (March 7, 1807). Hillgrove, *Art of Dancing*, 32–3; Cooper, *Home as Found*, 68.

15. Margaret Armstrong, *Five Generations: Life and Letters of an American Family 1750–1900* (New York: Harper & Brothers, 1930), 194.

16. See 'The Grand Fancy Ball,' *Morning Courier*, March 5, 1829, 2; 'The Second Masquerade,' March 21, 1829, 2 and 'The Bowery Masquerade,' March 27, 1829, 2; 'Fancy Ball,' Jan. 23, 1829, 2; 'A Ball in the Eighteenth Century, and a Ball in the Nineteenth,' *The Lady's Book*, 1 (Jan. 1830), 26–7. The authors of the *Lady's Book* letters were British aristocrats.

17. Abigail Adams to Miss Lucy Cranch, 2 April 1786, *Letters of Mrs. Adams . . . with an Introductory Memoir by Charles Francis Adams*, 2nd edn., 2 vols. (Boston: Charles C. Little & James Brown, 1840), II, 130–4.

18. Angus Davidson, *Miss Douglas of New York* (London: Sidgwick & Jackson, 1952), 40–1, who does not indicate the author of the verse epistle. There is a substantial quotation from this verse in Marian Gouverneur, *As I Remember*, 111–13, who attributes the authorship to Miss Anne Macmaster. The Douglas papers reached Davidson from his cousin, Mrs. Theodore Douglas Robinson, *née* Helen Roosevelt, daughter of Corinne Roosevelt, who was a younger sister of Theodore Roosevelt.

19. Mrs. Basil Hall, *The Aristocratic Journey*, 23–4. Malibran (1808–36), slandered by Mrs. Hall's bad judgment, was remembered for decades by New Yorkers as the 'all-time, peerless goddess of song.' The adoration in which 'the Signorina' was held in New York runs through Lawrence, *Strong on Music*, Vol. I.

20. *The Fancy Ball Given by Mrs. S***********. A Description of the Characters, Dresses, &c. &c. Assumed on the Occasion* (New York: To be had at Dubois & Stodart's Music Store, 167 Broadway . . . , 1829), NYPL; the *Morning Courier* published the complete text on Feb. 16, 1829, 2; *A Hasty Sketch of the Late Fancy Ball at G.G. Howland's, March 3rd, 1830*, Mss. Notebook, bound in green leather with 'Mrs. G.G. Howland' stamped in gold leaf on the cover. *Description of the Fancy Ball given by Mrs Hxxlxxd*, a second otherwise identical green-leather-bound notebook in a different hand, without a name embossed on the cover, and which contains six delicate watercolors tipped-in, signed 'R.C. Long del',

and a carte-de-visite of Mrs. Gardiner G. Howland by Disdéri, Paris. 21 pages. NYHS. The account of the Ballston spa fancy ball is among the longer entries in the early volumes of Hone's diary. It was neither quoted from nor mentioned by Allan Nevins, editor of the most substantial published selection of Hone's diary. Hone's account of the ball was initially written for the *Crumb Basket*, a small newspaper produced for the amusement of the Hone party at the Ballston, and subsequently transcribed in Hone's diary. The account of the fancy ball is arch, self-mocking, comical, unlike Hone's normally subdued and largely factual entries. The length of the material (occupying fifteen folio pages) suggests that the ball was an event which they all wished to recall in some detail. Other balls which they attended (at the Waddingtons, Nov. 4, 1830, and the de Rhams, Feb. 10, 1831) receive a sentence, or less, in the diary. His entry on the Brevoort ball in 1840 is of comparable length.

21. Richard Schermerhorn, Jr., *Schermerhorn Genealogy and Family Chronicles* (New York: Tobias A. Wright, 1914), 167; Armstrong, *Five Generations*, 201; Hone, Mss. Diary, I, 218ff.

22. Henry Adams, *History of the United States of America during the Administrations of Thomas Jefferson and James Madison*, ed. Earl N. Harbert, 2 vols. (New York: Library of America, 1986), II, 1334.

23. N.P. Willis referred to Scott as 'the greatest spirit that has walked the world since Shakespeare' in *Pencillings By the Way* (London: T. Werner Laurie, n.d.), 497. First published 1835. The residents of Washington Square successfully petitioned the Common Council to rename 6th Street, from the eastern edge of the Square to Broadway, Waverley Place, in honor of the popular first novel by Scott. Pintard's letters, and the diary of George Templeton Strong, record the passionate enthusiasm for Scott among educated New Yorkers. See also John Henry Raleigh, 'What Scott Meant to the Victorians,' *Time, Place and Idea: Essays in the Novel* (Carbondale: Southern Illinois University Press, [1968]), 96–125. Until the 1840s, and the popular enthusiasm for Dickens, Scott was a near rival to Shakespeare in the familiarity of his heroes and heroines. For the American passion for Shakespeare, see Lawrence W. Levine, 'William Shakespeare in America,' *Highbrow/Lowbrow: The Emergence of Cultural Hierarchy in America* (Cambridge, MA: Harvard University Press, 1988), 11–82.

24. Washington Irving, *The Sketch Book of Geoffrey Crayon, Gent.* (1819–20), *History, Tales and Sketches*, 791.

25. Entry for March 3, 1830, Hone Mss. Diary, II, 268.

26. Entry for Sept. 7, 1832, ibid., V, 315; Nevins, I, 75. See also Schermerhorn, Jr., *Schermerhorn Genealogy*, and Alfred E. Schermerhorn to William Rhinelander Stewart, July 1, 1923, Archives, Grace Church, New York City.

27. For Copley's *The Red Cross Knight* see Emily Ballew Knight, *John Singleton Copley in England*, with an essay by William L. Pressly (London: Merrell Holberton, [1995]), 167–9. For the Bradley Martins, see *New York World*, Oct. 11, 1891, 22; 'Bradley Martin Dies in London,' *New York Times*, Feb. 6, 1913, 11; Edith Wharton, *Novels*, ed. R.W.B. Lewis (New York: Library of America, [1985]) 141–2. There is an account in a New York paper of such a tableau held at the seat of the Earl of Essex, 'Great Fancy Ball at Cassioburg,' *Morning Herald*, Feb. 27, 1840, 2. An aristocratic English imprimatur eased the adaptation of the tableau vivant by upper-class American society. For the portrait of Mrs. Lloyd, see Nicholas Penny, ed. *Reynolds* (London: Royal Academy of Arts and Weidenfeld & Nicolson, 1986), plate 103 and accompanying text. Wharton *The Age of Innocence* may also allude to a Reynolds' painting of a young girl titled *The Age of Innocence* (*Reynolds*, ed. Penny, 317–18), although Wharton dismisses the painter's *Discourses on Art* as 'such a mixture of drivel & insight' in a letter to W. Morton Fullerton in 1911, *The Letters of Edith Wharton*, ed. R.W.B. Lewis and Nancy Lewis (New York: Charles Scribner's Sons, 1988), 238. Halttunen, *Confidence Men and Painted Ladies*, ch. 6, situates the vogue for tableaux vivants in mid-nineteenth-century America in the context of an increasing theatricalization of domestic life.

28. Entry for Jan. 27, 1827, *Letters from John Pintard*, II, 327–8.

29. Robert Hamburger suggested the relevance of Poe's tale to this chapter. Edgar Allan Poe, 'The Masque of the Red Death,' *Poetry and Tales*, ed. Patrick F. Quinn (New York: Library of America, 1984), 485–90; Marie Bonaparte, *The Life and Works of Edgar Allan Poe: A Psycho-Analytic Interpretation*, trans. John Rodker (London: Imago Publishing, 1949), 515–20; Charles E, Rosenberg, *The Cholera Years: The United States in 1832, 1849, and 1866* (Chicago: University of Chicago Press, 1962), ch. 1.

30. 'Fashionable Intelligence,' *Herald*, Feb. 10, 1840, 2.

31. *Herald*, Nov. 27, 1839; Maud Howe Elliott, *Uncle Sam Ward*, 196–7; Francis Brown, *Raymond of the Times* (New York: W.W. Norton, 1951), 23.

32. *Memoirs of James Gordon Bennett and His Times by A Journalist* (New York: Stringer & Townsend, 1855), 264–81, which presents the 'Moral War' as Bennett regarded it; Merle M. Hoover, *Park Benjamin Poet & Editor* (New York: Columbia University Press, 1948), 106; entry for Sept. 2, 1843, Hone Mss. Diary, XXI, 165; Nevins, II, 668.

33. 'Is Vanderbilt a Public Man?' *The World*, Oct. 16, 1883, 4.

34. Entry for Feb. 28, 1840, Hone Mss. Diary, XVI, 309; Nevins, I, 464.

35. See Patricia Cline Cohen, *The Murder of Helen Jewett* (New York: Knopf, 1998), *passim*. Cohen's investigation of the Jewett case also sheds valuable light on Bennett and the *Herald*.

36. 'Brilliant Bal Costumé,' *New York Herald*, March 5, 1840, 2.

37. 'Charles King's Rehearsal Fancy Ball,' *Morning Herald*, Feb. 14, 1840, 2; 'Obituary: The Death of Dr. Charles King,' *New York Times*, Sept. 20, 1867, 5; Noah's comment on King in 'Fancy Balls of the Past,' *New York Times*, Jan. 31, 1897, 20. Preparations for the ball follow 'The Famous Fancy Dress Ball to be Given at Brevoort Hall,' *Morning Herald*, Feb. 13, 1840, 2.

38. Advertisement in *Morning Courier*, March 20, 1829, 2.

39. The Hoyts figure prominently in Hannah Maria Denning Duer (Mrs. William Alexander Duer), 'A Diary of Passing Events Which May Occur, 1838–1849,' typescript of original diary, made for May King Van Rensselaer and with her notes, 1909. Butler Library, Columbia University. The original Mss. Diary is in the Columbiana collection, Columbia University.

40. Brevoort to Irving, Nov. 6, 1829, *Letters of Henry Brevoort*, 203–7. Entry for Dec. 17, 1838, Hone, Mss. Diary, XV, 65; Nevins, I, 374. Brevoort to Irving, Jan. 1, 1827, *Letters of Henry Brevoort*, 152–64.

41. Entry for Dec. 17, 1838, Hone, Mss. Diary, XV, 65; Nevins, I, 374. Bryant to Ferdinand E. Field, May 6, 1840, *The Letters of William Cullen Bryant*, ed. W.C. Bryant II and Thomas G. Voss, 6 vols. (New York: Fordham University Press, 1977–92), II, 126–7. An account of the ball appears in the *Morning Herald*, March 2, 1840, 1.

42. The iconography of the Greek struggle for independence is recorded in Nina Athanassoglou-Kallmyer, *French Images from the Greek War of Independence 1821–1830* (New Haven: Yale University Press, 1989). Hone's 'preparatory gathering': entry for Feb. 29, 1840, Hone, Mss. Diary, XVI, 311–14. Nevins, I, 461–4, omitted a list of over 120 individuals and their costumes. The account of the Brevoort Ball in 'Fancy Balls of the Past,' *New York Times*, Jan. 31. 1897, 20, closely follows the Hone diaries.

43. 'Fashionable Intelligence,' *Morning Herald*, Feb. 10, 1840, 2.

44. Black, *The King of Fifth Avenue*, 36–40.

45. 'Death of Hon. John Van Buren,' clipping from an unidentified newspaper dated Oct. 17, 1866, in Tailer, *Journal*, vol. XV. NYHS. Anne Hollingsworth Wharton, *Social Life in the Early Republic* (Philadelphia: J.B. Lippincott, 1903), 270. See also Gouverneur, *As I Remember*, 83–4.

46. *Herald*, March 2, 1840, 1; Entry for Feb. 29, 1840, Hone, Mss. Diary, XVI, 315; Hannah Duer, 'A Diary of Passing Events', entry for Feb. 29, 1840: 'Mrs. Bridge returned from Mrs. Barclays[.] Miss Matilda B . . . married yesterday.' See also 'Fancy-Dress Balls of Other Days,' *The Season*, ed. Crandall, 33.

47. Haswell, *Reminiscences*, 237–8.

48. Accounts of Leiderkranz balls: see *New York Daily Tribune*, Feb. 21, 1868, 5, and Mrs. Ann S. Stephens' *Phemie Frost's Experiences* (New York: G.W. Carleton, 1874), 161–4. See also D.W. Fostle, *The Steinway Saga: An American Dynasty* (New York: Scribner, 1995). William Steinway was for many years president of the Leiderkranz.

49. 'Masked Balls,' *New York Times*, Jan. 2, 1876, and a brief follow-up, 'The Masked Ball Law,' *New York Times*, Jan. 7, 1876, 8. The Police Board's response to this agitation appears in 'Local Miscellany,' *New York Times*, Jan. 8, 1876, 2. See also Nadel, *Little Germany*, 104–21, on social life in Kleindeutschland.

50. 'The Megrim Ball' [poem], *The Knickerbocker*, 1, 2 (Feb. 1833), 209–10; James Fenimore Cooper, *Home as Found*, with an Introduction by Lewis Leary (New York: Capricorn Books, 1961), 42.

51. [Fawcett,] *The Buntling Ball*, 133–4.

52. Anna Cora Mowatt Ritchie, *Fashion, or Life In New York* (1849; New York: S. French & Son, n.d.), 13; 'Obituary: Anna Cora Mowatt,' *New York Times*, July 30, 1870, 1; Eric Wollencott Barnes, *The Lady of Fashion: The Life and the Theatre of Anna Cora Mowatt* (New York: Charles Scribner's Sons, 1954), 93–114. Feeling that the play was a sign of the emergence of a genuinely American drama, Poe attended *Fashion* for eight consecutive performances.

53. Entry for Jan. 27, 1846, Strong, *Diary*, I, 274. The diary contains his oft-repeated doubts about the promiscuousness of fancy dress balls, 98; he attends 'Pete's [Peter Remsen Strong] grand soirée,' 222; attends Mrs Mary Jones' ball and expresses his dislike of the polka, 269; attends Mrs Baker's rout in honor of his sister—determination to attend no more balls, 270; reluctantly (as part of the 'soirée-attending aristocracy') attends ball at Henry Parish's, 275–6; attends Fish rout, 288; attends Ruggles' soirée, 292; attends 'the great Grinnell party,' 337; attends 'magnificent' party given by Robert Ray, 344.

54. Strong, *Diary*, I, 269–70.

55. Entry for Jan. 23, 1834, Hone Mss. Diary, VIII, 4; Nevins, I, 110–11. Alice Duer Miller, 'The Story of My Great-Aunt,' Duer Family Papers, Box 1, file 11, p.[5], Barnard College Archives, New York. Strong at the Ray Party, Jan. 26, 1849, *Diary*, I, 344.

56. 'Dancing in New-York,' *New York Times*, Dec. 18, 1875, 2.

57. Ibid.; Nadel, *Little Germany*, ch. 6. Mary P. Ryan, *Civic Wars: Democracy and Public Life in the American City during the Nineteenth Century* (Berkeley: University of California Press, 1997), 226–34. Pickwick Ball: 'Balls,' *The Subterranean*, 3 (Jan. 17, 1846), 2. 'Young Guard' ball: entry for Dec. 24, 1844, Hone Mss. Diary, XXII, 344–5. Calhoun Association Ball: 'Balls,' *The Subterranean*, 3 (Jan. 10, 1846), 2. Americus Club Ball and other Tammany balls in Homberger, *Scenes from the Life of a City*, 187–9.

58. Lately Thomas, *Delmonico's: A Century of Splendor* (Boston: Houghton Mifflin, 1967), 147. 'The Balls of the Season,' *New York Times*, Dec. 28, 1874, 8. Hostility to the dance may be sampled in the Rev. Frank D. Altman, 'Harsh on Dancing,' *The Sun*, Feb. 8, 1891, 23, reprinted from the *Kansas City Times*. I have reversed the order of the quotations. Archbishop Corrigan supported attacks made from the pulpit of St. Patrick's on masquerade balls, and seems to have had no better luck with New Yorkers. The Archbishop was 'greatly annoyed and sorrowed that his wishes in regard to the matter had been treated with contempt by some of his parishioners, who had since attended a public masquerade ball given by a local club.' See 'Churchmen Denounce Mask Balls,' *New York Daily Tribune*, Jan. 21, 1896, 1.

Chapter 5 Ward McAllister

1. 'Mr. McAllister on Society,' *New York Daily Tribune*, Dec. 7, 1890, 17.

2. He is mentioned only twice in a recent study of the New York upper class, Maureen E. Montgomery's *Displaying Women*. The chapter devoted to McAllister in Jerry E. Patterson's *The First Four Hundred* adds little to McAllister's memoir *Society As I Have Found It*.

3. 'Mr. Ward McAllister: Some Questions Answered Concerning Him,' *The Epoch*, 7 (Feb. 14, 1890), 865–7.

4. 'Ward McAllister's Ancestry,' *New York Daily Tribune*, May 10, 1891, 22.

5. See 'McAllister's Book. What a Foreigner Says About It,' *New York Daily Tribune*, Nov. 2, 1890, 17, and 'The Autocrat of the Drawing-Room?' *Lippincott's Magazine*, 46 (Dec. 1890), 873–8.

6. Cleveland Amory, *Who Killed Society?* (New York: Harper & Brothers, 1960), 122.

7. See Florence Adele Sloane, *Maverick in Mauve: The Diary of a Romantic Age*, with a Commentary by Louis Auchincloss (Garden City: Doubleday, 1983).

8. *Deborah Turbeville's Newport Remembered: A Photographic Portrait of a Gilded Past*, text by Louis Auchincloss (New York: Harry N. Abrams, 1994), 35.

9. The Grace Church Archives list Mrs. Edward Snelling as the pew owner, having acquired pew 113 in 1878. McAllister does not appear in any of the church's records as a pew owner, though he may have rented the pew by private treaty.

10. Stewart, who had been a Republican State Senator in the previous decade, was an archetypal New York clubman: 'Tall, thin and courtly,' recalled Elizabeth Drexel Lehr, 'he was famed for the perfection of his manners and for his conceit' (*'King Lehr' and the Gilded Age*, Philadelphia: J.B. Lippincott, 1935, 119). In addition to holding various civic posts of a ceremonial nature, he was active in the Republican Party. See also *Representative Men of New York*, ed. John Heney Mowbray, 2 vols. (New York: New York Press, 1898), II, 145–7. Dyer, son of the Governor of Rhode Island in the late 1850s, was one of the best men at the Astor–Willing marriage in 1891. There is a sketch of him in the *New York World*, Feb. 18, 1891, 1, and a revealing comment ('Elisha Dyer, Jr. is a power in a ballroom when he lays himself out to lead a graceful, genial and enjoyable cotillion') in 'What Is Going On in Society,' *The Sun*, Jan. 20, 1895, 6. See 'That Gold Again! Our Society Millionaires Want a Club,' *New York World*, March 8, 1891, 15, for the current form sheet on eligible society bachelors.

11. There is a vivid description of Mamie Fish in Richard O'Connor, *The Golden Summers: An Antic History of Newport* (New York: G.P. Putnam's Sons, 1974), 199–215. See also Jerry E. Patterson, *The First Four Hundred*, 199–205.

12. This was noted by Frederick Townsend Martin, who was present at the funeral, in *Things I Remember* (London: Eveleigh Nash, 1913), 227–9.

13. Funeral remark in 'Society in Mourning,' *New York Times*, Feb. 3, 1895, 19. It has occasionally been suggested that *Society As I Have Found It* was ghost-written by Jeanette Gilder, founder of the *Critic* and a novelist, as well as being a sister of the influential editor Richard Watson Gilder. In the absence of any proof, an examination of the style of McAllister's journalism might suggest that 'all the pompous, passé and ridiculous aphorisms that made him the laughingstock of society' were indeed of his own devising. The unsourced claim appears in Lewis, *Ladies and Not-so-gentle Women*, 35.

14. Ward McAllister to the editor of the *World*, July 15, 1893, The *World* Papers, Columbia University Library.

15. 'Guests of the Patriarchs,' *New York Daily Tribune*, Feb. 18, 1896, 7.

16. Richard Grant White, 'The Unsociableness of Society,' *The Galaxy*, 8 (Sept. 1869), 406.

17. 'The Old Families: They Are Arrayed Against the Millionaires,' *New York World*, March 1, 1891, 20.

18. The world of clubs and associations in New York is described in Edward Pessen, *Riches, Class, and Power*, ch. 11, and Brandt, *An American Aristocracy*, 210; Frederic Cople Jaher, *The Urban Establishment* (Urbana: University of Illinois Press, 1982), 276. Martin, *Things I Remember*, 227–9.

19. Henry Cabot Lodge, *Early Memories*, cited Amory, *Who Killed Society?*, 23.

20. 'I was an Updike, and this distinctive name conveyed that I was somebody, from a line of somebodies.' John Updike, *Self-Consciousness: Memoirs* (New York: Knopf, 1989), 197; Meaning of 'family' in Lawrence Stone, *Road to Divorce: England 1530–1987* (New York: Oxford University Press, 1990), 46; see also Nathaniel Burt, *First Families: The Making of an American Aristocracy* (Boston: Little, Brown, 1970), 3–11. James K. Paulding to Gasherie DeWitt, Dec. 28, 1827, *Letters of James Kirke Paulding*, 93. [George William Curtis,] 'Our New Livery, and Other Things,' *Putnam's Monthly*, 1 (April 1853), 389, collected as the second chapter of Curtis' *The Potiphar Papers* (1853).

21. In 1916 the Committee on Heraldry of the New England Historic Genealogical Society confirmed that the Winthrop family crest was, as it were, entirely kosher. See Dorothy B. Wexler, *Reared in a Greenhouse: The Stories—and Story—of Dorothy Winthrop Bradford* (New York: Garland, 1998), 6–7.

22. 'Official Society,' *New York World*, Feb. 15, 1891, 18.

23. Julia Rush Ward's keepsake album, and her collection of poetical quotations, are in the Beinecke Library, Yale University. '[Matthew Hall McAllister] Obituary,' *New York Times*, Dec. 23, 1865, 8; Maud Howe Elliott, *Uncle Sam Ward*, 9.

24. N.P. Willis, *Health Trip to the Tropics* (New York: Charles Scribner, 1854), 311–27. Frances Anne Kemble, *Journal of a Residence on a Georgian Plantation in 1838–1839*, ed. John A. Scott (New York: Knopf, 1961), 46. Noting the improvement in commerce in

Savannah over the winter, she wrote '. . . trade with Liverpool is very considerable, particular[ly] since the Carolinians have passed that offensive law that "all back seamen from any country shall on their arrival in Charleston be imprisoned, and remain so during their stay—or that the vessel containing them shall anchor below the city, and unload there—"' Louisa McAllister to Samuel Ward, Savannah, April 18, 1826, Ward Papers, NYPL.

25. Davis was also the architect of William Paulding's Lyndhurst, a Gothic extravaganza which Hone did not admire. For his comment on the Stevens residence, see entry for Feb. 3, 1849, Hone Mss. Diary, XXVII, 83–4; Nevins, II, 861. There is an architect's perspective drawing of the Stevens home in the Arnold Collection, Museum of the City of New York, reproduced in Russell Lynes, *The Art-Makers of Nineteenth-Century America* (New York: Atheneum, 1970), 169. See also Gouverneur, *As I Remember*, 166–7; Pessen, *Riches, Class and Power*, 237.

26. Ward McAllister, 'The City's Water Front,' *New York Daily Tribune*, Feb. 24, 1891, 10.

27. 'Newport. Hotel Life,' *New York Times*, July 11, 1873, 2.

28. 'Saratoga,' *The Knickerbocker*, 54 (Sept. 1859), 241–56; 'Saratoga Sprints: Race Week,' *New York Times*, July 21, 1873, 1; George Waller, *Saratoga: Saga of an Impious Era* (Englewood Cliffs, NJ: Prentice-Hall, 1966), 78–9. For recent scholarship, see Mary Murphy-Schlichting, 'A Summer Salon: Literary and Cultural Circles in Newport, Rhode Island, 1850–1890' (Ph.D., New York University, 1992), and Jon R. Sterngass, 'Cities of Play: Saratoga Springs, Newport, and Coney Island in the Nineteenth Century' (Ph.D., City University of New York, 1998).

29. Mary Gay Humphreys, 'Saratoga,' *The Epoch*, 2, 27 (Aug. 12, 1887), 9–10; Black, *The King of Fifth Avenue*, 61; Henry James, 'Saratoga,' *The Nation*, Aug. 11, 1870, *Collected Travel Writings: Great Britain and America*, ed. Richard Howard (New York: The Library of America, 1993), 752.

30. Marian Gouverneur (*As I Remember*, 69–70), was at Mrs. Clinton's side when she cut the President. The snub, long meditated, was a rebuke for Van Buren's hostility to DeWitt Clinton. Van Buren and his 'Bucktail' allies prevented Clinton from running for governor in 1822, and later had him dismissed as an Erie Canal commissioner.

31. Clipping about Saratoga from an unidentified newspaper, July 18, 1866, in Tailer, *Journal*, vol. XV. NYHS. 'Putting on Airs,' *Boston Weekly Voice*, 2 (Sept. 19, 1867), 4.

32. The Hilton–Seligman scandal is sensitively analyzed

in Stephen Birmingham, *'Our Crowd': The Great Jewish Families of New York* (New York: Harper & Row, 1967), 141–50, with additional material in Leonard Dinnerstein, *Antisemitism in America* (New York: Oxford University Press, 1994), 39–42. Three essays in John Higham's *Send These to Me: Immigrants in Urban America*, rev. edn. (Baltimore: Johns Hopkins University Press, 1984), 95–174, set the 1877 exclusion in a broad context. Robert McElroy, *Levi Parsons Morton: Banker, Diplomat and Statesman* (New York: G.P. Putnam's Sons, 1930), 20, mentions Mrs. Parsons' embarrassment at the name 'Levi.' Hilton's stewardship of the A.T. Stewart empire deserves closer scrutiny than it has yet received. He donated Meissonier's *Friedland, 1807* to the Metropolitan Museum in 1887; the painting is still on display.

33. Reaction to Stowe: Waller, *Saratoga*, 117. *Uncle Tom's Cabin* was repeatedly adapted for the stage. See, for example, '*Uncle Tom* Among the Bowery Boys,' *New York Times*, July 27, 1853, 1. Two decades later the English aristocrat Lord Rosebery attended a performance of *Uncle Tom* in Salt Lake City ('The play was long and dreary and Uncle Tom was intolerable.') See *Lord Rosebery's North American Journal—1873*, ed. A.R.C. Grant with Caroline Combe (London: Sedgwick & Jackson, [1967]), 48–9.

34. [John Dix,] *A Hand-Book of Newport and Rhode Island* (Newport: C.E. Hammett, Jr., 1852), 21.

35. Henry James, 'Newport,' *The Nation*, Sept. 15, 1870, *Collected Travel Writings*, 761. The sharp-eyed English diplomat's observations appear in *The Letters and Friendships of Sir Cecil Spring Rice: A Record*, ed. Stephen Gwynn, 2 vols. (London: Constable, 1929), I, 108. Louis Auchincloss makes the point about the female domination of Newport in *Deborah Turbeville's Newport Remembered*, 23–4. On the casino see Alan T. Schumacher, *The Newport Casino* (Newport: Bulletin of the Newport Historical Society, 1987). 'Newport: A Backward Season,' *New York Times*, July 14, 1873, 5; 'Life at Our Watering Places,' *Mrs. Grundy*, 7 (July 19, 1865), 72; Bourget, *Outre-Mer*, 55, concurs that there were no adventurers in Newport; on Hurlbert, see Louis Auchincloss, 'Crisis in Newport—August, 1857,' *Reflections of a Jacobite* (London: Gollancz, 1961), 184.

36. [Dix,] *A Hand-Book of Newport*, 72–3.

37. Elliott, *Newport*, 132–3; Edith Wharton, *A Backward Glance* (New York: D. Appleton-Century, 1934), 82. The occasional sight of female bathers in open carriages 'without stockings, collars or muslin sleeves' was a disgrace to proper Newport: such women

seemed 'ugly, undressed, cross, and coarse.' See *More than Common Powers of Perception*, 116–17.

38. Louise Hall Tharp, *The Appletons of Beacon Hill* (Boston: Little, Brown, 1973), 158–9.

39. Diana de Marly, *Worth: Father of Haute Couture*, 2nd edn. (New York: Holmes & Meier, 1990), ch. 7; corsets from Lord & Taylor, 1881, and Atelier Polonaise, 'Dressing the Victorian Lady from the 1850s,' from http://www.victoriana.com (Sept. 17, 1999). *Frank Leslie's Gazette of Fashion and the Beau Monde*, 6 (Oct. 1856), 62. Seashore wear at Bailey's Beach in O'Connor, *The Golden Summers*, 264–5; see also Consuelo Vanderbilt Balsan, *The Glitter and the Gold* (London: Heinemann, 1953), 20–1. The number and cost of gowns for Newport in Cleveland Moffett, 'Luxurious Newport,' *Cosmopolitan*, 43 (Aug. 1907), 349–58.

40. Wharton, *A Backward Glance*, 82–3. William Dean Howells. 'Confessions of a Summer Colonist,' *Atlantic Monthly*, 82 (Dec. 1898), 742–3. On the Howells' summer vacations, see Kenneth S. Lynn, *William Dean Howells: An American Life* (New York: Harcourt Brace Jovanovich, 1971), 233.

41. Bette Roth Young, *Emma Lazarus in Her World: Life and Letters* (Philadelphia: The Jewish Publication Society, 1995), 7. T.W. Higginson attended discourses on jellyfishes and polyps, and on the planet Jupiter. The Town and Country held picnics at Paradise Rocks, where there would be 'a little botanical lecture.' On another occasion, Alexander Agassiz gave a talk on natural history at a picnic on the shoreline. After listening to a talk from an officer on the US Navy training ship the *New Hampshire*, the captain provided practical demonstrations of modern explosives. Mrs. Julia Ward Howe was invited, as president of the club, to press the button which fired the first torpedo. Distinguished guests at Town and Country picnics included Mark Twain and ex-Vice-President Schuyler Colfax. *Letters and Journals of Thomas Wentworth Higginson 1846–1906*, ed. Mary Thacher Higginson (Boston: Houghton Mifflin, 1921), 230–1, 228, 226, 229.

42. Florence Howe Hall, 'Glimpses of Summer Life at Newport.—No. II,' *The Epoch*, 6 (Sept. 6, 1889), 496–7.

43. McAllister, *Society As I Have Found It*, 110. Quotations about McAllister's entertainments in Newport are drawn from this source. Charles Eliot Norton to A.H. Clough, Aug. 16, 1858, *Letters of Charles Eliot Norton*, with Biographical Comment by His Daughter Sara Norton and M.A. De Wolfe Howe, 2 vols. (Boston: Houghton Mifflin, 1913), I, 192.

44. Julia Ward Howe, *Is Polite Society Polite? And Other Essays* (Boston: Lanson, Wolffe, 1895), 26, 129.

45. Osgood's 'Discourse Delivered before the New York Historical Society,' Nov. 20, 1866. Cited I.N. Phelps Stokes, *Iconography*, V, 1925.

46. 'August Belmont is Dead,' *New York Times*, Nov. 25, 1890, 1–2.

47. Talbot Hamlin, *Greek Revival Architecture in America* (New York: Oxford University Press, 1944; reprinted New York: Dover, 1964), 132.

48. Niall Ferguson, *The World's Banker: The History of the House of Rothschild* (London: Weidenfeld & Nicolson, 1998), 391–4, 493, 575–6; Black, *The King of Fifth Avenue*, 53, 55–6, for Belmont's letter to Babette, and for Alphonse de Rothschild's visit to New York.

49. Fritz Stern, *Gold and Iron: Bismarck, Bleichröder, and the Building of the German Empire* (London: George Allen & Unwin, 1977), 166–8. W.E. Mosse, *The German-Jewish Economic Elite 1820–1935* (Oxford: Clarendon Press, 1989), ch. 8, sensitively discusses the complexities of the position of Jewish financiers and industrialists in Prussia-Germany. I would like to thank Paul Kennedy for pointing out to me the relevance of Bleichröder's experience. Crook, *The Rise of the "Nouveaux Riches"*, builds upon a substantial body of historical work showing how new money in the nineteenth century achieved social position in Britain by pursuing the ideal of the country gentleman. Lady Paget quoted in Crook, 160.

50. 'The Coming Revolution in the Fashionable World,' *New York Herald*, Oct. 1, 1861.

51. McAllister, *Society*, 126–7; Black, *The King of Fifth Avenue*, 171–2; entry for June 26, 1860, Strong, *Diary*, III, 36.

52. William Howard Russell, *My Diary North and South*, 2 vols. (London: Bradbury & Evans, 1863), I, 32–3. Russell was accompanied to the Belmonts on the evening of March 19, 1861, by Democratic politicians Horatio Seymour and Samuel J. Tilden.

53. Caroline S. Perry Belmont and August Belmont, Photographic Album (latched leather album for cartes-de-visite, tooled in gold, sold by D. Appleton & Co., New York City), Photography Room, NYPL. See Erving Goffman, 'Symbols of Class Status,' *British Journal of Sociology*, 2 (Dec. 1951), 294–304, on the many uses for status symbols.

54. J.S., 'Class Distinctions a Social Necessity,' *New-York Illustrated*, June 1, 1861, 51.

55. Elizabeth Duer, 'New York Society a Generation Ago,' *Harper's Monthly*, 105 (June 1902), 110; Black, *The King of Fifth Avenue*, 173. Entry for Jan, 30, 1858, Strong, *Diary*, II, 383–4.

56. Belmont to Tweed, Jan. 31, 1871, Misc. Mss. Tweed, NYHS; unidentified press clipping on the Viaduct Railway and the Tweed Ring in the 'Black Notebook,' #18, Robert B. Roosevelt Papers, NYHS; see also Black, *The King of Fifth Avenue*, 360–1, 374–5, 381.

57. Before the local elections in November 1870 men of wealth and integrity such as Moses Taylor, Marshall O. Roberts, and John Jacob Astor III had been recruited by Tweed and his Comptroller, Richard B. Connolly, to investigate the state of the city's finances. They concluded that affairs were in order, a verdict of monumental whitewashing naiveté. They were all to a degree compromised by their involvement with Tweed. For Astor's endorsement of Connolly's books, see *New York Times*, Jan. 25, 1875, 4. The role of the Seligmans and the Rothschilds is clarified in Seymour J. Mandelbaum, *Boss Tweed's New York* (Chicago: Ivan R. Dee, 1990), 77–8. The marriage of Amelia Tweed at Trinity Chapel in May 1871, and the reception at Tweed's mansion on Fifth Avenue at 43rd Street, catered by Charles Delmonico, were events which revealed how close Tweed had come to entering the social milieu of the city's wealthiest. His relations with the city's financial elite may be traced *inter alia* in Black, *The King of Fifth Avenue*, Alexander B. Callow, Jr., *The Tweed Ring* (London: Oxford University Press, 1965), and Harvey O'Connor, *The Astors* (New York: Knopf, 1941). There is no modern biography of Stewart.

58. McAllister, *Society*, 175.

59. [Abby Buchanan Longstreet,] *Social Etiquette of New York* (New York: D. Appleton, 1879), 18–19. McAllister, *Society*, 118–19.

60. McAllister, *Society*, 133.

61. Entry for May 22, 1865, Strong, *Diaries*, III, 600. The scrapbooks Strong refers to, compiled by Thomas Seaman Townsend, were donated to the Columbia University Library in 1895.

62. On the luxury of the city see 'The Extravagance of the Day,' *New York Herald*, Sept. 3, 1864.

63. Stockbrokers: *The New York Stock Exchange: The First 200 Years*, ed. James E. Buck (Essex, CT: Greenwich Publishing Group, 1992); the scale of post-war entertaining is cited in Black, *The King of Fifth Avenue*, 272; see also T.W., 'Our Millionaires,' *Galaxy*, 5 (May 1868), 529–38, and a letter from S. Weir Roosevelt denouncing this incursion into what 'was formerly considered to be the sacred domain of private life,' *New York Times*, April 25, 1868, 2. Sir Morton's banquet is recounted in Thomas, *Delmonico's*, 147; Peto, *The Resources and Prospects of America* (London: Alexander Strahan, 1866). On the

scale of the city's new mansions, see 'Mr. Stewart's New Residence,' *Harper's Weekly*, 13 (Aug. 14, 1869), 526. Theaters in New York are recorded in *Miller's New York As It Is; or Stranger's Guide-Book* (New York: James Miller, 1866), 63–5, and 'The Era of Amusements,' *New York Times*, Jan. 31, 1867, 4.

64. 'Leonard Jerome Dead,' *New York World*, March 5, 1891, 5. Clipping about Belmont Park from an unidentified newspaper, Sept. 28, 1866, in Edward Neufville Tailer, *Journal*, vol. XV. NYHS.

65. 'Ziska,' 'New York Letter,' *Weekly Voice* [Boston], 1 (Jan 24, 1867), 2.

66. Mrs. John King Van Rensselaer, 'The Basis of Society in New York City,' *Cosmopolitan*, 27 (Aug. 1899), 362.

67. 'Society,' *New York Times*, April 11, 1897, 15.

68. The 'engulfed' old fortunes: Jaher, *The Urban Establishment*, 253. Census figures: Ira Rosenwaike, *Population History of New York City* (Syracuse, NY: Syracuse University Press, 1972), 42, 67. The absolute numbers of the foreign-born rose throughout the rest of the century, but the rate of increase of the population as a whole slightly outstripped the immigration rate. Comparison of elites: Jaher, *The Urban Establishment*, 254 (table 7). Jaher's 'Style and Status in Late Nineteenth-Century New York', 258–84, a study of the social and geographical origins of the 'Four Hundred,' is the basis for this argument. The lineage of New York fortunes in Jaher, *The Urban Establishment*, 281.

69. For contemporary discussions of this point, see L. Melbourne, 'American Aristocracy,' *The Epoch*, 1, 39 (Nov. 4, 1887), 246–7; Paul R. Cleveland, 'The Millionaires of New York,' *Cosmopolitan*, 5 (Sept.–Oct. 1888), 385–98, 521–8; Milford Wriarson Howard, *The American Plutocracy* (New York: Holland, 1895); George Montfort Simonson, 'Have We Got a Landed Aristocracy?' *Munsey's Magazine*, 13 (Aug. 1895), 528–31; Harry Thurston Peck, 'The New American Aristocracy,' *Cosmopolitan*, 25 (1898), 701–8; 'Is America Developing an Aristocracy?' *Everybody's Magazine*, 10 (June 1904), 722–84; Gertrude Atherton, 'The New Aristocracy,' *Cosmopolitan*, 40 (April 1906), 621–7; T.W. Higginson, 'Aristocracy of the Dollar,' *Part of a Man's Life* (Boston and New York: Houghton, Mifflin, 1905), 94–113; Charles Edward Russell, 'The Growth of Caste in America,' *Cosmopolitan*, 42 (March 1907), 524–34; and Ernest Crosby, 'Our American Oligarchy,' ibid., 549–50.

70. R.W.B. Lewis, *Edith Wharton: A Biography* (London: Constable, 1975), 23; Wharton, *A Backward Glance*, 92–5. Intellectual barrenness: Jaher, *The Urban Establishment*, 270. Louis Auchincloss is the historian

of this world in the twentieth century.

71. Howard Crosby, 'The Dangerous Classes,' *North American Review*, 136 (April 1883), 345–52; quote 351. See on this theme Henry Adams to Henry Cabot Lodge, Nov. 15, 1881, *Henry Adams Selected Letters*, ed. Ernest Samuels (Cambridge, MA: Belknap Press of Harvard University Press, 1992), 165. Levine, *Highbrow/Lowbrow* and Helen Horowitz, *Culture and the City: Cultural Philanthropy in Chicago from the 1880s to 1917* (Chicago: University of Chicago Press, 1976) are among the historians rooting the late nineteenth-century institutions of culture in the class values of the philanthropists.

72. Frigidity of demeanor: *Frank Leslie's Gazette of Fashion*, 1 (Jan. 1854), 16; see also Boni de Castellane's account of a visit to the Long Island home of George Gould in the 1890s, in *Confessions of the Marquis de Castellane*, 108–9. Air of hauteur: 'Our Disregard of Good Breeding,' *Frank Leslie's Lady's Journal*, 1 (Dec. 2, 1871), 43. See also Mrs. John Sherwood, *Manners and Social Usages*, 131. There are conventional judgments which suggest an outcome of a different kind. With the exception of Roosevelt (whose social credentials were impeccable, but who disliked society and kept aloof from the clubs and balls once his public life began in earnest), the political careers of New York aristocrats were, in truth, modest; the writers mostly lightweight; the quality of the Metropolitan Opera and the benevolence bestowed upon the Metropolitan Museum were, until the next century, of more local than international importance. Nonetheless, the New York elite did not share such judgments.

73. McAllister, *Society*, 216–17, 157.

74. Charles Loring Brace, 'New York Society,' *The Nation*, 1 (Nov. 9, 1865), 587–8. See Brace's 'The Rich and the Poor: Opportunities for the Charitable,' *New York Times*, Nov. 5, 1859, 2; 'A Children's Friend Dead,' *New York Times*, Aug. 14, 1890, 8 (obituary).

75. Richardson, *Social Dances*, 23–5; J. Frances Scoffern, 'The Dowager Countess of Jersey,' *Belgravia*, 2 (March 1867), 343–50. [G. Yates,] *The Ball; or, A Glance at Almack's in 1829* (London: Henry Colburn, 1829), ch. 3, laments the decline of standards in the conduct of balls, and in particular deplores the waltz: 'It is nothing in short, but an outright romp . . .' (55); 'A Chaperon,' 'Recollections of Almack's,' *London Society*, Aug. 1863, 145–55. The Patriarchs' emulation of Almack's was commonly acknowledged: see 'A Brilliant Gathering at Delmonico's,' *New York Daily Tribune*, Dec. 21, 1880, 5; 'Second Ball of the Patriarchs,' *New York Times*, Jan. 18, 1881, 8. N.P.

W[illis]., 'Jottings Down in London, *The Corsair*, 1, 20 (July 13, 1839), 312–14; McAllister, *Society*, 211–12.

76. Nadel, *Little Germany*, 114–15, 157. 'The Balls of the Season,' *New York Times*, Dec. 28, 1874, 8. McAllister, *Society*, 211–12. Entry for April 13, 1860, Strong, *Diary*, III, 20. In addition to Strong, the committee included some of his oldest friends, Walter Cutting, Judge Pendleton, Hamilton Fish, Anson Livingston, and William Colford Schermerhorn.

77. McAllister's discussion of the Patriarchs appears in *Society*, 210–17. Significance of the decision to hold the balls at Delmonico's: 'Guests of the Patriarchs,' *New York Times*, Dec. 24, 1884, 5. See also 'Patriarchs Who Dance,' *New York World*, Dec. 18, 1883, 5.

78. The first Patriarchs were John Jacob Astor III, William Astor, Frederick G. d'Hauteville, William Butler Duncan, C.C. Goodhue, John W. Hamersley, Lewis Colford Jones, De Lancey Kane, Archibald Gracie King, Walter Langdon, Eugene A. Livingston, Maturin Livingston, Ward McAllister, Royal Phelps, Edwin A. Post, Robert G. Remsen, Francis R. Rives, Lewis Morris Rutherfurd, William. C. Schermerhorn, Frederick Sheldon, Edward Templeton Snelling, William R. Travers, Alexander Van Rensselaer, George Henry Warren, and Benjamin S. Welles. Membership list in McAllister, *Society*, 213. The list is reproduced (without further analysis) in Dixon Wecter, *The Saga of American Society: A Record of Social Aspiration 1607–1937* (New York: Charles Scribner's Sons, 1937), 214; and Cleveland Amory, *Who Killed Society?* (New York: Harper & Brothers, 1960), 120; but there is little reference to the Patriarchs in more recent studies of the American 'upper strata,' such as Jaher, *The Urban Establishment*. Popular books on the upper class, such as Mary Cable's *Top Drawer: American High Society from the Gilded Age to the Roaring Twenties* (New York: Atheneum, 1984), have been equally incurious about this first census of the self-proclaimed American aristocracy. August Belmont was admitted to the Patriarchs later in the 1870s, and his son August Jr. succeeded to membership when the senior Belmont largely withdrew from social life in the next decade. Elections to the society: 'Dancing Patriarchs,' *New York Herald*, Dec. 11, 1888, 6. For the hereditary trend see 'The Patriarchs' Dance,' *New York Times*, Dec. 11, 1894, 9; the waiting list is noted in 'Guests of the Patriarchs,' *New York Times*, Dec. 24, 1884, 5.

79. For the early leadership of the Metropolitan Museum, see Howe, *History of the Metropolitan Museum of Art*, 123. Club memberships in Townsend, *Mother of Clubs: The Century: 1847–1946* (New York: The Century Association, 1947), William J. Dunn,

Knickerbocker Centennial: An Informal History of the Knickerbocker Club, 1871–1971 (New York: The Knickerbocker Club, 1971) and Will Irwin et al., *A History of the Union League Club of New York City* (New York: Dodd, Mead, 1952), 20–1.

80. Entry for Feb. 28, 1872, Strong, *Diary*, IV, 413; Satterlee, *Morgan*, 93; for a recollection of Mrs. Rutherfurd, see Mrs. Burton Harrison, *Recollections Grave and Gay* (New York, 1911; London: Smith, Elder, 1912), 280–1; Armstrong, *Five Generations*, 389. See McAllister, *Society*, 207–8.

81. 'Fine Arts: Assignee's Sale of Works of Art Belonging to William Butler Duncan,' *Herald*, Jan. 13, 1876, 6; 'Petition of William Butler Duncan,' *New York Times*, Jan. 9, 1876, 7; 'Sale of the Duncan Collection of Paintings,' *New York Times*, Jan. 15, 1876, 10.

82. For Vanderbilt's collection of paintings, see 'Vanderbilt's Pictures,' *The World*, Dec. 21, 1883, 1, and W.A. Croffut, *The Vanderbilts and the Story of Their Fortune* (London: Griffith, Farrar, Okeden & Walso, 1886), 166. Hooper to General Charles Loring, Jan. 26, 1889, cited in Sarah Burns, *Inventing the Modern Artist: Art and Culture in Gilded Age America* (New Haven: Yale University Press, 1996), 317. Carolus-Duran had similar problems with a painting sold to a Brooklyn brewer. When the painting of an 'exceedingly nude lady' reached the New York Customs House, the brewer got cold feet, refused to pay the duty, and had the picture shipped back to the painter in Paris. Richard Morris Hunt helped broker an agreement by which Carolus-Duran added drapery sufficient for Brooklyn, and the picture was re-shipped to America. See Paul R. Baker, *Richard Morris Hunt* (Cambridge, MA: MIT Press, 1980), 324–5.

83. Entries for May 6 and Aug. 18, 1863, Strong, *Diary*, III, 319, 349. In Feb. 1863 the Marquis of Huntington, who later became the eighth Duke of Devonshire, visited New York, and was taken up by Mrs. Antonio Yznaga, Duncan and Belmont. Strong believed it was their pro-Southern attitudes which gave Huntington the idea that sympathy for the rebellion was widespread in New York. See Strong, *Diary*, III, 300–1. Duncan's possible candidacy for mayor in 1874 appears in Mark D. Hirsch, *William C. Whitney: Modern Warwick* (New York: Dodd, Mead, 1948), 80.

84. T.W., 'Our Millionaires,' *Galaxy*, 5 (May 1868), 529–38.

85. Glyndon G. Van Deusen, *Horace Greeley: Nineteenth-Century Crusader* (Philadelphia: University of Pennsylvania Press, 1953), 339–40, citing *New York Daily Tribune*, June 26, 29, and July 10, 1869.

86. Wharton, *A Backward Glance*, 11.

87. 'The Americus Club House,' *New York Times*, Aug. 6, 1873, 1.

88. Mrs. Astor's remark cited in Lehr, 'King Lehr', 86. On the social embargo of Gould, see Matthew Josephson, *The Robber Barons* (1934; London: Eyre & Spottiswoode, 1962), 205; Maury Klein forcefully rebuts the portrayal of Gould in Josephson's influential work in *The Life and Legend of Jay Gould* (Baltimore: Johns Hopkins University Press, 1986), and, *inter alia*, 'The Robber Baron's Bum Rap,' *City Journal*, 5 (Winter 1995). See also T.S. Hebard, 'Prominent American Families. IV. The Goulds,' *Munsey's Magazine*, 15 (July 1896), 448–57.

89. Bristed, *The Upper Ten Thousand*, 133.

90. George W. Smalley, *London Letters and Some Others*, 23. Smalley, who had made his name as one of the *Tribune*'s battlefield correspondents during the Civil War, established the paper's London bureau. Smalley's dandyism, and the completeness with which he adapted himself to the environment of aristocratic Tory circles, earned him considerable resentment in America, and admiration in London. He was hired by *The Times* as American correspondent in 1890. See Harry W. Baehr, Jr., *The New York Tribune since the Civil War* (New York: Dodd, Mead, 1936), 131.

91. McAllister, *Society*, 230–1. Cotillion attendance in 'The Last of the Cotillions,' *New York Times*, Feb. 21, 1884, 5; *Town Topics*, 18 (Dec. 15, 1887), 1. Attendance had its own rhythm, with the second Patriarchs always less well attended than the first or third.

92. 'Patriarchs Who Dance,' *New York World*, Dec. 18, 1883, 5.

93. Guests: see 'A Brilliant Gathering at Delmonico's,' *New York Daily Tribune*, Dec. 21, 1880, 7; 'Third Patriarchs' Ball,' *New York Daily Tribune*, Feb. 15, 1881, 5; 'Patriarchs Who Dance,' *New York World*, Dec. 18, 1883, 5

94. McAllister, *Society*, 229–32.

95. 'Dancing at Delmonico's. The First Ball of the Family Circle Dancing Class,' *New York Times*, Dec. 5, 1882, 12; 'Enjoying the Cotillion. The Last Ball of the Family Circle Dancing Class,' *New York Times*, Jan. 3, 1883, 8; 'Launched into Society,' *New York Times*, Dec. 9, 1884, 4; 'The World of Society,' *New York Times*, Sept. 20, 1885, 14.

96. 'Two Amateur Leaders,' *The German: How to Give It, How to Lead It, How to Dance It* (Chicago: Jansen, McClurg, 1879), 126–9; *How to Lead a German* (New York: Dick & Fitzgerald, 1895), 11; 'Third Patriarchs' Ball,' *New York Daily Tribune*, Feb. 15, 1881, 5.

97. [Fawcett,] *The Buntling Ball*, 65–6.

98. 'Two Amateur Leaders,' *The German*, 33, 47, 49. The leader as autocrat: *How to Lead a German*, 6.

99. 'Expert Opinion on Leading Cotillions,' *New York Herald*, Jan. 16, 1898, V, 5; 'First of the Cotillions,' *New York Times*, Dec. 19, 1884, 5; two 'youthful' members of the Knickerbocker Club were rumored to be the authors of *Gentleman*, an anonymous etiquette book for gentlemen in society published in 1891. See H.S.H., 'Rules for Gentlemen,' *New York World*, March 18, 1891, 10. For the 'Bouncers' Ball' see Mrs. John King Van Rensselaer, *The Social Ladder*, 56, 58. 165; Thomas, *Delmonico's*, 194–5. 'The Bachelor's Ball,' *New York Times*, April 18, 1884, 2. For the rivalry between Lehr and Dyer, see Elizabeth Drexel Lehr, 'King Lehr,' 68–9. G.P.A. Healy's portrait of his wife, Mrs. Alexander Van Rensselaer is reproduced in Patterson, *The First Four Hundred*, 88.

100. 'The Past Week in Society,' *New York Times*, Jan. 16, 1898, 3; 'In the World of Fashion,' *The Sun*, Jan. 9, 1895, 7; 'Tuesday Evening Club,' *New York Times*, Jan. 27, 1898, 7; 'Tuesday Evening Club: Fashionable Members and Guests Attend the Second Meeting at Mrs. J.J. Astor's,' *New York Times*, Jan. 27, 1898, 7. For the Thursday Evening Club, see *Town Topics*, 18 (Dec. 8, 1887), 2; Karen J. Blair, *The Clubwoman as Feminist: True Womanhood Redefined, 1868–1914* (New York: Holmes & Meier, 1880), ch. 2 on Sorosis. See also Nancy F. Cott, *The Grounding of Modern Feminism* (New Haven: Yale University Press, 1987) on the role of upper-class women in the feminist movement in the early twentieth century. Less useful is Anne F. Cox, *The History of the Colony Club 1903–1984* (New York: Privately printed for the Colony Club, 1984). In addition to a full range of civic, charitable, and benevolent activities, the experience of balls organized by women, of the evening clubs, and then the formation of the Colony Club, and the support which club members gave to Mrs. O.H.P. Belmont's Political Equality Association, established the powerful strain of aristocracy in the American women's movement.

101. For the 'howling swells' see 'Society Events of the Week,' *New York Times*, Jan. 10, 1897, 10; a list of the guests, and a description of the dresses worn, appears in 'Dance of the "Howling Swells",' *New York Herald*, Jan. 12, 1898, 9; 'The Past Week in Society,' *New York Times*, Jan. 16, 1898, 3; Blanche Wiesen Cook, *Eleanor Roosevelt*, vol. I: *1884–1933* (New York: Viking Penguin, 1992), 23.

102. The fortunes of the Bend family are noted in Sloane, *Maverick in Mauve*, 14. 'Patriarchs Who Dance,' *New York World*, Dec. 18, 1883, 5; 'Dancing Patriarchs,' *New York Herald*, Dec. 11, 1888, 6; 'Dance of the "Howling Swells",' *New York Herald*, Jan. 12, 1898, 9.

103. On the stupidity of a Patriarchs' ball, see *Town Topics*, 25 (Jan. 8, 1891), 1; on the use of the term 'Matriarchs' see 'The First Assembly Ball,' *New York Times*, Dec. 16, 1898, 7.

104. 'The Saunterer,' *Town Topics*, 26 (Oct. 29, 1891), 3.

105. The discussion which follows—and otherwise unattributed quotations—of the New York press and society draws upon the manuscripts of George Wotherspoon, a man who was a fixture in society and one of the earliest society journalists. Wotherspoon's sharply observed and well-informed 'I Hunt the Attic' (typescript, NYHS), is an invaluable insider's account of the transformation of social visibility in the world of McAllister.

106. Marie Ganz, in collaboration with Nat J. Ferber, *Rebels: Into Anarchy—and Out Again*, with illustrations by M. Leone Bracker (New York: Dodd, Mead, 1919), 97–8.

107. *The Money-Makers: A Social Parable* (New York: D. Appleton, 1885), 103–5.

108. Logan, *The Man Who Robbed the Robber Barons*, tells the story of the irrepressible Colonel Mann and his many well-heeled society victims. See also Robert R. Rowe, 'Mann of Town Topics,' *American Mercury*, 8 (July 1926), 271–80, and obituaries of E.D. Mann and Colonel Mann in *New York Times*, March 31, 1902, 9, and May 18, 1920, 11.

109. 'Jenny June' was the pen-name of Jane Cunningham Croly, an English-born journalist who wrote one of the first syndicated ladies' columns. She managed the Woman's Department of the *World* from 1862 to 1872, and for many years wrote for *Demorest's Monthly Magazine, Frank Leslie's Weekly* and other magazines. She was a founder of Sorosis, and author of a *History of the Woman's Club Movement in America*. Her columns in the *Cosmopolitan* reached a wide audience. See 'The Etiquette of Ladies' Luncheons' (Jan. 1887) and 'The Art of Dinner-Giving' (March 1887). Blair, *The Clubwoman as Feminist*, passim, gives an account of her career. On the use of *noms de plume* by women writers in this period, see the acerbic comment by Ann Douglas, *The Feminization of American Culture* (New York: Knopf, 1977), 186.

110. 'Our Aristocracy,' *New York World*, May 13, 1883, 4; 'Our Crested Nobility,' *New York World*, Dec. 9, 1883, 1. The last of the series appeared on Dec. 30. See W.A. Swanberg, *Pulitzer* (New York: Charles Scribner's Sons, 1967), 73–144, for Pulitzer's *World* in the 1880s.

111. 'Society Events of the Week,' *New York Times*, Jan. 10,

1897, 10. Harry Lehr was the author of a similar comment which was directed at Mrs. Astor; handing her a bouquet of red roses, he said: 'You look like a walking chandelier. Put them on. You need color.' *Deborah Turbeville's Newport Remembered*, 35.

112. 'Mrs. Paran Stevens Dead,' *New York Times*, April 4, 1895, 1.

113. McAllister, *Society*, 245.

114. McAllister, *Society*, ch. 24.

115. 'Secrets of Ball-Giving,' *New York Daily Tribune*, March 25, 1888, 11.

116. The city press carried the names of the 'Four Hundred' on Feb. 2, 1892. Patterson, *The First Four Hundred*, 207–34, provides brief biographical details.

117. Emmett Dedmon, *Fabulous Chicago* (New York: Random House, 1953), 222–5.

118. Mamie Fish quoted Elizabeth Drexel Lehr, '*King Lehr*,' 169.

119. 'Mr. McAllister Resigns,' *New York Daily Tribune*, April 15, 1889, 1–2; Moran Tudury, 'Ward McAllister,' *American Mercury*, 8 (June 1926), 141–3.

120. 'Our "Society Leader",' *New York Times*, Oct. 19, 1890, 19.

121. 'Patriarchs Not Quite Up to the Mark,' *New York Herald*, Dec. 9, 1890, 5; *Town Topics*, Jan. 8 and 22, 1891; 'Official Society,' *New York World*, Feb. 15, 1891, 18; 'Is Ward McAllister a Gentleman?' *Illustrated American*, 6 (Feb. 21, 1891), 5; *Town Topics*, Feb. 12, 1891.

122. 'Steward McGuzzler' [pseud. Alfred Thompson,] *Society As It Found Me Out* (New York: Carlton-Regaud, 1890); the Huntington squabble was revealed in *Town Topics*, Feb. 26 and March 12, 1891. Huntington's gifts to the Metropolitan Museum, and its list of trustees, appear in Calvin Tomkins, *Merchants and Masterpieces: The Story of the Metropolitan Museum of Art*, rev. edn. (New York: Henry Holt, 1989); Lehr's and Martin's commercial dealings appear in Elizabeth Drexel Lehr, '*King Lehr*' and Eve Brown, *The Plaza: Its Life and Times* (New York: Meredith Press, 1967), 38.

123. M'Hustler was mocked in *Town Topics*, Oct. 29, 1891. The prospect of an invitation for Pulitzer appears in *Town Topics*, Nov. 19 and 26, 1891. See McAllister in the *New York World*, Oct. 4, 14, 18, and 25, 1891 Among his later columns, see April 26, 1892, on a society marriage, and Jan. 27, 1895, on American snobs.

124. 'Ward McAllister's Triumph,' *New York Times*, Dec. 15, 1893, 9; 'Society's Great Ball,' *New York Times*, Dec. 9, 1894, 19. The report after the dance followed the same jubilant note: 'The Patriarchs' Dance,' *New York Times*, Dec. 11, 1894, 9. The absentees were noted: 'In the World of Fashion,' *New York Times*, Jan. 15, 1895, 7.

125. See Kernochan's explosive reaction to the elopement of his daughter with Clarence Pell, in the diary of Rev. Morgan Dix, entries for Feb. 22 and 23, 1883, Trinity Church Archives, New York City. See also 'James P. Kernochan Dead,' *New York Daily Tribune*, March 6, 1897, 1.

Chapter 6 Being Mrs. Astor

1. Poultney Bigelow, *Seventy Summers*, 2 vols. (New York: Longmans, Green, 1925), II, 7–8.

2. Patterson, *The First Four Hundred*, 40–1. Her distinctive handwriting, social knowledge, and Mrs. Astor's patronage made de Barril a valuable resource for hostesses planning entertainments. She was yet another of those who were well paid for their personal services to New York society.

3. Rebecca H. Insley, 'An Interview with Mrs. Astor,' *Delineator*, 72 (Oct. 1908), 549–50, 638–9. Further citations are to this source. The substance of the interview was reprinted as 'Mrs. Astor Censures Some Society Women,' *New York Times*, Sept. 15, 1908, 5. The interview appeared two weeks before her death, and betrays no hint of the declining mental powers which played so prominent a role in her obituaries.

4. O'Connor, *The Golden Summers*, 252; 'Consul, Chimpanzee, Mr. Belmont's Guest,' *New York Times*, July 27, 1907. Far more notorious was Stanford White's Pie Girl dinner on May 20, 1895, a celebration of a friend's tenth wedding anniversary. A nearly nude blonde served white wine, and red was served by a brunette. The *pièce de résistance* came when a naked young girl emerged, accompanied by a flock of canaries and nightingales, out of a large pie. The celebrated architect never quite managed to shed the 'penumbra of depravity' which he acquired after word of this dinner leaked out. It was Pulitzer's *World* which broke the story. The evening is described in detail in Michael Macdonald Mooney, *Evelyn Nesbit and Stanford White: Love and Death in the Gilded Age* (New York: William Morrow, 1976), ch. 13. Alva Belmont has attracted a great deal of scholarly attention: see Rebecca T. Keeler, 'Alva Belmont: Exacting Benefactor for Women's Rights' (Ph.D., University of South Alabama, 1987), Peter Geidel, 'Alva E. Belmont: A Forgotten Feminist' (Ph.D., Columbia University, 1993).

5. Mrs. Astor's enthusiasm for Meissonier placed her in the dead center of New York upper-class taste. In the

year before his death in 1876, A.T. Stewart acquired Meissonier's enormous *Friedland, 1807*. Members of the Rothschild family, Napoleon III, and assorted British aristocrats owned Meissoniers. Other New Yorkers, including August Belmont, William Henry Vanderbilt, and the first president of the Metropolitan Museum, James Taylor Johnston, were also collecting Meissonier, whose popularity was at its peak during the Second Empire.

6. 'Eugene Benson' [Charles Astor Bristed,] 'Meissonier,' *Appleton's Journal*, 2 (Sept. 11, 1869), 118–19.

7. Bigelow, *Seventy Summers*, II, 7–8. The green livery and Tyrolean hats worn by gamekeepers at Tuxedo seemed, to the younger generation, something like the 'chorus of a musical comedy.' See Edwin Post, Jr., *Truly Emily Post*, 11.

8. 'Our Musical Carnival,' *The World*, Oct. 23, 1883, 1–2.

9. In the late 1880s half of all performances at the Met were of Wagner's work. The box-holders disliked the length of Wagnerian opera, and also resisted German solemnity about art. The predominantly German audience demanded that the box-holders cease their chattering during performances, and were sharply reproved for their pains. See Joseph Horowitz, *Wagner Nights: An American History* (Berkeley: University of California Press, 1994), *passim*; Martin Mayer, *The Met: One Hundred Years of Grand Opera* (New York: Simon & Schuster and The Metropolitan Opera Guild, 1983), 63; 'Mrs. Astor Dies at her City Home,' *New York Times*, Oct. 31, 1908, 1–2.

10. See George E. Waring, Jr., 'The Cleaning of a Great City,' *McClure's Magazine*, 9 (Sept. 1897), 911–24; and Waring's *Street Cleaning* (New York: Doubleday & McClure Co., 1899). Innovative publicity techniques were used by reformers to sell their approach to the problem of street cleaning. See 'Mayor Strong Speaks Again,' *New York Times*, Oct. 20, 1897, 3.

11. Croker's gibe in 'Character Sketch: Mr. Richard Croker and Greater New York,' *Review of Reviews*, 16 (1897), 345. See 'Roosevelt Drank with Laborers,' *New York Evening Journal*, Jan. 28, 1897, 6. An account of the meeting at Clarendon Hall appears in Riis, *Theodore Roosevelt*, 152–4. The political consequences of the Bradley Martin ball are suggested in Burrows and Wallace, *Gotham: A History of New York City to 1898*, 1206. 'It is impossible to measure the depths of his loathing for Roosevelt,' writes David Nasaw in *The Chief: The Life of William Randolph Hearst* (Boston: Houghton Mifflin, 2000), 147.

12. Description of Mrs. Astor and the dress of others present at the opera in 'Society at the Opera,' *New York Times*, Nov. 30, 1898, 6.

13. Astor, Bishop, Bowdoin, J.T. and J.A. Burden, Cutting, Gerry, Goelet, Haven, Iselin, Morgan, A. Phelps Stokes, Cornelius Vanderbilt, Whitney, Buchanan, and Egerton Winthrop were Patriarchs in 1897.

14. See Joel Tyler Headley, *The Great Riots of New York, 1712 to 1873* (New York: Dover, 1971). First published 1887. Moody, *The Astor Place Riot*.

15. Spann, *The New Metropolis*, 219–20.

16. Pamphlet announcing Academy of Music season, 1883–4, Box 2, file 1, Belmont Papers, NYPL.

17. Belmont to Morton, May 7, 1878; to Mapleson, June 17, 1878: Correspondence relating to the Academy of Music, 1878, Belmont Papers, NYPL.

18. Black, *King of Fifth Avenue*, 550.

19. Black, *King of Fifth Avenue*, 666–7.

20. Mark D. Hirsch, *William C. Whitney: Modern Warwick* (New York: Dodd, Mead, 1948), 191–2.

21. Irving Kolodin, *The Metropolitan Opera 1883–1939*, 2nd edn. (New York: Oxford University Press, 1940), 4.

22. Nilsson did, apparently, sing at the Academy of Music in the early 1870s: see *Lord Rosebery's North American Journal—1873*, ed. A.R.C. Grant with Caroline Combe (London: Sidgwick & Jackson, [1967]). Opening night description in Richard O'Connor, *Gould's Millions* (Garden City, N.Y.: Doubleday, 1962), 200–1, citing the *Dramatic Mirror*.

23. The occupants of the boxes at the Met were listed in 'The New Opera-House,' *New York Times*, Oct. 23, 1883, 1; both houses are listed in 'Our Musical Carnival,' *The World*, Oct. 23, 1883, 1–2; see also Frank Crowninshield, 'The House of Vanderbilt,' *Vogue*, Nov. 15, 1941; reprinted in *Vogue's First Reader*, with an Introduction by Frank Crowninshield (New York: Julian Messner, 1942), 528. Kolodin, *The Metropolitan Opera*, 16, suggests that the schism was more fictitious than real. But the widespread contemporary belief that there was a split in the aristocracy remains powerful evidence that the division seemed real enough.

24. Reprinted Mayer, *The Met*, 50–1.

25. 'Grandeur': ibid., 40. A more qualified judgment of the structure (describing it as 'utilitarian' and 'unmajestic') is Mariana Griswold Van Rensselaer's 'Recent Architecture in America. II. Public Buildings,' *Century Magazine*, 28 (July 1884), 323–34. Montgomery Schuyler was distinctly more enthusiastic in 'The Metropolitan Opera-House,' *Harper's New Monthly Magazine*, 67 (Nov. 1883), 877–89.

26. Dizikes, *Opera in America*, 218–19.

27. 'There were new forms and faces in some of the

boxes and seats, and there were ghosts in other boxes, and seats, and who even walked the corridors, unseen by the many, but whose presence was felt by the few.' 'Society at the Opera,' *New York Times*, Nov. 30, 1898, 6.

28. Suzannah Lessard, *The Architect of Desire: Beauty and Danger in the Stanford White Family* (London: Weidenfeld & Nicolson, 1997), 118. Samuel G. White, *The Houses of McKim, Mead & White*, photographs by Jonathan Wallen (New York: Rizzoli, 1998), 75.

29. 'What Is Going On in Society,' *The Sun*, Feb. 8, 1891, 6.

30. *Town Topics*, 26 (July 23, 1891), 4.

31. 'Mrs. Astor, Ruler of Society for 20 years, Dead,' *The World*, Oct. 31, 1908, 1–2.

32. 'Mrs. Astor's Annual Ball,' *New York Times*, Jan. 30, 1900, 3.

33. Bourget, *Outre-Mer*, 50. The stem of the American Beauty was extraordinarily long, reaching six feet. It made possible a much more imposing display than the tight formal bouquet appropriate for weak-stemmed tea roses. On the introduction of the American Beauty see Thomas Christopher, *In Search of Lost Roses* (New York: Summit Books, 1989), 225–34.

34. *Town Topics*, 18 (Dec. 22, 1887), 2.

35. Biographical details of the family in 'Famous New York Families. 22. The Schermerhorns,' *Evening Post*, July 13, 1901 (clipping in Genealogy and Local History Division, NYPL), and Richard Schermerhorn, Jr., *Schermerhorn Genealogy*; Alfred E. Schermerhorn to William Rhinelander Stewart, July 13, 1923, Grace Church archives; William Rhinelander Stewart, *Grace Church*.

36. J.F. Cooper to Horatio Greenough, Feb. 26, 1830, *The Letters and Journals of James Fenimore Cooper*, ed. James Franklin Beard, 6 vols. (Cambridge: Belknap Press of Harvard University Press, 1960), I, 404. The Hone diaries are a particularly rich source of information on the Schermerhorn family. See entry for Jan. 14, 1845, Hone Mss. Diary, XXII 365–6; entry for June 27, 1852, Strong, *Diary*, II, 87.

37. Entry for Feb. 18, 1855, Strong, *Diary*, II, 212. W.C. Schermerhorn was chairman of the board when Columbia College moved to Morningside Heights, and donated $300,000 to erect a building on the new campus. Schermerhorn, *Schermerhorn Genealogy*, 48. Property holdings noted in 'Low Prices for Real Estate,' *New York Times*, Jan. 31, 1883, 3. The partition and sale of the estate of Abraham Schermerhorn produced prices so low that the sale was abandoned before all the properties were offered at auction.

38. Abraham Schermerhorn's Gowanus property was sold in 1835 for $102,000. With the opening of the Gowanus Canal in the late 1840s, the value of real estate in that part of Brooklyn greatly increased. Among his other real estate holdings were lots at 68 Broadway, 97 Wall Street, 8 Fulton Street, 1 Beaver Street, and 237 Water Street, as well as a one-fifth interest in Pier no. 5 on the Hudson.

39. Brief genealogical details from 'Mrs. Astor Dead; Many of Family at Her Bedside,' *New York World*, Oct. 31, 1908, 1, 4, and Marilyn Elizabeth Perry, 'Caroline Astor,' *American National Biography*, general eds. John A. Garraty and Mark C. Carnes, 24 vols. (New York: Oxford University Press, 1999), I, 695–6. There is a photograph of Mrs. Abraham Schermerhorn in her later years in Cleveland Moffett, 'Luxurious Newport,' *Cosmopolitan*, 43 (Aug. 1907), 351.

40. Entry for July 15, 1851, Strong, *Diary*, II, 58. The struggle between the proponents of the park and the Jones and Schermerhorn families is told in Roy Rosenzweig and Elizabeth Blackmar, *The Park and the People: A History of Central Park* (Ithaca, N.Y.: Cornell University Press, 1992), and Homberger, *Scenes from the Life of a City*, ch. 4. W.C. Schermerhorn to James Beekman, Dec. 18, 1852, Beekman Papers, NYHS, cited M. Christine Boyer, *Manhattan Manners: Architecture and Style 1850–1900* (New York: Rizzoli, 1985), 15.

41. Entry for Oct. 5, 1873, *Lord Rosebery's North American Journal*, 37.

42. Diary entry Nov. 1820, *Diary of James Gallatin*, 167–8.

43. [James Parton,] 'John Jacob Astor,' *Harper's New Monthly Magazine*, 30 (Feb. 1865), 315, 320.

44. Diary entry for Nov. 27, 1815, *Diary of James Gallatin*, 80; Lieber to Matilda Lieber, Sept. 1, 1841, Frank Friedel, *Francis Lieber: Nineteenth-Century Liberal* (Baton Rouge: Louisiana State University Press, 1947), 206–7. Anna Bridgen to Hannah Maria Denning Duer, Paris, Feb. 25, 1834. Duer Family Papers, Columbia University Library. This startling and frank letter seems to have escaped the notice of Astor's biographers.

45. Parton, '"John Jacob Astor,"' 323; *Letters of James Kirke Paulding*, 478–9.

46. Gouverneur, *As I Remember*, 72; Mrs. Basil Hall, *The Aristocratic Journey*, 129–30. The dinner took place on Nov. 27, 1827.

47. Entry for April 1, 1848, Tailer, 'Journal', vol. II. In 1833 William Backhouse became the residuary legatee of the estate of his uncle Henry Astor, and received $350,000.

48. Robert Baird, *Transplanted Flowers, or Memoirs of Mrs. Rumpff, Daughter of John Jacob Astor, Esq., and*

the Duchess de Broglie, Daughter of Madame de Stael, with an Appendix (New York: Baker & Scribner, 1846), 40–1; 'Death of a Noted Citizen,' *New York Times*, Nov. 25 , 1875, 1; 'William B. Astor,' *New York Herald*, Nov. 25, 1875, 3.

49. Hale Smith, *Sunshine and Shadow in New York*, 187.

50. [William Waldorf Astor,] *Silhouettes*, 27.

51. Lately Thomas, *A Pride of Lions: The Astor Orphans* (New York: William Morrow, 1971), 11; Brandt, *An American Aristocracy*, 191.

52. Entry for Dec. 16, 1846, Hone Mss. Diary, XXIV, 334–5; Nevins, II, 781. Nevins misdates the entry, and by deleting much of Hone's brutal sarcasm without indicating the omissions, manages to distort Hone's meaning. The passage from 'some with smooth faces' to 'masses of black hair' was omitted by Nevins.

53. If Cogswell's letters to Julia and Annie Ward in 1838–41 are anything to go by, he must have been a most tedious schoolmaster companion for John Jacob Astor III. See Julia Ward Howe Papers, Beinecke Library, Yale University. The harsh treatment of Henry Astor is recalled in 'An Odd, Forgotten Astor,' *The World*, April 17, 1892, 26.

54. Charles Loring Brace, 'Walks Among the New York Poor: The Eleventh Ward,' *New York Times*, March 4, 1853.

55. 'John Jacob Astor Dead,' *New York Times*, Feb. 23, 1890, 1 (obituary).

56. *The Life of Charles Loring Brace, Chiefly Told in his Own Letters*, edited by his daughter (New York: Scribner's Sons, 1894), 71–2; Sinclair, *Dynasty: The Astors and Their Times*, 178; [William Waldorf Astor,] *Silhouettes*, 4.

57. Kavaler, *The Astors*, 121.

58. Entry for June 13, 1853, Strong, *Diary*, II, 126.

59. Sinclair, *Dynasty*, 185.

60. 'Death of William Astor,' *The Sun*, April 27, 1892, 7.

61. Balsan, *The Glitter and the Gold*, 40.

62. For the emerging doctrine of romantic marriage, see Karen Lystra, *Searching the Heart: Women, Men and Romantic Love in Nineteenth-Century America* (New York: Oxford University Press, 1989).

63. Virginia Cowles argues that she married William Astor for his money in *The Astors* (New York: Knopf, 1979), 90. On the absence of love in their marriage, see Wilson, *The Astors*, 95.

64. Descriptions of Mrs. Astor in Kavaler, *The Astors*, 116 (quoting Alida Chanler Emmet); Sinclair, *Dynasty*, 189, 186; 'The Willing–Astor Wedding,' *New York Times*, Feb. 17, 1891, 5; 'Mrs. Astor Dies at her City Home,' *New York Times*, Oct. 31, 1908, 1–2; Frank Crowninshield, 'The Mrs. Astor I Remember,'

Vogue's First Reader, 93.

65. There is a description of Van Alen in Elizabeth Drexel Lehr, *'King Lehr' and the Gilded Age*, 124–9.

66. *Last Will and Testament, dated Jan 12, 1882, and codicils . . . of William Astor, Jan. 6, 1888*. Copy in NYPL. Sent on Astor's death in 1892 to the Trustees of the Astor Library to inform them of the will's provisions.

67. Noted by Girouard, *Cities & People*, 314.

68. *New York Daily Tribune*, Nov. 28, 1859, cited I.N. Phelps Stokes, *Iconography*, V, 1882.

69. 'Ziska,' 'Our New York Correspondence,' *Boston Weekly Voice*, Feb. 17, 1866; *Harper's Weekly*, Aug. 14, 1869; Van Rensselaer, 'Recent Architecture in America. V. City Dwellings,' *Century Magazine*, 31 (Feb. 1886), 552–3. The décor and structure of the Stewart house are described in *The Opulent Interiors of the Gilded Age*, with new text by Arnold Lewis, James Turner, and Steve McQuillin (New York: Dover, 1987), 33–9. 'Disposing of Stewart's Furniture,' *New York Daily Tribune*, Nov. 8, 1890, 7. There is a valuable account of the mansion in its later life in Henry M. Stevens, 'How Clubs Grew, I.—The Manhattan Club,' *Home & Country*, 8 (April 1893), 825–40.

70. Willis on Stewart's (which he misspells as Stuart's): Willis, *Dashes at Life with a Free Pencil*, 120. Paul R. Cleveland, 'The Millionaires of New York,' *Cosmopolitan*, 5 (Sept. 1888), 385–98; (Oct. 1888), 521–8.

71. For Stewart as a hard-faced employer, see C. E[dgar]. Rogers, 'Journal 1864,' NYPL. At the age of twenty, Rogers worked in Stewart's retail store. For Stewart's comment to Cooper, see 'Death of A.T. Stewart,' *New York Herald*, April 11, 1876, 4.

72. 'Death of A.T. Stewart,' *New York Times*, April 11, 1876, 1; Jay E. Cantor, 'A Monument of Trade: A.T. Stewart and the Rise of the Millionaire's Mansion in New York,' *Winterthur Portfolio*, 10 (1975), 165–97; Matthew Hale Smith, *Bulls and Bears of New York, with the Crisis of 1873, and the Cause* (Hartford: J.B. Burr, 1875), 195; on Stewart as parvenu, see Mabel Osgood Wright, *My New York*, 27.

73. Elizabeth Eliot, *Heiresses and Coronets: The Story of Lovely Ladies and Noble Men* (New York: McDowell, Obolensky, 1959), 58.

74. M.E.W. Sherwood, 'New York in the Seventies,' *Lippincott's Monthly Magazine*, 62 (Sept. 1898), 394. Martin, *Things I Remember*, 218.

75. Sinclair, *Dynasty*, 189–90; 'State dinner': entry for March 19, 1863, Strong, *Diary*, III, 306; Entry for Feb. 17, 1871, Tailer, *Journal*, XVI.

76. Cowles, *The Astors*, 109.

77. John Upton Terrell, *Furs by Astor* (New York: William Morrow, 1963), 105n. In 1911, in a similar expression of secretiveness and imperiousness, J.P. Morgan burned the letters containing Wall Street information he had sent over three decades to his father Junius in London. See Chernow, *The Death of the Banker*, 90.

78. Elias makes this distinction in *The Civilizing Process*, 501ff.

79. Cited Kavaler, *The Astors*, 125.

80. Chernow, *The Death of the Banker*, 27.

81. For a judgment on the 1883 ball see Smith, *Elsie de Wolfe*, 17–18, and, for example, Howard Mumford Jones, *The Age of Energy: Varieties of American Experience 1865–1915* (New York: The Viking Press, 1971), 134–5; Edwin P. Hoyt, *The Vanderbilts and Their Fortunes* (London: Frederick Muller, 1963), 254–9; and Scott C. Steward, 'Alva Vanderbilt's Ball,' *Social Register Observer*, Summer 1997, 58–63, and Steward's 'The Vanderbilt Ball of 1883: New York Society in the Age of Innocence,' New England Historic Genealogical Society Public Lecture Series, Oct. 14, 1998. The following account of the ball is based on contemporary press reports of March 27, 1883.

82. The story of Morgan's uncomfortable call on Rockefeller is vividly told in Chernow, *The Death of the Banker*, 39, and Chernow's *Titan: The Life of John D. Rockefeller, Sr.* (Boston: Little, Brown, 1998), 390–1, but does not appear in Jean Strouse, *Morgan: American Financier* (New York: Random House, 1999), 396.

83. 'Mrs. Astor Dies at her City Home,' *New York Times*, Oct. 31, 1908, 1–2. Mrs. Astor on the Vanderbilts quoted in Sinclair, *Dynasty*, 191.

84. 'Mrs. Astor's Reception,' *New York Times*, Dec. 19, 1890, 5 (the guests at this reception were an interesting example of 'Old New York' and a large number of people who had seldom appeared in the society pages); 'Mrs. Astor Dead; Many of Family at Her Bedside,' *New York Herald*, Oct. 31, 1908, 1, 4.

85. Mrs. John King Van Rensselaer, *The Social Ladder*, 49. 'Mrs. Astor, Ruler of Society for 20 Years, Dead,' *The World*, Oct. 31, 1908, 1–2.

86. Elizabeth Drexel Lehr, *'King Lehr,'* 166–8, and often repeated (see Kavaler, *The Astors*, 114, 132). The issue of Jewish membership of New York clubs is discussed in Birmingham, *'Our Crowd,'* 241–2.

87. 'Mr. Martin's Analysis of New York Society: Chaos, He Declares, Followed the Retirement of Mrs. Astor, Resulting in More Marked Social Divisions and Greater Boredom,' *New York Times*, May 3, 1908, V, 6; 'Society Stirred by 1,100 Dictum,' *New York Times*, April 28, 1908, 7.

88. 'Society Stirred by 1,100 Dictum,' *New York Times*, April 28, 1908, 7. Subletting the Astor box, and the quote from *Town Topics* cited in Kolodin, *The Metropolitan Opera*, 429–30.

89. N. Parker Willis, 'Gossiping Letter,' *The Rag-Bag, a Collection of Ephemera* (New York: Charles Scribner, 1855), 41; Willis, *Dashes at Life with a Free Pencil*, 87.

90. Rosemary Levy Zumwalt, *Wealth and Rebellion: Elsie Clews Parsons, Anthropologist and Folklorist*, publication of the American Folklore Society (Urbana: University of Illinois Press, 1992), 22–3, 36; Desley Deacon, *Elsie Clews Parsons: Inventing Modern Life* (Chicago: University of Chicago Press, 1997), 14–35. See Deacon, ch. 6, for Parsons in Greenwich Village. Parsons' sharp-edged portrayal of 'American "Society," ' appeared in the *New Republic*, Dec. 16–23, 1916.

91. Christine Stansell, *American Moderns: Bohemian New York and the Creation of a New Century* (New York: Henry Holt, 2000), is the latest, and in some ways the best, of a tidal wave of books about the Village in the early twentieth century. The Astors and Vanderbilts do not figure in her index.

SELECT BIBLIOGRAPHY

All place of publication New York City unless otherwise indicated.

NYHS   New-York Historical Society
NYPL   New York Public Library

Unpublished sources

Henry Bruere, interview, Oral History Project, Columbia University.
Anne Marie Dolan, 'The Literary Salon in New York, 1830–1860' (Ph.D., Columbia University, 1957)
Herbert Kriedman, 'New York's Philip Hone' (Ph.D., New York University, 1965)
Audrey Joyce Roberts, 'The Letters of Caroline M. Kirkland' (Ph.D., University of Wisconsin, 1976)
Peter George Buckley, 'To the Opera House: Culture and Society in New York City, 1820–1860' (Ph.D., State University of New York–Stony Brook, 1984)
David M. Scobey, 'Empire City: Politics, Culture, and Urbanism in Gilded-Age New York' (Ph.D., Yale University, 1989)
Mary Murphy-Schlichting, 'A Summer Salon: Literary and Cultural Circles in Newport, Rhode Island, 1850–1890' (Ph.D., New York University, 1992)
Peter Geidel, 'Alva E. Belmont: A Forgotten Feminist' (Ph.D., Columbia University, 1993)
Jon R. Sterngass, 'Cities of Play: Saratoga Springs, Newport, and Coney Island in the Nineteenth Century' (Ph.D., City University of New York, 1998)

Manuscript sources

A Hasty Sketch of the Late Fancy Ball at G.G. Howland's, March 3rd, 1830, notebook, bound in green leather with 'Mrs. G.G. Howland' stamped in gold leaf on the cover, NYHS

Description of the Fancy Ball given by Mrs Hxxlxxd, notebook, bound in green leather in a different hand to the above, without a name embossed on the cover, but otherwise identical, and which contains 6 delicate watercolors tipped in, signed 'R.C. Long del,' and a *carte-de-visite* of Mrs. Gardiner G. Howland by Disdéri, Paris, NYHS
Astor Family papers, NYPL
Beekman papers, NYHS
Caroline S. Perry Belmont and August Belmont, Photographic Album, Photography Room, NYPL
Belmont Family papers, NYPL
Elizabeth DeHart Bleecker, 'New York Journal for the Year 1799,' NYPL
Morgan Dix diary, Trinity Church Parish Archives
Duer Family papers, Butler Library, Columbia University
Gansevoort-Lansing papers, NYPL
Grace Church Archives, New York City
Philip Hone diary, 28 vols., NYHS
Julia Ward Howe papers, Beinecke Library, Yale University
Ward McAlister, Belmont and Pulitzer papers, Butler Library, Columbia University
Metropolitan Opera Archive, New York City
Alice Duer Miller papers, Barnard College Archives, New York City
Joseph Pulitzer papers, Butler Library, Columbia University
Charles Edgar Rogers, 'Journal 1864,' NYPL
Robert B. Roosevelt papers, NYHS
Edward Neufville Tailer, 'Journal of Some of the Events which have occured in my Life time,' NYHS
Trinity Church Archives, New York City
Vanderbilt Family papers, NYHS
Ward Family papers, NYPL
Julia Rush Ward keepsake album and poetical quotations, Beinecke Library, Yale University
Richard Ward Green Welling diary, NYPL
Edith Wharton papers, Beinecke Library, Yale University
George Wotherspoon, 'I Hunt the Attic,' tss., NYHS

Reference

Samuel Ward Francis, *Biographical Sketches of Distinguished Living New York Physicians* (Putnam & Son, 1867)

James Grant Wilson and John Fiske, eds., *Appleton's Encyclopedia of American Biography*, 6 vols. (D. Appleton, 1887–9)

Henry Hall, ed., *America's Sucessful Men of Affairs: An Encyclopedia of Contemporaneous Biography* (New York Tribune, 1895)

New York Biographical Dictionary: People of All Times and All Places Who Have Been Important to the History and Life of the State (Wilmington: American Historical Publications, 1896)

Lyman Horace Weeks, ed., *Prominent Families of New York*, rev. edn., 2 vols. (New York Historical Co., 1898)

John Henry Mowbray, ed., *Representative Men of New York*, 2 vols. (New York Press, 1898)

James Bronson Reynolds, *Civic Bibliography of Greater New York* (Charities Publishing Committee, 1911)

Margherita Arlina Hamm, *Famous Families of New York City* (Putnam, 1902; Heraldic Publishing Co., 1970)

Kenneth T. Jackson, ed., *Encyclopedia of New York City* (New Haven and London: Yale University Press, 1995)

John A. Garraty and Mark C. Carnes, gen. eds., *American National Biography*, 24 vols. (Oxford University Press, 1999)

Published works

The Fancy Ball, Given by Mrs. S***********. A Description of the Characters, Dresses, &c. &c. Assumed on the Occasion (reprinted from the *New-York Morning Courier*, 1829), NYPL

Andrew Alpern, *Apartments for the Affluent: New York's Fabulous Luxury Apartments: with original floor plans from the Dakota, River House, Olympic Tower and other Great Buildings*, Foreword by Harman H. Goldstone (Dover, 1987)

Cleveland Amory, *The Last Resorts* (Harper & Brothers, 1952)

——, *Who Killed Society?* (Harper & Brothers, 1960)

Wayne Andrews, *The Vanderbilt Legend: The Story of the Vanderbilt Family, 1794–1940* (Harcourt, Brace, 1941)

Margaret Armstrong, *Five Generations: Life and Letters of an American Family 1750–1900* (Harper & Brothers, 1930)

William Armstrong, *The Aristocracy of New York: Who They Are and What They Were; Being a Social and Business History of the City for Many Years, by an Old Resident* (New York Publishing Co., 1848)

——, *Stocks and Stock-Jobbing in Wall-Street, with Sketches of the Brokers and Fancy Stocks . . . by A Reformed Stock-Gambler* (New York Publishing Co., 1848)

Clive Aslet, *The American Country House* (New Haven: Yale University Press, 1990)

William Waldorf Astor, 'John Jacob Astor,' *Pall Mall Magazine*, 18 (1899), 171–84

Louis Auchincloss, *The Vanderbilt Era: Profiles of a Gilded Age* (Charles Scribner's Sons, 1989)

Paul R. Baker, *Richard Morris Hunt* (Cambridge, MA: MIT Press, 1980)

Consuelo Vanderbilt Balsan, *The Glitter and the Gold* (London: William Heinemann, 1953)

E. Digby Baltzell, *The Philadelphia Gentleman: The Making of a National Upper Class* (Free Press, 1958)

'Walter Barrett,' *The Old Merchants of New York City*, 3rd ser. (Carleton, 1865)

Michael and Ariane Batterberry, *On the Town in New York* (Charles Scribner's Sons, 1973; Routledge, 1999)

[Moses Y. Beach] *Wealth and Wealthy Citizens of New York City. Comprising an Alphabetical Arrangement of Persons Estimated to be Worth $100,000, and Upwards, with the sums appended to each name. Being Useful to Banks, Merchants, and Others* (The Sun Office, 1842)

Sven Beckert, *The Monied Metropolis: New York City and the Consolidation of the American Bourgeosie, 1850–1896* (Cambridge: Cambridge University Press, 2001)

James W. Beekman, *Founders of New York: An Address Delivered Before the Saint Nicholas Society of the City of New York . . . Saturday December 4, 1869* (The Saint Nicholas Society, 1870)

Eleanor Belmont, *The Fabric of Memory* (Farrar, Straus & Cudahy, 1957)

Rev. William Berrian, D.D., *An Historical Sketch of Trinity Church, New-York* (Stanford & Swords, 1847)

William Betts, LL.D., *The Causes of the Prosperity of New-York: An Anniversary Address, Delivered Before the St. Nicholas Society of New-York, December 3D, 1850* (Stanford & Swords, 1851).

Poultney Bigelow, *Seventy Summers*, 2 vols. (Longmans, Green, 1925)

Stephen Birmingham, *'Our Crowd': The Great Jewish Families of New York* (Harper & Row, 1967)

——, *America's Secret Aristocracy* (Boston: Little, Brown, 1987)

David Black, *The King of Fifth Avenue: The Fortunes of August Belmont* (Dial Press, 1981)

Elizabeth Blackmar, *Manhattan for Rent, 1785–1850* (Ithaca: Cornell University Press, 1989).

Pierre Bourdieu, *Distinction* (Cambridge, MA: Harvard University Press, 1984)

M. Christine Boyer, *Manhattan Manners: Architecture and Style 1850–1900* (Rizzoli, 1985)

Clare Brandt, *An American Aristocracy: The Livingstons* (Garden City, NY: Doubleday, 1986)

Leo Braudy, *The Frenzy of Renown: Fame & Its History* (Oxford University Press, 1986)

Letters of Henry Brevoort to Washington Irving, ed. George S. Hellman (G.P. Putnam's Sons, 1918)

Amy Beth Bridges, 'Another Look at Plutocracy and Politics in Antebellum New York City,' *Political Science Quarterly*, 97 (Spring 1982), 57–71

——, *A City in the Republic: Antebellum New York and the Origins of Machine Politics* (Cambridge: Cambridge University Press, 1984)

John Briggs, *Requiem for a Yellow Brick Brewery: A History of the Metropolitan Opera* (Boston: Little, Brown, 1969)

C[harles]. A[stor]. Bristed, *The Upper Ten Thousand: Sketches of American Society* (Stringer & Townsend, 1852)

——, 'Eugene Benson,' 'Meissonier,' *Appleton's Journal*, 2 (Sept. 11, 1869), 118–19.

——, 'Eugene Benson,' 'New York Journalists. Parke Godwin, of the Evening Post,' *The Galaxy*, 7 (Feb. 1869), 230–6.

James Brough, *Consuelo: Portrait of an American Heiress* (Coward, McCann & Geoghegan, 1979)

Clifford Browder, *The Money Game in Old New York: Daniel Drew amd His Time* (Lexington: University Press of Kentucky, 1986)

Peter G. Buckley, 'Culture, Class and Place in Antebellum New York,' in John Hull Mollenkopf, ed., *Power, Culture and Place: Essays on New York City*, (Russell Sage Foundation, 1988), 25–52

J[ames]. W[illiam]. Buel, *Mysteries and Miseries of America's Great Cities, embracing New York, Washington City, San Francisco, Salt Lake City, and New Orleans* (St. Louis and Philadelphia: Historical Publishing Co., 1883)

Edwin G. Burrows and Mike Wallace, *Gotham: A History of New York City to 1898* (Oxford University Press, 1999)

Nathaniel Burt, *First Families: The Making of an American Aristocracy* (Boston: Little, Brown, 1970)

Richard L. Bushman, *The Refinement of America: Persons, Houses, Cities* (Alfred A. Knopf, 1992)

William Allen Butler, *A Retrospect of Forty Years, 1825–1865* (Charles Scribner's Sons, 1911)

Mary Cable, *Top Drawer: American High Society from the Gilded Age to the Roaring Twenties*, Introduction by Oliver Jensen (Atheneum, 1984)

Edwin Harrison Cady, *The Gentleman in America* (Syracuse: Syracuse University Press, 1949)

Jay E. Cantor, 'A Monument of Trade: A.T. Stewart and the Rise of the Millionaire's Mansion in New York,' *Winterthur Portfolio*, 10 (1975), 165–97

Gerald Carson, *The Polite Americans: 300 Years of More or Less Good Behaviour* (London: Macmillan, 1967)

Betty Boyd Caroli, *The Roosevelt Women* (Basic Books, 1998)

Confessions of the Marquis de Castellane (London: Thornton Butterworth, 1924, published in New York as *How I Discovered America*, 1924)

David Castronovo, *The American Gentleman: Social Prestige and the Modern Literary Mind* (Continuum, 1991)

The Century Association, *The Century 1847–1947* (The Century Association, 1944)

Mrs. Winthrop Chanler [Margaret Chanler], *Roman Spring: Memoirs* (Boston: Little, Brown, 1934)

Ron Chernow, *The House of Morgan: An American Banking Dynasty and the Rise of Modern Finance* (Simon & Schuster, 1990)

——, *The Death of the Banker: The Decline and Fall of the Great Financial Dynasties and the Triumph of the Small Investor* (London: Pimlico, 1997)

Howard P. Chudacoff, *The Age of the Bachelor: Creating an American Subculture* (Princeton, NJ: Princeton University Press, 1999)

Allen Churchill, *The Roosevelts: American Aristocrats* (Harper & Row, 1965)

——, *The Upper Crust: An Informal History of New York's Highest Society* (Englewood Cliffs, NJ: Prentice-Hall, 1970)

——, *The Splendor Seekers: An Informal Glimpse of America's Multimillionaire Spender—Members of the $50,000,000 Club* (Grosset & Dunlap, 1974)

Henry Clews, *Twenty-Eight Years in Wall Street* (J.S. Ogilvie, 1887)

——, 'How to Make Money in Wall Street,' *Cosmopolitan*, 5 (Sept. 1888), 436–7.

——, *Fifty Years in Wall Street* (Irving Publishing Co., 1908)

The American Diaries of Richard Cobden, ed. Elizabeth Hoon Crawley (Princeton, NJ: Princeton University Press, 1952)

Virginia Cowles, *The Astors: Story of a Transatlantic Family* (London: Weidenfeld & Nicolson, 1979)

Anne F. Cox, *The History of the Colony Club 1903–1984* (The Colony Club, 1984)

Albert Stevens Crockett, *Peacocks on Parade* (Sears Publishing Co., 1931)

William A. Croffut, *The Vanderbilts and the Story of Their Fortune* (Belford, Clarke & Co., 1886)

Francis W. Crowninshield, *Manners for the Metropolis: An Entrance Key to the Fantastic Life of the 400*, decorations by Louis Fancher (D. Appleton, 1910)

Frank Crowninshield, 'The House of Vanderbilt,' *Vogue*, Nov. 15, 1941.

——, 'The Mrs. Astor I Remember,' *Vogue's First Reader*, Introduction also by Frank Crowninshield (Julian Messner, 1942), 93–8

Amos J. Cummings, *Scrapbook of Newspaper Clippings on Miscellaneous Subjects*, 4 vols. NYPL. Vol. II on New York

314

city politics, 1889–90; vol. III on miscellaneous foreign news, social, obituaries, spirit photographs, Siamese twins, executions; vol. IV on Wall Street

Kenneth A, Davis, *FDR: The Beckoning of Destiny 1882–1928: A History* (Putnam, 1972)

Julia Delafield, *Biographies of Francis Lewis and Morgan Lewis*, 2 vols. (Anson D.F. Randolph, 1877)

Desley Deacon, *Elsie Clews Parsons: Inventing Modern Life* (Chicago: University of Chicago Press, 1997)

John A. Dix, *A History of the Parish of Trinity Church in the City of New York* (Columbia University Press, 1950)

Rev. Morgan Dix, *Historical Recollections of St. Paul's Chapel, New York* (F.J. Huntington, 1867)

John Dizikes, *Opera in America: A Cultural History* (New Haven: Yale University Press, 1993)

Allen Dodworth, *Dancing and Its Relations to Education and Social Life* (London: Sampson Low Marston, 1885)

William Alexander Duer, LL.D., *New-York as it was, During the latter part of the last Century: An Anniversary Address, Delivered Before the St. Nicholas Society of New-York, December 1st, 1848* (Stanford & Swords, 1848)

M.H. Dunlop, *Gilded City: Scandal and Sensation in Turn-of-the-Century New York* (William Morrow, 2000)

William J. Dunn, *Knickerbocker Centennial: An Informal History of the Knickerbocker Club, 1871–1971* (Knickerbocker Club, 1971)

Norbert Elias, *The Civilizing Process: The History of Manners and State Formation and Civilization*, trans. Edmund Jephcott (Oxford: Blackwell, 1994)

Maude Howe Elliott, *Uncle Sam Ward and His Circle* (Macmillan, 1938)

——, *This Was My Newport* (Cambridge, MA: Mythology Co., 1944)

Edgar Fawcett, *The Adventures of a Widow: A Novel* (Boston: James R. Osgood, 1884)

——, *The Buntling Ball: A Graeco-American Play* (Funk & Wagnalls, 1884)

——, 'Plutocracy and Snobbery in New York,' *The Arena*, 4 (July 1891), 142-51.

Michael Feldberg, *The Turbulent Era: Riot and Disorder in Jacksonian America* (Oxford University Press, 1981)

Niall Ferguson, *The World's Banker: The History of the House of Rothschild* (London: Weidenfeld & Nicolson, 1998)

Stephen Fiske, *Off-Hand Portraits of Prominent New Yorkers* (Geo. R. Lockwood & Son, 1884)

Milton E. Flower, *James Parton, The Father of Modern Biography* (Durham, NC: Duke University Press, 1951)

John Foreman and Robbe Pierce Stimson, *The Vanderbilts and the Gilded Age: Architectural Aspirations, 1879–1901* (St. Martin's Press, 1991)

Ella M. Foshay, *Mr. Luman Reed's Picture Gallery: A Pioneer Collection of American Art* (Harry N. Abrams, Inc. in

Association with the New-York Historical Society, 1990)

Dixon Ryan Fox, *Yankees and Yorkers* (New York University Press, 1940)

——, *The Decline of Aristocracy in the Politics of New York 1801–1840*, ed. Robert V. Remini (Harper & Row, 1965)

John W. Francis, M.D., LL.D., *New York During the Last Half Century: A Discourse in Commemoration of the Fifty-third Anniversary of the New-York Historical Society, and of the Dedication of their New Edifice (November 17, 1857)* (NYHS, 1857)

——, *Old New York; or, Reminiscences of the Past Sixty Years*, with a Memoir of the Author by Henry T. Tuckerman, rev. and enlarged edn. of the 1857 discourse, 110 copies printed for subscribers (New York: W.J. Widdleton, 1865), NYPL (1 vol. expanded to 5 and extra-illustrated by Thomas Addis Emmet with 1,029 portraits and views, 79 letters and documents, and 8 broadsides)

John Fraser, *America and the Patterns of Chivalry* (Cambridge: Cambridge University Press, 1982)

Robert H. Fuller, *Jubilee Jim: The Life of Colonel James Fisk, Jr.* (Macmillan, 1928)

P.N. Furbank, *Unholy Pleasure: The Idea of Social Class* (Oxford: Oxford University Press, 1985)

C.J. Furness, ed., *The Genteel Female* (Alfred A. Knopf, 1931)

Frédéric Gaillardet, *L'Aristocratie en Amérique* (Paris: E. Dentu, 1883)

Frank Otto Gatell, 'Money and Party in Jacksonian America: A Quantitative Look at New York City's Men of Quality,' *Political Science Quarterly*, 82 (June 1967), 235-52

Timothy J. Gilfoyle, *City of Eros: New York City, Prostitution and the Commercialization of Sex 1790–1920* (W.W. Norton, 1992)

Gregory F. Gilmartin, *Shaping the City: New York and the Municipal Art Society* (Clarkson Potter, 1995)

Rufus Wilmot Griswold, *Republican Court, or, American Society in the Days of Washington* (D. Appleton, 1855)

Francis J. Grund, *Aristocracy in America: From the Sketch-Book of a German Nobleman*, Introduction by George E. Probst (Harper & Brothers, 1959; first published in London, 1839)

John Denis Haeger, *John Jacob Astor: Business and Finance in the Early Republic* (Detroit: Wayne State University Press, 1991)

The Aristocratic Journey: Being the Outspoken Letters of Mrs. Basil Hall Written during a Fourteen Months' Sojourn in America 1827–1828, ed. Una Pope-Hennessey (G.P. Putnam's Sons, 1931)

Karen Halttunen, *Confidence Men and Painted Women: A Study of Middle-Class Culture in America, 1830–1870* (New Haven and London: Yale University Press, 1982)

Allen McLane Hamilton, *The Intimate Life of Alexander Hamilton* (London: Duckworth, 1910)

Reminiscences of James A. Hamilton; or, Men and Events, at Home and Abroad, During Three Quarters of a Century (Charles Scribner, 1869)

David C. Hammack, *Power and Society: Greater New York at the Turn of the Century* (Russell Sage Foundation, 1982)

Alvin F. Harlow, *Old Bowery Days: The Chronicle of a Famous Street* (D. Appleton, 1931)

Mrs. J. Borden Harriman, *From Pinafores to Politics* (Henry Holt, 1923)

Constance Cary Harrison (Mrs. Burton Harrison), *The Well-Bred Girl in Society* (Garden City, N.Y.: Doubleday, Page, 1904)

——, *Recollections Grave and Gay* (London: Smith, Elder, 1912)

Chas. H. Haswell, *Reminiscences of an Octogenarian of the City of New York (1816 to 1860)* (Harper & Brothers, 1897)

Catherine Elizabeth Havens, *Diary of a Little Girl in Old New York* (Henry Collins Brown, 1919)

T.W. Higginson, 'Aristocracy of the Dollar,' *Part of a Man's Life* (Boston: Houghton, Mifflin, 1905), 94–113

——, *Book and Heart: Essays on Literature and Life* (Harper & Brothers, 1897)

Marilyn Wood Hill, *Their Sisters' Keeper: Prostitution in New York City, 1830–1870* (Berkeley: University of California Press, 1996)

Laura G. Holloway, *Famous American Fortunes and the Men Who Have Made Them: A Series of Sketches* (J.A. Hill, 1889)

Eric Homberger, *Scenes from the Life of a City: Corruption and Conscience in Old New York* (New Haven and London: Yale University Press, 1994)

The Diary of Philip Hone 1828–1851, ed. Allan Nevins, 2 vols. (Dodd, Mead, 1927)

David Sanctuary Howard, *New York and the China Trade*, with an essay by Conrad Edick Wright (NYHS, 1984)

Milford Wriarson Howard, *The American Plutocracy* (Holland Publishing Co., 1895)

Julia Ward Howe, *Is Polite Society Polite? And Other Essays* (Boston: Samson, Wolfe, 1895)

——, *Reminiscences 1819–1899* (Boston: Houghton Mifflin, 1899)

Winifred E. Howe, *A History of the Metropolitan Museum of Art* (Metropolitan Museum of Art, 1913)

William Dean Howells, 'Equality as the Basis of Good Society,' *The Century*, 51, n.s. 29 (Nov. 1895), 63–7

——, 'Are We a Plutocracy?,' *North American Review*, 158 (Feb. 1894), 185–96

Edwin P. Hoyt, *The Vanderbilts and Their Fortunes* (London: Frederick Muller, 1963)

——, *The Goulds: A Social History* (Weybright & Talley, 1969)

——, *The Guggenheims and the American Dream* (Funk & Wagnalls, 1977)

Freeman Hunt, *Lives of American Merchants*, 2 vols. (Derby & Jackson, 1858)

Rebecca H. Insley, 'An Interview with Mrs. Astor,' *The Delineator*, 72 (Oct. 1908), 549–50, 638–9.

Will Irwin *et al.*, *A History of the Union League Club of New York City* (Dodd, Mead, 1952)

Kathryn Allamong Jacob, *Capital Elites: High Society in Washington, DC, after the Civil War* (Washington, DC: Smithsonian Institution Press, 1995)

Frederic Cople Jaher, 'Style and Status in Late Nineteenth-Century New York' in Jaher, ed., *The Rich, the Well Born, and the Powerful: Elites and Upper Classes in History* (Secaucus, NJ: Citadel Press, 1975), 258–84

——, *The Urban Establishment: Upper Strata in Boston, New York, Charleston, Chicago, and Los Angeles* (Urbana: University of Illinois Press, 1982)

——, *A Scapegoat in the Wilderness: The Origins and Rise of Anti-Semitism in America* (Cambridge, MA: Harvard University Press, 1994)

Henry James, 'Saratoga,' *The Nation*, (Aug. 11, 1870), and 'Newport,' *The Nation*, (Sept. 15, 1870) in *Collected Travel Writings: Great Britain and America*, ed. Richard Howard (Library of America, 1993), 750–8, 758–66

Thomas A. Janvier, *In Old New York* (Harper & Brothers, 1894; reissued with an introduction by Edwin G. Burrows, St. Martin's Press, 2000)

H. Paul Jeffers, *Commissioner Roosevelt: The Story of Theodore Roosevelt and the New York City Police, 1895–1897* (John Wiley, 1994)

'Joseph,' *New York Aristocracy; or Gems of Japonica-dom* (Charles B. Norton, 1851)

John F. Kasson, *Rudeness & Civility: Manners in Nineteenth-Century Urban America* (Hill & Wang, 1990)

Lucy Kavaler, *The Astors: A Family Chronicle of Pomp and Power* (Dodd, Mead, 1966)

George Kennan, *E.H. Harriman: A Biography*, 2 vols. (Boston: Houghton, Mifflin, 1922)

Cynthia A. Kierner, *Traders and Gentlefolk: The Livingstons of New York, 1675–1790* (Ithaca: Cornell University Press, 1992)

Robert B. King, *The Vanderbilt Homes* (Rizzoli, 1989)

The Rt. Rev. William Ingraham Kip, *The Olden Time in New York* (G.P. Putnam's Sons, 1872)

Edward C. Kirkland, *Business in the Gilded Age: The Conservatives' Balance Sheet* (Madison, WI: University of Wisconsin Press, 1952)

Maury Klein, *The Life and Legend of Jay Gould* (Baltimore, MD: Johns Hopkins University Press, 1986)

Irving Kolodin, *The Metropolitan Opera 1883–1935*, 2nd edn. (Oxford University Press, 1940)

Ellen Kramer, 'Contemporary Descriptions of New York City and Its Public Architecture,' *Journal of the Society of*

Architectural Historians, 27 (Dec. 1968), 270–71

Mrs. Martha J. Lamb, 'Life in New York Fifty Years Ago,' *Magazine of American History*, 23 (March 1890), 177–209

John Lambert, 'A Description of the City of New York, 1807–1808,' *Manual of the Corporation of the City of New York* (John Hardy, Clerk of the Common Council, 1870), 847–67

Wheaton J. Lane, *Commodore Vanderbilt: An Epic of the Steam Age* (Alfred A. Knopf, 1942)

Lewis Lapham, *Money and Class in America: Notes and Observations on Our Civil Religion* (Weidefeld & Nicolson, 1988)

William Leach, 'Transformations in a Culture of Consumption: Women and Department Stores, 1890–1925,' *Journal of American History*, 71 (Sept. 1984), 319–42

T. Jackson Lears, *No Place of Grace: Antimodernism and the Transformation of American Culture 1880–1920* (Pantheon, 1981)

Elizabeth Drexel Lehr, *'King Lehr': and the Gilded Age* (Philadelphia: J.B. Lippincott,, 1935)

Gustav Lening, *The Dark Side of New York Life and Its Criminal Classes from Fifth Avenue down to the Five Points. A Complete Narrative of the Mysteries of New York* (Fred'k. Gerhard, 1873)

Anita Leslie, *The Fabulous Leonard Jerome* (London: Hutchinson, 1954)

——, *The Marlborough House Set* (Doubleday, 1973)

Suzannah Lessard, *The Architect of Desire: Beauty and Danger in the Stanford White Family* (Dial Press, 1996)

Lawrence W. Levine, *Highbrow/Lowbrow: The Emergence of Cultural Hierarchy in America* (Cambridge, MA: Harvard University Press, 1988)

Arnold Lewis, *American Country Houses of the Gilded Age* (Dover, 1982)

Charles Lockwood, 'The Bond Street Area,' *New-York Historical Society Quarterly*, 56 (Oct. 1972), 309–20.

——, *Bricks & Brownstone: The New York Row House, 1783–1929* (Abbeville Press, 1972)

——, *Manhattan Moves Uptown: An Illustrated History* (Barnes & Noble, 1995)

Andy Logan, *The Man Who Robbed the Robber Barons* (W.W. Norton, 1965)

Mrs. Abby Buchanan Longstreet, *Social Etiquette of New York* (D. Appleton, 1879)

[——], *Cards: Their Significance and Proper Uses as Governed by the Usages of New York Society, by the Author of 'Social Etiquette of New York'* (Frederick A. Stokes, 1889)

Myron H. Luke, 'Some Characteristics of the New York Business Community, 1800-1810,' *New York History*, 34 (Oct. 1953), 393–405

Ferdinand Lundberg, *America's 60 Families* (Vanguard Press, 1937)

Ward McAllister, *Society as I Have Found It* (Cassell, 1890)

James D. McCabe, Jr., *Great Fortunes and How They Were Made; or the Struggles and Triumphs of our Self-Made Men* (Cincinnati: E. Hannaford, 1871)

James Remington McCarthy, in collaboration with John Rutherford, *Peacock Alley: The Romance of the Waldorf-Astoria* (Harper & Brothers, 1931)

Robert McElroy, *Levi Parsons Morton: Banker, Diplomat and Statesman* (G.P. Putnam's Sons, 1930)

James T. Maher, *The Twilight of Splendor: Chronicles of the Age of American Palaces* (Boston: Little, Brown, 1975)

——, *Social Silhouettes (Being the Impressions of Mr. Mark Manhattan)*, ed. by Edgar Fawcett (Boston: Ticknor, 1885)

[Col. W. d'A. Mann,] *Fads and Fancies of Representative Americans of the Twentieth Century, being a Portrayal of their Tastes, Diversions and Achievements* (Town Topics Co., 1905)

Frederick Townsend Martin, *The Passing of the Idle Rich* (Doubleday, Page, 1911; Arno, 1973)

——, *Things I Remember* (London: Eveleigh Nash, 1913)

'Ik Marvel' [Donald G. Mitchell], *The Lorgnette; or, Studies of the Town*, 2 vols. (Stringer & Townsend, 1850)

——, *Fudge Doings: Being Tony Fudge's Record of the Same. In Forty Chapters*, 2 vols. (Charles Scribner, 1855)

Roger S. Mason, *Conspicuous Consumption: A Study of Exceptional Consumer Behavior* (Farnborough, Hants.: Gower, 1981)

Martin Mayer, *The Met* (Simon & Schuster/The Metropolitan Opera Guild, 1983)

James Knowles Medbery, *Men and Mysteries of Wall Street* (Boston: Fields & Osgood & Co., 1870)

Douglas T. Miller, *Jacksonian Aristocracy: Class and Democracy in New York 1830–1860* (Oxford University Press, 1967)

Edwin Havilland Miller, *Melville* (George Braziller, 1975)

Henry Wise Miller, *All Our Lives: Alice Duer Miller* (Coward McCann, 1945)

Maureen E. Montgomery, *Gilded Prostitution: Status, Money, and Transatlantic Marriages, 1870–1914* (Routledge, 1989)

——, *Displaying Women: Spectacles of Leisure in Edith Wharton's New York* (Routledge, 1998)

Charles C. Moreau, *A Collection of Scraps, Programmes and Portraits about the New York Academy of Music* (1887), Boston Public Library

Anne Morgan, *The American Girl: Her Education, Her Responsibility, Her Recreation, Her Future* (Harper & Brothers, 1915)

Anna Cora (Ogden) Mowatt Ritchie, *Fashion, or Life in New York* (1849; S. French & Son, 1854)

Gustavus Myers, *The History of Tammany Hall*, 2nd edn., new Introduction by Alexander B. Callow, Jr. (Dover, 1971)

——, *The Ending of Hereditary American Fortunes* (Julian Messner, Inc., 1939)

Roger Hale Newton, *Town and Davis, Architects: Pioneers in American Revival Architecture, 1812–1870* (Columbia University Press, 1942)

Rev. C.W. de Lyon Nicholls, *The 469 Ultra-Fashionables of America* (Broadway, 1912)

Harvey O'Connor, *The Astors* (Alfred A. Knopf, 1941)

Richard O'Connor, *Gould's Millions* (Garden City, NY: Doubleday, 1962)

——, *The Golden Summers: An Antic History of Newport* (G.P. Putnam's Sons, 1974)

Susan A. Ostrander, *Women of the Upper Class* (Philadelphia: Temple University Press, 1984)

Elsie Clews Parsons, 'American "Society",' *New Republic*, 9 (Dec. 16, 23, 1916), 184–6, 214–16

——, *The Journal of a Feminist*, new Introduction and Notes by Margaret C. Jones (Bristol: Thoemmes Press, 1994)

——, *Fear and Conventionality*, new Introduction by Desley Deacon (Chicago: University of Chicago Press, 1997)

[James Parton,] 'John Jacob Astor,' *Harper's Magazine*, 30 (Feb. 1865), 308–23

——, *et al.*, *Sketches of Men of Progress* (New York and Hartford Publishing Co., 1870–1)

Jerry E. Patterson, *The Vanderbilts* (Abrams, 1989)

——, *The Best Families: The* Town & Country *Social Directory, 1846-1996*, ed. Anthony T. Mazzola and Frank Zachary (Harry N. Abrams, in Association with Hearst Magazines, 1996)

——, *Fifth Avenue: The Best Address* (Rizzoli, 1998)

——, *The First Four Hundred: Mrs. Astor's New York in the Gilded Age* (Rizzoli, 2000)

Virginia Tatnall Peacock, *Famous American Belles of the Nineteenth Century* (Freeport, NY: Books for Libraries Press, 1970; first published 1900)

Philippe Perrot, *Fashioning the Bourgeoisie: A History of Clothing in the Nineteenth Century* (Princeton, NJ: Princeton University Press, 1994)

Stow Persons, *The Decline of American Gentility* (Columbia University Press, 1973)

Edward Pessen, *Most Uncommon Jacksonians: Radical Leaders of the Early Labor Movement* (Albany: State University of New York Press, 1967)

——, *Jacksonian America: Society, Personality, and Politics* (Homewood, IL, 1969; rev. edn. 1978)

——, 'The Wealthiest New Yorkers of the Jacksonian Era,' *New-York Historical Society Quarterly*, 54 (April 1970), 148–52

——, 'The Egalitarian Myth and the American Social Reality: Wealth, Mobility, and Equality in the "Era of the Common Man",' *American Historical Review*, 76 (Oct. 1971), 989–1034

——, 'Philip Hone's Set: The Social World of the New York City Elite in the "Age of Egalitarianism",' *New-York Historical Society Quarterly*, 56 (Oct. 1972), 285–308

——, *Riches, Class and Power before the Civil War* (Lexington, MA: D.C. Heath, 1973)

Ernest De Lancy Pierson, ed., *Society Verse* (Benjamin & Bell, 1887)

Letters from John Pintard to His Daughter Eliza Noel Pintard Davidson, 1816–1833, ed. Dorothy C. Barck, 4 vols. (NYHS, 1940)

Kenneth Wiggins Porter, *John Jacob Astor: Business Man* (Cambridge, MA: Harvard University Press, 1931)

Edwin Post, Jr., *Truly Emily Post* (Funk & Wagnalls, 1961)

Emily Post [Mrs. Price Post], *Etiquette: 'The Blue Book of Social Usage'*, new edn. (Funk & Wagnalls, 1945; first published 1922)

Marie Caroline Post, *The Life and Mémoirs of Comte Régis de Trobriand* (E.P. Dutton, 1910)

Henry C. Potter, D.D., *Sermons of the City* (E.P. Dutton, 1881)

Samuel Irenaeus Prime, *Life in New York* (Robert Carter, 1847)

——, *Irenaeus Letters* (The Outlook, 1881)

Henry F. Pringle, *Theodore Roosevelt: A Biography* (Harcourt, Brace, 1931)

Ralph Pulitzer, *New York Society on Parade* (Harper & Brothers, 1910)

William S. Rainsford, *The Story of a Varied Life* (Doubleday, Page, 1922)

Monica Randall, *The Mansions of Long Island's Gold Coast* (Hastings House, 1979)

Sidney Ratner, ed., *New Light on the History of Great American Fortunes: American Millionaires of 1892 and 1902* (Augustus M. Kelley, 1953)

Margaret Hayden Rector, *Alva, That Vanderbilt-Belmont Woman: Her Story as She Might have Told It* (Wickford, RI: Dutch Island Press, 1992)

Harry E. Ressequie 'The Decline and Fall of the Commercial Style of A.T. Stewart,' *Business History Review*, 36 (August 1962), 255–86

Laura E. Richards and Maud Howe Elliott, *Julia Ward Howe*, 2 vols. (Boston: Houghton Mifflin, 1915)

Jacob A. Riis, *How the Other Half Lives: Studies Among the Tenements of New York*, new Preface by Charles A. Madison (Dover, 1971; first published by Charles Scribner's Sons, 1890)

Reginald W. Rives, *The Coaching Club: Its History, Records and Activities* (Privately Printed, 1835)

Solon Robinson, *Hot Corn: Life Scenes in New York Illustrated* (De Witt and Davenport, 1853)

Robert R. Rowe, 'Mann of *Town Topics*,' *American Mercury*, 8 (July 1926), 271–80

Charles Edward Russell, 'England's System of Snobbery,' *Cosmopolitan*, 52 (Jan. 1907), 277–85

——, 'Caste in Various Countries,' *Cosmopolitan*, 52 (Feb. 1907), 448–56

——-, 'The Growth of Caste in America,' *Cosmopolitan*, 42 (March 1907), 524–34

Mary P. Ryan, *Civic Wars: Democracy and Public Life in the American City during the Nineteenth Century* (Berkeley: University of California Press, 1997)

Aline B. Saarinen, *The Proud Possessors* (London: Weidenfeld & Nicolson, 1959)

Herbert L. Satterlee, *J. Pierpont Morgan: An Intimate Portrait* (Macmillan, 1939)

Richard Schermerhorn, Jr., *Schermerhorn Genealogy and Family Chronicles* (Tobias A. Wright, 1914)

Kenneth A. Scherzer, *The Unbounded Community: Neighborhood Life and Social Structure in New York City, 1830–1875* (Durham, N.C.: Duke University Press, 1992)

Mary Elizabeth Wilson Sherwood, *Manners and Social Usages* (Harper, 1884; rev. edn. 1897)

Martin Simmons, *Union Club of the City of New York: The History of the Club from the year of its Founding to the year of its Sesquicentennial 1836 to 1986* (Union Club, 1986)

David Sinclair, *Dynasty: The Astors and Their Times* (London: J.M. Dent, 1983)

Florence Adele Sloane, *Maverick in Mauve: The Diary of a Romantic Age,* Commentary by Louis Auchincloss (Garden City, NY: Doubleday, 1983)

Arthur D. Howden Smith, *John Jacob Astor: Landlord of New York* (Philadelphia: J.B. Lippincott, 1929)

Jane S. Smith, *Elsie de Wolfe: A Life in the High Style* (Atheneum, 1982)

Matthew Hale Smith, *Bulls and Bears of New York, with the Crisis of 1873 and the Cause* (Hartford, Conn.: J.B. Burr, 1875)

Edward K. Spann, *The New Metropolis: New York City, 1840–1857* (Columbia University Press, 1981)

Christine Stansell, *City of Women: Sex and Class in New York, 1789–1860* (Alfred A. Knopf, 1986)

Clarice Stasz, *The Vanderbilt Woman: Dynasty of Wealth, Glamour, and Tragedy* (St. Martin's Press, 1991)

Henry Stevens, *Recollections of Mr James Lenox of New York and the Formation of His Library* (London: Henry Stevens & Son, 1886)

William Rhinelander Stewart, *Grace Church and Old New York* (Dutton, 1924)

I.N. Phelps Stokes, *Iconography of Manhattan Island, 1498–1909*, 6 vols. (Robert H. Dodd, 1915–28)

The Diary of George Templeton Strong, 1835–1875, ed. Allan Nevins and Milton Halsey Thomas, 4 vols. (Macmillan, 1952)

Jean Strouse, *Morgan: American Financier* (Random House, 1999)

Mrs. Jonathan Sturges, *Reminiscences of a Long Life* (F.E. Parrish, 1894)

W.A. Swanberg, *Jim Fisk: The Career of an Improbable Rascal* (London: Longmans, 1960)

——, *Pulitzer* (Charles Scribner's Sons, 1967)

——, *The Rector and the Rogue* (Charles Scribner's Sons, 1968)

——, *Whitney Father, Whitney Heiress* (Charles Scribner's Sons, 1980)

Thomas de Witt Talmage, *The Night Side of New York Life* (Chicago: J. Fairbanks Co., 1878)

Lately Thomas, *Sam Ward: 'King of the Lobby'* (Boston: Houghton Mifflin, 1965)

——, *Delmonico's: A Century of Splendor* (Boston: Houghton Mifflin, 1967)

——, *A Pride of Lions: The Astor Orphans: The Chanler Chronicle* (William Morrow, 1971)

Grant Thorburn, *Fifty Years' Reminiscences of New-York, or, Flowers from the Garden of Laurie Todd* (Daniel Fanshaw, 1845)

Calvin Tomkins, *Merchants and Masterpieces: The Story of the Metropolitan Museum*, rev. edn. (Henry Holt, 1989)

Reginald Townsend, *Mother of Clubs, Being the History of the First Hundred Years of the Union Club of the City of New York, 1836–1936* (Union Club, 1936)

Alan Trachtenberg, *Reading the American Photograph: Images as History, Matthew Brady to Walker Evans* (Hill & Wang, 1989)

Frances Trollope, *Domestic Manners of the Americans*, ed. Richard Mullen (Oxford University Press, 1984)

A Season in New York 1801: Letters of Harriet and Maria Trumbull, ed. and Introduction by Helen M. Morgan (Pittsburgh: University of Pittsburgh Press, 1969)

Deborah Turbeville's Newport Remembered: A Photographic Portrait of a Gilded Past, text by Louis Auchincloss (Harry N. Abrams, 1994)

Moran Tudury, 'Ward McAllister,' *American Mercury*, 8 (June 1926), 138–43

R.W.G. Vail, *Knickerbocker Birthday: A Sesqui-Centennial History of the New-York Historical Society 1804–1954* (New-York Historical Society, 1954)

Alan Valentine, *Lord Stirling* (Oxford University Press, 1969)

Arthur T. Vanderbilt II, *Fortune's Children: The Fall of the House of Vanderbilt* (William Morrow, 1989)

Cornelius Vanderbilt, Jr., *The Vanderbilt Feud: The Fabulous Story of Grace Wilson Vanderbilt* (London: Hutchinson, 1957)

Mrs. John King Van Rensselaer, 'The Basis of Society in New York City,' *Cosmopolitan*, 27 (August, 1899), 350–68

——, *Newport: Our Social Capital* (Philadelphia: J.B. Lippincott, 1905)

——, in Collaboration with Frederic Van de Water, *The Social Ladder* (London: Eveleigh Nash & Grayson, 1925)

Mariana Griswold Van Rensselaer, *Accent as Well as Broad Effects: Writings on Architecture, Landscape, and the Environment, 1876–1925*, ed. David Gebhard (Berkeley: University of California Press, 1996)

Thorstein Veblen, *Theory of the Leisure Class: An Economic Study of Institutions*, Foreword by Stuart Chase (Modern Library, 1934; first published Macmillan, 1899)

Catherine Hoover Voorsanger and John K. Howat, eds., *Art and the Empire City: New York, 1825–1861* (New Haven and London: Yale University Press, 2000)

[Reuben Vose,] *Reuben Vose's Wealth of the World Displayed* (Reuben Vose, 1859)

Stanley Walker, *Mrs. Astor's Horse* (Frederick A. Stokes, 1936)

Altina L. Waller, *Reverend Beecher and Mrs. Tilton: Sex and Class in Victorian America* (Amherst: University of Massachusetts Press, 1982)

George Waller, *Saratoga: Saga of an Impious Era* (Englewood Cliffs, NJ: Prentice-Hall, Inc., 1966)

Charles Dudley Warner, 'What Is Your Culture to Me?', *Scribner's Monthly*, 4 (August 1872), 470–8

Robert Irving Warshow, *Jay Gould* (Greenberg, 1928)

Dixon Wecter, *The Saga of American Society: A Record of Social Aspiration 1607–1937* (Charles Scribner's Sons, 1937)

Richard Welling, *As the Twig is Bent* (G.P. Putnam's Sons, 1942)

Edith Wharton, *A Backward Glance* (D. Appleton-Century, 1934)

—— and Ogden Codman, Jr., *The Decoration of Houses*, Introductory Notes by John Barrington Bayley and

William A. Coles (Charles Scribner's Sons, 1978; reprint of 1902 edn.)

Robert H. Wiebe, *The Opening of American Society: From the Adoption of the Constitution to the Eve of Disunion* (Random House, 1984)

Susan Williams, *Savory Suppers and Fashionable Feasts: Dining in Victorian America* (Pantheon, 1985)

N. Parker Willis, *People I Have Met; or Pictures of Society and People of Mark, Drawn under a Thin Veil of Fiction* (Baker & Scribner, 1850)

——, *Fun-Jottings; or, Laughs I Have Taken a Pen To* (Charles Scribner, 1853)

——, *Health Trip to the Tropics* (Charles Scribner, 1854)

——, *The Rag-Bag: A Collection of Ephemera* (Charles Scribner, 1855)

Derek Wilson, *The Astors 1763–1992: Landscape with Millionaires* (St. Martin's Press, 1993)

George Wilson, compiler, *Portrait Gallery of the Chamber of Commerce of the State of New York* (Chamber of Commerce, 1890)

Albert Foster Winslow, *Tuxedo Park: A Journal of Recollections* (Tuxedo Park: Tuxedo Historical Society, 1992)

Elsie de Wolfe, 'The Well-Dressed Woman,' *Cosmopolitan*, 24 (Dec. 1897), 125–130

——, *The House in Good Taste* (The Century Co., 1915)

——, *After All* (Harper & Brothers, 1935)

Helen Worden, *Society Circus* (Covici, Friede, 1936)

Mabel Osgood Wright, *My New York* (Macmillan, 1926)

John Zukowsky, 'Castles on the Hudson,' *Winterthur Portfolio*, 14 (Spring 1979), 73–92

INDEX

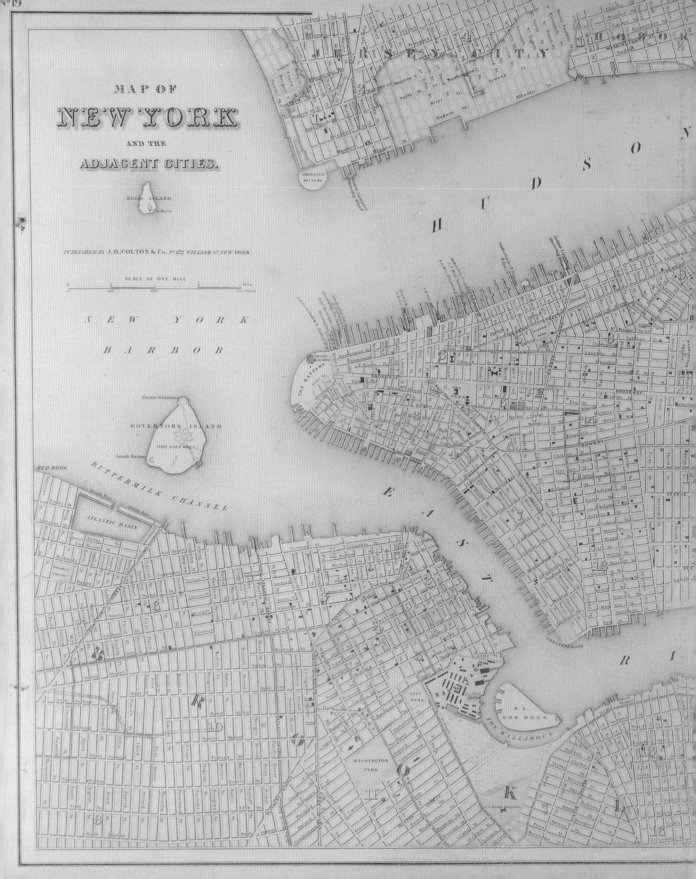

MAP OF
NEW YORK
AND THE
ADJACENT CITIES.

PUBLISHED BY J.H. COLTON & Co. Nº 172 WILLIAM St. NEW YORK.

SCALE OF ONE MILE